Frommer's®

P9-DFK-273

San Antonio & Austin

9th Edition

by David Baird

Wiley Publishing, Inc.

ABOUT THE AUTHOR

When not traveling, **David Baird** hangs his hat in Austin. Upon leaving college he took a vow of poverty and has faithfully kept it through a variety of pursuits, including anthropology and travel writing. He's something of a homebody but will occasionally rouse himself for an evening out, always for the selfless purposes of research.

Published by:

WILEY PUBLISHING, INC.

111 River St.
Hoboken, NJ 07030-5774

ISBN 978-1-118-00285-8 (paper); ISBN 978-1-118-07189-2 (ebk); ISBN 978-1-118-07208-0 (ebk); ISBN 978-1-118-07209-7 (ebk)

Editor: Jessica Langan-Peck
Production Editor: Erin Amick
Cartographer: Andrew Murphy
Production by Wiley Indianapolis Composition Services

Front Cover Photo: San Antonio, Texas, The Alamo, side angle wide angle view of façade ©Richard Nowitz / National Geographic / Getty Images

Back Cover Photo: Artwork on the wall of the "Intellectual Property" store on the Drag near the University of Texas ©Peter Tsai Photography / Alamy Images

For information on our other products and services or to obtain technical support, please contact our Customer Care Department within the U.S. at 877/762-2974, outside the U.S. at 317/572-3993 or fax 317/572-4002.

Wiley also publishes its books in a variety of electronic formats. Some content that appears in print may not be available in electronic formats.

Manufactured in the United States of America

5   4   3   2   1

CONTENTS

List of Maps vii

1 THE BEST OF SAN ANTONIO & AUSTIN 1

The Best Unforgettable Experiences 2

The Best Splurge Hotels 3

The Best Moderately Priced Hotels 3

The Best Dining Experiences 4

The Best Things to Do for (Almost) Free 5

The Best San Antonio Shopping 6

The Best Hour in Austin 6

The Best Austin Outdoor Activities 7

The Best Places to Hang with Austinites 7

The Best Plunges into Excess 7

THE BEST OF SAN ANTONIO & AUSTIN ONLINE 8

2 SAN ANTONIO & AUSTIN IN DEPTH 10

San Antonio & Austin Today 11

Looking Back: San Antonio & Austin History 14

GLOSS'RY: HOW TO TALK LIKE A TEXAN 16

SAN ANTONIO: DATELINE 18

AUSTIN: DATELINE 22

San Antonio & Austin in Pop Culture 23

Eating & Drinking 26

When to Go 27

SAN ANTONIO CALENDAR OF EVENTS 28

AUSTIN CALENDAR OF EVENTS 30

Lay of the Land 32

Responsible Travel 33

Tours 34

3 SUGGESTED SAN ANTONIO ITINERARIES 35

NEIGHBORHOODS IN BRIEF 35

THE BEST OF SAN ANTONIO IN 1 DAY 39

THE BEST OF SAN ANTONIO IN 2 DAYS 43

THE BEST OF SAN ANTONIO IN 3 DAYS 44

4 WHERE TO STAY IN SAN ANTONIO 46

DEAL WELL, SLEEP WELL 47

The Best San Antonio Hotel Bets 48

Downtown 49

King William Historic District 56

FAMILY-FRIENDLY HOTELS 58

Monte Vista Historic District 59

Fort Sam Houston Area 60

West/Northwest 61

North Central (Near the Airport) 64

5 WHERE TO DINE IN SAN ANTONIO 66

The Best San Antonio Dining
  Bets 67

Restaurants by Cuisine 68

Downtown 69

IT'S ALWAYS CHILI IN SAN ANTONIO 75

King William/Southtown 76

Monte Vista Area 78

*WHAT'S COOKING AT THE OLD PEARL
  BREWERY* 79

FAMILY-FRIENDLY RESTAURANTS 81

Alamo Heights Area 82

Northwest 84

FROZEN ASSETS 85

6 EXPLORING SAN ANTONIO 87

The Top Attractions 87

THE ALAMO: THE MOVIE(S) 92

More Attractions 97

Parks & Gardens 103

Especially for Kids 104

Special-Interest Sightseeing 106

OLD MOVIE PALACES OF SAN ANTONIO 107

Strolling Downtown San
  Antonio 108

WALKING TOUR: DOWNTOWN 108

Organized Tours 112

Staying Active 113

Spectator Sports 115

7 SHOPPING IN SAN ANTONIO 117

The Shopping Scene 117

Shopping A to Z 118

LOVE POTION NO. 9 124

8 SAN ANTONIO AFTER DARK 128

The Performing Arts 128

The Club & Music Scene 131

CONJUNTO: AN AMERICAN CLASSIC 134

The Bar Scene 135

Movies 136

9 SIDE TRIPS FROM SAN ANTONIO 137

New Braunfels & Gruene 137

Small-Town Texas 145

Corpus Christi & Beyond 147

BIRDING ALONG THE TEXAS COAST 148

TEXAS'S MOST DESERTED BEACH 150

*WHOOPING CRANES: BACK FROM THE
  BRINK OF EXTINCTION* 151

10 SUGGESTED AUSTIN ITINERARIES 154

NEIGHBORHOODS IN BRIEF 154

THE BEST OF AUSTIN IN 1 DAY 158

THE BEST OF AUSTIN IN 2 DAYS 159

THE BEST OF AUSTIN IN 3 DAYS 162

11 WHERE TO STAY IN AUSTIN 164

The Best Austin Hotel Bets 165

Downtown 166

South Austin 171

IT PAYS TO STAY 173

Central 173

Northwest 175

Westlake/Lake Travis 178

FAMILY-FRIENDLY HOTELS 179

At the Airport 180

12 WHERE TO DINE IN AUSTIN 181

The Best Austin Dining Bets 182

Restaurants by Cuisine 182

Downtown 184

GROCERY STORE DINING 187

South Austin 188

West Austin 193

Central 195

FOOD TRUCKS PARK IN AUSTIN 195

FAMILY-FRIENDLY RESTAURANTS 197

East Side 198

Northwest 200

Westlake/Lake Travis 201

Only in (or Around) Austin 202

13 EXPLORING AUSTIN 204

The Top Attractions 204

GOING BATTY 208

More Attractions 211

Especially for Kids 221

Special-Interest Sightseeing 223

Strolling the University of Texas 223

WALKING TOUR OF THE UNIVERSITY OF TEXAS 224

Organized Tours 229

Staying Active 232

Spectator Sports 234

14 SHOPPING IN AUSTIN 236

The Shopping Scene 236

FIRST THURSDAYS 240

Shopping A to Z 240

15 AUSTIN AFTER DARK 251

AUSTIN CITY LIMITS 252

The Performing Arts 252

The Club & Music Scene 256

NAVIGATING AUSTIN'S DOWNTOWN BAR SCENE 257

LABEL IT SUCCESSFUL—AUSTIN'S S×SW 260

The Bar Scene 261

Films 263

CELLULOID AUSTIN 263

16 SIDE TRIPS FROM AUSTIN 265

Small Towns & Texas Barbecue 265

EXPERIENCING CENTRAL TEXAS BARBECUE 266

San Marcos 270

LOST PINES 274

17 TOURING THE TEXAS HILL COUNTRY 276

Boerne 276

THE HILL COUNTRY WINE TRAIL 280

A TASTE OF ALSACE IN TEXAS 282

Bandera 283

Kerrville 287

OLD ENGLAND FINDS THE OLD WEST 288

BATS ALONG A BACK ROAD TO FREDERICKSBURG 290

Fredericksburg 291

GOING BACK (IN TIME) TO LUCKENBACH 296

Lyndon B. Johnson Country 297

The Northern Lakes 299

VIEWING BLUEBONNETS & OTHER WILDFLOWERS 299

18 PLANNING YOUR TRIP TO SAN ANTONIO & AUSTIN 304

Getting There: San Antonio 304

Getting There: Austin 306

Getting Around: San Antonio 307

Getting Around: Austin 311

Fast Facts: San Antonio 313

Fast Facts: Austin 320

Airline Websites 325

Index 327

General Index 327

Accommodations Index 339

Restaurant Index 340

LIST OF MAPS

San Antonio at a Glance   36

The Best of San Antonio in 1, 2 & 3
Days   40

Downtown San Antonio
Accommodations   51

Greater San Antonio Accommodations &
Dining   62

Downtown San Antonio Dining   71

Downtown San Antonio Attractions   89

Greater San Antonio Attractions   90

Walking Tour: Downtown San
Antonio   109

Downtown San Antonio Shopping   119

Greater San Antonio Shopping   120

New Braunfels   139

Corpus Christi   149

Austin at a Glance   156

The Best of Austin in 1, 2 & 3 Days   160

Downtown Austin Accommodations   167

Greater Austin Accommodations &
Dining   176

Downtown Austin Dining   185

SoCo Dining   189

Downtown Austin Attractions   205

Greater Austin Attractions   206

Walking Tour: The University of Texas   225

Downtown Austin Shopping   237

Greater Austin Shopping   238

Austin After Dark   253

Small Town Texas Barbecue   267

The Texas Hill Country   278

Fredericksburg   293

The Northern Lakes   301

HOW TO CONTACT US

In researching this book, we discovered many wonderful places—hotels, restaurants, shops, and more. We're sure you'll find others. Please tell us about them, so we can share the information with your fellow travelers in upcoming editions. If you were disappointed with a recommendation, we'd love to know that, too. Please write to:

Frommer's San Antonio & Austin, 9th Edition
Wiley Publishing, Inc. • 111 River St. • Hoboken, NJ 07030-5774
frommersfeedback@wiley.com

AN ADDITIONAL NOTE

Please be advised that travel information is subject to change at any time—and this is especially true of prices. We therefore suggest that you write or call ahead for confirmation when making your travel plans. The authors, editors, and publisher cannot be held responsible for the experiences of readers while traveling. Your safety is important to us, however, so we encourage you to stay alert and be aware of your surroundings. Keep a close eye on cameras, purses, and wallets, all favorite targets of thieves and pickpockets.

FROMMER'S STAR RATINGS, ICONS & ABBREVIATIONS

Every hotel, restaurant, and attraction listing in this guide has been ranked for quality, value, service, amenities, and special features using a **star-rating system.** In country, state, and regional guides, we also rate towns and regions to help you narrow down your choices and budget your time accordingly. Hotels and restaurants are rated on a scale of zero (recommended) to three stars (exceptional). Attractions, shopping, nightlife, towns, and regions are rated according to the following scale: zero stars (recommended), one star (highly recommended), two stars (very highly recommended), and three stars (must-see).

In addition to the star-rating system, we also use **seven feature icons** that point you to the great deals, in-the-know advice, and unique experiences that separate travelers from tourists. Throughout the book, look for:

special finds—those places only insiders know about

fun facts—details that make travelers more informed and their trips more fun

kids—best bets for kids and advice for the whole family

special moments—those experiences that memories are made of

overrated—places or experiences not worth your time or money

insider tips—great ways to save time and money

great values—where to get the best deals

The following abbreviations are used for credit cards:

AE American Express	DISC Discover	V Visa
DC Diners Club	MC MasterCard	

FROMMERS.COM

Frommer's travel resources don't end with this guide. Frommer's website, **www.frommers. com**, has travel information on more than 4,000 destinations. We update features regularly, giving you access to the most current trip-planning information and the best airfare, lodging, and car-rental bargains. You can also listen to podcasts, connect with other Frommers. com members through our active-reader forums, share your travel photos, read blogs from guidebook editors and fellow travelers, and much more.

THE BEST OF SAN ANTONIO & AUSTIN

Composing best-of lists is a subjective exercise, but it can lead you to some objective truths. In this case, it can lead you to realize just how many entertaining activities San Antonio and Austin afford the visitor. Both cities aren't so big as to be daunting but are large enough and have enough personality that they can offer one-of-a-kind experiences. The residents of both cities are open and personable and eager to help out-of-towners, so even the process of getting acquainted with these cities is fun.

In San Antonio, of course, the major attraction is the River Walk, which is absolutely stunning and gives downtown San Antonio its partylike atmosphere. The river meanders through the city and passes by museums, missions, theaters, and many outdoor restaurants and bars. But to get to know the real San Antonio, you have to drag yourself away from the River Walk and into one of the interesting neighborhoods nearby. Walking down the streets of King William, Southtown, or Monte Vista, poking your head into shops, and grabbing a bite at one of the neighborhood restaurants will put you into contact with the locals, and they can be a quirky bunch. Sometimes encounters with local characters can be the most memorable part of a trip.

Austin, as the "Live Music Capital of the World," offers its own vibe. Music is everywhere in this town. It's so easy to find that you may stumble on a free concert while you're checking out the sites. And then there's simply strolling down Sixth Street, keeping an ear out for any particularly enticing music and an eye out for colorful people. In this area you never know what to expect, which is part of its charm.

Of course, Austin has its own body of water downtown, Lady Bird Lake, encircled by the Hike and Bike Trail, which offers great views of the water, the trees, and the downtown skyline. If more fresh air is required, you can head out to the surrounding area, studded with limestone caverns and natural springs. Finding plenty to do is easy; but make sure you find the time to kick back and experience Austin's relaxed vibe.

THE most UNFORGETTABLE EXPERIENCES

o **Strolling the Grounds of the Alamo** (San Antonio): In the middle of this bustling city, the grounds of the Alamo (holy grounds, if you consider yourself a Texan) can seem curiously quiet on some days, when the crowds have abated—so quiet you can hear the wind blowing through the oak trees. Perhaps it was that quiet in the moments before the final siege. See p. 87.

o **Walking the River** (San Antonio): The first planned urban green space in Texas, the River Walk, is still the best. Follow the original course of the river as it meanders through this old city, a city that owes its origin, its layout, and, now, even its prosperity, to this river. Old bridges, some quite low, span the river at varying angles. It's an urban canyon, with buildings rising up along both banks. See it both at daytime and at nighttime. See p. 93.

o **Lazing in the Courtyard at the Marion Koogler McNay Art Museum** (San Antonio): As fine as many of the paintings here are, when it comes to transcendent experiences, you can't beat sitting out on the lovely tree-shaded patio of the McNay. See p. 94.

o **Riding a Bike Through the King William Historic District and Upper South Side** (San Antonio): Riding through this area just south of downtown is a trip through time and across cultures, from the opulent mansions built here by German merchants in the 19th century to the artsy and ethnic Hispanic areas south and east. See chapter 6.

o **Splashing Around Barton Springs Pool** (Austin): The bracing waters of this natural pool have been drawing Austinites to its banks for more than 100 years. If there's one thing that everyone in town can agree on, it's that there's no better plunge pond on a hot day than this one. See p. 209.

o **Joining the Healthy Hordes on Austin's Hike and Bike Trail** (Austin): Head over to the shores of Lady Bird Lake to see why *Walking* magazine chose Austin as America's "Most Fit" city. Walkers and runners share the path with cyclists and strollers. You get good vistas of the city and the lake and see quite a bit of local society, too. See p. 232.

o **Sipping a Margarita While Watching the Sun Set over Lake Travis** (Austin): Relax at the Oasis on one of the many decks that stretch across a hillside high above Lake Travis, order a large margarita, and congratulate yourself on living the high life. Laid out before you are miles of watery landscape. If conditions are right, a soft redness will tint the view and create a warm, fuzzy feeling of oneness with the world. See p. 202.

o **Attending a Taping of Austin City Limits** (Austin): This will be a matter of luck, but if you come to town at the right time, and the show that will be taped happens to be music you like, then there's nothing better than getting tickets to be part of the show. And then, sometime later, when the show airs, you can relive the experience. See p. 252.

o **Checking Out Who Is Playing at the Continental Club** (Austin): While you're in town, there will be some act playing at the Continental Club that you positively can't miss. It might be a happy hour show; it might be an evening show; it might be somebody you haven't even heard of yet. But take my word for it, with the variety and quality of acts that perform at this famous little club on South Congress Avenue, there's no better place to expand your musical tastes. See p. 172.

THE best SPLURGE HOTELS

- **Omni La Mansión del Río** (San Antonio): There's no hotel more San Antonio than this luxurious palace on the River Walk. Graceful buildings and courtyards, balconies overlooking the river amid tall cypress trees, handsome rooms decorated in traditional San Antonio style—La Mansión has it all. See p. 50.
- **Mokara Hotel & Spa** (San Antonio): Also on the river, this hotel, sister to La Mansión, specializes in pampering with style. A spa takes care of the details. See p. 52.
- **Hyatt Regency Hill Country Resort and Spa** (San Antonio): Visiting San Antonio with the family? Hole up in this place and the kids will forever be in your debt. With tubing and many other outdoor activities on the property and SeaWorld in the neighborhood, there's plenty to keep them busy while you enjoy your own relaxing activities or sneak off to the more urbane pleasures of the city. See p. 61.
- **Hotel Contessa** (San Antonio): With its great location on the river and its bold design, this hotel offers a promising setting for an enjoyable stay. The guest rooms offer comfort and views of either the River Walk or the skyline. See p. 49.
- **Four Seasons Austin** (Austin): Settle into one of the large guest rooms overlooking the lake, have the front desk schedule a massage at the highly regarded spa, get the concierge to line up dinner reservations at your favorite restaurant, and then pinch yourself to make sure you're not dreaming. The only thing that could make a stay at this hotel any more special would be billing someone else for it. See p. 166.
- **The Driskill** (Austin): This hotel is Austin's jewel. It's got all the history, all the character, and now, all the comfort that you could want. In the original building, where big cattle baron Jesse Driskill still surveys the scene (in stone effigy), you'll find suites with the most character. See p. 212.
- **Mansion at Judges Hill** (Austin): Splurge and reserve one of the large signature rooms on the second floor of the original mansion. These have access to the sweeping upper porch, which is one of the mansion's best features and a great place to relax and have a cocktail. Lots of amenities and personal service make this place perfect for any kind of visit to Austin, but especially a pleasure trip. See p. 173.
- **Lake Austin Spa Resort** (Austin): This spa resort gets more write-ups by the national press than any other lodging in town. Most of the articles do a good job conveying how relaxing and serene the place is, but not many do justice to its beauty. It's a rare combination of all these things. See p. 178.
- **Hotel Saint Cecilia** (Austin): This new hotel captures what's fun about the South Congress scene but takes comfort to an entirely new level. Sleep deeply on a handmade Swedish mattress; greet the morning with whatever your favorite crepe is. Lounge on the private deck or patio of your room, or spin some vinyl on your in-room turntable. The only inherent problem with this arrangement is getting the motivation to leave the hotel. See p. 171.

THE best MODERATELY PRICED HOTELS

- **Riverwalk Vista** (San Antonio): Lots of character, space, and amenities are what this independent, moderately priced hotel is known for. And the downtown location is central for those wanting to enjoy all the city has to offer. See p. 56.

o **O'Brien Hotel** (San Antonio): Near La Villita and the River Walk, the location is great. Rooms are attractive and contain extras such as robes and good-quality linens not usually seen at this price level. See p. 56.

o **Beckmann Inn and Carriage House** (San Antonio): Get the full bed-and-breakfast experience in the beautiful Victorian-era neighborhood of the King William District. Built in 1886, in Queen Anne style, the house features a lovely wraparound porch, perfect for enjoying the afternoon in this quiet spot near the San Antonio River. See p. 57.

o **Bonner Garden** (San Antonio): In an Italianate Villa with a rooftop deck and panoramic views, you'll find lovely rooms that steer clear of the cluttered look. You'll also find that rarest of features in a bed-and-breakfast—a large pool. Just north of downtown, the location is central and convenient. See p. 59.

o **Austin Motel** (Austin): In Austin's cool SoCo district is this hip, funky, completely remodeled old motel. The place keeps an air of the past about it, but the rooms have been individually furnished, many with fun and flair. See p. 172.

o **Austin Folk House** (Austin): This bed-and-breakfast, in addition to a great location on the west side of the university campus, offers rooms with plenty of character. Check out the artwork and enjoy some of the uncommon architectural features of this house. You're close to both downtown and the shops and restaurants of Lamar Boulevard. See p. 173.

o **Habitat Suites** (Austin): Several hotels in Austin take ecoconsciousness beyond the old "we won't wash your towels" option, but no one takes it nearly as far as Habitat Suites. Almost everything here is ecofriendly. It's also guest friendly, with quality linens and amenities, and lots of extras you don't see in other hotels. See p. 174.

o **Holiday Inn Austin Town Lake** (Austin): Okay, it's a freeway hotel, but you're also on the lake. Get a room facing the lake and you'll have gorgeous views. The location is close to all the central Austin attractions. See p. 170.

THE best DINING EXPERIENCES

o **Las Canarias** (San Antonio): For a romantic dinner for two, dine either along the River Walk or inside one of the cozy, softly lit dining rooms, accompanied by the soft music of a guitar or piano. Start off with one of the aperitifs, for which the bar has a good reputation. Then move on to a meal that, like San Antonio, represents the melding of unlikely cultural influences. See p. 70.

o **Silo** (San Antonio): This place serves New American cooking exactly the way it should be done—with much art and little fuss. The surroundings are spacious, low-key, and comfortable. And the service is attentive and knowledgeable, but without attitude. See p. 83.

o **Liberty Bar** (San Antonio): This is the place for letting your hair down and enjoying a little local society. There are few other places in San Antonio that so effortlessly reflect the culture of their town, especially in matters of eating and drinking. See p. 76.

o **Uchi** (Austin): Don't think of Uchi as just a great place for sushi and Japanese cuisine. It's a great restaurant, period, with creative cooking that transcends its humble roots. The setting, in a beautifully revamped 1930s house, is transcendent too. See p. 189.

- **Threadgill's** (Austin): As the locals say about this place, "It's world famous, at least in Austin." What's so famous about it is the honest, old-style cooking that Austinites have been praising for years: the chicken-fried steak with cream gravy, the fried okra, and the ham steak with Jezebel sauce. Local musicians love playing here; the owner is one of the city's biggest supporters of live music. There is no restaurant more Austin than this one. See p. 197.

- **Kreuz Market** (Lockhart): It's a short, pleasant drive to Lockhart and to this pilgrimage site for the barbecue faithful. Kreuz has amazing sausage and ribs. But don't expect to be putting any sauce on your meat. That would be an insult to the cook, and they take these things personally down here. If you positively must have that rich and tangy Texas barbecue sauce, then steer your car toward Black's, also in Lockhart, and held in high esteem by the must-have-sauce crowd. See p. 266.

- **Curra's Grill** (Austin): It's not the decor (or maybe it's the absence of decor) that brings people from all walks of life to this homey eatery in South Austin. It's for Curra's particular style of Mexican cooking that is, for locals, a delicious departure from standard Tex-Mex, without getting too far away from Tex-Mex's comfort food aspect. Not that the visitor would recognize them, but the place gets a lot of local celebrities. See p. 191.

THE best THINGS TO DO FOR (ALMOST) FREE

- **Scouting the Alamo and the River Walk** (San Antonio): How many other cities have freebies as their two major attractions? All the more reason for seeing the Alamo—and for seeing it more than once—until you find just the right moment to savor within its ancient walls. It's hard to say whether the River Walk is better at night or during the day, so see it both ways and make up your own mind. See chapter 6.

- **Visiting San Antonio Missions National Historical Park/Attending Mariachi Mass at San José** (San Antonio): See these as a day trip or break them up into a couple of visits. Now with the hike-and-bike path completed, you can see them as part of a 12-mile physical and religious exercise. On Sundays at noon, a Mass is held by the community of San José to the accompaniment of a mariachi band. Now that's pure San Antonio. See chapter 6.

- **Exposing Yourself to Art at the Blue Star Contemporary Art Center** (San Antonio): Enter this huge warehouse at the south end of San Antonio's downtown area, and you'll find thousands of square feet of studio and gallery space. In the thick of it all is the artist-run Contemporary Arts Center—a fertile home for whatever's new in the local art scene. See chapter 6.

- **Taking Austin's Visitor Center Walking Tour** (Austin): These history excursions are provided free by the city and are superb. See chapter 13.

- **Visiting the LBJ Library** (Austin): There's a lot to interest the visitor here, including an animatronic replica of the former President. LBJ was often very quotable, as the exhibits make clear. See chapter 13.

o **Touring Central Market or Whole Foods** (Austin): According to the Austin Visitor's Bureau, these two supermarkets are among the top five most popular attractions in Austin. While you're there, take a break and have lunch or dinner. Dining in grocery stores has become de rigueur in Austin. See chapter 12.

o **Touring the Capitol** (Austin): Definitely take the free tour rather than the self-guided tour. You'll have an easy time remembering you're in Texas; the place is loaded with state icons, and the size—bigger than all other state capitols—says it all. See chapter 13.

o **Enjoying Free Outdoor Concerts** (Austin): There are so many free outdoor concerts in Austin sponsored by both public and private money that you will probably have a chance to catch one. Check the local papers for info. See chapter 15.

THE best SAN ANTONIO SHOPPING

o **Buying Day of the Dead Souvenirs in Southtown:** The Day of the Dead (actually 2 days, Nov 1–2) is commemorated throughout the largely Hispanic Southtown, but you can buy T-shirts with dancing skeletons and folk-art tableau typical of the holiday year-round. See p. 122.

o **Checking out the Headgear at Paris Hatters:** Even if you're not in the market for a Stetson, you should at least wander over to this San Antonio institution that has sold hats to everyone from Pope John Paul II and Queen Elizabeth to lesser lights such as TV's Jimmy Smits. See how big your head is compared to those of the stars. See p. 127.

o **Shopping for Handmade Boots at Lucchese:** For the adult male Texan of a certain class, and especially for the San Antonian, getting fitted for Lucchese (pronounced Loo-*kaiz*-ee) boots is a sign that one has made it in the world. For establishment Texas, these boots are a symbol of Texas roots and should be worn both with suits and jeans. See p. 126.

o **Buying "Easy-Life" Potion from a Neighborhood Botanica:** Okay, you might prefer the standard love potion, but for my money, getting the easy-life mojo up and running is far more important. Truth be told, there is a lot more to explore in these places than simple potions. Stores like Papa Jim's are fertile grounds for the amateur urban anthropologist. Check them out. See p. 124.

THE best HOUR IN AUSTIN

o **Enjoying a Massage:** With a little planning ahead for that idle hour, you can change the whole complexion of the rest of your day. This is very much a common practice here, and when in Rome (er, Austin) . . . Most independent hotels can arrange an appointment with a massage therapist. See chapter 11.

o **Strolling up South Congress:** You never know what you're going to find when walking along this row of shops, eateries, and galleries. It's the best window-shopping in Austin. You'll be hard-pressed to keep it to just an hour. See chapter 14.

o **Browsing through Tesoros:** This store is one of a kind, but, as it deals in imports, has nothing in the way of local goods. Still, visitors and locals are fascinated by the variety of crafts and folk art for sale. There's plenty to capture the eye across a wide range of prices. See chapter 14.

THE best AUSTIN OUTDOOR ACTIVITIES

- **Feasting your Eyes on the Colorful Gardens at the Lady Bird Johnson Wildflower Center:** Spring is prime viewing time for the flowers, but Austin's mild winters ensure that there will always be bursts of color at Lady Bird Johnson's pet project. See p. 209.
- **Playing in the Water at Lake Travis:** The longest of the seven Highland Lakes, Travis offers the most opportunities for watersports, including jet-skiing, snorkeling, and angling. See p. 219.
- **Going Batty:** From late March through November, thousands of bats emerge in smokelike clouds from under the Congress Avenue Bridge, heading out for dinner. It's an intriguing sight, and you can thank each of the little mammals for keeping the air pest-free—a single bat can eat as many as 600 mosquitoes in an hour. See p. 208.
- **Having Coffee at Mozart's:** Picture a deck overlooking Lake Austin. Add to the picture the delights of coffee and baked goods, and perhaps a good book, and you have nature and civilization in perfect balance. See p. 203.

THE best PLACES TO HANG WITH AUSTINITES

- **The B Scene at the Blanton Museum:** On the first Friday of every other month, local art lovers socialize over wine and finger food at the new Blanton Museum. Music, too, is provided, but not so much that it puts a damper on the conversation. See p. 210.
- **Early Evenings at Scholz Garten:** At Austin's oldest drinking establishment, you can buy a pint of draft beer and claim your spot at one of the large picnic tables that fill the outdoor patio. People show up after work to slow down and enjoy some casual conversation. On Thursday evenings in cool weather, a brass band will play for beer, and they're not bad. See p. 262.
- **First Thursdays in SoCo:** The first Thursday of every month is a lively time on South Congress. Crowds show up to hear the free music, look over the goods at the street stalls, and enter the shops that stay open late for the occasion. You never know who or what will show up, and everyone is in the mood to have a good time. See p. 240.
- **The Broken Spoke:** There are a lot of dance halls in central Texas, but you would be hard-pressed to find a better, more fun place to go than this one. You'll see lots of local color and enjoy the easygoing society that Austin is known for. Everybody has a good time. See p. 257.

THE best PLUNGES INTO EXCESS

The following is not for everyone. To enjoy these experiences for what they are requires a certain appreciation for irony and absurdity.

THE best OF SAN ANTONIO & AUSTIN ONLINE

- **The Handbook of Texas Online** (www.tsha.utexas.edu/handbook/online): The Handbook is an encyclopedia offering concise entries that explain who's who, what's what, and where's where in Texas. It's easy to use and has information on just about everything, from the locations of towns and counties to explanations of some of the state's legends, to biographical data on the many characters who left their mark on Texas history.

- **Texas Department of Transportation** (www.traveltex.com): The state's official tourism website is practically the only site you'll need to type in—everything else will be a link. I especially like the section that offers easily printable discount coupons, primarily for lodging and attractions.

- **Texas Outside** (www.texasoutside.com): This is a great resource for planning outdoor activities for just about anywhere in the state. It breaks Texas down into different regions and has separate pages for Texas's largest cities. You'll find maps and information on all sorts of outdoor sports, such as hiking, hunting, fishing, biking, and canoeing.

- **MySanAntonio.com:** The website of the city's only mainstream newspaper, the *San Antonio Express-News,* not only provides the daily news, but also links to local businesses such as dry cleaners and florists (via its Power Pages) and to movie, nightlife, and dining listings and reviews.

- **Austin 360** (www.austin360.com): Movie times, traffic reports, restaurant picks, homes, jobs, cars. . . . This site, sponsored in part by the

- **Best Stereotype Wrapped Up in a Caricature** (San Antonio): A visit to the Buckhorn Saloon & Museum makes you ponder some of the deeper questions, such as "Why don't more museums sell beer?" There are no easy answers. Yes, much is made of the Old West's culture of violence. You can see gunfights enacted and exhibits on blood-thirsty desperadoes. It's all good family fun. But to those who would still cock an eyebrow at this place, I have one thing to say: costumed fleas. They must be seen (barely) to be believed. See p. 98.

- **Best Sensory Overload** (San Antonio): Excess, thy name is mariachi. To set the scene perfectly, you need a table by the river, a rather large platter of Tex-Mex food in front of you, a frozen margarita at your right hand, and the aforesaid mariachis, belting out some standard, such as "Guadalajara, no te rajes," with great bravado. They must of course be topped with their large sombreros and one of them plucking the strings of one of those large bass guitars. Lesser mortals might well recoil from the stimulation of so many nerve cell receptors. But you can placidly take it all in, comfortable in the knowledge that you have reached the promised land of travel brochures. Congratulations.

- **Best Way to Take the "Walk" out of River Walk** (San Antonio): Big boats on a small river—there's something very Texas about this, as there is about the boat captain's monologue. See p. 93.

Austin American-Statesman, the city's main newspaper, is a one-stop clicking center for a variety of essentials. It's easy to navigate, too.

o **www.sanantonio.gov**: The City of San Antonio's website offers timely information on such topics as traffic and street closures. Most of the other sections that would be of interest to visitors, such as the city-sponsored arts events and public parks, can be found in the "Recreation" section.

o **www.visitsanantonio.com**: You're not going to get honest critiques of hotels and attractions on the San Antonio Convention and Visitors Bureau's website; however, you are going to get useful links to many of them. The "Discounts" section is especially good if you're looking for discounts on everything from accommodations to theme parks. This is not the easiest site to navigate, but once you click on "Visitors," you should be able to find what you need.

o **www.sanantonio.citysearch.com**: I don't always agree with this site's reviews, but it's always good to have a variety of opinions about dining, nightlife, and shopping (even if mine are ultimately right). And there are a few things I can't do—such as provide you with an up-to-date weather report or Yellow Pages information—that this site can.

o **www.texasmonthly.com**: You won't necessarily find San Antonio stories on the *Texas Monthly* site, but the state's best magazine offers in-depth treatments of lots of interesting topics, so you'll be keyed into a Texas mindset. And the site sometimes highlights hot new San Antonio dining spots.

o **Best White Elephant Souvenirs** (San Antonio): Are you in the market for a souvenir with no redeeming aesthetic value? Are you looking for that perfect something to quiet forever those pesky requests to bring something back from your trips? Souvenir stores can be found scattered throughout the touristy areas of downtown, but there is an especially fertile hunting ground along the west side of Alamo Plaza. Take your pick of such gems as an Alamo ashtray, a beer can wind chime, or a barbed wire candle, just to name a few.

SAN ANTONIO & AUSTIN IN DEPTH

2

Though they are only 80 miles apart and share the same climate, soil, and natural resources, San Antonio and Austin have grown into two very different cities. San Antonio is much older and has been more static. Austin is young and always in flux. In short, while the former is all about structure, the latter is all about flow.

The city of San Antonio is a collection of tightly knit, structured communities. Some residents can trace their lineage all the way back to the original Canary Islanders who settled here in 1731. Others have family going back to the days of the *empresarios* of the early 19th century, the Anglos who contracted with the Mexican government to bring settlers to Texas from the United States.

San Antonio has always had a special relationship with the army. The city is home to a lot of career military, both active and retired, and they add another layer of networking to the social fabric of the city. The military has its own channels of communication: listserves, newsletters, and bulletins. And retired military personnel socialize frequently and, in the way of any subculture, share information about their surroundings, including San Antonio. And then there are the neighborhoods, which provide a strong sense of identity to their members. This is especially the case on the south side but is true of neighborhoods on the north and east sides, too.

With these microcosms in place, San Antonio has a placid air about it, which masks the city's economic dynamism. It doesn't feel at all like the boomtown that it is, and this could be because much of the change of the last 20 years has been growth at the city's periphery. At its core, San Antonio still feels like a small town. Moving through neighborhoods in Central San Antonio, one gets the impression that nothing of much importance has happened since 1960.

Austin makes the opposite impression on the visitor—that nothing of real importance occurred before 1960. Austin residents move around a lot—the typical Austin resident has lived in at least three or four different parts of the city—and as a result, few people identify themselves by their neighborhood. In the last 50 years, Austin has gone from a sleepy state capital and university town to a national center for high-tech manufacturing and software development.

Mobility is a key factor in Austin's identity. The city's three biggest elements are the state government, which sees politicians, lobbyists, and functionaries come and go as their careers take them to larger or smaller political stages; the university, with its large and mobile student body; and the tech industry, which is always in flux. All of this gives the city a more wide-open feel than San Antonio.

SAN ANTONIO & AUSTIN TODAY

San Antonio

San Antonio, home of the Alamo and the River Walk, has more character than any other big city in Texas. Indeed, it is often lumped together with New Orleans, Boston, and San Francisco as one of America's most distinctive cities. And, if you're looking for a destination for the whole family, you can't go wrong with San Antonio. It has a downtown area that is attractive and comfortable and safe, a couple of large theme parks—SeaWorld and Fiesta Texas—and resorts that cater specifically to families.

There is a richness in San Antonio that goes beyond the images often seen in posters and brochures. Visitors today will encounter a city with a strong sense of community, a city whose downtown shows its age and its respect for the past.

The eighth-largest city in the United States (pop. approx. 1.2 million), and one of the oldest, is undergoing a metamorphosis. For a good part of the past century, San Antonio was a military town that happened to have a nice river promenade running through its decaying downtown area. Now, with the growth in tourism, San Antonio's second biggest industry—it has an annual economic impact of approximately $7.2 billion—the city is now seen by outsiders as a fun city and unique destination.

Although the city's outlying theme parks and attractions are benefiting from increased visitation, downtown is by far the most affected section. The city's Henry B. Gonzalez Convention Center doubled in size at the end of the 1990s followed by strong growth in downtown hotels. But the biggest trend in the last decade or so has been recovering the past: Historic became hot. It started a bit earlier, with the renovation of the Majestic Theatre, which was reopened in the late 1980s after many years of neglect. This proved a great success and a point of civic pride, and resulted in the birth of several projects. The Empire Theatre came back in the late 1990s, and several hotels were restored to their former grandeur. And now, every time you turn around, some reclamation project is in the works.

Residential development in the suburbs was, until the bursting of the bubble, moving at a fast pace, and the city's growth has kept the excess of housing stock to a manageable level. The local economy relies on much more than just tourism and the convention business. In fact, the city's top industries, healthcare and bioscience, have a total economic impact of at least $12.9 billion, including medical conferences and the many people who travel to San Antonio for medical treatment. Boeing and Lockheed Martin are among the aviation companies that have been attracted to the former Kelly Air Force Base, now KellyUSA. And an $800-million Toyota truck manufacturing plant brought more than 2,000 jobs into the area when it began producing full-size pickups. Though the effects of the economic downturn have been felt here, the city has been cushioned by its diversity.

The North American Free Trade Agreement (NAFTA), signed in 1994, has been a boon for San Antonio, which hosts the North American Development Bank—the financial arm of NAFTA—in its downtown International Center. Representatives from the various states of Mexico are housed in the same building as part of the

"Casas" program. With its large Hispanic population, regular flights to Mexico City, cultural attractions such as the Latin American wing of the San Antonio Museum of Art, the Centro Alameda project, and a history of strong business relations with Mexico, San Antonio is ideally positioned to take advantage of the economic reciprocity between the two nations. And the fact that Meximerica Media, which is starting a chain of Spanish-language newspapers, established its headquarters in San Antonio strengthens the city's status as a major center for marketing and media aimed at the U.S. Hispanic population.

Even with its rosy outlook, the city is facing some major problems. San Antonio and Austin are 80 miles and political light-years apart, but the two cities are growing ever closer. Although they haven't yet melded to form the single metropolis that futurists predict, the increasing suburban sprawl and the growth of New Braunfels and San Marcos, two small cities that lie between San Antonio and Austin, are causing a great deal of congestion on I-35, which connects all four cities.

An even more serious concern is the city's water supply. Currently, the Edwards Aquifer is the city's main source of water, and ominously, no one knows exactly how many years' worth of water it contains. San Antonio is the largest city in the country that is so dependent on groundwater. The city is looking for ways to draw surface water from neighboring utility districts, but the effort is slow going.

Austin

In almost anything you read or hear about Austin, you will be told that it is a laid-back city. "Laid-back" has become Austin's defining trait. First-time visitors get here and expect to find a city whose denizens all move about and express themselves in the unhurried manner of Willie Nelson. They must feel a little put upon when they drive into town only to find bearish traffic and pushy drivers and a downtown that is looking uncomfortably similar to Houston or Dallas.

Over the years, Austin has gotten bigger and busier, but it hasn't lost its essential nature. Stay here for a couple of days and you'll feel the laid-back quality you've heard about. Austinites are personable, gracious, and open, and for them the enjoyment of the simple pleasures of life holds a great deal more attraction than the rat race. At times it seems that everyone you meet is either a musician, a massage therapist, or has some other sort of alternative career.

Austinites of all walks of life enjoy the outdoors. Barton Springs is the preferred spot for a swim; the popular hike-and-bike trail that encircles Town Lake is a favorite place for either a leisurely walk or a serious run. The city streets and bike lanes are filled with Austin's many cyclists. Just outside of town are several parks, nature preserves, and rivers and lakes that can be enjoyed. Hand in hand with this love of the outdoors comes a strong environmental consciousness, which is reflected in the local government. Austin leads the nation in green energy production, has the most aggressive recycling and energy conservation programs in the state, and, though starting late, it has instituted programs to reduce traffic and urban sprawl.

One can't talk about Austin for very long without mentioning the rather large university at its center. The University of Texas feeds the Austin scene. It has brought thousands of bright students here, some of whom don't wish to leave once they've received their degrees. They stay and add to a large pool of educated people looking for a livelihood. This in turn has attracted high-tech companies that seek a large educated workforce.

During the 1990s, Austin's population increased by 41% (from 465,600 to 656,600). Many of the new residents moved to the suburban west and northwest, but the economic expansion also fueled a resurgence in the older central city.

Downtown projects of the last 15 years include the restoration of the capitol and its grounds, the refurbishing of the State Theatre, the renovation of the Driskill Hotel, and the reopening of the Stephen F. Austin Hotel, two grand historic properties. The convention center doubled in size and the Bob Bullock Texas History Center, a major tourist attraction, opened in 2001.

The downtown area has become popular as residential space, too. It began with a move to convert former warehouses and commercial lofts into residential housing. A popular farmers' market has sprouted up Saturday mornings on Republic Square, which, along with the flagship store (and corporate headquarters) of the Austin-based Whole Foods Markets at Sixth and Lamar, makes living downtown easy and convenient, if not cheap.

Just across the river, South Congress Street (aka SoCo, of course) continues to see the development of a hip retail and restaurant district with one-of-a-kind galleries and boutiques, which stay open late once a month to take part in the First Thursdays block party. The popularity of SoCo has altered the rest of South Austin, sending house prices up and increasing the number of apartments and town houses under construction.

This boom in real estate is disquieting to many Austinites. There's now a gated residential complex right down the street from the famed Continental Club, and, because of increased rent, many of the struggling musicians who gave Austin's music scene its vitality can no longer afford to live here. And although the new airport prides itself on its use of local concessionaires, the restaurants and hotels that are springing up alongside the facility are chains. Indeed, locals are sufficiently worried about the city's evolving character that they've spawned a small industry of bumper stickers and T-shirts pleading KEEP AUSTIN WEIRD.

One of the most pressing problems is out-of-control traffic. Streets are filling with cars, and the freeways, especially I-35, are seeing frequent jams and delays. A new toll road (Hwy. 130) has been built to the east of town that seems to be siphoning off some of the traffic, and government planners hope more will follow when another 40-mile segment is completed in 2012.

Another solution to the traffic is a commuter rail service that now runs from the northern satellite community of Cedar Park to downtown. Completed in 2010, it should ease some of the traffic that clogs the northern freeways during rush hour, but ridership so far has not been as high as expected. Plans are currently on the table for an electric streetcar system to circulate through downtown and connect it to the university, Zilker Park, Austin-Bergstrom airport, and some of the central neighborhoods on the eastside.

The burst in the housing bubble has made for a glut of condos in the downtown market. Several planned developments, including a few hotel/condo towers, have been postponed or canceled. But the downturn has not stopped the construction of new housing in other areas in the central city.

2 LOOKING BACK: SAN ANTONIO & AUSTIN HISTORY

San Antonio

San Antonio's past is the stuff of legend—if it were a movie, the story of the city would be an epic with an improbable plot, encompassing the end of a great empire, the rise of a republic, and the rescue of the river with which the story began.

For most of its history, San Antonio was the largest city in Texas and the "cosmopolitan" center, where multiple cultures came together and coexisted. At the time of the arrival of the Spanish, the land was inhabited by native Indians called Coahuiltecans, who eventually populated the first Franciscan missions; 15 families from the Canary Islands, sent by order of the King of Spain; and a small garrison of soldiers. The settlement prospered. The church eventually built five missions. Later, during the fights for Mexican Independence and Texan Independence (1821 and 1836, respectively), San Antonio saw several hard-fought battles, including the famous siege of the Alamo. This greatly reduced the population for more than a decade until it began to attract thousands of German settlers fleeing the revolutions in Europe. So many came that by 1860, German speakers in the city outnumbered both Spanish and English speakers. Through the following decades, these different immigrant groups would accommodate each other and forge a unique local culture.

MISSION SAN ANTONIO

At the time of the first mission's founding, the Spanish Empire in America stretched from Texas to Tierra del Fuego. Administering such a vast territory was difficult. Spain divided the continent into viceroyalties. The viceroyalty of New Spain included all of Mexico, Guatemala, and large stretches of the southwestern United States, where it had a minimum presence.

In 1691, an early reconnaissance party passed through what is now San Antonio and found a wooded plain watered by a clear river, called Yanaguana by the native Coahuiltecan Indians. They named it San Antonio de Padua, after the saint's day on which they arrived. The Coahuiltecans, by that time, were suffering the depredations of the Apaches and looked to the Spaniards for protection. They asked to be converted to Christianity and invited the Spanish to establish missions there.

In 1718, Mission San Antonio de Valero—later known as the Alamo—was founded. To protect the religious complex from Apache attack, the presidio (fortress) of San Antonio de Béxar went up a few days later. In 1719, a second mission was built nearby, and in 1731, three ill-fated missions in East Texas, which were nearly destroyed by French and Indian attacks, were moved hundreds of miles to the safer banks of the San Antonio River. In March of that same year, the Canary Island settlers arrived and established the village of San Fernando de Béxar close by the garrison.

Thus, within little more than a decade, what is now downtown San Antonio became home to three distinct, though related, settlements: a mission complex, the military garrison designed to protect it, and the civilian town known as Béxar, which was officially renamed San Antonio in 1837. To irrigate their crops, the early settlers were given narrow strips of land stretching back from the river and from the nearby San Pedro Creek, and centuries later, the paths connecting these strips, which followed the winding waterways, were paved and became the city's streets.

REMEMBER THE ALAMO

As the 18th century wore on, bands of Apache Indians would frequently attack the village, but these attacks killed fewer of the native population than did the diseases brought from Europe, for which the Coahuiltecans had little resistance. By the beginning of the 19th century, the Spanish missions were sorely depopulated. In 1794, Mission San Antonio de Valero was secularized, its farmlands redistributed. In 1810, recognizing the military potential of the thick walls of the complex, the Spanish authorities turned the former mission into a garrison. The men recruited to serve here all hailed from the Mexican town of San José y Santiago del Alamo de Parras. The name of their station was soon shortened to the Alamo (Spanish for "cottonwood tree").

> **Impressions**
>
> *From all manner of people, business men, consumptive men, curious men, and wealthy men, there came an exhibition of profound affection for San Antonio. It seemed to symbolize for them the poetry of life in Texas.*
> —Stephen Crane, *Patriot Shrine of Texas*, 1895

By 1824, all five missions had been secularized and Mexico had gained its independence from Spain. Apache and Comanche roamed the territory freely, and it was next to impossible to persuade more Spaniards to live there. Although the political leaders of Mexico were rightly suspicious of Anglo-American designs on their land, they entered into an agreement with Moses Austin to settle some 300 Anglo-American families in the region to the east of San Antonio. Austin died before he could carry out his plan, and it was left to his son Stephen to bring the settlers into Texas. Shortly afterward, others (now called *empresarios*) made similar agreements with the Mexican government.

The Mexicans wanted a buffer between the Indians and their settlements in northern Mexico, but eventually grew nervous about the large numbers of Anglos entering their country from the north. Having already repealed many of the tax breaks they had initially granted the settlers, they now prohibited all further U.S. immigration to the territory. When, in 1835, General Antonio López de Santa Anna abolished Mexico's democratic 1824 constitution, Tejanos (Mexican Texans) and Anglos alike balked at his dictatorship, and a cry rose up for a separate republic.

One of the first battles for Texas independence was fought in San Antonio when the insurgents attacked the garrison there. The battle was intensely fought, much of it door-to-door combat. Eventually, Mexican general Martín Perfecto de Cós surrendered on December 9, 1835. Under terms of the surrender, the Mexicans were allowed to leave, as no one had food for so many prisoners.

But the Mexican army, under General Santa Anna, would return in force the next year to retake the Alamo, in a lopsided battle against the Texan forces that would capture the American imagination. The siege lasted from February 23 through March 6, 1836. Some 180 volunteers—among them Davy Crockett and Jim Bowie—serving under the command of William Travis, died in the final attack, defending the Alamo against a force that was 10 times their number. The delay allowed Sam Houston to

gloss'ry: HOW TO TALK LIKE A TEXAN

It may be true that Texans talk differently, but it's tough to pin down a true Texas accent—a reality evident in virtually any Hollywood picture about the place. Most Texans don't speak with the Southern drawl of the deep South. It's more of a Western twang. And because Texas is such a big place, influenced by the language of adventurers heading west and newly arrived immigrants (Yankees from the north, Mexicans from south of the border), Texans have adopted a rich vocabulary and colorful manner of speaking.

It's not just how they say it, but what they say that makes Texans stand out. Their folksy language and homespun hyperbole seem to come effortlessly. Former CBS news anchor Dan Rather, a native of Wharton, Texas, was both ridiculed and celebrated for his colorful language; one election night he described a candidate who "tore through Dixie like a big wheel through a cotton field." Evocative phrases, such as "that dawg don't hunt," also spilled effortlessly from the sharp tongue of the late former Texas governor Ann Richards, who famously chided George Bush, Sr., for having been born "with a silver foot in his mouth." Another tried-and-true method of talkin' Texan is to sprinkle in Spanish words and Anglicize the Spanish names of towns and streets. Even non-Hispanic Texans liberally toss around phrases like "Hola," "Qué pasa?" and "Adiós, amigo" in their everyday patter. Keep an ear out for things like "Guada-loop" (for Guadalupe) and "Man-shack" (for Manchaca).

o **All the fixin's** Accompaniments—beans, mashed potatoes, gravy, and the like—to go with chicken-fried steak. The plate should groan under their weight.

o **Awl** Texas's largest industry. As in, awl 'n' gas.

muster his forces and eventually defeat the Mexican army at San Jacinto with the battle cry "Remember the Alamo!"

AFTER THE FALL

Ironically, few Americans came to live in San Antonio during Texas's stint as a republic (1836–45), but settlers came from overseas in droves: By 1850, 5 years after Texas joined the United States, Tejanos and Americans were outnumbered by European, mostly German, immigrants. The Civil War put a temporary halt to the city's growth—in part because Texas joined the Confederacy and most of the new settlers were Union sympathizers—but expansion picked up again soon afterward. As elsewhere in the West, the coming of the railroad in 1877 set off a new wave of immigration. Riding hard on its crest, the King William district of the city, a residential suburb named for Kaiser Wilhelm, was developed by prosperous German merchants.

Some of the immigrants set up Southern-style plantations, others opened factories and shops, and more and more who arrived after the Civil War earned their keep by driving cattle. The Spanish had brought Longhorn cattle and *vaqueros* (cowboys) from

- **Big ol'** Large; esteemed.
- **Buffalo chip** What cowboys kick around out in the fields—cow dung.
- **Coke** Generic term for soft drink. Dr. Pepper, Pepsi, RC Cola—they're all just "Coke" to Texans.
- **Dadgummit** and **dadburnit** Common expletives.
- **Fixin' to** A general state of preparedness or intent to carry out an act ("I'm fixin' to eat that chicken-fried steak of yours").
- **Gimme cap** Freebie baseball caps with logos of awl 'n' gas and other companies on the bill; redneck uniform to be worn as an alternative to cowboy hat. The name is derived from the frequent request, "Gimme one them thar caps."
- **Give a holler** A plea to call, write, or e-mail.
- **Good ol' boy** A true Texan.

- **Gussied up** The look necessary for going out; dolled up 'n' pretty.
- **Hook 'em** The cry and hand signal (index finger and pinkie raised like horns) of University of Texas graduates everywhere—as in, "Hook 'em, horns."
- **Howdy, y'all** The one-size-fits-all greeting—singular, plural, who cares? Y'all is a contraction of "you all," but is actually just Texan for "you." Howdy is pronounced "high-dee."
- **I reckon** The act of thinking out loud.
- **Kicker** Cowboy who puts his pointy-toed boots to good use.
- **Over yonder** Where you'll likely be when you give a holler.
- **Yankee** A northerner; outsider; opponent of Texas statehood.
- **Yes, ma'am** The polite way to respond to any woman over 20.
- **Yessir** and **nossir** The polite way to respond to a Texan man.

By Janis Turk

Mexico into the area, and now Texas cowboys drove herds north on the Chisholm Trail from San Antonio to Kansas City, where they were shipped east. Others moved cattle west, for use as seed stock in the fledgling ranching industry.

As early as 1849, the Alamo was designated a quartermaster depot for the U.S. Army, and in 1876, the much larger Fort Sam Houston was built to take over those duties. Apache chief Geronimo was held at the clock tower in the fort's Quadrangle for 40 days in 1886, en route to exile in Florida, and Teddy Roosevelt outfitted his Rough Riders—some of whom he recruited in San Antonio bars—at Fort Sam 12 years later.

As the city marched into the 20th century, Fort Sam Houston continued to expand. In 1910, it witnessed the first military flight by an American, and early aviation stars such as Charles Lindbergh honed their flying skills here. From 1917 to 1941, four Army air bases—Kelly Field, Brooks Field, Randolph Field, and Lackland Army Air Base—shot up, making San Antonio the largest military complex in the United States outside the Washington, D.C., area. Although Kelly was downsized and privatized, the military remains the city's major employer today.

Frederick Law Olmsted's description in his 1853 *A Journey Through Texas* is poetic. San Antonio, he writes, "lies basking on the edge of a vast plain, through which the river winds slowly off beyond where the eye can reach. To the east are gentle slopes toward it; to the north a long gradual sweep upward to the mountain country, which comes down within 5 or 6 miles; to the south and west, the open prairies, extending almost level to the coast, a hundred and fifty miles away."

A RIVER RUNS THROUGH IT

The city continued to grow. In the early 1900s, it showcased the first skyscraper in Texas. But San Antonio wasn't growing fast enough to keep up with Houston or Dallas. By the 1920s, it had become Texas's third-largest city and had arrived at a crossroads. Was it to follow Houston and Dallas in their bull-rush toward growth and modernism? Or was it to go its own way, preserving what it thought most valuable? This dilemma took the form of a political dispute over the meandering San Antonio River. In 1921, during a violent storm, the river overflowed its banks and flooded the downtown area, killing 50 people and destroying many businesses. A city commission recommended draining the riverbed and channeling the water through underground culverts to remove the threat of flooding and free up space for more downtown buildings. This outraged many locals. A group of women's clubs formed to save the river and create an urban green space along its banks. (And this was decades before anyone in Texas had ever heard of urban planning.) The women's campaign was multipronged and even included a puppet-show dramatization. They won the battle, and the river was saved.

In 1927, Robert H. H. Hugman, an architect who had lived in New Orleans and studied that city's Vieux Carré district, came up with a detailed design for improving

SAN ANTONIO: DATELINE

1691 On June 13, feast day of St. Anthony of Padua, San Antonio River was discovered and named by the Spanish; governor of Spanish colonial province of Texas makes contact with Coahuiltecan Indians.

1718 Mission San Antonio de Valero (later nicknamed the Alamo) founded; presidio San Antonio de Béxar established to protect it and other missions to be built nearby.

1720 Mission San José founded.

1731 Missions Concepción, San Juan Capistrano, and Espada relocated from East Texas to San Antonio area; 15 Canary Island families, sent by Spain to help populate Texas, establish the first civil settlement in San Antonio.

1793–94 The missions are secularized by order of the Spanish crown.

1820 Moses Austin petitions Spanish governor in San Antonio for permission to settle Americans in Texas.

the waterway. His proposed River Walk, with shops, restaurants, and entertainment areas buttressed by a series of floodgates, would render the river profitable as well as safe, and also preserve its natural beauty. The Depression intervened, but in 1941, with the help of a federal Works Project Administration (WPA) grant, Hugman's vision became a reality.

Still, for some decades more, the River Walk remained just another pretty space. It was not until the 1968 HemisFair exposition drew record crowds to the rescued waterway that the city really began banking on its banks.

Austin

A vast territory that rejected foreign rule to become an independent nation, Texas has always played a starring role in the romance of the American West. So it's only fitting that Texas's capital should spring, full-blown, from the imagination of a man on a buffalo hunt.

A CAPITAL DILEMMA

The man was Mirabeau Buonaparte Lamar, who had earned a reputation for bravery in Texas's struggle for independence from Mexico. In 1838, Lamar was vice president of the 2-year-old Republic of Texas, and Sam Houston, the even more renowned hero of the Battle of San Jacinto, was president. Although they shared a strong will, the two men had very different ideas about the future of the republic. Houston tended to look eastward, toward union with the United States, while Lamar saw independence as the first step to establishing an empire that would stretch to the Pacific.

That year, an adventurer named Jacob Harrell set up a camp called Waterloo at the western edge of the frontier. Lying on the northern banks of Texas's Colorado River (not to be confused with the larger waterway up north), it was nestled against a series of gentle hills. Some 100 years earlier, the Franciscans had established a temporary mission here. In the 1820s, Stephen F. Austin, Texas's earliest and greatest land developer, had the area surveyed for the smaller of the two colonies he was to establish on Mexican territory.

1821	Mexico wins independence from Spain.	1861	Texas secedes from the Union.
1835	Siege of Béxar: first battle in San Antonio for Texas independence from Mexico.	1876	Fort Sam Houston established as new quartermaster depot.
		1877	The railroad arrives in San Antonio, precipitating new waves of immigration.
1836	The Alamo falls after 13-day siege by Mexican general Santa Anna; using "Remember the Alamo!" as a rallying cry, Sam Houston defeats Santa Anna at San Jacinto. Republic of Texas established.	1880s	King William, first residential suburb, begins to be developed by German immigrants.
		1939–40	Works Project Administration builds River Walk, based on plans drawn up in 1929 by architect Robert H. H. Hugman.
1845	Texas annexed to the United States.		

continues

But the place had otherwise seen few Anglos before Harrell arrived. The natural springs in the area had attracted various Indian tribes, including the Comanche, Lipan Apaches, and Tonkawas, but none settled there. Thus, it was to a rather pristine spot that, in the autumn of 1838, Harrell invited his friend Mirabeau Lamar to take part in a shooting expedition. The buffalo hunt proved extremely successful, and when Lamar gazed at the rolling, wooded land surrounding Waterloo, he thought it was an ideal place to settle.

In December of the same year, Lamar became president of the Republic. He ordered the congressional commission that had been charged with the task of selecting a site for a permanent capital to check out Waterloo. This news was not well received by the residents of Houston, who were hoping to keep their city as the republic's capital. They argued that Waterloo was a dangerous and inconvenient outpost unsuitable for being a capital. The commission was made up of those who wanted to push Texas's westward expansion, and thought that moving the capital to the west would help this endeavor, so it recommended Lamar's pet site.

In early 1839, Lamar's friend Edwin Waller was dispatched to lay out a new capital city to be named in honor of Stephen F. Austin—the only one in the United States besides Washington, D.C., designed to be an independent nation's capital. The first public lots went on sale on August 1, 1839, and by November of that year, Austin was ready to host its first session of Congress.

Austin's position as capital was far from entrenched, however. Attacks from the republic by Mexico in 1842 gave Sam Houston, now president again, sufficient excuse to order the national archives to be relocated out of remote Austin. Resistant Austinites greeted the 26 armed men who came to repossess the historic papers with a cannon. After a struggle, the men returned empty-handed, and Houston abandoned his plan, thus ceding to Austin the victory in what came to be called the Archive War.

Although Austin won this skirmish, it was losing a larger battle for existence. President Houston refused to convene the Congress in Austin. By 1843, Austin's population had dropped down to 200 and its buildings lay in disrepair. Help came in the person of Anson Jones, who succeeded to the presidency in 1844. The constitutional

1968 HemisFair exposition—River Walk extension, Convention Center, Mansión del Río, and Hilton Palacio del Río completed for the occasion, along with Tower of the Americas and other fair structures.	1998 Opening of the Nelson A. Rockefeller Center for Latin American Art, a three-story, $11-million addition to the San Antonio Museum of Art; reopening of the Empire Theatre.
1988 Rivercenter Mall opens.	1999 San Antonio Spurs outgrow the Alamodome; funding approved for the new SBC Center. Spurs win the NBA championship.
1989 Premier of the newly refurbished Majestic Theatre.	
1993 Alamodome, huge new sports complex, completed.	2001 Completion of Convention Center expansion.
1995 Southbank and Presidio complexes open on the river.	2002 Opening of SBC Center, new home to the Spurs, the rodeo, and more; now called AT&T center.

convention he called in 1845 not only approved Texas's annexation to the United States, but also named Austin the capital until 1850, when voters of what was now the state of Texas would choose their governmental seat for the next 20 years. In 1850, Austin campaigned hard for the position and won by a landslide.

A CAPITAL SOLUTION

Austin thrived under the protection of the U.S. Army. The first permanent buildings to go up during the 1850s construction boom following statehood included an impressive limestone capitol, which no long exists. But two of the buildings in its complex, the General Land Office and the Governor's Mansion, are still standing today.

The boom was short-lived, however. Although Austin's Travis County voted against secession, Texas decided to join the Confederacy in 1861. By 1865, Union army units—including one led by General George Armstrong Custer—were sent to restore order in a defeated and looted Austin.

But once again Austin rebounded. With the arrival of the railroad in 1871, the city's recovery was secured. The following year Austin won election as state capital.

Still, there were more battles for status to be fought. Back in 1839, the Republic of Texas had declared its intention to build a "university of the first class," and in 1876, a new state constitution mandated its establishment. Through yet another bout of heavy electioneering, Austin won the right to establish the flagship of Texas's higher educational system on its soil. In 1883, the classrooms not yet completed, the first 221 members of what is now a student body of more than 50,000 met the eight instructors of the University of Texas.

The university wasn't the only Austin institution without permanent quarters that year. The old limestone capitol had burned in 1881, and a new, much larger home for the legislature was being built. In 1888, after a series of mishaps, the current capitol was completed. The grand red-granite edifice towering above the city symbolized Austin's arrival.

2003	Spurs win the NBA championship.
2005	Spurs win the NBA championship again.
2006	Large Toyota plant opens. First pickup truck rolls off the line.
2008	AT&T moves corporate headquarters from San Antonio to Dallas.
2010	San Antonio's City Council approves smoking ban.

DAMS, OIL & MICROCHIPS

The new capitol notwithstanding, the city was once again in a slump. Although some believed that quality of life would be sacrificed to growth—a view still widely held today—most townspeople embraced the idea of harnessing the fast-flowing waters of the Colorado River as the solution to Austin's economic woes. A dam, they thought, would not only provide a cheap source of electricity for residents, but also supply power for irrigation and new factories. Dedicated in 1893, the Austin Dam did indeed fulfill these goals—but only temporarily. The energy source proved to be limited, and when torrential rains pelted the city in April 1900, Austin's dreams came crashing down with its dam.

Another dam, attempted in 1915, was never finished. It wasn't until the late 1930s that a permanent solution to the water power problem was found. The successful plea to President Roosevelt for federal funds on the part of young Lyndon Johnson, the newly elected representative from Austin's 10th Congressional District, was crucial to the construction of six dams along the lower Colorado River. These dams not only afforded Austin and central Texas all the hydroelectric power and drinking water they needed, but also created the seven Highland Lakes—aesthetically appealing and a great source of recreational revenue.

Still, Austin might have remained a backwater capital seat abutting a beautiful lake had it not been for the discovery of oil on University of Texas (UT) land in 1923. The huge amounts of money that subsequently flowed into the Permanent University Fund—worth some $4 billion today—enabled Austin's campus to become truly first class. While most of the country was cutting back during the Depression, UT went on a building binge and began hiring a faculty as impressive as the new halls in which they were to hold forth.

The indirect effects of the oil bonus reached far beyond College Hill. In 1955, UT scientists and engineers founded Tracor, the first of Austin's more than 250 high-tech companies. Lured by the city's natural attractions and its access to a growing bank of young brainpower, many outside companies soon arrived: IBM (1967), Texas Instruments (1968), and Motorola's Semiconductor Products Section (1974). In the 1980s,

AUSTIN: DATELINE

1730 Franciscans build a mission at Barton Springs, but abandon it within a year.

1836 Texas wins independence from Mexico; Republic of Texas established.

1838 Jacob Harrell sets up camp on the Colorado River, calling the settlement Waterloo; Mirabeau B. Lamar succeeds Sam Houston as president of Texas.

1839 Congressional commission recommends Waterloo as site for new capital of the republic.

Waterloo's name changes to Austin.

1842 Sam Houston succeeds Lamar as president, reestablishes Houston as Texas's capital, and orders nation's archives moved there. Austinites resist.

1844 Anson Jones succeeds Houston as president and returns capital to Austin.

1845 Constitutional convention in Austin approves annexation of Texas by the United States.

two huge computer consortiums, MCC and SEMATECH, opted to make Austin their home. And wunderkind Michael Dell, who started out selling computers from his dorm room at UT in 1984 and is now the CEO of the hugely successful Austin-based Dell Computer Corporation, spawned a new breed of local "Dellionaires" by rewarding his employees with company stock.

Willie Nelson's return to Austin from Nashville in 1972 didn't have quite as profound an effect on the economy, but it certainly had one on the city's live-music scene. Hippies and country-and-western fans could now find common ground at the many clubs that began to sprout up along downtown's Sixth Street, which had largely been abandoned. These music venues, combined with the construction that followed in the wake of the city's high-tech success, helped spur a general downtown resurgence.

SAN ANTONIO & AUSTIN IN POP CULTURE

San Antonio

For a quick and easy look at what Texas is all about, try *All Hat & No Cattle,* a collection of somewhat irreverent observations on Texas fashions, cuisine, music, animals, and the like by humorist Anne Dingus. Before Frederick Law Olmsted became a landscape architect—New York's Central Park is among his famous creations—he was a successful journalist, and his 1853 *A Journey Through Texas* includes a delightful

1850s Austin undergoes a building boom; construction of the capitol (1853), Governor's Mansion (1856), and General Land Office (1857).

1861 Texas votes to secede from the Union (Travis County, which includes Austin, votes against secession).

1865 General Custer is among those who come to restore order in Austin during Reconstruction.

1871 First rail line to Austin completed.

1883 University of Texas opens.

1923 Santa Rita No. 1, an oil well on University of Texas land, strikes a gusher.

1937 Lyndon Johnson elected U.S. representative from 10th Congressional District, which includes Austin.

Late 1930–early 1950s Six dams built on the Colorado River by the Lower Colorado River Authority, resulting in formation of the Highland Lakes chain.

1960s High-tech firms, including IBM, move to Austin.

continues

section on his impressions of early San Antonio. William Sidney Porter, better known as O. Henry, had a newspaper office in San Antonio for a while. Two collections of his short stories, *Texas Stories* and *Time to Write*, include a number of pieces set in the city, among them "A Fog in Santone," "The Higher Abdication," "Hygeia at the Solito," "Seats of the Haughty," and "The Missing Chord."

O. Henry wasn't very successful at promoting his newspaper *Rolling Stone* (no, not *that* one) in San Antonio during the 1890s, but there's a lively literary scene in town today. Resident writers include Sandra Cisneros, whose powerful, critically acclaimed short stories in *Women Hollering Creek* are often set in the city; and mystery writer Jay Brandon, whose excellent *Loose Among the Lambs* kept San Antonians busy trying to guess the identities of the local figures they (erroneously) thought had been fictionalized therein. Rick Riordan, whose hard-boiled detective novels *Tequila Red* and *Southtown* take place in an appropriately seamy San Antonio, is also a resident.

Two Austin writers use San Antonio settings: Novelist Sarah Bird's humorous *The Mommy Club* pokes fun at the yuppies of the King William district, while Stephen Harrigan's *The Gates of the Alamo* is a gripping, fictionalized version of Texas's most famous battle.

Austin

The foibles of the Texas "lege"—along with those of Congress and the rest of Washington—are hilariously pilloried by Molly Ivins, who, until she died in 2007, was Austin's resident scourge. Her syndicated newspaper columns have been published in two collections: *Molly Ivins Can't Say That, Can She?* and *Nothin' But Good Times Ahead*. George W. Bush was a more recent target in Ivins's *Shrub: The Short but Happy Political Life of George W. Bush*. Austinite Lou Dubose and Jan Reid give more insight into the inner workings of Texas (and national) politics with *The Hammer: Tom DeLay, God, Money, and the Rise of the Republican Congress*. Serious history buffs might want to dip into Robert Caro's excellent multivolume biography of Lyndon B. Johnson, the consummate Texas politician, who had a profound effect on the Austin area.

1972	Willie Nelson moves back to Texas from Nashville; helps spur live-music scene on Sixth Street.
1976	PBS's *Austin City Limits* airs for the first time.
1980s	Booming real-estate market goes bust, but South by Southwest (S×SW) Music Festival debuts (1987).
1993	S×SW adds interactive (tech) and film components to its festival.
1995	Capitol, including new annex, reopens after massive refurbishing.
1997	Completion of the refurbishing of the capitol's grounds and of the Texas State Cemetery.
1999	Opening of Austin-Bergstrom International Airport.
2000	The Driskill revamp completed, and the Stephen F. Austin Hotel reopens.
2001	The Bob Bullock Texas State History Museum opens.
2002	The tech recession hits, but Austin's still partying like it's 2000, as the Austin City Limits Music Festival debuts.

For background into the city's unique music scene, try Jan Reid's *The Improbable Rise of Redneck Rock.* Barry Shank's *Dissonant Identities: The Rock 'n' Roll Scene in Austin, Texas,* does a more scholarly take on the same topic.

William Sydney Porter, better known as O. Henry, published a satirical newspaper in Austin in the late 19th century. Among the many short tales he wrote about the area—collected in *O. Henry's Texas Stories*—are four inspired by his stint as a draftsman in the General Land Office. Set largely in Austin, Billy Lee Brammer's *The Gay Place* is a fictional portrait of a political figure loosely based on LBJ.

Sarah Bird has published a recent novel that pokes light fun at what passes for society in Austin. It's called *How Perfect is That.* She uses her insider knowledge and a novelist's eye to explore the values and contradictions of Austin's Terrytown set. In his newest novel, *Next,* author James Hynes looks at Austin through the eyes of a visitor from Ann Arbor, and finds that the local scene offers often absurd and ironic material.

The city's most famous resident scribe, the late James Michener, placed his historical epic *Texas* in the frame of a governor's task force operating out of Austin. The city is also the locus of several of Austin resident Mary Willis Walker's mysteries, including *Zero at the Bone* and *All the Dead Lie Down;* it is also the setting for *The Boyfriend School,* a humorous novel by San Antonian Sarah Bird. Shelby Hearon, who attended the University of Texas, lovingly and humorously contrasts old and new Austin in *Ella in Bloom.* Her novel *Armadillo in the Grass* is also set in Austin.

It's only logical that the king of cyberpunk writers, Bruce Sterling, should live in Austin; he gets megabytes of fan mail each week for such books as *Islands in the Net, The Difference Engine* (with William Gibson), and *Holy Fire.* His nonfiction work, *The Hacker Crackdown,* details a failed antihacker raid in Austin. His latest, *Tomorrow Now: Envisioning the Next 50 Years,* moves him from cyberpunk to prognostication. For a unique take on Austin, check out *The Great Psychedelic Armadillo Picnic: A "Walk" in Austin,* a travel guide and music history of the city where the writer grew up, by Kinky Friedman—a mystery writer, musician (his most famous band was Kinky Friedman and the Texas Jewboys), aspiring politician (he ran for governor of Texas in 2006), and all-around curmudgeon.

2003 Samsung announces major 3-year expansion.

2004 Debut of Austin's tallest building, the Frost Bank Tower, on Congress Avenue. *Austin City Limits* celebrates 30 years on-air as the longest running music program in American TV history.

2006 The new Blanton Museum of Art is inaugurated with a weekend-long celebration.

2008 Completion of Hwy. 130 bypass for Austin, intended to reduce the volume of traffic on I-35, the main transit route between the Mexico–U.S. border and central United States.

2010 A plan to bring Formula 1 racing to Austin is announced and gains credibility as the city council approves several changes to zoning and transportation necessary for the project to move forward.

EATING & DRINKING

Visitors to San Antonio, Austin, and the Hill Country will surely want to sample the local fare, especially some of the most famous dishes that the region is known for, such as its local style of barbecue, Tex-Mex food, chicken-fried steak, and even chili con carne. The common denominator here is beef; other ingredients and other meats may be involved in making these foods, but beef remains the spotlight attraction, as befits this region with so much ranching heritage.

Of course, the last dish mentioned—chili—has become popular from coast to coast and even beyond America's borders, thanks to the efforts of people like William Gebhardt, an early chili enthusiast from the town of New Braunfels. The chili that you'll find in central Texas isn't that much different from what is served up in other parts, so you shouldn't make any special effort to sample some. Although if you spend any time in the town of **New Braunfels** (see chapter 9), just for kicks, you might order a bowl of chili at the **Phoenix Saloon,** the original site of Gebhardt's grand project (and an excellent chili it is).

The rest of the dishes I mentioned haven't made it out of Texas without suffering significant alterations. So be sure to try some of these when you get a chance. San Antonio, of course, is at the center of the Tex-Mex universe. And it offers various renditions of Tex-Mex tacos, beef and cheese enchiladas with chili gravy, and the famous fajita. You could dine on Tex-Mex for your entire visit without having to stray outside of central San Antonio. Austin, too, has several good Tex-Mex joints, and you won't lack for options there.

But, Austin has a leg up over San Antonio in the matter of barbecue, both in variety and quality. The best places in town are discussed in the dining chapter for Austin, and if you read through the reviews, I'm pretty sure you'll find something that suits your personal tastes. But if you want to expand your horizons and try some of the most unforgettable barbecue found anywhere, you're going to have to leave the city and get out to one of the small towns that ring Austin and feature the old-time barbecue joints. Often, people who aren't accustomed to eating barbecue cooked using the dry method don't appreciate its virtues, but with time (and repeated sampling) many come to prefer this style to all others. (See chapter 16 for more info.)

Good chicken-fried steak can be found both in the city and the country. It's usually served smothered in cream gravy with mashed potatoes on the side. In both San Antonio and Austin you can find excellent interpretations. But in the Hill Country, it

---

 And the Beat Goes On . . .

Both Janis Joplin, who attended the University of Texas for a short time, and Stevie Ray Vaughan, enshrined in a statue overlooking Town Lake, got their starts in Austin clubs in the 1960s. During the 1970s, the area was a hotbed for "outlaw" country singers Willie Nelson, Waylon Jennings, and Jerry Jeff Walker. During the 1980s, there was a national surge of interest in local country-folk artists Lyle Lovett, Eric Taylor, Townes Van Zandt, Darden Smith, Robert Earl Keen, and Nanci Griffith. And the tradition continues with Austin's current musical residents, including Grammy Award winners Shawn Colvin and the Dixie Chicks, among others.

alone can establish a restaurant's reputation among the locals. You practically have to go out of your way not to try it in towns such as Bandera and Kerrville. And, for the visitor, it is a safe choice that is rarely a disappointment.

WHEN TO GO

Most tourists visit San Antonio and Austin in summer, though it's not the ideal season. The weather is hot, and restaurants and attractions tend to be crowded. That said, there are plenty of places to cool off around town, and hotel rates are slightly lower (conventioneers come in the fall, winter, and spring). Also consider that some of the most popular outdoor attractions, such as SeaWorld and Six Flags Fiesta Texas, either open only in summer or keep far longer hours in summer.

In fall and spring, temperatures are comfortable for exploring. If there's a large convention in **San Antonio,** downtown hotels will have high occupancy rates and, consequently, higher prices. *Tip:* If you have some flexibility, check hotel rates for different weeks or go online to the San Antonio CVB website (www.visitsanantonio. com) and click on "Meeting Professionals," then go to the calendar. By entering dates, you can see the meetings planned for that time period and just how many hotel rooms each meeting is projected to fill. Winter is a slow season for San Antonio hotels, and good deals can be had. December, in particular, is a great time to see San Antonio, if you don't mind running the risk of cold weather (see below). The River Walk is all lit up with lights, and piñatas can be seen everywhere.

San Antonio is the most popular in-state destination for Texans, many of whom come for the weekend. This, too, can raise room rates for hotels on the River Walk, but not necessarily for the pure business hotel, such as those that are downtown, but not on the river, and those just north of downtown, in the vicinity of the airport. Try these options on weekends for discount rates.

Try to avoid coming to **Austin** in March unless you're planning to come to the S×SW Music Festival. This is the busiest month of the year, and rooms are expensive and hard to come by. Summer season is typically busy, and legislative sessions (the first half of odd-numbered years) and University of Texas events (graduation, say, or home football games) can also fill up the town's lodgings.

Weather

From late May through September, expect regular high temperatures and often high humidity.

Fall and spring are prime times to visit; the days are pleasantly warm and, if you come in late March or early April, the wildflowers in the nearby Hill Country will be in glorious bloom. Temperate weather combined with the lively celebrations surrounding Christmas also make November and December good months to visit. Sometimes a "Norther" wind blows in, dropping daytime temperatures to between 40 and 50 degrees Fahrenheit (4°–10°C). January and February can be colder, but not necessarily—it's a matter of luck.

San Antonio/Austin Average Daytime Temperature (°F & °C) & Monthly Rainfall (Inches)

	JAN	FEB	MAR	APR	MAY	JUNE	JULY	AUG	SEPT	OCT	NOV	DEC
Avg. Temp. (°F)	51	55	62	70	76	82	85	85	80	71	60	53
Avg. Temp. (°C)	11	13	17	21	24	28	29	29	27	22	16	12
Rainfall (in.)	1.7	1.9	1.6	2.6	4.2	3.6	1.9	2.5	3.2	3.2	2.1	1.7

Holidays

Banks, government offices, post offices, and many stores, restaurants, and museums are closed on the following legal national holidays: January 1 (New Year's Day), the third Monday in January (Martin Luther King, Jr., Day), the third Monday in February (Presidents' Day), the last Monday in May (Memorial Day), July 4 (Independence Day), the first Monday in September (Labor Day), the second Monday in October (Columbus Day), November 11 (Veterans Day/Armistice Day), the fourth Thursday in November (Thanksgiving Day), and December 25 (Christmas). The Tuesday after the first Monday in November is Election Day, a federal government holiday in presidential-election years (held every 4 years, and next in 2012).

San Antonio Calendar of Events

Please note that the information contained below is always subject to change. For the most up-to-date information on these events, call the number provided, or check with the **Convention and Visitors Bureau** (✆ **800/447-3372,** ext. 4; www.sanantoniovisit.com).

For an exhaustive list of events beyond those listed here, check http://events.frommers.com, where you'll find a searchable, up-to-the-minute roster of what's happening in cities all over the world.

JANUARY

Michelob ULTRA Riverwalk Mud Festival, River Walk. Every year, when the horseshoe bend of the San Antonio River Walk is drained for maintenance purposes, San Antonians cheer themselves up by electing a king and queen to reign over such events as Mud Stunts Day and the Mud Pie Ball (✆ 210/227-4262; www.thesanantonioriverwalk.com). Mid-January.

FEBRUARY

Stock Show and Rodeo, AT&T Center. In early February, San Antonio hosts more than 2 weeks of rodeo events, livestock judging, country-and-western bands, and carnivals. It's been going (and growing) since 1949 (✆ 210/225-5851; www.sarodeo.com). Early February.

San Antonio CineFestival, Guadalupe Cultural Arts Center. The nation's oldest and largest Chicano/Latino film festival screens more than 70 films and videos (✆ 210/271-3151; www.guadalupeculturalarts.org). Mid-to late February.

MARCH

Dyeing O' the River Green Parade. Are leprechauns responsible for turning the San Antonio River into the green River Shannon? Irish dance and music fill the Arneson River Theatre from the afternoon on (✆ 210/227-4262; www.thesanantonioriverwalk.com). St. Patrick's Day weekend.

APRIL

Starving Artist Show, River Walk and La Villita. Part of the proceeds from the works, sold by nearly 900 local artists, goes to benefit the Little Church of La Villita's program to feed the hungry (✆ 210/226-3593; www.lavillita.com). First weekend of the month.

Fiesta San Antonio. What started as a modest marking of Texas's independence in 1891 is now a huge event, with an elaborately costumed royal court presiding for 9 or 10 days of revelry: parades, balls, food-fests, sporting events, concerts, and art shows all over town. Call ✆ 877/723-4378 or 210/227-5191 for details on tickets and events, or log on to www.fiesta-sa.org. Late April (always includes Apr 21, San Jacinto Day).

MAY

Tejano Conjunto Festival, Rosedale Park and Guadalupe Theater. This annual festival, sponsored by the Guadalupe Cultural Arts Center, celebrates the lively and unique blend of Mexican and German music born in south Texas. The best conjunto musicians perform at the largest event of its kind in the world. Call

© **210/271-3151** for schedules and ticket information, or check the website, www.guadalupeculturalarts.org. Early May.

Return of the Chili Queens, Market Square. An annual tribute to chili, which originated in San Antonio, with music, dancing, crafts demonstrations, and (of course) chili aplenty. Bring the Tums. (© **210/207-8600;** jessemo@sanantonio.gov). Memorial Day weekend.

JUNE

Texas Folklife Festival, Institute of Texas Cultures. Ethnic foods, dances, crafts demonstrations, and games celebrate the diversity of Texas's heritage (© **210/458-2224;** www.texancultures.utsa.edu). Four days in early June.

Juneteenth, various venues. The anniversary of the announcement of the Emancipation Proclamation in Texas in 1865 is the occasion for a series of African-American celebrations, including an outdoor jazz concert, gospelfest, parade, picnic, and more. Call the San Antonio Convention and Visitors Bureau for details at © **800/447-3372.** June 19.

JULY

Contemporary Art Month, various venues. More than 400 exhibitions at more than 50 venues make this month a contemporary art lover's heaven (especially inside the air-conditioned galleries). To find out what's showing where, call © **210/212-7082** or log on to www.camsanantonio.org.

SEPTEMBER

Diez y Seis, various venues. Mexican independence from Spain is feted at several different downtown venues, including La Villita, the Arneson River Theatre, and Guadalupe Plaza. Music and dance, a parade, and a *charreada* (rodeo) are part of the fun (© **210/223-3151;** www.agatx.org). Weekend nearest September 16.

Jazz'SAlive, Travis Park. Bands from New Orleans and San Antonio come together for a weekend of hot jazz (© **210/212-8423;** www.saparksfoundation.org). Third weekend in September.

OCTOBER

Oktoberfest, Beethoven Halle and Garten. San Antonio's German roots show at this festival with food, dance, oompah bands, and beer (© **210/222-1521;** www.beethovenmaennerchor.com/oktoberfest.htm). Early October.

International Accordion Festival, La Villita. Inaugurated in 2001, this squeezebox fest was such a success that it became an annual event. More than a dozen ensembles play music from around the globe, from Cajun, merengue, zydeco, and conjunto to klezmer, Basque, and Irish music. There are also dancing and workshops for all ages (© **210/865-8578;** www.international accordionfestival.org). Mid-October.

NOVEMBER

New World Wine and Food Festival, various venues. Celebrity chefs from around Texas help celebrate San Antonio's culinary roots with everything from tequila tastings and chocolate seminars to cooking classes. It's a taste treat, and it's all for charity (© **210/930-3232;** www.newworldwine food.org). First weekend in November.

Ford Holiday River Parade and Lighting Ceremony. Trees and bridges along the river are illuminated by some 122,000 lights. Celebrities, duded-up locals, and lots of bands participate in this floating river parade, which kicks off the Paseo del Rio Holiday Festival (© **210/227-4262;** www.thesanantonioriverwalk.com). Friday following Thanksgiving.

DECEMBER

Fiestas Navideñas, Market Square. The Mexican market hosts piñata parties, a blessing of the animals, and surprise visits from Pancho Claus (© **210/207-8600;** www.sanantonio.gov/sapar). First 3 weekends in December.

La Gran Posada, Milam Park to San Fernando Cathedral. Dating back to the 1800s, when it was staged in the same area, this candlelit procession reenacts Mary and Joseph's search for shelter in a moving rendition of the Christmas story (© **210/227-1297;** www.sanantonio.gov/sapar). Third Sunday in December.

The Fiesta City

San Antonio's nickname refers to its huge April bash, but it also touches on the city's tendency to party at the drop of a sombrero. It's only natural that a place with strong Southern, Western, and Hispanic roots would know how to have a good time. Elaborately costumed festival queens, wild-and-woolly rodeos, and parades and mariachis are rolled out year-round.

Austin Calendar of Events

Many of Austin's festivals capitalize on the city's large community of local musicians and/or on the great outdoors. The major annual events are listed here. See also chapter 15 for information on the various free concerts and other cultural events held every summer. Additional local events may also be found by logging on to www.austintexas.org, www.austin360.com, and www.auschron.com.

For an exhaustive list of events beyond those listed here, check http://events.frommers.com, where you'll find a searchable, up-to-the-minute roster of what's happening in cities all over the world.

JANUARY

Red Eye Regatta, Austin Yacht Club, Lake Travis. The bracing lake air at this keelboat race should help cure what ails you from the night before (✆ 512/266-1336; www.austinyachtclub.net). New Year's Day.

FEBRUARY

Carnival Brasileiro, Palmer Events Center. Conga lines, elaborate costumes, samba bands, and confetti are all part of this sizzling Carnavale-style event, started in 1975 by homesick Brazilian students at the University of Texas (✆ 512/452-6832; www.sambaparty.com). First or second Saturday of February.

MARCH

Kite Festival, Zilker Park. Colorful handmade kites fill the sky during this popular annual contest, one of the oldest of its kind in the country (✆ 512/647-7488; www.zilkerkitefestival.com). First Sunday in March.

South by Southwest (S×SW) Music and Media Conference & Festival, various venues. The Austin Music Awards kick off this huge conference, which organizes hundreds of concerts at more than two dozen city venues. Aspiring music-industry and high-tech professionals sign up months in advance (✆ 512/467-7979; www.sxsw.com). Usually around third week in March (during University of Texas's spring break).

Star of Texas Fair and Rodeo, Travis County Exposition Center. This 2-week Wild West extravaganza features rodeos, cattle auctions, a youth fair, a parade down Congress Avenue, and lots of live country music (✆ 512/919-3000; www.staroftexas.org). Mid- to late March.

Jerry Jeff Walker's Birthday Weekend, various locations. Each year, singer/songwriter Walker performs at such venues as the Broken Spoke and the Paramount Theatre; proceeds of related events—perhaps a silent auction or golf tournament—benefit a foundation to establish a music school for at-risk youth. It's a good cause—and the man knows how to throw a party (✆ 512/477-0036; www.jerryjeff.com). Late March, early April.

Statesman Capitol 10,000, downtown. Texas's largest 10K race winds its way from the state capitol through West Austin, ending up at Town Lake (✆ 512/445-3598; www.statesman.com/cap10k). Late March, early April.

Austin Fine Arts Festival, Republic Square. The major fundraiser for the Austin Museum of Art, this show features a large juried art show, local musicians, and lots of kids' activities (✆ 512/458-6073; www.austin fineartsfestival.org). First weekend in April.

Saveur Texas Hill Country Wine and Food Festival, most events at the Four Seasons Hotel. Book a month in advance for the cooking demonstrations, beer, wine, and food tasting, and celebrity chef dinners. For the food fair, just turn up with an appetite (✆ 512/542-WINE [9463]; www.texas wineandfood.org). Third or fourth weekend in April.

Old Settlers Music Festival, Salt Lick BBQ Pavilion. More than two dozen bluegrass bands descend on nearby Driftwood to take part in this Americana roots music fest, which also includes songwriter workshops, arts and crafts booths, and children's entertainment (✆ 512/346-0999, ext. 3; www.oldsettlersmusicfest.org). Mid-to late April.

MAY

Old Pecan Street Spring Arts and Crafts Festival, Sixth Street. Eat and shop your way along Austin's restored Victorian main street while bands play in the background (✆ 512/441-9015; www.roadstar productions.com). First weekend in May.

Cinco de Mayo Music Festival, Fiesta Gardens and other locations. Norteño, Tejano, and other rousing music, as well as food, arts and crafts, and competitions—for example, a jalapeño-eating contest—are all part of this 4-day family-friendly event to celebrate Latin American culture (✆ 512/867-1999; www.austin-cincodemayo.com). Around May 5.

O. Henry Museum Pun-Off, O. Henry Museum. One of the "punniest" events around, this annual battle of the wits is for a wordy cause—the upkeep of the O. Henry Museum (✆ 512/472-1903; www.punpun pun.com). Mid-May.

JUNE

Republic of Texas Biker Rally, Sixth Street and Congress. The city fills with the sound of rolling thunder as hordes of bikers descend on Austin for a weekend of partying. The rally provides an opportunity for enthusiasts to show off their rides. Famous custom bike makers from around the country bring their newest creations to be put on display and admired. Sixth Street becomes a giant parking lot of choppers and hogs, each one fancier than the next (www.rotrally.com). Usually the second weekend of the month.

Juneteenth, various venues, mostly in East Austin. The celebration of African-American emancipation, which became a Texas state holiday in 1980, generally includes a parade, gospel singing, and many children's events. The best source of information is the George Washington Carver Museum and Cultural Center (✆ 512/472-4809; www.ci.austin.tx.us/carver). June 19.

JULY

Austin Symphony Orchestra, Auditorium Shores. Cannons, fireworks, and of course a rousing rendition of the "1812 Overture" contribute to the fun at this noisy freedom celebration (✆ 888/4-MAESTRO [888/4-6237876] or 512/476-6064; www.austin symphony.org). July 4th.

AUGUST

Austin Chronicle **Hot Sauce Festival,** Waterloo Park. The largest hot-sauce contest in the world features more than 300 salsa entries, judged by celebrity chefs and food editors. The bands that play this super party are *muy caliente,* too (✆ 512/454-5766; www.austinchronicle.com). Last Sunday in August.

SEPTEMBER

Fall Jazz Festival, Zilker Hillside Theater. Zilker Park swings with 2 days of free concerts by top local jazz acts (✆ 512/442-2263). Second weekend of September.

Diez y Seis, Plaza Saltillo and other sites. Mariachis and folk dancers, conjunto and Tejano music, as well as fajitas, piñatas, and clowns, help celebrate Mexico's independence from Spain. The highlight is the crowning of the Fiestas Patrias Queen (✆ 512/974-2264 for Plaza Saltillo events or 476-7502 for other events). Four days, usually starting around September 16.

Austin City Limits Music Festival, Zilker Park. Yet more evidence of Austin's devotion to live music, this 3-day music extravaganza kicked off in 2002 and has grown exponentially every year since. Expect a superb lineup of musical talent (✆ **866/GO-AUSTIN** [462-8784]; www.aclfestival.com). Late September.

OCTOBER

Austin Film Festival, Paramount Theatre and other venues. If you like the idea of sitting in the dark and watching 80 films in 8 days—everything from restored classics to new indie releases—or are an aspiring screenwriter or filmmaker, this one's for you (✆ **800/310-FEST** [3378] or 512/478-4795; www.austinfilmfestival.com). Eight days in mid-October.

Texas Book Festival, State Capitol. One of the largest literary events in the Southwest, this 2-day fundraiser for Texas public libraries draws literati from all over the U.S., though Texas authors rule the roost (✆ **512/477-4055;** www.texasbookfestival.org). Late October.

Halloween, Sixth Street. Nearly 100,000 costumed revelers take over 7 blocks of historic Sixth Street (✆ **866/GO-AUSTIN** [462-8784]). October 31.

NOVEMBER

Chuy's Christmas Parade, Congress Avenue. With giant balloons, marching bands, floats, and gifts for needy kids, what better way is there to ring in the season (✆ **888/439-2489;** www.chuysparade.com)? Saturday after Thanksgiving.

DECEMBER

Zilker Park Tree Lighting. The lighting of a magnificent 165-foot tree is followed by the Trail of Lights, a mile-long display of life-size holiday scenes. This being Austin, a 5K run is also involved (✆ **512/974-6700;** www.cityofaustin.org/tol). First Sunday of the month (tree lighting); second Sunday through December 23 (Trail of Lights).

Armadillo Christmas Bazaar, Austin Music Hall. Revel in Tex-Mex food, live music, and a full bar at this high-quality art, craft, and gift show (✆ **512/447-1605;** www.armadillobazaar.com). Begins approximately 2 weeks before Christmas.

LAY OF THE LAND

San Antonio and Austin lie on the boundary between two distinct geographical regions of Texas: the coastal prairies and the Hill Country. The coastal prairies extend from the Gulf Coast all the way into Central Texas. They are mostly flat, with gentle undulations as they stretch inland. In the descriptions of early settlers, this prairie land was metaphorically described as a sea of grass, for its vastness, uniformity, and lack of natural features. When the wind would blow, the metaphor was even more striking, as the tall grass would bend to and fro in waves that rolled across the landscape.

The Hill Country is situated on a large limestone shelf that has been pushed up over 1,000 feet by volcanic uplifting. The entire raised area is known as the Edwards Plateau. And it is the eastern side of this plateau that is labeled the Texas Hill Country, where the warping of the earth's crust produced the hilly terrain.

The boundary between the coastal prairie and Hill Country is the Balcones Fault, which crosses central Texas in a diagonal line from southwest to northeast, roughly paralleling the interstate highway I-35. In this fault zone the limestone shelf is fractured, and the water pouring off the plateau on its way to the Gulf seeps into the fissures and returns to the surface in the form of natural springs, which are abundant in this region. Water coursing through the limestone has also carved out caverns and formed stalactites and other mineral formations. Most of these caverns are not far from the interstate highway, and can make for enjoyable breaks from driving.

The higher altitude of the Hill Country makes for slightly milder, less humid summer weather. Whereas San Antonio and Austin are roughly 600 feet above sea level, Kerrville and Fredericksburg, the two largest towns of the Hill Country, are at an altitude of more than 1,700 feet The soil is generally thin and more appropriate for ranching than farming, but certain areas, especially the land around the German farming community of Fredericksburg, are rich enough to sustain intensive agriculture. Indeed, Fredericksburg peaches, harvested from May to July, are famous in Texas for their quality. But the real agricultural boom these days is in grapes for wine-making. Several vineyards are now well established in the Hill Country, and their number increases annually.

RESPONSIBLE TRAVEL

Both San Antonio and Austin are Sunbelt cities organized around the personal automobile. But this doesn't mean that using a rental car is necessarily the best way to explore them. Most of their attractions are located at their cores, which can be explored on foot or by bus. San Antonio's downtown is so attractive and enjoyable it invites walking—and having a car is, in fact, a liability, not an advantage. And when you need to go slightly farther out, to the Southtown or Monte Vista areas, you can take one of the three trolley bus lines which are color-coded, easy to use, and cost efficient ($1.10). At the visitor center you can pick up a pamphlet with the routes.

Austin's downtown is not quite as attractive as San Antonio's, but it is just as walkable. And if you're not a big walker, any number of buses can get you around downtown and a bit farther south to the SoCo district, or north to the university campus. The city's new light rail line, as it is presently operated, doesn't offer much utility to visitors, but there are plans to build a light rail line between Austin's downtown and the airport. If this project gets approval, it won't be completed until 2015. At present, several buses in Austin Metro's fleet are powered by propane to reduce pollution, and a few more have hybrid power systems. Austin also has an advantage over San Antonio in that it is very bicycle friendly and growing more so each year. There are bike lanes on several downtown streets. From downtown, riders can cross Lady Bird Lake into South Austin very safely. The South First St. Bridge has separate lanes for bikes and pedestrians that are completely removed from car traffic, and next to the South Lamar Bridge is a bridge built solely for runners, walkers, and cyclists. Heading north from downtown, riders can use one of several bike lanes leading into the University of Texas campus. From there, bike lanes lead in all directions, blanketing central Austin.

Austin prides itself on being a green city. In electrical use and generation, Austin leads the country with its conservation programs and investment in wind energy. Austin Energy, the municipal utility company, has won recognition for its work from the utility industry associations and the Department of Energy. The city is generally ranked among America's greenest cities by several organizations, including the Green Guide and *Popular Science,* who include several energy-usage factors in making their determination.

Though San Antonio isn't at quite the same level of greenness as Austin, it excels in one particular area—water conservation. This came about more through need than initiative, because San Antonio is dependent for its water on the Edwards Aquifer, a finite resource. To control its water usage, San Antonio has built the largest water recycling and distribution system in the nation. It has also put in place several programs to promote private efforts at water conservation.

TOURS

Tourism in San Antonio and Austin hasn't gotten to the point where companies are arranging packaged coach tours of the region, but some companies do offer special-interest tours for a day or half-day to sites in the Hill Country. **Gray Line Tours** (© **800/341-6000;** www.grayline.com) offers a daylong bus tour of the Hill Country from San Antonio and another through the same area focusing on Hill Country wineries.

Si Texas Tours (© **888/748-3927** or 840/460-4565; www.sitexastours.com), which operates out of the Hill Country town of Bandera, occasionally offers bus tours of the Hill Country, but usually serves as a charter service for groups.

From Austin, **Wine Tours of Texas** (© **877/693-0800** or 512/458-5466; www.winetoursoftexas.com) offers a variety of winery tours through the Texas Hill Country, either half-day or full-day trips. They can accommodate almost any size of group. **Texas Toast Culinary Tours** (www.texastoastculinarytours.com), based in Fort Worth, Texas, will occasionally offer tours to small-town barbecue joints in central Texas around Austin.

Historic Texas Tours (© **210/467-2534;** www.sanantoniofoodietours.com), based just outside of San Antonio, offers half-day food tours of the city.

SUGGESTED SAN ANTONIO ITINERARIES

The following itineraries are merely suggestions for how to see San Antonio if your time is limited. The first itinerary is structured for people with only 1 day. On this tour, you'll see all that makes San Antonio unique, and you'll leave town with an appreciation for what San Antonio is all about. People with more time can tack on the second day's activities. Unlike the first itinerary, this one requires a car, but the driving is easy. By adding on a third day, you can embellish your San Antonio experience with a taste of the Texas Hill Country.

If you're coming with kids (San Antonio is a big family destination), and you're considering one of the theme parks, allow a full day for it and get your money's worth. Most kids won't be able to handle any more excitement in a day than what these parks provide. If old enough, they may enjoy the first itinerary, and, should it be necessary, you can make some substitutions using some of the downtown entries in the "Especially for Kids" section of chapter 6.

But first, I should give a brief description of the different areas of San Antonio where the attractions are located. For information on moving through San Antonio, see the "Getting Around: San Antonio" section of chapter 18.

Neighborhoods in Brief

The older areas described here, from downtown through Alamo Heights, are all "in the Loop" (410). The Medical Center area in the Northwest lies just outside it, but the rest of the Northwest, as well as North Central and the West, is expanding beyond even Loop 1604.

Downtown The site of San Antonio's original Spanish settlements, this area includes the Alamo and other historic sites, along with the River Walk, the Alamodome, the convention center, the Rivercenter Mall, and many high-rise hotels, restaurants, and shops. It's also the center of commerce and government, so many banks and offices, as well as the county courthouse and City Hall buildings, are located here. Downtown is fun and vibrant. The River Walk is the centerpiece, but there's a lot more that can be seen and appreciated that takes a bit of exploring.

King William The city's first suburb, this historic district directly south of

San Antonio at a Glance

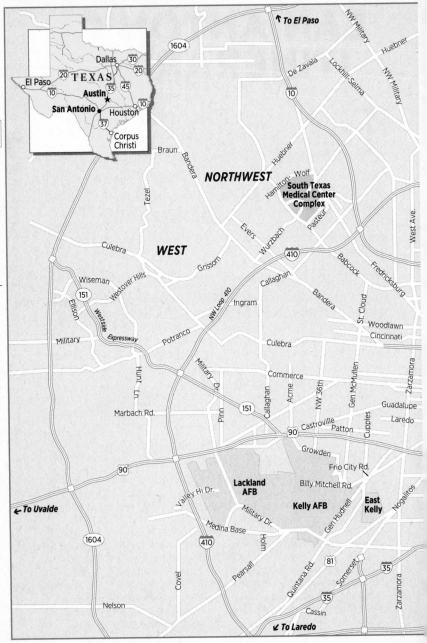

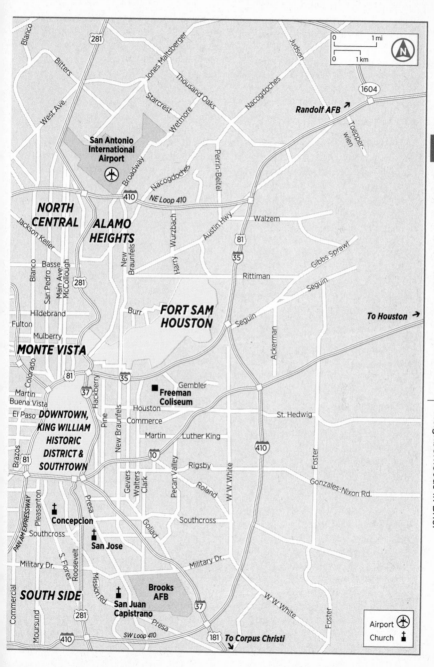

downtown was settled in the mid- to late 1800s by wealthy German merchants who built some of the most beautiful mansions in town. It started to decline in 1950s, but over the last few decades was saved. Only three of the area's many restored homes are open to the public, but a number have been turned into bed-and-breakfasts. As you might imagine, the location is ideal for those who want to explore the central city.

Southtown Southtown is the larger area that surrounds King William. It's a mixed residential/commercial area, which has become quite popular with artists and gallery owners over the last 15 years. You'll find a good mix of restaurants and galleries here, but few hotels worth staying in. If you're in San Antonio during the first Friday of the month, you can experience **Artwalk,** a street fair that takes over South Alamo Street.

South Side The old, largely Latin American southeast section of town that begins where Southtown ends (there's no agreed-upon boundary, but I'd say it lies a few blocks beyond the Blue Star Arts Complex) is home to four of the city's five historic missions. This is one of the many areas of the central part of the city where time seems to have stood still.

Monte Vista Area Immediately north of downtown, Monte Vista was established soon after King William by a conglomeration of wealthy cattlemen, politicos, and generals who moved "on to the hill" at the turn of the 20th century. A number of the area's large houses have been split into apartments for students of nearby Trinity University and San Antonio Community College, but many lovely old houses have been restored in the past 30 years. It hasn't reached King William status, but this is already a highly desirable (read: pricey) place to live. Monte Vista is close to the once thriving, but now less lively, restaurant and entertainment district along North St. Mary's Street between Josephine and Magnolia known locally as the **Strip.**

Fort Sam Houston Built in 1876 to the northeast of downtown, Fort Sam Houston boasts a number of stunning officers' homes. Much of the working-class neighborhood surrounding Fort Sam is now run-down, but renewed interest in restoring San Antonio's older areas is beginning to have some impact here, too.

Alamo Heights Area In the 1890s, when construction in the area began, Alamo Heights was at the far northern reaches of San Antonio. This is now home to San Antonio's well-heeled residents and holds most of the fashionable shops and restaurants. **Terrell Hills** to the east, **Olmos Park** to the west, and **Lincoln Heights** to the north are all offshoots of this area. The latter is home to the Quarry, once just that, but now a ritzy golf course and popular shopping mall. Shops and restaurants are concentrated along two main drags: Broadway and, to a lesser degree, New Braunfels. Most of these neighborhoods share a single zip code ending in the numbers "09"—thus the local term "09ers," referring to the area's affluent residents. The Witte Museum, San Antonio Botanical Gardens, and Brackenridge Park are all in this part of town.

Northwest The mostly characterless neighborhoods surrounding the South Texas Medical Center (a large grouping of health-care facilities referred to as the **Medical Center**) were built relatively recently. The area includes lots of condominiums and apartments, and much of the shopping and dining is in strip malls (the trendy, still-expanding Heubner Oaks retail center is an exception). The farther north you go, the nicer the housing complexes get. The high-end Westin La Cantera resort, the exclusive La Cantera and Dominion residential enclave, several tony golf courses, and the Shops at La Cantera, San Antonio's fanciest new retail center, mark the direction that development is taking in the far northwest part of town. It's becoming one of San Antonio's prime growth areas.

North Central San Antonio is inching toward Bulverde and other Hill Country towns via this major corridor of development clustered from Loop 410 north to Loop 1604, east of I-10 and west of I-35, and bisected by U.S. 281. The airport and many developed industrial strips line U.S. 281 in the southern section, but the farther north you go, the more you see the natural beauty of this area, hilly and dotted with small canyons. Recent city codes have motivated developers to retain trees and native plants in their residential communities.

West Although SeaWorld has been out here since the late 1980s, and the Hyatt Regency Hill Country Resort settled here in the early 1990s, other development was comparatively slow in coming. Now the West is booming with new midprice housing developments, strip malls, schools, and businesses. Road building hasn't kept pace with growth, however, so traffic can be a bear.

THE BEST OF SAN ANTONIO IN 1 DAY

This itinerary is a bit like the walking tour of downtown in chapter 6. The biggest differences between the two are that this one hits only the big attractions and leaves the Alamo for late afternoon (btw. 4:30 and 5pm) and the Tower of the Americas for later in the day when the sun is low and the view is at its best. Both tours were designed so that you'll avoid the crowds at the Alamo, which are largest during the midday hours. Also, this itinerary includes a stop at the IMAX that could not be put in any self-respecting "walking" tour, even though I feel it helps make for a more enjoyable experience at the Alamo. See which one works best for you. It's usually warm in San Antonio, so you may want to take a hat to protect yourself from the sun. Fortunately, downtown San Antonio is compact, and this itinerary isn't taxing. You can stroll along easily, even with kids in tow.

1 Market Square ★

If you haven't eaten breakfast, you can begin by having a bite at **Mi Tierra** (p. 74), a restaurant in the middle of Market Square that is very much a reflection of the local culture. The same can be said of this market area. It's a blend of Mexican and Texas styles and is enjoyable in the mornings, when it's semideserted. Facing Market Square is a large building, the modern and attractive **Museo Alameda** (p. 99), recognizable by its singular metal screen facade bordered by elaborate ironwork.

Walk 1½ blocks east on Commerce Street. On your right will be the:

2 Spanish Governor's Palace ★

Don't let the word "palace" lead you to expect something grandiose. It's a translation of *palacio*, which in Mexico means any building used as the seat of government. This was the house of the garrison's captain. It's a handsome building constructed of adobe and stone that dates from 1722. Look for the keystone above the entrance that bears the double-headed eagle—a symbol of Habsburg rule—as well as the date of 1749, when the first addition was added. The palace sits on the old Military Plaza, or Plaza de Armas, which was the center of town after Texas became independent. The famous chili queens would set up their stalls in this plaza until they were moved to Market Square in 1886. See p. 100.

Walk 2½ blocks east. You will come to the city's **Main Plaza** and the:

3 San Fernando Cathedral ★

The San Fernando Cathedral had humble beginnings as a parish church. It was commissioned as a simple stone church in 1738. The colonial society of the day

The Best of San Antonio in 1, 2 & 3 Days

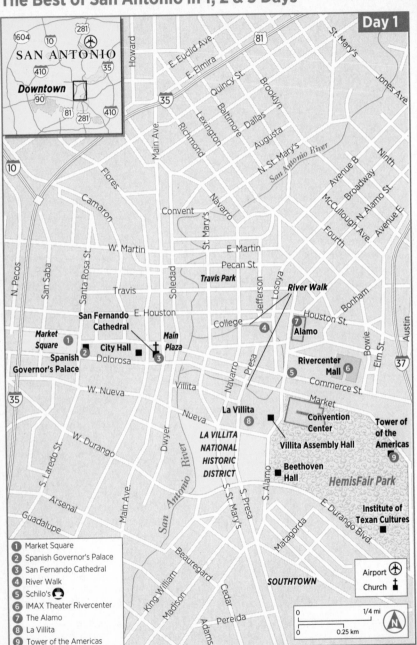

Day 1

SAN ANTONIO
Downtown

1 Market Square
2 Spanish Governor's Palace
3 San Fernando Cathedral
4 River Walk
5 Schilo's
6 IMAX Theater Rivercenter
7 The Alamo
8 La Villita
9 Tower of the Americas

Airport
Church

0   1/4 mi
0   0.25 km

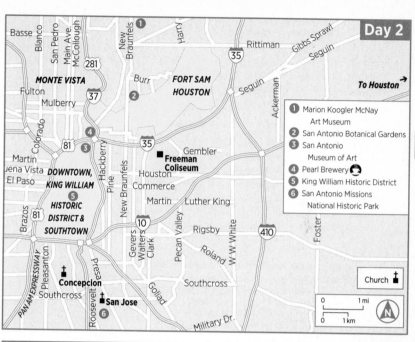

Day 2

1. Marion Koogler McNay Art Museum
2. San Antonio Botanical Gardens
3. San Antonio Museum of Art
4. Pearl Brewery
5. King William Historic District
6. San Antonio Missions National Historic Park

Church ✝

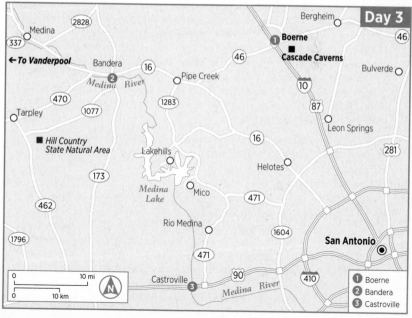

Day 3

1. Boerne
2. Bandera
3. Castroville

was divided into two principal classes: the Canary Islanders, who, having been born in the Old World, were above those of Spanish descent born in the New World, which included most of the garrison and their families. But the project of building a church united them, and in choosing the patron saints, they selected one from each continent—from Europe, Our Lady of Candlemas, and from the Americas, Our Lady of Guadalupe. What you see today mostly dates from the 1870s when the church was elevated to cathedral. Changes continue into the present century. Enter and have a look at the gilt altarpiece that was introduced only a few years ago. See p. 100.

Walk a couple of blocks farther east; you will come to the:

4 River Walk ★★★

The section you see was man-made and is the plainest part of the River Walk. Cross the bridge over the river and turn right. Follow the river and you'll soon find an access stairway leading down to the walkway that follows the original riverbank. Continue in the same direction and you'll come to the prettiest section of the River Walk, with tall cypress and palm trees, patches of flowers, ornamental bushes, and bridges crisscrossing the river this way and that. See p. 93.

5 Take a Break

Take a breather at this fun and fine old German restaurant, Schilo's, where Commerce Street crosses the river. You can fill up on one of their moderately priced sandwiches or a slice of the cheesecake. 424 E. Commerce. ℂ 210/223-6692. See p. 74.

Head 1 block west on Commerce Street to the Rivercenter Mall.

6 IMAX Theater Rivercenter ★

The main course of the Rivercenter Mall was built over a section of Blum Street, where the house of a famous desperado and scalp hunter named John Glanton, fictionalized in Cormack McCarthy's novel *Blood Meridian,* once stood. The IMAX theater has multiple showtimes (almost hourly) of a 45-minute documentary about the siege of the Alamo. This and the diorama in front of the ticket counter give you good context for what you're about to see at the Alamo. The movie schedule is subject to change, so call ahead for times and ticket reservations. Or buy your tickets at the theater and spend time exploring this pleasant mall while you wait. See p. 105.

When you exit the theater, turn right and walk down the main concourse to the door leading to Blum Street. Make another right at the corner. Walk a block and on your right you'll see:

7 The Alamo ★★

By midafternoon, the crowds will have thinned here. The church and long barrack are good examples of frontier colonial Spanish architecture, whose traits were to give shape to the region's architecture. The grounds are lovely and reflect the fact that San Antonio is on the cusp of four different ecological zones: Hill Country, Gulf coast plains, South Texas chaparral, and West Texas desert. Thus you'll find magnificent live oak trees, gnarled mesquites, fronded palms, and prickly cacti and ocotillo, all growing within the walls of the mission. In addition to the native species, here and there grow patches of flowering ornamentals to lend more color and please the eye. What today is Alamo Plaza was the original *atrio* of the church—a walled plaza for celebrating Mass when the celebrants numbered too many to fit into the church. It played a prominent part in the battle. See p. 87.

Head south on Alamo Street and in 4 blocks you'll see a group of buildings on your left. This is:

8 La Villita ★

In colonial society, even on the frontier, society's divisions shaped settlement patterns. While the Canary Islanders settled on the west side of the river, the families of the garrison soldiers settled on the east side in what is now La Villita. In the mid–19th century, La Villita became a popular residential area with the Europeans (Germans, Swiss, and French), giving the Spanish village some European flavor. Its well preserved architecture earned it its designation as a historical district. Though it has been a craft center since the 1930s, my favorite thing about it is the architecture. I like it best when the shops are closing and there's just enough bustle to give it a lived-in feeling. See p. 92.

Across Alamo Street, at about 2 blocks' distance, you'll see the needle that is a distinctive part of San Antonio's skyline.

9 Tower of the Americas ★

Built for the HemisFair world exposition of 1968, the Tower of the Americas is still the tallest building in San Antonio. The observation deck on top provides a grand view of the city in every direction, and the glass elevators provide the rush. See p. 101.

THE BEST OF SAN ANTONIO IN 2 DAYS

This trip makes use of the morning to see the best art museums while the mind and spirit are still fresh. The second half of the day takes the visitor to the residential King William District and then to the outlying missions that dot the Mission Trail. If, by this time of day, it's feeling more like *Mission Impossible,* you can abbreviate the trip by seeing only San José and Espada. Between museum stops, I've sandwiched a visit to the city's impressive botanical garden, where you can replenish your energies gazing on all varieties of foliage. **Note:** This trip is best done with a car.

1 Marion Koogler McNay Art Museum ★★★

I love the building, the landscaping, and the view, but also the collection. It holds works by many of the great artists of the late 19th and early 20th centuries, including Cézanne, Matisse, and O'Keeffe. See p. 94.

2 San Antonio Botanical Garden ★

Here you'll find wonderful gardens, a great variety of habitats, and plenty of literature about xeriscaping. The city of San Antonio faces serious water problems. It's the largest city in America to use an aquifer as its main water source. See p. 103.

3 San Antonio Museum of Art ★★

Housed in the old Lone Star Beer Brewery, the San Antonio Museum of Art is an excellent recycling of old structures to create a distinctive museum. Concentrate on the Rockefeller Center of Latin American Art, and if you still have energy left, follow your tastes. If you like Asian art, the museum's Brown Collection is rather good; if you prefer antiquities, there's a small but handsome collection of Egyptian and Greek pieces. See p. 94.

4 Take a Break

I like mixing up high culture and natural beauty with good food in relaxing surroundings. The old **Pearl Brewery,** 100 Pearl Pkwy., just off Broadway (www.pearlbrewery.com), which is only a few blocks from the museum, has become a gourmet center for San Antonio and home to a cooking school and some of the town's best restaurants. Take your pick of Mexican, Italian, seafood, or the Culinary Institute's cafe. See p. 79.

5 King William Historic District ★

After lunch, stretch your legs in this neighborhood, where there are about 25 blocks of houses. You can do a self-guided tour by picking up a booklet at the offices of the San Antonio Conservation Society, located at 107 King William St., or simply take in the views along King William Street, where you'll see the majority of the grandest houses. See p. 88.

6 San Antonio Missions National Historical Park ★★

These missions depict the story of an incredible human endeavor—Franciscan friars walking all the way from central Mexico (riding horseback or in carriages was forbidden by their vows of poverty) into the wilds of central Texas, hoping to build here a community of God, free from the corruptions then occurring in the heart of colonial Mexico. The trail starts with Concepción. The missions are within 2 or 3 miles of each other, never very far from the river. In each you will find a park station that provides tourist info and driving directions. Of the four, make sure to see San José, the most historical and architecturally interesting, and Espada, which is still the center of a local community. See p. 95.

THE BEST OF SAN ANTONIO IN 3 DAYS

Now that you've been cooped up in the city for 2 days, it's time to see a bit of the Hill Country. The driving distances in this loop north and west of San Antonio are quite comfortable, which is really saying something in Texas. You can easily see these three towns in a day, do a little strolling around, browse through some antiques stores, and even get in a horseback ride. I like this trip best in the fall and winter months and in the middle of the week, when traffic and crowds are light.

1 Boerne

Take I-10 northwest out of San Antonio. In 30 miles, you arrive at the town of Boerne (pronounced *bur*-nee), a German settlement known for its quaint buildings and antiques stores. It's a good place for walking around, talking to the locals, and enjoying the slow rhythm of life here. See p. 276.

Take Hwy. 46 west to Hwy. 16 west to the town of:

2 Bandera

Bandera is one of the main centers for cowboy culture in Texas, and it holds an important annual rodeo. It's also the dude ranch capital of Texas. But you don't have to stay the night to enjoy a horseback ride. See p. 283.

3 Castroville

South of Bandera is an oddity for the Texas Hill Country—an old Alsatian settlement from the 1840s. For the first few decades of its existence, it remained an isolated community, with residents not often venturing to neighboring towns. Even today, Alsatian speakers remain here. See p. 282.

4 Take a Break

You've probably already stopped for lunch in **Bandera,** but you might still want to pass by Haby's Alsatian Bakery to pick up some wonderful baked goods for the drive back to San Antonio. 207 U.S. 90 East, Castroville. ℂ **830/931-2118.** See p. 282.

3

SUGGESTED SAN ANTONIO ITINERARIES | The Best of San Antonio in 3 Days

WHERE TO STAY IN SAN ANTONIO

4

Most visitors to San Antonio want to stay downtown so that they can be close to the River Walk and many of the major attractions. Staying downtown is a lot of fun, and you will have all kinds of dining and entertainment options nearby. But if you prefer staying at B&Bs, or you're visiting San Antonio for the second or third time and want to change the way you experience the town, consider staying in the King William neighborhood or in Monte Vista. Both are interesting places in their own right, both are close to downtown, and both also have dining and entertainment options nearby. In addition, you get a feel for San Antonio—one you don't get by staying downtown.

If the main objective is a relaxing family vacation, then another option would be to stay at one of the resorts or hotels on the west/northwest side of San Antonio, near the two big theme parks: SeaWorld and Fiesta Texas. Then you can combine swimming, golfing, and shopping with spa treatments and the amusement parks and make the drive into San Antonio when you're up for a change of pace.

DOWNTOWN There are a lot of hotel rooms downtown because, well, it's a fun place to stay. It has variety, too. Besides the River Walk, you can explore distinctive areas, such as La Villita or the area surrounding Market Square, which have an entirely different feel from the rest of downtown—La Villita exhibits a more modest architecture. The houses are two-story buildings surfaced in unadorned limestone tiles. The streets are narrow and predominantly pedestrian. Market Square is somewhat similar, contrasting sharply with the exuberant skyscrapers that fill much of the rest of downtown. There are more street vendors than in the rest of downtown. And then there's the street scene, which features interesting facades, and curious examples of buildings being adapted to new uses. People are open and helpful, and the vibe is unintimidating. Much of the city's downtown was built when architects were still having fun and weren't shy about adding decoration. The architectural details, both outside and inside these old buildings, make exploring downtown highly enjoyable, day or night.

With so many hotel rooms, it's important to shop around. Rates float up and down depending upon occupancy, and occupancy is driven by

DEAL WELL, sleep well

In large hotels, room rates vary quite a bit based on occupancy, so don't automatically write off hotel choices because of their price category without doing a little checking on prices. The prices listed here are the hotel's "rack rates," the room rate charged without any discount, and you can almost always do better. The San Antonio Convention and Visitors Bureau's annual **SAVE (San Antonio Vacation Experience)** promotion features discounts on hotel rooms (more than 50 properties participate) as well as on dining and entertainment. Some bed-and-breakfasts and hotels offer better rates to those who book for at least 4 days, although a week is usually the minimum.

In addition, ask about any discounts you can think of—corporate, senior, military, Internet, AAA, entertainment/hotel coupon books, your Uncle Morty's high-school friendship with the manager—and about packages such as family, romance, or deals that include meals or sightseeing tours. *Bottom line: Always ask for the lowest-priced room with the most perks available.* Reservation agents are eager to sell rooms, so you shouldn't have a problem getting a good deal.

conventions and smaller corporate or professional gatherings. These have their quirks—convention people will tend to group in certain hotels, and many conferences are based at a particular property. So hotels do not fill up evenly, hence, you should do some checking at different properties, and, if you have flexibility, you should inquire about different dates. If you want to see the big picture, check out this website, where you can find what meetings are taking place during your travel dates: www.meetings.visitsanantonio.com/meeting-calendar. The high seasons for conventions in San Antonio are fall and spring.

And now a few words about the listing info: The rates included here are those that are prevalent for most of the year, before taxes (16.75%). They can go both higher and lower, again, depending on occupancy. By now, almost all large hotels are nonsmoking properties; when smoking rooms are available, I say so in the review. Parking fees are always per day. Pet fees and Wi-Fi fees are per visit, unless the listing specifies otherwise. Wi-Fi is free unless specified otherwise.

KING WILLIAM There's no doubt that this neighborhood and the larger Southtown area are happening places these days—more about the arts and leisure than business, this is a perfect choice for a couple of grown-ups wanting to spend a relaxing weekend, or longer if possible. And the monthly street fair on South Alamo (first Fridays) is quite popular with visitors. If you're going to stay in this part of town, you'll want to lodge in one of the grand old houses in King William. Downtown is only a 15-minute walk away, via the River Walk or along South Alamo Street, with its galleries and stores. As with B&Bs in the Monte Vista area, prices don't fluctuate as much as those at the large hotels. For a larger selection of properties, check out the website of the **San Antonio Bed & Breakfast Association:** www.sanantoniobb.org.

MONTE VISTA B&Bs in this neighborhood offer an especially good value. The houses are beautiful, the neighborhood is quiet, despite its central location, and there are some interesting neighborhoods on all sides. It's either a 30-minute walk or a short and easy bus ride to downtown. And there are several new things happening nearby, including the redevelopment of the old Pearl Brewery. And B&B innkeepers, both here and in King William, are great at giving tips and answering questions during your stay. You can also expect B&Bs to provide fax and other business services, and these days most offer wireless Internet connections.

With a few other exceptions detailed here, the vast majority of the other lodgings around town are low-priced chains. The most convenient are clustered in the northwest, near the Medical Center, and in the north central area, around the airport. For a full alphabetical listing of the accommodations in the city, mapped by area and including rate ranges as well as basic amenities, phone the **San Antonio Convention and Visitors Bureau** (© **800/447-3372**) and request a lodging guide. The "Accommodations" section of **www.sanantoniovisit.com** is also a good resource.

Wherever you decide to stay, try to book as far in advance as possible—especially if the property is located downtown. And don't even think about coming to town during **Fiesta** (the third week in Apr) if you haven't reserved a room 6 months in advance.

THE best SAN ANTONIO HOTEL BETS

- **Best Place for the Trendy to Be Seen:** The **Hotel Valencia Riverwalk,** 150 E. Houston St. (© **866/842-0100** or 210/227-9700), hosts Vbar and Citrus, two of the hottest hangouts in town. And flanking the hotel are Acenar and Sip, two other top stylish spots. See p. 49.
- **Best Value for Business Travelers:** Such features as a location near the convention center and high-speed Internet access in the room make the **O'Brien Hotel,** 116 Navarro St. (© **800/257-6058** or 210/527-1111), convenient for all business travelers, while low rates and perks such as free local phone calls make it especially appealing to those whose companies aren't picking up the tab. See p. 56.
- **The Best Place to See (or Feel) a Ghost:** San Antonio's got plenty of historic hotels—the kind where haunts tend to linger—but only the **Menger,** 204 Alamo Plaza (© **800/345-9285** or 210/223-4361), claims to have 32 ghosts. You can take your pick of the spirits you want to sleep with—or drink with. The bar where Teddy Roosevelt recruited his Rough Riders is in this hotel, too. See p. 53.
- **Best for Families:** If you can afford it, the **Hyatt Regency Hill Country Resort and Spa,** 9800 Hyatt Resort Dr. (© **800/233-1234** or 210/647-1234), just down the road from SeaWorld, is ideal for a family getaway. Kids get to splash in their own shallow pool, go tubing on a little river, and participate in a kids' camp, and you get to relax in the resort's spa or play a few holes on its expanding golf course. See p. 61.
- **Best Riverside Bargain:** The **Drury Inn & Suites,** 201 N. St. Mary's St. (© **800/DRURY-INN** [378-7946] or 210/212-5200), is a good, economical downtown bet located in a historic building right on the river. Breakfast and afternoon cocktails are included in the room rate, and in-room fridges and microwaves mean you can cut down on food costs in this pricey area even further. See p. 54.
- **Best Budget Lodging:** How do I love the savings at the **Best Western Sunset Suites,** 1103 E. Commerce St. (© **866/560-6000** or 210/223-4400)? Let me count the ways: Low room rates, lots of freebies, and a convenient location near downtown, plus very attractive rooms, make staying here a super deal. See p. 54.

- **Best B&B:** The King William area abounds with B&Bs, but the **Ogé House,** 209 Washington St. (© **800/242-2770** or 210/223-2353), stands out as much for its rooms as for the gorgeous mansion and extensive grounds. See p. 57.

- **Best One-Stop Lodging:** You never have to wander far from the **Marriott Rivercenter,** 101 Bowie St. (© **800/228-9290** or 210/223-1000), with its excellent health club (on the same floor as the hotel's free washers and dryers, no less); its proximity to the Rivercenter Mall and to water taxis that take you along the River Walk; and its abundant on-site eateries. See p. 50.

- **Best Place to Spot Celebrities:** Everyone from Paula Abdul to ZZ Top (hey, they're big in Texas) has stayed at **Omni La Mansión del Río,** 112 College St. (© **800/292-7300** or 210/518-1000); discretion, a willingness to cater to special requests, and a location that's just slightly away from the action might explain why. See p. 50.

- **Best for River Views:** The River Walk is best viewed from a modest height, because you lose something from 12 stories up. At **Omni La Mansión del Río,** 112 College St. (© **800/292-7300** or 210/518-1000), the views from the hotel's balconies are ideal. The hotel is only six stories tall, and this stretch of the river, bordered by tall cypress trees, evokes a sense of calm. See p. 50.

DOWNTOWN
Very Expensive

Hotel Contessa ★★   This is one of the newest hotels to be built on the river, and its location makes you wonder why someone waited so long to build here. Fronting the property is a massive cypress tree crowning a small bit of land that creates a slight bend in the river—a popular wedding spot. The architecture and decor are less traditional than that of the neighboring Westin. Rooms surround a soaring atrium with lots of light and bold colors. Glass elevators take you up the 12 stories of rooms, all of them suites. All have good-size sitting rooms, Southwestern accents, and bedrooms with either a river or a city view. The best river views are down low, at level with the cypress trees, and the best city views are up high. Each room comes with either a king-size or two double beds.

The decision between staying this hotel or at the Westin next door would depend largely on the rates, the availability of "riverview" rooms, and the importance of having a balcony (Westin).

306 W. Market St. (at Navarro), San Antonio, TX 78205. © **866/435-0900** or 210/229-9222. Fax 210/229-9228. www.thehotelcontessa.com. 265 units. $219–$289 suite; executive suites from $260. AE, DC, DISC, MC, V. Valet parking $28. Pets no larger than 50 lb. for a fee of $50 per night. **Amenities:** Restaurant; bar; babysitting; concierge; fitness room; Jacuzzi; outdoor heated pool; room service; spa. *In room:* A/C, TV, hair dryer, minibar, Wi-Fi.

Hotel Valencia Riverwalk   The Valencia is the hippest hotel on the River Walk. It's a good choice for the design-conscious traveler or anyone who feels in a rut. The hotel's aesthetic avoids the grandiose, with subdued light and a sonic background of falling water. The hotel is a modern statement made with primitive materials and lots of texture (stone, clay, bamboo). The drama is provided in subtle ways, such as the play of light and shadow. Guest rooms work equally well for business or leisure travelers. They are large and comfortable and made to feel larger by the lack of clutter and the use of solid colors. A heavy built-in counter running the length of the room provides ample desk and counter space. The priciest rooms offer river views from narrow balconies. In addition to the hotel's own restaurant, Citrus, there is the popular **Acenar** (not associated with the hotel) on the bottom floor (p. 73).

150 E. Houston St. (at St. Mary's), San Antonio, TX 78205. ℭ **866/842-0100** or 210/227-9700. Fax 210/227-9701. www.hotelvalencia.com. 213 units. $199–$239 double; suites from $350. Web discounts often available. AE, DC, DISC, MC, V. Valet parking $29. **Amenities:** Restaurant; bar; concierge; fitness room; room service; spa. *In room:* A/C, TV, hair dryer, minibar, Wi-Fi.

Hyatt Regency San Antonio on the River Walk ★

We all know the look of classic Hyatts: soaring atriums of glass and steel accented with vegetation here and there and glass elevators that seem always in motion. In 2010, the hotel remodeled the lobby, and all the common areas, making it a lot more impressive looking. It also added a spa. The guest rooms still look sharp, with sleek modern furniture of rich, dark wood, and modern, attractive decor. The Hyatt gets business and leisure travelers alike, who both enjoy its great location on the River Walk at the point where it passes closest to the Alamo. Rooms have interior views, Alamo views ($30 extra), and river views ($60 extra).

123 Losoya St. (at College St.), San Antonio, TX 78205. ℭ **800/233-1234** or 210/222-1234. Fax 210/227-4925. www.sanantonioregency.hyatt.com. 632 units. $269–$349 double; $328–$768 suite. AE, DC, DISC, MC, V. Self-parking $21; valet parking $27. **Amenities:** Restaurant; bar; concierge; club-level rooms; 24-hr. health club; outdoor heated pool; room service; spa. *In room:* A/C, TV, hair dryer, minibar, Wi-Fi ($11).

Marriott Rivercenter

This is a massive hotel rising high above the Rivercenter Mall. It has access to the river and is close to HemisFair Park and the convention center. It's mainly a convention hotel, but it works great for shoppers and sightseers, who can get good rates when no big convention is in town.

Guest rooms are attractive and comfortable, and most afford views of the city. But they aren't readily distinguishable from Marriott hotel rooms anywhere else in the country. Convenience is definitely a plus here; for example, free washers and dryers on the same floor as the health club allow you to bicycle while your clothes cycle. If you don't like mega hotels, you can opt to stay at the hotel's smaller sister, the Marriott Riverwalk, across the street. This older and less-expensive hotel has comfortable Southwest-style rooms, and its guests have access to all the facilities of the Rivercenter.

101 Bowie St. (at Commerce St.), San Antonio, TX 78205. ℭ **800/228-9290** or 210/223-1000. Fax 210/223-6239. www.marriott.com. 1,001 units. $249–$349 double; suites from $450. AE, DC, DISC, MC, V. Self-parking $25; valet parking $33. **Amenities:** 3 restaurants; babysitting; concierge; club-level rooms; health club; Jacuzzi; indoor pool; outdoor pool; room service; sauna. *In room:* A/C, TV, hair dryer, Wi-Fi ($14 per day; complimentary in lobby).

Omni La Mansión del Río ★★★

This hotel is pure San Antonio and is the favorite choice of Texan out-of-towners. The core of the building was constructed in 1852 for a seminary, which later became old St. Mary's College. Architectural elements such as old-style Mexican tile floors, wrought-iron work, and beamed ceilings lend the hotel a sense of place instead of a sense of corporate concept. Moreover, La Mansión makes being on the river more enjoyable than its high-rise neighbors. The balconies of the river-view rooms are level with the tall cypress and palm trees that line the riverbank and look out over a particularly attractive stretch of the River Walk. I could idle away many hours on one of those balconies. Other rooms have courtyard views and, though not quite as much fun, are preferable to many of the standard rooms of other hotels. Rooms are for the most part large, are comfortably furnished, and don't go overboard with the decor. The Omni chain took over the property in

Downtown San Antonio Accommodations

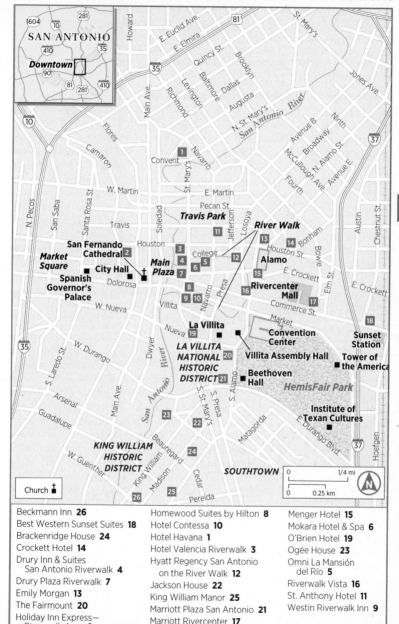

Beckmann Inn **26**
Best Western Sunset Suites **18**
Brackenridge House **24**
Crockett Hotel **14**
Drury Inn & Suites
  San Antonio Riverwalk **4**
Drury Plaza Riverwalk **7**
Emily Morgan **13**
The Fairmount **20**
Holiday Inn Express—
  Riverwalk Area **2**

Homewood Suites by Hilton **8**
Hotel Contessa **10**
Hotel Havana **1**
Hotel Valencia Riverwalk **3**
Hyatt Regency San Antonio
  on the River Walk **12**
Jackson House **22**
King William Manor **25**
Marriott Plaza San Antonio **21**
Marriott Rivercenter **17**

Menger Hotel **15**
Mokara Hotel & Spa **6**
O'Brien Hotel **19**
Ogée House **23**
Omni La Mansión
  del Río **5**
Riverwalk Vista **16**
St. Anthony Hotel **11**
Westin Riverwalk Inn **9**

2006 and provides attentive, personal service. Guests have signing privileges at the Mokara (another Omni property on the opposite bank) for that hotel's restaurant, fitness room, spa, and salon.

112 College St. (btw. St. Mary's and Navarro), San Antonio, TX 78205. © **800/292-7300** or 210/518-1000. Fax 210/226-0389. www.omnilamansion.com. 338 units. $169–$229 double; $219–$279 ambassador rooms; suites from $750. AE, DC, DISC, MC, V. Valet parking $32. Pets under 25 lb. accepted for $50. **Amenities:** Restaurant; bar; babysitting; children's program; concierge, outdoor heated pool; room service. *In room:* A/C, TV, hair dryer, minibar, Wi-Fi.

Mokara Hotel & Spa ★★★ This hotel is the best choice for anyone wishing to add pampering and relaxation to the San Antonio experience. Everything about this hotel is relaxing, and the spa is large, elaborate, and highly rated. Guest rooms have high ceilings; walls painted in light, cool shades of elemental colors; and lots of soft, natural light. Many have balconies overlooking the river, large enough to accommodate a couple of chairs. Marble bathrooms are oversized and offer jetted tubs and separate showers. The rooftop cafe and pool area offers yet another way to take in San Antonio in a relaxing way. And to all this add the easy, personal, and unobtrusive attention of the staff, and you have the total experience. The location is on one of my favorite stretches of the River Walk—quiet, yet close to the main restaurant section, as well as the restaurants along East Houston Street. If you think you'll be making much use of the spa, consider getting one of the spa-level rooms, which come with hardwood floors and direct access to the facilities. A full-service salon is also on the premises.

212 W. Crockett St. (at St. Mary's), San Antonio, TX 78205. © **866/605-1212** or 210/396-5800. www.mokarahotelsandspas.com. 99 units. $259–$289 double; $359–$389 riverview double. AE, DC, DISC, MC, V. Valet parking $32. **Amenities:** Restaurant; cafe; babysitting; concierge; gym; Jacuzzi; outdoor pool; sauna; spa; room service. *In room:* A/C, TV, hair dryer, minibar, MP3 docking station, Wi-Fi.

Westin Riverwalk Inn ★★ ☺ This property was designed to blend in architecturally with its older neighbors on this (relatively) quiet section of the river bend, while its clean lines reflect a more modern aesthetic. Rooms, however, are furnished in a traditional style and are large and comfortable. All the "riverview" rooms have balconies. My favorites are on the fourth floor, where the balconies are a tad larger and you're a little closer to the river. There are nice details for the business traveler, such as an ample desk with stone countertop and convenient connections. Of course, the property includes Westin's signature "Heavenly Beds," which in my opinion are just that. Perhaps in a nod to its many high-end Latin American business visitors, the hotel has a traditional Merienda Wednesday to Friday evenings, which includes Mexican hot chocolate, sweet bread, cookies, and refreshments (it's free to hotel guests). This Westin has also nicely incorporated several kid-friendly features (see "Family-Friendly Hotels" on p. 179).

420 W. Market St. (at Navarro), San Antonio, TX 78205. © **800/WESTIN-1** (937-8461) or 210/224-6500. Fax 210/444-6000. www.westin.com/riverwalk. 473 units. $339–$429 double; $419 and up suite. AE, DC, DISC, MC, V. Valet parking $30. Pets under 40 lb. accepted without fee or deposit. **Amenities:** Restaurant; bar; babysitting; children's program; concierge; fitness room; outdoor heated pool; room service; spa. *In room:* A/C, TV, hair dryer, minibar, Wi-Fi ($13).

Expensive

Emily Morgan ★★ ✦ This hotel is located next to the Alamo and is housed in a Gothic skyscraper from the 1920s (once the tallest building in the western U.S.). The location is ideal for visitors: close to the attractions, the shopping, the restaurants, and the River Walk. The guest rooms are contemporary, plush, and streamlined. Black lacquer finishes, flat-panel TVs, and sliding doors to the bathroom add to the sleek appearance. The Emily Morgan is considerably less expensive than many comparable hotels on the river, and the combination of style, comfort, and history is hard to beat. The hotel is popular with repeat visitors and has been voted one of the top hotels by a couple of travel magazines. This is a fun place to stay—the lobby bar during happy hour can be a lively scene (the bartenders make a good margarita).

705 E. Houston St. (at Ave. E), San Antonio, TX 78205. ✆ **800/824-6674** or 210/225-5100. Fax 210/225-7227. www.emilymorganhotel.com. 177 units. $169–$269 double; $229–$279 suite. Special rates often available. AE, DC, DISC, MC, V. Valet parking $26. Pets permitted with $75 fee. **Amenities:** Restaurant; bar; concierge; fitness room; Jacuzzi; outdoor heated pool; sauna; room service. *In room:* A/C, TV, CD player, hair dryer, Wi-Fi ($9.95).

The Fairmount ★★ Not to be confused with the Fairmont luxury hotels, this is a small San Antonio original, independently owned and one of a kind. Built in 1906 for the benefit of railroad passengers, the entire three-story, redbrick Victorian was moved 6 blocks (in one piece) to its present site in 1985. The move made headlines and the *Guinness Book of World Records.* Elaborate decorative details in the hotel's interior were thus preserved and add to the charm of staying here. The rooms, which are decorated in period style and furnished with antiques, vary a great deal, but most are of comfortable size and have lovely marble bathrooms. The junior suites are a good bargain and worth an upgrade. What doesn't vary is the personal service. Staying here, you won't be lost among the masses, as can be the case at larger hotels; and you'll be greeted by Luke, the hotel mascot, a friendly retriever rescued from a shadowy past.

401 S. Alamo St. (at E. Nueva), San Antonio, TX 78205. ✆ **877/229-8808** or 210/224-8800. Fax 210/224-2767. www.fairmountsa.com. 37 units. $179–$249 double; suites $189–$409. AE, DC, DISC, MC, V. Valet parking $21. Pets permitted with $75 fee. **Amenities:** Restaurant; bar; concierge; fitness room; room service. *In room:* A/C, TV, hair dryer, Wi-Fi.

Marriott Plaza San Antonio Tucked away in an isolated corner of the south end of downtown, this hotel feels like an island of tranquillity in the busy downtown scene. It's close by La Villita and the King William district, and it shares the relaxed feel of those two older parts of town. The hotel incorporates four buildings from the 19th century, which were saved from the bulldozer in 1968 during the creation of HemisFair Park. One houses the health club and the spa; the others are offices and conference centers. The main hotel building (seven floors) is pure Marriott, decorated in a Southwestern style. Rooms are larger than the norm and brightly decorated. Most come with a balcony overlooking the hotel's manicured grounds. This Marriott is one of the few hotels in town that have lit tennis courts, and the only one with a croquet lawn.

555 S. Alamo St. (at Durango), San Antonio, TX 78205. ✆ **800/421-1172** or 210/229-1000. Fax 210/229-1418. www.plazasa.com. 251 units. $169–$274 double; suites from $400. AE, DC, DISC, MC, V. Self-parking $23; valet parking $29. **Amenities:** Restaurant; bar; babysitting; concierge; concierge-level floor; health club; Jacuzzi; outdoor pool; room service; 2 lit tennis courts. *In room:* A/C, TV, hair dryer, Wi-Fi ($13/day).

Menger Hotel ★ In the late 19th century, no one who was anyone would consider staying anywhere but the Menger, which opened its doors in 1859 and has never closed them. Ulysses S. Grant, Sarah Bernhardt, and Oscar Wilde were among those who walked—or, rumor has it, in the case of Robert E. Lee, rode a horse—through the halls, ballrooms, and gardens. Successfully combining the original, restored building with myriad additions, the Menger now takes up an entire city block. The hotel's location is terrific—between the Alamo and the Rivercenter Mall, a block from the River Walk. And its public areas, particularly the Victorian lobby, are gorgeous. The **Menger Bar** (p. 135) is one of San Antonio's historic taverns, and while nearly every historic hotel in town boasts a ghost, this one claims to have no fewer than 32. Rooms in the modern sections tend to be a bit plain. Those in the original Victorian section, furnished with period pieces, are much more entertaining, though more costly. These tend to fill up first, so if you intend to book one, book well in advance.

204 Alamo Plaza (at Crockett St.), San Antonio, TX 78205. © **800/345-9285** or 210/223-4361. Fax 210/228-0022. www.mengerhotel.com. 316 units. $169–$229 double; $250–$495 suite. Internet specials sometimes available. AE, DC, DISC, MC, V. Valet parking $25. Pets accepted with $50 fee. **Amenities:** Restaurant; bar; fitness room; Jacuzzi; outdoor pool; room service; spa. *In room:* A/C, TV, hair dryer, high-speed Internet access.

Moderate

Best Western Sunset Suites–Riverwalk ★ 🖋   This hotel is a rare combination of economy and location. The reception and lobby area are in a two-story brick building from around 1900. The rooms are in a new building next door. They are large and comfortable and are equipped with sleeper sofas, microwaves, and minifridges. The hotel is located next to the freeway, but the rooms are quiet. Two blocks away are the Rivercenter Mall, the River Walk, and the convention center. This part of downtown near the old train station is just opposite the freeway from the rest of downtown. Known as Sunset Station, it has been redeveloped to include several restaurants and entertainment venues.

1103 E. Commerce St. (at Hwy. 281), San Antonio, TX 78205. © **866/560-6000** or 210/223-4400. Fax 210/223-4402. www.bestwesternsunsetsuites.com. 64 units. $109–$165 double. Internet specials available. AE, DC, DISC, MC, V. Free parking. **Amenities:** Fitness room. *In room:* A/C, TV, fridge, hair dryer, Wi-Fi.

Crockett Hotel ★ 🖋   This hotel is a bit of a hybrid, consisting of the original historical landmark building (expanded in 1927) and several low-slung, motel-style units that surround what may be downtown's nicest swimming pool. Rooms in both sections of the hotel are attractive; all were remodeled recently and have a clean, uncluttered look to them. Check for deals; rooms here are discounted for every imaginable reason. Its location, close to the Alamo, the Rivercenter Mall, and the river, is excellent.

320 Bonham St. (at Crockett St.), San Antonio, TX 78205. © **800/292-1050** or 210/225-6500. Fax 210/225-7418. www.crocketthotel.com. 204 units. Rooms $139–$157; suites from $345. Various discounts (including Internet booking and specials). AE, DC, DISC, MC, V. Valet parking $20. **Amenities:** Restaurant; bar; outdoor pool; room service. *In room:* A/C, TV, hair dryer, Wi-Fi.

Drury Inn & Suites San Antonio Riverwalk/Drury Plaza Riverwalk 🖋   Both of these properties occupy old San Antonio skyscrapers. Rooms at the Inn & Suites can have river views (for which you pay a little extra) and are a little smaller than their counterparts at the Plaza Riverwalk, which run about $10 more. Some offer good views of San Fernando Cathedral, which looks lovely at night. I'm not a fan of the way guest rooms are decorated at Drury Inns, but this chain does a good job of offering comfort and location at a good price. The suites are a worth the extra money. Both properties have direct access to the River Walk and have preserved the original lobbies. Be sure to take note of the Plaza Riverwalk's lobby. It was built in 1929, the heyday of exuberance right before the big stock market crash—50-foot ceilings, travertine marble, gold accents—it's a magnificent vision.

201 N. St. Mary's St. (at Commerce St.), San Antonio, TX 78205. ℂ **800/DRURY-INN** (378-7946) or 210/212-5200. Fax 210/352-9939. www.druryhotels.com. 150 units. $129–$164 double; $164–$199 suite. AE, DC, DISC, MC, V. Self-parking $14. Small pets accepted. **Amenities:** Restaurant; fitness room; Jacuzzi; outdoor pool. *In room:* A/C, TV, fridge and microwave (in king rooms and suites), hair dryer, Wi-Fi.

Holiday Inn Express–Riverwalk Area 🦺 This hotel occupies the old Bexar (pronounced *bear*) County Jail, which explains the stout, fortresslike appearance of the building. The interior was gutted, so you're not going to see vestiges of the jail; only the bars on the front windows remain. Rooms are a good size and well kept up. The largest rooms come with two queen beds and are quite comfortable. Other options are a king bed and the studio king. Service here is attentive if minimal, in keeping with the "express" concept of the hotel. The location is in the western part of downtown San Antonio. It's a safe area and is only 3 blocks from the River Walk and several more to the Alamo and the main restaurant area.

120 Camaron St. (btw. Houston and Commerce), San Antonio, TX 78205. ℂ **800/HOLIDAY** (800/465-4329) or 210/281-1400. Fax 210/228-0007. www.hiexpress.com. 82 units. $109–$129 double. Rates include continental breakfast. AE, DC, DISC, MC, V. Off-site parking (1 block away) $16. **Amenities:** Exercise room; Jacuzzi; outdoor heated pool. *In room:* A/C, TV, fridge, hair dryer, microwave, Wi-Fi.

Homewood Suites by Hilton 🦺 ☺ Occupying the former San Antonio Drug Company building (built in 1919), this all-suites hotel is a good downtown deal. Located on a central stretch of the river, it's convenient to most of the downtown attractions. Rooms have a homey feel, without much flash, but they are large, comfortable, and pragmatically furnished. In-room amenities, such as microwaves, refrigerators with ice makers, and dishwashers, appeal to business travelers and families alike. The dining area can double as a work space, and there's a sleeper sofa in each suite as well as two TVs. On weekdays in the early evening/late afternoon, the hotel offers refreshments and a light supper free of charge. One drawback, and part of the reason the hotel offers such a good deal is that, despite being on the river, there are no rooms with river views. The rooftop pool area offers attractive views of San Antonio and the river.

432 W. Market St. (at St. Mary's St.), San Antonio, TX 78205. ℂ **800/CALL-HOME** (800/225-5466) or 210/222-1515. Fax 210/222-1575. www.homewood-suites.com. 146 units. $169–$199 suite; $309–$339 2-bedroom suites. Rates include breakfast and afternoon refreshments (Mon–Thurs). AE, DC, DISC, MC, V. Valet parking $22. **Amenities:** Fitness room; Jacuzzi; outdoor pool. *In room:* A/C, fan, 2 TVs, hair dryer, kitchen, Wi-Fi.

Hotel Havana ★ Liz Lambert, the owner of **Saint Cecilia** (p. 171) and **San José** (p. 172) in Austin, recently purchased this classic, three-story hotel located by the River Walk in the northern part of downtown. She has removed the clutter and decorated the rooms in a spare manner that lets the cool white walls, dark-wood trim, and handsome wood floors take center stage. Rooms, as with the owner's other properties, received a careful eye toward design. The rooms don't have closets, but they are now equipped with large retro fridges. At present, there is no functioning restaurant, but this is scheduled to change in 2011. For now, you can request to have a continental breakfast served in your room.

1015 Navarro (btw. St. Mary's and Martin sts.), San Antonio, TX 78205. ℂ **210/222-2008.** Fax 210/222-2217. www.havanasanantonio.com. 27 units. $149–$199 double; $209–$599 suite. AE, DC, DISC, MC, V. Self-parking $10. Pets accepted for $25 fee. **Amenities:** Bar; concierge; limited room service. *In room:* A/C, fan, TV, fridge, hair dryer, minibar, Wi-Fi.

O'Brien Hotel 🛥 Though this small hotel occupies an old, three-story brick building (1904), nothing remains of the past except for the facade. Its major draw is a combination of comfortable rooms and good location at a low price. Some rooms offer balconies and/or whirlpool tubs. The hotel works for business and leisure travelers; it's near La Villita and a quiet part of the River Walk, and it's close to both the heart of downtown and the King William district. The staff is friendly and accommodating.

116 Navarro St. (at St. Mary's), San Antonio, TX 78205. ℂ **800/257-6058** or 210/527-1111. Fax 210/527-1112. www.obrienhotel.com. 39 units. $99–$139 double. Rates include continental breakfast. AE, DC, DISC, MC, V. Self-parking $10. **Amenities:** Exercise room. *In room:* A/C, TV, hair dryer, Wi-Fi.

Riverwalk Vista ★★ 🛥 Intimacy, history, amenities—that's a tough combination to beat. The 17 rooms in the 1883 Dullnig building are extremely attractive, with beautifully finished pine floors, large windows, high ceilings, and elegant reproduction pieces. They come with all the modern fittings, including flatscreen TVs with DVD players, as well as such posh touches as plush robes, makeup mirrors, and umbrellas. The location (near the River Walk, Alamo, and other top downtown sights) and lack of parking make this hotel a good choice for those without a car. In this area, you're far better off without one anyway. Rooms can be a little noisy but come equipped with a white-noise machine.

262 Losoya (at Commerce St.), San Antonio, TX 78205. ℂ **866/898-4782** or 210/223-3200. www.riverwalkvista.com. 17 units. $120–$210 double; $180–$270 suite; midweek convention discounts often available. Rates include continental breakfast. AE, DC, DISC, MC, V. **Amenities:** Passes to nearby fitness center. *In room:* A/C, TV/DVD player, fridge, hair dryer, high-speed Internet access.

St. Anthony Hotel ★ 🛥 More than any of the other old hotels in San Antonio, the St. Anthony (1909) conveys the feel of old-time grandeur. Chandeliers, elaborate moldings, distinctive furniture—all are artifacts of a bygone era—but they make staying here a unique experience. The guest rooms vary widely in size and floor plan. In several cases, the hotel has torn down a wall between two singles to create what they call a "double-double." These are of good size, are reasonably priced, and have two queen beds and two bathrooms. I enjoy the historical touches, but others might find them a bit inconvenient and will need to balance character vs. convenience when choosing lodgings. Service is attentive; this hotel is a Wyndham property.

300 E. Travis St. (across from Travis Park), San Antonio, TX 78205. ℂ **877/999-2332** or 210/227-4392. Fax 210/222-1896. www.thestanthonyhotel.com. 352 units. $109–$179 double; $152–$259 suite. AE, DC, DISC, MC, V. Self-parking $19; valet parking $25. **Amenities:** Restaurant; bar; concierge; exercise room; outdoor pool; room service. *In room:* A/C, TV, hair dryer, Wi-Fi ($9.95).

KING WILLIAM HISTORIC DISTRICT

Expensive

Jackson House ★★ Built in a restrained Victorian style, the Jackson House (1894) is in my mind one of the most beautiful and distinctive properties in the area. It has been restored with great care and imagination by Liesl and Donald Noble, both of whom come from families who have lived in the King William neighborhood and San Antonio for generations. The common rooms exhibit original fixtures and rare Texas long-leaf pine flooring. This is a comfortable place to stay, too. There is a large, enclosed Jacuzzi behind the house, and afternoon snacks and refreshments are offered. The rooms are uncluttered and have all the modern conveniences. All come with gas fireplaces and mantelpieces. Four are furnished with a queen-size bed; two with king-size.

107 Madison St. (off St. Mary's St.), San Antonio, TX 78204. ℂ **800/242-2770** or 210/223-2353. www. nobleinns.com. 6 units. $149–$225 double; $199–$245 suite. Rates include full breakfast, afternoon snacks, and beverages. Corporate, Mon–Fri discounts available. AE, DC, DISC, MC, V. Free off-street parking. **Amenities:** Jacuzzi. *In room:* A/C, fan, TV, hair dryer, Wi-Fi.

Ogé House and Pancoast Carriage House ★★   These are two separate properties owned by the same people who own the Jackson House. The Ogé House is a massive house built in 1856 in antebellum neoclassical style. It's furnished with European antiques of similar or complementary style and sits on a large landscaped property that backs up to the river. The common areas, the yard, and the 10 guest rooms are more spacious than those of the Jackson House. The bathrooms are much more than what you would expect at a B&B—large, with showers and tubs; some with oversize spa showers and/or Jacuzzi tubs. Many rooms also have fireplaces and views of the grounds, and one looks out on the river from its own balcony. The units downstairs aren't as light as those on the upper two floors, but they're larger and more private, with separate entrances. An ample breakfast is served at individual tables, either in the stately dining room or out on the veranda; in-room breakfast service can be arranged for the suites.

The Pancoast Carriage House (1896) is across the street from the Ogé house and has three suites with full kitchens. It would work well for small groups traveling together, business travelers, or those who prefer the privacy of guesthouses. The rates here include a continental breakfast. Rooms are attractive and spacious. There is a pool on the property.

209 Washington St. (at Turner St.), San Antonio, TX 78204. ℂ **800/242-2770** or 210/223-2353. www. nobleinns.com. 13 units. $179–$269 double; suites $259–$349 ($159–$259 suites in Carriage House). Rates include full breakfast (continental breakfast in Carriage House). Corporate rates available for single business travelers. 2-night minimum stay Sat–Sun; 3 nights during holidays and special events. AE, DC, DISC, MC, V. Free off-street parking. *In room:* A/C, TV/DVD, fridge, hair dryer, Wi-Fi.

Moderate

Beckmann Inn and Carriage House   This 1886 Queen Anne house has a beautiful wraparound porch, which is perfect for enjoying the serenity of the King William area. The house is located at the southern end of the neighborhood, right by the river, which in this particular spot is unpopulated by tourists. You couldn't find a more relaxing spot so close to downtown. The common rooms are trimmed in elegant woodwork and furnished with antiques of the period, and evoke times past.

Guest rooms are also furnished in antique period pieces, including carved wooden beds. Two of them, as well as the carriage house, have private entrances. A full breakfast—perhaps cranberry French toast topped with orange twist—is served in the formal dining room, but you can also enjoy your coffee in a cheerful sunroom.

222 E. Guenther St. (at Madison St.), San Antonio, TX 78204. ℂ **800/945-1449** or 210/229-1449. Fax 210/229-1061. www.beckmanninn.com. 5 units. $109–$199. Rates include full breakfast. AE, DC, DISC, MC, V. Free off-street parking. *In room:* A/C, fan, TV, fridge, hair dryer, Wi-Fi.

Brackenridge House 🛏   It's not just that this bed-and-breakfast is homey rather than fancy—although it's got its fair share of antiques—but that owners Sue and Bennie (aka the King of King William) Blansett instantly make you feel welcome. They also offer little extras and are quick to help you find whatever you need. I especially

family-friendly HOTELS

Hilton San Antonio Hill Country Hotel & Spa (p. 64) Seasonal specials, such as the Ultimate SeaWorld Adventure package, providing passes, transportation, and complimentary souvenirs for both you and the kids, make this an excellent option.

Homewood Suites (p. 55) This reasonably priced all-suites hotel near the River Walk, with in-room kitchen facilities and two TVs per suite—not to mention a guest laundry—is extremely convenient for families.

Hyatt Regency Hill Country Resort and Spa (p. 61) In addition to its many great play areas (including a beach with a shallow swimming area), and its proximity to SeaWorld, this hotel offers Camp Hyatt—a program of excursions, sports, and social activities for children ages 3 to 12. The program fills up fast during school breaks and other holidays, making reservations mandatory.

O'Casey's Bed & Breakfast (p. 59) Usually B&Bs and family vacations are

a contradiction in terms, but O'Casey's is happy to host well-behaved kids. ***Best bet:*** Stay in the separate guesthouse with the fold-out bed, and then join the main-house guests for breakfast in the morning.

Omni San Antonio (p. 64) This hotel's proximity to the theme parks as well as in-room Nintendo and various other Omni Kids features makes the Omni appealing to families.

Westin La Cantera (p. 61) It's close to Six Flags Fiesta Texas, it's got two pools just for children, and it offers the Enchanted Rock Kids Club—an activities program for ages 5 through 12—from May through Labor Day.

Westin Riverwalk Inn (p. 52) Though not as family-friendly as the Westin La Cantera, this Westin on the River Walk still offers such amenities as free in-room movies, a kids' treat pack upon check-in, and bedtime stories told over the phone.

like sitting on the upstairs deck attached to the back of the house. Guest rooms are located in the main house (four), the cottage (one), and carriage house (two), which are two doors down. These latter rooms afford more privacy and work well for those traveling with kids and/or a pet.

230 Madison St. (btw. Beauregard and Turner sts.), San Antonio, TX 78204. © **800/221-1412** or 210/271-3442. www.brackenridgehouse.com. 7 units. $120–$250 double; $140–$275 suites and carriage house. Rates include breakfast (full in main house, continental in cottage and carriage house). Corporate, state, and federal rates; extended stay plans available for the carriage house. 2-night minimum stay required Sat–Sun. AE, DC, DISC, MC, V. Free off-street parking. Small pets accepted in carriage house. **Amenities:** Outdoor heated pool; hot tub. *In room:* A/C, fan, TV w/DVD, fridge, hair dryer, microwave, Wi-Fi.

King William Manor This Greek revival mansion (1892) with an adjacent house (1901) was recently purchased by a young couple, Alison and Craig Clingan. They live on the property and hope to install a workshop for Craig, who is a glass blower. The common rooms are large and light and have long-leaf pine floors, and unusual walk-through windows leading to a veranda. Most of the guest rooms are in the second house. There is a good bit of variety, including some large rooms. One of the biggest and most private is the cottage attached to the guesthouse. Rooms are uncluttered and furnished with a mix of modern and period pieces. Both houses are set well back from Alamo Street and enjoy and extensive fenced yard and an outdoor pool. Access to the River Walk is just a block away.

1037 S. Alamo St. (at Sheridan, 5 blocks south of Durango), San Antonio, TX 78210. ℭ **800/405-0367** or 210/222-0144. www.kingwilliammanor.com. 12 units. $119–$175 double. Rates include full breakfast. AE, DISC, MC, V. Free off-street parking. **Amenities:** Outdoor pool. *In room:* A/C, fan, TV, fridge, hair dryer, Wi-Fi.

MONTE VISTA HISTORIC DISTRICT
Moderate

The Inn at Craig Place ★　This 1891 mansion-turned-B&B appeals to history, art, and architecture buffs alike. It was built by one of Texas's most noted architects, Alfred Giles, for H. E. Hildebrand, a major public figure at the time. The living room holds a mural by Julian Onderdonk, an influential Texas landscape artist, who grew up in Monte Vista in the 1880s.

But that's all academic. More to the point, this place is gorgeous, with forests of gleaming wood and clean Arts and Crafts lines, as well as cushy couches and a wrap-around porch. Rooms are equipped for modern needs but still very luxurious; all have working fireplaces and hardwood floors, and come with robes, slippers, feather pillows, and down comforters. The inn offers several packages; be sure to check their website.

117 W. Craig Place (off N. Main Ave.), San Antonio, TX 78212. ℭ **877/427-2447** or 210/736-1017. Fax 210/737-1562. www.craigplace.com. 5 units. $125–$199 double; $160–$210 suites. Corporate rates available. Rates include full breakfast. AE, DC, DISC, MC, V. Free off-street parking. No children 11 or younger. *In room:* A/C, TV/DVD player, hair dryer, no phone, Wi-Fi.

Inexpensive

Bonner Garden ★ 🕯　This is a fascinating house built in 1910 for Louisiana artist Mary Bonner. She'd experienced two house fires before moving to San Antonio, so she had this one built of solid cement and plaster—though there is beautiful wood trim work, including the staircase, the moldings, and door and window jambs, inside. Rooms are large, well furnished, and uncluttered. The downstairs Portico Room has a painted blue sky with billowing clouds on the ceiling, and it enjoys a private poolside entrance. The two upstairs corner rooms are quite large and comfy, and one room has a large Jacuzzi tub.

Most of the rooms feature European-style decor, but Mary Bonner's former studio, separate from the main house, is done in an attractive Santa Fe style. A rooftop deck affords a sparkling nighttime view of downtown. All in all, this is a very comfortable place to stay. It also has something not commonly found at B&Bs: a large 45-foot swimming pool. Margi, one of the owners, bakes her own pastries for breakfast.

145 E. Agarita (at McCullough), San Antonio, TX 78212. ℭ **800/396-4222** or 210/733-4222. Fax 210/733-6129. www.bonnergarden.com. 6 units. $115–$165 double. Rates include full breakfast. Extended-stay discount (minimum 3 nights) and corporate rates available. 2-night minimum stay Sat–Sun. AE, DISC, MC, V. Free off-street parking. **Amenities:** Outdoor pool. *In room:* A/C, TV/VCR, hair dryer, Wi-Fi.

O'Casey's Bed & Breakfast ☺ 🕯　If there's a twinkle in John Casey's eye when he puts on a brogue, it's because he was born on U.S. soil, not the auld sod. But he and his wife Linda Fay exhibit a down-home friendliness that's no blarney. This Irish-themed

B&B is one of the few around that welcomes families and is well equipped to handle them. One suite in the main house has a sitting area with a futon large enough for a couple of youngsters; another has a trundle bed for two kids in a separate bedroom. Studio apartments in the carriage house both offer full kitchens. Rooms in the main house, a gracious structure built in 1904, feature hardwood floors and antiques, and many bathrooms display claw-foot tubs. There's a wraparound balcony upstairs, too. For a treat, ask Linda (a professional pianist) and John (a choir director and singer) to perform a few numbers for you.

225 W. Craig Place (btw. San Pedro Ave. and Main St.), San Antonio, TX 78212. ② **800/738-1378** or 210/738-1378. www.ocaseybnb.com. 7 units. $89–$110 double (single-night stays Sat–Sun may be slightly higher). Rates include full breakfast. Extended-stay discounts sometimes available. DISC, MC, V. Street parking. Pets allowed in apts only; $10 for up to a week. *In room:* A/C, TV, kitchen (in apts), Wi-Fi.

Ruckman Haus   The accommodations in this pretty turn-of-the-20th-century stucco home, just a block from San Pedro Springs Park, are comfy but elegant, with lots of antiques and plenty of light. Two rooms offer showers with three body jets— almost as good as an in-room massage. Two rooms share a large covered deck with ceiling fans; the Sun Room Suite has a private uncovered deck. Another room, the Highlands, is large enough to sleep three. Breakfasts are generous, and you can bond with fellow guests over afternoon drinks on either the covered deck or the shaded side patio with fountain. The in-room refrigerators come stocked with water and soft drinks. Hey, it can get toasty in San Antonio, and your friendly hosts don't want you to dehydrate! Designated smoking areas are outside.

629 W. French St. (at Breeden, 1 block west of San Pedro Ave.), San Antonio, TX 78212. ② **866/736-1468** or 210/736-1468. Fax 210/736-1468. www.ruckmanhaus.com. 5 units. $100–$120 double; $150–$170 suite. Rates include full breakfast. Corporate rates for single travelers. AE, DISC, MC, V. Free off-street parking. *In room:* A/C, fans, TV/DVD, fridge, hair dryer, Wi-Fi.

FORT SAM HOUSTON AREA

Inexpensive

Bullis House Inn   This graceful neoclassical mansion, just down the street from the Fort Sam Houston quadrangle and easily accessible from the airport and downtown by car, is an excellent bed-and-breakfast bargain, especially for those who don't mind sharing bathrooms. It was built from 1906 to 1909 for General John Lapham Bullis, a frontier Indian fighter who played a key role in capturing Geronimo (some claim the Apache chief's spirit still roams the mansion). More concerned with creature comforts when he retired, the general had oak paneling, parquet floors, crystal chandeliers, and marble fireplaces installed in his home, which is now often used for wedding receptions. Guest rooms all have 14-foot ceilings and are furnished with some period antiques along with good reproductions; three of them feature fireplaces, and one offers a private bathroom. The family room, which sleeps up to six, also has a refrigerator. VCR and video rentals are among the other perks.

621 Pierce St. (at Grayson, directly across from Fort Sam Houston), San Antonio, TX 78208. ② **877/477-4100** or 210/223-9426. Fax 210/299-1479. www.bullishouseinn.com. 7 units. $75–$135 double with shared bathroom. Weekly rates available; rates reduced if you opt out of breakfast. Rates include continental breakfast. AE, MC, V. Free off-street parking. **Amenities:** Outdoor pool. *In room:* A/C, TV, no phone.

WEST/NORTHWEST
Very Expensive

Hyatt Regency Hill Country Resort and Spa ★★★ ☺ This resort and the **Westin La Canterra** (see below) target the exact same public—families (and when school is in session, groups and conferences). They offer a lot of the same things: easy access to theme parks (the Hyatt is built by SeaWorld, the Westin by Six-Flags Fiesta, Texas), lots of swimming pools and tennis courts, and plenty of organized activities for kids and teens. I would say that the Hyatt puts in a little more effort with kid and family activities than the Westin. It is a homier property, and it has one feature that seems to delight everybody—the 950-foot-long Ramblin' River (entirely man-made), where you can relax in the water while letting the current pull you along. The setting, on 200 acres of former ranch land on the far-west side of San Antonio, is idyllic, and there is a 27-hole golf course on-site.

Rooms are large and comfortable. Some ground-floor rooms have direct access to the grounds so that you don't have to go through the lobby. New to the Hyatt are 16 "respire rooms" built for people who have a difficult time with the pollen of the Texas Hill Country. These are equipped with enhanced air scrubbers, special coatings on all the surfaces to repel pollen, and hypoallergenic everything. There are also seven rooms for smokers that come with the same air filtering. The spa is low-key and has a full range of treatments. The Hyatt also has a small spa for teenagers. There are free laundry facilities and a country store for supplies on the property.

9800 Hyatt Resort Dr. (off Hwy. 151, btw. Westover Hills Blvd. and Potranco Rd.), San Antonio, TX 78251. ✆ **800/55-HYATT** (49288) or 210/647-1234. Fax 210/520-4075. www.hillcountry.hyatt.com. 500 units. $249–$400 double; $450–$2,550 suite. Rates lower late Nov to early Mar; packages available. AE, DC, DISC, MC, V. Free self-parking; valet parking $15. **Amenities:** 6 restaurants; 2 bars; children's programs; concierge; club level; golf course; 24-hr. health club; 5 Jacuzzis; 4 outdoor pools; room service; sauna; spa and youth spa; 3 tennis courts (1 lit). *In room:* A/C, TV, fridge, hair dryer, MP3 docking station (in suites), Wi-Fi ($9.95 per day).

Westin La Canterra ★★★ ☺ This resort is grander and less homey than the Hyatt. Golfers will be drawn to its two championship courses (in addition to the much-praised La Canterra, there's a newer Arnold Palmer–designed course) plus a golf academy. In addition to being close to the theme park Six Flags Fiesta Texas, the Westin is also near the newest and best shopping mall in San Antonio—the **Shops at La Canterra.** This resort is more romantic, too, with rocky outcroppings and gorgeous views from its perch on one of the highest points in the San Antonio area. Remnants of the limestone quarry on which the resort was built were incorporated into the four swimming pools interconnected with bridges and channels and a dramatic waterfall.

Rooms are large and are decorated in mix of modern and traditional furnishings. And, as with other Westins, the bed is quite comfortable. Bathrooms are large, and there's plenty of closet space. If you want to go larger, the junior suites offer quite a bit more for the extra cost. Many rooms have balconies with views of the neighboring hills. The "casitas" are units in a section set apart from the main building, which has its own pool. These are larger, quieter, and more private. Each comes with its own patio.

16641 La Canterra Pkwy. (take the La Canterra Pkwy. exit off I-10 and turn left; resort entrance is ¾ mile ahead, on the right), San Antonio, TX 78256. ✆ **800/WESTIN-1** (937-8461) or 210/558-6500. Fax 210/641-0721. www.westinlacanterra.com. 508 units. $259–$369 double; suites from $380; casitas from

Greater San Antonio Accommodations & Dining

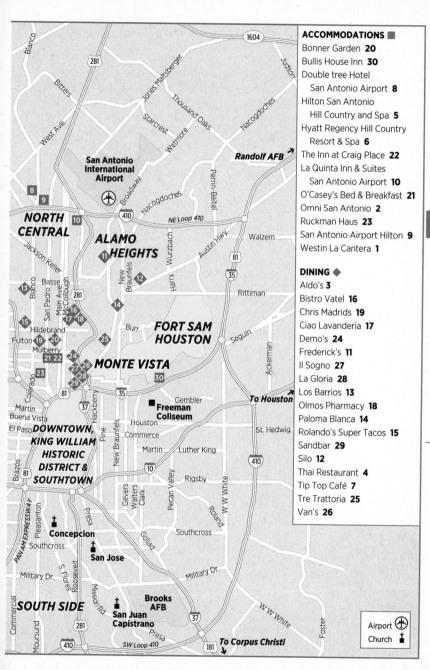

ACCOMMODATIONS ■

Bonner Garden **20**
Bullis House Inn **30**
Double tree Hotel
  San Antonio Airport **8**
Hilton San Antonio
  Hill Country and Spa **5**
Hyatt Regency Hill Country
  Resort & Spa **6**
The Inn at Craig Place **22**
La Quinta Inn & Suites
  San Antonio Airport **10**
O'Casey's Bed & Breakfast **21**
Omni San Antonio **2**
Ruckman Haus **23**
San Antonio Airport Hilton **9**
Westin La Cantera **1**

DINING ◆

Aldo's **3**
Bistro Vatel **16**
Chris Madrids **19**
Ciao Lavanderia **17**
Demo's **24**
Frederick's **11**
Il Sogno **27**
La Gloria **28**
Los Barrios **13**
Olmos Pharmacy **18**
Paloma Blanca **14**
Rolando's Super Tacos **15**
Sandbar **29**
Silo **12**
Thai Restaurant **4**
Tip Top Café **7**
Tre Trattoria **25**
Van's **26**

$350. AE, DC, DISC, MC, V. Free self-parking; valet parking $14. **Amenities:** 5 restaurants; 2 bars; children's program; concierge; club level; 2 golf courses; health club; Jacuzzi; 5 outdoor pools; room service; sauna; spa; 2 tennis courts; Wi-Fi in lobby. *In room:* A/C, TV, hair dryer, high-speed Internet, minibar.

Expensive

Hilton San Antonio Hill Country Hotel and Spa ★ ☺ After becoming a Hilton property in 2009, this family hotel continues to be a less-expensive alternative to the nearby **Hyatt Regency Hill Country Resort and Spa** (see above). It has some of the same features as the Hyatt, including an understated Texas-themed decor, and an upscale convenience store. It's really meant for families who have come to visit SeaWorld, as it's less than a mile from the theme park. Rooms are large and traditional in decoration, and the bathrooms are a cut above what's normal for this price range. Suites offer jetted tubs and rainforest shower heads, and all accommodations feature Hilton's "Serenity" bedding.

9800 Westover Hills Blvd. (off Hwy. 151), San Antonio, TX 78251. ☎ **800/774-1500** or 210/509-9800. Fax 210/767-5329. www.hilton.com. 227 units. $120–$220 double; $240–$300 suite. Internet rates available. AE, DISC, MC, V. Free parking. **Amenities:** Restaurant; bar; health club; Jacuzzi; 2 outdoor pools; room service; spa. *In room:* A/C, TV, fridge (suites only), hair dryer, high-speed Internet.

Omni San Antonio ★ ☺ This polished granite high-rise off I-10 W. is convenient to SeaWorld, Six Flags Fiesta Texas, the airport, and the Hill Country, and the shops and restaurants of the 66-acre Colonnade complex are within easy walking distance. Guest rooms are furnished comfortably in traditional style. The hotel gets a lot of business travelers, but the proximity to the theme parks, the various Omni Kids features at the hotel, and the large pool make it a good choice for families. The exercise facilities are quite good, and guests can get treadmills brought into their rooms as part of the Omni "Get Fit" program. Even at the busiest of times, service here seems prompt and courteous.

9821 Colonnade Blvd. (at Wurzbach), San Antonio, TX 78230. ☎ **800/843-6664** or 210/691-8888. Fax 210/691-1128. www.omnihotels.com. 326 units. $169–$249 double; suites from $289. A variety of discount packages available. AE, DC, DISC, MC, V. Free self-parking; valet parking $12. Pets 25 lb. or less permitted for $50 fee. **Amenities:** Restaurant; bar; free airport transfer; concierge; club-level rooms; health club; Jacuzzi; indoor pool; outdoor pool; room service; sauna. *In room:* A/C, TV, hair dryer, high-speed Internet access, minibar.

NORTH CENTRAL (NEAR THE AIRPORT)

Moderate

Doubletree Hotel San Antonio Airport ★ For an airport hotel, the Doubletree is surprisingly serene. Moorish arches, potted plants, stone fountains, and colorful tile create a Mediterranean mood in the public areas. Intricate wrought-iron elevators descend from the guest floors to the lushly landscaped pool patio, eliminating the need to tramp through the lobby in a swimsuit. Guest rooms are equally appealing, with brick walls, wood-beamed ceilings, draped French doors, and colorful contemporary art. And because this hotel gets a large business clientele from Mexico, most of the staff is bilingual.

37 NE Loop 410 (McCullough exit), San Antonio, TX 78216. ☎ **800/535-1980** or 210/366-2424. Fax 210/341-0410. www.doubletree.com. 290 units. $139–$229 double; $250–$350 suite. Packages available.

AE, DC, DISC, MC, V. Free self-parking. **Amenities:** Restaurant; 2 bars; concierge; club-level rooms; exercise room; Jacuzzi; outdoor pool; sauna; spa. *In room:* A/C, TV, hair dryer, high-speed Internet ($10/day).

San Antonio Airport Hilton ★   The rooms at this airport Hilton offer a bit of local character, with a few Southwestern decorative touches. They're attractive and spacious. The hotel is straight west of the airport, on the north side of Loop 410, making it easy to get to and easy to find. Of course, it's predominantly a business traveler's hotel, but it doesn't have that feel, thanks to such things as the cheerful lobby with colorful Texas mural, the large outdoor pool, and the family-oriented **Tex's Grill,** which serves some mean Texas barbecue. Such nongeneric features as an outdoor putting green also help make your stay enjoyable. But while this hotel may be playful, it also knows how to get down to business.

611 NW Loop 410 (San Pedro exit), San Antonio, TX 78216. © **800/HILTONS** (445-8667). Fax 210/377-4674. www.hilton.com. 386 units. $139–$199 double; suites from $175. AE, DC, DISC, MC, V. Self-parking $10; valet parking $15. **Amenities:** Restaurant; bar; club-level rooms; outdoor pool; room service. *In room:* A/C, TV, hair dryer, Wi-Fi ($11).

Inexpensive

La Quinta Inn & Suites San Antonio Airport   Bunched up around the intersection of Hwy. 281 and Loop 410 are a number of airport hotels. Among them is this property, which is nicely located so that it doesn't front either freeway. It's still easy to find, has an airport shuttle that can also take you to any restaurant in a 2-mile radius, and has easy access to Hwy. 281 South, which leads to downtown. The property was recently built and is well maintained. Guest rooms are plain but comfortable and functional.

850 Halm Blvd., San Antonio, TX 78216. © **800/753-3757** or 210/342-3738. Fax 210/348-9666. www.lq.com. 276 units. $100–$155 double. Rates include free breakfast buffet. AE, DC, DISC, MC, V. Free parking. Pets accepted for free. **Amenities:** Airport shuttle; outdoor pool. *In room:* A/C, TV, hair dryer, high-speed Internet access.

WHERE TO DINE IN SAN ANTONIO

5

Visitors to San Antonio usually have Tex-Mex food on their minds, and for good reason. There is a wealth of variety here and lots of tradition. But the restaurant scene in San Antonio is a lot more sophisticated and cosmopolitan than many people realize. Good French, Italian, and new American food abounds, and there are some one-of-a-kind restaurants that will make any stay here memorable. You can also find some down-home cooking, local taquerías, and neighborhood dives that are genuine to the core and offer an experience that can't be found elsewhere.

The downtown dining scene, especially that found along the River Walk, sees the most visitors; and because most out-of-towners either stay downtown or spend the day there, I devote a good deal of space to restaurants in this area. (To locate restaurants downtown, see the map on p. 71.)

Keep in mind, however, that there are many excellent restaurants in other parts of town that can add to your range of dining choices. There are two areas within walking distance of downtown that merit special mention. Both are easily reached by bus, too.

One is the old Pearl Brewery (a 20-min. stroll up the river from downtown). The developers are making this a major gourmet focal point for the city. First, they persuaded the Culinary Institute of America to open a school here, which was recently inaugurated in October 2010. And they've lured San Antonio's most famous chef, Andrew Weissman, from downtown—he moved his seafood restaurant, Sandbar, here in 2009. In addition to other restaurants, there is a farmers' market and plans to open a microbrewery.

The second hotspot is Southtown, the eclectic, vivacious area just downstream from the city center (a 15-min. walk down the river). It is predominantly Mexican American, with neighborhood eateries and taquerías, and has become a popular place for artists, gallery owners, and innovative restaurateurs. One well-known fixture on the San Antonio scene, the Liberty Bar, which used to occupy the iconic leaning saloon north of downtown, has moved here and set up business in a former convent. You'll have several places to choose from when visiting the sights of King William or shopping the galleries.

There is a wealth of restaurants farther afield, surrounding the prosperous neighborhoods to the north of the city center. Many are on or around Broadway, starting a few blocks south of Hildebrand, extending north to Loop 410. This area caters to the denizens of the wealthy neighborhoods nearby. Here you'll also find several attractions, including Brackenridge Park, the zoo, the botanical gardens, and the Witte and McNay museums. A car is handy when exploring this neighborhood. (To locate restaurants outside of Downtown, see the map on p. 71.)

Restaurant Categories

Rather than trying to make fine distinctions between overlapping labels such as Regional American, New Southwestern, and American Fusion, which generally identify the kind of cooking that tweaks classic American dishes using out-of-the-ordinary ingredients—roast chicken with tamale stuffing, coffee-crusted tenderloin, blue cheese fritters with pesto dipping sauce—I lump them all into the category of **New American.** Tex-Mex is, of course, **Tex-Mex,** and should not be confused with the cooking in the heart of Mexico, which is labeled **Mexican.**

The price categories into which the restaurants have been divided are only rough approximations, based on the average costs of the appetizers and entrees. By ordering carefully or splurging, you can eat more or less expensively at almost any place you choose.

THE best SAN ANTONIO DINING BETS

○ **Best for a Romantic Dinner:** On a quiet stretch of the River Walk, **Las Canarias,** at La Mansión del Río, 112 College St. (© **210/518-1063**), is a haven from the hustle and bustle experienced at other restaurants on the River Walk. You'll enjoy candlelight and superb, unobtrusive service. See p. 70.

○ **Best Movable Feast:** It used to be that you could dine on the river only if you were with a group, but among the restaurants that now offer reservations on communal tables to individuals and couples, **Boudro's,** 421 E. Commerce St./River Walk (© **210/224-8484**), tops the meals-on-river-barge-wheels list. See p. 72.

○ **Best Place for Fat Expense Accounts:** If you need to wine and dine someone in San Antonio, whether for business or personal reasons, you will really impress them at **Bohanan's,** 219 E. Houston St. (© **210/472-2600**). Not only is it considered one of the best steakhouses in Texas, but it also completely looks the part—soft lights, white tablecloths, lots of woodwork, and a serious menu. See p. 69.

○ **Best Seafood:** Andrew Weissman's small seafood restaurant, **Sandbar,** at the Pearl Brewery, Ste. 117 (© **210/222-2426**), serves the best seafood in town. Like his other restaurant, it's all about the food. See p. 79.

○ **Best Place to Listen to Music While You Dine:** Enjoy creative South American, Mexican, and Caribbean fare at Southtown's **Azuca,** 713 S. Alamo St. (© **210/225-5550**), while listening to salsa, merengue, and other Latin sounds. See p. 76.

○ **Best Blast from the Past:** Schilo's, 424 E. Commerce St. (© **210/223-6692**), not only serves up German deli in portions that date back to pre-cholesterol-conscious days, but also retains prices from that era. See p. 74.

- **Best Fine Dining Kept Simple:** It's a tie: Not only do I like the food at both of these places, but I also appreciate the lack of ostentation and the effort to keep things simple. **Silo,** 1133 Austin Hwy. (© **210/824-8686**), offers enough variety to please just about anyone, while steering clear of strangely worded descriptions and playing at one-upmanship. The dining experience at the new **Liberty Bar,** 1111 S. Alamo St. (© **210/227-1187**), is comfortable and casual and belies all the effort going on back in the kitchen to create this kind of cuisine. The atmosphere is quite in keeping with its new Southtown location. See p. 76.

RESTAURANTS BY CUISINE

AMERICAN
Boudro's ★ (Downtown, $$$, p. 72)
Guenther House ★ (Southtown, $, p. 77)
Little Rhein Steak House (Downtown, $$$$, p. 70)
Olmos Pharmacy (Alamo Heights Area, $, p. 84)
Tip Top Cafe (Northwest, $$, p. 85)
Zinc ★ (Downtown, $$, p. 73)

BARBECUE
County Line ★ (Downtown, $$, p. 73)

BURGERS
Chris Madrids (Monte Vista Area, $, p. 81)

CHINESE
Van's (Alamo Heights Area, $$, p. 84)

DELI
The Filling Station (Southtown, $, p. 77)
Madhatters (Southtown, $, p. 78)
Schilo's (Downtown, $, p. 74)
Twin Sisters (Downtown and Alamo Heights Area, $, p. 75)

ECLECTIC
The Filling Station (Southtown, $, p. 77)
Madhatters (Southtown, $, p. 78)

FRENCH
Bistro Vatel ★★ (Alamo Heights Area, $$$, p. 82)
Frederick's ★★★ (Alamo Heights Area, $$$, p. 82)
Le Midi ★★★ (Downtown, $$$, p. 72)

FUSION
Frederick's ★★★ (Alamo Heights Area, $$$, p. 82)

GERMAN
Schilo's (Downtown, $, p. 74)

GREEK
Demo's (Monte Vista Area, $$, p. 80)

HEALTH FOOD
Twin Sisters (Downtown and Alamo Heights Area, $, p. 75)

ITALIAN
Aldo's (Northwest, $$$, p. 84)
Ciao Lavanderia ★ (Alamo Heights Area, $$, p. 83)
Il Sogno ★★★ (Pearl Brewery, $$$, p. 78)
Paesano's Riverwalk (Downtown, $$$, p. 72)
Tre Trattoria ★ (Alamo Heights Area, $$, p. 84)

JAPANESE
Sushi Zushi (Downtown, $$, p. 73)
Van's (Alamo Heights Area, $$, p. 84)

MEXICAN
Acenar ★ (Downtown, $$, p. 73)
Cascabel ★ (Southtown, $, p. 77)
La Gloria ★ (Pearl Brewery, $$, p. 80)
Paloma Blanca ★ (Alamo Heights Area, $$, p. 83)

NEW AMERICAN
Biga on the Banks ★★★ (Downtown, $$$$, p. 69)
Las Canarias ★★★ (Downtown, $$$$, p. 70)

Key to Abbreviations: $$$$ = Very Expensive $$$ = Expensive $$ = Moderate $ = Inexpensive

Liberty Bar ★★ (Southtown, $$, p. 76)

Silo ★★ (Alamo Heights Area, $$$, p. 83)

NUEVO LATINO
Azuca ★ (Southtown, $$, p. 76)

SEAFOOD
Bohanan's ★★★ (Downtown, $$$$, p. 69)

Ostra ★★★ (Downtown, $$$$, p. 70)

Sandbar ★★★ (Pearl Brewery, $$$, p. 79)

Sushi Zushi (Downtown, $$, p. 73)

STEAKS
Bohanan's ★★★ (Downtown, $$$$, p. 69)

Little Rhein Steak House (Downtown, $$$$, p. 70)

TEX-MEX
Casa Rio (Downtown, $, p. 74)

Los Barrios (Monte Vista Area, $$, p. 80)

Mi Tierra (Downtown, $, p. 74)

Rolando's Super Tacos (Monte Vista Area, $, p. 81)

Rosario's ★★ (Southtown, $$, p. 76)

Tito's (Southtown, $, p. 78)

THAI
Thai Restaurant ★ (Northwest, $$, p. 85)

VIETNAMESE
Van's (Alamo Heights Area, $$, p. 84)

DOWNTOWN
Very Expensive

Biga on the Banks ★★★ NEW AMERICAN   This is one of the only fine-dining spots on the River Walk worth visiting. Biga on the Banks serves international cuisine with a nod to local flavors. Fittingly, it's located on the ground floor of the International Center building. You'll enter a dining room that is modern and airy with high ceilings, clean lines, and large windows looking out over the river. The chef/owner is Bruce Auden, a Brit who found his way to San Antonio, where he has won much acclaim from the national press for his cooking.

The menu changes daily, but you're certain to find his popular Angus beef rib-eye served with Shiner Bock–battered onion rings and habañero catsup. You'll also find a number of Asian-inspired dishes, including lettuce wraps of minced venison, buffalo, ostrich, and pheasant accompanied by two spicy dipping sauces, or duck confit *bao* buns (those unearthly doughy balls filled with seasoned meat that can be slightly salty, spicy, and sweet). For dessert, order the signature sticky toffee pudding from Mr. Auden's homeland. If you're willing to eat before 6:30pm or after 9pm, you can enjoy a three-course prix fixe for $37 per person or four-course for $43.

International Center, 203 S. St. Marys St./River Walk. ✆ **210/225-0722.** www.biga.com. Reservations recommended. Main courses $27–$40. AE, DC, DISC, MC, V. Sun–Thurs 5:30–10pm; Fri–Sat 5:30–11pm.

Bohanan's ★★★ STEAKS/SEAFOOD   Considered by many to be the best steakhouse in the state, Bohanan's has everything a proper Texas steakhouse should: comfortable chairs, white tablecloths, lots of dark woodwork, and a good bar. The upstairs dining room (with elevator) has an air of establishment, soft lighting, and a hint of nostalgia for the good old days. The cuts of prime beef come from Allen Bros. of Chicago, the pork is Kurobuta, and if you want Akaushi beef, they have that, too. Steaks are beautifully grilled over mesquite. Seafood is flown in from different suppliers, and the way they grill a red snapper topped with crabmeat makes me nostalgic for the good old days, when quality seafood prepared this way was more common. Service is provided by an experienced waitstaff.

As with many steakhouses in this class, all sides are a la carte. You might consider splitting one or two with a dining companion, but try not to fill up on the fresh bread. Lunch is served downstairs in the bar area. The restaurant is located in the central downtown area just a block or two from the River Walk.

219 E. Houston St. © **210/472-2600.** www.bohanans.com. Reservations recommended. Steaks $34–$125. AE, DC, DISC, MC, V. Mon–Thurs 11am–2pm and 5–10pm; Fri 11am–2pm and 5–11pm; Sat 5–11pm; Sun 5–9pm.

Las Canarias ★★★ NEW AMERICAN   This is the perfect place for celebrating either a special occasion or the simple fact that you're wandering free in San Antonio. At night the multi-tiered dining room is softly lit and in the background you hear someone strumming a Spanish guitar. There are also some tables outside on the River Walk. Las Canarias is the hotel restaurant of **Omni La Mansión del Río** (p. 50), and is located on a part of the river that isn't too noisy. The menu changes seasonally and is fairly adventurous, with a flair for presentation, but you will always find some standard options such as beef tenderloin or a traditional pasta. When I was last there, the menu featured caramelized scallops with a bit of pork belly and a garnish of pickled watermelon, also a duck confit with a cherry *guajillo* sauce. The kitchen will cook for special needs, but you should give advance notice. Also, even if there are vegetarian options on the menu, ask about off-menu dishes. If you really feel like exploring, check out the tasting menu, both with ($150) and without ($100) wine pairings. And there is a reasonably priced five-course prix fixe for $39.

La Mansión del Río, 112 College St./River Walk. © **210/518-1063.** Reservations recommended. Main courses $26–$38; champagne Sun brunch $40 adults, $20 children. AE, DC, DISC, MC, V. Daily 6:30am–10:30pm; Sun brunch 10:30am–2:30pm.

Little Rhein Steak House STEAKS   If you're looking for a steakhouse that's on the River Walk, or one that's homey and less formal, this place will work for you. The restaurant has a terraced dining area on the river, which is quite popular. Or you can eat indoors the old stone house that dates from 1847. The dining room has rustic stone walls covered in old photos and artifacts of San Antonio's past, and a rough-cut wooden ceiling. This part of town was once known as the Rhein district, as it was popular with many German émigrés.

All the steaks are prime beef and are grilled over hardwood. Side dishes are a la carte. The quality isn't what you would find at Bohanan's, but there's something special about having steak outdoors on the river. The restaurant is located next door to the Hilton.

231 S. Alamo St. at Market St. © **210/225-2111.** www.littlerheinsteakhouse.com. Reservations recommended. Steaks $24–$46. AE, DC, DISC, MC, V. Daily 5–10pm.

Ostra ★★★ SEAFOOD   This riverside restaurant at the **Mokara Hotel** (p. 52) has some outdoor tables on a lovely spot on the river, and a large, modern, understated dining room with comfortable booths and a sharp-looking glass oyster bar. The executive chef, John Brand, who also supervises **Las Canarias,** has definite ideas about seafood and keeps the dishes simple, yet with contrasts. Such was the case with the lobster bouillabaisse, which features a fish-flavored broth and a whole lobster, added late in the cooking process. At the oyster bar you can choose between various East Coast oysters. The menu changes every 2 months, though it will always have seafood favorites, such as pan-seared flounder. And there will always be

Downtown San Antonio Dining

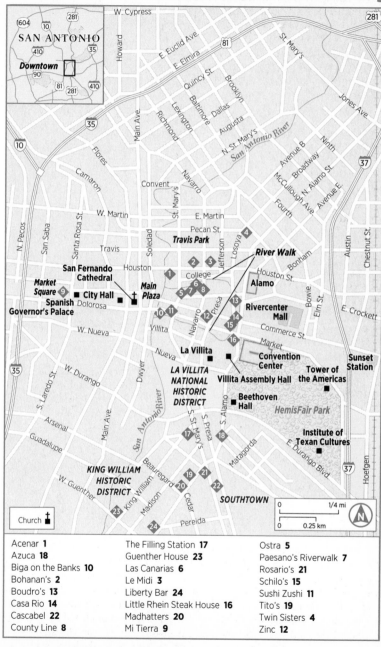

Acenar **1**
Azuca **18**
Biga on the Banks **10**
Bohanan's **2**
Boudro's **13**
Casa Rio **14**
Cascabel **22**
County Line **8**

The Filling Station **17**
Guenther House **23**
Las Canarias **6**
Le Midi **3**
Liberty Bar **24**
Little Rhein Steak House **16**
Madhatters **20**
Mi Tierra **9**

Ostra **5**
Paesano's Riverwalk **7**
Rosario's **21**
Schilo's **15**
Sushi Zushi **11**
Tito's **19**
Twin Sisters **4**
Zinc **12**

non-seafood offerings, such as a Kobe beef burger or a vegetarian pasta. Also of note is the large selection of tequilas (about 65).

212 W. Crockett St. (Mokara Hotel). ✆ **210/396-5817.** www.mokarahotels.com. Reservations recommended, particularly Fri–Sun. Main courses $30–$45. AE, DC, DISC, MC, V. Daily 6:30am–10:30pm.

Expensive

Boudro's ★ AMERICAN   Everybody loves this old standby on the River Walk. The kitchen uses fresh local ingredients—Gulf Coast seafood, Texas beef, Hill Country produce—and the preparations and presentations do them justice. The setting is also out of the ordinary, in a turn-of-the-20th-century limestone building with hardwood floors and a handmade mesquite wood bar.

You might start with the guacamole, prepared tableside and served with tostadas, or the "seacakes" (pan-fried Texas crab cakes). Both options are well prepared. The prime rib, blackened on a pecan-wood grill, is deservedly popular, as is the Black Angus rib-eye served with roasted rosemary potatoes. Portions are hearty. Lighter alternatives include the tortilla soup, the coconut shrimp with orange horseradish, and the rosemary-grilled yellowfin tuna. For dessert, the whiskey-soaked bread pudding is a good choice, and the lime chess pie with a butter pastry crust is divine. Service is attentive, but, if you can, I would suggest going for a late lunch to avoid the crowd.

421 E. Commerce St./River Walk. ✆ **210/224-8484.** www.boudros.com. Reservations recommended. Main courses $20–$33. AE, DC, DISC, MC, V. Sun–Thurs 11am–11pm; Fri–Sat 11am–midnight.

Le Midi ★★★ FRENCH   This new restaurant is part of the burgeoning dining scene on Houston Street, a couple of blocks off the River Walk. It offers classic country French food from the south of France. Chef/owner Nicolas Lebas is adept at layering contrasting tastes and textures, but knows when to let the food speak for itself. I enjoyed a delicious green salad that was simplicity itself, followed by a plate of the house pâté that combined sweet, salty, and acidic flavors on a background rich in what is often called *umami*. The small menu changes often, but you will always find well-known classics, such as lemon sole or coq au vin. This being Texas, there are a couple of steaks on the menu as well, including a small hangar steak served with a bit of caramelized onion in a beef stock reduction.

The small dining room has glass windows on two sides and feels airy. Across the street you can see the old Majestic theater. On show nights, Le Midi offers a $29 three-course prix fixe from 5 to 7pm. Make a reservation, and I suggest you go early and allow lots of time for the meal. Le Midi has a small cocktail bar that is my favorite (see chapter 8).

301 E. Houston St. (at Navarro). ✆ **210/858-7388.** www.lemidirestaurant.com. Reservations recommended. Main courses $20–$34. AE, DISC, MC, V. Tues–Fri 11:30am–2:30pm and 5–10pm; Fri 11:30am–2:30pm and 5–11pm; Sat 5–11pm.

Paesano's Riverwalk ITALIAN   This River Walk incarnation of a longtime San Antonio favorite relinquished its old Chianti bottle–kitsch decor for a soaring ceiling, lots of inscrutable contemporary art, and a more up-to-date menu. But the one thing the restaurant couldn't mess with, at the risk of a local insurrection, was the signature shrimp Paesano's. These are as good as their devotees claim. Also on the menu are reasonably priced pizzas, including the one topped with grilled chicken, artichokes, basil pesto, and feta cheese. The hearty southern Italian staples such as lasagna with meat sauce are good but not great. Standouts among the pricier entrees include the grilled pork chops with potato gnocchi or the sautéed sea bass with eggplant and lemon butter. Locals tend to go to the newer—and somewhat quieter—Paesano's, across from the Quarry Golf Club, at 555 Basse Rd., Ste. 100 (*℗* **210/828-5191**).

111 W. Crockett, Ste. 101/River Walk. *℗* **210/227-2782.** www.joesfood.com. Reservations accepted for 10 or more only. Pizzas $14; pastas $13–$19; main courses $24–$28. AE, DC, DISC, MC, V. Sun–Thurs 11am–10pm; Fri–Sat 11am–11pm.

Moderate

Acenar ★ MEXICAN   This restaurant on the River Walk below the Hotel Valencia is a collaboration between Lisa Wong of **Rosario's** (see below) and Bruce Auden of **Biga.** It's a large, casual restaurant decorated in bold, modern Mexican colors. You can dine indoors or outdoors on a couple of terraces above the river. The "updated" Mexican fare includes such standards as *ceviche* (fish "cooked" in lime juice marinade) or guacamole made at the table, as well as some original dishes, such as crepes with duck in a tamarind-cherry-grilled-onion sauce or the ever-popular *camarones al Diablo* (shrimp in butter with a hint of chipotle served over cilantro-flavored rice). I also wouldn't hesitate to order the fish tacos, which are served with a sweet and spicy mayo and shredded cabbage. For steak lovers, Acenar serves *arrachera* (fajitas) on a sizzling skillet with tortillas and all the sides.

146 E. Houston St. (next to the Hotel Valencia). *℗* **210/222-CENA** (222-2362). www.acenar.com. Reservations not accepted (priority seating for large parties). Lunch $7–$13; dinner $15–$25. AE, DC, MC, V. Sun–Thurs 11am–10pm, Fri–Sat 11am–11pm.

County Line ★ BBQ   This place serves the best barbecue on the River Walk. It's a well-known outfit from Austin that doesn't take shortcuts, cooks everything slowly with indirect heat, and does a good job with side dishes. The kitchen also bakes its own bread, an uncommon occurrence at bbq joints. I believe the cooks do their best work with the pork ribs and the brisket, which come with sauce on top (you can always ask for the sauce on the side). If you're feeling like something with less of a smoke flavor, they offer grilled steaks, too. You have the option to dine outside by the river or inside; I would opt for outside.

111 W. Crockett St., Ste. 104. *℗* **210/229-1941.** Reservations not accepted. AE, DISC, MC, V. Lunch $10–$17; dinner $13–$22; steaks $15–$28. Daily 11:30am–10:30pm.

Sushi Zushi 🌶 JAPANESE/SEAFOOD   For a Japanese food fix in a congenial atmosphere, you can't beat this clean, well-lit place. You'll find sushi in all its variety, including a My Spurs roll—yellowtail, cilantro, avocado, chives, and *serro* chilies— but far more is on the menu. Choose from rice bowls, soba noodle bowls, soups, teppanyakis, tempuras—a mind-boggling array of food options, not to mention a long list of sakes. This spot is popular with downtown office workers.

   Three more branches of Sushi Zushi are in the Northwest, at the Colonnade Shopping Center, 9867 I-10 W. (*℗* **210/691-3332**); in the Northeast, at Stone Oak Plaza II, 18720 Stone Oak Pkwy., at Loop 1604 (*℗* **210/545-6100**); and in Lincoln Heights, at 999 E. Bosse, at Broadway (*℗* **210/826-8500**).

203 S. St. Mary's St. (The International Center). *℗* **210/472-2900.** www.sushizushi.com. Reservations recommended Sat–Sun. Sushi rolls and sashimi $8–$15; bowls, tempuras, and other hot entrees $8–$17. AE, DISC, MC, V. Mon–Thurs 11:30am–10pm; Fri 11:30am–11pm; Sat 12:30–11pm; Sun 5–9pm.

Zinc ★ AMERICAN   Ask locals about this restaurant and wine bar and you'll hear about the Zinc burger, popularly known as the "crack burger" because it's supposedly so addictive. In fact, it could be habit-forming (smoked cheddar, Bibb lettuce, and spicy tomato aioli), but don't order it as such—the restaurant staff has heard it before and isn't fond of the moniker. I particularly like the steak and frites, where the steak is pan-seared and finished with a cognac pan sauce. Zinc occupies an old brick building. The wine bar area is a long narrow room with the bar running the length of one wall, to the right is the main dining room, and there's a small patio in back. All of these options are attractive. In the evening many patrons come just for the wine (see chapter 8).

209 N. Presa St. 🕐 **210/224-2900.** Reservations recommended. AE, DISC, MC, V. Pizzas, burgers, sandwiches $8–$12; main courses $10–$22. Mon–Fri 11am–midnight; Sat–Sun 3pm–midnight.

Inexpensive

Casa Rio TEX-MEX   I often hear the question, "Where's the best place to eat Tex-Mex at a good table by the river?" The answer is that your options are many and few; many bad options and a few passable ones. Of these, my choice would be Casa Rio. When the weather is glorious, few things are more enjoyable than getting a table at the water's edge, ordering a big platter of something spicy, meaty, and crispy, and sipping down a frozen margarita. This place has an excellent location, not as crowded as most, and, so long as you stick to the Tex-Mex classics, you'll do fine. Steer clear of the tortilla soup and the tamales (which aren't really a Tex-Mex forte) and go with something like flautas, enchiladas, tacos, or fajitas. Enjoy. This is San Antonio, after all, and you're supposed to do these things.

430 E. Commerce St./River Walk. 🕐 **210/225-6718.** www.casa-rio.com. Reservations not accepted. AE, MC, V. Main courses $7–$9; fajitas and steaks $10–$17. Daily 11am–11pm (weather permitting).

Mi Tierra 📷 TEX-MEX   If you've come to San Antonio with the idea of tasting traditional Tex-Mex, this is a great place. Sure, you do see out-of-towners finding their way here because the restaurant is so famous, but you see a lot more locals than anybody else—locals who know their city and know their restaurants. The atmosphere is unselfconsciously *so* San Antonio. I love it. Past the bar are three dining rooms. I like the first one the best, but walk around; in the last room is a big mural with famous San Antonians.

Don't order the *mole* or the fine cuts of steak—that's not why you should be here. Order the Tex-Mex and bring your appetite. You can start with the *botanas* platter, which offers a good smattering of such dishes as *flautas* and *minitostadas*. The top-shelf margarita makes a nice accompaniment. Then move on to the classic Tex-Mex enchiladas bathed in chili gravy.

Mi Tierra is also noted for its bakery, which produces all the baked sweet breads of Mexico collectively known as *pan dulce*. Try one, along with a cup of coffee or hot chocolate Mexican style. I would suggest an *oreja,* made of pastry dough, or a sugar cookie known as a *polvorón.*

You may pay a couple of dollars more here than you would at a Tex-Mex joint in the barrio, but it's well worth it—for the food, for the atmosphere, and for the convenience. The place is open 24/7, so you don't have to check your watch or your calendar before heading on over.

218 Produce Row (Market Sq.). 🕐 **210/225-1262.** www.mitierracafe.com. Reservations accepted for large groups only. Breakfast $7–$10; lunch and dinner plates $8–$19. AE, DISC, MC, V. Daily 24 hr.

Schilo's 🍴 ☺ GERMAN/DELI   This place looks like it has been here since they built the Alamo. The large, open room with its worn wooden booths is classic. It's a good place to stop, rest your feet, and enjoy a hearty bowl of split-pea soup or a piece

IT'S ALWAYS chili IN SAN ANTONIO

It ranks up there with apple pie in the American culinary pantheon, but nobody's mom invented chili. The iconic stew of meat, chilies, onions, and a variety of spices was likely conceived around the 1840s by Texas cowboys who needed to make tough meat palatable while covering up the taste as it began to go bad. The name is a Texas corruption of the Spanish *chile* (chee-leh), after the peppers—which are not really peppers at all, but that's another story—most conventionally used in the stew.

The appellation chili *con carne* is really redundant in Texas, where chili without meat isn't considered chili at all. Indeed, most Texans think that adding beans is only for wimps. Beef is the most common base, but everything from armadillo to venison is acceptable.

No one really knows exactly where chili originated, but San Antonio is the prime candidate for the distinction. There are written accounts from the mid-19th century that describe the town's "chili queens," women who ladled steaming bowls of the concoction in open-air markets and on street corners. They were dishing out chili in front of the Alamo as late as the 1940s.

William Gebhardt helped strengthen San Antonio's claim to chili fame when he began producing chili powder in the city in 1896. His Original Mexican Dinner package, which came out around 20 years later, included a can each of chili con carne, beans, and tamales, among other things, and fed five for $1. This precursor of the TV dinner proved so popular that it earned San Antonio the nickname "Tamaleville."

Oddly enough, chili isn't generally found on San Antonio restaurant menus. But modern-day chili queens come out in force for special events at Market Square, as well as for Nights in Old San Antonio, one of the most popular bashes of the city's huge Fiesta celebration. And there's not a weekend that goes by without a chili cook-off somewhere in the city.

of the signature cherry cheesecake. They also make a mean Reuben sandwich. German live bands play on Saturday from 5 to 8pm. The menu has a large kid-friendly selection and retro low prices. Come Friday or Saturday evening if you want to be serenaded by accordion music.

424 E. Commerce St. 📞 **210/223-6692.** Reservations for large groups for breakfast and dinner only. Sandwiches $5–$7; hot or cold plates $5–$7; main dishes (served after 5pm) $7–$8.95. AE, DC, DISC, MC, V. Mon–Sat 7am–8:30pm.

Twin Sisters 📭 HEALTH FOOD/DELI   This bakery/cafe isn't a bad choice if you've overindulged on Tex-Mex during your stay and are looking for something light and wholesome. Eggless and meatless doesn't mean tasteless here; you can get great Greek salads, spicy tofu scrambles, and salsa-topped veggie burgers. Carnivores can also indulge in the likes of ham, pastrami, and salami sandwiches on the excellent bread made on the premises.

Tip: This place serves a lot more locals than visitors, and fills up by 11:30am but empties after 12:45pm, so plan your visit accordingly. A branch in Alamo Heights, 6322 N. New Braunfels (📞 **210/822-2265**), has longer hours (Mon–Fri 7am–9pm; Sat 7am–3pm; Sun 9am–2pm) and live music on Friday nights.

124 Broadway St. at Travis St. 📞 **210/354-1559.** www.twinsistersbakeryandcafe.com. Reservations not accepted. Breakfast $4–$6; lunch $5–$9. MC, V. Mon–Fri 8am–3pm.

KING WILLIAM/SOUTHTOWN
Moderate

Azuca ★ NUEVO LATINO   "Azuca!" (short for *azucar*—sugar) was the trademark rallying cry of the late, great Cuban diva Celia Cruz. And this Southtown restaurant brings the same kind of verve to the table that she would bring to the stage. The menu incorporates dishes from all over Latin America, which is known for, among other things, dishes highlighting fresh tropical ingredients, bright colors, and bold flavors. There's a large sampling of Caribbean dishes, several of which include characteristic ingredients of the region, such as brightly colored *achiote* and fried plantains. From South America you have the grilled meats of southern Brazil and Argentina, as well as some delicious Bolivian *empanadas*. Mexico is, of course, heavily featured, too. The menu is large and has several original dishes inspired by traditional Latin American cooking and adapted to Texan tastes.

The setting is colorful, with contrasting bold tones and modern lines. On weekends, live salsa and merengue gets cranking, and a lot of people show up to drink *mojitos*. On Thursday evenings, Azuca offers a slightly milder entertainment, flamenco dancing.

713 S. Alamo St. ✆ **210/225-5550.** www.azuca.net. Reservations recommended. Lunch (salads and sandwiches) $7–$11; dinner main courses $14–$27. AE, DC, DISC, MC, V. Mon–Thurs 11am–9:30pm; Fri–Sat 11am–10:30pm. Bar Mon–Thurs 11am–11pm; Fri–Sat 11am–2am.

Liberty Bar ★★ NEW AMERICAN   The Liberty Bar has just completed the move from the old, leaning saloon building on Josephine Street to its new location on South Alamo. The new home makes for a completely different atmosphere, but how could it be otherwise when moving from a former brothel to a former convent? The new location is actually more comfortable and less cramped, with dining areas on the ground floor and upstairs by the bar. The rustic, hewn chairs are actually solid and comfortable, and the tables well separated.

The cooking remains about the same, making an innovative use of many ingredients. Prices are reasonable and portions are generous. On my last visit, I sampled a goat cheese appetizer in a sauce made with *chile cascabel* and *piloncillo* (Mexican raw brown sugar), served with griddled bread; a perfectly dressed green salad with roasted hazelnuts, apples, and bits of pecorino cheese and prosciutto; and a grilled chicken breast wrapped in *hoja santa* (Mexican herb). Pay attention to the daily specials, which I've had good luck with. For something lighter, try one of the innovative sandwiches, such as the portobello with smoked Gouda and saffron aioli. Bread is made in house and is used in the classic bread pudding with hard sauce. The Liberty Bar is a great option for vegetarians.

1111 S. Alamo St. ✆ **210/227-1187.** www.liberty-bar.com. Reservations accepted. Main courses $10–$16; sandwiches $9–$14. AE, DISC, MC, V. Sun–Thurs 11am–9pm; Fri–Sat 11am–10pm, bar until midnight.

Rosario's ★★ TEX-MEX   This colorful restaurant is a favorite meeting place for happy hour and dinner. Owner Lisa Wong succeeded in pulling Tex-Mex out of its traditional setting—the typical Mexican food restaurant, decorated with bullfight posters, Mexican calendars, and mariachi sombreros. Rosario's is modern and fun. The dining rooms have lots of natural light, cheerful colors, a splash of neon light, and polished cement floors. And the contemporary Tex-Mex fare, prepared with fresh ingredients lures locals and visitors alike. The ceviche (whitefish, onions, and jalapeños marinated in lime juice) tastes fresh, or the fish tacos would make for a good light meal. For something more substantial, you have several options, including the chicken chipotle or the chile relleno. The large size of the rooms means that you generally don't have to wait long for a table, but it also means that the noise level can make conversation difficult. I like to go at midafternoon on a weekday, when the place is uncrowded, and happy hour is about to begin (4pm). On Friday and Saturday nights, there's live music starting at 8 or 9pm.

910 S. Alamo St. 📞 **210/223-1806.** www.rosariossa.com. Reservations not accepted. Lunch $6–$9; dinner main courses $8–$23. AE, DC, DISC, MC, V. Mon–Sat 11am–11pm; Sun 11am–9pm.

Inexpensive

Cascabel ★ MEXICAN   Inside a brightly colored modest frame house that's slightly off square is a small kitchen and dining room where you can get delicious genuine Mexican food. The owner is a Mexican woman from the northern state of Coahuila, but she enjoys cooking the classic dishes of central and southern Mexico, such as *mole* (rich, dark sauce made of nuts, sweet meats, bitter chocolate, and several chilies), *pipián verde* (a dish of ground tomatillos, herbs, and pumpkin seeds), and *cochinita pibil*. She also makes Mexico's fast foods, such as tacos, tostadas, and *huaraches* (a large masa cake topped with a variety of ingredients) with your choice of topping/filling. The corn tortillas are made in house, and the cooking is first rate. I enjoyed the signature dish *puerco a la cascabel* (pork in a *chile cascabel* sauce) and will make a point of going back on my next visit to San Antonio.

1000 S. St. Mary's St. 📞 **210/212-6456.** Reservations accepted. Main courses $7–$12. AE, DISC, MC, V. Mon–Fri 10:30am–2pm and 6–9pm; Sat 10:30am–3pm.

The Filling Station 🍴 DELI/ECLECTIC   If you get a little hungry while wandering about the King William district, try this tiny place where you can get quality food for not much money. A young couple, Stacie and Jon Rowe, make soups and salads and bake bread and pizza in this old abandoned gas station. Everything here is made from scratch. You have your choice of several standard pizzas as well as an uncommon Southwestern version, with chicken, black olives, red onion, poblano pepper slices, and black bean sauce. Similarly, among several standard hot sandwiches is a habañero roast beef with melted provolone and a garlic habañero aioli. You can get your food to eat on the premises (only six chairs inside and a small picnic bench area outside), or you can get the food to go and enjoy a picnic in the little park across the way.

701 S. St. Mary's St. (at King William St.). 📞 **210/444-2200.** Reservations not accepted. Pizza slices $2.25–$2.75; sandwiches $4.95–$5.75. AE, DISC, MC, V. Mon–Fri 11am–9pm.

Guenther House ★ AMERICAN   If you're not staying in a King William B&B, this is the easiest way to visit one of the neighborhood's historic homes and have a good meal at the same time. Hearty breakfasts and light lunches are served both indoors—in a bright, cheerful old-style dining room added on to the Guenther family residence (1860)—and outdoors on a trellised patio. The Guenther family owns the old Pioneer Flour Mill, which is in plain sight right across the river, its old-fashioned crenelated tower adding a certain amount of charm to the view. So it's fairly natural that the restaurant would emphasize baked goods. If you're looking for the maximum old southern experience, order the biscuits and gravy, but if you're not in the mood for something different, the waffles and pancakes are quite good. For something less filling, try the breakfast tacos. Breakfast is served till closing at 3pm. The lunch menu is on the light side and includes an excellent chicken salad (made with black olives) and mild chicken enchiladas made with flour tortillas. Adjoining the restaurant are a small museum, a Victorian parlor, and a mill store featuring baking items, including mixes, cookbooks, and kitchen gear. The house fronts a lovely stretch of the San Antonio River.

205 E. Guenther St. ℭ **210/227-1061.** www.guentherhouse.com. Reservations not accepted. Breakfast $4–$8; lunch $6–$8. AE, DC, DISC, MC, V. Daily 7am–3pm (house and mill store Mon–Sat 8am–4pm; Sun 8am–3pm).

Madhatters 🎒 ☺ DELI/ECLECTIC   This colorful, sprawling storefront attracts everyone from nouveau hippies to buttoned-down office workers, to the occasional clutch of housewives out for lunch. They come for Age-of-Aquarius-meets-south-of-the-border food: granola bowls and breakfast burritos in the morning, veggie and deli sandwiches for lunch, and pork tamales in the evening. The rambling house has several indoor and outdoor dining areas, all with a comfortable lived-in feel. The main dining area, where you place your order, has cold cases full of reasonably priced wines and beers. You can also bring the kids to have afternoon tea, which can include peanut-butter-and-jelly sandwiches (crusts cut off, naturally). The NO CELLPHONES sign seems to be taking effect, so you no longer have to retreat from the bustling front room to have a conversation without hearing ringing in your ears (though the back room is pleasant and still quieter).

320 Beauregard St. (at S. Alamo). ℭ **210/212-4832.** www.madhatterstea.com. Reservations not accepted. Breakfast $4–$10; sandwiches and salad plates $7–$10; high tea for 2 $18. AE, DISC, MC, V. Mon–Thurs 7am–10pm; Fri 7am–11pm; Sat 8am–11pm; Sun 9am–9pm.

Tito's 🍴 TEX-MEX   This is one of several typical neighborhood joints that have existed here since before the area started to get trendy. It occupies a slightly run-down building that is attractive and comfortable none the less, with lots of natural light pouring through the big windows. If you're there in the morning (before 10am), the best deal is three breakfast tacos for $2. For lunch or dinner, the thing to order is the enchiladas. The *Tejanas* with chili gravy, the *verdes*, and the *chipotle* cream are all worthy selections.

995 S. Alamo St. (at Beauregard). ℭ **210/212-8226.** Reservations not accepted. Breakfast $2–$6; main courses $7–$13. AE, DISC, MC, V. Sun–Thurs 8am–10pm; Fri–Sat 8am–11pm.

MONTE VISTA AREA
Expensive

Il Sogno ★★★ ITALIAN   When Andrew Weissman made the move from downtown, he decided to close his highly acclaimed Le Reve and open a simpler Italian restaurant instead. Despite the name being an Italian translation of Le Reve, do not expect this restaurant to be the Italian equivalent of the old one, which was a formal French restaurant with several fixed options. It has a simpler concept and more straightforward menu. The daily menu offers pastas, pizzas, and main courses, and there are always some specials. The ingredients are fresh and of the highest quality, and the wine list is an extensive exploration of Italy's winemaking culture. Il Sogno has only 19 tables indoors and doesn't take reservations, but you can call ahead to be put on the waiting list.

what's cooking AT THE OLD PEARL BREWERY

The old Pearl Brewery, occupying about 6 square blocks just north of downtown, is becoming a gastronomical center for San Antonio. First, developers negotiated with the Culinary Institute of America (the other CIA) to establish a school here that would give greater attention to Latin American cooking than either its East Coast school in Hyde Park, N.Y., or its West Coast school in Napa Valley, California. Though it has been operating at a low level for quite a while, the school was officially inaugurated in October 2010. In 2011, it will be offering occasional weekend classes for the non-professional cook. Go to www.ciachef.edu/enthusiasts to explore what's available. The CIA will also be opening a cafe for the public in March 2011.

Next, the developers persuaded San Antonio's most acclaimed chef, Andrew Weissman, to set up two restaurants here—the **Sandbar**, which he moved from a small space downtown, and **Il Sogno**, a new endeavor offering Italian food. In the same manner, they brought in another chef, Johnny Hernandez, who recently opened his Mexican food restaurant called **La Gloria.** These three restaurants are reviewed below.

Other gastronomical activities include a farmers' market on Saturday mornings and Wednesday afternoons, and an excellent cooking store with a Latin American slant called **Melissa Guerra** (see "Shopping in San Antonio," chapter 7). Plans for the future include a microbrewery, stores, apartments, a boutique hotel, and more restaurants. You can walk from downtown to the Pearl Brewery (20 min.) by heading north on the River Walk or taking a river taxi. If you're driving from downtown, take Broadway, and as soon as you've driven under the I-35 overpass, look for a sign on your left.

200 E. Grayson, Pearl Brewery. (℃) **210/223-3900.** Reservations not accepted. Main courses $20–$30. AE, DC, MC, V. Tues–Fri 7:30–10am, 11:30am–2pm, and 6–9:30pm; Sat 8:30–10am, 11:30am–2pm, and 6–9:30pm; Sun 9pm–9pm.

Sandbar ★★★ SEAFOOD   Andrew Weissman's new restaurant is a modern, minimally decorated affair; its white tile wainscoting and commercial light fixtures remind me of old fish markets. In contrast to the casual surroundings is the food, which excels in its variety, its freshness, and its preparation. Using various suppliers, the restaurant receives 10 to 15 kinds of oysters flown in from the East and West coasts. Lobster, caviar, diver scallops—the sea's bounty is rarely so well represented. The top half of the daily menu celebrates to the sea in its purest state: oysters on the half shell, sashimi, boiled shrimp, and ceviche. There's a nod to a few traditional dishes, too: chowder, lobster rolls, fish and chips, and whole fried fish. In the lower half of the menu, you'll see the day's prepared dishes, which strive to complement the freshness of the seafood. Chef Chris Carlson believes in keeping preparation to a minimum. Though reservations aren't accepted, you can call ahead and get on the waiting list.

Pearl Brewery, Ste. 117. (℃) **210/222-2426.** Reservations not accepted. Main courses $20–$36. AE, DC, DISC, MC, V. Tues–Sat 11:30am–10pm.

Moderate

Demo's ✦ GREEK   Demo's is a little bit of Greece in San Antonio. Located across the street from a Greek Orthodox church, it's a favorite among members of the local Greek community. Occasionally you might see a belly-dancing show (not only here, but in the other two locations as well). You can dine on the airy patio or in the dining room, decorated with murals of Greek island scenes. The menu includes gyros, Greek burgers, *dolmas*, *spanakopita*, and other Mediterranean specialties. If you go for the Dieter's Special—a Greek salad with your choice of gyros or souvlakia—you might be able to justify the baklava. In addition to this location, the original (but more characterless) restaurant is at 7115 Blanco Rd. (✆ **210/342-2772**), near Loop 410, across from what used to be Central Park Mall; a third location is farther out at Blanco and Loop 1604 (✆ **210/798-3840**).

2501 N. St. Mary's St. ✆ **210/732-7777.** www.demosgreekfood.com. Reservations accepted for parties of 10 or more only. Main courses $10–$18. AE, DC, DISC, MC, V. Mon–Thurs 11am–9pm; Fri–Sat 11am–midnight.

La Gloria ★ MEXICAN   If you're not going to Mexico (and these days, who is?) you can still enjoy that country's delicious street food at this attractive, playfully decorated eatery at the Pearl Brewery. You're not going to see yellow cheddar or American cheese here; this place does it up Mexican style, finishing several dishes with a light crumbling of a fresh farmer's cheese or a dried *cotija* and perhaps a light drizzle of Mexican cream. Get in line to place your order from a wide-ranging menu that includes dishes from across the country. On the back of the menu is a bit of explanation of the different items, and the staff is happy to explain further. It's clear that chef-owner Johnny Hernandez and his staff put a lot of thought into how to bring these Mexican delicacies to America. Not everything is exactly how you would get it in its native land, but who of us can resist temptation to improve dishes according to our own tastes? The only thing I would avoid are the *tlayudas*, which are near impossible to reproduce outside of Oaxaca.

100 E. Grayson, Pearl Brewery. ✆ **210/267-9094.** www.lagloriaicehouse.com. Reservations not accepted. Dishes $5–$14. AE, DISC, MC, V. Sun–Mon 11am–10pm; Wed–Thurs 11am–10pm; Fri–Sat 11am–midnight.

Los Barrios TEX-MEX   This very popular Tex-Mex joint has been around since the '70s, when it first opened in a former Dairy Queen. Remnants of a big expansion in the '80s can still be in seen in the peach-and-green color combination. All in all, it has the unpretentiousness necessary for popular local restaurants in San Antonio.

The excellent Tex-Mex enchiladas are made of red tortillas and cheese bathed in a hearty chili gravy. Or you could go for the five-enchilada plate, with one of every variety served here. Departures from Tex-Mex include *cabrito* (goat) in salsa and the *milanesa con papas*, described on the menu (accurately) as a Mexican-style chicken-fried steak. If you're really hungry, try the Los Barrios deluxe special platter, which includes two beef tacos, two cheese enchiladas, a strip of steak, rice, beans, and guacamole. Portions are large. If you're watching what you eat, you can easily satisfy hunger pangs with a *chalupa Vallarta* a la carte ($4), and you'll get a large red tortilla stacked with chicken, lettuce, tomato, guacamole, carrot strips, jalapeños, cheese, and sour cream. Nothing at Los Barrios is too spicy.

Chris Madrids (p. 81)   The kid-friendly menu includes burgers, nachos, fries, and various combinations thereof; and the casual atmosphere and down-home cooking make it popular with families.

Madhatters (p. 78)   Even if your kids aren't up for an entire children's tea, they'll be happy to find their faves on the menu, from PB&J to plain turkey or cheese sandwiches. The chocolate-chip cookies and brownies won't be sneezed at, either.

Olmos Pharmacy (p. 84)   Bring your kids to this old-time soda fountain and you can relive the pleasures of your childhood vicariously through them. There are a couple of items on the drinks menu and artifacts behind the counter that most kids won't be familiar with. You can tell them about the old days.

Schilo's (p. 74)   A high noise level, a convenient location near the River Walk (but with prices far lower than anything else you'll find there), and a wide selection of familiar food make this German deli a good choice for the family.

Mondays and Tuesdays are popular for "Fajita Nights," when you can get a pound of fajitas with all the sides for $14 ($18 regular price). Wednesdays are "Margarita Nights," and on Thursdays, there's a special on longnecks.

4223 Blanco Rd. ℰ **210/732-6017.** Reservations accepted for large groups only. Dinners $9–$14. AE, DISC, MC, V. Mon–Thurs 10am–10pm; Fri–Sat 10am–11pm; Sun 9am–10pm.

Inexpensive

Chris Madrids ☺ BURGERS   This is a fun, down-home hamburger joint where Tex-Mex meets Americana. It's been around forever and is known for its extra-large "macho" burger, which is a supersized version of any of their standard burgers. Two burgers merit special mention. The ever popular "tostada burger" comes with crushed tortilla chips, refried beans, and real cheddar. The other is the "cheddar cheesy" burger, which in its "macho" state is quite intimidating (and I've never been intimidated by a burger before). The cheddar oozes out over the large burger engulfing even the platter. The french fries are made in-house and are well worth ordering. The kid-friendly menu also includes chicken sandwiches, nachos, and chalupas. The main dining area is a large room with cement floor and a high-framed ceiling. There is also an outdoor patio in back.

1900 Blanco Rd. (just south of Hildebrand Ave.). ℰ **210/735-3552.** www.chrismadrids.com. Reservations not accepted. Burgers $5–$8. AE, DC, DISC, MC, V. Mon–Sat 11am–10pm.

Rolando's Super Tacos ✦ TEX-MEX   Rolando's is one of the many small businesses that pack both sides of West Hildebrand between I-10 and Trinity University. It offers further proof that once you get out of the downtown tourist zone, you'll find San Antonio a dining bargain. Next door to a Chevron gas station, Rolando's is a rambling shack painted in vivid red and green. It doesn't look that big, especially when you walk through the door into a small room, but the dining room beyond goes way back and turns a corner. The surroundings aren't spectacular. In fact, this place is a real dive, but it's representative of old San Antonio: a blue-collar, old-time Tejano eatery.

Rolando's is open only for breakfast and lunch and is famous for its extra-large "super tacos," which can be had in corn or flour tortillas with a variety of fillings. One makes a meal. Also popular are the *carne guisada* (beef stewed in a chili sauce) plate and the puffy tacos.

919 W. Hildebrand Ave. (just west of Blanco Rd.) ✆ **210/732-6713.** Reservations not accepted. Super tacos $5.50; plates $7–$10. DC, DISC, MC, V. Mon and Wed–Fri 7am–2pm; Sat 7am–4pm; Sun 8am–3pm.

ALAMO HEIGHTS AREA

Expensive

See also **Paesano's,** in the "Downtown" section, p. 69.

Bistro Vatel ★★ 🍴 FRENCH In 1671, the great French chef Vatel killed himself out of shame because the fish for a banquet he was preparing for Louis XIV wasn't delivered on time. Fortunately, his descendant, Damian Watel, has less stress to contend with in San Antonio, where diners are very appreciative of the chef's efforts to bring them classic French cooking at reasonable prices. Comfortable furniture, ample space, white tablecloths, and excellent service make for a satisfying dining experience.

You can't go wrong with the rich escallop of veal with foie gras and mushrooms, and fans of sweetbreads will be pleased to find them here beautifully prepared in truffle crème fraîche sauce. Your best bet is the prix-fixe dinner; choose one each from four appetizers (perhaps shrimp *vol au vent*) and entrees such as roasted quail, then enjoy the dessert of the day.

218 E. Olmos Dr. at McCullough. ✆ **210/828-3141.** www.bistrovatel.com. Reservations recommended on weekends. Main courses $15–$27; prix-fixe dinner $35. AE, MC, V. Tues–Sat 11am–9pm; Sun 5–9pm.

Frederick's ★★★ 🍴 FRENCH/FUSION Year in and year out, this restaurant serves outstanding food with admirable consistency. Not as well-known as many of San Antonio's glitzier culinary establishments, it has its own large body of loyal customers who know of its semi-hidden location, at the back of a Broadway strip mall. I like the sedate dining room with low ceiling, soft lights, comfortable furniture, and the non-fussy atmosphere. It's a refreshing combination of great food served without a lot of show.

Chef-owner Frederick Costa was born in Vietnam, but moved to France early on. His cooking combines elements from both cultures. For starters, consider caramelized pork ribs with a spicy sauce; the delicate and crispy spring rolls of shrimp, pork, and mushrooms; or a zesty crab salad with avocado. Entrees might include baked sea bass in truffle oil with artichoke hearts, or a duck breast cooked in a sauce of green peppercorns and cognac. The large wine list is mostly French and Californian.

7701 Broadway, Ste. 20 (in the back of Dijon Plaza). ✆ **210/828-9050.** www.frederickssa.com. Reservations recommended on weekends. Main courses $20–$30. AE, DC, MC, V. Mon–Thurs 11:30am–2pm and 5:30–10pm; Fri 11:30am–2pm and 5:30–10:30pm; Sat 5:30–10:30pm.

Silo ★★ NEW AMERICAN   For my money, this is one of the best places for fine dining when you want something other than French food. In contrast with many chic restaurants that try to get attention by creating fanciful sounding dishes, Silo quietly goes about its business, focusing on creating satisfying dishes that deliver something new without gimmickry. The menu changes often, but some representative examples include the chipotle marinated pork tenderloin with white cheddar andouille grits and peach chutney, the crab spring rolls with shiitake mushrooms and tantalizing dipping sauces, pan-seared scallops treated very simply, and wonderful mango-wasabi crab cakes.

1133 Austin Hwy. Ⓒ **210/824-8686.** www.siloelevatedcuisine.com. Reservations recommended. Main courses $20–$40; prix fixe (salad, entree, dessert) $25–$35 (5:30-6:30pm nightly). AE, DC, DISC, MC, V. Lunch daily 11am-2:30pm; dinner Sun-Thurs 5:30-10pm, Fri-Sat 5:30-10:30pm.

Moderate

Ciao Lavanderia ★ ITALIAN   In an open, cheery storefront with post-mod tributes to the business that used to reside here (exposed ductwork, an old washing machine), you can savor the expert renditions of some of the classic dishes of Italy—pastas, thin-crust pizzas (baked in a wood-burning brick oven), and risotto. The calzone or the panini would make for a satisfying lunch, as would one of the wide variety of salads offered here. The dinner options include a mouthwatering pork tenderloin wrapped in prosciutto and served with creamy polenta. Everything's fresh and delicious, and the portions reflect a normal human appetite. This restaurant is an excellent choice for vegetarians, and the kitchen can make gluten-free versions of all but a few of the pastas. A good selection of wines enhances an already optimal experience.

226 E. Olmos Dr. Ⓒ **210/822-3990.** www.ciaofoodandwine.com. Reservations accepted for large parties only. Pastas and pizzas $8–$18; main courses $15–$23. AE, DC, DISC, MC, V. Mon-Thurs 11am-2pm and 5-9:30pm; Fri 11am-2pm and 5-10pm; Sat 5-10pm.

Paloma Blanca ★ MEXICAN   Something about this place reminds me of a certain class of restaurant you'd find in the fashionable neighborhoods of Mexico City. Perhaps it's the large windows facing a walled patio area graced with fountain and decorative plants, or the modern leather furniture in the bar area. On the menu are some great soups, such as the cream soup flavored with *poblano chile* (if you like that combination of cream and poblano but want to forgo a soup course, try the *pollo en crema poblana*). Several mainstays of Mexican cooking are offered: enchiladas in a dark, earthy *mole* sauce, or in a tangy *salsa verde;* steak *a la tampiqueña* (which must be the most commonly found menu item in Mexico); and a red snapper cooked in the style of Veracruz. Of course, Tex-Mex standards are on the menu, too, and you can find some hearty vegetarian dishes such as a great vegetable chile relleno. A separate gluten-free menu is available for anyone who requests it. The bar is comfortable and has a full margarita menu, which I'm pretty sure is gluten-free as well. Keep this place in mind if you just want to enjoy some savory finger food with drinks in attractive surroundings. The bar area is comfortable and the menu has plenty of appetizers and finger foods.

5600 Broadway St. Ⓒ **210/822-6151.** www.palomablanca.net. Reservations recommended for large groups only. Main courses $10–$25. AE, MC, V. Mon-Wed 11am-9pm; Thurs-Fri 11am-10pm; Sat 10am-10pm; Sun 10am-9pm.

Tre Trattoria ★ ITALIAN   This restaurant on Broadway is the perfect place to enjoy a leisurely meal. Casual and modern, with a cozy bar/lounge and a good selection of wines, you can get comfortable in the overstuffed chairs while you wait for your table. Sit inside in a well-lit, not-too-noisy dining room or outside on an inviting deck sufficiently distant from the street noise. The dinner menu is organized in typical Italian style with first and second courses; the second courses are served family-style, to be shared among up to four people. The grilled rainbow trout with crispy skin is marvelous. Another option is the small pizzas; three or four varieties have out-of-the-ordinary combinations of toppings. Quite good.

4003 Broadway St. (next to the Witte Museum). ✆ **210/805-0333.** www.tretrattoria.com. Reservations accepted. Main courses $15-$20. AE, MC, V. Mon–Thurs 11am–10pm; Fri–Sat 11am–11pm.

Van's CHINESE/JAPANESE/VIETNAMESE   Talk about Pan-Asian. The sign outside announces that Van's is a "Chinese Seafood Restaurant and Sushi Bar," but you'll also find Vietnamese dishes on the huge menu. The dining room is low-key but appealing, with crisp green-and-white cloth table coverings. If you like seafood, go for the shrimp in a creamy curry sauce or the fresh crab with black-bean sauce. Alternatively, consider one of the meal-size soups—beef brisket with rice noodles, say, or a vegetable clay pot preparation—or tasty versions of such Szechuan standards as spicy kung pao chicken with carrots and peanuts. Van's also has a surprisingly large wine list.

3214 Broadway St. ✆ **210/828-8449.** Reservations for large parties only. Main courses $9–$15. AE, DISC, MC, V. Daily 11am–10pm.

Inexpensive

Olmos Pharmacy 🍴 ☺ AMERICAN   When was the last time you drank a rich chocolate malt served in a large metal container—with a glass of whipped cream on the side? Grab a stool at Olmos's Formica counter and reclaim your childhood. Olmos Pharmacy, opened in 1938, also scoops up old-fashioned ice-cream sodas, Coke or root beer floats, sundaes, banana splits . . . if it's cold, sweet, and nostalgia-inducing, they've got it. This is also the place to come for filling American and Mexican breakfasts, an array of tacos, and classic burgers and sandwiches, all at seriously retro prices.

3902 McCullough Ave. ✆ **210/822-3361.** Main courses $4–$7. AE, MC, V. Mon–Fri 7am–5pm (fountain until 6pm); Sat 8am–4pm (fountain until 5pm).

NORTHWEST

Expensive

Aldo's ITALIAN   A northwest San Antonio favorite, Aldo's offers good, old-fashioned Italian food in a pretty, old-fashioned setting. You can enjoy your meal outside on a tree-shaded patio or inside a 100-year-old former ranch house in one of a series of Victorian dining rooms. The scampi Valentino, sautéed shrimp with a basil cream sauce, is a nice starter, as are the lighter steamed mussels in marinara sauce, available seasonally. A house specialty, sautéed snapper di Aldo, comes topped with fresh lump crabmeat, artichoke hearts, mushrooms, and tomatoes in a white-wine sauce.

FROZEN assets

Austin has long had Amy's ice cream, but when it comes to homegrown frozen desserts, San Antonio has been, well, left out in the cold. But that's all changed with the new century and the introduction of **Brindles Awesome Ice Cream,** 11255 Huebner Rd. (© **210/641-5222**). Brindles features more than 200 varieties of creative ice creams, gelati, and sorbets. About 45 to 50 flavors are available on any given day. You might find such unique creations as spice apple brandy or bananas Foster ice cream; white chocolate Frangelico or candied ginger gelato; and champagne or cranberry sorbet—as well as, in every category, far more traditional flavors for ice-cream purists. Among the best-selling ice creams is the signature

Brindles, a butterscotch fudge crunch inspired, like the store's name, by the multicolored coat of the owners' pet boxer. And don't miss "The Kick" ice cream whenever it's available. This mixture of pineapple, coconut, mint, and habañero chili doesn't taste hot initially, but it packs a bit of a wallop afterward.

If you don't want to have to trek all the way to Brindles' mother ship, the espresso and ice-cream parlor in the Strand shopping center on San Antonio's northwest side, you can also sample Brindles products at several of San Antonio's finest restaurants, including Acenar, Biga on the Banks, Bistro Vatel, and Boudro's, all covered elsewhere in this chapter.

8539 Fredericksburg Rd. © **210/696-2536.** Reservations recommended, especially on weekends. Pastas $12–$18; main courses $19–$34. AE, DC, DISC, MC, V. Mon–Thurs 11am–10pm; Fri 11am–11pm; Sat 5–11pm; Sun 5–10pm.

Moderate

See also Sushi Zushi, in the "Downtown" section of this chapter.

Thai Restaurant ★ 🍴 THAI   The cooking is marvelous at this small, family-owned restaurant in a small strip center just outside Loop 410. The menu offers many of Thailand's most famous dishes, and these are cooked with great care and fresh ingredients. The pad Thai (not too sweet, noodles cooked to the perfect texture, very fresh bean sprouts), the pad kra pao (generous with the basil leaves), and the panang curry (nicely scented, with just the right hint of lime and shrimp paste) were all hits with me. So, too, were the rolls, and an uncommon appetizer of fried stuffed tofu. The latter was served with a delicious peanut and cilantro dipping sauce. And last but not least is the *yum nua,* a cold beef salad with fresh butter lettuce, red onion, tomato, and cucumber, covered in a citric dressing. The attentive service, the low prices, and the quiet dining room (quiet until 9pm, when music from the bar next door begins to seep through the wall) also make this place an attractive choice.

1709 Babcock Rd. (at Callaghan) © **210/341-0606.** Reservations accepted. Main courses $9–$12. DISC, MC, V. Mon–Fri 11am–3pm and 5–9:45pm; Sat 11am–9:45pm.

Tip Top Cafe 🎁 AMERICAN   This place has remained unchanged for years. Since I first wrote about it, it has become popular outside its traditional clientele. But it still has the same faux adobe and neon exterior, the same wood-paneled walls (with both real and imitation paneling), and the same dusty decorations, including everything from antlers to letters of recognition. It also has the same comfortable old-style tables and chairs, classic booths, and a solid wood lunch counter. The staff has been here forever. Example: My waitress mentions that she's the "new kid," having worked here for only 8 years.

Comfort food is the draw here. Favorites include chicken-fried steak (and the chicken-fried steak sandwich), fried shrimp, and onion rings, not to mention the meatloaf on Thursdays, and chicken and dumplings—the ultimate in comfort food—served on Fridays starting at 5pm and ending sometime on Saturday when it runs out. All the pies are made in-house. Among them, there's always an apple and at least one other fruit pie, as well as a cream pie or two, and usually a pecan pie. Note that this isn't the place for people who are in the habit of dining late. The locals come early, and the place closes by 8pm.

2814 Fredericksburg Rd. (btw. Santa Anna and Santa Monica). (© **210/735-2222.** Reservations not accepted. Sandwiches $4-$7; main courses $8-$13. No credit cards. Tues-Sat 11am-8pm; Sun 11am-7pm.

EXPLORING SAN ANTONIO

San Antonio has a wide selection of attractions that can satisfy a variety of interests. You could easily fill your visit hitting each one on your list, but I suggest that you set aside at least a little time for aimlessly strolling about the city's downtown. You'll come across unexpected sights such as, for instance, the Bexar (pronounced bear) County Court House, which, though not remarkable enough to merit specific listing among the city's attractions, is still quite attractive and exemplifies the city's character. Also, a couple of plazas lie almost forgotten, one of which was the scene of a battle with a Comanche raiding party.

Before you visit any of the paid attractions, stop in at the **San Antonio Visitor Information Center,** 317 Alamo Plaza (© **210/207-6748**), across the street from the Alamo, and ask for their *SAVE San Antonio* discount book; it includes coupons for everything from the large theme parks to some city tours and museums. Many hotels also have a stash of discount coupons for their guests.

THE TOP ATTRACTIONS

Downtown Area

The Alamo ★★ Upon seeing the Alamo for the first time, most visitors react with surprise at how small it is. Though the shape of the facade of the Alamo is widely recognized, most Americans think of it as a large fortress. This only underscores the heroic and desperate actions of the Alamo's defenders, who in 1836 held off a siege by a large Mexican army for 13 days. Also, it should be noted, the defenses for the battle were much larger than what you see today on the mission grounds. Back in those days, missions often had large enclosed areas in front of the church, known as *atrios*. The wall enclosed all of what is now Alamo Plaza and extended even a bit farther in the direction of the river.

The Alamo today is more a shrine than a museum. Its main purpose is to honor the actions of its defenders, which, whether real or imagined, went a long way toward creating the larger-than-life mystique that Texas was eventually to acquire. Among the famous defenders were Davy Crockett and Jim Bowie, and the idea of their sacrifice for Texas independence gave added meaning to the struggle almost immediately. "Remember the Alamo!" became the battle cry at San Jacinto, when the Texans finally defeated the Mexican army and captured its general, López de Santa Anna.

The Daughters of the Republic of Texas, who saved the crumbling mission from being turned into a hotel by a New York syndicate in 1905, have long been the Alamo's stewards. They have installed exhibits to display the various roles the mission played, including serving as a Native American burial ground. The Alamo's original name was Mission San Antonio de Valero, and many converted Indians from a variety of tribes lived and died here. The complex was secularized by the end of the 18th century and leased out to a Spanish cavalry unit; however, by the time the famous battle took place, it had been abandoned. **A Wall of History,** erected in the late 1990s, provides a chronology of these events.

The outlying buildings of the original mission are gone. Only the **Long Barrack** (formerly the *convento,* or living quarters for the missionaries) and the much-photographed **mission church** are still here. The former houses a museum detailing the history of Texas in general and the battle in particular, and the latter includes artifacts of the Alamo fighters, along with an information desk and a small gift shop. The exhibit doesn't do the best job of explaining how the battle developed. If you want to understand more, see the IMAX show in the nearby Rivercenter Mall.

A larger **museum** and gift shop are at the back of the complex. A peaceful **garden** and an excellent **research library** (closed Sun) are also on the grounds. All in all, though, the complex is fairly small. You won't need to spend more than an hour here. Interesting historical presentations are given every half-hour by Alamo staffers; for private, after-hour tours, phone © **210/225-1391,** ext. 34.

300 Alamo Plaza. © **210/225-1391.** www.thealamo.org. Free admission (donations welcome). Mon-Sat 9am–5:30pm; Sun 10am–5:30pm. Closed Dec 24-25. Streetcar: Red or Blue line.

King William Historic District ★
San Antonio's first suburb, King William was settled in the 19th century by prosperous German merchants who displayed their wealth through extravagant homes and named the 25-block area after Kaiser Wilhelm of Prussia. (The other residents of San Antonio were rather less complimentary about this German area, which they dubbed "Sauerkraut Bend.")

The neighborhood fell into decline in the middle of the 20th century, as the affluent abandoned the inner city for prosperous neighborhoods and suburbs to the north. Property values, and hence investment, fell. King William could easily have been lost but was saved largely through the efforts of one man, Walter Mathis, a local investment banker. He bought his house here in 1967 and then purchased several others in the '70s. To these he made structural repairs to arrest the decay and then sold them with interest-free loans to other preservationists wanting to live in the neighborhood. By the 1990s it was again flourishing. Mr. Mathis's house, **Villa Finale,** is now a National Trust property (the only one in Texas) and is open to the public (see later in this chapter). So many houses have been restored that the area has become popular with visitors. Though tour buses frequent the area, if the weather's agreeable, it's much more pleasant to be on foot here than on a bus. You can stroll down tree-lined streets and admire the old houses and their various architectural styles.

Stop at the headquarters of the **San Antonio Conservation Society,** 107 King William St. (© **210/224-6163;** www.saconservation.org), and pick up a self-guided walking tour booklet outside the gate. *Tip:* At the Visitor Center for Villa Finale, 122 Madison St., you can get a pamphlet with instructions for a cellphone audio tour of the neighborhood. If you go at a leisurely pace, the stroll should take a little more than an hour. If you want to see Villa Finale or the **Steves Homestead Museum** (see

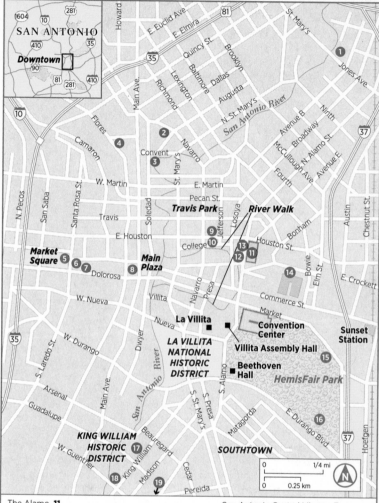

The Alamo **11**
ArtPace **4**
Blue Star Contemporary Art Center **19**
Buckhorn Saloon & Museum **10**
Casa Navarro State Historic Site **7**
Institute of Texan Cultures **16**
Louis Tussaud's Wax Works
   & Ripley's Believe It or Not **12**
Museo Alameda **5**
Ripley's Haunted Adventure, Guinness
   World Records Museum, and Tomb Rider 3D **13**

San Antonio Central Library **3**
San Antonio Children's Museum **9**
San Antonio IMAX Theater **14**
San Antonio Museum of Art **1**
San Fernando Cathedral **8**
Southwest School of Art and Craft **2**
Spanish Governor's Palace **6**
Steves Homestead Museum **18**
Tower of the Americas **15**
Villa Finale **17**

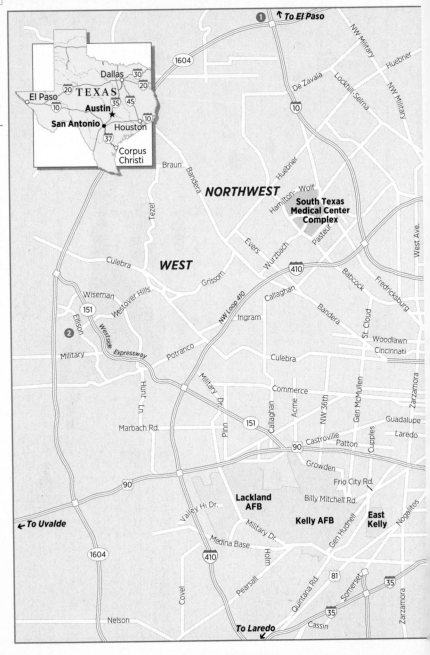

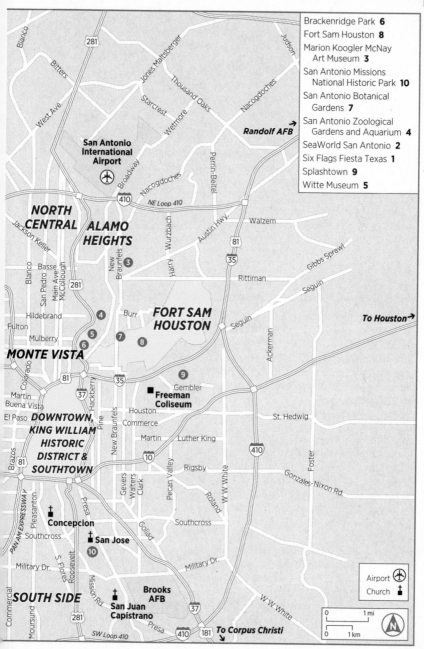

Brackenridge Park **6**
Fort Sam Houston **8**
Marion Koogler McNay
  Art Museum **3**
San Antonio Missions
  National Historic Park **10**
San Antonio Botanical
  Gardens **7**
San Antonio Zoological
  Gardens and Aquarium **4**
SeaWorld San Antonio **2**
Six Flags Fiesta Texas **1**
Splashtown **9**
Witte Museum **5**

the alamo: THE MOVIE(S)

At least one weighty tome, Frank Thompson's *Alamo Movies,* has been devoted to the plethora of films featuring the events that occurred at San Antonio's most famous site. Some outtakes:

Most famous movie about the Alamo not actually shot at the Alamo: *The Alamo* (1959), starring John Wayne as Davy Crockett. Although it has no San Antonio presence, it was shot in Texas. Wayne considered shooting the film in Mexico, but was told it wouldn't be distributed in Texas if he did.

Latest controversy-ridden attempt to tell the story of the Alamo: A 2004 Disney version, also called *The Alamo,* that was originally supposed to be directed by Ron Howard but was eventually only co-produced by him.

Directed by John Lee Hancock and starring Dennis Quaid, Billy Bob Thornton, and Jason Patric, among others, it was not a complete success in any shape or form, but it wasn't an embarrassment, either.

Most accurate celluloid depiction of the Alamo story (and also the largest): *Alamo—The Price of Freedom,* showing at the San Antonio IMAX Theater Rivercenter. According to writer and historian Stephen Harrigan in an interview on National Public Radio, it's "90% accurate."

Least controversial film featuring the Alamo: *Miss Congeniality,* starring Sandra Bullock and Benjamin Bratt. A beauty pageant presided over by William Shatner takes place in front of the shrine to the Texas martyrs.

later in this chapter), you need to do a little planning, but the **Guenther House** is easily accessible and doesn't require a guided tour. If you're staying downtown and are a good walker, you can get to the neighborhood in 15 minutes by following the recently completed extension of the River Walk. It's a pleasant hike. If you're hungry, choose from quite a few options for lunch in the neighborhood and on South Alamo Street (see chapter 5).

East bank of the river, just south of downtown. Streetcar: Blue line.

La Villita National Historic District ★ Developed by European settlers along the east bank of the San Antonio River in the late 18th and early 19th centuries, La Villita (the Little Village) was on the proverbial wrong side of the tracks until natural flooding of the west-bank settlements made it fashionable again. It fell back into poverty by the beginning of the 20th century, only to be revitalized in the late 1930s by artists and craftspeople and the San Antonio Conservation Society. Now boutiques, crafts shops, and restaurants occupy this historic district, which resembles a Spanish/Mexican village, replete with shaded patios, plazas, brick-and-tile streets, and some of the settlement's original adobe structures. You can see (but not enter, unless you rent it for an event) the house of General Cós, the Mexican military leader who surrendered to the Texas revolutionary army in 1835, or attend a performance at the **Arneson River Theatre** (p. 129). Walking tour maps of these and other historical structures are available throughout the site. It'll take you only about 20 minutes to do a quick walk-through, unless you're an inveterate shopper—in which case, all bets are off.

Bounded by Durango, Navarro, and Alamo sts. and the River Walk. © **210/207-8610.** www.lavillita. com. Free admission. Shops daily 10am–6pm. Closed Thanksgiving, Dec 25, and Jan 1. Streetcar: Red, Purple, or Blue line.

Market Square ★ It may not be quite as colorful as it was when live chickens squawked around overflowing, makeshift vegetable stands, but Market Square will still transport you south of the border. Stalls in the indoor El Mercado sell everything from onyx paperweights and manufactured serapes to high-quality crafts from the interior of Mexico. Across the street, the Farmers' Market, which formerly housed the produce market, has carts with more modern goods. If you can tear yourself away from the merchandise, take a look around at the buildings in the complex; some date back to the late 1800s.

Bring your appetite along with your wallet: In addition to two Mexican restaurants (see p. 74 for **Mi Tierra** review), almost every weekend sees the emergence of food stalls selling specialties such as *gorditas* (chubby corn cakes topped with a variety of goodies) or funnel cakes (fried dough sprinkled with powdered sugar). Most of the city's Hispanic festivals are held here, and mariachis usually stroll the square. The **Museo Alameda** (see "More Attractions," later in this chapter) provides historic context for an area that can seem pretty touristy.

Bounded by Commerce, Santa Rosa, Dolorosa, and I-35. © **210/207-8600.** www.marketsquaresa. com. Free admission. El Mercado and Farmers' Market Plaza summer daily 10am–8pm; winter daily 10am–6pm; restaurants and some shops open later. Closed Thanksgiving, Dec 25, Jan 1, and Easter. Streetcar: Red or Yellow line.

The River Walk (Paseo del Río) ★★★ Below the streets of downtown San Antonio lies another world, alternately soothing and exhilarating, depending on where you venture. The quieter areas of the 5 miles of winding riverbank, shaded by cypresses, oaks, and willows, exude a tropical, exotic aura. The River Square and South Bank sections, chockablock with sidewalk cafes, tony restaurants, bustling bars, high-rise hotels, and even a huge shopping mall, have a festive, sometimes frenetic feel. Tour boats, water taxis, and floating picnic barges regularly ply the river, and local parades and festivals fill its banks with revelers.

Although plans to cement over the river after a disastrous flood in 1921 were stymied, it wasn't until the late 1930s that the federal Works Project Administration (WPA) carried out architect Robert Hugman's designs for the waterway, installing cobblestone walks, arched bridges, and entrance steps from various street-level locations. In the late 1960s, when the River Walk proved to be one of the most popular attractions of the HemisFair exposition, its commercial development began in earnest.

The River Walk may run the risk of becoming overdeveloped, with new restaurants and entertainment complexes opening every year, but plenty of quieter spots still exist. The city has extended the River Walk a couple of miles in each direction so that it's now fairly long. These extensions are quiet places perfect for walking, but they lack some of the features of the core, especially the majestic trees. Mornings are a good time to see the main part of the River Walk, when the crowds are smaller and the light filters softly through the trees. At night the River Walk takes on a different character; if you're caught up in the sparkling lights reflected on the water, you might forget anyone else is around.

All the streetcars stop somewhere along the river's route. The River Walk Streetcar Station at Commerce and Losoya is accessible to travelers with disabilities.

San Antonio Museum of Art ★★   This may not be at the top of everyone's list of San Antonio attractions, but I enjoy museums with interesting architecture and collections related to the cities in which they're located. This one definitely fits the bill on both scores. Several old buildings of the 1904 Lone Star Brewery were gutted, connected, and transformed into a unique exhibition space in 1981, which offers terrific views of downtown from the windows of the crosswalk between the structures. Although holdings range from early Egyptian, Greek, Oceanic, and Asian to 19th- and 20th-century American, it's the Nelson A. Rockefeller Center for Latin American Art, opened in 1998, that is the jewel of the collection. This 30,000-square-foot wing hosts the most comprehensive collection of Latin American art in the United States, with pre-Columbian, folk, Spanish colonial, and contemporary works. You'll see everything here from magnificently ornate altarpieces to a whimsical Day of the Dead tableau. The contemporary art in this collection is particularly strong. Computer stations add historical perspective to the collection, which is a nationwide resource for Latino culture. Allot at least 2 hours for your visit.

The Lenora and Walter F. Brown Asian Art Wing represents another major collection, the largest Asian art collection in Texas and one of the largest in the Southwest. To see everything, which I don't particularly recommend, would take more than 4 hours.

200 W. Jones Ave. ✆ **210/978-8100.** www.samuseum.org. Admission $8 adults, $7 seniors, $5 students with ID, $3 children 4–11, free for children 3 and under. Free general admission Tues 4–9pm (fee for some special exhibits). Tues 10am–9pm; Wed–Sat 10am–5pm; Sun noon–6pm. Closed Thanksgiving Day, Dec 25, Jan 1, Easter Sunday, and Fiesta Friday. Bus: 7, 8, 9, or 14.

Alamo Heights Area

Marion Koogler McNay Art Museum ★★★   Well worth a detour from downtown, this museum is one of my favorite spots. A knockout setting on a hill north of Brackenridge Park with a panoramic view of the city is home to a sprawling Spanish Mediterranean–style mansion (built in 1929) so picturesque that it's often used as a backdrop for weddings and photo shoots. The art collection, though not perhaps the equivalent of collections in bigger cities, is quite good if you enjoy modern art. It has at least one work by most American and European masters of the past 2 centuries, including van Gogh, Manet, Gauguin, Degas, O'Keeffe, Hopper, Matisse, Modigliani, Cézanne, and Picasso, to name just a few of the artists.

The McNay recently finished a modern addition that nearly doubles its gallery space, yet the museum manages to retain an intimate feel. The addition, designed by French architect Jean Paul Viguier, is modern and airy and quite enjoyable, adding variety to the original gallery space. It has an innovative roof and ceiling that allows it to filter and adjust the lighting according to the needs of a particular exhibit. The McNay occasionally hosts major traveling shows and, with the new addition, will probably host more of these exhibits. It'll take you 2 hours to go through this place at a leisurely pace, longer if it's cool enough for you to stroll the beautiful 23 acres of landscaped grounds dotted with sculpture. You might also enjoy the 15-minute orientation film about oil heiress and artist Marion Koogler McNay, who established the museum. And, of course, there's a gift shop.

6000 N. New Braunfels Ave. ℂ **210/824-5368.** www.mcnayart.org. Admission $8 adults, $5 seniors, $5 students w/ID, free for children 12 and under. Tues–Wed 10am–4pm; Thurs 10am–9pm; Fri 10am–4pm; Sat 10am–5pm; Sun noon–5pm. Closed Jan 1, July 4th, Thanksgiving, and Dec 25. Bus: 14.

Witte Museum ★ ☺ A family museum that adults will enjoy, too, the Witte focuses on Texas history, natural science, and anthropology, with occasional forays as far afield as the Berlin Wall. Your senses will be engaged along with your intellect: You might hear bird calls as you stroll through the Texas Wild exhibits, or feel rough-hewn stone carved with Native American pictographs beneath your feet. Children especially like exhibits devoted to mummies and dinosaurs, as well as the EcoLab, where live Texas critters range from tarantulas to tortoises. But the biggest draw for kids is the terrific HEB Science Treehouse, a four-level, 15,000-square-foot science center that sits behind the museum on the banks of the San Antonio River; its hands-on activities are geared to all ages. Also on the grounds are a butterfly and hummingbird garden and three restored historic homes. *Note:* Several years ago the museum acquired the wonderful Herzberg Circus Collection, and parts of it are regularly incorporated into the museum's exhibits.

3801 Broadway (adjacent to Brackenridge Park). ℂ **210/357-1900.** www.wittemuseum.org. Admission $8 adults, $7 seniors, $6 children 4–11, free for children 3 and under. Free Tues 3–8pm. Tues 10am–8pm; Mon and Wed–Sat 10am–5pm; Sun noon–5pm. Closed 3rd Mon in Oct, Thanksgiving, and Dec 24–25. Bus: 7, 9, or 14.

South Side

San Antonio Missions National Historical Park ★★ The Alamo was just the first of five missions established by the Franciscans along the San Antonio River to Christianize the native population. The four other missions, which now fall under the aegis of the National Park Service, are still active parishes, run in cooperation with the Archdiocese of San Antonio. But the missions were more than churches: They were whole communities. The Park Service has assigned each mission an interpretive theme to educate visitors about the roles they played in early San Antonio society. You can visit them separately, but if you have the time, see them all; they were built uncharacteristically close together and—now that you don't have to walk there or ride a horse—it shouldn't take you more than 2 or 3 hours to see them.

The easiest way to see them is to drive. The missions are about 3 miles apart from each other. Each has an information office with free maps and can give you driving instructions to the next mission. New signs make touring the missions easier. If you ever get turned around, remember that all the missions are built along the river. The main information office is at Mission San José. The other option for touring the missions is a 12-mile hike-and-bike trail that for the most part follows the river as it passes close by each mission. If you want to try biking it, see later in this chapter for bike rentals.

The first of the missions you'll come to as you head south, **Concepción,** 807 Mission Rd., at Felisa, was built in 1731. The oldest unrestored Texas mission, Concepción looks much as it did 200 years ago. We tend to think of these old missions as somber and austere places, but traces of color on the facade and restored wall paintings inside show how cheerful this one originally was.

San José ★★, 6701 San José Dr., at Mission Road, established in 1720, was the largest, best known, and most beautiful of the Texas missions. It was reconstructed to give visitors a complete picture of life in a mission community—right down to the granary, mill, and Indian quarters. The beautiful rose window is a big attraction, and popular mariachi Masses are held here every Sunday at noon (come early if you want a seat). This is also the site of the missions' excellent visitor center. If you're going to visit only one of the missions, this is it.

Moved from an earlier site in east Texas to its present location in 1731, **San Juan Capistrano,** 9101 Graf, at Ashley, doesn't have the grandeur of the missions to the north—the larger church intended for it was never completed—but the original simple chapel and the wilder setting give it a peaceful air. A short (.3-mile) interpretive trail, with a number of overlook platforms, winds through the woods to the banks of the old river channel.

The southernmost mission in the San Antonio chain, **San Francisco de la Espada** ★, 10040 Espada Rd., also has an ancient, isolated feel, although the beautifully maintained church shows just how vital it still is to the local community. Be sure to visit the Espada Aqueduct, part of the mission's original *acequia* (irrigation ditch) system, about 1 mile north of the mission. Dating from 1740, it's one of the oldest Spanish aqueducts in the United States.

Headquarters: 2202 Roosevelt Ave. Visitors Center: 6701 San José Dr., at Mission Rd. ✆ **210/932-1001.** www.nps.gov/saan. Free admission (donations accepted). All missions open daily 9am–5pm. Closed Thanksgiving, Dec 25, and Jan 1. National Park Ranger tours daily. Bus: 42 stops at Mission San José (and near Concepción).

Far Northwest

Six Flags Fiesta Texas ★ ☺ Every year brings another thrill ride to this theme park, set on 200 acres in an abandoned limestone quarry and surrounded by 100-foot cliffs. Among the extreme rides are the Tornado, an exhilarating wet and wild tunnel and funnel tubing experience; the Superman Krypton Coaster, nearly a mile of twisted steel with six inversions; the Rattler, one of the world's highest and fastest wooden roller coasters; the 60-mph-plus Poltergeist roller coaster; and Scream!, a 20-story space shot and turbo drop. Laser games and virtual reality simulators complete the technophilia picture. Feeling more primal? Wet 'n' wild attractions include the Lone Star Lagoon, the state's largest wave pool; the Texas Treehouse, a five-story drenchfest whose surprises include a 1,000-gallon cowboy hat that tips over periodically to soak the unsuspecting; and Bugs' White Water Rapids.

If you want to avoid both sogginess and adrenaline overload, check out a vast variety of food booths, shops, crafts demonstrations, and live shows of everything from 1950s musical revues to the laser-fireworks shows (held each summer evening). This theme park still has some local character, dating back to the days when it was plain old Fiesta Texas: Themed areas include a Hispanic village, a western town, and a German town. But when it came under the aegis of Six Flags, a Time Warner company, Looney Tunes cartoon characters such as Tweety Bird became ubiquitous, especially in the endless souvenir shops. Sometimes you can get discounts through some hotels, and there's usually a discount for buying tickets online.

17000 I-10 W. (corner of I-10 W. and Loop 1604). ✆ **800/473-4378** or 210/697-5050. www.sixflags. com/parks/fiestatexas. Admission $55 general admission, $40 children under 48 in., free for children 2 and under. Discounted 2-day and season passes available. Parking $15 per day. The park opens at 10am; closing times vary depending on the season, as late as 10pm in summer. The park is generally open daily late May to mid-Aug; Sat–Sun Mar–May and Sept–Oct; closed Nov–Feb. Call ahead or visit website for current information. Bus: 94 (summer only). Take exit 555 (La Cantera Pkwy.) on I-10 W.

West Side

SeaWorld San Antonio ★ ☺   Leave it to Texas to provide Shamu, the performing killer whale, with his most spacious digs: At 250 acres, this SeaWorld is the largest of the Anheuser-Busch–owned parks, which also makes it the largest marine theme park in the world. Fascinating walk-through habitats house penguins, sea lions, sharks, tropical fish, and flamingos. But if you're a theme park fan, you might find even more fun in the aquatic acrobatics at such stadium shows as Shamu Adventure, combining live action and video close-ups, and Viva, where divers and synchronized swimmers frolic with whales and dolphins.

You needn't get frustrated just looking at all that water because there are loads of places here to get wet. The Lost Lagoon has a huge wave pool and water slides aplenty, and the Texas Splashdown flume ride and the Rio Loco river-rapids ride also offer splashy fun. Younger children can cavort in Shamu's Happy Harbor and the "L'il Gators" section of the Lost Lagoon or take a ride on the Shamu Express kiddie coaster.

Nonaquatic activities abound, too. You can ride the Steel Eel, a huge "hyper-coaster" that starts out with a 150-foot dive at 65 mph, followed by several bouts of weightlessness, or Great White, the Southwest's first inverted coaster—which means riders will go head-over-heels during 2,500 feet of loops (don't eat before either of them). It's well worth sticking around for the shows offered in the evening during the peak summer season or for the Halloween activities held on October weekends—if you're not too tuckered from the rides. Hotels in the area sometimes offer discounts, and there's usually a discount for buying tickets online.

10500 SeaWorld Dr., 16 miles northwest of downtown San Antonio at Ellison Dr. and Westover Hills Blvd. ℂ **800/700-7786.** www.seaworld.com. 1-day pass $59 adults, $54 seniors (55 and older), $50 children ages 3–9, free for children 2 and under. Discounted 2-day and season passes available. Internet purchase discounts. Parking $12 per day. Early Mar to late Nov. Days of operation vary. Open at 10am on operating days, closing times vary. Call ahead or check website for current information. Bus: 64. From Loop 410 or from Hwy. 90 W., exit Hwy. 151 W. to the park.

MORE ATTRACTIONS
Downtown Area

ArtPace   San Antonio's contemporary art gallery features rotating shows, displaying the work of artists selected by a guest curator for 2-month residencies at the facility. One artist must be from Texas, one from anywhere else in the United States, and one from anywhere else in the world. The result has been a fascinating mélange, including everything from twists on the traditional—such as a monumental drawing of a winter landscape populated by men in black tracksuits and a lenticular print (an image that shows depth and motion when the viewing angle changes) in which the Alamo vanishes before one's eyes—to the more cutting edge: an installation of 5,500 pounds of airplane parts or rooftop speakers that sing until the sun sets. Lecture series by the artists as well as public forums to discuss the work have also helped make this a very stimulating art space.

445 N. Main Ave. ℂ **210/212-4900.** www.artpace.org. Free admission. Wed–Sun noon–5pm. Check local listings or call for lectures and other special events. Bus: 2, 82, or 88.

First Fridays

On the first Friday of every month, San Antonio closes off a section of South Alamo Street in the artsy Southtown district and holds something between an "art walk" and a street carnival, which centers around the Blue Star Contemporary Art Center (see below) and extends northward, almost to downtown. It's a popular activity that attracts a lot of people, and with the people come street vendors, sidewalk artists, and street performers. Local merchants and restaurants get involved, too. For the visitor, it can be an entertaining pastime. If you're staying in the King William District, you'll be right next to the action.

Buckhorn Saloon & Museum 🖐 If you like your educational experiences accompanied by a tall cold brew, this is the place for you. With its large stuffed animals, mounted antlers, and wax museum version of history, this collection fulfills every out-of-stater's stereotype of what a Texas museum might be like. Many will find it overpriced, but what sets the Buckhorn apart and will make it of interest to others is the age of the collection, started back in the 1880s, which lends it the character of an old curio museum. It's been modernized somewhat, which has removed some of the old charm, but much remains. A lot of the items on exhibit are precisely the kind of objects that would have been of interest to an earlier public: artwork made with rattlesnake rattles, dressed fleas, freaks of nature such as a two-headed calf, cowboy and Indian memorabilia, shrunken heads. Many of these things are stuck in the corners of the exhibition rooms because they defy the semblance of order that the curators have imposed. But it's this character (and the saloon) that really sets the Buckhorn apart from any other museum I know.

318 E. Houston St. ✆ **210/247-4000.** www.buckhornmuseum.com. Admission $18 adults, $17 seniors (55 and older), $14 children age 4-12. Labor Day to Memorial Day daily 10am–5pm; rest of year daily 10am–6pm (later hours in summer). Closed Thanksgiving and Dec 25. Streetcar: Red or Blue line.

Casa Navarro State Historic Site A key player in Texas's transition from Spanish territory to American state, José Antonio Navarro participated in several legislatures and assemblies. He was a signer of the 1836 Texas Declaration of Independence, one of only two native Texans to do so. He also participated in the convention that ratified the annexation of Texas to the United States in 1845. He made his living as a merchant and landholder and bought this property in the 1830s, but didn't make it his residence until the 1850s. The three buildings you see were all probably built then. The single-story main house with attic (to which additions were later constructed) is typical of San Antonio houses of the period. The two-story stone building served as a store and office and was built a few years later. The simplest of the three, made of adobe and limestone, may have existed earlier. It was converted to a kitchen, and an extra room was later added. The house doesn't get many visitors, and the staff are only too happy to point out the most interesting features of the site and provide historical context to what you are seeing.

228 S. Laredo St. ✆ **210/226-4801.** Admission $4 adults, $3 children ages 6-12, free for children 5 and under. Tues–Sun 9am–4pm. Streetcar: Purple line.

Institute of Texan Cultures ☺ It's the rare visitor who won't discover here that his or her ethnic group has contributed to the history of Texas: 26 different ethnic and cultural groups are represented in the imaginative, hands-on displays of this educational center, which is one of three campuses of the University of Texas at San Antonio. Outbuildings include a one-room schoolhouse, an adobe home, a windmill, and the multimedia Dome Theater, which presents images of Texas on 36 screens. A variety of heritage festivals and kid-friendly shows and events, such as pioneer life reenactments, holography exhibits, and ghost-tale storytellers at Halloween are always on tap; phone or check the institute's website for a current schedule. An excellent photo archive here, open to the public by appointment, holds more than three million images. Call ℂ **210/458-2298** for information on using it.

801 S. Bowie St. (at Durango St., in HemisFair Park). ℂ **210/458-2300.** www.texancultures.utsa.edu. Admission $8 adults; $7 seniors; $6 military (with ID) and children ages 3–12. Mon–Sat 9am–5pm; Sun noon–5pm. Dome shows presented at 11am, 12:30, 2, and 4pm (Thurs–Sat 6pm shows also, Sun no 11am show). Closed Thanksgiving, Dec 24–25, Jan 1, and for 3 days during the Texas Folklife Festival (held in June). Streetcar: Yellow or Purple line.

Museo Alameda Inaugurated in April 2007, the Museo Alameda is the nation's largest museum celebrating Hispanic American culture. It has 20,000 square feet of exhibition space divided into 11 galleries. Though the museum doesn't have a permanent collection, it has many resources, including a close association with the Smithsonian Institute. The exhibits, each running about 4 months, seek to illuminate some aspect of the Latino experience in America; to explore through art and artifact what America represents for Hispanic Americans; and what the old homeland, be it Mexico or another country, comes to signify, as well. Such a broad purpose embraces art and history to piece together its narrative on Latino culture. It necessarily leans heavily on the expertise of the curators who will create these exhibitions. The building proper is an attractive addition to the area around Market Square. It injects color and bold modern lines. The main decorative feature is some elaborate stainless steel panels that variously bring to mind the wrought-iron work of colonial Latin America and the humble decorative practice of cutting designs into folded paper (*papel picado*).

101 S. Santa Rosa Blvd. (at Commerce, in Market Square). ℂ **210/299-4300.** www.thealameda.org. Admission $4 adults, $2 seniors, students, and children 5 and under. Tues admission is free. Tues–Sat noon–6pm. Streetcar: Red, Purple, or Yellow line.

San Antonio Central Library San Antonio's main library, opened in the mid-1990s at a cost of $38 million, has a number of important holdings (including part of the Hertzberg Circus Collection, scattered when it lost its museum home in 2001), but it is most notable for its architecture. Ricardo Legorreta, renowned for his buildings throughout Mexico, created a wildly colorful and whimsical public space that people apparently love to enter—by the second month after the library opened, circulation had gone up 95%. The boxy building, painted what has been called "enchilada red," is designed like a hacienda around an internal courtyard. A variety of skylights, windows, and wall colors (including bright purples and yellows) afford a different perspective from each of the six floors. A gallery offers monthly exhibits of paintings, photography, textiles, and more.

600 Soledad St. ℂ **210/207-2500.** www.sanantonio.gov/library. Free admission. Mon–Thurs 9am–9pm; Fri–Sat 9am–5pm; Sun 11am–5pm. Bus: 3, 4, 90, 91, or 92.

San Fernando Cathedral ★   Construction of a church on this site, overlooking what was once the town's central plaza, was begun in 1738 by San Antonio's original Canary Island settlers and completed in 1749. Part of the early structure—the oldest cathedral sanctuary in the United States and the oldest parish church in Texas—is incorporated into the cathedral built in 1868. Jim Bowie got married here, and General Santa Anna raised the flag of "no quarter" from its roof during the siege of the Alamo in 1836. The cathedral underwent major interior and exterior renovations in 2002; its most impressive new addition, a 24-foot-high gilded *retablo* (altarpiece), was unveiled in 2003.

115 Main Plaza. ✆ **210/227-1297.** www.sfcathedral.org. Free admission. Daily 6am–7pm; gift shop Mon–Fri 9am–4:30pm, Sat until 5pm. Streetcar: Purple or Yellow line.

Southwest School of Art and Craft ★   A stroll along the River Walk to the northern corner of downtown will lead you into another world: a rare French-designed cloister where contemporary crafts are now being practiced. An exhibition gallery and artist studios–cum–classrooms (not open to visitors) occupy the garden-filled grounds of the first girls' school in San Antonio, established by the Ursuline order in the mid–19th century. Learn about both the school and the historic site at the Visitors Center Museum in the First Academy Building. The Ursuline Sales Gallery carries unique crafts items, most made by the school's artists. You can enjoy a nice, light lunch in the Copper Kitchen Restaurant (Mon–Fri 11:30am–2pm, closed national holidays). The adjacent Navarro Campus, built in the late 1990s, is not as architecturally interesting, but it's worth stopping there for its large contemporary art gallery—and for the Art*O*Mat (sic), a converted vending machine selling local artists' work for $5 a pop. What a steal!

300 Augusta St. ✆ **210/224-1848.** www.swschool.org. Free admission. Mon–Sat 9am–5pm (galleries on both campuses), Sun 11am–4pm (Navarro Campus gallery only); Mon–Sat 10am–5pm (gift shop); Mon–Sat 10am–5pm, Sun 11am–4pm (museum). Streetcar: Blue line.

Spanish Governor's Palace ★★ 📷   This is the oldest, best-preserved structure in San Antonio. It began as a one-room house built in 1722. Three other rooms were added in 1749 (the date is shown on one of the doorways, along with the insignia of Spanish King Ferdinand VI). It served as the residence and headquarters for the captain of the Spanish garrison and became the seat of Texas government in 1772, when San Antonio was made capital of the Spanish province of Texas. It remained as such until 1821 when Mexico gained its independence. The last captain of San Antonio de Béxar, Juan Ignacio Pérez, and his descendants remained in the house until the 1860s. By 1928, when the city purchased the house, it had served as the residence for several businesses, including a tailor's shop, barroom, and schoolhouse.

It's not a palace—this was just a bit of aggrandizement that came about in the 1920s to promote its purchase and restoration by the city. Up until then, it had been known simply as *la casa del capitán.* The building, with high ceilings supported by protruding beams, is typical of the way houses were constructed back then. The walls are a mix of adobe and rubblework, with a stucco finish. The five rooms are furnished in the way they might have been in the 18th century. There's a shaded garden and patio in back with a stone fountain and mosaic flooring. It was a 19th-century addition and remains quite attractive. If your visit elicits questions, talk to the staff, who are very helpful and know a great deal about the house's history.

105 Plaza de Armas. ✆ **210/224-0601.** www.spanishgovernorspalace.org. Admission $4 adults, $3 seniors, $2 children ages 7–13, free for children 6 and under. Tues–Sat 9am–5pm; Sun 10am–5pm. Closed Jan 1, San Jacinto Day (Apr 21), Thanksgiving, and Dec 25. Streetcar: Purple line.

Tower of the Americas ★ For a good take on the lay of the land, just circle the eight panoramic panels on the observation deck of the Tower of the Americas. The 750-foot-high tower was built for the HemisFair in 1968. The deck sits at the equivalent of 59 stories and is lit for spectacular night viewing. The tower also hosts a rotating restaurant with surprisingly decent food (for the revolving genre) as well as a thankfully stationary cocktail lounge.

600 HemisFair Park. ✆ **210/207-8615.** www.toweroftheamericas.com. Admission $11 adults, $10 seniors 55 and older, $9 children ages 4–11, free for children 3 and under. Sun–Thurs 10am–10pm; Fri–Sat 10–11pm. Streetcar: Yellow or Purple line.

Southtown/King William

Blue Star Contemporary Art Center This huge former warehouse in Southtown hosts a collection of working studios and galleries, along with a performance space for the Jump-Start theater company. The 11,000-square-foot artist-run Contemporary Art Center is its anchor. The style of work varies from gallery to gallery—you'll see everything from primitive-style folk art to feminist photography—but the level of professionalism is generally high. One of the most interesting spaces is SAY Si, featuring exhibitions by talented neighborhood high-school students that might include collages or book illustrations. A number of galleries are devoted to (or have sections purveying) arty gift items such as jewelry, picture frames, and crafts. And there's a strategically placed brew pub, where you can put your feet up and rest from your exertions.

> ## Impressions
>
> *We have no city, except, perhaps, New Orleans, that can vie, in point of picturesque interest that attaches to odd and antiquated foreignness, with San Antonio.*
>
> —Frederick Law Olmsted, *A Journey Through Texas*, 1853

116 Blue Star (bordered by Probandt, Blue Star, and South Alamo sts. and the San Antonio River). ✆ **210/227-6960.** www.bluestarart. org. Free admission ($2 suggested donation for art center). Hours vary from gallery to gallery; most are open Wed–Sun noon–6pm, with some opening at 10am. Streetcar: Blue line.

Steves Homestead Museum ★ Don't be mislead by the word "homestead." This is a Victorian mansion built in 1876 for lumber magnate Edward Steves. It was restored by the San Antonio Conservation Society, to whom it was willed by Steves's granddaughter. Believed to have been built by prominent San Antonio architect Alfred Giles and one of the few houses in the King William Historic District open to the public, it gives a fascinating glimpse into the life of the local upper class in the late 19th century. The 45-minute-long tour is made more entertaining by the wealth of local color and gossip provided by the guides. *Tip:* You can view this mansion only by tour. The number of docents present at any given day affects the frequency of the tours, and the only set tour time is 3:30pm (the last tour of the day). Don't wait for that one, because you could get bumped if too many visitors show up. Instead, call ahead the day you wish to visit and make an informal arrangement with the staff.

509 King William St. ✆ **210/225-5924.** www.saconservation.org. Admission $6 adults, $4 seniors, $3 students and active-duty military with ID, free for children 11 and under. Daily 10am–4:15pm (last tour at 3:30pm). Closed major holidays. Streetcar: Blue line.

Villa Finale ★ The house of Walter Mathis, now a property of the National Trust, opened for tours in October 2010. Walter Mathis was the investment banker who saved the King William neighborhood from decay and promoted its restoration. The mansion he bought for his home dates from 1876 and was built in the style of an Italian villa. Mathis was a great collector of the fine and decorative arts. He enjoyed the works of artist Mary Bonner and was an admirer of French culture. The collection has several works of hers and lots of French furniture and art objects. Evidently, he was intrigued by Napoleon and even acquired one of the emperor's death masks. Tours of the house and the collection last about an hour and are limited to six people. You need to call ahead to make reservations. I expect that changes in scheduling will occur as this museum acquires a routine, and accommodates public interest—check the website before going to San Antonio.

401 King William St. (Visitor Center, 122 Madison St.). ✆ **210/223-9800.** www.villafinale.org. Admission $10 adults, $7.50 seniors, students, and active-duty military with ID. Tues 12:30 and 1:30pm; Wed–Sat 9:30am–1:30pm. Tours every hour on the half-hour. Streetcar: Blue line.

Alamo Heights Area

San Antonio Zoological Gardens and Aquarium ☺ This zoo is considered one of the top facilities in the country because of its conservation efforts and its successful breeding programs (it produced the first white rhino in the U.S.). Home to more than 700 species, it has one of the largest animal collections in the United States. Kids will get a kick out of many critters (the Lory Encounter is especially popular), and parents will appreciate the fact that they won't run into an expensive gift shop around every corner.

3903 N. St. Mary's St., in Brackenridge Park. ✆ **210/734-7183.** www.sazoo-aq.org. Admission $10 adults, $8 seniors 62 and older and children ages 3–11, free for children 2 and under. Daily 9am–5pm (until 6pm in summer). Bus: 7 or 8.

Fort Sam Houston Area

Fort Sam Houston Since 1718, when the armed Presidio de Béxar was established to defend the Spanish missions, the military has played a key role in San Antonio's development, and it remains one of the largest employers in town today. The 3,434-acre Fort Sam Houston affords visitors an unusual opportunity to view the city's military past (the first military flight in history took off from the fort's spacious parade grounds) in the context of its military present—the fort currently hosts the Army Medical Command and the headquarters of the Fifth Army. Most of its historic buildings are still in use and thus off-limits, but three are open to the public. The **Fort Sam Houston Museum,** 1210 Stanley Rd., Bldg. 123 (✆ **210/221-1886;** free admission; Wed–Sun 10am–4pm), details the history of the armed forces in Texas, with a special focus on San Antonio. The **U.S. Army Medical Department Museum,** 2310 Stanley Rd., Bldg. 1046 (✆ **210/221-6277** or 221-6358; www.ameddgiftshop.com/museum.htm; free admission; Tues–Sat 10am–4pm), displays army medical equipment and American prisoner-of-war memorabilia. The oldest building on the base, the **Quadrangle ★**, 1400 E. Grayson St. (no phone; free admission; Mon–Fri 8am–5pm, Sat–Sun noon–5pm), an impressive 1876 limestone structure, is centered on a brick clock tower and encloses a grassy square where peacocks and deer roam freely. The Apache chief Geronimo was held captive here for 40 days in 1886. Free self-guided tour maps of the historic sites are available in all three buildings. Anyone wishing to visit the fort must enter through the Walters Gate (take the Walters St. exit off I-35) and present a driver's license.

Grayson St. and New Braunfels Ave., about 2½ miles northeast of downtown. ✆ **210/221-1151** (public affairs). There is no longer public transportation to the Quadrangle.

PARKS & GARDENS

Brackenridge Park ★ With its rustic stone bridges and winding walkways, the city's main park has a charming, old-fashioned feel and serves as a popular center for such recreational activities as golf, polo, biking, and picnicking. I especially like the **Japanese Tea Garden** ★ (also known as the Japanese Sunken Garden), created in 1917 by prison labor to beautify an abandoned cement quarry. (The same quarry furnished cement rock for the state capitol in Austin.) You can still see a brick smoke-stack and a number of the old limekilns among the beautiful flower arrangements—lusher than those in most Japanese gardens. After Pearl Harbor, the site was officially renamed the Chinese Sunken Garden, and a Chinese-style entryway was added on. Not until 1983 was the original name restored. Just to the southwest, a bowl of lime-stone cliffs found to have natural acoustic properties was turned into the **Sunken Garden Theater** (p. 131). A 60-foot-high waterfall and water lily–laced ponds are among its lures. Across from the entrance to the **San Antonio Zoological Gardens** (see above), you can buy tickets for the **Brackenridge Eagle** (© 210/734-7183), a miniature train that replicates an 1863 model. The pleasant 2-mile ride through the park takes about 20 minutes (tickets $2.50 for adults, $2 for children 3–11; daily 9:30am, weather permitting, to when zoo gate closes).

Main entrance 2800 block of N. Broadway. © **210/207-3000.** www.sanantonio.gov/sapar. Daily dawn-dusk. Bus: 7, 8, or 9.

HemisFair Park Built for the 1968 HemisFair, an exposition celebrating the 250th anniversary of the founding of San Antonio, this urban oasis boasts **water gardens** and a **wood-and-sand playground** constructed for children (near the Alamo St. entrance). Among its indoor diversions are the **Institute of Texan Cultures** and the **Tower of the Americas** (both detailed above). Be sure to walk over to the Henry B. Gonzales Convention Center and take a look at the striking mosaic **mural** by Mexican artist Juan O'Gorman. The **Schultze House Cottage Garden** ★, 514 HemisFair Park (© **210/229-9161**) is also worth checking out for its heirloom plants, varietals, tropicals, and xeriscape area. Look for it behind the Federal Building.

Bounded by Alamo, Bowie, Market, and Durango sts. No phone. Streetcar: Blue, Yellow, or Purple line.

San Antonio Botanical Garden ★ Take a horticultural tour of Texas at this gra-cious 38-acre garden, encompassing everything from south Texas scrub to Hill Country wildflowers. Fountains, pools, paved paths, and examples of Texas architecture provide visual contrast to the flora. The formal gardens include a garden for the blind, a Japa-nese garden, an herb garden, a biblical garden, and a children's garden. Perhaps most

 Stone Oak Park's Diamond in the Rough

One of the fastest-growing urban development areas in town is in the area called Stone Oak, which these days is known for heavy traffic jams during rush hours, quickly built "McMansions," and Starbucks-style strip centers northwest of town. But what you may not know about Stone Oak is that it's also home to a delight-ful park, with hiking trails, pavilions, and picnic spots. Leave the ugly urban sprawl behind—scenery like this is why folks moved to Stone Oak in the first place.

outstanding is the $6.9-million Lucile Halsell Conservatory complex, a series of greenhouses replicating a variety of tropical and desert environments. The 1896 Sullivan Carriage House, built by Alfred Giles and moved stone-by-stone from its original downtown site, serves as the entryway to the gardens. It houses a gift shop (© **210/829-1227**) and a restaurant (© **210/821-6447**) offering salads, quiches, sandwiches, and outrageously rich desserts, open Tuesday to Sunday from 11am to 2pm.

555 Funston Place © **210/207-3250.** www.sabot.org. Admission $8 adults; $6 seniors, students, and military; $5 children 3–13; free for children 2 and under. Daily 9am–5pm. Closed Dec 25 and Jan 1. Bus: 7, 9, or 14.

ESPECIALLY FOR KIDS

Without a doubt, the prime spots for kids in San Antonio are **SeaWorld** and **Six Flags Fiesta Texas.** They'll also like the hands-on, interactive **Witte Museum** and the various ethnic-pride kids' programs at the **Institute of Texan Cultures.** There's a children's area in the **zoo,** which vends food packets so kids can feed the fish and the ducks. The third floor of the main branch of the **San Antonio Public Library** is devoted to children, who get to use their own catalogs and search tools. Story hours are offered regularly, and there are occasional puppet shows.

In addition to these sights, detailed in "The Top Attractions" and "More Attractions" sections, earlier in this chapter, and the **Magik Theatre** (p. 129), the following should also appeal to the sandbox set and up.

Louis Tussaud's Waxworks & Ripley's Believe It or Not ★ Adults may get the bigger charge out of the wax stars—Dustin Hoffman and Dallas Cowboy coach Tom Landry are among those in an impressive array—and some of the oddities collected by the globe-trotting Mr. Ripley, but there's plenty for kids to enjoy at this twofer attraction. The walk-through wax Theater of Horrors, although low on gore compared to *Friday the 13th*–type adventures, usually elicits some shudders. At Believe It or Not, there are three floors of "unbelievable" stuff. Half of the second floor has to do with the Titanic. Youngsters generally get a kick out of learning about people around the world whose habits—such as sticking nails through their noses— are even weirder than their own. There are also a few interactive displays.

301 Alamo Plaza. © **210/224-9299.** www.plazawaxmuseum.com. Either attraction $19 adults, $10 children ages 4–12; both attractions $22 adults, $13 children 4–12. Memorial Day to Labor Day daily 9am–10pm; remainder of the year Sun–Thurs 10am–7pm, Fri–Sat 10am–9pm (ticket office closes 1 hr. before listed closing times). Streetcar: Red or Blue line.

Ripley's Haunted Adventure, Guinness World Records Museum, and Tomb Rider 3D ★ Of these three attractions, Ripley's Haunted Adventure is the most popular. It's a 10,000-square-foot, state-of-the-art haunted house (if that's not a contradiction in terms), combining live actors, animatronics, and lots of special effects. The Guinness Museum brings the famed record book to life with such hands-on exhibits as a drum set that lets you see how hard it is to best the most-drum-beats-per-minute record and a multiple-choice quiz room where you can guess at the actual world record. Tomb Rider 3D combines a theme park–style ride through ancient tombs, with an interactive video game format where you shoot the mummies and spirits you encounter on the trip.

329 Alamo Plaza. ⓒ **210/226-2828.** www.alamoplazaattractions.com. Admission $19 for any 1 attraction, $22 for 2, $27 for all 3 for adults; $11 for 1, $14 for 2, $17 for 3 for children ages 4–12; $1 off any rate for seniors. Labor Day to Memorial Day Sun–Thurs 10am–10pm, Fri–Sat 10am–midnight; off season Sun–Thurs 10am–7pm, Fri–Sat 10am–10pm. Call ahead to verify hours and prices.

San Antonio Children's Museum San Antonio's children's museum offers a terrific, creative introduction to the city for the pint-size and grown-up alike. San Antonio history, population, and geography are all explored through such features as a miniature River Walk, a multicultural grocery store, a bank where kids can use their own ATM, and even a miniature dentist's office (more fun than you'd imagine). Activities range from crawl spaces and corn-grinding rocks to a weather station and radar room. For children younger than age 10.

305 E. Houston St. ⓒ **210/21-CHILD** (212-4453). www.sakids.org. Admission $7, free for children under age 2. Mon–Fri 9am–5pm; Sat 9am–6pm; Sun noon–5pm; 3rd Thurs of month 5–7pm. Bus: 7 or 40. Streetcar: Red line.

San Antonio IMAX Theater Rivercenter ★ Having kids view this theater's main attraction, *Alamo—The Price of Freedom,* on a six-story-high screen with a stereo sound system is a surefire way of getting them psyched for the historical battle site (which, although it's just across the street, can't be reached without wending your way past lots and lots of Rivercenter shops). It's a reasonably accurate rendition of the historical events, to boot. The first commercial IMAX venue to double its viewing pleasures by introducing a second megascreen (this one with 3-D capability and a state-of-the-art sound system) at the beginning of the 21st century, this theater also shows thrilling—and educational—nature and scientific adventure movies produced especially for the large screen.

849 E. Commerce St., in the Rivercenter Mall. ⓒ **800/354-4629** or 210/247-6429. www.imax-sa.com. You can reserve seats by phone. Admission $12 adults, $11 seniors and youth 12–17, $9 children 3–11. Times of daily shows vary, but generally the first show is screened at 10am, the last at 8:45pm. Streetcar: All lines.

Splashtown Cool off at this 20-acre waterpark, which includes a huge wave pool, hydro tubes nearly 300 feet long, a Texas-size water bobsled ride, more than a dozen water slides, and a two-story playhouse for the smaller children. A variety of concerts, contests, and special events are held here.

3600 I-35 N. (exit 160, Splashtown Dr.). ⓒ **210/227-1100** (recorded info) or 227-1400. www.splash townsa.com. Admission $33 adults and kids, $25 children under 48 in. (after 5pm, $15 for any age), free for seniors over 65 and children under 2. Call ahead or check website for exact dates and closing times.

SPECIAL-INTEREST SIGHTSEEING

For Military History Buffs

San Antonio's military installations are crucial to the city's economy, and testaments to their past abound. Those who aren't satisfied with touring Fort Sam Houston (see "More Attractions," earlier in this chapter) can also visit the **Hangar 9/Edward H. White Museum** at Brooks Air Force Base, Southeast Military Drive, at the junction of I-37 (© **210/536-2203;** www.brooks.af.mil). The history of flight medicine, among other things, is detailed via exhibits in the oldest aircraft hangar in the Air Force. Admission is free, and it's open Monday to Friday 8am to 3pm, except the last 2 weeks of December.

Lackland Air Force Base (12 miles southwest of downtown off U.S. 90, at Southwest Military Dr. exit; www.lackland.af.mil) is home to the **Air Force History and Traditions Museum,** 2051 George Ave., Bldg. 5206 (© **210/671-3055**), which hosts a collection of rare aircraft and components dating back to World War II. Admission is free; it's open Monday to Friday 8am to 4:30pm. At the **Security Forces Museum,** about 3 blocks away, at Bldg. 10501 (on Femoyer St., corner of Carswell Ave.; © **210/671-2615**), weapons, uniforms, and combat gear dating up to Desert Storm days are among the security police artifacts on display. Admission is free; it's open Monday to Friday 8am to 3pm. Inquire at either museum about the 41 static aircraft on view throughout the base. With current security measures in place, the bases are sometimes restricted to retired military, their families, and those sponsored by someone who works at the base. But you can try phoning the museums or the Public Affairs Office at Brooks (© **210/536-3234**) or the visitor center at Lackland (© **210/671-6174**) to inquire about visitation status. In any case, phone ahead to find out if anyone is permitted on the base on the day you're planning to visit. As may be expected, the museums are closed all national holidays.

For Those Interested in Hispanic Heritage

A Hispanic heritage tour is almost redundant in San Antonio, which is a living testament to the role Hispanics have played in shaping the city. **Casa Navarro State Historic Site, La Villita, Market Square, San Antonio Missions National Historical Park,** and the **Spanish Governor's Palace,** all detailed earlier in this chapter, give visitors a feel for the city's Spanish colonial past, while the Nelson A. Rockefeller wing of the **San Antonio Museum of Art,** also discussed earlier, hosts this country's largest collection of Latin American art. The sixth floor of the main branch of the **San Antonio Public Library** (see earlier in this chapter) hosts an excellent noncirculating Latino collection, featuring books about the Mexican-American experience in Texas and the rest of the Southwest. It's also the place to come to do genealogical research into your family's Hispanic roots.

The city is in the process of exploring its Hispanic roots and evolving Latino culture. The **Centro Alameda cultural zone** on downtown's west side includes the old **Alameda Theater** at 310 W. Houston St. This theater dates from 1949 and has many great features of the old grand movie palaces. First, there's the spectacular 86-foot-high sign adorning the marquee. Lit by rare cold cathode technology, not neon, it's one of a kind and a spectacular sight at night. Other features are mentioned above. The Alameda was one of the last of its kind and the largest movie palace ever dedicated to Spanish-language entertainment. It has been described as being "to U.S.

old movie palaces OF SAN ANTONIO

In the first half of the 20th century, Old San Antone was a movie-going town, and four grand old movie palaces have survived. Each deserves to be an attraction in its own right. Back then theaters were in the business of selling glamour and fantasy. They were also expressions of local pride, so the fantastical decorations most often had some tie-in with the heritage of the city.

Two of the theaters—the **Empire** and the **Majestic**—have been fully restored to their former glory and now function as venues for a wide range of performances and entertainment. Unfortunately, no one gives tours of them; to see them you would need to attend an event, many of which are fun and worth seeing (p. 130). Both theaters were designed and decorated with exuberance. Just to get an idea, visit the website www.majesticempire.com. The Empire is smaller and older (1913) and is on the historic registry of buildings. The walls are thickly textured with molded plaster and gold leaf. The Majestic (1929) is larger and grander. Its imaginative decoration incorporates Moorish and Spanish design. Any performance here will feel like a special occasion.

The old **Aztec Theater** was built in 1926 and completely refurbished in 2006 (© 877/43-AZTEC [432-9832]; www.aztecontheriver.com). The theater lobby is a fanciful rendition of an Aztec temple, with pre-Columbian iconography blanketing the columns and walls with great Art Deco touches.

Finally, there is the **Alameda,** which is not yet open to the public, but might be the most original of the four theaters. It was built much later than the others, in 1949, and was a center for the Hispanic community. In the late '40s, Mexican cinema was in its heyday, and big stars would come from Mexico to attend film premières. The only part of the theater you can see now is the exterior decoration, including a marvelous terrazzo mosaic on the sidewalk that flows into the theater lobby, a beautiful and unique tile facade made here in the city, and a large marquee that's brilliantly illuminated at night. Inside the auditorium are two black-light murals in need of restoration. Revolutionary in their day, the murals had a deep blue background decorated in Day-Glo paints (p. 106).

Latinos what Harlem's Apollo Theater is to African Americans." The theater is scheduled for restoration. The work is to be done by an arts organization called the Alameda National Center of Latino Arts and Culture, which also operates the Museo Alameda. For additional information, log on to **www.thealameda.org**.

Cultural events and blowout festivals, many of them held at Market Square, abound. The **Guadalupe Cultural Arts Center,** which organizes many of them, is detailed in chapter 8. In HemisFair Park, the **Instituto Cultural Mexicano/Casa Mexicana,** 600 HemisFair Plaza Way (© 210/227-0123), sponsored by the Mexican Ministry of Foreign Affairs, hosts Latin American film series, concerts, conferences, performances, contests, and workshops—including ones on language, literature, and folklore as well as art. The institute also hosts shifting displays of art and artifacts relating to Mexican history and culture, from pre-Columbian to contemporary (free admission; Tues–Fri 10am–5pm, Sat–Sun noon–5pm).

For information on the various festivals and events, contact the **San Antonio Hispanic Chamber of Commerce** (© 210/225-0462; www.sahcc.org). Another roundup resource for Latin *cultura* is the **"Guide to Puro San Antonio,"** available from the San Antonio Convention and Visitors Bureau (© **800/447-3372**).

STROLLING DOWNTOWN SAN ANTONIO

One of downtown San Antonio's gifts to visitors on foot is its wonderfully meandering early pathways—they were not laid out by drunken cattle drivers as has been wryly suggested, but formed by the course of the San Antonio River and the various settlements that grew up around it. Turn any corner in this area and you'll come across some fascinating testament to the city's historically rich past.

Note: Stops 1, 5, 6, 7, 9, 11, 13, and 14 are described earlier in this chapter. Entrance hours and admission fees (if applicable) are listed there. See chapter 4 for additional information on stop no. 2.

WALKING TOUR: DOWNTOWN

START:	**The Alamo.**
FINISH:	**Market Square.**
TIME:	**Approximately 1½ hours, not including stops at shops, restaurants, or attractions.**
BEST TIMES:	**Early morning during the week, when the streets and attractions are less crowded. If you're willing to tour the Alamo museums and shrine another time, consider starting out before they open (9am).**
WORST TIMES:	**Weekend afternoons, especially in summer, when the crowds and the heat render this long stroll uncomfortable. (If you do get tired, you can always pick up a streetcar within a block or two of most parts of this route.)**

Built to be within easy reach of each other, San Antonio's earliest military, religious, and civil settlements are concentrated in the downtown area. The city spread out quite a bit in the subsequent 290 years, but downtown still functions as the seat of the municipal and county government, as well as the hub of tourist activities.

Start your tour at Alamo Plaza (bounded by E. Houston St. on the north); at the plaza's northeast corner, you'll come to the entrance for:

1 The Alamo

Originally established in 1718 as the Mission San Antonio de Valero, the first of the city's five missions, the Alamo was moved twice before settling at this site. The heavy limestone walls of the church and its adjacent compound later proved to make an excellent fortress. In 1836, fighters for Texas's independence from Mexico took a heroic, if ultimately unsuccessful, stand against Mexican general Santa Anna here.

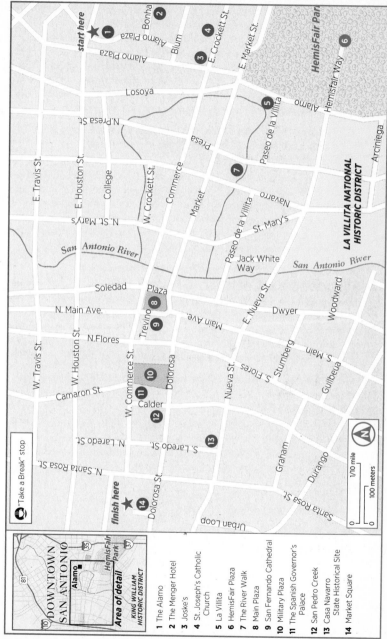

start here

Bonha

Alamo Plaza

Blum

E. Crockett St.

E. Market St.

HemisFair Par

HemisFair Way

Alamo Plaza

Losoya

N.Presa St.

Paseo de la Villita

Alamo

Arciniega

Presa

LA VILLITA NATIONAL HISTORIC DISTRICT

E. Travis St.

E. Houston St.

College

W. Crockett St.

Commerce

Market

Paseo de la Villita

Navarro

N. St. Mary's

St. Mary's

San Antonio River

Jack White Way

San Antonio River

Soledad

Plaza

N. Main Ave.

Trevino

Main Ave.

E. Nueva St.

Dwyer

Woodward

N.Flores

W. Houston St.

N.Flores

W. Commerce St.

Dolorosa

Nueva St.

S. Flores

S. Stumberg

S. Main

Guilbeua

W. Travis St.

Camaron St.

Calder

N. Laredo St.

S. Laredo St.

Graham

Durango

N. Santa Rosa St.

W. Commerce St.

finish here

Dolorosa St.

Urban Loop

Santa Rosa St.

"Take a Break" stop

1/10 mile

0

100 meters

0

DOWNTOWN SAN ANTONIO

35

HemisFair Park

37

81

Alamo

Area of detail

KING WILLIAM HISTORIC DISTRICT

10

1 The Alamo
2 The Menger Hotel
3 Joske's
4 St. Joseph's Catholic Church
5 La Villita
6 HemisFair Plaza
7 The River Walk
8 Main Plaza
9 San Fernando Cathedral
10 Military Plaza
11 The Spanish Governor's Palace
12 San Pedro Creek
13 Casa Navarro State Historical Site
14 Market Square

When you leave the walled complex, walk south along the plaza to:

2 The Menger Hotel

German immigrant William Menger built this hotel in 1859 on the site of Texas's first brewery, which he opened with partner Charles Deegan in 1855. Legend has it that Menger wanted a place to lodge hard-drinking friends who used to spend the night sleeping on his long bar. Far more prestigious guests—presidents, Civil War generals, writers, stage actors, you name it—stayed here over the years, and the hotel turns up in several short stories by frequent guest William Sidney Porter (O. Henry). The Menger has been much expanded since it first opened but retains its gorgeous, three-story Victorian lobby.

On the south side of the hotel, Alamo Plaza turns back into North Alamo Street. Take it south 1 block until you reach Commerce Street, where you'll spot:

3 Joske's (now empty)

This was San Antonio's oldest department store. The modest retail emporium, opened by the Joske Brothers in 1889, was enlarged in successive stages until, in 1939, it became the large Art Deco building you see now, distinctive for its intricate Spanish Renaissance–style details; look for the miniaturized versions of Mission San José's sacristy window on the building's ground-floor shadow boxes. This was the first department store in Texas to be fully air-conditioned.

Walk a short way along the Commerce Street side of the building to:

4 St. Joseph's Catholic Church

This church was built for San Antonio's German community in 1876. The Gothic revival–style house of worship is as notable for the intransigence of its congregation as it is for its beautiful stained-glass windows. The worshipers' refusal to move from the site when Joske's department store was rising up all around it earned the church the affectionate moniker "St. Joske's."

Head back to Alamo Street and continue south 2 blocks past the San Antonio Convention Center to reach:

5 La Villita

Once the site of a Coahuiltecan Indian village, La Villita was settled over the centuries by Spanish, Germans, and, in the 1930s and '40s, a community of artists. A number of the buildings have been continuously occupied for more than 200 years. The "Little Village" on the river was restored by a joint effort of the city and the San Antonio Conservation Society, and now hosts a number of crafts shops and two upscale restaurants in addition to the historic General Cós House and the Arneson River Theatre.

Just south of La Villita, you'll see HemisFair Way and the large iron gates of:

6 HemisFair Park

This park was built for the 1968 exposition held to celebrate the 250th anniversary of San Antonio's founding. The expansive former fairgrounds are home to two museums, a German heritage park, and an observation tower—the tallest structure in the city and a great reference point if you get lost downtown. To explore the entire park would take more than 2 hours, so for the purposes of this tour, you might want to confine yourself to the observation tower and the German heritage park.

Retrace your steps to Paseo de la Villita and walk 1 block west to Presa Street. Take it north for about half a block until you see the Presa Street Bridge, and descend from it to:

7 The River Walk

You'll find yourself on a quiet section of the 2⅗-mile paved walkway that lines the banks of the San Antonio River through a large part of downtown and the King William Historic District. The bustling cafe, restaurant, and hotel action is just behind you on the stretch of the river that winds north of La Villita.

Stroll down this tree-shaded thoroughfare until you reach the St. Mary's Street Bridge (you'll pass only one other bridge, the Navarro St. Bridge, along the way) and ascend here. Then walk north half a block until you come to Market Street. Take it west 1 long block, where you'll find:

8 Main Plaza (Plaza de Las Islas)

This is the heart of the city, established in 1731 by 15 Canary Island families sent by King Philip V of Spain to settle his remote New World outpost. Much of the history of San Antonio—and of Texas—unfolded on this modest square. A peace treaty with the Apaches was signed (and later broken) on the plaza in 1749. In 1835, the Texan forces battled Santa Anna's troops here before barricading themselves in the Alamo across the river. Much calmer these days, the plaza still sees some action as home to the Romanesque-style Bexar County Courthouse.

Walk along the south side of Main Plaza to the corner of Main Avenue. Across the street and just to the north you'll encounter:

9 San Fernando Cathedral

This is the oldest parish church building in Texas and site of the earliest marked graves in San Antonio. Three walls of the original church started by the Canary Island settlers in 1738 can still be seen in the rear of the 1868 Gothic revival cathedral, which recently underwent a massive renovation. Among those buried within the sanctuary walls are Eugenio Navarro, brother of José Antonio Navarro (see stop no. 13, below), and Don Manuel Muñoz, first governor of Texas when it was a province of a newly independent Mexico.

On the north side of the cathedral is Trevino Street; take it west to the next corner and cross the street to reach:

10 Military Plaza (Plaza de Armas)

This used to be the parade grounds for the Spanish garrison charged with guarding San Antonio de Béxar. The garrison was stationed here in 1718, the same year the mission San Antonio de Valero (the Alamo) was established. After Texas won its independence, Military Plaza became one of the liveliest spots in Texas, where cowboys, rangers, and anyone passing through would come to obtain local news. In the 1860s, it was the site of vigilante lynchings, and after the Civil War, it hosted a bustling outdoor market. At night, the townsfolk would come to its open-air booths to buy chili con carne from their favorite chili queen. The plaza remained completely open until 1889, when the ornate City Hall was built at its center.

The one-story white building you'll see directly across the street from the west side of the plaza is the:

11 Spanish Governor's Palace

This was the former residence and headquarters of the captain of the Presidio de Béxar (but not of any Spanish governors). From here, the commander could watch his troops drilling across the street.

From the front of the Governor's Palace, walk south until you come to the crosswalk; just west across Dolorosa Street is a drainage ditch, the sad remains of:

12 San Pedro Creek

The west bank of this body of water—once lovely and flowing, but now usually dry—was the original site of both Mission San Antonio de Valero and the Presidio de Béxar. At the creek's former headwaters, approximately 2 miles north of here, San Pedro Park was established in 1729 by a grant from the king of Spain; it's the second-oldest municipal park in the United States (the oldest being Boston Common).

Continue west along Dolorosa Street to Laredo Street and take it south about three-quarters of a block until you come to:

13 Casa Navarro State Historic Site

The life of José Antonio Navarro, for whom the park is named, traces the history of Texas itself: He was born in Spanish territory, fought for Mexico's independence from Spain, and then worked to achieve Texas's freedom from Mexico. (He was one of only two Texas-born signatories to the 1836 Texas Declaration of Independence.) In 1845, Navarro voted for Texas's annexation to the United States, and a year later, he became a senator in the new Texas State Legislature. He died here in 1871, at the age of 76.

Trace your steps back to Laredo and Dolorosa, and go west on Dolorosa Street; when you reach Santa Rosa, you'll be facing:

14 Market Square

This square was home to the city's Market House at the turn of the 20th century. When the low, arcaded structure was converted to El Mercado in 1973, it switched from selling household goods and personal items to crafts, clothing, and other more tourist-oriented Mexican wares. Directly behind and west of this lively square, the former Haymarket Plaza has become the Farmers' Market and now sells souvenirs instead of produce. You can enjoy a well-deserved lunch here at Mi Tierra, reviewed in chapter 5. At the entryway to Market Square is the Museo Alameda. The stainless-steel screen that fronts it is inspired by the Mexican craft of *hojalatería* (tin work); the 30-foot-high screen consists of a series of panels that incorporate cultural symbols, from the Pre-Columbian headdress of the Aztec god Quetzalcoatl to the Smithsonian sun logo.

ORGANIZED TOURS

In addition to the tours listed below, you can always opt for a carriage ride around downtown ($25). You can find them lined up around Alamo Plaza. You'll also see pedicabs (bicycle rickshaws) circulating. These don't have set routes or prices, but are generally inexpensive.

Bus Tours

Alamo Sightseeing Tours   This company serves up a menu of long and short guided bus tours. There's one for the downtown area, another for the missions, and another that leaves town and goes out to the Hill Country.

122 Losoya St. ℂ **210/492-4144.** www.alamosightseeingtours.com. Half-day tours $35 adults, $32 seniors, $17 children 4–10, free for children 3 and under. Full-day tours $55 adults, $50 seniors, $27 children 4–10. Earliest tours depart at 9am, latest return is 6pm daily (including holidays).

Trolley Tours

Grand Trolley Tours   This is a good way to sightsee without a car. The trolley tour touches on all the downtown highlights, plus two of the missions in the south. If you want to get off at any of these sights, you can pick up another trolley (they run every 45 min.) after you're finished. At the least, you get oriented and learn some of the city's history.

321 Alamo Plaza (in front of Alamo). ℂ **210/492-4144.** www.grandtrolleytours.com. Tickets for 60-min. tour are $20 adults, $26 for "hopper" pass (good for 2 days); $10 children 3–11, $13 for the pass. Daily 9:30am–4:15pm.

River Cruises

Rio San Antonio Cruises ★   Maybe you've sat in a River Walk cafe looking out at people riding by in open, flat-bottom barges. Go ahead—give in and join 'em. An amusing, informative tour, lasting from 35 to 40 minutes, will take you more than 2 miles down the most built-up sections of the Paseo del Río, with interesting sights pointed out along the way. You'll learn a lot about the river and find out what all those folks you watched were laughing about. There are four spots on the river where you can buy a ticket and board a boat.

Ticket offices: Under Market St. Bridge (at Alamo St.), at Rivercenter Mall, at Aztec Theatre (at Crocket and St. Mary's), and Museum Reach by Brooklyn St. Bridge (closes early). ℂ **210/244-5700.** www.riosanantonio.com. (Tickets can be purchased online.) Tickets $8 adults, $6 seniors and active-duty military with ID, $3 children 5 and under. Boats depart daily every 15–20 min. Nov to mid-Mar Sun–Thurs 10am–8pm, Fri–Sat 10am–9pm; extended hours rest of the year.

Segway Tours

SegCity Tours   See some of downtown San Antonio while trying to master using one of these horseless chariots. Before the tour there's a little teaching session. Tours vary in length and price. Exercise caution. I once saw a rider almost go off a curb and into traffic. Sidewalks in San Antonio can be narrow.

124 Losoya St. ℂ **210/224-0773.** www.segcity.com/sanantonio. 2-hr. tours $65 adults; 1-hr. tours $50. Earliest tours depart at 9am (sometimes earlier).

STAYING ACTIVE

Most San Antonians head for the hills—that is, nearby Hill Country—for outdoor recreation. Some suggestions of sports in or around town follow; see chapter 17 for more on Hill Country.

BIKING   With the creation and continuing improvements of the biking paths along the San Antonio River, part of the larger **Mission Trails** project (see the San Antonio Missions National Historical Park listing earlier in this chapter), local and visiting cyclists will finally have a good place within the city to spin their wheels (it's not quite there yet, but soon . . .). Other options within San Antonio itself include **Bracken-ridge Park; McAllister Park** on the city's north side, 13102 Jones-Maltsberger (© **210/207-PARK** [207-7275] or 207-3120); and around the area near **SeaWorld of Texas.** If you didn't bring your own, **Blue Star Bike Shop,** in Southtown at 1414 S. Alamo (© **210/212-5506;** www.bluestarbrewing.com), will rent cruisers and other bikes ($20 for 6 hours). Another bike rental place is **Brackenride** (© **210/826-7433**), at 3619 Broadway. Perhaps the best resource in town is the website of the San Antonio Wheelmen, **www.sawheelmen.com**, with details on local organized rides, links to bicycle shops in the area, and more (it's even got an essay on the history of bicycling).

FISHING   For good angling close to town, try **Braunig Lake,** a 1,350-acre, city-owned reservoir, a few miles southeast of San Antonio off I-37, and **Calaveras Lake,** one of Texas's great bass lakes, a few miles southeast of San Antonio off U.S. 181 South and Loop 1604. A bit farther afield but still easy to reach from San Antonio are **Canyon Lake,** about 20 miles north of New Braunfels, and **Medina Lake,** just south of Bandera. Fishing licenses—sold at most sporting-goods and tackle stores and sporting-goods departments of large discount stores such as Wal-Mart or Kmart, as well as county courthouses and Parks and Wildlife Department offices—are required for all nonresidents; for current information, call © **512/389-4800,** ext. 3, or go to www.tpwd.state.tx.us/publications/annual/fish/fishlicense.phtml. **Tackle Box Outfitters,** 6330 N. New Braunfels (© **210/821-5806;** www.tackleboxoutfitters.com), offers referrals to private guides for fishing trips on area rivers and on the Gulf coast ($250–$400 per person).

GOLF   Golf has become a big deal in San Antonio, with more and more visitors coming to town expressly to tee off. Of the city's six municipal golf courses, two of the most notable are **Brackenridge,** 2315 Ave. B (© **210/226-5612**), the oldest (1916) public course in Texas, featuring oak- and pecan-shaded fairways; and north-west San Antonio's $4.3-million **Cedar Creek,** 8250 Vista Colina (© **210/695-5050**), repeatedly ranked as South Texas's best municipal course in golfing surveys. For details on both and other municipal courses, log on to www.sanantonio.gov/sapar/golf.asp. Other options for unaffiliated golfers include the 200-acre **Pecan Valley,** 4700 Pecan Valley Dr. (© **210/333-9018**), which crosses the Salado Creek seven times and has an 800-year-old oak near its 13th hole; the high-end **Quarry,** 444 E. Basse Rd. (© **800/347-7759** or 210/824-4500; www.quarrygolf.com), on the site of a former quarry and one of San Antonio's newest public courses; and **Canyon Springs,** 24405 Wilderness Oak Rd. (© **888/800-1511** or 210/497-1770; www. canyonspringsgc.com), at the north edge of town in the Texas Hill Country, lush with live oaks and dotted with historic rock formations. There aren't too many resort courses in San Antonio because there aren't too many resorts, but the two at the **Westin La Cantera,** 16401 La Cantera Pkwy. (© **800/446-5387** or 210/558-4653; www.lacanteragolfclub.com)—one designed by Jay Morish and Tom Weiskopf, the other by Arnold Palmer—have knockout designs and dramatic hill-and-rock out-croppings to recommend them. Expect to pay $55 to $60 per person for an 18-hole round at a municipal course with a cart, from $70 to as much as $130 (Sat–Sun) per person at a private resort's course. Twilight (afternoon) rates are often cheaper. To get a copy of the free *San Antonio Golfing Guide,* call © **800/447-3372** or log on to www.sanantoniovisit.com/visitors/things_golfhome.asp.

HIKING   The 240-acre **Friedrich Wilderness Park,** 21480 Milsa (© **210/698-1057;** wildtexas.com/parks/fwp.php), operated by the city of San Antonio as its only nature preserve, is crisscrossed by 5.5 miles of trails that attract bird-watchers as well as hikers; a 2-mile stretch is accessible to people with disabilities. **Enchanted Rock State Natural Area,** near Fredericksburg, is the most popular spot for trekking out of town (see chapter 17).

RIVER SPORTS   For tubing, rafting, or canoeing along a cypress-lined river, San Antonio river rats head 35 miles northwest of downtown to the 2,000-acre **Guadalupe River State Park,** 3350 Park Rd. 31 (© **830/438-2656;** www.tpwd.state.tx. us/park/guadalup), near Boerne (see chapter 17 for more details about the town). Five miles north of Hwy. 46, just outside the park, you can rent tubes, rafts, and canoes at the **Bergheim Campground,** FM 3351 in Bergheim (© **830/336-2235**). Standard tubes run $10 per person (but the ones with a bottom, at $12, are better), rafts are $15 per person ($10 for ages 12 and younger), and canoes go for $35. The section of the Guadalupe River near Gruene is also extremely popular; see the "New Braunfels & Gruene" section of chapter 9 for details.

SWIMMING/WATERPARKS   Most hotels have swimming pools, but if yours doesn't, the Parks and Recreation Department (© **210/207-3113;** www.sanantonio. gov/sapar/swimming.asp) can direct you to the nearest municipal pool. Both SeaWorld and Six Flags Fiesta Texas, detailed in the section "The Top Attractions," earlier in this chapter, are prime places to get wet (the latter has a pool in the shape of Texas and a waterfall that descends from a cowboy hat). Splashtown water recreation park is described in the "Especially for Kids" section, earlier in this chapter. Many San Antonians head out to New Braunfels to get wet at Schlitterbahn, the largest waterpark in Texas; see the "New Braunfels" section of chapter 9 for additional information.

TENNIS   You can play at the 22 lighted hard courts at the **McFarlin Tennis Center,** 1503 San Pedro Ave. (© **210/732-1223**), for the very reasonable fee of $3 per hour per person ($1 for students and seniors), $3.50 per hour ($2 for students and seniors) after 5pm. Log on to www.sanantonio.gov/sapar/tennis.asp for additional information about McFarlin, which requires reservations for you to play, and for a list of other city facilities (all operate on a first-come, first-served basis).

SPECTATOR SPORTS

BASEBALL   From early April through early September, the minor-league **San Antonio Missions** play at the Nelson Wolff Stadium, 5757 Hwy. 90 W. Most home games for this farm club for the San Diego Padres start at 7:05pm, except Sunday games, which start at 4:05pm. Tickets range from $8 for adult general admission to $12 for seats in the lower box. Call © **210/675-7275** for schedules and tickets, or check the website at www.samissions.com.

BASKETBALL   Spurs madness hits San Antonio every year from mid-October through May, when the city's only major-league franchise, the **San Antonio Spurs,** shoots hoops. At the end of 2002, the Spurs found a new home at the AT&T Center. Ticket prices range from $20 for nosebleed-level seats to $100 for seats on the corners of the court. Tickets are available at the Spurs Ticket Office in the AT&T Center, which is at One AT&T Center Pkwy. (© **210/444-5819**), or via Ticketmaster San Antonio (© **210/224-9600;** www.ticketmaster.com). Get schedules, players' stats, and promotional news—everything you might want to know or buy relating to the team—online at www.nba.com/spurs.

GOLF   The **AT&T Championship,** an Official Senior PGA Tour Event, is held each October at the Oak Hills Country Club, 5403 Fredericksburg Rd. ((C) **210/698-3582**). One of the oldest professional golf tournaments, now known as the **Valero Texas Open,** showcases the sport in May. Log on to www.pgatour.com/r/schedule for information about both.

HORSE RACING   **Retama Park,** some 15 minutes north of San Antonio, in Selma ((C) **210/651-7000;** www.retamapark.com), is the hottest place to play the ponies; take exit 174-A from I-35, or the Lookout Road exit from Loop 1604. The five-level Spanish-style grandstand is impressive, and the variety of food courts, restaurants, and lounges is almost as diverting as the horses. Live racing is generally from late April through mid-October on Wednesday or Thursday through Sunday. Call or check the website for thoroughbred and quarter horse schedules. Simulcasts from top tracks around the country are shown year-round. General admission for live racing is $2.50 adults, $1.50 seniors; for clubhouse, $3.50 adults, $2.50 seniors; for simulcast, $2. Kids 15 and younger and members of the military, active or retired, can enter gratis.

ICE HOCKEY   San Antonio has had professional hockey only since 1994, when the Central Hockey League's San Antonio Iguanas appeared on the scene. Disbanded after the 2001–02 season, they were replaced by the American Hockey League's **San Antonio Rampage,** who dropped their first puck at the AT&T Center (One AT&T Center Pkwy.) in 2002. AHL tickets cost $10 to $65. Try (C) **210/444-5554** or www.sarampage.com for schedules and other information.

RODEO   If you're in town in early February, don't miss the chance to see 2 weeks of Wild West events like calf roping, steer wrestling, and bull riding at the annual **San Antonio Stock Show and Rodeo.** You can also hear huge amounts of major live country-and-western talent—Reba McEntire, Toby Keith, Randy Rogers Band, and Lady Antebellum are scheduled for the 2011 roster—and you're likely to find something to add to your luggage at the AT&T Center's exposition hall, packed with Texas handicrafts. Call (C) **210/225-5851,** or log on to www.sarodeo.com for information on schedules. Smaller rodeos are held throughout the year in nearby **Bandera,** the self-proclaimed "Cowboy Capital of the World." Contact the Bandera County Convention and Visitors Bureau ((C) **800/364-3833** or 830/796-3045; www.banderacowboycapital.com) for more information.

SHOPPING IN SAN ANTONIO

San Antonio offers the shopper a nice balance of large malls and little enclaves of specialized shops. You'll find everything here from the utilitarian to the unusual: a huge Sears department store, a Saks Fifth Avenue fronted by a 40-foot pair of cowboy boots, a mall with a river running through it, and some lively Mexican markets.

You can count on most shops around town being open from 9 or 10am to 5:30 or 6pm Monday through Saturday, with shorter hours on Sunday. Malls are generally open Monday through Saturday 10am to 9pm and on Sunday noon to 6pm. Sales tax in San Antonio is 8.25%.

THE SHOPPING SCENE

Most out-of-town shoppers will find all they need **downtown,** between the large Rivercenter Mall, the boutiques and crafts shops of La Villita, the colorful Mexican wares of Market Square, the Southwest School of Art and Craft, and assorted shops and galleries on and around Alamo Plaza. More avant-garde boutiques and galleries, including Blue Star, can be found in the adjacent area known as Southtown.

Most mainstream San Antonians prefer to shop in the malls along Loop 410, especially Alamo Quarry Market, the Shops at La Cantera, North Star, and Heubner Oaks. The Shops at La Cantera is the city's newest large-scale mall. It's also the farthest away from downtown (15 miles), out along the outer loop (Loop 1604) just west of I-10. This is now the fanciest mall in town, having secured the city's only Neiman Marcus and only Nordstrom, and it has plenty of smaller retail stores to match the same well-heeled customer base. More upmarket retail outlets can be found closer to downtown in the fancy strip centers that line Broadway, where it passes through Alamo Heights (the posh Collection and Lincoln Heights are particularly noteworthy). Weekends might see locals poking around a number of terrific **flea markets.** For bargains on brand labels, they head up to San Marcos (35 miles north on I-35), home to two large **factory outlet malls** (see chapter 16).

SHOPPING A TO Z

Antiques

In addition to the places that follow, a number of antiques shops line Hildebrand between Blanco and San Pedro, and McCullough between Hildebrand and Basse.

Alamo Antique Mall   The easiest way for visitors to go antiques shopping is to try this downtown collection of 100 independent dealers distributed among three floors in the old Anderson Building. It's just a few blocks from the Alamo. Inside, you'll find for sale just about anything that is collected, from jewelry to furniture, from military memorabilia to glassware. 125 Broadway. © **210/224-4354.**

The Land of Was   Every inch of space on the two floors of this shop is crammed with stuff—some of it strange and funky, more of it rare and pricey. The store is especially strong on 18th-century furniture and chandeliers. If you're seeking an altarpiece or a treasure chest, try here first. 3119 Broadway. © **210/822-5265.**

Art Galleries

ArtPace, in the northern part of downtown, and the **Blue Star Contemporary Arts Center** in Southtown (see "More Attractions," in chapter 6, for details on both), are the best venues for cutting-edge art, but **Finesilver Gallery,** 816 Camaron St., Ste. 1–2, just north of downtown (© 210/354-3333; www.finesilver.com), assembles some impressive shows with talented artists. And **Galería Ortiz Contemporary,** 4026 McCullough (© **210/826-8623**), represents several up-and-coming artists, and it has a downtown space in Market Square, 102 Concho St. Much of what it sells is Southwestern art. Another gallery specializing in this work is **Nanette Richardson Fine Art,** 555 E. Basse Rd. (© **210/930-1343;** www.nanetterichardson fineart.com), with a wide array of oils, watercolors, bronzes, ceramics, and hand-crafted wood furnishings. Also, keep in mind the smaller galleries in **La Villita.** You'll find a good bit of variety, and the area is so laid back and relaxing that it makes for enjoyable viewing.

For more information on other galleries and the art scene in general, visit the Office of Cultural Affairs' website, www.sahearts.com, with listings of several local galleries, and schedules for events held during July's **Contemporary Art Month** (see chapter 2).

Crafts/Folk Art

Again, since most people happen upon La Villita while exploring downtown, take a little time to explore the crafts stores there. You never know what you might come across. Another top option is the Ursuline Sales Gallery in the **Southwest School of Art and Craft** (see chapter 6). See also **Alamo Fiesta** in "Gifts/Souvenirs," below.

Casa Salazar   This colorful store next door to the Majestic Theatre's box office has a wide selection of Mexican crafts, including crosses, jewelry, *milagros,* and a little furniture. 216 E. Houston St. © **210/472-2272.** www.themajestic.com/casa.

Garcia Art Glass, Inc.   This store has some wild and colorful glass bowls, wall sconces, mobiles, and more. Often, especially in the morning, the glass blowers are at work behind the store, manipulating molten glass while they listen to Chicano music on the radio. The bracelets and other pretty baubles made out of glass beads are the most portable. 715 S. Alamo St. © **210/354-4681.** www.garciaartglass.com.

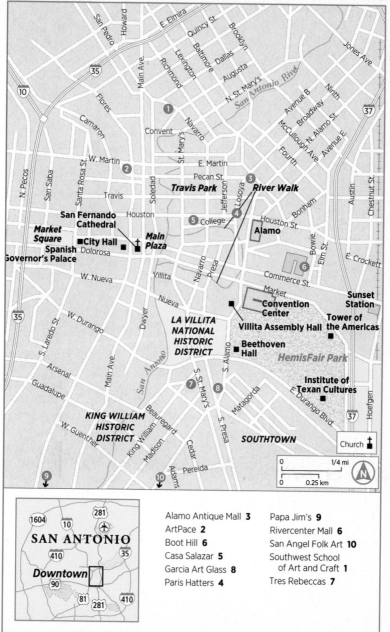

Alamo Antique Mall **3**
ArtPace **2**
Boot Hill **6**
Casa Salazar **5**
Garcia Art Glass **8**
Paris Hatters **4**

Papa Jim's **9**
Rivercenter Mall **6**
San Angel Folk Art **10**
Southwest School
 of Art and Craft **1**
Tres Rebeccas **7**

Greater San Antonio Shopping

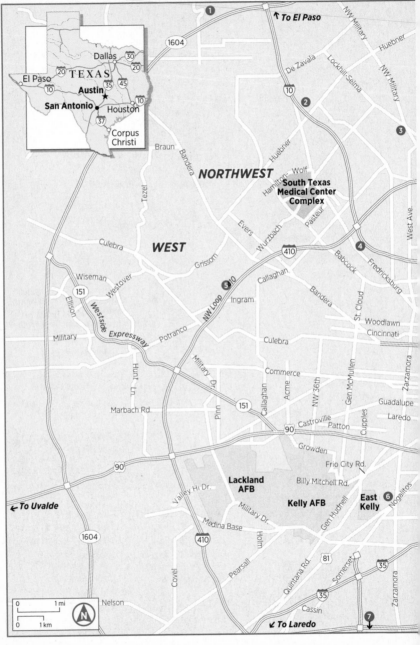

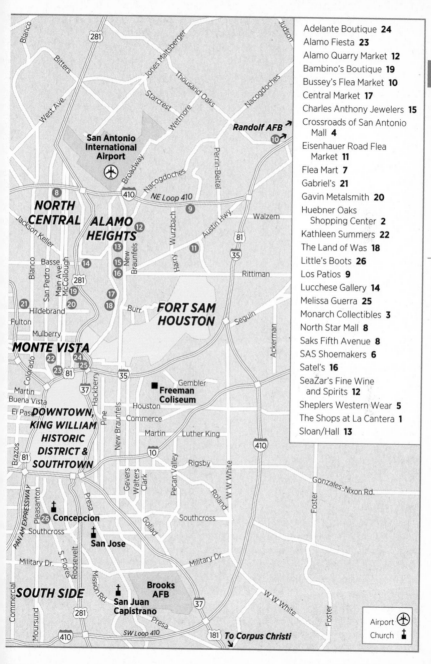

Adelante Boutique **24**
Alamo Fiesta **23**
Alamo Quarry Market **12**
Bambino's Boutique **19**
Bussey's Flea Market **10**
Central Market **17**
Charles Anthony Jewelers **15**
Crossroads of San Antonio Mall **4**
Eisenhauer Road Flea Market **11**
Flea Mart **7**
Gabriel's **21**
Gavin Metalsmith **20**
Huebner Oaks Shopping Center **2**
Kathleen Summers **22**
The Land of Was **18**
Little's Boots **26**
Los Patios **9**
Lucchese Gallery **14**
Melissa Guerra **25**
Monarch Collectibles **3**
North Star Mall **8**
Saks Fifth Avenue **8**
SAS Shoemakers **6**
Satel's **16**
SeaZar's Fine Wine and Spirits **12**
Sheplers Western Wear **5**
The Shops at La Cantera **1**
Sloan/Hall **13**

San Angel Folk Art   This is one of the best folk art stores in Texas. It has a sizable collection of pieces from Mexico and Latin America, and the work of American folk artists, including some talented local artists. Pottery, baskets, textiles, clothing, tin work, wood carvings—there's much to look at. And if you have questions, the manager, Leigh Anne Lester, can answer them. 1404 S. Alamo, Ste. 110, in the Blue Star Arts Complex. ☏ **210/226-6688.** www.sanangelfolkart.com.

Tres Rebecas   This is a difficult store to categorize. Yes, it sells handmade textiles, pottery, and jewelry from Mexico. But it has a broader view of crafts than most stores—for example, it sells traditional cooking implements and cookbooks, as well as children's fiction, in Spanish and English. It also sells yarn and needles, the raw material that encourages customers to get creating. 711 S. St. Mary's St. ☏ **210/224-5733.** www.3rebecas.com.

Department Stores

Saks Fifth Avenue   Forget low-key and unobtrusive; this is Texas. Sure, this department store has the high quality, upscale wares, and attentive service one would expect from a Saks Fifth Avenue, but it also has a 40-foot-high pair of cowboy boots standing out front. 650 North Star Mall. ☏ **210/341-4111.**

Fashion

The following stores offer clothing in a variety of styles; if you're keen on the cowpuncher look, see "Western Wear," below.

CHILDREN'S

Bambinos Boutique   Whether your child goes for the English-country look or veers more toward punk rocker, you'll find clothing to suit his or her (okay, your) tastes at this delightful store, which also carries maternity clothes and a great selection of kiddie room furnishings and toys. The focus is on the younger set—infants to age 12. 4216 McCullough Ave. ☏ **210/824-7676.**

MEN'S

Satel's   This family-run Alamo Heights store has been the place to shop for menswear in San Antonio since 1950; classic, high-quality clothing and personal service make it a standout. A newer location in the Colonnade, 9801 I-10 W. (☏ **210/694-0944**), offers the same fine goods and attention to customer needs. The staff is both helpful and knowledgeable about various styles of clothing. 5100 Broadway. ☏ **210/822-3376.** www.satels.com.

SHOES

SAS Shoemakers   This San Antonio footwear store is such an institution that the website for the VIA bus line lists it among the city's attractions. Men and women have been coming here to buy comfortable and handsome shoes and sandals since 1976. The brand is well known for making shoes without cutting corners. Most of the inventory is casual shoes and sandals. The factory store, on the south side of town, is the one to visit; you can even take one of three daily tours Monday through Thursday. Call in advance to make a reservation and to get directions. Other branches are located at Westlake Village, 1305 Loop 410 (☏ **210/673-2700**); Shoemakers Inn, 16088 San Pedro (☏ **210/494-1823**); and Garden Ridge, in Shertz, 17885 I-35 N. (☏ **210/651-5312**). 101 New Laredo Hwy. ☏ **210/921-7415** or 924-6507 (tour reservations).

WOMEN'S

Adelante Boutique   The focus here is on handmade clothes, which have colorful, natural fabrics and free-flowing lines. There's a good bit of embroidery and hand-woven articles. You'll also find a good selection of artistic jewelry, leather belts, and other accessories. 211 E. Grayson, Ste. 116, Pearl Brewery. ✆ **210/826-6770.** www.adelanteboutique.com.

Kathleen Sommers ★   This small shop on the corner of Main and Woodlawn has been setting trends for San Antonio women for years. Kathleen Sommers, who works mainly in linen and other natural fabrics, designs all the clothes, which bear her label. The store also carries eye-catching bags and purses, great jewelry, bath items, books, fun housewares, and a selection of unusual gifts. 2417 N. Main. ✆ **210/732-8437.** www.kathleensommers.com.

Food

Central Market   Free valet parking at a supermarket? On Saturday and Sunday, so many locals converge here to take advantage of the huge array of delectable samples that it's easy to understand why the store is willing to alleviate parking stress. You'll feel as though you've died and gone to food heaven as you walk amid gorgeous mounds of produce, cheeses, and other dairy products, sauces, pastas, and more. If you don't want to just graze, there are freshly prepared hot and cold gourmet foods, including a soup and salad bar, and a seating area in which to enjoy them. Wine tastings and cooking classes draw crowds in the evenings. 4821 Broadway. ✆ **210/368-8600.** www.centralmarket.com.

Gifts/Souvenirs

Alamo Fiesta 👜   Head just north of downtown to this two-level store near Monte Vista for a huge selection of Mexican folk art and handicrafts—everything from tin-work to colorful masks and piñatas—at extremely reasonable prices. Less touristy than most such shops, Alamo Fiesta is geared to local Hispanic families looking to celebrate special occasions. 2025 N. Main at Ashby. ✆ **210/738-1188.** www.alamofiesta.com.

Sloan/Hall   A cross between The Body Shop, Sharper Image, and Borders, only more concentrated and more upscale, this addictive boutique carries an assortment of toiletries, gadgets, books, and those uncategorizable items that you probably don't need but may find you desperately want. 5922 Broadway. ✆ **210/828-7738.** www.sloanhall.com.

Jewelry

See also "Crafts/Folk Art" and the Women's boutiques under "Fashion," above.

Charles Anthony Jewelers   This store sells vintage and antique jewelry. You never know what you'll find, but it's a good bet that whatever you do find will be out of the ordinary. Occasionally, you'll find some unique piece in a style long since abandoned. You never know, which makes shopping here interesting. 5320 Broadway. ✆ **210/804-6300.** www.charlesanthonyjewelers.com.

Gavin Metalsmith   For contemporary metal craft with a flair, come to this small gallery, where the exquisite original pieces range from wedding rings to salt-and-pepper shakers. The work sold here incorporate lots of unusual stones into silver and white-gold settings. 4024 McCullough Ave. ✆ **210/821-5254.**

love potion NO. 9

Ask a proprietor of a **botanica,** "What kind of store is this?" and you'll hear anything from "a drugstore" to "a religious bookstore." But along with Christian artifacts (including glow-in-the-dark rosaries and dashboard icons), botanicas carry magic floor washes, candles designed to keep the law off your back, wolf skulls, amulets, herbal remedies, and, of course, love potions. The common theme is happiness enhancement, whether by self-improvement, prayer, or luck.

Many of San Antonio's small botanicas specialize in articles used by *curanderos,* traditional folk doctors or medicine men and women. Books directing laypersons in the use of medicinal herbs sit next to volumes that retell the lives of the saints. It's easy enough to figure out the use of the *santos* (saints), candles in tall glass jars to which are affixed such labels as "Peaceful Home," "Find Work," and "Bingo." *Milagros* (miracles) are small charms that represent parts of the body—or mind—that a person wishes to have healed. Don't worry that many of the labels are in Spanish, as the person behind the counter will be happy to translate.

Papa Jim's, 5630 S. Flores (© **210/ 922-6665;** www.papajimsbotanica. com), is the best known of all the botanicas. (Papa Jim, who used to bless the various artifacts he sold, died a few years ago.) Can't make it to the shop? Order online or get a copy of the more comprehensive print catalog by phoning or ordering through the Papa Jim's website.

Kitchenware

Melissa Guerra   In addition to the upscale cookware and appliances sold in most kitchen stores, you'll find specialty implements and ingredients for cooking Latin American food. The owner, who is a cookbook author, also stocks her favorite dishes, apparel, and decorative objects. 200 E. Grayson, Ste. 122, Pearl Brewery. © **877/875-2665.** www. melissaguerra.com.

Malls/Shopping Complexes

Alamo Quarry Market   Alamo Quarry Market may be its official name, but no one ever calls this popular mall anything but "The Quarry" (from the early 1900s until 1985, the property was in fact a cement quarry). The four smokestacks, lit up dramatically at night, now signal play, not work. There are no anchoring department stores, but a series of large emporiums (Old Navy, Bed Bath & Beyond, Pottery Barn, and Borders) and smaller upscale boutiques (Ann Taylor, Jos. A. Bank, and Lucchese Gallery—see "Western Wear," below) will keep you spending. A multiplex cinema and an array of refueling stations—Chili's and Starbucks, as well as the more upscale Fleming's, and Piatti's, an Italian eatery well liked by locals—add food and entertainment to the shopping options. 255 E. Basse Rd. © **210/824-8885.** www.quarrymarket.com.

Crossroads of San Antonio Mall   Located near the South Texas Medical Center, this is San Antonio's bargain mall, featuring Burlington Coat Factory, Super Target, and Stein Mart department stores alongside smaller discount stores. Some glitzier shops and performances at the food court are part of an effort to draw San Antonians to this low-profile shopping destination. 4522 Fredericksburg Rd. (off Loop 410 and I-10). © **210/735-9137.**

Huebner Oaks Shopping Center This upscale open-air mall, in the north central part of town, houses a variety of yuppie favorites, including Old Navy, Banana Republic, Victoria's Secret, and Eddie Bauer. When your energy flags, retreat to one of several casual dining spots, such as La Madeleine, serving good fast French food, or head straight to Starbucks for a caffeine boost. 11745 I-10. © **210/697-8444.**

Los Patios The self-proclaimed "other River Walk" features about a dozen upscale specialty shops in a lovely 18-acre wooded setting. You'll find shops carrying imported clothing, crafts, jewelry, and antique furniture among other offerings here. None are chain stores, and all are locally owned. 2015 NE Loop 410, at the Starcrest exit. © **210/655-6171.** www.lospatios.com.

North Star Mall Starring Saks Fifth Avenue and such upscale boutiques as Abercrombie & Fitch, J. Crew, and Williams-Sonoma, this is the crème de la crème of the San Antonio indoor malls. It also has highly desired outlets, such as an Apple Store. But there are many sensible shops here, too, including a JCPenney department store. Food choices also climb up and down the scale, ranging from a Godiva Chocolatier to a Luby's Cafeteria. Loop 410, btw. McCullough and San Pedro. © **210/340-6627.** www.north starmall.com.

Rivercenter Mall There's a festive atmosphere at this bustling, light-filled mall, fostered, among other things, by its location on an extension of the San Antonio River. You can pick up a ferry from a downstairs dock or listen to bands play on a stage surrounded by water. Other entertainment options include the IMAX theater, the multiple-screen AMC, and the Rivercenter Comedy Club. The shops—more than 130 of them, anchored by Macy's—run the price gamut, but tend toward upscale casual. Food picks similarly range from Dairy Queen and Cinnabon to Morton's of Chicago and Fogo de Chao. This can be a great place to shop, but remember that it's thronged with teeny-boppers Friday and Saturday nights. 849 E. Commerce, btw. S. Alamo and Bowie. © **210/225-0000.** www.shoprivercenter.com.

The Shops at La Cantera The newest, fanciest mall is in far northwest San Antonio, off Loop 1604, beside the Six Flags Fiesta Texas theme park. This, too, is an outdoor mall, and it's nicely designed. All the stores face a central pedestrian concourse, and the parking is kept separate, behind the stores. As was mentioned earlier, it has two of San Antonio's fanciest department stores: Neiman Marcus and Nordstrom, and several boutiques, jewelers, and cosmetics stores. 15900 La Cantera Pkwy. © **210/582-6255.** www.theshopsatlacantera.com.

Markets

Market Square Two large indoor markets, El Mercado and the Farmers' Market—often just called, collectively, the Mexican market—occupy adjacent blocks on Market Square. Competing for your attention are more than 100 shops and pushcarts and an abundance of food stalls. The majority of the shopping booths are of the border-town sort, filled with onyx chess sets, cheap sombreros, and the like, but you can also find a few higher quality boutiques, including **Galería Ortiz** (see above). Come here for a bit of local color, good people-watching, and food—in addition to the sit-down **Mi Tierra,** detailed in chapter 5, and La Margarita, there are loads of primo places for street snacking. You'll often find yourself shopping to the beat of a mariachi band. 514 W. Commerce St. (near Dolorosa). © **210/207-8600.**

Flea Markets

Bussey's Flea Market Unless you're heading to New Braunfels or Austin, Bussey's is a bit out of the way. But these 20 acres of vendors selling goods from as far afield as Asia and Africa are definitely worth the drive (about a half-hour north of downtown). Crafts, jewelry, antiques, incense—besides perishables, it's hard to imagine anything you couldn't find at this market. 18738 I-35 N. ✆ **210/651-6830.**

Eisenhauer Road Flea Market The all-indoors, all air-conditioned Eisenhauer, complete with snack bar, is a good flea market to hit at the height of summer. You'll see lots of new stuff here—purses, jewelry, furniture, toys, shoes—and everything from houseplants to kinky leather-wear. Closed Monday and Tuesday. 3903 Eisenhauer Rd. ✆ **210/653-7592.**

Flea Mart On weekends, Mexican-American families make a day of this huge market, bringing the entire family to exchange gossip, listen to live bands, and eat freshly made tacos. There are always fruits and vegetables, electronics, crafts, and new and used clothing—and you never know what else. 12280 Hwy. 16 S. (about 1 mile south of Loop 410). ✆ **210/624-2666.**

Toys

If your child is especially hard on playthings or your cash supply is running low, consider buying used toys at **Kids Junction Resale Shop,** 2267 NW Military Hwy. (✆ **210/ 340-5532**), or **Too Good to Be Threw,** 7115 Blanco (✆ **210/340-2422**).

Monarch Collectibles ☺ Welcome to doll heaven. Many of the models that fill Monarch's four rooms—about 3,000 dolls in all—are collectible and made from such delicate materials as porcelain and baked clay, but others are cute and cuddly. Some come with real hair and eyelashes, and some are one of a kind. Doll furniture is also sold here—with a 6,000-square-foot dollhouse to showcase it—along with plates and a few stuffed animals. An entire room is devoted to Barbies. (Maybe the other dolls don't want to play with them?) 2012 NW Military Hwy. ✆ **210/341-3655.** www.dollsdolls.com.

Western Wear

Boot Hill This one-stop shopping center for all duds Western, from Tony Lama boots to Stetson hats and everything in between, is one of the few left in town that's locally owned. Arnold Schwarzenegger and Ashley Judd are among the stars who have been outfitted here. Rivercenter Mall, 849 E. Commerce, Ste. 213. ✆ **210/223-6634.**

Little's Boots 👢 Lucchese (see below) is better known, but this place—established in 1915—uses as many esoteric leathers and creates fancier footwear designs. You can get anything you like bespoke if you're willing to wait a while—possibly in line behind Reba McEntire and Tommy Lee Jones, who have had boots handcrafted here. Purchase some just so you can tell your friends back home, "Oh, Lucchese is so commercial. Little's is still the real thing." 110 Division Ave. ✆ **210/923-2221.** www.dave littleboots.com.

Lucchese Gallery The name says it all: Footwear is raised to the level of art at Lucchese. If it ever crawled, ran, hopped, or swam, these folks can probably put it on your feet. The store carries boots made of alligator, elephant, ostrich, kangaroo, stingray, and lizard. Come here for everything from executive to special-occasion boots, all handmade and expensive and all still serious Texas status symbols. Lucchese also carries jackets, belts, and sterling silver belt buckles. 255 E. Basse, Ste. 800. © **210/828-9419.** www.lucchese.com.

Paris Hatters   What do Pope John Paul II, Prince Charles, Jimmy Smits, and Dwight Yoakam have in common? They've all had headgear made for them by Paris Hatters, in business since 1917 and still owned by the same family. About half of the sales are special orders, but the shelves are stocked with high-quality, ready-to-wear hats, including Kangol caps from Britain, Panama hats from Ecuador, Borsolina hats from Italy, and, of course, Stetson, Resistol, Dobbs, and other Western brands. A lot of them can be adjusted to your liking while you wait. Check out the pictures and newspaper articles in the back of the store to see which other famous heads have been covered here. 119 Broadway. © **210/223-3453.** www.parishatters.com.

Sheplers Western Wear   If you want instant (as in trying on the clothes) gratification rather than waiting to get your duds in the mail from what has turned into the world's largest online western store (www.sheplers.com), come to this Ingram Mall Super Store branch of the national chain founded in Wichita, Kansas, during the 1950s. 6201 NW Loop 410. © **210/681-8230.** www.sheplers.com.

Wines

See also Central Market, under "Food," above.

Gabriel's   A large, warehouse-style store, Gabriel's combines good selection with good prices. You never know what oenological bargains you'll find on any given day. The Hildebrand store is slightly north of downtown; there's also another location near the airport at 7233 Blanco (© **210/349-7472**). 837 Hildebrand. © **210/735-8329.** www.gabrielsonline.com.

SeaZar's Fine Wine & Spirits   A temperature-controlled wine cellar, a large selection of beer and spirits, a cigar humidor, and a knowledgeable staff all make this a good choice for aficionados of the various legal vices. 6422 N. New Braunfels, in the Sunset Ridge Shopping Center. © **210/822-6094.**

SAN ANTONIO AFTER DARK

San Antonio is the home of several performance companies, a symphonic orchestra, a continuous flow of road shows, and recurring performances by local talent. Much of what San Antonio has to offer has a strong Latin influence, which lends spice to some of the best local nightlife. San Antonio is America's capital for Tejano music, a unique blend of German polka and northern Mexico ranchero sounds. You shouldn't miss the Ballet Folklórico, a colorful dance troupe with Mexican roots.

Keep in mind, too, that the Fiesta City throws big public parties year-round: Fiestas Navideñas and Las Posadas around Christmastime, Fiesta San Antonio and Cinco de Mayo events in spring, the Texas Folklife Festival in summer, and Oktoberfest and the International Accordion Festival in autumn (see the "San Antonio Calendar of Events," in chapter 2).

For the most complete listings of what's on while you're visiting, pick up a free copy of the weekly alternative newspaper, the *Current,* or the Friday "Weekender" section of the *San Antonio Express-News.* You can also check out the website of **San Antonio Arts & Cultural Affairs:** www.sanantonio.gov/art. There's no central office in town for tickets, discounted or otherwise. You'll need to reserve seats directly through the theaters or clubs, or, for large events, through **Ticketmaster** (© **210/224-9600;** www.ticketmaster.com). Generally, box office hours are Monday to Friday 10am to 5pm, and 1 to 2 hours before performance time. The **Majestic** and **Empire** (p. 130) also have hours on Saturday from 10am to 3pm.

THE PERFORMING ARTS

The San Antonio Symphony is the city's largest resident performing arts company. There are also a few theaters with their own professional companies who keep the local arts scene lively, and cultural organizations that bring well-known performing artists to San Antonio. The city provides some unique venues—such as the elegant Majestic and Empire theaters, the Arneson outdoor theater on the River Walk, and the state-of-the-art AT&T Center. See "Major Arts Venues," below.

Classical Music

San Antonio Symphony The city's symphony orchestra was founded in 1939. It celebrated its 50th anniversary by moving into the Majestic Theatre, the reopening of which was planned to coincide with the event.

The symphony still plays there, but it may move to the Municipal Auditorium in 2011 or 2012. The symphony's season runs from September to May and usually has two concert series, one classical and the other pops. The Music Director is Sebastian Lang-Lessing, a German native, who has conducted orchestras around the world, including the Tokyo Philharmonic and the Orchestre de Paris. He is particularly well known for his opera direction, including work with the opera companies of San Francisco, Houston, and Los Angeles, as well as the Washington National Opera.

222 E. Houston St. (C) **210/554-1000** or 554-1010 (box office). www.sasymphony.org. Tickets $19–$90 classical, $19–$62 pops.

Theater

Most of San Antonio's major road shows turn up at the Majestic or Empire theater (see "Major Art Venues," below), but several smaller theaters are of interest too. The **Actors Theater of San Antonio,** 1920 Fredericksburg Rd. ((C) **210/738-2872**), uses local talent for its productions, which tend to be in the less commercial, off-Broadway tradition. Their venue is the Woodlawn Theatre, opened as a movie house in 1945. The community-based **Josephine Theatre,** 339 W. Josephine St. ((C) **210/734-4646;** www.josephinetheatre.org), puts on an average of five productions a year—mostly musicals—at the Art Deco–style theater, only 5 minutes from downtown.

Whether it's an original piece by a member of the company or a work by a guest artist, anything you see at the **Jump-Start Performance Company,** 108 Blue Star Arts Complex (1400 S. Alamo; (C) **210/227-JUMP** [5867]; www.jump-start.org), is likely to push the social and political envelope. This is the place to find performance artists such as Karen Finley or Holly Hughes.

Magik Theatre, Beethoven Hall, 420 S. Alamo, in HemisFair Park ((C) **210/227-2751;** www.magiktheatre.org), puts on shows exclusively for children and families. It's one of very few such organizations to have its own professional company and venue. The theater, Beethoven Hall, used to belong to an old German singing society and has 600 seats. Shows are popular, so you need to reserve in advance, especially on weekends. Magik Theatre performs a full season of plays, mostly adaptations from children's books.

San Antonio's first public theater, the **San Pedro Playhouse,** 800 W. Ashby ((C) **210/733-7258;** www.sanpedroplayhouse.com), presents a wide range of plays in a neoclassical-style performance hall built in 1930. For information on other small theaters in San Antonio and links to many of those listed in this section, log on to the website of the **San Antonio Theater Coalition** at www.satheatre.com.

Major Arts Venues

See the "For Those Interested in Hispanic Heritage" section of chapter 6 for information on the Alameda Theater.

Arneson River Theatre   If you're visiting San Antonio in the summer, try seeing something at the Arneson. It was built by the Works Project Administration in 1939 as part of architect Robert Hugman's design for the River Walk. The stage for this unique theater sits on one bank of the river, while the audience sits in the amphitheater on the opposite bank. Most of the year, performance schedules are erratic and include everything from opera to Tejano, but the summer brings a stricter calendar: the Fandango folkloric troupe performs every Tuesday and Thursday in June and July, and the Fiesta Noche del Río takes the stage on Friday and Saturday May through July. Both offer lively music and dance with a south-of-the-border flair. La Villita. (C) **210/207-8610.** www.lavillita.com/arneson.

The Aztec Theater   This grand old theater dates from 1926. At present, it's home to a country music revue called San Antonio Rose Live. Performances are Friday through Monday nights at 7:30 and a Saturday afternoon matinee at 2pm. Tickets range from $25 to $35. 104 N. St. Mary's St. ✆ **210/213-7638.** www.majesticempire.com.

Beethoven Halle and Garten   San Antonio's German heritage is celebrated at this venue, a converted 1894 Victorian mansion in the King William area. It's open Tuesday through Saturday as a beer garden, with bands playing everything from oom-pah to rock. Among the regular performers is the Mannerchor (men's choir), which dates back to 1867. Lots of traditional German food, drink, and revelry make Okto-berfest an autumn high point. In December, a *Kristkrindle Markt* welcomes the holi-day season with an old country–style arts-and-crafts fair. 422 Pereida. ✆ **210/222-1521.** www.beethovenmaennerchor.com.

Carver Community Cultural Center   Located near the Alamodome on the east edge of downtown, the Carver theater was built by the city's African-American com-munity in 1929, and hosted the likes of Ella Fitzgerald, Charlie "Bird" Parker, and Dizzy Gillespie over the years. It continues to serve the community while providing a widely popular venue for an international array of performers in a variety of genres, including drama, music, and dance. In 2004, the center completed a major renova-tion, so performances that had been held elsewhere returned for the 2005 season to a newly spiffy—and structurally sound—venue. 226 N. Hackberry. ✆ **210/207-7211** or 207-2234 (box office). www.thecarver.org. Tickets $25.

Guadalupe Cultural Arts Center   There's always something happening at the Guadalupe Center. Visiting and local directors put on six or seven plays a year; the resident Guadalupe Dance Company might collaborate with the city's symphony or invite modern masters up from Mexico City. The Xicano Music Program celebrates the popular local conjunto and Tejano sounds; an annual book fair brings in Spanish-language literature from around the world; and the CineFestival, running since 1977, is one of the town's major film events. And then there are always the parties thrown to celebrate new installations at the theater's art gallery and its annex. 1300 Guadalupe. ✆ **210/271-3151.** www.guadalupeculturalarts.org.

Laurie Auditorium   Some pretty high-powered people turn up at the Laurie Audi-torium, on the Trinity University campus in the north-central part of town. Everyone from former weapons inspector David Kay to Fox news correspondent Brit Hume has taken part in the university's Distinguished Lecture Series, subsidized by grants and open to the public free. The 2,700-seat hall also hosts major players in the popular and performing arts: Chick Corea and the Preservation Hall Jazz Band were among those who took the stage in recent years. Dance recitals, jazz concerts, and plays, many with internationally renowned artists, are held here, too. Trinity University, 715 Stadium Dr. ✆ **210/999-8117** (box office information line) or 999-8119. www.trinity.edu/departments/Laurie.

Majestic and Empire Theatres   The Majestic Theatre introduced air-condition-ing to San Antonio—the hall was billed as "an acre of cool, comfortable seats"—and society women wore fur coats to its opening, held on a warm June night in 1929. The Empire Theatre, which is just around the corner, is a little smaller but is not far behind in swankiness. Nowadays, they are managed by the same company and host a variety of performances, including the symphony, traveling Broadway productions, and a variety of musical and theater acts, mostly roadshows. 230 E. Houston. ✆ **210/226-3333.** www.majesticempire.com.

A Theater that Lives Up to Its Name

Everyone from Jack Benny to Mae West played the **Majestic,** one of the last "atmospheric" theaters to be built in America. The stock market crashed 4 months after its June 1929 debut, and no one could afford to build such expensive showplaces afterward. Designed in baroque Moorish/Spanish revival style by John Eberson, this former vaudeville and film palace features an elaborate village above the sides of the stage and, overhead, a magnificent night sky dome, replete with twinkling stars and scudding clouds. Designated a National Historic Landmark, the Majestic affords a rare glimpse into a gilded era (yes, there's genuine gold leaf detailing).

Sunken Garden Theater   Built by the WPA in 1936 in a natural acoustic bowl in Brackenridge Park, the Sunken Garden Theater boasts an open-air stage set against a wooded hillside; cut-limestone buildings in Greek revival style hold the wings and the dressing rooms. This appealing outdoor arena, open from March through October, offers a little bit of everything—rock, country, hip-hop, rap, jazz, Tejano, Cajun, and sometimes even the San Antonio Symphony. Annual events include Taste of New Orleans (a Fiesta event in Apr), the Margarita Pour-Off in August, and a biannual Bob Marley Reggae Festival. Brackenridge Park, 3875 N. St. Mary's St. (Mulberry Ave. entrance). (C) **210/207-7275.**

THE CLUB & MUSIC SCENE

The closest San Antonio comes to having a club district is the stretch of North St. Mary's between Josephine and Magnolia—just north of downtown and south of Brackenridge Park—known as the Strip. This area was hotter about 15 years ago, but it still draws a young crowd to its restaurants and lounges on the weekend. The River Walk clubs tend to be touristy, and many of them close early because of noise restrictions. Downtown's **Sunset Station,** 1174 E. Commerce ((C) **210/474-7640;** www.sunset-station.com), a multivenue entertainment complex in the city's original train station, has yet to take off when there are no events in the nearby Alamodome. When there are, you can get down at Club Agave, where the movement has a Latin flavor. More regular action occurs on Sunday at noon, when the House of Blues lays on a gospel brunch buffet in a covered outdoor pavilion. Call the Sunset Station office or check the website for details.

In addition to the **Alamodome,** 100 Montana St. ((C) **210/207-3663;** www.sanantonio.gov/dome), the major concert venues in town include **Verizon Wireless Amphitheater,** 16765 Lookout Rd., north of San Antonio just beyond Loop 1604 ((C) **210/657-8300;** www.vwatx.com), and, when the Spurs aren't playing there, downtown's **AT&T Center,** One AT&T Center Pkwy. ((C) **210/444-5000;** www.nba.com/spurs).

Country & Western

Floores Country Store ★★   John T. Floore, the first manager of the Majestic Theatre and an unsuccessful candidate for mayor of San Antonio, opened up this country store in 1942. A couple of years later, he added a cafe and a dance floor—at

Latin American music and dancing is all the rage in the **Southtown Arts and Entertainment District** along South Alamo Street near the King William District. Several clubs swing to a Cuban, Argentinian, Mexican, and Brazilian beat. Whether you come to dance to *cumbia* at a Mexican ballroom or you try the merengue, there's a place for you in San Antonio most every night and weekend. First Fridays of the month are the main event in Southtown, of course—shops, galleries, restaurants, and clubs stay open late, and special openings and art events flood the area.

half an acre, the largest in south Texas. And not much has changed since then. Boots, hats, and antique farm equipment hang from the ceiling of this typical Texas roadhouse, and the walls are lined with pictures of Willie Nelson; Hank Williams, Sr.; Conway Twitty; Ernest Tubb; and other country greats who have played here. There's always live music on weekends, and Dwight Yoakum, Robert Earl Keen, and Lyle Lovett have all turned up along with Willie. The cafe still serves homemade bread, homemade tamales, old-fashioned sausage, and cold Texas beer. 14464 Old Bandera Rd./ Hwy. 16, Helotes (2 miles north of Loop 1604). ✆ **210/695-8827.** www.liveatfloores.com. Cover $5–$35.

Leon Springs Dancehall This lively 1880s-style dance hall can—and often does—pack some 1,200 people into its 18,000 square feet. Lots of people come with their kids when the place opens at 7pm, though the crowd turns older (but not much) as the evening wears on. Some of the best local country-and-western talent is showcased here on Friday and Saturday nights, the only 2 nights the dance hall is open. Get a group of more than 10 together and you can order barbecue from the original Rudy's, just down the road. 24135 I-10 (Boerne Stage Rd. exit). ✆ **210/698-7072.** www.leon springsdancehall.com. Cover usually $5, kids 11 and under.

Rock

White Rabbit One of the few alternative rock venues on the Strip—and one of the only ones large enough to have a raised stage—the Rabbit attracts a mostly young crowd to its black-lit recesses. Those 18 to 20 years old are allowed in for a higher cover. 2410 N. St. Mary's St. ✆ **210/737-2221.** www.sawhiterabbit.com. Cover $6.

Eclectic

Casbeers at the Church Casbeers, in Southtown, offers two different ways to hear music. Downstairs in the cafe, you can hear local acts for free from Tuesday through Saturday nights. The kitchen serves burgers and enchiladas (the enchiladas are popular) and has a full bar. Upstairs, in the nave of the old church, you can hear larger acts for somewhere between $5 and $20, depending on the band. Most of the bands that play here are roots rock, blues, Tejano, country, or folk, anything from the Texas Tornados to Michele Shocked. The setting isn't much different from when it functioned as a Methodist church. The pews and the stained-glass windows are still intact. It wasn't a large church, so even the pews in back offer good views of the stage. You can buy tickets in advance online. 1150 South Alamo. ✆ **210/271-7791.** www.casbeersat thechurch.com. No cover in cafe, cover for some shows $5–$20.

Tycoon Flats ☺ This friendly outdoor venue is a fun place to kick back and listen to blues, rock, acoustic, reggae, or jazz. The burgers and such Caribbean specialties as jerk chicken are good, too. There's rarely any cover for the almost nightly live music. 2926 N. St. Mary's St. ℂ **210/320-0819.** Cover $5 or less when there is one.

Jazz & Blues

The Landing ★★ You might have heard cornetist Jim Cullum on the airwaves. His American Public Radio program, *Riverwalk, Live from the Landing,* is now broadcast on more than 160 stations nationwide, and his band has backed some of the finest jazz players of our time. If you like big bands and Dixieland, there's no better place to listen to this music. Check the website for performance dates—you might want to make reservations. The Landing Cafe features a fairly basic steak and seafood menu, with a few Mexican/Southwest touches. Hyatt Regency Hotel, River Walk. ℂ **210/223-7266.** www. landing.com. Cover $5 Mon–Sat, free Sun (outdoor stage only, when other bands entertain).

Salute! Like the crowd, the music at this red-lit little wonder is eclectic, to say the least. The live jazz at this tiny club tends to have a Latin flavor, but you never know what you're going to hear—anything from synthesized '70s sounds to conjunto. There is no set cover, but some nights it can be as much as $10 to get in the door. So, call ahead or pocket a 10-spot, just in case. 2801 N. St. Mary's St. ℂ **210/732-5307.**

Comedy

Rivercenter Comedy Club This club books such big names in stand-up as Dennis Miller and Garry Shandling, but it also takes advantage of local talent on Mondays (Comedy Potpourri nights) and Fridays (open-mic night in the Ha!Lapeno Lounge 5–7:30pm; no cover). The late, late (12:20am) adult-oriented shows on Friday nights are also free. 849 E. Commerce St. (Rivercenter Mall, 3rd level). ℂ **210/229-1420.** www.rivercenter comedyclub.com. Cover $8 Mon–Tues, $10 Wed–Thurs, $13 Fri–Sun.

The Gay Scene

In addition to the **Bonham** (see below), Main Street just north of downtown has three gay men's clubs in close proximity (it's been nicknamed the "gay bar mall"). **Pegasus,** 1402 N. Main (ℂ **210/299-4222**), is your basic cruise bar. The **Silver Dollar,** 1418 N. Main (ℂ **210/227-2623**), does the country-and-western thing. And the **Saint,** 1430 N. Main (ℂ **210/225-7330**), caters to dancing fools. Covers are low to nonexistent at all three. Popular lesbian bars include **Bermuda Triangle** (119 El Mio; ℂ **210/342-2276**) and **Petticoat Junction** (1812 N. Main; ℂ **210/737-2344**).

Bonham Exchange Tina Turner, Deborah Harry (aka Blondie), and LaToya Jackson—the real ones—have all played this high-tech dance club near the Alamo. While

Smoking in San Antonio

The San Antonio City Council recently passed a nonsmoking ordinance that will apply to most restaurants and bars but is not scheduled to go into effect until August 2011. Smoking will no longer be allowed in indoor areas of restaurants and bars or out in public areas, but there will be exemptions for the River Walk and Alamo Plaza, and inside cigar bars.

conjunto: AN AMERICAN CLASSIC

Cruise a San Antonio radio dial or go to any major city festival, and you'll most likely hear the happy, boisterous sound of conjunto. Never heard of it? Don't worry, you're not alone. Although conjunto is one of our country's original contributions to world music, for a long time few Americans outside Texas knew much about it.

Conjunto evolved at the end of the 19th century, when South Texas was swept by a wave of German immigrants who brought with them popular polkas and waltzes. These sounds were easily incorporated into—and transformed by—Mexican folk music. The newcomer accordion, cheap and able to mimic several instruments, was happily adopted, too. With the addition at the turn of the 20th century of the *bajo sexto,* a 12-string guitarlike instrument used for rhythmic bass accompaniment, conjunto was born.

Tejano (Spanish for "Texan") is the 20th-century offspring of conjunto. The two most prominent instruments in Tejano remain the accordion and the *bajo sexto,* but the music incorporates more modern forms, including pop, jazz, and country-and-western, into the traditional conjunto repertoire. At clubs not exclusively devoted to Latino sounds, what you're likely to hear is Tejano.

Long ignored by the mainstream, conjunto and Tejano were brought into America's consciousness by the murder of Hispanic superstar **Selena.** Before she was killed, Selena had already been slotted for crossover success—she had done the title song and put in a cameo appearance in the film *Don Juan de Marco* with Johnny Depp—and the movie based on her life boosted awareness of her music even further.

San Antonio is to conjunto music what Nashville is to country. The most famous *bajo sextos,* used nationally by everyone who is anyone in conjunto and Tejano music, were created in San Antonio by the Macías family—the late Martín and now his son, Alberto. The undisputed king of conjunto, **Flaco Jiménez**—a mild-mannered triple-Grammy winner who has recorded with the Rolling Stones, Bob Dylan, and Willie Nelson, among others—lives in the city. And San Antonio's **Tejano Conjunto Festival,** held each May (see the "San Antonio Calendar of Events," in chapter 2), is the largest of its kind, drawing aficionados from around the world—there's even a conjunto band from Japan.

Most of the places to hear conjunto and Tejano are off the beaten tourist path, and they come and go fairly quickly. Those that have been around for a while—and are visitor-friendly—include **Arturo's Sports Bar & Grill,** 3310 S. Zarzamora St. (📞 **210/923-0177**), and **Cool Arrows,** 1025 Nogalitos St. (📞 **210/227-5130**). For live music schedules, check the Tejano/Conjunto section under "Entertainment" and "Music" of www.mysanantonio.com, the website of the *San Antonio-Express News.* You can also phone **Salute!** (see above) to find out which night of the week they're featuring a Tejano or conjunto band. Best yet, just attend one of San Antonio's many festivals—you're bound to hear these rousing sounds.

you may find an occasional cross-dressing show here, the mixed crowd of gays and straights, young and old, comes mainly to move to the beat under wildly flashing lights. All the action—five bars, three dance floors, three levels—takes place in a restored German-style building dating back to the 1880s. Roll over, Beethoven. 411

Bonham. ✆ **210/271-3811** or 224-9219. www.bonhamexchange.net. No cover for ages 21 and older before 10pm, then $5 Fri–Sat, $3 Sun.

THE BAR SCENE

Most bars close at 2am, although some alternative spots stay open until 3 or 4am. Some of the hottest bars in town are also in restaurants: See **Acenar** and **Azuca** in chapter 5.

Blue Star Brewing Company Restaurant & Bar   Preppies and gallery types don't often mingle, but the popularity of this brewpub in the Blue Star Arts Complex with college kids demonstrates the transcendent power of good beer. (The King William ale, a barleywine style of ale, is especially fine.) And if a few folks who wouldn't know a Picasso from a piccolo happen to wander in and see some art after dinner, then the owners have performed a public service. You can get a beer sampler for $10, which includes five samples of your choice (there are usually about eight beers to choose from). 1414 S. Alamo, #105 (Blue Star Arts Complex). ✆ **210/212-5506.** www.bluestarbrewing.com.

Cadillac Bar & Restaurant   This bar near the Bexar County Courthouse gets a lot of lawyers and businesspeople on the weekdays. Set in an old saloon, it's an enjoyable place to relax after a day of walking around town. On the weekends it's a little noisier with live music on Fridays and recorded music on Saturday. You might hear anything from cover bands to Tejano and conjunto music. Full dinners are served on a patio out back. 212 S. Flores. ✆ **210/223-5533.**

Howl at the Moon Saloon   This well-known piano bar attracts a slightly older crowd who can listen to dueling piano players hash out oldies from the '60s, '70s, and '80s. 111 W. Crockett St. ✆ **210/212-4695.** www.howlatthemoon.com. Cover $5 Sun–Thurs, $7 Fri–Sat until 10pm, $10 after 10pm.

Le Midi Bar   The cocktail, that most American of inventions, lost its way somewhere around the middle of the last century, but now it's making a comeback thanks to specialty bars such as this one. Forget the flash, forget the show. What a good cocktail requires is quality ingredients and a conscientious and knowledgeable bartender. This small bar at Le Midi restaurant has both. If it's too crowded, try the bar at Bohanan's, just down the street. 301 E. Houston St. ✆ **210/858-7388.**

Menger Bar   More than 100 years ago, Teddy Roosevelt recruited men for his Rough Riders unit at this dark, wooded bar (they were outfitted for the Spanish-American War at nearby Fort Sam Houston). Constructed in 1859 on the site of William Menger's earlier successful brewery and saloon, the bar was moved from its original location in the Victorian hotel lobby in 1956, but 90% of its historic furnishings remain intact. Spanish Civil War uniforms hang on the walls. It's still one of the prime spots in town to toss back a few. Menger Hotel, 204 Alamo Plaza. ✆ **210/223-4361.**

Stone Werks Cafe and Bar   At this offbeat venue—a 1920s building that used to be the Alamo Cement Company's office—a 30-something crowd moves to local cover bands from Wednesday through Saturday. A fence, hand-sculpted from cement by Mexican artist Dionicio Rodríguez, surrounds an oak-shaded patio. 7300 Jones-Maltsberger. ✆ **210/828-3508.**

When it premièred in 1947, the screen of the **Mission Drive-In**, 3100 Roosevelt Ave. ((C) 210/532-3259 or 496-2221), was framed with a neon outline of nearby Mission San Jose, replete with moving bell, burro, and cacti. San Antonio's last remaining open-air movie house, refurbished and reopened in 2001, now has four screens and features first-run films. It's as much fun to come here for a family film fest or romantic under-the-stars evening as it ever was.

Swig Martini Bar   This martini and cigar bar is quite popular. It also has single-barrel bourbon, single-malt scotch, and a wide selection of beer and wines, but James Bond's preferred poison is always the top seller. The big cigars are the draw here. This place was so popular it spawned a national chain. 111 W. Crockett, #205. (C) **210/476-0005.** www.swigmartini.com.

Tex's Grill   If you want to hang with the Spurs, come to Tex's, regularly voted San Antonio's best sports bar in the *Current* readers' polls. Three satellite dishes, two large-screen TVs, and seventeen smaller sets keep the bleachers happy, as do the killer margaritas and giant burgers. Among Tex's major collection of exclusively Texas sports memorabilia are a signed Nolan Ryan jersey, and a football used by the Dallas Cowboys in their 1977 Super Bowl victory. San Antonio Airport Hilton and Conference Center, 611 NW Loop 410. (C) **210/340-6060.**

Waxy O'Connors Irish Pub   Sit in the pub or out on the river. This is your typical Irish-style pub—friendly, loud, and with lots of pub grub. Most nights someone is singing songs to the accompaniment of an acoustic guitar. 234 River Walk. (C) **210/229-9299.**

Zinc   This chic wine bar makes for a nice watering hole in the afternoon when it's half empty. Hardwood floors, brick walls, and racks of wines make the indoor space appealing, but when the place fills, you might head for the pretty back patio. 209 N. Presa St. (C) **210/224-2900.** www.zincwine.com.

MOVIES

The alternative cinemas in San Antonio are not in the most trafficked tourist areas, but if you're willing to go out of your way for an indie fix you can get one at the **Regal Fiesta Stadium 16,** 12631 Vance Jackson ((C) **210/641-6906**). The city also boasts a cinema that not only screens offbeat films, but also allows you to munch on more than popcorn and licorice while viewing them. An Austin import (its name notwithstanding), the **Alamo Drafthouse Westlakes,** 1255 SW Loop 410 ((C) **210/677-8500;** www.originalalamo.com), shows mostly first-run films but accompanies them with seat-side food service.

The **Guadalupe Cultural Arts Center** (see "Major Arts Venues," earlier in this chapter) and the **McNay** and **Witte museums** (see chapter 6) often have interesting film series; and the **Esperanza Center,** 922 San Pedro ((C) **210/228-0201;** www.esperanzacenter.org), usually offers an annual gay and lesbian cinema festival. In addition to *Alamo, the Price of Freedom,* the **San Antonio IMAX Theater Rivercenter,** 217 Alamo Plaza ((C) **210/225-4629;** www.imax-sa.com), shows such high-action films as *Spider-Man* or *Into the Deep* suited to the big, big screen.

SIDE TRIPS FROM SAN ANTONIO

S hould you decide that you want to get out of town for a short spell, you have options besides the Hill Country (chapter 17). Here are three possible trips. The first—to New Braunfels—involves the least amount of travel but offers several activities. The second is a driving tour of small towns that don't see many visitors—offers a visit to a famous old brewery, an old county jail, and a factory where they build small houses using recycled materials for those who like to live small. The third is a trip to the Gulf coast, where you can enjoy all the activities that a beach resort offers and a few that are unique to the central part of the Texas coast. It all depends on what you want to do and how much time you have.

NEW BRAUNFELS & GRUENE

New Braunfels is an old German town only 35 miles up the interstate in the direction of Austin. On the way there, you can take a side trip to visit a large, impressive cavern, and when you get to the town you can do some tubing on the Guadalupe River or spend the day at the biggest, best-known waterpark in Texas—**Schlitterbahn**—considered to be the best waterpark in the country. And, if you're curious about German customs and crafts, there are a couple of good museums that make for enjoyable visits. You can also find some Texas-style nightlife here in the form of old dance halls. And, if you elect to do that, you can stay the night at one of several hotels in town, including a couple of old properties with character.

New Braunfels was founded in 1845 by Prince Carl of Solms-Braunfels, a well-connected German nobleman. He was appointed the commissioner general of the *Adelsverein*, or the Society for the Protection of German Immigrants in Texas, the same group that later founded **Fredericksburg** (see chapter 17). The German way of founding settlements was a more organized endeavor than the Anglo way. The society chose artisans and tradesmen for their potential benefit to the new community. It set aside money and supplies for the first years. And, among the first things Prince Carl did was see to the layout of the settlement, and the construction of a stockade and a fort. After seeing to these necessities, he left for Germany and never returned. New Braunfels, however, grew quickly with the flood of immigrants from Germany, especially with the revolution of 1848. By the mid-1850s, it was the fourth-largest city in Texas after Houston, San Antonio, and Galveston. But growth slowed soon after that. Today it's a town of about 36,000 inhabitants. The town owes much of its recent growth to its proximity to San Antonio. It's one of the few towns in Texas that doesn't have a courthouse square; instead, it has a large traffic circle, with the courthouse on one corner, crowded by other buildings. Most of the old town lies within 5 blocks of this circle.

Tip: Unless you have a particular interest in German heritage, avoid New Braunfels during its annual Wurstfest, a 10-day festival that starts at the end of October. Wurstfest lures 100,000 people to town, fills the streets with traffic, packs the hotels and restaurants, and makes it impossible to get acquainted with New Braunfels.

If you go to New Braunfels, consider driving the 15 miles farther up I-35, to **San Marcos** (see chapter 16), if you want to do some kayaking or shop at two large outlet malls, which are en route.

Nearby Caverns

On the way to New Braunfels, you'll probably see a billboard or two advertising **Natural Bridge Caverns,** 26495 Natural Bridge Caverns Rd. (© **210/651-6101;** www.naturalbridgecaverns.com). These caverns are beautiful and make for an enjoyable side trip. Take exit 175 off of I-35 and go under the freeway and head north on FM 3009. Signs will point the way; the cavern is 8 miles from the interstate. From there the shortest route to New Braunfels is to continue north for 2 miles, then make a right on FM 1863. The caverns hold more than a mile of huge rooms and passages, some of which are filled with stunning, multihued formations—still being formed, as the dripping water attests. The daring—and physically fit—can opt to join one of the Adventure Tours, which involve crawling and, in some cases, rappelling, in an unlighted cave not open to the general public ($100 for 3–4 hr.), while those who prefer their adventures outdoors can opt for the Watchtower Challenge, a 40-foot climbing tower with a zipline (prices vary, subject to weather and availability). The caverns are open 9am to 7pm June through Labor Day, 9am to 4pm the rest of the year; closed Thanksgiving Day, Christmas Day, and New Year's Day; two different tours cost the same, $18 adults, $10 children ages 3 to 11. The **Discovery Tour** explores a half-mile of the cavern, viewing many formations of all types. The **Illuminations Tour** focuses on two chambers with lots of delicate formations, which are dramatically lit.

Just down the road is the **Natural Bridge Wildlife Ranch,** 26515 Natural Bridge Caverns Rd. (© **830/438-7400;** www.nbwildliferanchtx.com), one of those safari parks where you drive through the reserve and can view exotic animals from the safety of your car. The park covers 400 acres, with some 50 species from around the world; there's also a shorter (and equally safe) walking safari. Packets of food sold at the entryway inspire even some generally shy types to amble over to your vehicle. It is open daily 9am to 4:30pm, with extended summer hours until 6:30pm; admission costs $17 adults, $16 seniors 65 and older, $8.50 children ages 3 to 11.

New Braunfels

If you want to head to old town New Braunfels, take exit 187 from I-35 and turn left. This will put you on to South Seguin Street. Only a block from the interstate, you'll see a CVS pharmacy, and behind it, in a white building, is the Visitors Center, but it's easier to pass that by and continue down Seguin until you see on your left the **New**

ACCOMMODATIONS
Faust Hotel 11
Gruene Mansion Inn 17
Prince Solms Inn 1

ATTRACTIONS
Braunfels Railroad Museum 6
Comal County Courthouse 2
Conservation Plaza 15
Henne Hardware 5
Heritage Village 16
Jacob Schmidt Building 4
Lindheimer Home 13
Sophienburg Museum 12
Museum of Texas Handmade Furniture 16

DINING
Huisache Grill 7
Myron's 3
New Braunfels Smokehouse 14
Naeglin's Bakery 10
Phoenix Saloon 8

NIGHTLIFE
Brauntex Performing Arts Theatre 4

Braunfels Chamber of Commerce, 390 S. Seguin, New Braunfels, TX 78130 (© **800/572-2626** or 830/625-2385; www.nbjumpin.com). It's open weekdays 8am to 5pm. The staff can answer questions and give you a map and brochures.

South Seguin Street runs straight to the courthouse circle. Before you get there you'll pass the **Faust Hotel** (and brewpub), a handy place to spend the night (see "Where to Stay in New Braunfels & Gruene," below) and/or stop for a sampling of local flavor. It was built with that exuberance for decoration typical of the buildings of the 1920s and was completed just before the stock market crash of 1929. It's said to be haunted, probably by the hotel's original investors. A few blocks farther down is the **Comal County Courthouse** (1898). Like the courthouses in San Antonio and nearby Gonzales (see "Small-Town Texas," below), it was built by J. Riely Gordon, but this was obviously not his best work or the best location.

If from here you take West San Antonio Street (¾ of a revolution around the circle from S. Seguin St.), you'll come to a large old commercial building built of red brick, the **Jacob Schmidt Building** (193 W. San Antonio). It was here, in 1896, that William Gebhardt took his love for Texas chili and developed a way to popularize it in the rest of the country, an endeavor that eventually made chili the internationally recognized dish that it is today. You can see a mural on the side wall that commemorates the event. The ground floor of the building was a saloon, a grocery store, and a saloon again; after a fire, the saloon reopened as the Phoenix Saloon, rising, as it were, from the ashes. The building was later closed up for years but was recently reopened, again as the **Phoenix Saloon** (© **830/660-6000**), by owners who obviously have a sense of history. Here you can get a righteous bowl of chili and honor the memory of Mr. Gebhardt. You can also taste the chili in the form of a chili burger, or in a Frito pie (served in an updated version of the original dish—using the Frito bag as a container). The Phoenix is an enjoyable place to pass an evening. It has live music almost every night and usually without a cover charge.

If you walk down a little farther and across the street, you'll find **Henne Hardware,** 246 W. San Antonio (© **830/606-6707**). This is a classic old hardware store with tall shelves lining the walls from floor to ceiling, reached by using ladders attached to an old rail. Henne bills itself as the oldest hardware store in Texas (1893) and sells everything most hardware stores do, in addition to cookware, toys, and a number of traditional items not commonly found, such as old locks and doorplates for refurbishing old buildings.

A bit farther down are the railroad tracks and the site of the **New Braunfels Railroad Museum,** 302 W. San Antonio St. (© **830/627-2447**), an all-volunteer effort, which is open from Thursday to Monday from noon to 4pm. The museum suggests a $2 donation to see the old depot, restored to its early-20th-century condition, the collection of train memorabilia, an elaborate model train set, and the four antique rail cars in its possession: a locomotive, caboose, dining car, and boxcar.

Just on the other side of the tracks (but not visible from the street) is the **Huisache Grill,** which probably has the best food in New Braunfels (see below). If you're in the mood for baked goods, return to the courthouse circle and make a right back on to South Seguin Avenue. **Naeglin's Bakery,** 129 S. Seguin Ave. (© **830/625-5722**), will be on your left. It opened in 1868 and stakes its claim as the state's longest-running bakery. For something different, try the *kolaches*—Czech pastries filled with cheese, fruit, poppy seeds, sausage, or ham, among other delicious fillings.

MUSEUMS

In addition to the railroad museum mentioned above, New Braunfels has a few others. First, there's the **Sophienburg Museum,** 401 W. Coll St. (© **830/629-1572;** www.sophienburg.org), located on the hill where the original Sophienburg fort was built by Prince Carl in honor of his fiancé Sophia. The museum has one room of rotating exhibits portraying life in the town during the 19th and early 20th centuries. The museum has a few interesting artifacts, but I don't think it's worth the time for most people, or the $5 general admission. It's open Tuesday to Saturday 10am to 4pm. Students 17 and under only pay $1. Take West San Antonio Street a few blocks past the railroad tracks and turn left on Clemens Avenue. The museum is 3 blocks down on the right.

There are two related museums, next door to each other on the east side of New Braunfels, which do a better job of describing the life of early residents. Take South Seguin back toward the interstate; make a left onto Business 35, go 1 mile to Hwy. 46 and make a left, then your first right. The **Museum of Texas Handmade Furniture,** 1370 Church Hill Dr. (© **830/629-6504;** www.nbheritagevillage.com), offers tours of the 1858 Breustedt-Dillon Haus, filled with period furniture made in the area, including some beautiful examples of Texas Biedermeier by local craftsmen of the last half of the 19th century. The house's *fachwerk* construction will also be something new for most visitors. *Fachwerk* consists of solidly built wooden frames filled in with a variety of materials, including brick, stone, and earth. The 11-acre **Heritage Village** complex, which is the site of the furniture museum, also includes an 1848 log cabin and a barn that houses a reproduction of a cabinetmaker's workshop. The museum is open Tuesday through Sunday from 1 to 4pm from February 1 through November 30, closed December and January. The last tour begins at 3:30pm. Admission costs $5 for adults, $4 for seniors, $1 for children ages 6 to 12.

Right next to the entrance to the furniture museum is **Conservation Plaza,** 1300 Church Hill Dr. (© **830/629-2943**), a collection of seventeen 19th-century structures that were preserved and moved onto this site. Guided tours (included in admission) are offered from Tuesday to Friday, 10am to 2:30pm, and Saturday and Sunday, 2 to 5pm; adult admission costs $2.50, while children 6 to 17 pay 50¢. The site is closed on Mondays. The tour includes viewing an original 1870 schoolhouse, a store, a music studio, and several houses. On the grounds is a gazebo and garden with more than 50 varieties of antique roses.

Conservation Plaza is a project of the New Braunfels Conservation Society, which also owns the 1852 **Lindheimer Home** at 491 Comal Ave. (© **830/608-1512**). It's a particularly good example of an early *fachwerk* house. Ferdinand J. Lindheimer, one of the town's first settlers, was an internationally recognized botanist and editor of the town's German-language newspaper. Call ahead to request a tour, or to wander the grounds planted with Texas natives (38 species of plants were named for Lindheimer).

HISTORIC GRUENE

To get to Gruene, take exit 189 off of I-35 and turn left onto Hwy. 46, then follow the signs. Actually part of New Braunfels, **Gruene** (pronounced "green") is only 4 miles north of downtown. It was first settled by German farmers in the 1840s and stayed small. It was virtually abandoned during the Depression in the 1930s and remained a ghost town until the mid-1970s, when two investors realized the value of its intact historic buildings and sold them to businesses. These days, tiny Gruene is crowded with day-trippers browsing the specialty shops in the restored structures, which

Tubing is a favorite pastime during Central Texas summers. It's very simple. You drift lazily down the river in an oversize tube and occasionally enjoy a very little bit of white water. This stretch of the Guadalupe River below Canyon Dam, and the San Marcos River below Aquarena Springs, are the preferred areas for spending time in the river. They are a bit different, and the experience you will have depends a good deal on local factors. For the Guadalupe, one of the biggest factors is the Canyon Dam flow rate. When the flow rate is low, you hardly move on the water; when it's high, the ride can be a lot more fun. What you're looking for is something around 100 cubic feet per second or higher. Call ahead to either of the outfitters listed above to inquire about the flow rate before you make the trip, or visit www.guadalupefly.com/flow.html. Another thing to keep in mind is that the water is released from the bottom of the lake and is pretty cold—good during the summer, less so during spring and autumn. Also, sometimes this area is affected by flooding. In 2010, it was closed for more than a month. The San Marcos River isn't affected by most of these factors. The river is spring-fed and doesn't flood or slow down as much as the Guadalupe. The water is also a couple of degrees warmer, and can be enjoyed for a little longer into the autumn. But the tubing runs are shorter. I prefer tubing on the Guadalupe when the conditions are ideal because there is more variety and more time in the river. When conditions are less than ideal, San Marcos is preferable.

include a smoked-meat shop, lots of cutesy gift boutiques, several antiques shops, and an old Texas dance hall.

The **New Braunfels Museum of Art & Music,** 1259 Gruene Rd., on the river behind Gruene Mansion (ⓒ 800/456-4866 or 830/625-5636), focuses on popular arts in the West and South (as opposed to, say, high culture and the classics). Subjects of recent exhibits, which change quarterly and combine music and art, have included Texas accordion music, central Texas dance halls, and cowboy art and poetry. Live music throughout the year includes an open mic on Sunday afternoons, and the recording of *New Braunfels Live* radio show of roots music on Thursday evenings. The museum is open Wednesday through Sunday from noon to 6pm from September 1 through April 30; and Monday through Thursday from 10am to 6pm, Friday and Saturday from 10am to 8pm, Sunday noon to 8pm the rest of the year. Free admission, though donations are gratefully accepted (and you can contribute by shopping at the museum's excellent gift shop).

Watersports

Gruene is upriver on the Guadalupe, close to many outfitters who can help you ride the Guadalupe River on a raft, tube, canoe, or inflatable kayak, including **Rockin' R River Rides** (ⓒ 800/553-5628 or 830/629-9999; www.rockinr.com) and **Gruene River Company** (ⓒ 888/705-2800 or 830/625-2800; www.toobing.com), both on Gruene Road just south of the Gruene bridge.

The other popular option for fun in the water is **Schlitterbahn ★**, Texas's largest waterpark and perhaps the best in the country, 305 W. Austin St., in New Braunfels (ⓒ 830/625-2351; www.schlitterbahn.com). If there's a way to get wet 'n' wild, this place has got it. Six separate areas feature gigantic slides, pools, and rides, including

Master Blaster, one of the world's steepest uphill water coasters. The combination of a natural river-and-woods setting and high-tech attractions makes this splashy 65-acre playland a standout. The park usually opens in late April and closes in mid-September; call or check the website for the exact dates. All-day passes cost $45 for adults, $36 for children 3 to 11; children 2 and under enter free. The park has grown a lot over the years and now is in two distinct sections, linked by shuttles: the original park, and the new additions. If you're going straight to Schlitterbahn from San Antonio, take exit 187, turn left and drive to the courthouse circle, make a right onto East San Antonio Street, and drive 5 blocks.

Those who like their water play a bit more low-key might try **New Braunfels's Landa Park** (© 830/608-2160), where you can either swim in the largest spring-fed pool in Texas or calmly float in an inner tube down the Comal River—at 2½ miles the "largest shortest" river in the world, according to *Ripley's Believe It or Not*. There's also an Olympic-size swimming pool, and you can rent paddle boats, canoes, and water cycles. Even if you're not prepared to immerse yourself, you might take the lovely 22-mile drive along the Guadalupe River from downtown's Cypress Bend Park to Canyon Lake.

For more details about all the places where camping, food, and water toys are available along the Guadalupe River, pick up the Water Recreation Guide pamphlet at the New Braunfels Visitors Center.

Perhaps you want to buy your own toys—and learn how to use them. The 70-acre **Texas Ski Ranch,** 6700 I-35 N. (© 830/627-2843; www.texasskiranch.com), is paradise for those interested in wake, skate, and motor sports. Features of this expanding complex include a cable lake, boat lake, skate park, and motor track—at all of which you can test the equipment you want to purchase or rent (you can also bring your own). Training clinics and private lessons for a variety of sports are offered. Costs depend on the use of facilities and classes. The complex is open Tuesday through Thursday from 10am to 8pm, Friday and Saturday 10am to 9pm, Sunday 10am to 6pm.

Where to Stay in New Braunfels & Gruene

The **Prince Solms Inn,** 295 E. San Antonio St., New Braunfels, TX 78130 (© 800/625-9169 or 830/625-9169; www.princesolmsinn.com), was built to be a small hotel. It has been in continuous operation since 1898. A prime downtown location, tree-shaded courtyard, and florid, High Victorian–style sleeping quarters have put accommodations at this charming bed-and-breakfast in great demand. Three Western-themed rooms in a converted 1860 feed store next door work for families, and there's an ultraromantic separate cabin in the back of the main house. Rates range from $125 to $195.

The **Faust Hotel,** 240 S. Seguin St. (© 830/625-7791; www.fausthotel.com), has standard rooms going from $69 to $99. Rates go up when there's a festival in town. This is in many ways a classic old hotel with an ornate lobby and welcoming brewpub.

For a bed-and-breakfast experience, consider the **Gruene Mansion Inn,** 1275 Gruene Rd., New Braunfels, TX 78130 (© 830/629-2641; www.gruenemansioninn.com). The barns that once belonged to the opulent 1875 plantation house were converted to rustic elegant cottages with decks; some also offer cozy lofts (if you don't like stairs, request a single-level room). Accommodations for two go from

New Braunfels & Gruene

$170 to $240 per night, including breakfast served in the plantation house. Two separate lodges, suitable for families, are available, too ($260–$340).

The nearby **Gruene Apple Bed and Breakfast,** 1235 Gruene Rd. (© **830/643-1234;** www.grueneapple.com), set on a bluff overlooking the Guadalupe River, is less historic, more upscale. This opulent limestone mansion, built expressly to serve as an inn, hosts 14 luxurious theme rooms, from "Wild West" and "Shady Lady" to the more decorous "1776"; many look out on the river from private balconies. On-site recreation includes a natural stone swimming pool, hot tub, pool table, player piano—even a small movie theater. Doubles range from $175 to $235; midweek discounts available.

If you're planning to come to town during the Wurstfest sausage festival (late Oct–early Nov), be sure to book well in advance, no matter where you stay—that is high season here.

Where to Dine in New Braunfels & Gruene

The **New Braunfels Smokehouse,** 1090 N. Business 35 (© **830/625-2416;** www.nbsmokehouse.com), opened in 1951 as a tasting room for the meats it started hickory smoking in 1943. Savor it in platters or on sandwiches, or have some shipped home as a savory souvenir. It's open daily for breakfast, lunch, and dinner; prices are moderate. For my money, the **Huisache Grill,** 303 W. San Antonio St. (© **830/620-9001;** www.huisache.com), has the best food in town. The American menu has classic and original dishes. The pecan-crusted pork chop, the mixed grill, and the blue cheese steak are among my favorites. Lunch and dinner are served daily; prices are moderate to expensive. The restaurant is broken into several different dining areas, each with its own character. To find it, take West San Antonio from the courthouse and take the first driveway to the left after you cross the tracks.

If you want just steak, **Myron's,** 136 Castell Rd. (© **830/624-1024;** www.myronsprimesteakhouse.com), serves perfectly prepared Chicago prime in a retro dining room (a converted 1920s movie palace). Prices are big-city expensive, but the outstanding food and service, combined with the atmosphere, make any meal here a special occasion. Myron's is open for dinner nightly. Reservations are recommended.

In Gruene, the **Gristmill River Restaurant & Bar,** 1287 Gruene Rd. (© **830/625-0684;** www.gristmillrestaurant.com), a converted 100-year-old cotton gin, includes burgers and chicken-fried steak as well as healthful salads on its Texas-casual menu. Kick back on one of its multiple decks and gaze out at the Guadalupe River. Lunch and dinner daily; prices are moderate.

New Braunfels & Gruene After Dark

At the **Brauntex Performing Arts Theatre,** 290 W. San Antonio (© **830/627-0808;** www.brauntex.org), a restored 1942 movie theater in midtown New Braunfels, you can expect to see anything from Frula, an eastern European folk-dancing extravaganza that played Carnegie Hall, to such local acts as the Flying J. Wranglers.

Lyle Lovett and Garth Brooks are just a few of the big names who have played **Gruene Hall ★★**, Gruene Road, corner of Hunter Road (www.gruenehall.com), the oldest country-and-western dance hall in Texas and still one of the state's most outstanding spots for live music. If you don't like the act playing at Gruene Hall, try the **Phoenix Saloon,** 193 W. San Antonio St. (© **830/660-6000;** www.the phoenixsaloon.com).

SMALL-TOWN TEXAS

If you want to get out of San Antonio and away from the crowds, and you want to see a less touristy part of Texas, then consider this day trip to a few of the old towns to the east of San Antonio. The trip includes a smattering of things: a little history, an old county jail, a little antiques shopping, a tour of Texas's last independent brewery, and some award-winning barbecue, plus a good amount of local color. It's best to go on a weekday, when the brewery is open for tours. This is a relaxing trip—the roads are good, the traffic is light, and the driving is easy. There won't be any crowds, which is especially important during wildflower season in the spring. Visitors show a strong preference for the Hill Country, but the wildflowers do not.

Gonzales

Start by heading out of San Antonio east on I-10 to Hwy. 183 (60 miles), then south to the town of **Gonzales** (12 miles). One of the original Anglo settlements made under agreement with the Mexican government, Gonzales was a hotbed for Texas independence and saw the first hostilities of the war. While driving around the town, you're sure to see signs and banners with the words "Come and take it" below an image of a canon. This was the battle cry of the local settlers when, in October 1835, a regiment of Mexican cavalry came to collect a small cannon that had been lent to the settlement to fend off the Comanche. What followed was more of a skirmish than a battle, but it set Texas on the road to independence. A few months later, the town was burned to the ground by orders of General Sam Houston when the Texan army retreated eastward, during the so-called Runaway Scrape.

In the oldest part of Gonzales (pop. 7,000), the streets are still named after saints, following the original layout proposed by the Mexican government. There's a relatively large business sector with old brick storefronts, which tells of past prosperity. Occupying a few of these (and a couple of warehouses, too) is **Discovery Architectural Antiques** (© **830/672-2428;** www.discoverys.com) at 409 St. Francis St. It sells all manner of old building materials and details, including original lumber, doors, windows, and hardware, stained glass, and small details, such as doorknobs, for instance.

The **town courthouse** is one of the prettiest in Texas. It was built in 1898 in Richardsonian Romanesque (a style named after the architect who built Trinity Church in Boston). It was designed by J. Riely Gordon, who also designed Bexar County Courthouse in San Antonio and the Comal County Courthouse in New Braunfels. This is the best of the three and is one of the best-preserved courthouses in the state, having retained its clock tower and original roof. The interior is well preserved, too. It contains a few paintings, one of which depicts the town circa 1925. The **old jailhouse,** which sits at the opposite corner of the square (facing St. Lawrence St.), is home of the chamber of commerce and visitor center. It dates from 1887 and is open to visitors. It must have been a grim sight for prisoners, to judge by the way the cells were built and by the gallows room, which was used for executions until the 1920s, when capital punishment was brought under state control. Gonzalez did have a criminal element, and its most famous member was John Wesley Harden (son of a Methodist preacher). He killed several men in the Sutton-Taylor feud, which raged throughout several counties in this part of Texas during the 1870s. For a while he was jailed in Gonzales (in an earlier jailhouse) but managed to escape.

Gonzales has several large houses in the old part of town, as well as a **Pioneer Village** (℡ 830/672-2157; www.gonzalespioneervillage.com), which is at the north end of town, on 2122 N. St. Joseph St. It holds a collection of 19th-century buildings brought here from different parts of the county and restored, including a ranch house, a cabin, and a saloon. It's open from 10am to 2pm Tuesday to Saturday. Admission is $5 per adult, $3 for children 4 to 13, free for children 3 and under. It's probably a good idea to call ahead to make sure someone is there. You also need to be mindful of the time because you'll want to get to the next town, Shiner, before either 11:30am or 1pm, when the brewery tours start. It's 20 minutes away.

Shiner

Shiner (pop. 2,000) is home to the **Spoetzl brewery,** the makers of Shiner beer. This is the last independent brewery in Texas, and in 2009 celebrated its 100th anniversary. Take Hwy. 90 E. for 18 miles. When you drive into Shiner, the brewery will be on your left. It's the highest structure in town.

Shiner Bock beer, sold in brown longnecks, is now available in various parts of the country, but, as late as the 1970s it was available only seasonally and only in central and southeast Texas. But it soon shot up in popularity until it's now the default beer in Austin, San Antonio, and most other parts of central Texas.

Free tours are offered Monday to Friday, at 11:30am and 1pm, and take about 30 minutes, with beer tastings before and after in the hospitality room. It's an impressive tour—especially the bottling plant. You can see the bottles move along a conveyor that looks like a long amusement ride. It loops around the entire brewery, guiding bottles in and out of several machines, until capped, labeled, and filled with beer; then they are deposited in boxes ready for shipping.

All the Shiner beer sold is made at this small brewery; no production is contracted out to other plants.

Flatonia

After your immersion in German/Czech beer culture, it's time to move on. From the brewery, take a left on Hwy. 95 N. and drive 18 miles to **Flatonia** (pop. 1,000). This is a small agricultural town and railroad depot. Really, the main reason to come here is that firstly, it's on the way to the next destination, and secondly, so that you can tell your friends back home that you were in Flatonia, Texas. (The name doesn't actually refer to its lack of topography, but you don't have to mention that.) If you want to know more about the town, you will pass right by the **town archives and museum** (on your right). It's occasionally open, and you can stretch your legs while examining a few antiques.

Luling

From Flatonia, head back west on I-10. Your destination is **Tiny Texas Houses** (℡ 830/875-2500; www.tinytexashouses.com). The owner builds small, fully functional, energy-efficient houses, using recycled lumber and hardware. Examples of his houses are on view for anyone who stops by. They're beautiful and distinctive, and are small enough to transport by truck. The business is on the southeast corner of the intersection of I-10 and Hwy. 80 (exit 628).

Luling (pop. 5,000) has some of the best barbecue in the state. The town is divided down the middle by the railroad tracks. Where the highway crosses the tracks, look for **City Market** (℡ 830/875-9019) on the left, a few doors down at 633 E. Davis St.

Small-Town Texas | SIDE TRIPS FROM SAN ANTONIO

(It's reviewed, and its barbecue is discussed, on p. 268.) It's open Monday through Saturday until 6pm. Luling is also known for watermelon, and they have a festival the last week of June called the **Watermelon Thump.** If you arrive during the festival, you will have a hard time scoring some barbecue, as the town gets crowded.

In the 1920s and '30s, Luling was at the center of a central Texas oil boom. After you finish your barbecue, you can stroll down Davis Street to no. 421, where you'll find the **Central Texas Oil Patch Museum** (✆ 830/875-1922; www.oilmuseum. org). This very large space is filled with artifacts of the early days of oil extraction and of the city of Luling. It's an interesting exhibit, and the building itself, with its old-time tin ceiling, is a pleasure to see. While you are there, you can pick up a brochure and map for the **Pumpjack Tour.** Within the city are several pumpjacks (those rocking-horse-like machines that bob up and down in oil fields). Denizens of Luling started dressing up the pumpjacks for fun, and then the local chamber of commerce commissioned Texas sign artist George Kalesik to decorate some. The pumpjacks are located close enough together that you can see the majority on foot.

After your visit to Luling, you can return to San Antonio or head to San Marcos or New Braunfels.

CORPUS CHRISTI & BEYOND

If you're in San Antonio, you're only 2½ hours from the ocean and some of the best stretches of Texas coastline. The communities around **Corpus Christi** and **Copano Bays** have a lot going for them. In the summer, you can do some kayaking, windsurfing, fishing, and other watersports. And, with Texas's mild weather, you can do most these activities in other seasons as well. In spring and autumn, birders flock to this area for the migrations, when birds rest up before and after hopping the Gulf of Mexico. Another attraction in the region is the Aransas National Wildlife Refuge, the winter home of the whooping crane, the largest bird in North America, and the rarest, too. For a more detailed view of this region, search "Gulf Coast Texas" at frommers.com.

Corpus Christi is a major deepwater seaport, with a population of just under 300,000, but it has the feel of a much smaller place. The downtown is easy to enjoy, and everything is pretty close together. The two biggest attractions are the State Aquarium and the USS *Lexington* aircraft carrier, which are right next to each other on the bay just north of downtown, across Harbor Bridge.

How to Get There

Take I-37 straight to Corpus Christi. If you're headed for Rockport, from I-37, take Hwy. 181 over the Bay Causeway, then continue on Tex. 35. To get to the beach town of Port Aransas, follow the signs for Aransas Pass, and from there take the causeway that leads to the Port Aransas ferry. Another nice beach is on Mustang Island. As you approach central Corpus Christi on I-37, look for signs reading Tex. 358 or "S.P.I.D." (South Padre Island Dr.).

What to Do

Corpus Christi's top two attractions are on the east side of the tall bridge that spans the Nueces River: The **Texas State Aquarium** (✆ 800/477-4853; www.texas stateaquarium.org), at 2710 N. Shoreline Blvd., and the **USS** *Lexington* (✆ 800/523-9539; www.usslexington.com), an old aircraft carrier docked at 2914 N. Shoreline Blvd.

birding ALONG THE TEXAS COAST

The coastal plains of Texas are a haven for birds. The area is rich in resident species and is the winter home to many more. It offers a variety of habitats—freshwater and saltwater marshes, tidal zones, prairies, and woodlands—and abundant food sources. It's also smack in the middle of the great flyway for birds migrating from the northern parts of the U.S. and Canada to Central and South America. On their southward journey this is the last chance for R & R before they have to hop the Gulf of Mexico, and on the return it's the first landfall.

All of this is why the Texas Gulf Coast attracts lots of birders and sponsors several birding events. The reader can take for granted that throughout this chapter there are plenty of birding opportunities, even when none is specifically mentioned. The best times to visit are during the migration seasons and in winter. Most of the annual events are held in the Brazosport and the Corpus Christi areas. Here are a few highlights: The towns of Lake Jackson and Rockport hold festivals for viewing hummingbirds (lots of them) when they pass through here in September. Also in late September or early October, local birders in Corpus hold the annual hawk count at Hazel Bazemore County Park, where tens of thousands of raptors of various species fly through here following the Nueces River. And in April, Brazosport holds its annual Migration Celebration, when local birders serve as guides on birding walks. For specific information, contact local visitor centers listed in this chapter. The state publishes three helpful maps called **"The Great Texas Coastal Birding Trail,"** one for each section of the Texas coast. These list 300 viewing sites and give driving directions and descriptions for each. Call ℂ **888/900-2577** or check out the maps at the following website: www.tpwd.state.tx.us/huntwild/wild/wildlife_trails/coastal.

Admission to the Texas State Aquarium is $16 adults, $15 seniors, and $11 for children ages 3 to 12. It has several large tanks displaying different saltwater and freshwater habitats. You can see and participate in dolphin training, and chat with some of the staff. Each day there's a schedule of presentations. Check it when you first arrive. To see the USS *Lexington* costs a little less: $13 adults, $11 seniors, and $8 for children 4 to 12. Touring the boat requires a good bit of stair climbing. This aircraft carrier saw service in the Pacific during World War II. It shows its age, which conveys to a great degree the difficulty and risk of being a crewman or a pilot back in those days. Part of the hangar deck has been converted into a large-format film theater, which offers shows, not necessarily about the ship. Both the aquarium and the USS *Lexington* are open daily, with slightly longer hours during the summer season.

If you're in Corpus Christi during baseball season, you might want to check out the local minor league baseball team, called the **Corpus Christi Hooks** (ℂ **361/866-TEAM** [866-8326]; www.cchooks.com). They are a AA farm club for the Houston Astros and play in the Texas League. Their ballpark, **Whataburger Field,** is the most attractive farm-club ballpark you'll ever see. It's at the water's edge, at the foot of the tall bridge, but on the south side (the same side as central Corpus Christi). Tickets run from $5 to $12. (Whataburger is a chain of fast-food restaurants, which began in Corpus and still keeps its corporate offices here.)

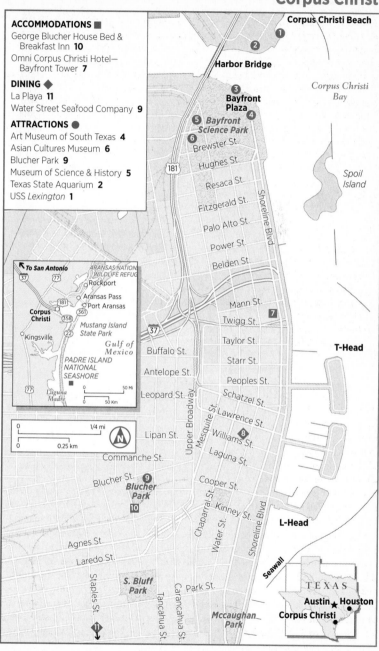

ACCOMMODATIONS ■
George Blucher House Bed &
    Breakfast Inn **10**
Omni Corpus Christi Hotel—
    Bayfront Tower **7**

DINING ◆
La Playa **11**
Water Street Seafood Company **9**

ATTRACTIONS ●
Art Museum of South Texas **4**
Asian Cultures Museum **6**
Blucher Park **9**
Museum of Science & History **5**
Texas State Aquarium **2**
USS *Lexington* **1**

Corpus Christi Beach

Harbor Bridge

Corpus Christi Bay

Bayfront Plaza

Bayfront Science Park

Brewster St.

Hughes St.

Resaca St.

Fitzgerald St.

Palo Alto St.

Power St.

Belden St.

Shoreline Blvd.

Spoil Island

181

To San Antonio

37 77

ARANSAS NATION WILDLIFE REFUG

Rockport

Aransas Pass
Port Aransas

181

Corpus Christi

361

358

Mustang Island State Park

22

Kingsville

Gulf of Mexico

PADRE ISLAND NATIONAL SEASHORE ■

77

Laguna Madre

0   50 Mi
0   50 Km

0   1/4 mi
0   0.25 km

Mann St.

Twigg St.   **7**

Taylor St.

Starr St.

Peoples St.

Schatzel St.

Lawrence St.

Williams St.   **8**

Laguna St.

Cooper St.

Kinney St.

T-Head

Buffalo St.

Antelope St.

Leopard St.

Upper Broadway

Mesquite St.

Lipan St.

Commanche St.

Blucher St.   **9**
Blucher Park

10

Agnes St.

Laredo St.

S. Bluff Park

Staples St.

Chaparral St.

Water St.

Shoreline Blvd.

L-Head

Seawall

Park St.

Carancahua St.

Tancahua St.

Mccaughan Park

11

T E X A S

Austin ★ Houston
Corpus Christi

Heading down the coast toward Corpus Christi, you come to Matagorda Bay, one of the least developed areas of the coast, with lots of small fishing towns and farming communities. This region has its charm, and life here is really laid-back. Protecting the coast is Matagorda Island, a 38-mile-long strip of land covering almost 44,000 acres. It's mostly federal and state land set aside as a wildlife refuge. Aside from a small state park with camping areas and a historic lighthouse, there is little development. But there are plenty of beaches, pristine and deserted, on which you will see no motorized vehicles; they are prohibited. You can swim, hike, ride a bike (if you brought one), do some bird-watching (more than 300 species of birds have been spotted here, including the whooping crane), or look for shells.

Fishing is also popular. Many locals fish in the surf here.

But if you decide to visit the island, you'll have to bring your own water and food; none can be purchased on the island. Primitive campsites at the state park cost $6 per night (up to four people). An outdoor cold-water rinse is available near the boat docks. The state used to operate a passenger ferry (📞 361/983-2215) to the island from the town of Port O'Connor, but for the past couple of years, it's been inoperative. Call to see if it's running again. Another option is to hire a boat at Port O'Connor. For more information, contact **Matagorda Island State Park and Wildlife Management Area** (📞 979/244-6804; www.tpwd.state.tx.us/park/matagisl/matagisl.htm).

OUTDOOR ACTIVITIES

Most visitors come to this area either for some relaxing beach time or for one of the many activities offered here, or both.

DOLPHIN AND WHOOPING CRANE CRUISES   These tours are done in large shallow-draft boats that go out for 3 to 4 hours. Tours to see the whooping cranes run from November through March. Boats depart from the Fulton Harbor, which is in the Rockport area. Fulton is a township next to Rockport and it's difficult to tell where one town ends and the other begins. There are a number of small outfits, and they usually charge about $40 per person. The best thing to do is go down to the piers and inquire about which company might have a boat departing imminently.

FISHING   Most visitors wanting to fishing go to Port Aransas. There are several outfits and many guides. Try **Woody's Sports Center** (📞 361/749-5271; www.gulfcoastfishing.com) at 136 W. Cotter, on the main pier of Port Aransas.

SEA KAYAKING   There are several good places to explore by kayak in the bays surrounding Corpus Christi, and most are in the vicinity of Rockport. You might want to try Rockport Adventures (📞 877/892-4737; www.rockportadventures.com). It offers rentals and tours. Tours require a minimum of four people, but you might be able to hook up with another group or do a self-guided tour on your own with a map provided by the store. The staff can haul you and your kayaks to a drop-off spot and pick you up later.

WINDSURFING   The best place to learn windsurfing or hone your skills is in the sheltered water of the Laguna Madre, on North Padre Island, which is south of Mustang Island. Inside the Padre Island National Seashore, you'll find a small but well-known concessionaire called **Worldwinds Windsurfing** (© **361/949-7472;** www.worldwinds.net), which sells and rents windsurfing equipment and wet suits, and in summer, offers windsurfing lessons.

OTHER ATTRACTIONS

Just north of downtown is the city's striking convention center. Nearby are a visitor center at 1823 N. Chaparral St. and a handful of small museums, including the **Art Museum of South Texas,** the **Asian Cultures Museum,** and the **Museum of Science and History.** Before going to any of these, first step into the visitor center to see if any coupons are available. Visiting these museums, which are small to medium size, is a nice way to spend a rainy afternoon.

whooping cranes: BACK FROM THE BRINK OF EXTINCTION

By and large, there are two kinds of tourists who come to the Rockport area in winter: winter Texans fleeing the harsh cold of their northern homes and nature enthusiasts who come to visit another sort of winter Texan, the magnificent whooping cranes. The largest birds in America, these cranes fly in from northwest Canada in October/November and leave again in the spring. An adult male stands 5 feet high and can have a wingspan of 8 feet. They are elegant, too: Elongated legs and throat give them dramatic lines, and the plumage has a classic appeal that never goes out of fashion—solid white with black wing tips, black eyeliner, and just a touch of red accent on the top of the head. It would be a tremendous blow to lose these creatures to oblivion, but that is almost what happened—and their comeback story is probably the most famous of all the cases of wildlife conservation.

Before the arrival of the Europeans, these birds inhabited the Gulf and Atlantic shores in winter and northern Midwest and Canada in summer. But hunting and loss of habitat dwindled the population until, by 1941, only 15 birds survived. All were members of the flock that winters here on the central Texas coast. A concerted effort requiring the contributions of many dedicated biologists and fieldworkers was launched to save them.

The team first pushed for laws preserving the summer and winter nesting grounds and all the major stopover points along the 2,400 miles of the migration route. The cranes were slow to come back, but through protection and public education, their mortality rates decreased and the population began to grow. This was difficult and took time because these cranes are slow to mature and don't reproduce until their fourth year. And even then the female lays only two eggs and raises only one chick. Worried that with only one flock the species was vulnerable, biologists began stealing the second eggs and hatching them elsewhere. They have established a nonmigrating population in south central Florida and another population that they've been "teaching" to migrate between Wisconsin and western Florida. So far it's working, but the Aransas flock is still the largest and only natural population of "whoopers" in the world. In 2010 their numbers hit an all-time high of 224.

The best way to view the birds is from the deck of a boat. Several boats specialize in birding and whooping crane tours. They skirt along the coast of the refuge, which is the favorite feeding grounds for the cranes. A few are listed below.

This 3,954-acre state park is home to about 5 miles of beach on the Gulf of Mexico in Nueces County, just south of Port Aransas. Mustang Island is a coastal barrier island with a unique and complex ecosystem, dependent upon its numerous sand dunes, some of which reach as much as 35 feet in height (15×20 ft. is average). Activities here include swimming, fishing, kayaking, camping, hiking, mountain biking, bird-watching, and sunbathing. From downtown Port Aransas, take Alister Street/Hwy. 361 south to Mustang Island State Park (© **361/749-4573**; www.tpwd.state.tx.us).

Adding to Corpus Christi's small-town amusements is a minor-league baseball team in the Texas league called the **Corpus Christi Hooks** (© **361/561-4665;** www.cchooks.com). Home games are played at Whataburger Field, which is a beautiful ballpark at the water's edge near the foot of the tall bridge that spans the Nueces River. (Whataburger is a successful chain of burger joints with restaurants all across the South and Southwest. It began in Corpus in 1950. During your stay here, you'll see lots of these restaurants with their trademark orange-and-white roofs.)

Where to Stay

If you're staying in Corpus Christi and want a hotel with a view, inquire about a room in the Bayfront Tower of the **Omni Corpus Christi Hotel** (© **800/843-6664;** www.omnihotels.com) at 900 N. Shoreline Blvd. Rates run from $160 to $220 for a double, depending on the season and the day of the week.

Corpus Christi has a lovely bed-and-breakfast called the **George Blucher House** (© **866/884-4884;** www.georgebluucherhouse.com), at 211 N. Carrizo, in an old residential area close by the city's downtown. The location is good, and the rooms and the house in general have lots of character. Rates run from $120 to $190.

If you're looking for an inexpensive motel, there is a concentration of them in the vicinity of the Texas State Aquarium and USS *Lexington*. This is not a bad location for visitors. One inexpensive independent motel among the chain properties is the **Sea Shell Inn** (© **361/888-5291**) at 202 Kleberg Place, with rates for a double from $50 to $125.

In Rockport, the nicest full-service hotel is the **Lighthouse Inn** (© **866/790-8439;** www.lighthousetexas.com) at 200 S. Fulton Beach Rd. Rates run from $140 to $220, depending upon the season. A good bed-and-breakfast is **Hoope's House** (© **800/924-1008;** www.hoopeshouse.com), at 417 N. Broadway, where rates are $160 for a double.

In Port Aransas and all the barrier islands in this area, the predominant form of lodging is condo towers. These almost always rent by the week and advertise heavily on the Internet. One agency that represents many condos is **Starkey Properties** (© **888/951-6381;** www.starkeyproperties.com). If you want hotel lodging, there's a great old hotel called the **Tarpon Inn** (© **361/749-5555;** www.thetarponinn.com) in Port Aransas at 200 E. Cotter. As this is an old place, the double rooms are awfully small but economical, at $69 to $99. The premium rooms are a substantial upgrade ($110–$130) and worth the extra money, but the suites ($145–$250), especially the FDR suite, have the style and size to warrant the extra money and are one of a kind.

For roomy, inexpensive lodging, try the **Balinese Flats** (© **888/951-6381;** www. balineseflats.com), at 121 Cut-off Rd., in Port Aransas. It offers 2-bedroom apartments for $75 in winter, $95 in spring and fall, and $155 in summer.

Where to Dine

In downtown Corpus Christi, you can't go wrong with **Water Street Seafood Company** (© **361/882-8683**) at 309 N. Water St. It's easy to find and is very popular, but it's big enough that you usually don't have to wait long for a table. Good and cheap Tex-Mex can be had at **La Playa** (© **361/853-4282**), at 4201 S.P.I.D., which isn't as easy to find but is worth the extra trouble.

For Tex-Mex in Rockport, try **Los Comales** (© **361/729-3952**) at 431 Hwy. 35. It offers several kinds of enchiladas, which are all good. It also offers a few dishes from central Mexico, which is a bit surprising for being a small-town restaurant on the Texas coast. **Latitude 28°02'** (© **361/727-9009**) serves locally caught seafood; there's no shortage of appealing dishes on the menu in addition to the nightly chef's specials.

Port Aransas has plenty of good restaurants, and a favorite is **La Playa Mexican Grille** (© **361/749-0022**), at 222 Beach St., which has no connection with La Playa Restaurant in Corpus Christi. For something of a surprise for Port Aransas, there's **Venetian Hot Plate** (© **361/749-7617**), just down the way at 232 Beach St. The Italian owners care about food and care about wine. The menu has some wonderful northern Italian dishes.

SUGGESTED AUSTIN ITINERARIES

T here is an old joke that circulates among Austinites about what to do with family and friends who come to town wanting to see the sights. Anytime someone mentions plans to take visitors sightseeing, another person present is supposed to ask, "So when are you taking them to San Antonio?"

It's not that Austin doesn't have places of interest; it's just that most of these aren't sights in the traditional sense. A trip here is more about absorbing the atmosphere than it is about sightseeing. Don't get me wrong: There are places to see, such as the state capitol and the LBJ Library. And there are plenty of local activities to indulge in, such as swimming in Barton Springs and watching the bats take flight from the Congress Avenue Bridge, though both of those can usually only be enjoyed seasonally. The following itineraries should allow visitors to take in the attractions and experience the laid-back Austin vibe. Day 1 hits all the major sights. Day 2 is more an exploration of city life—a day of bohemian Austin, taken to its utopian extreme, in which you'll hit some of the centers of local culture. Day 3 gets you out of Austin to see some nearby towns, where you can enjoy a variety of activities.

But first, I describe the principal parts of town, where you'll find these attractions. For more information about navigating the city, see the "Getting Around: Austin" section of chapter 18.

Neighborhoods in Brief

Although Austin, designed to be the capital of the independent Republic of Texas, has a planned, grand city center similar to that of Washington, D.C., the city has spread out far beyond those original boundaries. These days, with a few exceptions, detailed below, locals tend to speak in terms of landmarks (the University of Texas) or geographical areas (East Austin) rather than neighborhoods.

Downtown The original city, laid out by Edwin Waller in 1839, runs roughly north from the Colorado River. The river has been dammed in several places, forming a series of lakes. The section near downtown is called Lady Bird Lake. Downtown extends north up to 11th Street, where the capitol building is. The main north-south street is **Congress Avenue.** It runs from the river to the capitol. Downtown's eastward limit is the I-35 freeway, and its westward limit is Lamar Boulevard. This is a prime

10

sightseeing area (it includes the capitol and several historic districts), and a hotel area, with music clubs, restaurants, shops, and galleries. There are a lot of clubs on **Sixth Street,** just east of Congress, in the **Warehouse District,** centered on Third and Fourth streets just west of Congress, and in the **Red River District,** on (where else?) Red River, between 6th and 10th streets.

South Austin For a long time, not a lot was happening south of Lady Bird Lake. This was largely a residential area—a mix of working class and slackers lived here. **South Congress,** the sleepy stretch of Congress Avenue running through the middle of South Austin, was lined with cheap motels. In the 1980s, the area became attractive to store and restaurant owners who liked the proximity to downtown without the high rents. Trendy shops moved into the old storefronts. Yuppies started buying houses in the adjoining neighborhoods. And now South Austin is booming.

Fairview Park and **Travis Heights,** adjoining neighborhoods between Congress and I-35, are perhaps the most popular for young professionals who can afford the high prices. They were Austin's first settlements south of the river, because Austin residents realized they were not as likely to be flooded as the lower areas on the north bank. Farther south and west, toward the Lady Bird Johnson Wildflower Center, South Austin begins to reassert its rural roots, with less construction and more businesses that serve the local populace.

Central Austin This is a larger area that includes downtown and the university campus. It's not precisely defined. If you were to travel north from Lady Bird Lake through the downtown area and past the capitol, you would come across a complex of state government office buildings (btw. 15th and 19th sts.). Past that would be the UT campus (19th to 26th sts.). Farther north, you get to the **Hyde Park** neighborhood (35th to 51st sts.). Hyde Park got its start in 1891 as one of Austin's first planned suburbs; renovation of its Victorian and early Craftsman houses began in the 1970s, and now it has a real neighborhood feel. Neighbors socialize a good bit here and are out tending their gardens or walking to one of the many places here where people congregate.

Beyond Hyde Park, numbered streets disappear. You pass through a couple of neighborhoods, and eventually you come to Research Boulevard. For a lot of Austinites, this is where central Austin ends and north Austin begins.

West Austin West of Lamar is **Clarksville,** formerly a black community founded in the 1870s by freed slaves. It's now a neighborhood of small, old houses that command high prices. To the west of Clarksville, on the other side of the Mo-Pac Freeway, is a tony neighborhood called **Tarrytown,** which extends as far as Lake Austin (upstream from downtown, the Colorado river bends around in a more northerly direction, where another dam creates this long, narrow lake).

West Lake The name denotes the townships that are on the opposite side of Lake Austin from West Austin. This is an affluent suburban area that includes the communities of **Rollingwood** and **Westlake Hills.** If you head upstream to the next dam, you come to Lake Travis, a large lake with lots of marinas and lakeside communities, such as **Lakeway.** But you don't have to live here to play here: This is also where those who live in Central Austin come to splash around and kick back on nice weekends.

East Side East of I-35 are several neighborhoods, which are predominantly Hispanic and African American. The parts closest to downtown and the university area are increasing in popularity, forcing many of the poorer denizens of East Austin to move farther east.

Northwest This is where most of the high-tech industry is located. It is largely suburban and includes the Arboretum, a large mall, and a newer mall called the Domain. Farther north are the bedroom communities of Round Rock and Cedar Park.

Austin at a Glance

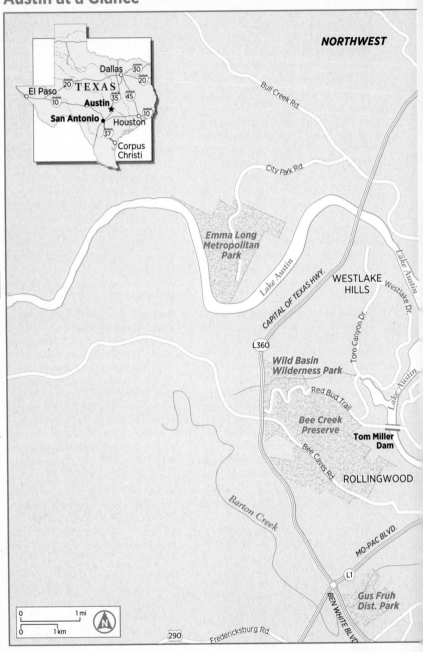

NORTHWEST

Dallas 30
20 **TEXAS**
El Paso 35 45
10 **Austin** ★
San Antonio 10
Houston
37
Corpus Christi

Bull Creek Rd.

City Park Rd.

Emma Long Metropolitan Park

Lake Austin

CAPITAL OF TEXAS HWY.

WESTLAKE HILLS

Lake Austin

Westlake Dr.

L360

Wild Basin Wilderness Park

Toro Canyon Dr.

Red Bud Trail

Bee Creek Preserve

Tom Miller Dam

Bee Caves Rd.

ROLLINGWOOD

Barton Creek

MO-PAC BLVD.

L1

BEN WHITE BLVD.

Gus Fruh Dist. Park

290 Fredericksburg Rd.

0 — 1 mi
0 — 1 km

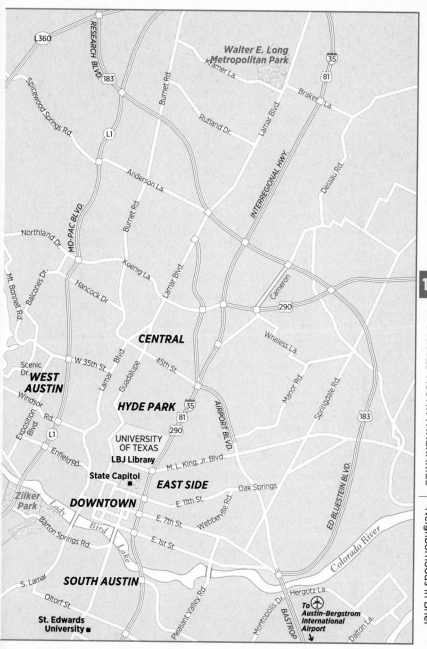

THE BEST OF AUSTIN IN 1 DAY

Between March and November, the bats will be in town. If you're here at the cusp of one of those months, call the Bat Hotline to check and to get the estimated time that they take flight. See p. 208. **Note:** This itinerary requires a car.

1 LBJ Library and Museum ★

If you're in town for just a short time, visiting the LBJ Library may afford you the best view of campus that you'll get. From the stone platform, you can see the campus to the west of you sloping down the hill and then rising up on the next one. There's no mistaking the well-known University Tower. Inside the library, behind glass windows, you'll see the presidential papers boxed in red Moroccan leather. But it's the museum you'll really want to head toward. Be sure not to miss the animatronic version of LBJ. See p. 210.

2 Blanton Museum of Art ★

The new Blanton has a gracious interior and a good bit of space to show its works. Of its holdings, the Latin American art is probably the most fun, and the Renaissance collection is probably the most important. There might also be a visiting show. See p. 210.

3 Bob Bullock Texas State History Museum ★

This museum was built more with Texans in mind than out-of-staters. Outsiders are welcome, but the museum does delve into some Texas history minutiae that might not be so interesting to others. The exhibits are beautifully done, and some have a sense of humor. There are a lot of choices to consider at the ticket booth: exhibits, IMAX, the Texas Spirit Theater. You might have time to do all of them if you haven't lollygagged at the earlier stops. The combo ticket package includes a decent discount, and the Texas Spirit Theater, with its multiculturalist message, doesn't take long to see. See p. 210.

South of the Bob Bullock Museum, and so obvious that you can't miss it, is the:

4 State Capitol ★★

This is fun for everyone. The biggest capitol building (but not the tallest) in the 50 states has seen a lot of shenanigans. Take the guided tour, which is free and is more interesting than the self-guided tour. See p. 204.

5 Take a Break

Step into this delightful Congress Avenue restaurant, the Roaring Fork, on the ground floor of the old Stephen F. Austin Hotel (now the InterContinental). Lunches are hearty and reasonably priced. 701 Congress Ave. ✆ 512/583-0000. See p. 184.

6 Lady Bird Johnson Wildflower Center ★★★

You can end up spending a lot more time here than you planned, especially if you come in the spring when most of the wildflowers are in bloom. Watch the clock to ensure that you're back in town in time to catch the next (and last) stop on this itinerary. There are some attractions indoors worth your attention, and don't miss the gift shop. See p. 209.

7 Evening Bat Flight

When the largest urban bat colony in North America takes wing out from under downtown's Congress Avenue Bridge, it's an impressive act of nature. Call the Bat Hotline (© **512/416-5700,** ext. 3636) for the daily estimated flight time. If you arrive early, get a space on the east side of the bridge close by the southern bank of Town Lake. You should also check out the information module set up by Bat Conservation International; it explains something about the habits and life of a bat colony. See p. 208.

THE BEST OF AUSTIN IN 2 DAYS

Think of this itinerary as a cultural exploration. The idea is less about accomplishing a set of tasks than it is about blending into Austin's easygoing culture. This trip should be done in midweek; otherwise, you'll have to work your way through the crowd of workaday wage slaves who only come out on the weekends. I include a lot of stops to give you options. Should you linger at one place longer than most, you can pick up the trail as you see fit. I don't include any places to take a break because, in practice, this whole day amounts to taking a break.

---

1 Hike-and-Bike Trail

The first activity is a leisurely stroll along the hike-and-bike trail (unless you're a late riser, in which case move on to the second activity if you want to avoid the heat and the crowds). One of the most attractive sections of the path is the loop from Congress Avenue west to the pedestrian bridge next to the Lamar Bridge. See p. 232.

2 South Congress Cafe

Walk up South Congress to this popular brunch spot, where you can enjoy a local favorite—*migas* (eggs cooked with chopped tomato, onion, chili, and tortilla bits)—or try something out of the ordinary, such as the wild boar *pozole* (Mexican-style hominy stew). See p. 192.

3 Tesoros Trading Co.

Tesoros is a large import business that carries a huge variety of things large and small. You don't have to buy anything; just enjoy the showroom's unique mix of ethno-crafts and ethno-kitsch. See p. 244.

4 Barton Springs Pool ★★

By now, if it's gotten warm enough, it's time to relax at Barton Springs. A lot of folks show up at night in summer to cool off for free, but why not enjoy it during the hottest hours of the day? Catch some rays, or some shade on the grassy hillsides above the pool, then cool off in the clear water. Then repeat. See p. 209.

5 Shady Grove ★

This homey restaurant offers up some of the classics of Texas and American cuisine in a relaxed indoor/outdoor setting. The ample menu includes chili, meatloaf, and burgers. Perfect for a late lunch after a good swim. See p. 193.

The Best of Austin in 1, 2 & 3 Days

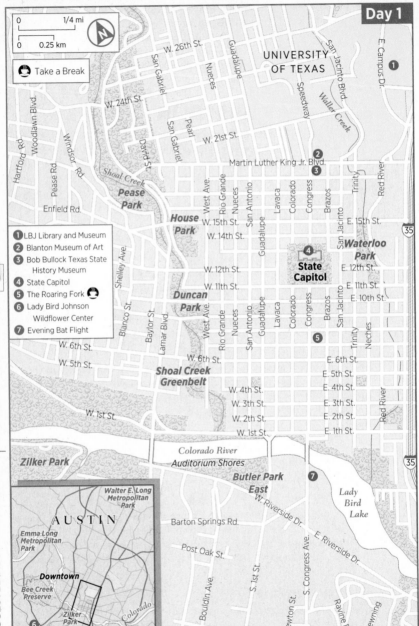

Day 1

0 — 1/4 mi
0 — 0.25 km

☺ Take a Break

1. LBJ Library and Museum
2. Blanton Museum of Art
3. Bob Bullock Texas State History Museum
4. State Capitol
5. The Roaring Fork ☺
6. Lady Bird Johnson Wildflower Center
7. Evening Bat Flight

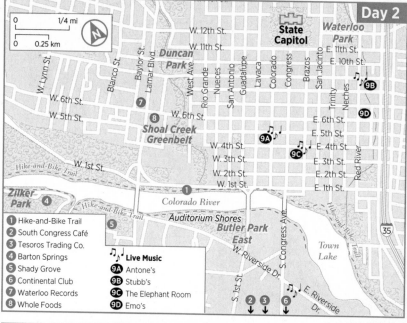

1 Hike-and-Bike Trail
2 South Congress Café
3 Tesoros Trading Co.
4 Barton Springs
5 Shady Grove
6 Continental Club
7 Waterloo Records
8 Whole Foods

♫ Live Music
9A Antone's
9B Stubb's
9C The Elephant Room
9D Emo's

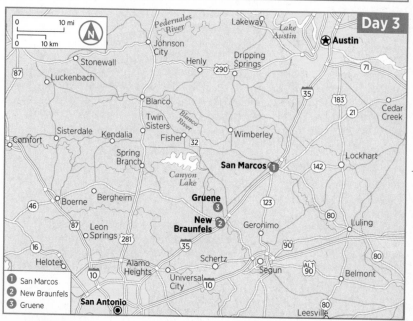

Day 3

1 San Marcos
2 New Braunfels
3 Gruene

6 Continental Club ★

By now it should be time for happy hour, and if reading the entertainment section of the paper didn't provide any guidance, make the Continental Club your default choice. Sometimes you get really lucky. See p. 259.

7 Waterloo Records

This is Austin's favorite music store. The staff is knowledgeable and can help you find what you didn't know you were missing. It's a great place just to browse through the CDs, and sample some of the music at one of the listening stations. See p. 247.

8 Whole Foods

Explore the flagship store of the chain of natural and organic foods. Whole Foods sells a lot besides food. It's also a great place to have a light lunch, as you can make your way through all the steam tables and food counters picking and choosing exactly what you want in just the right amount. It's perfect for eating light. There's a pretty little outdoor seating area, too. See p. 245.

9 Live Music

This stop is where your morning research should really be paying off. The clubs to pay special attention to are Antone's, Stubb's, the Elephant Room, and the Saxon Pub. Alternatively, you can decide to stroll through the downtown entertainment districts looking for the music that fits your taste. The entire area is compact enough to walk through it easily. See p. 257.

THE BEST OF AUSTIN IN 3 DAYS

The three towns on the following itinerary provide opportunities for any number of activities—strolling a town square, canoeing, shopping for discounts at outlet malls, visiting a waterpark, and even tubing on the Guadalupe River. If tubing strikes your fancy, the day trip is usually best done in the late spring to early summer, when the water in the lower Guadalupe is flowing fast and deep enough so you don't have to paddle and you won't scrape your backside on the rocks. If you have kids, they will enjoy Schlitterbahn, an extremely large waterpark that counts many faithful among central Texas's youth. ***Start:*** Head south from Austin on I-35.

1 San Marcos

Thirty miles south of Austin is San Marcos, a college town that some are calling the new Austin. San Marcos has a nicely restored courthouse and town square, making it a good stop for stretching your legs. If you're looking for a more active endeavor, San Marcos is a good place for canoeing or kayaking. Just past San Marcos on the interstate are two outlet malls, **Prime Outlets** (ⓒ **800/628-9465** or 512/396-2200) and **Tanger Factory Outlet Center** (ⓒ **800/408-8424** or 512/ 396-7446), which together boast a hundred name-brand stores and attract a lot of visitors. See p. 270.

Continue south on I-35 to reach:

2 New Braunfels

When you get to New Braunfels, drive through the center of town. It still has a small-town feel about it, despite the town having grown considerably in the last few years. New Braunfels is home to the Schlitterbahn waterpark, a great destination for families looking to get wet. If you'd rather do your cooling off in a less hectic environment, head to nearby Gruene (now practically a suburb of New Braunfels), the next (and last) stop on the itinerary. See p. 137.

3 Gruene

Gruene (pronounced *green*) is upstream from New Braunfels and is the lower end of the long stretch of the Guadalupe River. For many locals, it's a favorite spot for tubing. Drive up River Road, and you'll see one outfitter after another renting inner tubes. Rent one, and then plunk down into the refreshing Guadalupe. You'll see what all the fuss is about. See p. 137.

4 Take a Break

After tubing and changing clothes, you can grab a bite to eat at the traditional Gristmill River Restaurant & Bar, 1287 Gruene Rd. (© 830/625-0684). See p. 144.

WHERE TO STAY IN AUSTIN

Unlike San Antonio, Austin doesn't have a large stock of downtown hotel rooms dependent on large conventions, so discounted rates for downtown rooms are harder to come by. In slack times, the properties at the margins of the city feel the pinch; but the central properties don't because normal business and leisure travel can fill most of their rooms.

When looking for discounts, keep in mind the calendars of the state legislature and the University of Texas. Lawmakers and lobbyists converge on the capital from January through May of odd-numbered years, so you can expect tighter bookings. The beginning of fall term, graduation week, and football weekends—UT's football stadium now seats 100,000—will also fill lots of hotel rooms.

The busiest season, however, is the month of March, when the South by Southwest (S×SW) music festival fills entire hotels. It is designed to coincide with UT's spring break, usually the third week of the month. S×SW is the largest gathering of the year for the music industry. It attracts more than a hundred bands from all over the world trying to get record deals, thousands of music fans, and lots of producers and music company execs. And now there's a film and media festival the week before the music begins. To make matters worse, Austin often hosts regional playoffs for NCAA basketball, and the university likes to take advantage of spring break by hosting academic conferences. So, try to avoid coming in March of an odd-numbered year when UT's basketball team is in the regionals. Of course, there are a few other spots in the calendar when the city is busier than usual, such as in September for the Austin City Limits Music Festival. This festival has become immensely popular and attracts lots of out-of-towners.

If you're coming here to see what Austin's all about, consider staying somewhere in the central part of town. You'll enjoy your stay more because traffic in Austin can be bad, and making your way around an unfamiliar city can be trying. You don't have to stay downtown. Consider the hotels in South Austin in and around South Congress or close to Lady Bird Lake. This is a comfortable area to say in, with lively foot traffic, and most of the places of interest are very close. These areas are within walking distance of downtown. You don't need a car unless you're planning to visit sites outside central Austin.

If you're on a tight budget and looking for bargain discounts, you should know that there are two major clusters of budget hotels in Austin. One surrounds the intersection of I-35 and Ben White Blvd. (Hwy. 71), and the other is north of there, where I-35 intersects Hwy. 290 East. The latter cluster is a better location for three reasons: one, it's closer to downtown; two, it has better dining options; and three, you're not limited to using I-35—there are alternative routes for getting around. This cluster includes **Studio 6,** at 6603 I-35 (© 512/458-5453; www.staystudio6.com), and **Hawthorn Suites** at 935 La Posada Dr. (© 512/459-3335; www.hawthorn.com).

Also consider the areas near the University of Texas, such as Hyde Park, West Campus, and even a little farther to the north. Here, too, it's easy to get around, and you get a good feel for Austin.

Most hotels catering to business travelers offer weekend discounts and, of course, corporate discounts. You'll find lots of Austin room deals on the Internet, but don't stop there. Be sure to phone and ask about packages—which might include such extras as breakfast or champagne—and reduced rates for seniors, families, active-duty military personnel . . . whatever you can think of. Call the toll-free number and the hotel itself, because sometimes the central reservations agent doesn't know about local deals. Sure, calling is not as impersonal as the Internet, but don't be afraid of being a pain if the deal is worth it.

Please note that rates listed below do not include the city's 15% hotel sales tax, and they are the prevailing rates during normal times of the year. During festival times other occasions that fill hotels, the rates will rise.

Wherever you bunk in Austin, it is safe to expect air-conditioning and Internet connections. Even B&B rooms offer high-speed wireless Internet connections these days, and many hotels also offer WebTV, enabling you to retrieve e-mail and cruise the Internet via the tube. Most hotels in Austin are smoke-free; when smoking rooms are available, I mention them in the review.

THE best AUSTIN HOTEL BETS

- **Best for Conducting Business:** Located near the high-tech companies of northwest Austin, the **Renaissance Austin Hotel,** 9721 Arboretum Blvd. (© 800/HOTELS-1 [468-3571] or 512/343-2626), has top-notch meeting and schmoozing spaces, not to mention fine close-the-deal-and-party spots. See p. 175.
- **Best Place to Play Cattle Baron:** If you want to imagine you've acquired your fortune in an earlier era, bed down at the **Driskill,** 604 Brazos St. (© 800/252-9367 or 512/474-5911), where big meat mogul Jesse Driskill still surveys (via stone bust) the opulent 1886 hotel that bears his name. See p. 166.
- **Hippest Budget Hotel:** Look for the classic neon sign for the **Austin Motel,** 1220 S. Congress St. (© 512/441-1157), in Austin's cool SoCo district. The rooms have been individually furnished, many in fun and funky styles, but the place retains its 1950s character and its retro prices. See p. 172.

○ **Best New Arrival: Hotel Saint Cecilia,** 112 Academy Dr. (📞 **512/852-2400**), is a small one-of-a-kind hotel in the heart of SoCo. It has beautiful rooms, beautiful grounds, and amenities like no hotel in Austin, including mattresses that could have been made by Swedish elves. See p. 171.

○ **Best View of Lady Bird Lake:** Lots of downtown properties have nice water views, but the **Hyatt Regency's** location, 208 Barton Springs Rd. (📞 **800/233-1234** or 512/477-1234), on the lake's south shore gives it the edge. You get a panoramic spread of the city with the capitol as a backdrop. See p. 168.

○ **Best Place to Tee Off:** Austin isn't a major destination for duffers, but you'd never know it if you stay at **Barton Creek Resort,** 8212 Barton Club Dr. (📞 **800/336-6158** or 512/329-4000), featuring courses designed by a pantheon of golf greats—two by Tom Fazio, one by Ben Crenshaw, and one by Arnold Palmer—plus a golf school run by Austinite Chuck Cook. See p. 178.

○ **Greenest Hotel:** Several hotels in Austin take ecoconsciousness beyond the old "we won't wash your towels" option, but no one takes it nearly as far as **Habitat Suites,** 500 E. Highland Mall Blvd. (📞 **800/535-4663** or 512/467-6000). Almost everything here is ecofriendly. See p. 174.

○ **Best for Forgetting Your Troubles:** Stress? That's a dirty word at the **Lake Austin Spa Resort,** 1705 S. Quinlan Park Rd. (📞 **800/847-5637** or 512/372-7300). After a few days at this lovely, ultrarelaxing spot, you'll be ready to face the world again, even if you don't especially want to. See p. 178.

DOWNTOWN

Very Expensive

The Driskill ★★★ Opened in 1886, the Driskill is Austin's original grand hotel and national historic landmark. It has seen its share of history. Lyndon Johnson wrapped up his presidential campaign and received the election results here. The Daughters of the Republic of Texas, the saviors of the Alamo, met here to agree on their plan of action. It was here, too, that the Texas Rangers plotted their ambush on Bonnie and Clyde. Nothing in town comes close to the Driskill in character or magnificence, which draws locals and visitors alike to the hotel's cafe and piano bar (p. 263).

The Driskill offers guests a choice between rooms in the original 1886 building (labeled "historic") or in the 1928 addition ("traditional"); the latter are the better deal, especially those on the 12th floor, which have higher ceilings. Rooms are well lit, distinctively decorated, and furnished with period pieces. This hotel is on Austin's lively Sixth Street, and some of the "historic" rooms with balconies can catch street noise. The hotel recently refurbished all the rooms, including replacing all mattresses and installing flatscreen televisions. It has been awarded the Five Dog Bone Award for pet friendliness by the readers of *Animal Fair* magazine. The Driskill has a handful of smoking rooms.

604 Brazos St. (at E. Sixth St.), Austin, TX 78701. 📞 **800/252-9367** or 512/474-5911. Fax 512/474-2214. www.driskillhotel.com. 189 units. $250–$340 double; suites from $345. AE, DC, DISC, MC, V. Valet parking $26. Pets under 25 lb. accepted with $50 fee per pet per stay. **Amenities:** 2 restaurants; bar; concierge; health club; room service. *In room:* A/C, TV, hair dryer, Wi-Fi.

Four Seasons Austin ★★★ ☺ An ideal location on the north shore of Lady Bird Lake; comfortable rooms; an excellent spa; beautifully manicured grounds; and

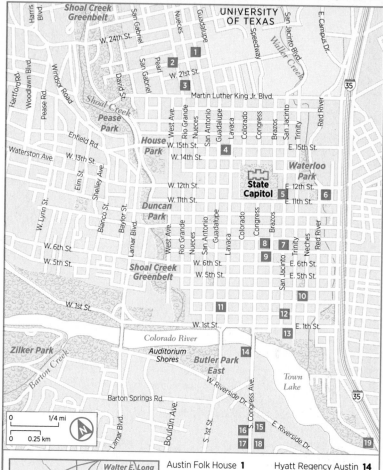

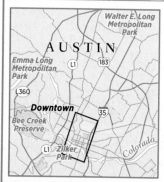

Austin Folk House **1**
Austin Motel **16**
Doubletree Guest
 Suites Austin **4**
The Driskill **9**
Four Seasons Austin **13**
Hampton Inn & Suites
 Austin-Downtown **12**
Hilton Austin **10**
Holiday Inn Austin Town
 Lake **19**
Hotel Saint Cecilia **15**
Hotel San José **18**

Hyatt Regency Austin **14**
InterContinental Stephen
 F. Austin **8**
Kimber Modern Boutique
 Hotel **17**
La Quinta Inn—Capitol **5**
Mansion at Judges Hill **3**
Omni Austin **7**
Sheraton Austin **6**
Star of Texas Inn **2**
W Austin **11**

167

direct access to Austin's Hike and Bike Trail are just a few reasons to stay here. And, of course, there's the famous Four Seasons service, which sets this hotel apart from all others. No place in Austin can make life easier.

The look of the place is part modern, part traditional, and part Texas. Polished stone floors, with plush area rugs, deep easy chairs and sofas, and a smattering of Western art form a muted blend. The hotel obviously knows the tastes of its clientele, but to my eye, the interiors lacks character. The guest rooms have the same plush and conservative feel. The city views are fine, but the ones of the lake are finer still. You can choose between rooms with balconies and rooms without.

If you're traveling with toddlers, the staff can provide such necessary gear as strollers and baby seats, and there are plenty of weekend activities. Older kids can enjoy complimentary treats, such as popcorn and soda or milk and cookies, if you notify the hotel when you make your reservations.

98 San Jacinto Blvd. (at First/Cesar Chavez St.), Austin, TX 78701. © **800/332-3442** or 512/478-4500. Fax 512/478-3117. www.fourseasons.com/austin. 291 units. $320–$480 double; suites from $570. Lower rates Sat–Sun; spa packages available. AE, DC, DISC, MC, V. Valet parking $25. Pets no taller than 12–15 in. accepted; advance notice to reservations department required. **Amenities:** Restaurant; bar; concierge; health club; outdoor heated saltwater pool; room service; spa. *In room:* A/C, TV/DVD, hair dryer, minibar, Wi-Fi.

Hyatt Regency Austin ★★★   Austin's Hyatt Regency may have the best location of any hotel in town. It sits on Lady Bird Lake's south shore (strictly speaking, this is South Austin, but its size and feel are downtown traits). This gives the north-facing rooms lake vistas with the downtown skyline as a backdrop. The most popular of these have balconies. Also, right below the hotel is the dock for boat tours to see the bats (under Congress Ave. bridge) and other Lady Bird Lake excursions. You can rent paddle boats and canoes from this dock, as well, or take advantage of the Hike and Bike Trail. The Hyatt rents bikes to guests who prefer riding to walking. Rooms have a comfortable, modern-functional look and are, for the most part, of average size. Hyatt has just completed installing "Respire Rooms" at this hotel for the benefit of allergy sufferers (Central Texas is the promised land for allergists). These come with beefed up air scrubbers, special coatings on all surfaces, and hypoallergenic everything. And for smokers, the hotel still offers a few rooms, which come with enhanced air-filtering technology.

208 Barton Springs Rd. (at S. Congress), Austin, TX 78704. © **800/233-1234** or 512/477-1234. Fax 512/480-2069. www.austin.hyatt.com. 446 units. $199–$314 double; $450–$650 suite. Sat–Sun specials, corporate, and government rates available. AE, DC, DISC, MC, V. Self-parking $12; valet parking $18. **Amenities:** Restaurant; bar; bike rental; concierge; club-level rooms; health club; Jacuzzi; outdoor pool; room service. *In room:* A/C, TV, hair dryer, Wi-Fi ($9.95 per 24 hr.).

Omni Austin   This is a cool hotel despite the fact that it caters to business travelers. The hotel occupies one of two towers (the other is an office building) enclosed in a giant cube of steel and glass. The rest of the area in the cube is free space, crating an airy atrium illuminated by natural light filtering in through the glass. Rooms have either interior or exterior views. Standard rooms are comfortable, with bathrooms slightly larger than the norm. The one-bedroom suites come with a full kitchen and dining area. I especially like the Omni's rooftop pool, sun deck, and Jacuzzi (with terrific city views), which are a big part of the hotel's attraction. The hotel's Get Fit program gives you incentive to exercise, offering free fitness kits and healthy snacks; for $25, a treadmill will be brought to your room. The location is great, just off the Sixth Street entertainment district.

700 San Jacinto Blvd. (at E. Eighth St.), Austin, TX 78701. ☏ **800/THE-OMNI** (843-6664) or 512/476-3700. Fax 512/397-4888. www.omnihotels.com. 375 units. $239–$279 double; $299–$389 suite. AE, DC, DISC, MC, V. Self-parking $18; valet parking $25. Pets up to 25 lb. accepted with $50 fee (pet menu available). **Amenities:** Restaurant; bar; children's program; concierge; club-level rooms; health club; Jacuzzi; heated outdoor pool; room service. *In room:* A/C, TV, hair dryer, minibar, Wi-Fi ($10 per 24 hr.).

W Austin   When this book went to press, this hotel was just about to open across the street from City Hall. Part of the building will be condos, and another part will be a concert venue and the new studio for Austin City Limits. The location is perfectly chosen for the brand's usual clientele—the young and affluent. The hippest and glitziest clubs and bars that Austin has to offer are in the neighboring Warehouse District, and West Second Street is practically door-to-door boutiques.

200 Lavaca St., Austin, TX 78701. ☏ **877/946-8357** or 512/542-3600. Fax 512/542-3625. www.whotelaustin.com. 251 units. $249–$384 double; suites from $550. AE, DISC, MC, V. Valet parking $27. Pets allowed with $100 fee and $25 per day. **Amenities:** Restaurant; bar; concierge; health club; heated outdoor pool; room service; spa. *In room:* A/C, TV/DVD, hair dryer, minibar, MP3 docking station, Wi-Fi ($15 per day).

Expensive

Doubletree Guest Suites Austin 🍴 ☺   If you're not going to be by the lake, you might as well be by the capitol. This hotel is one of the most comfortable places to stay in the downtown area and a favorite with lobbyists and state contractors. Standard one-bedroom suites are oversize and a bargain for the price. The two-bedroom suites all have balconies and are only $80 more. Many rooms have a capitol view. Full-size appliances with all the requisite cookware allow guests to prepare meals in comfort. And, unlike kitchens in many all-suite hotels, the ones here are separate—you don't have to stare at dirty dishes after you eat. (The housekeepers wash them every day, regardless.) These suites are attractively furnished with practical considerations for families. The hotel is planning to renovate all of the rooms starting in summer of 2011.

303 W. 15th St. (at Guadalupe), Austin, TX 78701. ☏ **800/222-TREE** (222-8733) or 512/478-7000. Fax 512/478-3562. www.doubletree.com. 189 units. 1-bedroom suite $179–$269; 2-bedroom suite $239–$319. Corporate, extended-stay, Internet, and other discounts available. AE, DC, DISC, MC, V. Self-parking $17; valet parking $21. Pets less than 50 lb. accepted for $40. **Amenities:** Restaurant; bar; health club; Jacuzzi; outdoor heated pool; room service; sauna. *In room:* A/C, TV, hair dryer, full-size kitchen, Wi-Fi ($12 per day).

Hilton Austin   This hotel, located directly across from the convention center, discounts rooms when there's no convention in town. Despite being relatively new, the hotel is already refreshing the rooms with new paint jobs and carpets. Regular rooms are average in size and attractively furnished. The service here is attentive, and there seems to be plenty of staff on hand to help. There is a full health club on the property. To use it costs an extra $10 for the first day and $5 for each day thereafter.

500 E. Fourth St., Austin, TX 78701. ☏ **800/HILTONS** (445-8667) or 512/482-8000. Fax 512/486-0078. www.hilton.com. 447 units. $189–$384 double; suites from $550. Weekend and online specials. AE, DC, DISC, MC, V. Valet parking $25; self-parking $16. **Amenities:** 2 restaurants; bar; health club; heated outdoor pool; room service. *In room:* A/C, TV, hair dryer, minibar, Wi-Fi ($14/24 hr.).

InterContinental Stephen F. Austin ★   Built in 1924 to compete with the Driskill (see above), the Stephen F. Austin was another favorite spot for state legislators, as well as celebrities like Babe Ruth and Frank Sinatra. It reopened in 2000 as an InterContinental property after years of sitting abandoned. Most of its clientele are business travelers, and the InterContinental offers lots of amenities aimed at this market.

The public areas are elegant and retro, if not nearly as grand as at the Driskill. The guest rooms are simply furnished but comfortable. Reserve a deluxe room as the standards are small. Corner suites are large and not much more pricey than deluxe rooms. Two other assets: **Stephen F's Bar and Terrace,** with great views of Congress Avenue and the capitol, and the **Roaring Fork** restaurant (p. 184).

701 Congress Ave. (at E. Seventh St.), Austin, TX 78701. © **800/327-0200** or 512/457-8800. Fax 512/457-8896. www.intercontinental.com. 189 units. $179–$329; suites from $399. Weekend and Internet discounts. AE, DC, DISC, MC, V. Valet (only) parking $25. **Amenities:** 2 restaurants; bar; club-level rooms; concierge; exercise room; Jacuzzi; indoor pool; room service; sauna. *In room:* A/C, TV, hair dryer, minibar, Wi-Fi ($10/24 hr.).

Sheraton Austin 🏷 The Sheraton is a good deal. It's 5 blocks east of the capitol and within easy walking distance of downtown and the university campus. The hotel mainly targets business travelers, but it has a certain amount of character that separates it from its competition. First, it has an indoor and outdoor pool, with the outdoor pool backing up to Waller creek. Large oak trees border the pool, an attractive feature unless you're trying to get a tan. Above the pool is another deck that gets more sun and connects to the restaurant. The glass walls of the atrium give the hotel's public areas good light and an open, airy feel. The guest rooms are of good size and offer views of downtown or the university campus. The corner rooms are a bit larger and offer a view of the capitol building.

701 E. 11th St. (at Red River), Austin, TX 78701. © **800/325-3535** or 512/478-1111. Fax 512/478-3700. www.starwoodhotels.com. 365 units. $149–$229 double; suites from $320. Weekend discounts, holiday rates. AE, DC, DISC, MC, V. Self-parking $15; valet parking $24. **Amenities:** Restaurant; bar; babysitting; concierge; concierge-level rooms; exercise room; Jacuzzi; indoor pool; outdoor pool; room service; sauna. *In room:* A/C, TV, hair dryer, Wi-Fi ($10 per 24 hr.).

Moderate

Hampton Inn & Suites Austin-Downtown 🏷 This conventioneer hotel is a cut above average. The rooms are ample and comfortable, decorated in an understated mix of modern and traditional—a bit bland. The generous hot-breakfast buffet is included in the room rate. Room service can be had from either P.F. Chang's or Fleming's. Other perks include free local phone calls and no surcharge for using a calling card. The location, a block from the convention center and close to all of downtown's sights, restaurants, and nightlife, is hard to beat. The pool is on the roof of the four-story garage and has a view of downtown.

200 San Jacinto Blvd. (at Second St.), Austin, TX 78701. © **800/560-7809** or 512/472-1500. Fax 512/472-8900. www.hamptoninn.com. 209 units. $139–$179 double; $159–$199 studio suite. Rates include breakfast buffet and happy hour (Mon–Thurs). AE, DC, DISC, MC, V. Valet (only) parking $23. **Amenities:** Restaurant; fitness room; heated outdoor pool; room service from neighboring restaurants. *In room:* A/C, TV, hair dryer, Wi-Fi.

Holiday Inn Austin Town Lake ☺ The most upscale Holiday Inn in Austin, this high-rise hotel is situated on the north shore of Lady Bird Lake, at the edge of downtown, and just off I-35. Rooms are in two towers: one round, one square. Many of the units have sofa sleepers, which draws families, especially because kids 17 and under stay free, and kids 11 and under eat at the hotel restaurant for free. Other amenities include a rooftop pool large enough for swimming laps, happy-hour specials, and a big-screen TV in the lounge. The hotel underwent a thorough renovation in 2007.

Furniture and appliances were changed out in the guest rooms, and the fitness center was re-equipped. Rooms in both towers are about the same size if not the same shape. Both can offer views of the lake.

20 I-35 N. (exit 233, Riverside Dr./Lady Bird Lake), Austin, TX 78701. ☎ **800/HOLIDAY** (465-4329) or 512/472-8211. Fax 512/472-4636. www.holiday-inn.com/austintownlake. 322 units. $129–$199 double. Weekend and holiday rates, corporate discounts. AE, DC, DISC, MC, V. Free self-parking. **Amenities:** Restaurant; bar; exercise room; outdoor pool; room service. *In room:* A/C, TV, hair dryer, Wi-Fi.

La Quinta Inn–Capitol ⚑ Practically on the grounds of the state capitol, this is a great bargain for both business and leisure travelers. Rooms are more attractive than those in your typical motel: TVs are larger, the furnishings are far from cheesy, and perks such as free local phone calls, free high-speed Internet access, and free continental breakfasts keep annoying extras off your bill. The sole drawback is the lack of a restaurant on the premises, and the closest restaurants are a few blocks away. If you don't want to leave the hotel, there's always pizza delivery. There are five rooms where smoking is permitted.

300 E. 11th St. (at San Jacinto), Austin, TX 78701. ☎ **800/NU-ROOMS** (687-6667) or 512/476-1166. Fax 512/476-6044. www.lq.com. 150 units. $119–$175 double; $185–$210 suite. Rates include continental breakfast. AE, DC, DISC, MC, V. Valet parking $13. Pets accepted (no deposit or extra fee). **Amenities:** Outdoor pool. *In room:* A/C, TV, hair dryer, Wi-Fi.

SOUTH AUSTIN

Very Expensive

Hotel Saint Cecilia ★★★ A small, private hotel, the Saint Cecilia (named after the patron saint of music) sits on a large property just off South Congress. The original house (1888) has five rooms, each with a different emphasis (the bathroom in one, bedroom in another, garden in a third). Behind the house is a modern, understated building with three guest rooms, hotel reception, and an indoor/outdoor lounge area, while across a landscaped yard set off by old oak trees are three modern bungalows located around a small pool area, each with an upstairs and a downstairs unit. Rooms are designed with clean lines and attractive spaces, and each has its own outdoor area. In each room, you'll find a turntable connected to a Geneva sound system. But the capper is the Swedish Hastens mattress, handmade with all-natural materials, which feels like nothing I've ever experienced. After spending the night on one of these, you can have breakfast crepes in the lounge area while gazing out at the old oak trees and ponder what you could possibly do to make your life any better.

112 Academy Dr. (a block east of S. Congress Ave.), Austin, TX 78704. ☎ **512/852-2400.** Fax 512/852-2401. www.hotelsaintcecilia.com. 14 units. $290–$610 double. Rates include full breakfast. AE, DC, DISC, MC, V. Free secure off-street parking. Pets under 25 lb. accepted with $25 fee per day. **Amenities:** Bar; concierge; outdoor pool; breakfast-only room service. *In room:* A/C, TV/DVD player, fridge, hair dryer, minibar, sound system, Wi-Fi.

Kimber Modern Boutique Hotel ★★★ This hotel should be the choice of design-conscious travelers who can't bear to be lodged in the standard cubical room off the standard long and dreary corridor. The hotel is strictly modern, but not the cookie-cutter kind of modern. You can easily see that thought and effort went into its construction, most evident in the way it is set on the property—a wedge-shaped lot on an incline. Five rooms and two suites surround a well-furnished, broad deck shaded by oak trees. This is a great place to relax and enjoy a little leisure time, which the hotel encourages with a free happy hour featuring beer and wine. The rooms are lovely and the bathrooms are just so, with handsome fixtures and good layouts. A continental breakfast featuring some Austin favorites is spread out in the lounge in the mornings. The staff is very accommodating.

110 The Circle (a block east of S. Congress Ave.), Austin, TX 78704. ✆ **512/912-1046.** www.kimber modern.com. 7 units. $250–$295 double; $295–$365 suite. Rates include continental breakfast and afternoon drinks. AE, MC, V. Free off-street parking. No kids 15 or under. *In room:* A/C, fans, TV, fridge, hair dryer, MP3 docking station, no phone, Wi-Fi.

Expensive

Hotel San José ★★ This revamped 1930s motor court gets a lot of attention from the national press for a design that weds beauty to simplicity. The San José is a good choice for design enthusiasts and hipsters, who enjoy both the nonconformist vibe and the social scene in South Austin. Other travelers may think that the mini-malist rooms are overpriced. Even if you don't stay here, you might enjoy coming here in the late afternoon/early evening to be in the comfortable surroundings of the hotel's wine bar. The rooms are indeed spare and come furnished with beds and chairs made from Texas pine, and most rooms have pleasant small outdoor sitting areas. The design achieves a certain serenity that evaporates the moment you step out on to South Congress Avenue's lively street scene. Right across the way is the famous **Continental Club,** a great place for happy hour. Book a room in the back to avoid the Congress Avenue traffic noise.

1316 S. Congress Ave. (south of Nelly), Austin, TX 78704. ✆ **800/574-8897** or 512/444-7322. Fax 512/444-7362. www.sanjosehotel.com. 40 units. $95–$105 double with shared bathroom; $180–$280 double with private bathroom; $300–$400 suite. AE, DISC, MC, V. Free parking. Dogs accepted for $10 per dog per day. **Amenities:** Bar/lounge; coffee shop; bike rentals; outdoor pool; breakfast-only room service. *In room:* A/C, TV/DVD player, CD player, hair dryer, Wi-Fi.

Inexpensive

Austin Motel ★ 🐾 This establishment, the best lodging bargain on South Congress, is one of the old motels that was built when this was the main road to San Antonio. Built in 1938, it has been in the hands of the same family since the 1950s. A convenient (but not quiet) location in the heart of SoCo and great rates make this place very popular. It has a classic kidney-shaped pool, a great neon sign, free HBO, free coffee in the lobby, and a certain quirkiness that's part of the local charm. It also has one of those rarities: real single rooms, so those traveling on their own don't have to pay for a bed they're not sleeping in. All rooms are different, many decorated with murals. For instance, room no. 257 has a cactus mural. You can check out pictures of the rooms before you make a reservation by going to the website.

1220 S. Congress St., Austin, TX 78704. ✆ **512/441-1157.** Fax 512/441-1157. www.austinmotel.com. 41 units. $70–$96 single; $87–$96 double; $119–$127 poolside and deluxe; $178 suite. AE, DC, DISC, MC, V. Free parking. Limited number of rooms for pets; one-time $15 fee. **Amenities:** Outdoor pool. *In room:* A/C, TV, fridge (in some rooms), hair dryer, Wi-Fi.

Hostelling International–Austin 🐾 Youth-, nature-, and Internet-oriented Austin goes all out for its hostellers at this winning facility, located on the hike-and-bike trail and boasting views of Lady Bird Lake that many would pay through the nose to get. Amenities not only include the standard laundry room and kitchen, but also a high-speed Internet kiosk (with a meager $1 fee per stay), not to mention the fact that the grounds are Wi-Fi, too. The former boathouse is solar paneled, and

IT pays TO STAY

If you're planning to settle in for a spell, two downtown accommodations at prime locations will save you major bucks. Rooms at **Extended Stay America Downtown,** 600 Guadalupe (at Sixth St.), Austin, TX 78701 (© **800/EXT-STAY** [398-7829] or 512/457-9994; www.extstay.com), within easy walking distance of both the Warehouse District and the Lamar and Sixth shops;

and at **Homestead Studio Suites Austin–Downtown,** 507 S. First St. (at Barton Springs), Austin, TX 78704 (© **888/782-9473** or 512/476-1818; www.homesteadhotels.com), near the Barton Springs restaurant row and the hike-and-bike trail, will run you from $400 to $500 per week. Full kitchens and coin-op laundries at both bring your costs down even more.

other ecofriendly features include low-flow shower heads. The entire hostel shares one bathroom and shower area.

2200 S. Lakeshore Blvd. (east of I-35, on the southern shore of Lady Bird Lake), Austin, TX 78741. © **512/444-2294.** Fax 512/444-2309. www.hiaustin.org. 39 beds in 4 dorms, all with shared bathrooms. $19 for AYH members, $3 additional for nonmembers; $50 private room with shared bathroom. AE, MC, V. Free parking. **Amenities:** Bike and kayak rentals; Internet kiosk; Wi-Fi in public areas. *In room:* A/C, no phone.

CENTRAL

Expensive

Mansion at Judges Hill ★★ All the rooms in this boutique hotel are furnished and decorated with more character than you'll find at any of the local chain hotels. This is true of the rooms in the modern building at the rear of the property and especially for the ones in the original mansion. In the mansion, the second-story signature rooms are the most fun; they all open onto a sweeping upstairs porch and have tall ceilings and large bathrooms with special amenities (including L'Occitane toiletries and bathrobes). Beds have particularly good mattresses and linens. The third-floor rooms are a little smaller, but lovely and with a real feel of the old house. The ground floor holds the bar and the restaurant.

The modern building is called the North Wing. Built in 1983 in the rear of the property, it offers rooms far from the traffic sounds coming from MLK. The rooms vary quite a bit. Most come without tubs. The deluxe king rooms are the nicest (particularly room no. 212). The West Campus location is convenient to the university and to downtown.

1900 Rio Grande (at MLK, Jr. Blvd./19th St.), Austin, TX 78705. © **800/311-1619** or 512/495-1800. www.judgeshill.com. 48 units. $169–$229 North Wing; $189–$299 Mansion. AE, DC, DISC, MC, V. Free off-street parking. Pets accepted with restrictions and $50 fee. **Amenities:** Restaurant; bar; fitness room; room service. *In room:* A/C, TV, CD player, hair dryer, Wi-Fi.

Moderate

Austin Folk House ★★ ✦ You get the best of both worlds at this appealing B&B that combines old-time charm with new plumbing. The sunny rooms have cheerfully painted walls and the wiring to accommodate megachannel cable TVs, private phone lines, broadband cable access, and radio/alarms with white-noise machines. At the same time, nice antiques and such amenities as fancy bedding and towels, candles, robes, expensive lotions, and soaps make you feel like you're in a small luxury inn. The lavish breakfast buffet is served in a dining room decorated with the folk art for which the B&B is named. Prices are reasonable for all this, while the free off-street parking, near the heart of UT, puts this place at a premium all by itself. Local phone calls are gratis.

506 W. 22nd St. (at Nueces), Austin, TX 78705. ✆ **866/472-6700** or 512/472-6700. www.austinfolk house.com. 9 units. $110–$225 double; Internet specials sometimes available. Rates include full break-fast. AE, DISC, MC, V. Free off-street parking. *In room:* A/C, fans, TV/VCR, Wi-Fi.

Doubletree Hotel Austin   Two miles north of the university, just off the I-35 freeway, is this large, five-story hotel decorated in the style of a Mexican hacienda. Rooms are arranged around a landscaped courtyard that is dotted with umbrella-shaded tables. Guest quarters are airy and spacious, if a bit dull. If you're driving around the city, this is a good choice for its convenient location and easy access to your vehicle. All the sleeping floors have direct access, via room key, to the parking garage. The hotel is located near the intersection with Hwy. 290 E./Hwy. 2222, which is one of the few convenient east-west corridors in the city, and is close by Highland Mall. The hotel keeps a few rooms for smokers.

6505 I-35 N. (btw. Hwy. 290 E. and St. Johns Ave.), Austin, TX 78751. ✆ **800/222-TREE** (222-8733) or 512/454-3737. Fax 512/454-6915. www.austin.doubletree.com. 350 units. $169–$209 double; $209–$229 suites. Weekend rates available. AE, DC, DISC, MC, V. Self-parking $8; valet parking $14. **Amenities:** Restaurant; bar; fitness center; Jacuzzi; outdoor pool; room service. *In room:* A/C, TV, hair dryer, Wi-Fi ($10/24 hr.).

Habitat Suites ★★ ☺ 🎒   This hotel just might represent the future of green businesses. The owners, who are also behind the **Casa de Luz** macrobiotic restau-rant (p. 191), strive to do all that a truly green hotel can: use natural materials and cleaning products over synthetics and chemicals; save, and even generate, electricity; recycle materials; conserve water; grow organic foods; and act in a socially conscious manner.

For guests, this means never running the risk of getting a room that reeks of chemicals. It also means friendly service—the hotel staff enjoys a profit-sharing arrangement; consequently, the staff retention rate is way above the industry norm. Staying here also means healthful food choices for breakfast; if you decide to cook for yourself, you can make use of some of the organically grown vegetables, when avail-able. All of these green activities are performed without fanfare, though the hotel quietly piles up awards for its ecoconsciousness. To the casual observer, the hotel looks like a standard three-story residential hotel. The rooms are oversized and come with complete kitchens. Sheets and towels are of natural materials. The furniture, though not of the latest style, is comfortable (pieces are refinished or reupholstered to avoid adding to the waste stream). Each room has a small separate outdoor area with chairs.

The location is central, just 2 miles north of the university campus. It's not noisy, and the hotel institutes quiet hours between 9pm and 9am. This hotel is one of the best-kept secrets in Austin's lodging scene.

500 E. Highland Mall Blvd. (take exit 222 off I-35 to Airport Blvd., take a right to Highland Mall Blvd.), Austin, TX 78752. ✆ **800/535-4663** or 512/467-6000. Fax 512/467-6000. www.habitatsuites.com. 96 units. $147 1-bedroom suite; $207 2-bedroom suite. Extended-stay rates available. Rates include full breakfast and afternoon wine and snacks (except for Sun). AE, DC, DISC, MC, V. Free parking. **Amenities:** Jacuzzi; outdoor pool. *In room:* A/C, TV, hair dryer, kitchen, Wi-Fi.

Star of Texas Inn ★   Longtime visitors to Austin might remember this as the Governor's Inn, a converted 1897 neoclassical residence. Bought and refurbished by the young owners of the **Austin Folk House,** Sylvia and Chris (see above), this B&B is a bit more traditional than its sister property a block away but still has friendly perks for the business traveler as well as upscale amenities. It also has more porch and deck space. Rooms vary quite a bit in size and layout, but most are a little larger than those at the Folk House. The Star of Texas also harbors that hard-to-find gem, a real single bedroom that's small but not claustrophobic. Three rooms open directly onto a very appealing covered porch, and the others have access to it.

611 W. 22nd St. (at Rio Grande), Austin, TX 78705. © **866/472-6700** or 512/472-6700. www.staroftexas inn.com. 10 units. $110–$225 double. Internet specials sometimes available. Rates include full breakfast. AE, DISC, MC, V. Free off-street parking. *In room:* A/C, fan, TV/VCR, Wi-Fi.

Inexpensive

The Adams House 🎁   Monroe Shipe, the developer of Hyde Park, designed his homes to be both attractive and affordable to the middle class. This B&B honors Shipe's egalitarian spirit. Built as a single-story bungalow and expanded into a two-story colonial revival in 1931, it was restored in the 1990s by a preservation architect. The house is beautifully furnished and has a friendly, open feel due to its 12-foot ceilings. Innkeepers Liz Lock and Eric Hughes are friendly and helpful and are happy to make suggestions for your stay. All the rooms are lovely, but the nicest is the suite with a king-size four-poster bed and a sun porch with a foldout couch. A separate house out back doesn't have as much character, but compensates with a TV/VCR and Jacuzzi. The house's location in leafy Hyde Park is not only attractive and restful, but is quite practical, as it is just a block away from a small neighborhood center that includes a small grocery, coffee bar, laundromat ("washateria" in Texas), and a few superb local restaurants.

4300 Ave. G (at 43rd St.), Austin, TX 85751. © **512/453-7696.** Fax 512/453-2616. www.theadamshouse. com. 5 units. $99–$110 double; $149 suite and bungalow. Monthly rates available. Rates include break-fast. MC, V. Free off-street parking. No children 11 or under. *In room:* A/C, TV (in 1 room).

NORTHWEST
Expensive

Renaissance Austin Hotel ★   Anchoring the upscale Arboretum mall on Austin's northwest side, the Renaissance caters to business travelers visiting nearby high-tech firms. But on weekends, rates are often discounted. Rooms and suites rise up nine stories around a massive square atrium lobby. Exterior rooms have attractive views of the heavily wooded rolling hills surrounding the mall. The hotel's location allows guests to explore the outdoor mall without having to get into their cars. It's a fairly large mall, so it works for getting exercise, too.

Guest rooms are larger than normal with comfortably upholstered furniture. Suites include extras such as wet bars and extra amenities.

9721 Arboretum Blvd. (off Loop 360, near Research Blvd.), Austin, TX 78759. © **800/HOTELS-1** (468-3571) or 512/343-2626. Fax 512/346-7945. www.marriott.com. 478 units. $229–$269 double; suites from $299. Weekend packages available. AE, DC, DISC, MC, V. Free self-parking; valet parking $14. Pets under 35 lb. accepted with $50 fee. **Amenities:** 3 restaurants; bar; nightclub; concierge; club-level rooms; fitness center; Jacuzzi; indoor pool; outdoor pool; room service; sauna. *In room:* A/C, TV, fridge (in some rooms), hair dryer, MP3 docking station, Wi-Fi ($12/day).

Greater Austin Accommodations & Dining

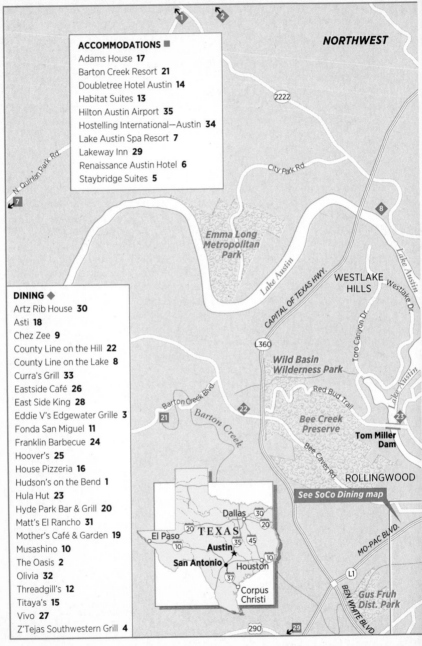

NORTHWEST

ACCOMMODATIONS ■
Adams House **17**
Barton Creek Resort **21**
Doubletree Hotel Austin **14**
Habitat Suites **13**
Hilton Austin Airport **35**
Hostelling International—Austin **34**
Lake Austin Spa Resort **7**
Lakeway Inn **29**
Renaissance Austin Hotel **6**
Staybridge Suites **5**

DINING ◆
Artz Rib House **30**
Asti **18**
Chez Zee **9**
County Line on the Hill **22**
County Line on the Lake **8**
Curra's Grill **33**
Eastside Café **26**
East Side King **28**
Eddie V's Edgewater Grille **3**
Fonda San Miguel **11**
Franklin Barbecue **24**
Hoover's **25**
House Pizzeria **16**
Hudson's on the Bend **1**
Hula Hut **23**
Hyde Park Bar & Grill **20**
Matt's El Rancho **31**
Mother's Café & Garden **19**
Musashino **10**
The Oasis **2**
Olivia **32**
Threadgill's **12**
Titaya's **15**
Vivo **27**
Z'Tejas Southwestern Grill **4**

Emma Long Metropolitan Park

WESTLAKE HILLS

Wild Basin Wilderness Park

Bee Creek Preserve

Tom Miller Dam

ROLLINGWOOD

See SoCo Dining map

Gus Fruh Dist. Park

TEXAS
El Paso
Dallas
Austin
San Antonio
Houston
Corpus Christi

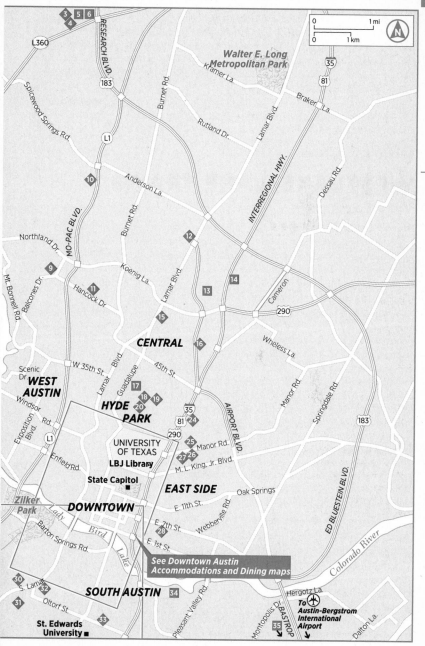

See Downtown Austin
Accommodations and Dining maps

To
Austin-Bergstrom
International
Airport

Moderate

Staybridge Suites ☺ 🍴   This cheery Holiday Inn property works well for families, who can take advantage of the kitchen in every suite, the multiple TVs (with DVDs), the complimentary breakfast buffet, the pool in a leafy courtyard, and the free laundry facilities that adjoin the exercise room (the latter is small but has some sturdy-looking cardio machines). The location is close to the Arboretum and the Domain shopping complexes, as well as the many restaurants in this burgeoning area. A few rooms are available for smokers.

10201 Stonelake Blvd. (btw. Great Hills Trail and Braker Lane), Austin, TX 78759. ✆ **800/238-8000** or 512/349-0888. Fax 512/349-0809. www.staybridge.com. 121 units. $165–$195 studio suite; $179–$209 1-bedroom suite; $205–$235 2-bedroom suite. Rates include breakfast. Extended-stay and Sat–Sun discounts. AE, DC, DISC, MC, V. Free parking. Pets accepted; $15 for 1st night, $10 per night afterward. **Amenities:** Fitness center; outdoor pool; tennis court. *In room:* A/C, TV/DVD, hair dryer, kitchen, Wi-Fi.

WESTLAKE/LAKE TRAVIS
Very Expensive

Barton Creek Resort ★★★ ☺   Austin's only real full-service resort—one that caters to business travelers, couples, singles, and families alike—Barton Creek would stand out even if it weren't alone. The facilities are top-notch, including four 18-hole championship golf courses and the Chuck Cook Golf Academy, tennis courts and a tennis clinic, and an excellent health club with an indoor track. Members of the affiliated country club share the recreational facilities.

With 4,000 gently rolling and wooded acres and relative proximity to Lake Travis, the resort feels rural, but it's close enough to central Austin (about 20 min. away) that you can easily sightsee or party there. Rooms are spacious in both the main buildings, one resembling a European château and the other a nine-story tower connecting the spa and the conference center. The custom-made Drexel Heritage furnishings are complemented by such Texas touches as cowhide chairs and work by local artists. Some rooms have balconies, and those in the back have superb views of the Texas Hill Country. The main restaurant of the resort does a great job with contemporary American cuisine, including some great steaks and seafood.

8212 Barton Club Dr. (1 mile west of the intersection of Loop 360 and R.R. 2244), Austin, TX 78735. ✆ **800/336-6158** or 512/329-4000. Fax 512/329-4597. www.bartoncreek.com. 300 units. $249–$380 double; suites from $500. Discounts in off season (winter). Spa and golf packages available. AE, DC, DISC, MC, V. Free self-parking; valet parking $25. **Amenities:** 2 restaurants; bar; babysitting; children's center and programs; 4 golf courses; health club; indoor pool; outdoor pool; room service; spa; 11 tennis courts. *In room:* A/C, TV, hair dryer, minibar, Wi-Fi.

Lake Austin Spa Resort ★★★   If you had to create the quintessential Austin spa, it would be laid-back, located on a serene body of water, offer lots of outdoor activities, and feature super-healthy food that lives up to high culinary standards. You can check off every item on that wish list here. The spa takes advantage of its proximity to the Highland Lakes and the Hill Country by offering such activities as combination canoe/hiking trips and excursions to view the wildflowers. The aromatic ingredients for soothing spa treatments, such as a honey-mango scrub, are grown in the resort's garden, also the source for the herbs used at mealtimes. Guest rooms, many in cottages with private gardens, fireplaces, and hot tubs, are casually elegant, with all-natural fabrics and locally crafted furniture.

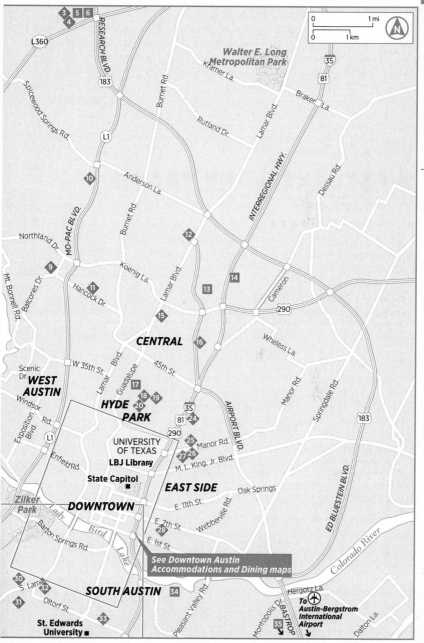

Moderate

Staybridge Suites ☺ ⚐ This cheery Holiday Inn property works well for families, who can take advantage of the kitchen in every suite, the multiple TVs (with DVDs), the complimentary breakfast buffet, the pool in a leafy courtyard, and the free laundry facilities that adjoin the exercise room (the latter is small but has some sturdy-looking cardio machines). The location is close to the Arboretum and the Domain shopping complexes, as well as the many restaurants in this burgeoning area. A few rooms are available for smokers.

10201 Stonelake Blvd. (btw. Great Hills Trail and Braker Lane), Austin, TX 78759. ② **800/238-8000** or 512/349-0888. Fax 512/349-0809. www.staybridge.com. 121 units. $165–$195 studio suite; $179–$209 1-bedroom suite; $205–$235 2-bedroom suite. Rates include breakfast. Extended-stay and Sat-Sun discounts. AE, DC, DISC, MC, V. Free parking. Pets accepted; $15 for 1st night, $10 per night afterward. **Amenities:** Fitness center; outdoor pool; tennis court. *In room:* A/C, TV/DVD, hair dryer, kitchen, Wi-Fi.

WESTLAKE/LAKE TRAVIS
Very Expensive

Barton Creek Resort ★★★ ☺ Austin's only real full-service resort—one that caters to business travelers, couples, singles, and families alike—Barton Creek would stand out even if it weren't alone. The facilities are top-notch, including four 18-hole championship golf courses and the Chuck Cook Golf Academy, tennis courts and a tennis clinic, and an excellent health club with an indoor track. Members of the affiliated country club share the recreational facilities.

With 4,000 gently rolling and wooded acres and relative proximity to Lake Travis, the resort feels rural, but it's close enough to central Austin (about 20 min. away) that you can easily sightsee or party there. Rooms are spacious in both the main buildings, one resembling a European château and the other a nine-story tower connecting the spa and the conference center. The custom-made Drexel Heritage furnishings are complemented by such Texas touches as cowhide chairs and work by local artists. Some rooms have balconies, and those in the back have superb views of the Texas Hill Country. The main restaurant of the resort does a great job with contemporary American cuisine, including some great steaks and seafood.

8212 Barton Club Dr. (1 mile west of the intersection of Loop 360 and R.R. 2244), Austin, TX 78735. ② **800/336-6158** or 512/329-4000. Fax 512/329-4597. www.bartoncreek.com. 300 units. $249–$380 double; suites from $500. Discounts in off season (winter). Spa and golf packages available. AE, DC, DISC, MC, V. Free self-parking; valet parking $25. **Amenities:** 2 restaurants; bar; babysitting; children's center and programs; 4 golf courses; health club; indoor pool; outdoor pool; room service; spa; 11 tennis courts. *In room:* A/C, TV, hair dryer, minibar, Wi-Fi.

Lake Austin Spa Resort ★★★ If you had to create the quintessential Austin spa, it would be laid-back, located on a serene body of water, offer lots of outdoor activities, and feature super-healthy food that lives up to high culinary standards. You can check off every item on that wish list here. The spa takes advantage of its proximity to the Highland Lakes and the Hill Country by offering such activities as combination canoe/hiking trips and excursions to view the wildflowers. The aromatic ingredients for soothing spa treatments, such as a honey-mango scrub, are grown in the resort's garden, also the source for the herbs used at mealtimes. Guest rooms, many in cottages with private gardens, fireplaces, and hot tubs, are casually elegant, with all-natural fabrics and locally crafted furniture.

Barton Creek Resort (p. 178) In addition to the great recreational activities here (including a basketball court), this resort also has an activity room for ages 6 months to 8 years, open from morning 'til evening. It's $10 per hour to drop your kids off here for a maximum of 4½ hours, with additional fees for longer periods.

Doubletree Guest Suites (p. 169), **Habitat Suites** (p. 174), and **Staybridge Suites** (p. 178) That "suites" is in the name of these properties says it all. These guest quarters all offer spacious, common-sense living quarters, plus the convenience (and economy) of kitchen facilities, so you don't have to eat out all the time.

Four Seasons Austin (p. 166) Tell the reservations clerk that you're traveling with kids, and you'll be automatically enrolled in the free amenities program, which offers age-appropriate snacks—cookies and milk for children 9 and under, popcorn and soda for those

older—along with various toys and games that will be waiting for you when you arrive. And you don't have to travel with all your gear, because the hotel will provide such items as a car seat, stroller, playpen, bedrails, disposable pacifiers, a baby bathtub, shampoo, powder and lotions, bib, bottle warmers, and disposable diapers.

Holiday Inn Austin (p. 170) You're near lots of the outdoor play areas at Lady Bird Lake, and kids 17 and under stay free, and kids 11 and under eat free. It's hard to beat that!

Lakeway Inn (below) There's plenty for kids to do here, and this property offers a Family Playdays Package, which includes a $100 credit toward recreational activities (such as boat rentals and tennis), plus a free meal and dessert for children 12 and under, with the purchase of an adult entree. Prices vary depending on the time of year.

Lake Austin Spa Resort has piled up awards and been included on virtually all top-ten spa lists (ranked as top destination spa by Condé Nast in 2010). If you go, you'll see why. It's simply an incredibly relaxing experience, with a winning combination of beauty; a welcoming, knowledgeable staff; and delicious, healthful food.

1705 S. Quinlan Park Rd. (5 miles south of Hwy. 620), Austin, TX 78732. ✆ **800/847-5637** or 512/372-7300. Fax 512/266-1572. www.lakeaustin.com. 40 units. 3-day packages available for $1,635 per person (double occupancy). Rates include all meals, classes, and activities. Spa treatments/personal trainers are extra. AE, DC, DISC, MC, V. Free parking. Dogs accepted in Garden Cottage rooms; $250 pet guest fee. Children 14 and up only. **Amenities:** Restaurant; health club; canoes; hydrobikes; kayaks; indoor pool; 2 outdoor pools; room service; spa. *In room:* A/C, TV/DVD player, CD player, hair dryer, Wi-Fi.

Expensive

Lakeway Inn ✦ ☺ Not as glitzy as Barton Creek, nor as picture-perfect as the Lake Austin Spa, this conference resort in a planned community on Lake Travis is for those seeking traditional recreation at prices that won't require a second mortgage.

There's something for everyone in the family. At the resort's marina, you can rent pontoons, ski boats, sculls, sailboats, water skis, WaveRunners, fishing gear and guides—just about everything but fish that promise to bite. Lakeway's excellent 32-court tennis complex, designed for indoor, outdoor, day, and night games, has a pro shop with trainers and even a racket-shaped swimming pool. Duffers can tee off from 36 holes of golf on the property, get privileges at other courses nearby, or brush up on their game at the Jack Nicklaus–designed Academy of Golf. Rooms are spacious and comfortable, with all the requisite conference attendee business amenities and, in many cases, lake views.

101 Lakeway Dr., Austin, TX 78734. © **800/LAKEWAY** (525-3929) or 512/261-6600. Fax 512/261-7322. www.lakewayinn.com. 178 units. $179–$289 double. Romance, golf, spa, and family packages available. AE, DC, DISC, MC, V. Free self-parking; valet parking $12. **Amenities:** Restaurant; bar; health club; 2 Jacuzzis; 3 outdoor pools; room service; spa; watersports rentals. *In room:* A/C, TV, hair dryer, Wi-Fi.

AT THE AIRPORT
Moderate

Hilton Austin Airport ★ This Hilton's circular shape gives Austin's only full-service airport hotel, formerly the headquarters of Bergstrom Air Force Base, a distinctively modern look. Although the hotel retains few of the features that made it one of three bunkers where the President of the United States might be spirited in the event of a nuclear attack, the building remains rock-solid—and blissfully soundproof. (If you stay here, ask for a sheet that details the fascinating history of "The Donut," which also served as a strategic air command center during the Vietnam War, the Persian Gulf War, and Desert Storm.) These days, the dome serves as a skylight for a bright and airy lobby. The theme throughout is Texas Hill Country, with lots of limestone and wood and plenty of live plants for good measure. Large, comfortable rooms are equipped with all the amenities.

9515 New Airport Dr. (½ mile from the airport, 2 miles east of the intersection of Hwy. 183 and Hwy. 71), Austin, TX 78719. © **800/445-8667** or 512/385-6767. Fax 512/385-6763. www.hilton.com. 263 units. $159–$199 double; suites from $190. Sat–Sun, online discounts. AE, DC, DISC, MC, V. Self-parking $11; valet parking $15. **Amenities:** Restaurant; lounge; club-level rooms; health club; outdoor pool; room service. *In room:* A/C, TV, hair dryer, minibar, Wi-Fi.

WHERE TO DINE IN AUSTIN

Austin has many one-of-a-kind establishments that serve regional cooking, international cuisine, or their own style of cooking, many of which are concentrated in and around downtown and the area immediately south of Lady Bird Lake. In other parts of the city, they tend to set up along the major commercial corridors, but in some old neighborhoods the most interesting of local restaurants are tucked away on quiet streets.

In the Hyde Park neighborhood (north of the university campus), one such cluster is at Duval Street and 43rd, where you'll find Asti, Hyde Park Bar & Grill, and Mother's Café & Garden; in the Clarksville neighborhood (west of downtown) is another cluster at West Lynn and 12th Street (Jeffrey's, Cipollina, and Zocalo); and in central East Austin, on the boundary between French Place and Blackland neighborhoods, is yet another cluster on Manor Road (Eastside Cafe, Hoover's, and Vivo). As neighborhood restaurants, these places are comfortable and welcoming, and reflect the tastes of the local community.

Also, a concentration of restaurants is located on Guadalupe Street, by the university campus. These cater to students and don't have to be good; they just have to be cheap. I would avoid them.

To locate restaurants outside of downtown, see the map on p. 189. Wherever you eat, think casual. There isn't a restaurant in Austin that requires men to put on a tie and jacket, and many upscale dining rooms are far better turned out than their rich tech-industry clientele.

In the past couple of years, it has become very popular to dine a la "cart" at one of the ever-increasing number of food carts parked around town. These offer a variety of foods, usually at lower than normal prices. When driving around Austin, you'll see them everywhere—downtown, along South Congress and South Lamar, and in a lot of unexpected places. I've included my three favorites (El Naranjo, East Side King, and Franklin Barbecue), but if you really want to explore this phenomenon more, go to www.austinfoodcarts.com.

Dining out can be a competitive sport in Austin. Make reservations wherever you can or dine at off hours. If you turn up at some of the most popular spots at around 7:30pm, you might wait an hour or more. Austin restaurants tend to be noisier than those of other cities. The locals seem to be okay with this, but, in my opinion, it's yet another reason to dine at off hours.

Finally, Austin has a large population of vegetarians and vegans, so local restaurants offer lots of vegetarian options, and there are a number of purely vegetarian restaurants.

THE best AUSTIN DINING BETS

o **The Best Food: Uchi,** 801 S. Lamar Blvd. (*C* **512/916-4808**), has received national attention and glowing reviews from just about everyone. See p. 189.

o **Most Impressive Vegetarian Cuisine:** Given all the dietary strictures of macrobiotics and veganism, it amazes me that **Casa de Luz,** 1701 Toomey Rd. (*C* **512/476-2335**), can produce the delicious meals that it does. Vegetarians of all stripes leave here completely sated. See p. 191.

o **Best Quintessentially Austin:** Its laid-back Texas menu, huge outdoor patio, and "unplugged" music series all make **Shady Grove** (1624 Barton Springs Rd.; *C* **512/474-9991**) the ideal Austin restaurant. See p. 193.

o **Best Brunch:** At **Fonda San Miguel,** 2330 W. North Loop (*C* **512/459-4121**), a large spread of cold and hot dishes explores the cuisines of central, southern, and eastern Mexico. See p. 196.

o **Best if You're Game for Game:** It's a bit of a drive and more than a bit of a wallet bite, but if you want to see how tasty venison or bison can be, you can't beat **Hudson's on the Bend,** 3509 Hwy. 620 N. (*C* **512/266-1369**). See p. 201.

o **Best View:** The easy winner is the **Oasis,** 6550 Comanche Trail, near Lake Travis (*C* **512/266-2442**), which has multiple decks that afford stunning views of Lake Travis and the Texas Hill Country. See p. 202.

o **Sweetest Contribution to the Dining Scene:** For years, **Amy's** has been Austin's favorite ice-cream stop. College-age servers put on a show for the customers, tossing scoops of ice cream about and crushing toppings into it with rhythmic glee. The ice cream is rich and the flavorings are natural and distinctive. There are 10 locations in Austin, including the airport. Central locations include 1012 W. Sixth St. (at Lamar; *C* **512/480-0673**); one in SoCo, 1301 S. Congress Ave. (by the Continental Club; *C* **512/440-7488**); and one just north of the UT campus, 3500 Guadalupe (*C* **512/458-6895**). See p. 190.

RESTAURANTS BY CUISINE

AMERICAN

Eastside Cafe ★★ (East Side, $$, p. 198)

Hoover's ★ (East Side, $$, p. 198)

Hula Hut (West Austin, $$, p. 194)

Hut's Hamburgers (Downtown, $, p. 188)

Hyde Park Bar & Grill ★ (Central and South Austin, $$, p. 196)

The Oasis (Lake Travis, $$, p. 202)

Shady Grove ★ (South Austin, $, p. 193)

Threadgill's ★ (Central and South Austin, $$, p. 197)

ASIAN/FUSION

East Side King ★ (East Side, $, p. 199)

Uchi ★★★ (South Austin, $$$, p. 189)

BARBECUE

Artz Rib House ★ (South Austin, $$, p. 191)

County Line on the Hill ★ (Westlake/Lake Travis, $$, p. 201)

Franklin Barbecue ★★ (East Side, $, p. 199)

The Iron Works ★ (Downtown, $, p. 188)

Key to Abbreviations: $$$$ = Very Expensive $$$ = Expensive $$ = Moderate $ = Inexpensive

BURGERS

Hut's Hamburgers (Downtown, $, p. 188)

CAJUN/CREOLE

Gumbo's ★ (Downtown, $$$, p. 184)

FRENCH

Chez Nous ★★ (Downtown, $$$, p. 184)

INDIAN

Clay Pit ★ (Downtown, $$, p. 186)

ITALIAN

Asti ★ (Central, $$$, p. 195)

Cipollina ★★ (West Austin, $$, p. 194)

Enoteca Vespaio ★ (South Austin, $$$, p. 190)

La Traviata ★ (Downtown, $$$, p. 184)

Vespaio ★ (South Austin, $$$, p. 190)

JAPANESE

Musashino ★★ (Northwest, $$$, p. 200)

Uchi ★★★ (South Austin, $$$, p. 189)

MEXICAN

Curra's Grill ★★ (South Austin, $$, p. 191)

El Naranjo ★★ (Downtown, $, p. 187)

El Sol y La Luna (Downtown, $, p. 188)

Fonda San Miguel ★ (Central, $$$, p. 196)

Manuel's ★ (Downtown and Northwest, $$, p. 186)

Zocalo (West Austin, $, p. 194)

NEW AMERICAN

Chez Zee ★ (Northwest, $$$, p. 200)

Cipollina ★★ (West Austin, $$, p. 194)

Hudson's on the Bend ★★ (Lake Travis, $$$$, p. 201)

Jeffrey's ★★★ (West Austin, $$$$, p. 193)

Olivia ★★★ (South Austin, $$$, p. 188)

PIZZA

Asti ★ (Central, $$$, p. 195)

Cipollina ★★ (West Austin, $$, p. 194)

House Pizzeria ★★ (Central, $$, p. 196)

SEAFOOD

Eddie V's Edgewater Grille ★★ (Downtown and Northwest, $$$$, p. 200)

SOUTHERN

Hoover's ★ (East Side, $$, p. 198)

Threadgill's ★ (Central and South Austin, $$, p. 197)

SOUTHWEST

Ranch 616 (Downtown, $$, p. 187)

Roaring Fork ★★ (Downtown, $$$, p. 184)

South Congress Cafe ★ (South Austin, $$, p. 192)

Z'Tejas Southwestern Grill ★ (Downtown and Northwest, $$, p. 201)

STEAKS

Eddie V's Edgewater Grille ★★ (Northwest, $$$$, p. 200)

TEX-MEX

Chuy's (South Austin and Northwest, $$, p. 191)

Güero's ★ (South Austin, $$, p. 192)

Hula Hut (West Austin, $$, p. 194)

Matt's El Rancho (South Austin, $$, p. 192)

The Oasis (Lake Travis, $$, p. 202)

Vivo ★ (East Side, $$, p. 198)

THAI

Titaya's ★ (Central, $$, p. 197)

VEGETARIAN

Casa de Luz ★ (South Austin, $$, p. 191)

Mother's Café & Garden (Central Austin, $, p. 197)

DOWNTOWN

Expensive

Chez Nous ★★ 🍴 FRENCH   This small bistro is a great choice for a quiet lunch or dinner. The setting is attractive and casual—small tables decorated with a few fresh flowers sticking out from old anisette bottles, *Folies Bergere* posters on the wall. The French owners have prospered by consistently providing high-quality service and food at reasonable prices. The most popular choice here is the prix-fixe dinner with a choice of soup, salad, or pâté; one of three designated entrees; and crème caramel, chocolate mousse, or brie for dessert. The main courses might include a *poisson poivre vert* (fresh fish of the day with a green-peppercorn sauce) or a simple but delicious roast chicken. Everything from the pâtés to the profiteroles is made on the premises. Of the main courses, one of my favorites is the lamb chops crusted in fine herbs and grilled.

510 Neches St. ☏ **512/473-2413.** www.cheznousaustin.com. Reservations accepted for parties of 6 or more only. Main courses $20–$30; prix fixe $27. AE, DC, DISC, MC, V. Tues–Fri 11:45am–2pm; Tues–Sun 6–10:30pm.

Gumbo's ★ CAJUN/CREOLE   People forget that Texas shares a border with Louisiana. During the oil boom years of the first half of the last century, many from southern Louisiana settled in Texas to make their fortune. They brought their cooking with them, and over the years Texans have developed quite a taste for such Creole dishes as blackened fish, spicy jambalaya, and rich crawfish étoufée. These and other dishes from the broader Gulf Coast region are on the menu at Gumbo's. The mainstay is seafood, but beef, duck, and chicken are also included. If you go for lunch, you can enjoy a New Orleans–style oyster po' boy. The dining room, with high ceilings and a black-and-white tiled floor, re-creates the atmosphere of a Louisiana cafe. The restaurant is in the renovated Art Deco Brown Building (1938), where LBJ used to have an office.

701 Colorado. ☏ **512/480-8053.** www.gumbosaustin.com. Reservations recommended on weekends. Main courses $16–$30. AE, DC, DISC, MC, V. Mon–Thurs 11am–2pm and 5:30–10pm; Fri 11am–2pm and 5:30–11pm; Sat 5:30–11pm.

La Traviata ★ ITALIAN   If you're tired of Italian restaurant clichés, you'll love this cozy, Euro-chic trattoria, with textured limestone walls complementing the hardwood floors, sleek bar, and sunny yellow walls. The food is just as unfussy and fresh. Chef/owner Marion Gilchrist allows the quality ingredients to take center stage, and creates sauces that are delicious without being overwhelming. That's why such classics as chicken Parmesan or spaghetti Bolognese remain so popular here. The same is true of the crispy polenta with Gorgonzola cheese or the duck confit. The narrow room bustles with energy, especially on weekend pretheater evenings, but the staff never seems overwhelmed. Service is both knowledgeable and friendly. Don't miss the tiramisu, wonderfully light with toasted hazelnuts and a dusting of espresso.

314 Congress Ave. ☏ **512/479-8131.** www.latraviata.net. Reservations highly recommended Sat–Sun. Pasta $14–$16; main courses $16–$26. AE, DISC, MC, V. Mon–Thurs 11:30am–2pm and 5:30–10pm; Fri 11:30am–2pm and 5:30–10:30pm; Sat 5:30–10:30pm.

Roaring Fork ★★ SOUTHWEST   If you're looking for some hearty eating, this would be a good choice. The dishes don't get too fancy but are executed with flair. Most involve grilling or roasting in a wood-burning oven. Favorites include a hearty

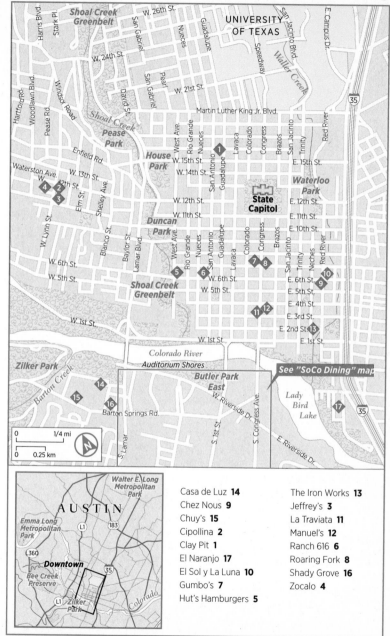

Casa de Luz **14**
Chez Nous **9**
Chuy's **15**
Cipollina **2**
Clay Pit **1**
El Naranjo **17**
El Sol y La Luna **10**
Gumbo's **7**
Hut's Hamburgers **5**

The Iron Works **13**
Jeffrey's **3**
La Traviata **11**
Manuel's **12**
Ranch 616 **6**
Roaring Fork **8**
Shady Grove **16**
Zocalo **4**

green chili pork, an extra-large hamburger, spit-roasted chicken, and some lovely steaks. The menu changes seasonally, but you'll always find these selections or something comparable, as well as at least one item flavored with green chili. Seafood is always available as well.

On my last visit, there was a delicious bacon-wrapped pork tenderloin served with cheese grits, and a rich tortilla soup, which seems to have acquired a semi-permanent status. Portions are generous; you can save money by going for lunch, which costs almost half what dinner does. The dining room is comfortable, softly lit, and quieter than your average Austin restaurant. Leave room for the margaritas. A new location in north Austin is at 10850 Stonelake Blvd. (© **512/342-2700**).

701 Congress Ave. (in the InterContinental Stephen F. Austin). © **512/583-0000.** www.roaringfork. com. Reservations recommended. Main courses $15–$30. AE, DC, DISC, MC, V. Mon–Thurs 11am–10pm; Fri 11am–11pm; Sat 4–11pm; Sun 4–9pm.

Moderate

Clay Pit ★ 🖉 INDIAN   The old building that houses this restaurant was a saloon for many years, as far back as the 1870s. The thick limestone walls and rough wood floors show their age, and the proportions of the large room still bring to mind the old saloon. But oh how the custom and wares have changed! The Clay Pit is known for Indian cooking with a bit of a twist. Try the perfectly cooked coriander calamari served with a piquant cilantro aioli as an appetizer. For an entree, consider *khuroos-e-tursh,* baked chicken breast stuffed with nuts, mushrooms, and onions, and smothered in a cashew-almond cream sauce; or one of the many dazzling vegetarian dishes.

At night, the dining room is softly lit, creating an attractive and romantic setting for dates or special occasions. During the day, it's something quite different—a place to grab a quick, economical lunch from the buffet of typical Indian standards. The restaurant is located near the courthouse and the state office buildings just north of the capitol. Keep this in mind should you get hungry while touring either the capitol or the university campus.

1601 Guadalupe St. © **512/322-5131.** www.claypit.com. Reservations recommended. $8 lunch buffet; main courses $10–$20. AE, DC, DISC, MC, V. Mon–Fri 11am–2pm and 5–10pm (till 11pm on Fri); Sat noon–3pm and 5–11pm.

Manuel's ★ MEXICAN   This is one of the few moderately priced holdouts to be found in a downtown dining scene that's been steadily heading uptown. Although there are some Tex-Mex dishes on the menu, most of the menu items are interior Mexican. You can get well-prepared versions of Mexican standards and some tweaked versions of the more common dishes, but Manuel's also offers hard-to-find specialties such as the *chile relleno ennogada* (chilies stuffed with pork and topped with walnut-cream sauce). A more common dish would be the *enchiladas banderas,* which are arrayed in the colors of the Mexican flag: a green *tomatillo verde* sauce, a white cream *suiza* sauce, and a red sauce. There's a delicious healthful option, *pescado con espinacas,* which is pan-seared fish with a bit of garlic served on a bed of sautéed spinach seasoned with a lime juice dressing.

In the evenings the small bar area is crowded with young professionals, and on weekends the wait for a table is about normal for Austin restaurants. The decor is assertively modern to draw a contrast with the building's original brick walls. There's a lively happy hour (daily 4–6pm), with half-price hors d'oeuvres and discounted drinks. (See "Only in (or Around) Austin," later in this chapter, for the musical Sun brunch).

GROCERY STORE dining

Austinites have a fondness for dining in grocery stores, and I'm not talking about grazing the produce aisle. Indeed, the city's two grocery palaces, **Central Market** and **Whole Foods,** have large dining areas. Austinites like the casual feel of a grocery store and the convenience of mixing dining with the opportunity to pick up a couple of things forgotten on the last shopping trip. But for visitors, it's a good choice, too. Both of these stores are popular sightseeing destinations, so you can grab a bite and explore Austin's utopian vision of fine grocery shopping. The food is good, quick, and wholesome, and you control the portions. The prices are moderate and compare favorably to sitting down in a full-service restaurant. In both stores, indoor and outdoor seating are available, sometimes with live music. Whole Foods probably has more variety, though it's more self-serve and can be a little confusing. Food at both places is available during regular store hours. For more information see "Food" in chapter 14.

A northwest branch is near the Arboretum, 10201 Jollyville Rd. (© **512/345-1042**). It presents live music Thursday nights.

310 Congress Ave. © **512/472-7555.** www.manuels.com. Reservations accepted for 5 or more only. Main courses $9–$23. AE, DISC, MC, V. Mon–Thurs 11am–10pm; Fri–Sat 11am–11pm; Sun 10am–10pm.

Ranch 616 SOUTHWEST   The huge snake logo on the outside of an otherwise nondescript building—created by Bob "Daddy-O" Wade, best known for the oversize boots that front San Antonio's North Star Mall—is your first hint that this place might be a bit, well, different. Inside, cowboy kitsch, 1950s diner decor, and Mexican folk art mingle, as do workers from the nearby county offices, local movers and shakers, and anyone else looking for food that, like the decor, defies easy categorization.

Call it South Texas gourmet. You can really taste the chipotle chilies in the tartar sauce that comes with some of the best crispy oysters this side of the Mason-Dixon line, and the Gulf fish tacos are gussied up with chili lime aioli and Tabasco jalapeño onions. You get the idea—lots of spicy dishes. More soothing and delicious are such desserts as the banana shortbread tart and any of the fried pies. In case you hadn't guessed from the description of the decor, this place is a hoot. On Tuesdays and Thursdays, the diners are serenaded with live country music, usually good, but often too loud for conversation.

616 Nueces St. © **512/479-7616.** www.theranch616.com. Reservations recommended. Lunch $7–$10; dinner $14–$22. AE, DC, DISC, MC, V. Mon–Thurs 11am–2:30pm and 5:30–10pm; Fri–Sat 11am–2:30pm and 5:30–11pm.

Inexpensive

El Naranjo ★★ MEXICAN   I first met Iliana de la Vega and her husband, Ernesto Torrealba, many years ago when I was in Oaxaca City researching for *Frommer's Mexico*. They had just opened a restaurant, which would eventually win acclaim from major publications both in Mexico and abroad and become a hot spot on the travel circuit through interior Mexico. But troubled times came to Oaxaca, forcing Iliana and her family to leave. They settled in Austin and have now opened another eatery, a decidedly more modest food trailer parked in the Rainey Street District, just south of Cesar Chavez and east of Red River Street. Here you can get a sampling of her cooking while sitting on picnic benches. If you're there on a weekend night, you can get the best tacos *al pastor* in Austin, with or without cheese. And any day of the week, you can get light and delicious fish or shrimp tacos. For something more substantial, try the *mole* (which varies depending on the day and the week), and for appetizers, I like the mushroom *empanadas*.

85 Rainey St. © **512/474-2776.** Plates $5–$11. AE, MC, V. Mon–Thurs 5–10pm; Fri–Sat 5–11pm.

El Sol y La Luna 🍴 MEXICAN   This is the best value in the area. It serves good, no-nonsense Mexican for low prices, especially considering its location. The menu is large. Ignore the outliers and stick to Mexican food. I like the chipotle enchiladas and the enchiladas de *mole*. The *ceviche* is light and fresh-tasting. And you can find an uncommon *jícama* and cucumber salad. This is also a good place for a late breakfast with migas, or that other Austin invention, the breakfast taco. If you like music with your dinner, go on a Friday (mariachi) or Saturday (different acts) or check out the flamenco show on Wednesday nights from 7:30 to 9pm. If you prefer quiet, eat early. The restaurant has a full bar and serves good margaritas.

600 E. Sixth St. (by Emo's). © **512/444-7770.** www.elsolylalunaaustin.com. Plates $7–$11. MC, V. Tues–Thurs 9am–10pm; Fri–Sat 9am–2am; Sun 9am–4pm.

Hut's Hamburgers 🍴 AMERICAN/BURGERS   This classic burger shack is very Austin. It opened its doors as Sammie's Drive-In in 1939, serving the traditional-style Texas burger with lettuce and onions. Now it offers 19 types of burgers, including a vegetarian garden burger (which is very Austin, too). As you might expect, you can also get fries and shakes, the usual burger complements; but for those who enjoy onion rings, this place is a special treat. Also on the menu are blue-plate specials of meatloaf, chicken-fried steak, and fried catfish. The decor is sports pennants and '50s memorabilia.

807 W. Sixth St. © **512/472-0693.** Sandwiches and burgers $5–$8; plates $8–$9. AE, DISC, MC, V. Daily 11am–10pm.

The Iron Works ★ BARBECUE   Some of the best barbecue in Austin is served in one of the most unusual settings. Until 1977, this building housed the ironworks of the Weigl family, who came over from Germany in 1913. You can see their ornamental craft all around town, including at the state capitol. Cattle brands created for Jack Benny ("Lasting 39"), Lucille Ball, and Bob Hope are displayed in front of the restaurant. The beef ribs are the most popular order, with the brisket running a close second. Lean turkey breast and juicy chicken are also smoked to perfection.

100 Red River (at E. First St.). © **800/669-3602** or 512/478-4855. www.ironworksbbq.com. Reservations accepted for large parties only. Sandwiches $3–$5; plates $6–$12; meat by the lb. $8–$13. AE, DC, MC, V. Mon–Sat 11am–9pm.

SOUTH AUSTIN
Expensive

Olivia ★★★ NEW AMERICAN   If you are in search of creative cooking capable of extending your gastronomical horizons, are fond of light and angular modern architecture, and want to sample some of the best that our local farmers have to offer, this would be the right choice. Olivia is far and away the brightest newcomer to Austin's fine dining scene. The entire dining experience—food, setting, and service—rivals

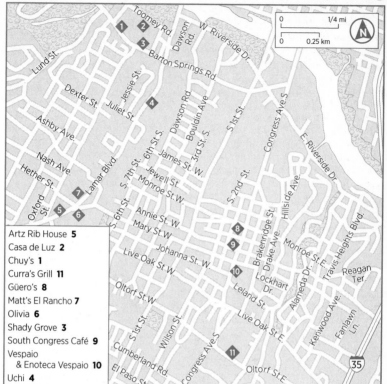

Artz Rib House **5**
Casa de Luz **2**
Chuy's **1**
Curra's Grill **11**
Güero's **8**
Matt's El Rancho **7**
Olivia **6**
Shady Grove **3**
South Congress Café **9**
Vespaio
   & Enoteca Vespaio **10**
Uchi **4**

any restaurant in Austin. The chef/owner, James Holmes, is intent on getting it all right, from the new building, to the staff, to the suppliers. His cooking has a Mediterranean influence, but with Austin sensibilities. More than any other restaurant in Austin, Olivia emphasizes local producers. The menu varies a bit every day and offers sufficient variety to satisfy just about any taste without sacrificing focus or quality. The building, with lots of glass and a soaring roof, has an open feel and presents many details that can be admired over the course of a meal; an outside patio also offers interesting perspectives.

2043 S. Lamar Blvd. © **512/804-2700.** www.olivia-austin.com. Reservations recommended. Main courses $20–$30. AE, MC, V. Mon–Thurs 5:30–10pm; Fri–Sat 11am–2pm and 5:30–11pm; Sun 10:30am–2:30pm and 5:30–10pm.

Uchi ★★★ ASIAN/JAPANESE   Chef/owner Tyson Cole has garnered all kinds of acclaim from the local and national press. He loves to play with ingredients Texans are familiar with to create Asian dishes that are beautifully presented and exciting to Austin's tastes. His Uchiviche—citrus-marinated whitefish and salmon mixed with tomato, peppers, cilantro, and chilies—will make a believer out of you. It's not only the seafood that gets the culinary crossover treatment: Brie, pumpkin, shiitake mushrooms, and asparagus are among the food items that you can order tempura-style. And the skewered Kobe beef should satisfy those who eschew vegetables and fish. Choose from a long list of cold sakes—especially the rare upmarket brands—for the perfect complement. Uchi has legions of fans among the public, which means that you need to make reservations a week in advance or enjoy waiting for a table at the bar. The space, a converted 1930s bungalow done up in Asian reds and blacks, is at once dramatic and spare.

801 S. Lamar Blvd. ✆ **512/916-4808.** www.uchiaustin.com. Reservations accepted (and strongly recommended) for Mon–Thurs 5:30–9pm and Fri–Sat 5:30–6:30pm. Main courses $18–$30; sushi (per piece) $3–$5; sashimi, hot and cold plates $5–$25. AE, DISC, MC, V. Mon–Thurs 5–10pm; Fri–Sat 5–11pm.

Vespaio & Enoteca Vespaio ★ ITALIAN   Austin isn't really known for its Italian food, but when Austinites want Italian, this is their preferred destination. Vespaio's swanked-up old storefront with lots of exposed brick and glass is an elegant setting, and the food is worth waiting for, but you can drop quite a bit of dough on expensive wines while you're doing so. Your best bet is to get an order of the crispy calamari (they're huge) while you're waiting for a table. The spaghetti alla carbonara is super, as is the veal scaloppine with mushrooms. Many come for the pizza. Try the *boscaiola,* topped with wild boar sausage and Cambozola cheese. Among the 10 chalkboard specials offered nightly, the mixed meat and seafood grills are usually top-notch. It's important to note that reservations are limited to off-peak hours and days (see below).

Next door is the Enoteca, which is more informal, a bit less expensive, and offers lighter fare. It's open for lunch and dinner. The dining room is a little more cramped but is a very attractive space, perfect for an afternoon coffee, a panini, or a glass of wine. There's a small outdoor patio, too. One of the starters served here is a plate of crispy fried risotto balls filled with fontina. There's a small cold case filled with Italian delicacies for those interested in taking something back to the hotel room.

1610 S. Congress Ave. ✆ **512/441-6100.** www.austinvespaio.com. Reservations accepted for Sun–Thurs 5:30–6:30pm only. Pizzas $17–$18; pastas and main courses $21–$28. AE, DISC, MC, V. Tues–Fri 5:30–10:30pm; Sat 5–10:30pm; Sun–Mon 5:30–10pm. (Bar 5pm–midnight.) **Enoteca Vespaio** ✆ **512/441-7672.** No reservations. Pizzas and pastas $12–$16. AE, DISC, MC, V. Mon–Sat 11am–10pm; Sun 10am–3pm.

 Sweet Tooth

Amy's, Austin's homegrown brand of ice cream, is wonderfully rich and creamy. But eating it is only half the fun. Watching the colorfully clad servers juggling the scoops is a kick. Amy's has nine Austin locations, including one on the west side of downtown, 1012 W. Sixth St., at Lamar Boulevard (✆ 512/480-0673); one in SoCo, 1301 S. Congress Ave. (✆ 512/440-7488); and one at the Arboretum, 10000 Research Blvd. (✆ 512/345-1006). And if you don't have a chance to try it in town, you can catch this tasty treat at the airport.

Another place to keep in mind is Hey Cupcake! (no phone), which sells over-size cupcakes from an Airstream trailer parked on the 1600 block of South Congress at Milton Street. It opens Tuesday to Saturday at noon and Sunday at 1pm, and it closes when the cupcakes run out. The place is so popular that when the land on which the trailer sits was sold recently, the new owners assured the public that Hey Cupcake! would remain. The most popular flavors are the red velvet and the "Michael Jackson."

Moderate

Artz Rib House ★ BARBECUE   If you want to be really efficient in your visit to Austin, you can get your fill of live music and bbq all in one convenient stop. Artz has some talented local musicians playing bluegrass and country music from 7:30 to 9:30pm just about every night (except Sunday, when they play from 6:30–8:30pm). The food merits a visit even if a band isn't playing. The country-style pork ribs are indeed the standout, but the brisket and sausage aren't far behind. Artz offers turkey and chicken, too, and really good burgers made with Angus beef. The plates come with a choice of the traditional sides, of which the cole slaw and the potato salad are my favorites. The decor is homey, and the staff is easygoing yet efficient. As with any barbecue joint, occasionally Artz sells out of meat, so don't go too late, especially if you want ribs.

2330 S. Lamar. ✆ **512/442-8283.** www.artzribhouse.com. Reservations not accepted. Sandwiches $5–$7; plates $11–$19. No credit cards. Mon–Sat 11am–10pm; Sun noon–9pm.

Casa de Luz ★ 🍴 VEGAN   Austin has a large vegetarian community, and this is one of its favorite restaurants. The dining experience is easy and relaxed. The restaurant is part of a larger environmentally sound project—from the Parkside Montessori school at the front of the property, a shaded walkway leads to the dining room in back, past a book/gift shop, massage rooms, and a yoga studio. The dining room is a large, attractive space with lots of windows shaded with bamboo. Lunch and dinner consist of a set menu of soup, salad, and entree for a fixed price. (Check the website or call to find out what's cooking.) All the food is organic, vegan, macrobiotic, and gluten-free. Those with a sweet tooth can grab a piece of pie or cake at the dessert bar. There is no waitstaff—you pick up the food from a counter—and no tipping, as you're expected to bus your own dishes.

1701 Toomey Rd. ✆ **512/476-2335,** ext. 3 (ext. 2 for menu). www.casadeluz.org. No reservations. Breakfast $7, lunch or dinner $11. MC, V. Daily 7–10am (starts an hour later on weekends), 11:30am–2pm, and 6–8:30pm.

Chuy's ☺ TEX-MEX   In the row of low-priced, friendly restaurants that line Barton Springs Road just east of Zilker Park, Chuy's stands out for its determinedly wacky decor—hubcaps lining the ceiling, Elvis memorabilia galore—and its sauce-smothered Tex-Mex food. You're not likely to leave hungry after specials such as Chuy's special enchiladas, piled high with smoked chicken and cheese and topped with sour cream, or one of the "big as yo' face" burritos, stuffed with ground sirloin, say, and cheese and beans.

Chuy's is popular and doesn't take reservations; most people wait for a table by grabbing a seat in the bar area and ordering appetizers and "Mexican martinis" (like margaritas, but bigger and with olives). Try to stay away from the free nacho bar . . . if you can. Other locations have sprouted up: in the north on 10520 N. Lamar Blvd. (✆ **512/836-3218**), in the northwest at 11680 N. Research Blvd. (✆ **512/342-0011**), and far south at 4301 William Cannon (✆ **512/899-2489**).

1728 Barton Springs Rd. ✆ **512/474-4452.** www.chuys.com. Reservations not accepted. Main courses $8–$12. AE, DISC, MC, V. Sun–Thurs 11am–10pm; Fri–Sat 11am–11pm.

Curra's Grill ★★ ☺ MEXICAN   This plain, unassuming restaurant has a strong local following for its large menu of interior Mexican dishes and moderate prices. The tortillas are handmade. The Mexican tamales (not the kind usually served in Texas) come in several flavors and are quite good, with moist, spongy *masa*. You can build your own enchiladas from a selection of sauces and fillings—I like the *mole* and the *chile pasilla*. The Yucatecan *cochinita pibil* (pork baked in a marinade of *achiote*, sour orange, and herbs and spices) is tender and complex. The *pescado veracruzano* is fish baked in a sauce of tomatoes, onions, olives, and capers. There are also a lot of Tex-Mex options as well, such as the tostadas, piled high with lettuce and crumbled fresh cheese. For dessert, the flan can't be beat.

614 E. Oltorf. ☏ **512/444-0012.** www.curras.com. Reservations recommended for large parties. Main courses $8–$17. AE, DISC, MC, V. Daily 7am–10pm.

Güero's ★ ☺ TEX-MEX   This is one of the main hangouts on South Congress. It occupies an old feed store that dates from the time when South Austin was a low-rent area at the margins of the city. The restaurant has retained as much of the old feed store as it could, capturing the feel of homey informality that Austinites love. Floors of worn wood and stained cement; brick walls coated in old, faded paint; tall ceilings; tin roof; cheap tables and chairs—it's welcoming and friendly. It's also popular, and noisy when crowded. I like it best during off-hours. The restaurant makes its own tortillas by hand for dishes such as tacos (and the tacos *al pastor,* served Mexican-style on small tortillas, folded around deliciously seasoned, grilled pork with pineapple, onion, and cilantro, is one of the dishes this place is known for). I like the chicken breast marinated in *achiote* and Mexican oregano, which can be served on a salad, in enchiladas, or in tacos. None of the food is particularly spicy.

1412 S. Congress. ☏ **512/447-7688.** www.guerostacobar.com. Reservations not accepted. Main courses $7–$19. AE, DC, DISC, MC, V. Mon–Fri 11am–11pm; Sat–Sun 8am–11pm.

Matt's El Rancho TEX-MEX   This old South Austin standby is avoided by the young, hip crowd, in favor of some of the seedier, "more authentic" Tex-Mex dives. But the rest of Austin comes here to chow down on dependable old-school Tex-Mex dishes such as enchiladas in chili gravy, flautas, or fajitas. The chiles rellenos and shrimp a la Mexicana (smothered with peppers, onions, tomato, ranchero sauce, and jack cheese) are perennial favorites. Or you can go for a bit of everything by ordering one of the combo plates.

The original restaurant was opened downtown in 1952 by Matt Martinez, a former prizefighter. In 1986, he moved to the present location in South Austin, and now his son, Matt, Jr., manages it. Matt's is large with lots of parking. It gets crowded on weekend nights, especially if there's a university event, and you might have to wait up to an hour. As luck would have it, there's a bar area and terrace where you can sip a fresh-lime margarita until your table is ready. If you don't want to wait, you would do well to show up by 6pm on weekends. There are several dining rooms, and the tables aren't bunched together. Service is excellent.

2613 S. Lamar Blvd. ☏ **512/462-9333.** www.mattselrancho.com. Reservations not accepted after 6pm on Sat–Sun, except for large groups. Dinners $9–$18. AE, DC, DISC, MC, V. Sun–Mon and Wed–Thurs 11am–10pm; Fri–Sat 11am–11pm.

South Congress Cafe ★ SOUTHWEST   A small, modern establishment in the heart of SoCo that caters mostly to South Austin's leisure crowd, the cafe opens for brunch and dinner. For brunch, order the *migas* (Austin's favorite breakfast—eggs scrambled with strips of tortillas, tomatoes, onions, and chilies), which are some of the best; avoid the omelets, which are rubbery. For something hearty, try the wild boar red *pozole* (a Mexican-style soup served as a main course) for either brunch or dinner. It's a great mix of flavors and textures—succulent bits of pork, dark red chili sauce, and spongy grains of hominy, garnished with finely shredded cabbage and minced onion. The dinner menu changes seasonally, but, as with most Southwestern cooking, you'll usually find a variety of grilled meats and updated versions of old comfort food standbys. The dining room is a bit cramped but has a high ceiling and tall windows facing South Congress that give it a light and airy feel. At the height of the dinner hour it can get noisy.

1600 S. Congress. © **512/447-3905.** www.southcongresscafe.com. Reservations not accepted. Main courses $12–$24. AE, DC, MC, V. Mon–Fri 10am–4pm and 5–10pm; Sat–Sun 9am–4pm and 5–10pm.

Inexpensive

Shady Grove ★ AMERICAN   This ironic salute to Americana evokes David Lynch's vision of small town "Twin Peaks," including the corny touches. Stonework and yellow pine planks make up a good bit of the dining room's interior. Deep booths lining the walls and windows covered by old-fashioned Venetian blinds complete the picture. And the menu adds to the ambience with classics like Freddie's Airstream chili, meatloaf, and fried catfish. Shady Grove is known for its burgers made with ground sirloin. A popular choice is the green chili cheeseburger. Also, the hippie sandwich (grilled eggplant, veggies, and cheese with pesto mayonnaise) is a good bet.

When the weather is agreeable most patrons sit out on the large patio shaded by trees. On Thursdays during spring and summer this is the site of a free concert series called Shady Grove Unplugged. It features popular local artists and runs from 7 to 10pm.

1624 Barton Springs Rd. © **512/474-9991.** www.theshadygrove.com. Reservations not accepted. Main courses $8–$13. AE, DC, DISC, MC, V. Sun–Thurs 11am–10pm; Fri–Sat 11am–11pm.

WEST AUSTIN

Very Expensive

Jeffrey's ★★★ NEW AMERICAN   This little bistro in the old Clarksville neighborhood west of downtown has been a destination for food lovers for over 25 years. Some locals feel that its arrival marked the first steps of the city's march toward a food and dining culture. In keeping with the tone set by the surrounding neighborhood, the restaurant and bar area are cozy, comfortable, and informal. The furniture and lighting are handled nicely, and you relax from the moment you ease into a dining chair.

Menu items rotate with seasons, but one appetizer in particular, a signature dish of Jeffrey's, will be there: the crispy oysters on yucca chips topped with habañero honey aioli. There's also an updated version, called "Octavia," created by the new chef, Deegan McClung. He likes to layer rich flavors together for the main courses, and he's good at it. The innovative menu includes several dishes that may be new terrain to most diners, and the popular "Jeffrey's burger"—ground sirloin on a brioche with grilled onions, red romaine, strong cheddar, house-cured bacon, and a side of *pommes frites*—is no different. For those wanting to save money and still sample the cuisine, Jeffrey's has a bar menu with several appetizers (and the aforementioned burger). And you can save even more during happy hour, from 5 to 7pm.

1204 W. Lynn. © **512/477-5584** or 477-5587. www.jeffreysofaustin.com. Reservations strongly recommended. Main courses $19–$44; tasting menu $75, with wines $107. AE, DC, DISC, MC, V. Mon–Thurs 6–10pm; Fri–Sat 5:30–11pm; Sun 6–9:30pm.

Moderate

Cipollina ★★ 🍴 ITALIAN/PIZZA/NEW AMERICAN   This neighborhood bistro has a past that it's never managed to shake, and that past involved pizza and sandwiches. This is what happens when you're a neighborhood business—people don't forget. Cipollina kept the pizzas on the menu, but it made them new and out of the ordinary (such as bacon with Gorgonzola, apples, and arugula, or prosciutto with truffle oil, Gruyère, and oregano). The new chef, Daniel Hunt, believes that quality ingredients shouldn't be overworked. The restaurant does its best to use local suppliers, but won't sacrifice quality. The oyster mushroom risotto and the duck confit tortellini exemplify both quality and restraint. The menu changes seasonally, and there's usually a reasonably priced prix fixe. Sandwiches have been relegated to the lunch menu, but they are out of the ordinary, too.

Simple elegance is the prevailing character of the dining room, which has comfortable furniture, lots of room, and subtle decoration. To finish off your meal, walk a block south to Caffé Medici for some of the best espresso in Austin.

1213 W. Lynn. ⓒ **512/477-5211.** www.cipollina-austin.com. Reservations not accepted. Pizzas $12–$16; sandwiches $7–$12; main courses $11–$19; 3-course prix fixe $35 with wine paring, $25 without. AE, MC, V. Sun–Thurs 11am–10pm; Fri–Sat 11am–10:30pm.

Hula Hut 📷 TEX-MEX/AMERICAN   This place is a big hit with my out-of-town friends. They want to enjoy some Tex-Mex in a festive setting, and this restaurant strikes the right note. The Hula Hut brings a slightly cheesy Hawaiian theme to Tex-Mex cooking. Nothing is taken seriously. Brash and colorful, the main dining room invites good cheer, but the best thing about this place is the outdoor dining on the pier extending out into Lake Austin, with a view of the hills across the way. The fajita plates are especially good, and the other Tex-Mex dishes are irreproachable. For a sampler, try the pu pu platter (nachos, flautas, tacos, and queso). This place is popular, and parking is sometimes a problem, so go early or late if you can.

3826 Lake Austin Blvd. ⓒ **512/476-4852.** www.hulahut.com. Reservations not accepted. Main courses $9–$15. AE, MC, V. Sun–Thurs 11am–10pm; Fri–Sat 11am–11pm.

Inexpensive

Zocalo 🏷 MEXICAN   This fast-food Mexican cafe in the Clarksville neighborhood offers light, healthful fare for reasonable prices. The ingredients are fresh, and the tortillas are handmade. The soft tacos, which come three to the order, accompanied by rice and beans, make for just the right amount to satisfy an appetite without being too much. The fillings vary between vegetables, fish, fowl, and fajitas. Unlike Tex-Mex tacos, they don't come topped with cheese. Specialties include the "Zocalo plate" (a version of *chilaquiles con pollo*), which is made of tortilla pieces cooked with chicken in a green sauce and topped with crumbled fresh cheese and sour cream. The "tostada salad" comes with black beans, avocado, cilantro, roasted jalapeños, and a lime dressing. Look for the daily specials offered every weekday. The dining area is flooded by natural light from tall windows, and an outdoor area is available when the weather is agreeable.

1110 W. Lynn St. ⓒ **512/472-8226.** www.zocalocafe.com. Plates $7–$10. AE, DISC, MC, V. Mon–Fri 11am–10pm; Sat–Sun 10am–10pm.

CENTRAL

Expensive

Asti ★ ITALIAN/PIZZA   This is the Italian place everyone wants in their neighborhood: casual, attractive, and consistently good. The dining room is modern with lots of light and a high ceiling. For my taste, the tables are a bit too close together, but the food is worth the trouble. The pizzas can make for a light meal (the best is the white pizza with truffle oil). And even the main course portions are reasonable. The seafood risotto, if on the menu, is deliciously prepared and perfumed with a little saffron. Save room for such desserts as the amazing bittersweet chocolate cannoli. For a little restaurant, Asti has an unexpectedly large and well-selected wine list (mostly Italian and Californian bottles). The beer list is smaller, but it's good that they have one at all.

408C E. 43rd St. ⓒ **512/451-1218.** www.astiaustin.com. Reservations recommended Thurs–Sat. Pizzas $9–$12; pastas and main courses $13–$28. AE, DISC, MC, V. Mon–Thurs 11am–10pm; Fri 11am–11pm; Sat 5–11pm.

---

food trucks PARK IN AUSTIN

Food concession trailers are all the rage across the U.S. these days, especially in late-night entertainment areas like SoCo. Here, "meals-on-wheels" has taken on a whole new meaning with a centrally located strip of Airstream and RV eateries on the Avenue. In laid-back Austin, no one is in a hurry to eat on the run, so here tables are set up and little lights hang above the gravel parking lot, making this food trailer court a place to gather with friends, grab good food, and stay a while. The *Wall Street Journal* called SoCo's Mighty Cone one of "The Top-10 Trailers in America." Currently located in the gravel parking lot next to Congress Avenue Baptist Church (1511 S. Congress Ave.), the trailers may soon find a new location on South Congress when a new boutique hotel is built on this spot. For more info, visit www.austinfoodcarts.com.

Here's a list of a few fun trailers to try:

- **The Mighty Cone:** Known for hot and crunchy fried wraps (or "cones") made with chicken, shrimp, or avocado and served with mango aioli and slaw. It's no wonder this place gets such raves—its haute cuisine counterpart is the elegant, highly acclaimed Hudson's on the Bend restaurant on Lake Travis, whose chefs helped launch this hot trailer stop.

- **Flip Happy Crepes:** Featuring tasty tarragon-mushroom crepes with goat cheese, caramelized onions, spinach, and tomatoes.

- **Love Puppies Brownies:** Homemade brownies made by people who love puppies. Voted Austin's Best Kept Secret in the 2009 Best of Austin readers' poll in *The Austin Chronicle.*

- **Torchy's Tacos:** Go for the green chili pork tacos topped with *queso fresco,* cilantro, onions, and lime.

- **Hey Cupcake!:** Among their quirky cupcakes is "The Michael Jackson"—chocolate on the inside with cream cheese icing.

- **Vaquero Cocina:** Yummy smoked brisket and sweet plantain chips.

- **The Holy Cacao:** Ooooh, I love their sweet S'mores on a Stick and chocolate mint Grasshopper cake-balls.

By Janis Turk

Fonda San Miguel ★ MEXICAN   This was one of the first restaurants to introduce fine dining a la Mexicana to Texas. It's a local landmark, but in the last couple of years it has been in a holding pattern, keeping the quality up but not showing much life. The swinging door to the kitchen has seen plenty of action as several chefs have come and gone since Miguel Rávago retired. Still, there's much to be said for a well-made *mole poblano* or *cochinita pibil*. And, though the dinner menu doesn't have much that's new, many like it that way. There's something about the graceful rooms, the rich colors, and the attractive lighting that makes for a charming evening. For the pleasure of this experience, you pay more than at other Mexican restaurants, but for a special evening it's worth it.

Sunday brunch is a big deal at Fonda, with a more interesting selection of dishes (such as fruit gazpacho and *chilaquiles*). If money were no object . . .

2330 W. North Loop. ✆ **512/459-4121** or 459-3401. www.fondasanmiguel.com. Reservations recommended. Main courses $18–$31; Sun brunch $50. AE, DC, DISC, MC, V. Mon–Thurs 5:30–9:30pm; Fri–Sat 5:30–10:30pm. Bar open 5pm–close Mon–Sat. Sun brunch 11am–2pm.

Moderate

House Pizzeria ★★ PIZZA   This is a pizzeria tailor-made for Austin. It makes delicious thin-crust Neapolitan-style pizza, has nothing but local small brews on tap (and several to choose from) and a jukebox with an eclectic Austin vibe. It offers vegetarians several options, and, when it uses meats, it buys locally whenever possible. Furthermore, the restaurant recycles and composts almost everything (and doesn't own a dumpster), and the squarish "house" that it occupies was constructed with recycled materials and green-building practices. Look for a nondescript cream-colored building with a weathered wood siding on top, partially hidden by a large oak tree. There's some outdoor seating, a closed-in porch, and the main dining room. Pizzas are cooked in a proper wood-burning brick oven, the cheese is high quality, and the staff is friendly. You will like this place.

5111 Airport Blvd. (at E. 52nd St.). ✆ **512/600-4999.** www.housepizzeria.com. Pizzas $9–$13. AE, DISC, MC, V. Tues–Sun 11am–10pm.

Hyde Park Bar & Grill ★ 🍴 AMERICAN   Situated in the Hyde Park neighborhood's little enclave of restaurants along Duval Street, this place is easy to spot owing to the giant fork out front. Not only is it easy to find, but it's also easy to get to, it's easy to park your car, and, at least during off hours, it's easy to get a table here. If you do have to wait, then it's easy to have a drink at the bar. On weekends, this place is popular, especially when there are events at the university. In addition to the chicken-fried steak (and more healthful options, such as the roast chicken or any one of the various salads), people come here for the battered french fries, which are perennially voted best fries in Austin. I enjoy the way the New York strip is prepared, with a light dusting of dried ancho chili—not enough to make it spicy, but enough to bring out the flavor of the meat. The dessert menu features a famously good banana cream pie, and a not-so-common peach pudding. The atmosphere at Hyde Park—formerly a one-story house now divided into different dining rooms—is cozy, and the service is quick and unobtrusive. There's a south location at 4521 W. Gate Blvd. (✆ **512/899-2700**), which is at the West Gate Shopping Center, on the southeast corner of the intersection of South Lamar and Ben White Blvd. (Hwy. 71).

4206 Duval St. ✆ **512/458-3168.** www.hydeparkbarandgrill.com. Reservations not accepted. Salads and sandwiches $5–$10; main courses $10–$16. AE, DC, DISC, MC, V. Daily 11am–midnight.

Threadgill's ★ ☺ AMERICAN/SOUTHERN   If you want a side of music history with your heaping plate of down-home food, this Austin institution is for you. When Kenneth Threadgill obtained Travis County's first legal liquor license after the repeal of prohibition in 1933, he turned his Gulf gas station into a club. His Wednesday-night shows were legendary in the 1960s, with performers such as Janis Joplin turning up regularly. In turn, the Southern-style diner that was added on in 1980 became renowned for its huge chicken-fried steaks, as well as its vegetables. You can get fried okra, broccoli-rice casserole, garlic-cheese grits, black-eyed peas, and the like in combination plates or as sides.

Eddie Wilson, the current owner of Threadgill's, was the founder of the now-defunct Armadillo World Headquarters, Austin's most famous music venue (the South Austin branch, 301 W. Riverside [✆ **512/472-9304**], is called Threadgill's World Headquarters). Across the street from the old Armadillo, it's filled with music memorabilia from the club and a state-of-the-art sound system. Unlike the original location, it lays on a Sunday brunch buffet and a "howdy" hour during the week. Both branches still double as live-music venues.

6416 N. Lamar Blvd. ✆ **512/451-5440.** www.threadgills.com. Reservations not accepted. Sandwiches and burgers $8–$9; main courses $10–$17. DISC, MC, V. Mon–Sat 11am–10pm; Sun 11am–9pm.

Titaya's ★ THAI   In a strip mall on North Lamar, you'll find some of the best Thai food in Austin. Look for a nondescript building on the east side of the street, by a large Half-Price Books (local chain that sells used and remaindered books). The Thai standards, such as pad Thai (not too sweet and with the right amount of tamarind) and pad kee mao are well prepared (more so on weekdays than weekends), as is the typical Vietnamese noodle bowl (called "vermicelli lover" on the menu). The green curry is highly aromatic and is perhaps the best of the curries. For something more off the beaten path, try the spicy fried catfish in garlic sauce.

5501 N. Lamar (just south of Koenig). ✆ **512/458-1792.** Reservations not accepted. Lunch specials $7.50–$8; main courses $8.50–$14. AE, MC, V. Mon–Fri 11am–3pm and 5–10pm; Sat–Sun noon–10pm.

Inexpensive

Mother's Café & Garden VEGETARIAN/VEGAN   This neighborhood vegetarian restaurant is attractive, spacious, and softly lit. The dining rooms are understated modern with touches of hominess. They conjure up Austin's laid-back mood in much the same way as the old place did before it was gutted by fire in 2007 (caused, in an ironic twist, by a homeless man who late one night was cooking some meat

---

☺ family-friendly RESTAURANTS

Curra's (p. 191), **Güero's** (p. 192), **Hoover's** (p. 198), and **Threadgill's** (p. 197) all have special menus for ages 12 and under, not to mention casual, kid-friendly atmospheres and food inexpensive enough to feed everyone without taking out a second mortgage. **Chuy's** (p. 191) is great for teens and aspiring teens, who love the cool T-shirts, Elvis kitsch, and green iguanas crawling up the walls. At the **County Line on the Hill** (p. 201), all-you-can-eat platters of meat (beef ribs, brisket, and sausage), and generous bowls of potato salad, cole slaw, and beans are just $5.95 for children 11 and under.

behind the restaurant). Vegetarians are among the mellowest of Austin's latent hippie culture, making this place welcome relief from some of the more frenetic eateries in town. If there's a signature dish, it might be the artichoke enchiladas with mushrooms and black olives. Many prefer the zingier barbecued tofu. Aside from these and other regionally inspired dishes, there are vegetarian standards such as spinach lasagna, a vegetable stir fry, and a popular veggie burger. If you order a salad, check out the cashew-tamari dressing, which is quite good. Desserts are made in house, and, if they can be faulted at all, it would be because they are too healthful. There's a popular Sunday brunch from 10am to 3pm.

4215 Duval St. ⓒ **512/451-3994.** www.motherscafeaustin.com. Reservations not accepted. Main courses $8–$10. DISC, MC, V. Mon–Fri 11:15am–10pm; Sat–Sun 10am–10pm.

EAST SIDE
Moderate

Eastside Cafe ★★ AMERICAN   This was one of the earliest eateries to open in this rapidly changing area just east of the university. Eastside Cafe remains popular with student herbivores and congressional carnivores alike. Diners enjoy eating on a tree-shaded patio or in one of a series of small, homey rooms in a classic turn-of-the-20th-century bungalow.

This restaurant gears its menu to all appetites. You can get half orders of such pasta dishes as the smoked salmon ravioli, of the mixed field green salad topped with warm goat cheese, and of entrees like the sesame-breaded catfish. There's also a daily blue-plate special, which is usually a good deal. Each morning, the gardener informs the head chef which of the vegetables from the restaurant's organic garden (and from the restaurant's farm, about 2 miles out of town) are ready for harvesting. An adjoining store carries gardening tools, cookware, and the cafe's salad dressings.

2113 Manor Rd. ⓒ **512/476-5858.** www.eastsidecafeaustin.com. Reservations recommended. Pastas $14–$18; main courses $10–$22. AE, DISC, MC, V. Mon–Thurs 11:15am–9:30pm; Fri 11:15am–10pm; Sat 10am–10pm; Sun 10am–9:30pm (brunch Sat–Sun 10am–3pm).

Hoover's ★ ☺ AMERICAN/SOUTHERN   This is down-home comfort food at its best. When native Austinite Alexander Hoover, long a presence on the local restaurant scene, opened up his own place near the neighborhood where he grew up, he looked to his mother's recipes and added a bit of Cajun and Tex-Mex for inspiration. Fried catfish, meatloaf, and gravy-smothered pork chops, with sides of mac and cheese or jalapeño-creamed spinach, come to the table in generous portions. If you're in the mood for a sandwich, try the muffuletta. And if you haven't yet tried that Texas standard, the chicken-fried steak, this is a great place to do so. Check the chalkboard for daily specials, seasonal side dishes, and available desserts. If coconut cream pie is on the list, making a decision is much easier. The crowd is a mix of the East Side African-American community, UT students, and food lovers from all around town.

2002 Manor Rd. ⓒ **512/479-5006.** www.hooverscooking.com. Reservations not accepted. Sandwiches (with 1 side) $8–$9; plates (with 2 sides) $10–$15. DC, DISC, MC, V. Mon–Fri 11am–10pm; Sat–Sun 8am–10pm.

Vivo ★ TEX-MEX   Vivo bills its food as "healthful Tex-Mex" and has brown rice and tofu on the menu. I'm not sure how healthful it really is, but I can vouch for the taste.

The first thing the diner is presented with—a smoky, garlicky salsa made with blackened serrano chilies—is superb. The tortilla soup is hearty and filled with crunchy bits of tortilla contrasting with smooth chunks of avocado. The puffy tacos—handmade tortillas that puff up when fried (in canola oil, of course)—are messy to eat, but are a little-known Tex-Mex classic. They come filled with spiced beef or chicken, lettuce, tomato, and cheese. The *enchiladas verdes,* stuffed with chicken and topped with a nicely spiked *tomatillo* sauce, are quite good. The sauce is plentiful, as it should be (often not the case in other restaurants). The service is good, and the margarita menu is complete (and includes an interesting cucumber margarita with black Hawaiian sea salt).

Vivo is a date place and gets crowded on Friday and Saturday nights. Indoors, the walls are painted bright yellow, purple, and red, and hung with provocative modern art, including a fun version of the usual mounted head of a longhorn bull. Outside, you can dine on a deck decorated with tropical plants and a gurgling fountain.

2015 Manor Rd. (✆ **512/482-0300.** Reservations not accepted. Main courses and combination plates $8–$16. AE, DC, DISC, MC, V. Mon–Thurs 11am–10pm; Fri–Sat 11am–10:30pm; Sun 5–9pm.

Inexpensive

East Side King ★ ASIAN   At this food cart, you get a lot of local color with your meal. It's parked in the rear patio of the Liberty Bar, a "classy" dive on East Sixth Street between Comal and Chicon streets. The bar is dark and picturesque, with pool table, jukebox, and pinball machines. But, in keeping with Austin fashion, there's more than a touch of irony, and things are a just a bit off kilter. Nothing more so than the small food cart in back serving up some exotic fare to a youngish clientele. Beet fries served with Japanese-style mayonnaise, pork belly *bao* with a cucumber *kimchee,* peanut butter curry in a fried bun. The cart is a side project of one of the chefs at Uchi, and, though the favorite method of cooking seems to be deep frying, aromatic herbs—cilantro, basil, and mint—feature prominently. It's a menu of contrasts. Delicious and highly improbable, like the setting.

1618 E. Sixth St. No phone. Main courses $5–$8. No credit cards. Mon–Wed 7pm–midnight; Thurs–Sat 7pm–2am.

Franklin Barbecue ★★ 🍴 BARBECUE   Look for a blue-and-white trailer parked at the back of a fenced vacant lot on the northbound feeder road of I-35. Aaron and Stacy Franklin have been serving food out of this trailer since winter 2010, and word of their old-style barbecue has spread like wildfire. Aaron cooks it for 18 hours, using a low-temperature oak fire. The problem is that until he finds a bigger smoker (which you can see in a second trailer standing behind the first), he sells out of meat by 1pm or so. The popularity is well founded. The ribs, brisket, and sausage taste very much like the small-town barbecue outside of Austin. And, if you don't want to drive that far, but want to sample traditional barbecue, you should schedule a trip here. Franklin also has a couple of twists: pulled pork, which is uncommon here, and an espresso-flavored bbq sauce in addition to a traditional one. The lot has a few picnic tables where you can enjoy the food. Also, you should check the website for changes; Aaron tells me that he's looking to move out of the trailer and into a full kitchen.

3421 I-35 N. (at Concordia St.). (✆ **512/653-1187.** www.franklinbarbecue.com. Plates $7.75–$8.75. AE, DISC, MC, V. Wed–Sun 11am–1pm.

NORTHWEST

Very Expensive

Eddie V's Edgewater Grille ★★ SEAFOOD/STEAK   This swanky restaurant in the Arboretum mall is one of the hottest dinner spots in northwest Austin. The supper club atmosphere—white tablecloths, lots of black accents—and the top-notch seafood are a winning combination. The crispy calamari appetizer and lump crab cake make great starters, but take care not to indulge too much; this place doesn't stint on portion sizes. And the Parmesan-crusted lemon sole or smoked salmon with horseradish butter might not cut it as breakfast the next day. Also, consider the steaks—prime black Angus, well aged, and perfectly grilled. Besides, you want to leave room for the hot bread pudding soufflé, large enough for a table (as long as you're not dining with an entourage). The downtown Eddie V's, 301 E. Fifth St. (© **512/472-1860**), has the same menu, the same decor, and the same "see and be seen" cachet, but it doesn't have this location's Hill Country views at sunset. Both offer good happy hours (4:30–7pm), with half-price appetizers and $1 off wines and cocktails.

9400-B Arboretum Blvd. © **512/342-2642.** www.eddiev.com. Reservations recommended. Main courses $20–$39. AE, DC, DISC, MC, V. Sun–Thurs 4:30-10pm; Fri–Sat 4:30-11pm.

Expensive

Chez Zee ★ 🎁 NEW AMERICAN   This is a charming bakery/bistro noted for its incredible desserts and weekend brunches. You should consider it for lunch or dinner if you find yourself anywhere near the Mo-Pac freeway. Simply take it to the Northland (2222) exit and go 1 block west, turning left on to Balcones. The dining room, with its whimsical artwork, its many windows, and enclosed front patio, is light and cheerful. And it would be tough to bring someone here who couldn't find something to like on the eclectic menu—crunchy, fried dill pickles, perhaps, or tasty tequila-lime grilled chicken. In fact, it's hard to find a culinary category in which Chez Zee doesn't shine. It topped the "Best American," "Best Dessert," and "Best Soup" categories in the *Austin Chronicle* readers' poll. The desserts are rich and varied. It's tempting to go for something chocolaty (there's plenty to choose from), but if you're in the mood for something different, request a slice of their lemon rosemary cake—it's a poorly kept secret.

5406 Balcones. © **512/454-2666.** www.chez-zee.com. Main courses $14–$19. AE, DC, DISC, MC, V. Mon–Thurs 11am-10:30pm; Fri 11am-midnight; Sat 9am-midnight; Sun 9am-10pm.

Musashino ★★ JAPANESE   This place has the freshest, best-prepared sushi in northwest Austin, and every sushi aficionado knows it—which is why, in spite of its inauspicious location (on the southbound access road of Mo-Pac) and less-than-stunning setting (beneath a Chinese restaurant called Chinatown), it's always jammed. A combination of Musashino's local star status and its policy of not accepting reservations means you're likely to have to wait awhile for a table, especially on Friday and Saturday nights. The cozy upstairs area, which has a sushi bar and table service but a shorter menu, is a good substitute. Be sure to ask your server what's special before you order; delicacies not listed on the regular menu are often flown in.

3407 Greystone Dr. © **512/795-8593.** www.musashinosushi.com. Reservations not accepted. Sushi $4–$12 (including maki); main courses $14–$27. AE, DC, DISC, MC, V. Mon–Fri 11:30am-2pm; Tues–Thurs and Sun 5:30-10pm; Fri–Sat 5:30-10:30pm.

Moderate

Z'Tejas Southwestern Grill ★ 🍴 SOUTHWEST   An offshoot of a popular downtown eatery (and the second link in what became a small chain), this Arboretum restaurant is notable not only for its zippy Southwestern cuisine, but also for its attractive dining space, featuring floor-to-ceiling windows, a soaring ceiling, Santa Fe–style decor, and, in cool weather, a roaring fireplace. Grilled shrimp and guacamole tostada bites make a great starter, and if you see it on a specials menu, go for the smoked chiles rellenos made with apricots and jack cheese. Entrees include a delicious crusted salmon with a green tomatillo sauce and a pork tenderloin stuffed with chorizo. Even if you think you can't eat another bite, order a piece of ancho chili fudge pie.

If you're staying downtown, try the original—and smaller—Z'Tejas at 1110 W. Sixth St. (📞 **512/478-5355**).

9400-A Arboretum Blvd. 📞 **512/346-3506.** www.ztejas.com. Reservations recommended. Main courses $11–$22. AE, DC, DISC, MC, V. Mon–Thurs 11am–10pm; Fri 11am–11pm; Sat–Sun 10am–11pm.

WESTLAKE/LAKE TRAVIS
Very Expensive

Hudson's on the Bend ★★ NEW AMERICAN   If you're game for game, served in a civilized setting, come to Hudson's. Soft candlelight, fresh flowers, and attentive service combine with out-of-the-ordinary cuisine to make this worth a special-occasion splurge. Set in an old house some 1½ miles southwest of the Mansfield Dam, near Lake Travis, Hudson's has several softly lit, romantic dining rooms. The restaurant is famous for serving game, including diamondback rattlesnake cakes, but most come for the mixed grill of venison, rabbit, quail, and buffalo. It's quite expensive, but where else will you be able to experience food like this? There's also a superb trout served with tangy mango-habañero butter and a memorable pecan-smoked duck breast. Hudson's indoor dining rooms can be noisy on weekends. Opt for the terrace if the weather permits.

3509 Hwy. 620 N. 📞 **512/266-1369.** www.hudsonsonthebend.com. Reservations recommended, essential Sat–Sun. Main courses $25–$50. AE, DC, DISC, MC, V. Sun–Thurs 6–9pm; Fri–Sat 5:30–10pm.

Moderate

County Line on the Hill ★ 😊 BARBECUE   Opened in 1975, this scenic hillside bbq restaurant is the original of the County Line chain. The original business on this site, dating from the 1920s, was a speak-easy, positioned strategically on the "county line." Some critics deride these restaurants as "suburban" barbecue, but that doesn't stop crowds from packing in here nightly; if you don't get here before 6pm for dinner, you can wait as long as an hour to eat. Should this happen, sit out on the deck and soak in the views of the Hill Country. County Line is known for its big beef ribs, but I like the pork ribs better. The brisket is lean unless you specify "moist," which I also recommend. Sausage and chicken are also good bets. The slow-cooking method employed here makes for consistently good bbq. The sides, beans, slaw, and potato salad aren't just afterthoughts, and the bread is baked in-house. The atmosphere is rustic country house with such nostalgic accents as old signs and photos. County Line on the Lake (northwest), 5204 FM 2222 (📞 **512/346-3664**), offers the same menu, and is also open for lunch and dinner.

6500 W. Bee Cave Rd. ℂ **512/327-1742.** Reservations not accepted. Plates $11–$20; all-you-can-eat platters $19–$27 ($6–$8 for children 11 and under). AE, MC, V. Mon–Thurs 11:30am–2pm and 5–9pm; Fri 11:30am–2pm and 5–10pm; Sat 11:30am–10pm; Sun 11:30am–9:30pm (closing times are a half-hour earlier in winter).

The Oasis 📷 AMERICAN/TEX-MEX   This is the required spot for Austinites to take out-of-town guests at sunset. From the multilevel decks nestled into the hillside hundreds of feet above Lake Travis, visitors and locals alike cheer—with toasts and applause—as the sun descends behind the hills on the opposite shores. No one ever leaves unimpressed. The food is another matter entirely: It can be erratic. Keep it simple—nachos, burgers—and you'll be okay. Then add a margarita, and kick back. It doesn't get much mellower than this.

In 2005, lightning struck the restaurant and burned most of the decking that extended across a good portion of the hillside, causing more than $1 million in damage. Two days later the restaurant was back open, and after a year's worth of restoration, it was returned to its former glory. Those who have been there before will recognize that some of the decks have been reconfigured in an effort to improve the overall arrangement.

6550 Comanche Trail, near Lake Travis. ℂ **512/266-2442.** www.oasis-austin.com. Reservations not accepted. Main courses $12–$20. AE, DC, DISC, MC, V. Mon–Fri 11:30am–10pm; Sat–Sun 11am–10pm; closing an hour earlier in fall/winter.

ONLY IN (OR AROUND) AUSTIN

For information on Austin's funky, original cafe scene, see "Late-Night Bites" in chapter 15.

World-Famous Barbecue

Austin is at the center of an area rich in classic barbecue joints. Head out of town in just about any direction, and you'll come upon small towns that are home to famous institutions. A list of the most famous of these would have to include Lockhart, 30 miles south, which might be considered the bbq capital of Texas. It's home to such landmarks as **Kreuz Market, Black's,** and **Smitty's Market.** Southwest of Austin, in the town of Driftwood (25 miles), is the **Salt Lick,** where friends go on weekends with ice chests full of beer to sit at the picnic tables and wait their turn for some brisket served up right out of the pit. For some context, more description, and greater detail, see "Small Towns & Texas Barbecue" in chapter 16.

Musical Brunches

For a spiritual experience on Sunday morning, check out the gospel brunch at **Stubb's Bar-B-Q,** 801 Red River St. (ℂ **512/480-8341**). The singing is heavenly, the pork ribs divine. **South Congress Cafe** (p. 192) has a popular soul brunch that also mixes in a little gospel. At **Threadgill's World Headquarters** (p. 197), you can graze at a Southern-style buffet while listening to live inspirational sounds; find out who's playing at www.threadgills.com. If you're more in the mood for jazz, check out the brunches at both locations of **Manuel's** (p. 186), where you can enjoy eggs with venison chorizo, or corn gorditas with garlic and cilantro, while listening to smokin' traditional or Latin jazz.

Coffeehouses

Coffeehouse culture, students, and the Internet seem to go together naturally. Austin has seen a steady growth of independent coffeehouses, each with its own feel, refreshingly different from the corporate designs of the national chains. All the following are wireless Internet hotspots.

In the downtown area, you can find **Little City** at 916 Congress Ave. (✆ **512/476-2489**). It's close to the capitol and other downtown tourist sights. **Caffé Medici** (see below) will soon open a branch of its well-known coffeehouse in the Austonian Condo tower at Congress and East Second Street.

In South Austin, at 1300 S. Congress, is **Jo's** (✆ **512/444-3800**), which is the meeting place for SoCo's coffee set at any time of day. In the mornings, they sell pastries and an old Austin standard, breakfast tacos. In the afternoon, simple sandwiches go with the coffee, which is quite good. You're apt to encounter one of Austin's several local characters here, including Leslie, the bearded transvestite and former mayoral candidate who can be seen around town wearing revealing garb. Also in South Austin, in the Zilker Park area, is **Flipnotics,** 1601 Barton Springs Rd. (✆ **512/322-9750**), a two-story, indoor/outdoor "coffee space," where you can sip great caffeine drinks or beer while listening to acoustic singer/songwriters most nights.

In West Austin, in the Clarksville neighborhood, is **Caffé Medici** at 1101 W. Lynn (✆ **512/524-5049**). It serves excellent espresso drinks, perhaps the best in town. Farther west is **Mozart's,** 3825 Lake Austin Blvd. (✆ **512/477-2900**). It enjoys a beautiful location on the shores of Lake Austin; on a pretty day, the views are lovely from the deck. Here you can get great white-chocolate-almond croissants.

In central Austin, across from the University of Texas campus, is a second branch of **Caffé Medici** (✆ **512/474-5730**) at 2222-B Guadalupe. Just north of campus, and just off Guadalupe, is an atmospheric coffee bar called **Spider House,** 2908 Fruth St. (✆ **512/480-9562**). It's frequented by a mix of students and artists. Besides coffee, it sells tempeh chili, Frito pies, smoothies, all-natural fruit sangrias, and beer. Farther north, in the homey Hyde Park neighborhood, is the **Flightpath** coffeehouse (✆ **512/458-4472**) at 5011 Duval St. It's furnished '50s mod style.

EXPLORING AUSTIN

have two pieces of advice for visitors to Austin. First, don't hesitate to ask locals for directions or advice. Austinites are friendly and approachable. It's common practice here for complete strangers to engage in conversation. Indeed, one of the great things about Austin is how welcoming the city is. And second, take full advantage of the city's Visitor Information Center at 209 E. Sixth Street. It offers free walking tours, has pamphlets for self-guided tours, and is the point of departure for the motorized city tours. The office will know if one of the daily tours is canceled for whatever reason.

What sets Austin apart from other Texas cities and what puts it on all those "most livable" lists is the amount of green space and outdoor activities available to its denizens, whose attitude toward the outdoors borders on nature worship. From bats and birds to Barton Springs, from the Highland Lakes to the hike-and-bike trails, Austin lays out the green carpet for its visitors. You'd be hard-pressed to find a city that has more to offer fresh-air enthusiasts.

THE TOP ATTRACTIONS

Downtown

State Capitol ★★ 🔥 The history of Texas's legislative center is as turbulent and dramatic as that of the state itself. The current capitol, erected in 1888, replaced a limestone statehouse that burned down in 1881. A land-rich but otherwise impecunious Texas government traded 3 million acres of public lands to finance its construction. Gleaming pink granite was donated to the cause, but a railroad had to be built to transport the material some 75 miles from Granite Mountain, near the present-day town of Marble Falls. Texas convicts labored on the project alongside 62 stonecutters brought in from Scotland.

It is the largest state capitol building in the country, covering 3 acres, and is second in size only to the U.S. Capitol—but still, in typical Texas style, measuring 7 feet taller. The cornerstone alone weighs 12,000 pounds, and the total length of the wooden wainscoting runs approximately 7 miles. A splendid rotunda and dome lie at the intersection of the main corridors. The House and Senate chambers are located at opposite ends of the second level. Go up to the third-floor visitors' gallery during the legislative sessions, which occur almost every weekday from January

Downtown Austin Attractions

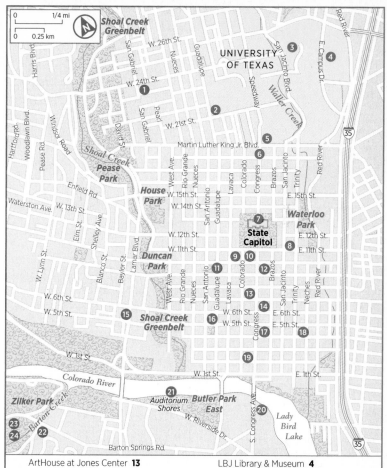

ArtHouse at Jones Center **13**
Austin Children's Museum **19**
Austin History Center **11**
Austin Museum of Art–Downtown **12**
Barton Springs Pool **23**
Bats **20**
Blanton Museum of Art **5**
Bob Bullock Texas State History
  Museum **6**
The Bremond Block **16**
Capitol Visitors Center **8**
Driskill Hotel **14**
Governor's Mansion **9**
Harry Ransom Humanities
  Research Center **2**

LBJ Library & Museum **4**
MEXIC-ARTE Museum **17**
Neill-Cochran Museum House **1**
O. Henry Museum **18**
Old Bakery & Emporium **10**
Philosopher's Rock **23**
Splash **23**
State Capitol **7**
Stevie Ray Vaughn Statue **21**
Texas Memorial Museum **3**
Treaty Oak **15**
Umlauf Sculpture Garden
  & Museum **22**
Zilker Zephyr Miniature Train **24**

Greater Austin Attractions

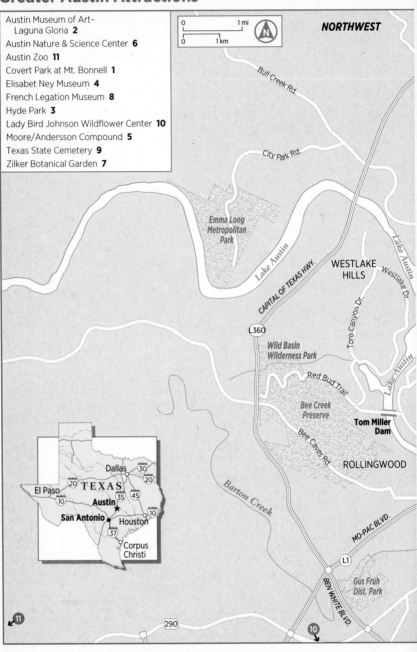

Austin Museum of Art–
Laguna Gloria **2**

Austin Nature & Science Center **6**

Austin Zoo **11**

Covert Park at Mt. Bonnell **1**

Elisabet Ney Museum **4**

French Legation Museum **8**

Hyde Park **3**

Lady Bird Johnson Wildflower Center **10**

Moore/Andersson Compound **5**

Texas State Cemetery **9**

Zilker Botanical Garden **7**

NORTHWEST

Bull Creek Rd.

City Park Rd.

Emma Long
Metropolitan
Park

Lake Austin

WESTLAKE
HILLS

Lake Austin

CAPITAL OF TEXAS HWY.

Westlake Dr.

L360

Toro Canyon Dr.

Wild Basin
Wilderness Park

Red Bud Trail

Lake Austin

Bee Creek
Preserve

**Tom Miller
Dam**

Bee Caves Rd.

ROLLINGWOOD

Barton Creek

TEXAS

Dallas

El Paso

Austin

San Antonio

Houston

Corpus
Christi

MO-PAC BLVD.

L1

Gus Fruh
Dist. Park

BEN WHITE BLVD.

290

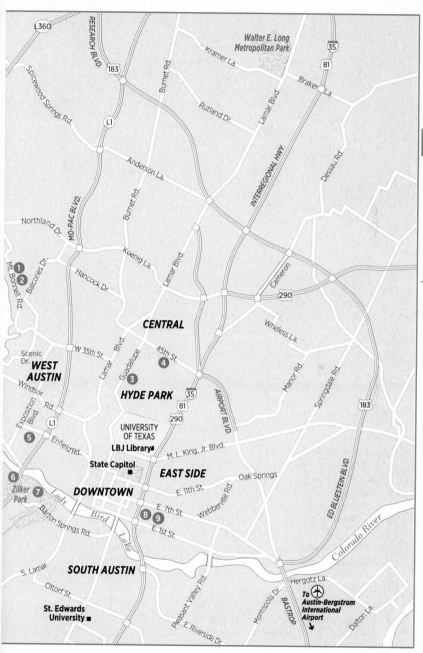

GOING batty

Austin has the largest urban bat population in North America. Some visitors are dubious at first, but it's difficult to be unimpressed by the sight of 1.5 million of the creatures, who emerge from under the Congress Avenue Bridge shortly before dusk and flitter through the air in a long winding ribbon floating above the river on the east side of the bridge.

Each March, free-tailed bats migrate from central Mexico to various roost sites in the Southwest. In 1980, when a deck reconstruction of Austin's bridge created an ideal environment for raising bat pups, some 750,000 pregnant females began settling in every year. Each bat gives birth to a single pup, and by August these offspring take part in nightly forays for bugs, usually around dusk. Depending on the size of the group, they might consume anywhere from 10,000 to 30,000 pounds of insects a night—one of the things that makes them so popular with Austinites. By November, these youngsters are old enough to fly back south with their group on the winds of an early cold front.

While the bats are in town, an educational kiosk designed to dispel some of the more prevalent myths about them is set up each evening on the south bank of the river, just east of the bridge. You'll learn, for example, that bats are not rodents, they're not blind, and they're not in the least interested in getting in your hair. **Bat Conservation International** (② 512/327-9721; www.batcon.org), based in Austin, has lots of information, as well as bat-related items for sale. Log on to the website or phone ② **800/538-BATS** (538-2287) for a catalog. To find out what time the bats are going to emerge from the bridge, call the *Austin American-Statesman* **Bat Hotline** (② **512/416-5700,** category 3636). A lot of people don't know this, but sometimes the bats don't leave all at once. If you can still hear bats chattering from beneath the bridge, sit tight; you may have an encore presentation.

through May of odd-numbered years, if you want see how politics are conducted Texas-style.

The building had become dingy and its offices overcrowded over the past century, but a massive renovation and expansion in the 1990s restored its grandeur. The expansion project was fascinating in its own right: Almost 700,000 tons of rock were chiseled from the ground to create an underground annex (often called the "inside-out, upside-down capitol"). It was constructed with similar materials and connected to the capitol and four other state buildings by tunnels. To prevent the expansion from seeming too much like a cave, extensive skylights were installed and the main corridors designed as atriums. You can opt for either a 30- to 45-minute free guided tour, or walk around on your own using self-guided tour pamphlets (you might want to use a pamphlet for the capitol grounds, but do take the guided tour of the building afterward; you're free to explore the building at your leisure). Include the Capitol Visitors Center (see "More Attractions," below), and figure on spending around 2 hours here. Wear comfortable shoes; you'll be doing a lot of walking.

11th and Congress sts. ② **512/463-0063.** www.tspb.state.tx.us. Free admission. Mon–Fri 7am–10pm; Sat–Sun 9am–8pm; hours extended during legislative sessions (held in odd years, starting in Jan, for 140 straight calendar days). Closed all major holidays. Free guided tours Mon–Fri 8:30am–4:30pm; Sat 9:30am–3:30pm; Sun noon–3:30. Bus: Multiple bus lines.

South Austin

Barton Springs Pool ★★ ☺ If the University of Texas is the seat of Austin's intellect, and the state capitol is its political pulse, Barton Springs is the city's soul. The Native Americans who settled near here believed these waters had spiritual powers, and today's residents still place their faith in the abilities of the spring-fed pool to soothe and cool.

Each day, approximately 32 million gallons of water from the underground Edwards Aquifer bubble to the surface here, and at one time, this force powered several Austin mills. Although the original limestone bottom remains, concrete was added to the banks to form uniform sides to what is now a swimming pool of about 1,000×125 feet. Maintaining a constant 68°F (20°C) temperature, the amazingly clear water actually feels colder in the summer than in the winter, when a few brave souls unwilling to do without their daily swim have the large pool all to themselves. Lifeguards are on duty for most of the day, and a large bathhouse operated by the Parks and Recreation Department offers changing facilities and a gift shop. For details about the Splash! environmental information center, see "Especially for Kids," later in this chapter.

Zilker Park, 2201 Barton Springs Rd. ⓒ **512/476-9044.** www.ci.austin.tx.us/parks/bartonsprings.htm. Admission $3 adults, $2 ages 12–17, $1 seniors and children 11 and under (admission charged only after 8am Mar 13–Oct; free for early birds). Daily 5am–10pm except during pool maintenance (Thurs 9am–7pm). Splash! Tues–Fri noon–6pm; Sat–Sun 10am–6pm. Bus: 30 (Barton Creek Sq.).

Lady Bird Johnson Wildflower Center ★★★ If you know anything about Lady Bird Johnson, then you've heard that her big cause was the preservation of wildflowers and native plants. She insisted that natural habitats and native species were beautiful in their own right, that they are part of what defines regional identity, and that they could even be economically beneficial. She was right, you know. And her efforts have had an enormous impact on the way gardeners practice their craft in central Texas. She also prevailed upon the state highway agency to seed the roadsides with wildflowers, which have flourished throughout the state but especially in central Texas where fields of bluebonnets, Indian paintbrush, evening primrose, and other wildflowers paint the landscape in rich colors, attracting visitors from far and wide.

To further the cause, Mrs. Johnson founded the Wildflower Center to research native species and habitat and educate the public on the benefits of gardening with these plants and wildflowers. The center has a large staff and scores of volunteers, 279 acres of land, large greenhouses, and an elaborate rainwater collection system. The facility's research library is the largest in the United States for the study of native plants. For visitors, the main attractions are the 12 acres of beautiful gardens displaying 650 species of native plants (most of which are labeled) in varying habitats, 2 miles of trails, and an observation tower. In 2010, the Wildflower Center received $1.4 million to create an arboretum featuring native trees. There is also a large and colorful gift shop and a cafe serving soups and sandwiches. Free lectures and guided walks are usually offered on the weekends—it's best to phone or check the website for current programs.

Once you get on Mo-Pac freeway, it's a 20-minute ride from West Austin. If you're really interested in gardening or botany, you can spend the better part of a day here.

4801 La Crosse Ave. ⓒ **512/292-4200.** www.wildflower.org. Admission $8 adults, $7 students and seniors 60 and older, $3 ages 5–12, free for children 4 and under. Tues–Sat 9am–5:30pm; Sun noon–5:30pm (rates sometimes increase during the height of wildflower season: Mar–Apr). Take Loop 1 (Mo-Pac) south to La Crosse Ave., and turn left.

Central

Blanton Museum of Art ★   Located on the University of Texas campus (across the street from the Bob Bullock Museum), the Blanton houses the university's art collection, which is ranked among the top university collections in the United States. Most notable is the Suida-Manning Collection, a gathering of Renaissance works by such masters as Veronese, Rubens, and Tiepolo that was sought after by many other museums. Other permanent holdings include the Mari and James Michener collection of 20th-century American masters, a large collection of Latin American art, and a collection of 19th-century plaster casts of monumental Greek and Roman sculpture.

The museum has been a big success in its first few years, attracting large crowds. The directors are working hard to increase public involvement through a variety of events. On the first Friday of every other month, it hosts a little happening called "B scene," which mixes art with live music, wine, finger foods, and socializing. It costs $12 and runs from 6 to 11pm. And on the third Thursday of every month the museum holds events that mix different activities with the arts, such as yoga or literature. These events start at 6:30pm. Check the website for other events. Across a small plaza from the museum's main door are the museum's store and cafe. The store offers entertaining shopping with a good variety of uncommon merchandise (including some good gift items), and the cafe is an attractive place to recharge with a coffee or bite to eat.

Martin Luther King, at Congress. ✆ **512/471-7324.** www.blantonmuseum.org. $9 adults, $7 seniors (65 and over), $5 youth (13–25), free for children 12 and under. Free admission Thurs. Parking is $3 with validation. Tues–Fri 10:30am–5pm; Sat 11am–5pm; Sun 1–5pm. Closed university holidays. Bus: UT Shuttle.

The Bob Bullock Texas State History Museum ★ ☺   This museum offers a view of Texas history that's different from the most common treatments. There's more emphasis on many contributions that came from unheralded groups, with many of the exhibits presenting some surprising and commonly unknown facets of life in Texas. The building that houses the museum is impressive. Three floors of exhibits are arrayed around a rotunda set off by a 50-foot, polished granite map of Texas. The permanent displays—everything from Stephen F. Austin's diary to Neil Armstrong's spacesuit—and rotating exhibits are interesting. Still, for all the interactive video clips and engaging designs (lots of different rooms to duck into), the presentations didn't strike me as dramatically different from those in other history museums. The real treat is the multimedia Spirit Theater, the only one of its kind in Texas, where you can experience the high-speed whoosh of the great Galveston hurricane and feel your seats rattle as an East Texas oil well hits a gusher. Austin's only IMAX Theater with 3-D capabilities is pretty dazzling too, though the films don't necessarily have a direct relation to Texas history. If you do everything, plan to spend at least 2½ to 3 hours here.

1800 N. Congress Ave. ✆ **512/936-8746.** www.thestoryoftexas.com. Exhibit areas $7 adults, $6 seniors 65 and over, $4 youth 5–18, free for children 4 and under. IMAX Theater $7 adults, $6 seniors, $5 youth. Texas Spirit Theater $5 adults, $4 seniors, $4 youth. Combination tickets for admission to exhibits and one or both theaters are available. Parking $8 (IMAX parking free after 6pm). Mon–Sat 9am–6pm; Sun noon–6pm. Phone or check website for additional IMAX evening hours. Closed Jan 1, Easter, Thanksgiving, and Dec 24–25. Bus: UT Shuttle.

LBJ Library and Museum ★ 🎖   A presidential library may sound like a big yawn, but this one's almost as interesting as the 36th president to whom it's devoted. Lyndon Baines Johnson's popularity in Texas and his many successes in Washington are often forgotten in the wake of his actions regarding the Vietnam War. The story of Johnson's long political career, starting with his early days as a state representative and continuing through to the Kennedy assassination and the groundbreaking Great Society legislation, is told through a variety of documents, mementos, and photographs. Johnson loved political cartoons, even when he was the object of their satire, and examples from his large collection are among the museum's most interesting rotating exhibits. You can take the elevator up to the top floor to view a replica of the oval office decorated in the same manner as during Johnson's presidency. The room is a bit smaller than the actual oval office. Other exhibits might include anything from photographs from the American civil rights era to a display of gifts to LBJ from various other world leaders. You'll also see an animatronic version of LBJ. Dressed in his clothes and speaking with the same folksy delivery that he used when talking to reporters, the life-size, gesticulating figure is either amusing or creepy, depending upon your perspective. From 1971, when the library was dedicated, until his death in 1973, Johnson himself kept an office in this building, which commands an impressive campus view. A large, free parking lot next to the library makes it one of the few UT campus sights that's easy to drive up to.

University of Texas, 2313 Red River. ✆ **512/721-0200.** www.lbjlib.utexas.edu. Free admission. Daily 9am–5pm. Closed Dec 25. Bus: 15 or UT shuttle.

MORE ATTRACTIONS

Downtown

Arthouse at Jones Center ★　The Jones Center is home to Arthouse, also known as the Texas Fine Arts Association, an organization whose purpose is to promote all forms of contemporary art in Texas. The building was originally a movie theater, which was converted into a department store in 1956. In late 2010, the center completed a large expansion and renovation, which more than doubled the exhibition space and added flexibility and functionality. Inside and outside, the new improved Arthouse offers interesting views from various perspectives. The exhibition space is dedicated temporary shows representing a wide variety of visual art forms. Check the website to see what will be on view during your visit.

700 Congress Ave. ✆ **512/453-5312.** www.arthousetexas.org. Free admission, suggested donation $5. Wed noon–11pm; Thurs–Fri noon–9pm; Sat–Sun noon–5pm.

Austin History Center/Austin Public Library　Next door to the modern public library, this center, which was the original city library, now holds various materials of Austin's past. Built in 1933, the Renaissance revival–style building displays lots of architectural details and rich materials, including beautiful work in stone, wood, and iron. In the main gallery, there's always an exhibit illustrating some facet of the city's history. This gallery leads back to the main reading room, where you'll often find genealogical researchers going over old public records. Among its other possessions, the center also has a large and interesting photographic collection.

810 Guadalupe St. ✆ **512/974-7480.** www.austinhistorycenter.org. Free admission. Tues–Sat 10am–6pm; Sun noon–6pm. Bus: 171.

Austin Museum of Art–Downtown　This has become the main gallery space for Austin's local art association. It represents a sizable expansion from the association's other location in the Laguna Gloria mansion in West Austin. The downtown gallery hosts some interesting, often highly original, exhibits. It's not formal at all and can be visited as an afterthought if you're downtown with some time on your hands. And you can always check what's currently on display by going to their website.

823 Congress Ave. (at Ninth St.). ✆ **512/495-9224.** www.amoa.org. Admission $5 adults, $4 seniors 55 and over and students, $1 for everyone on Tues, free for children 11 and under. Tues–Wed 10am–5pm; Thurs 10am–8pm; Fri 10am–5pm; Sat 10am–6pm; Sun noon–5pm.

Bremond Block ★ "The family that builds together, bonds together" might have been the slogan of Eugene Bremond, an early Austin banker who established a mini-real-estate monopoly for his own kin in the downtown area. In the mid-1860s, he started investing in land on what was once Block 80 of the original city plan. In 1874, he moved into a Greek revival home made by master builder Abner Cook. By the time Bremond was through, he had created a family compound, purchasing and enlarging homes for himself, two sisters, a daughter, a son, and a brother-in-law. Some of these private buildings were destroyed, but those that remain on what is now known as the Bremond Block are exquisite examples of elaborate late-19th-century homes.

Btw. Seventh and Eighth, San Antonio and Guadalupe sts.

Capitol Visitors Center ★ At the southeast corner of the capitol grounds is Texas's oldest state office building, the 1857 General Land Office. At present the building houses the visitor center for the capitol. It's a curious structure and looks a bit out of place with its Romanesque-medieval style and mock crenelated towers. Also uncommon is the surfacing of the exterior walls—scored stucco to imitate stone blocks. The short-story writer O. Henry worked in this building as a draftsman for the General Land Office (1887–91), and you'll find an exhibit on the first floor remembering him. He based two stories on his experiences here. Also on the first floor is a gift shop selling all kinds of books, decorative items, and merchandise commemorating aspects of the Texas capitol, and an information desk that is somewhat redundant. The second floor hosts rotating exhibits about some aspect of the Texas capitol.

Tip: The Texas Department of Transportation staffs an information desk on the first floor of the visitor center. If you're driving around Texas at all, you can pick up a state map and a helpful travel guide for free. The guide lists almost all the towns in Texas and tells what's of interest in each.

112 E. 11th St. (southeast corner of capitol grounds). ✆ **512/305-8400.** www.texascapitolvisitorscenter. com. Free admission. Mon–Sat 9am–5pm; Sun noon–5pm.

The Driskill Col. Jesse Driskill was not a modest man. When he opened a hotel in 1886, he named it after himself, put busts of himself and his two sons over the entrances, and installed bas-relief sculptures of longhorn steers to remind folks how he had made his fortune. Nor did he build a modest property. The ornate four-story structure, which originally boasted a sky-lit rotunda, has the largest arched doorway in Texas over its east entrance. It was so posh that the state legislature met here while the 1888 capitol was being built. The hotel has had its ups and downs over the years, but it was restored to its former glory in the late 1990s. You'll enjoy the magnificent retro lobby and can get coffee or food and sit at a table to take it in at your leisure. At the front desk, you can get a history of the hotel. For a full hotel review, see p. 166.

604 Brazos St. ✆ **512/474-5911.** www.driskillhotel.com.

Governor's Mansion ★ This venerable public building suffered serious damage when it was targeted by arsonists on the night of June 8, 2008. At the time, the mansion was closed for renovation. Officers of the Department of Public Safety, charged with guarding the building and grounds, did not detect the intruders, and apparently some of the closed-circuit cameras were not working. All of this will make it difficult to catch the vandals. Workers managed to stabilize the structure and protect it from the elements, but extensive restoration is necessary. With all the budget problems the state faces, there was some difficulty allocating funds. Work has begun on restoration, and the projected completion date is February 2012.

In ordinary times, this mansion is the governor's residence. State law requires that the governor live here whenever he or she is in Austin. The house was built by Abner Cook in 1856. Originally it had no indoor toilets (there are now seven). The nation's first female governor, Miriam "Ma" Ferguson, entertained her friend Will Rogers in the mansion, and Gov. John Connally recuperated here from gunshot wounds received when he accompanied John F. Kennedy on his fatal motorcade through Dallas. Among the many historical artifacts on display are a desk belonging to Stephen F. Austin and portraits of Davy Crockett and Sam Houston.

Tip: You know how iffy projected completion dates can be. If you will be in Austin after February 2012, you should check the website. If the mansion is open, only a limited number of visitors will be allowed to tour it, so make your required reservations as far in advance as possible.

1010 Colorado St. ℂ **512/463-5516** (recorded information) or 463-5518 (tour reservations). www.txfgm.org. Free admission. Tours generally offered every 20 min. Mon–Thurs 10am–noon (last tour starts 11:40am). Closed Fri–Sun, some holidays, and at the discretion of the governor; call the 24-hr. information line to see if tours are offered the day you want to visit.

MEXIC-ARTE Museum Though it has a small permanent collection of 20th-century Mexican art, photographs from the Mexican revolution, and a fascinating array of masks from the state of Guerrero, this museum is best known for the yearly "Young Latino Artists" show. This show isn't held at the same time every year, but it's usually a summer event. You'll have to check the website for dates. The show's curators choose different artists each year, and usually arrange an eye-catching exhibit. The other time of year when MEXIC-ARTE is especially entertaining is in and around *Día de los Muertos* (end of Oct/beginning of Nov), when the curators construct an altar to some recently deceased celebrity, and the museum store supplements its usual merchandise with some fun and traditional *calavera* (skull) artwork.

419 Congress Ave. ℂ **512/480-9373.** www.mexic-artemuseum.org. Admission $5 adults, $4 seniors and students, $1 children 11 and under. Mon–Thurs 10am–6pm; Fri–Sat 10am–5pm; Sun noon–5pm.

O. Henry Museum The short-story writer O. Henry had such a tremendous impact on American literature and culture that most people can retell one of his stories even if they can't identify the author. As mentioned earlier, he lived in Austin (1884–98), where he published a popular satirical newspaper called *Rolling Stone*. He also held down a string of jobs, including a stint as a teller at the First National Bank of Austin. After he left, he was accused of embezzling funds. We don't know whether he was guilty or not, but he did serve time for this crime in a prison in Ohio, where he finally had the leisure to develop his writing style and establish himself as a writer. He went on to write many stories and based several of them in Austin. The museum occupies a modest Victorian cottage where O. Henry resided with his wife and daughter from 1893 to 1895. About a third of the furniture and appointments in the house originally belonged to him; the rest is of the same period. There are quite a few things to marvel at, and the helpful staff answers questions that may come to mind in viewing the house. Visitors are asked to wear flat, soft-soled shoes to prevent damage to the original pine floors.

If you saw the cult-classic 1993 indie film *Dazed and Confused*, set in Austin, you may remember the line, "Party at the moon tower!" and the scene filmmaker Richard Linklater set under one of Austin's Moonlight Towers. So what's a "moon tower"? Standing 165 feet above their 15-foot base, these old-fashioned towers illuminate Austin with bright lights, creating a bright moonlight-like glow. Popular in the late 1800s across the U.S. and Europe, the original moonlight towers were established in Austin between 1884 and 1885. Today, Austin is the only city in the world still using moon tower lighting, though only 17 of the original 31 towers remain. Each tower originally contained six carbon arc lamps, illuminating a 1,500-foot-radius circle, which is said to have burned "brightly enough to read a watch from as far away as 1,500 feet." Originally, the towers were connected to generators on the Colorado River. Later, carbon arc lamps were added, but in the '20s, those were changed to incandescent lamps, and in the 1930s, mercury vapor lamps were lit by a switch at each tower's base. During World War II, a central switch controlled the lights, allowing citywide blackouts in case of air raids. As a part of a $1.3-million project in 1993, the City of Austin dismantled and meticulously restored each piece of the 17 towers. The towers were officially recognized as state archaeological landmarks in 1970 and were later collectively listed in the National Register of Historic Places in 1976. Austin's towers are scattered all over town, with the greatest concentration being near the capitol; however, the city's most popular tower may be a replica moonlight tower standing in Zilker Park.

409 E. Fifth St. ✆ **512/472-1903.** www.ci.austin.tx.us/parks/ohenry.htm. Free admission. Wed–Sun noon–5pm. Closed Thanksgiving, Dec 25, and Jan 1.

Old Bakery and Emporium   On the National Register of Historic Landmarks, the Old Bakery was built in 1876 by Charles Lundberg, a Swedish master baker, and continuously operated until 1936. You can still see the giant oven and wooden baker's spade inside. Rescued from demolition by the Austin Heritage Society and now owned and operated by Austin's Parks and Recreation Department, the brick-and-limestone building is one of the few unaltered structures on Congress Avenue. It houses a gift shop selling crafts handmade by seniors, a reasonably priced lunchroom (Mon–Fri 11am–1:30pm), and a hospitality desk with visitors' brochures.

1006 Congress Ave. ✆ **512/477-5961.** www.ci.austin.tx.us/parks/bakery1.htm. Free admission. Mon–Fri 9am–4pm; first 3 Sat in Dec 10am–2pm. Closed most holidays.

Sixth Street   Formerly known as Pecan Street (all the east-west streets in downtown were originally named for Texas trees while north-south streets continue to be named for Texas rivers), Sixth Street was the main connecting road to the older settlements east of Austin. During the Reconstruction boom of the 1870s, the wooden wagon yards and saloons of the 1850s and 1860s began to be replaced by the more solid masonry structures you see today. After the new state capitol was built in 1888, the center of commercial activity began shifting toward Congress Avenue, and by the middle of the next century, Sixth Street had become a skid row.

Restoration of the 9 blocks designated as a Historic District by the National Register of Historic Places began in the late 1960s. In the 1970s, the street thrived as a live-music center. Austin's former main street is now lined with restaurants, galleries, bars, and shops. Despite the makeover, East Sixth still retains an air of decadence that reminds many of Bourbon Street. (West Sixth is much more sanitized.) On any night, you'll find a mostly young crowd walking the sidewalks looking for just the right bar.

Btw. Lavaca Ave. and I-35.

Treaty Oak   Legend has it that Stephen F. Austin signed the first boundary treaty with the Comanche under the spreading branches of this 500-year-old live oak tree. (A live oak is a species of oak that doesn't lose its leaves in winter.) This is the sole remaining tree in what was once a grove known as Council Oaks. In the late 1980s, a mentally unstable man deliberately poisoned the tree and almost managed to kill it. The attack shocked the community, and led to the creation of a large international team of forestry experts who managed to save the tree through extraordinary efforts. The dried wood from major limbs that they removed was allocated to local artists, whose works were auctioned off for the tree's 500th anniversary in 1993. Now such items as pen sets, gavels, and clocks made out of the tree's severed limbs are for sale, with proceeds going to plant additional trees throughout public areas of Austin.

503 Baylor St., btw. W. Fifth and Sixth sts. ℘ **512/440-5194.** www.ci.austin.tx.us/treatyoak.

South Austin

Umlauf Sculpture Garden & Museum   This is a great museum for people who don't enjoy being cooped up in a stuffy, hushed space. A sculptor at the University of Texas for 40 years, Charles Umlauf donated his home, studio, and more than 250 pieces of artwork to the city of Austin, which maintains the wooded native garden where much of the sculpture is displayed. Umlauf, whose pieces reside in such places as the Smithsonian Institution and New York's Metropolitan Museum, worked in many media and styles. Though he used several models, the one you're likely to recognize is Farrah Fawcett, Umlauf's most famous UT student. The museum video is captioned for those who are hearing-impaired, and, with advance notice, "touch tours" can be arranged for those who are blind or visually impaired.

605 Robert E. Lee Rd. ℘ **512/445-5582.** www.umlaufsculpture.org. Admission $3.50 adults, $2.50 seniors, $1 students, free for children 5 and under. Wed–Fri 10am–4:30pm; Sat–Sun 1–4:30pm. Closed major holidays. Bus: 29 or 30.

West Austin

Austin Museum of Art–Laguna Gloria   This is the old home of Austin's fine arts community. It made for a small museum that hosted modest shows from the late 60s to the late 90s. Since the creation of the downtown gallery space (see above), the mansion houses a small arts school for kids and some exhibits focusing on the historic aspects of the mansion and grounds. It is a Mediterranean-style villa built in 1916 by Austin newspaper publisher Hal Sevier and his wife, Clara Driscoll, best known for her successful crusade to save the Alamo from commercial development. The villa sits on 13 wooded acres bordering Lake Austin. There is a small well-tended, attractive garden.

Tip: If the weather's nice, bring along a picnic lunch to enjoy by the lake. It's one of the prettiest spots in the city and, during the week, one of the most peaceful.

3809 W. 35th St. ℘ **512/458-8191.** www.amoa.org. At the end of W. 35th St., before it arrives at the lake.

Moore/Andersson Compound Those interested in architecture might enjoy checking out the compound where Charles Moore spent the last decade of his life. The peripatetic American architect, who kept a low profile but had a great influence on postmodernism, built five homes, but this one, which he designed with Arthur Andersson, perfectly demonstrates his combination of controlled freedom, whimsical imagination, and connection to the environment. The wildly colorful rooms are filled with folk art from around the world, while odd angles, bunks, and dividers render every inch of space fascinating. The compound now functions as a conference and lecture center. Tours are by appointment only, and no children under 12 are permitted.

2102 Quarry Rd. ✆ **512/220-7923.** www.charlesmoore.org. Tours by appointment only. $25 adults, $10 students.

Central

Elisabet Ney Museum ★ Elisabet Ney was a celebrated German sculptor who carved the likenesses of philosophers, statesmen, and kings (Schopenhauer, Garibaldi, Bismarck, Ludwig II, among others). She was also a woman of ideas and was part of a circle of intellectuals in Munich. With the rise of the anti-intellectual Prussians in Germany, she and her scientist husband decided to flee Europe just before the war of 1870, first to Georgia, then to Texas. Strong-willed and independent, she moved to Austin by herself in 1891 because she was bored with life on the family farm near Hempstead, Texas. She constructed the studio that is now part of the museum and got busy creating sculptures of Texas leaders, including Stephen F. Austin and Sam Houston. She also had an immediate impact on Austin society, entertaining all the local intelligentsia, politicians, and visiting celebrities, such as William Jennings Bryan and Enrico Caruso. After her death in 1907, her friends claimed the studio-residence for a museum. It's a great way to spend an hour or two, if you have the chance. You can see many full-size plaster studies, many of which she had shipped from Germany, some that she created in Texas, including the ones for Austin and Houston. You can also see some miniatures, some photos, and some personal effects. The building itself is worth a visit, too.

304 E. 44th St. ✆ **512/458-2255.** www.elisabetney.org. Free admission. Wed-Sat 10am-5pm; Sun noon-5pm. Bus: 1 or 5.

Harry Ransom Humanities Research Center ★ 🖋 The special collections of the Harry Ransom Center (HRC) contain approximately one million rare books (including a Gutenberg Bible, one of only five complete copies in the U.S.); 30 million literary manuscripts (including those by James Joyce, Ernest Hemingway, and Tennessee Williams); five million photographs, including the world's first; and more than 100,000 works of art, with several pieces by Diego Rivera and Frida Kahlo. Most of this wealth remains the domain of scholars, although anyone can request a look at it; but parts of the collection are regularly exhibited in the gallery on the ground floor. I've seen some fascinating exhibits here, covering everything from the Beat generation to the American '20s, to the technology of the written word. Check the website for the various lectures, plays, and poetry readings held here, too, and for displays at the affiliated Leeds Gallery.

University of Texas, Harry Ransom Center, 21st and Guadalupe sts. ✆ **512/471-8944.** www.hrc.utexas.edu. Free admission. Galleries Tues-Wed and Fri 10am-5pm; Thurs 10am-7pm; Sat-Sun noon-5pm; call for reading-room hours. Closed university holidays. Bus: UT shuttle.

Hyde Park Developer Monroe Martin Shipe laid out this neighborhood of graceful houses and tree-lined streets in the 1890s, in what was at that time the northern edge of Austin. A streetcar that passed through the university campus connected Hyde Park to downtown. It stopped operating in the 1940s, and, with the rising availability of cars, the neighborhood entered a slow decline. By the 1960s, many of the houses served as rental properties for students. But in the next 10 years, young professionals started moving here, charmed by the central location and the quiet, shady streets. Today Hyde Park is one of the most popular neighborhoods in Austin. This is a good place to take a relaxing walk. Most of the houses you'll see are cottages that express a sweet and simple domesticity, while a few lean more toward grandeur. Shipe's own architecturally eclectic home can be seen at 3816 Ave. G.

Btw. E. 38th and E. 45th, Duval and Guadalupe sts. Bus: 1 or 7.

Neill-Cochran Museum House   Abner Cook, the architect-contractor responsible for the governor's mansion and many of the city's other Greek Revival mansions, built this home in 1855. It bears his trademark portico with six Doric columns and a balustrade designed with crossed sheaves of wheat. Almost all its doors, windows, shutters, and hinges are original, which is rather astonishing when you consider the structure's history: The house was used as the city's first Blind Institute in 1856 and then as a hospital for Union prisoners near the end of the Civil War. The well-maintained furnishings, dating from the 18th and 19th centuries, are eye-catching, but many people come just to see the painting of bluebonnets that helped convince legislators to designate these native blooms as the state flower.

2310 San Gabriel St. (C) **512/478-2335.** Admission $5 adults, free for children 9 and under. Tues–Sat 2–5pm; free 20-min. tours given (with admission).

Texas Memorial Museum ★ ☺ ✦   Let me tell you flat out that the two biggest attractions here are well worth the price of admission to this free museum. Both are in the lobby. One is the skeleton of the largest flying creature on record—the Texas Pterosaur. It's suspended from the ceiling and, with its 40-foot wingspan, looks very threatening (something similar to how a hawk must appear to a mouse). The other is a blue cut topaz almost the size of a fist.

Since you're at the museum already, you might want to explore a little farther. On the floor below the lobby is the main paleontology exhibit, with several more impressive skeletons. It's designed to help you conceptualize the vastness of time, something quite difficult for us mortals to grasp. And the great thing about this museum is that just about any staff person you run into will have a Ph.D. and can provide an intelligent answer to any question you have. In fact, once or twice a year the museum holds "Identification Day," when the public is invited to bring in any fossil, stone, or other natural object and find out what it is. The floor above the lobby is dedicated to Texas natural history, and has some dioramas and other exhibits. The fourth floor is an exhibition on evolution and biodiversity. It's well put together and includes several interactive displays, including a model of the HIV virus. In Texas such an exhibit could be considered controversial, which is why I find it interesting to read some of the comments left by visitors, which are collected in a binder. The gift shop carries lots of science toys.

University of Texas, 2400 Trinity St. (C) **512/471-1604.** www.texasmemorialmuseum.org. Free admission (donations appreciated). Mon–Thurs 9am–5pm; Fri 9am–4:45pm; Sat 10am–4:45pm; Sun 1–4:45pm. Closed major holidays. Bus: UT shuttle.

University of Texas at Austin   In 1883, the 221 students and eight teachers who made up the newly established University of Texas in Austin had to meet in makeshift classrooms in the town's temporary capitol. At the time, the 2 million acres of dry west Texas land that the higher educational system had been granted barely brought in 40¢ an acre for grazing. Now, nearly 50,000 students occupy 120 buildings on UT's main campus alone, and that arid West Texas land, which blew a gusher in 1923, has raked in more than $4 billion in oil money—two-thirds of it have gone directly to the UT school system.

The **Texas Union Information Center,** on the West Mall (© **512/475-6636**), is the easiest place to get information about the campus; it's open Monday through Friday from 7am to 3am (really), Saturday from 10am to 3am, and Sunday from noon to 3am. There's also an information desk on the ground floor of the Main building/ UT Tower (near 24th and Whitis). Here you can get information about tours up to the top of the tower. Down the hall from the information desk is the admissions office, which hands out brochures for a self-guided tour of campus.

Guided tours of the campus are free and start at the **Visitor Center,** which is at the corner of Guadalupe and West 25th Street (405 W. 25th St.; © **512/471-1000**), about 3 blocks from the tower. These tours are for prospective students and their families, but anyone can come. These leave weekdays at 10am and 2pm (only at 2pm in Dec and May) and Saturday at 10am. It's a lot tougher to get on the free **Moonlight Prowl Tours,** packed with amusing anecdotes of student life and campus lore, because they're held only a few evenings a month and they fill up quickly; but if you want to give it a try, log on to www.utexas.edu/tours/prowl and fill out the registration form.

See also "The Top Attractions," earlier in this chapter, for more on the LBJ Library and Museum and the Blanton Museum of Art; also, the above listings in this section for the Harry Ransom Humanities Research Center and Texas Memorial Museum; the Walking Tour of university sights section, later; and information on visiting the UT Tower in the "Organized Tours" section, later in this chapter.

Guadalupe and I-35, Martin Luther King, Jr. Blvd. and 26th St. © **512/471-3434.** www.utexas.edu. Bus: UT shuttle.

East Side

French Legation Museum ★

Occupying 2½ acres on a hilltop above downtown, this small museum with attractive grounds is a good place to pass the odd moment and explore Austin's French connection. The only difficulty is making sure that the moment falls within the museum's limited hours. The main attraction is the original house dating from 1841, the oldest surviving house in Austin still standing in its original location. Its builder was Count Alphonse Dubois de Saligny, France's representative to the fledgling republic of Texas. He sold the house to the Robinson family in 1848, and it remained in their possession for close to 100 years. The house is furnished with antiques dating from the 1840s to the 1870s. Some of the pieces actually belonged to Count Dubois and the Robinsons. At the rear of the house is a reconstructed kitchen of the era, the original having burned down. The tour takes 45 minutes and is quite enjoyable, as you'll probably have a guide all to yourself.

802 San Marcos. © **512/472-8180.** www.frenchlegationmuseum.org. Admission $5 adults, $3 seniors, $2 students/teachers, free for children 5 and under. Tours Tues–Sun 1–4pm. Bus: 4 and 18 stop nearby (at San Marcos and Seventh sts.). Go east on Seventh St., then turn left on San Marcos St.

Texas State Cemetery ★

The city's namesake, Stephen F. Austin, is the best-known resident of this East Side cemetery, established by the state in 1851. Judge Edwin Waller, who laid out the grid plan for Austin's streets and later served as the city's mayor, also rests here, as do eight former Texas governors, various fighters in

Texas's battles for independence, and Barbara Jordan, the first black woman from the South elected to the U.S. Congress (in 1996, she became the first African American to gain admittance to these grounds). Perhaps the most striking monument is one sculpted by Elisabet Ney (see "Central," above), for the tomb of Confederate general Albert Sidney Johnston, who died at the Battle of Shiloh.

The narrow drive that runs through the cemetery is actually a state highway. In the 1990s, the cemetery grounds were refurbished and extensively landscaped. This was the pet project of Lt. Gov. Bob Bullock, a politician who was nothing if not resourceful. Unable to get funding from the state legislature, Bullock got the driveway designated as a highway so he could allocate funds from the Texas Department of Transportation. When you pay a visit, you can see the highway signs at the entrances. And you can check out a rather fancy tomb with Mr. Bullock's name on it. There are two self-guided-tour pamphlets at the visitor center/museum, which is designed to resemble the long barracks at the Alamo.

909 Navasota St. © **512/463-0605.** www.cemetery.state.tx.us. Free admission. Grounds daily 8am–5pm; visitor center Mon–Fri 8am–5pm. Bus: 4 and 18 stop nearby.

Austin Outdoors
LAKES
Highland Lakes   The six dams built by the Lower Colorado River Authority in the late 1930s through the early 1950s not only controlled the flooding that had plagued the areas surrounding Texas's Colorado River (not to be confused with the river of the same name that flows through the Grand Canyon), but also transformed the waterway into a sparkling chain of lakes, stretching some 150 miles northwest of Austin. The narrowest of them, Lady Bird Lake, is also the closest to downtown. The heart of urban recreation in Austin, its banks are lined by trails and a shoreline park. Lake Austin, just upstream, divides West Austin from Westlake Hills. On its banks is Emma Long Park (see "Parks & Gardens," below). Next in the series is Lake Travis, the longest lake in the chain. It offers the most possibilities for boating and general recreation. Together with the other Highland Lakes—Marble Falls, LBJ, Inks, and Buchanan, some of which are discussed in chapter 17—these compose the largest concentration of freshwater lakes in Texas. See "Staying Active," later in this chapter, for activity and equipment-rental suggestions.

MOUNTAINS
Covert Park at Mount Bonnell ★   For the best views of the city, Lake Austin, and some of the Hill Country stretching out westward, take a drive up to this hilltop park. It's 785 feet tall and the highest point in Austin. The oldest tourist attraction in town, it has also long been a favorite spot for romantic trysts, and rumor has it that any couple who climbed the 106 stone steps to the top together would fall in love (an emotion often confused with exhaustion). The peak was named for George W. Bonnell, Sam Houston's commissioner of Indian affairs in 1836, while the far-from-secret park at the summit gets its moniker from Frank M. Covert, Jr., who donated the land to the city in 1939.

3800 Mt. Bonnell Rd. No phone. Free admission. Daily 5am–10pm. Take Mt. Bonnell Rd. 1 mile past the west end of W. 35th St.

NATURE PRESERVES
For information on **Wild Basin Wilderness Preserve,** see "Organized Tours," later in this chapter.

City of Austin Nature Preserves   Highlights of the remarkably diverse group of natural habitats Austin boasts in its city-run nature preserves include the following: **Blunn Creek** (1100 block of St. Edward's Dr.) is 40 acres of upland woods and meadows traversed by a spring-fed creek. One of the two lookout areas is made of compacted volcanic ash. Spelunkers will like **Goat Cave** (3900 Deer Lane), which is honeycombed with limestone caves and sinkholes. You can arrange for cave tours by phoning the **Austin Nature Center** (✆ 512/327-8181). Lovely **Mayfield Park** (3505 W. 35th St.) directly abuts the Barrow Brook Cove of Lake Austin. Peacocks and hens roam freely around lily ponds, and trails cross over bridges in oak and juniper woods. Visitors to the rock-walled ramada (a shaded shelter) at the **Zilker Preserve** (Barton Springs Rd. and Loop 1), with its meadows, streams, and cliff, can look out over downtown Austin. All the preserves are maintained in a primitive state with natural surface trails and no restrooms. The preserves are free and open daily from dawn to dusk. For additional information, including directions, phone ✆ **512/327-7723,** or log on to www.ci.austin.tx.us/preserves.

Westcave Preserve   If you don't like the weather in one part of Westcave Preserve, you might like it better in another: Up to a 25° difference in temperature has been recorded between the highest area of this beautiful natural habitat, an arid Hill Country scrub, and the lowest, a lush woodland spread across a canyon floor. Because the ecosystem here is so delicate, the 30 acres on the Pedernales River may be entered only by guided tour. Reservations are taken for weekday visits, while on weekends, the first 30 people to show up at the allotted times are allowed in.

Star Rte. 1, Dripping Springs. ✆ **830/825-3442.** www.westcave.org. Sat–Sun for tours at 10am, noon, 2, and 4pm (weather permitting). $5 adults, $2 children 11 and under, or $15 per family. Take Hwy. 71 to Ranch Rd. 3238. Follow the signs 15 miles to Hamilton Pool, across the Pedernales River Bridge from the preserve.

OUTDOOR ART

Philosophers' Rock   Glenna Goodacre's bronze sculpture of three of Austin's most recognized personalities from midcentury—naturalist Roy Bedichek, raconteur J. Frank Dobie, and historian Walter Prescott Webb—captures the essence of the three friends who used to chew the fat together at Barton Springs Pool. No heroic posing here: Two of the three are wearing bathing trunks, which reveal potbellies, wrinkles, and sagging muscles, and all three are sitting down in mid-discussion. The casual friendliness of the pose and the intelligence of the men's expressions have made this piece, installed in 1994, an Austin favorite.

Zilker Park, 2201 Barton Springs Rd., just outside the entrance to Barton Springs Pool.

Stevie Ray Vaughan Statue   In contrast to the Philosophers' Rock (see above), Ralph Roehming's bronze tribute to Austin guitarist Stevie Ray Vaughan is artificial and awkward. Although he's wearing his habitual flat-brimmed hat and poncho, the stiffly posed Stevie Ray looks more like a frontiersman with a gun than a rock star with a guitar. But his devoted fans don't seem to mind, as evidenced by the flowers and devotions that almost always can be found at the foot of the statue.

South side of Lady Bird Lake, adjacent to Auditorium Shores.

PARKS & GARDENS

Emma Long Metropolitan Park   More than 1,100 acres of woodland and a mile of shore along Lake Austin make Emma Long Park—named after the first woman to sit on Austin's city council—a most appealing space. You'll find boat ramps, a fishing dock, and a protected swimming area, guarded by lifeguards on summer weekends. This is the only city park to offer camping, with permits ($10 for open camping, $20 utility camping in addition to entry fee) available on a first-come, first-served basis. If you hike through the stands of oak, ash, and juniper to an elevation of 1,000 feet, you'll get a view of the city spread out before you. Note that the park closes whenever its maximum capacity is reached.

1706 City Park Rd. ℂ **512/346-1831** or 346-3807. Admission $5 per vehicle Mon–Thurs; $10 Fri–Sun and holidays. Daily 7am–10pm. Exit I-35 at 290 W., then go west (street names will change to Koenig, Allendale, Northland, and FM 2222) to City Park Rd. (near Loop 360). Turn south (left) and drive 6¼ miles to park entrance.

Zilker Botanical Garden ★ ☺ There's bound to be something blooming at the Zilker Botanical Garden from March to October, but no matter what time of year you visit, you'll find this a soothing outdoor oasis in which to spend some time. The Oriental Garden, created by the landscape architect Isamu Taniguchi when he was 70 years old, is particularly peaceful. Be sure to ask someone at the garden center to point out how Taniguchi landscaped the word "Austin" into a series of ponds in the design. A butterfly garden attracts gorgeous winged visitors during April and October migrations, and you can poke and prod the many plants in the herb garden to get them to yield their fragrances. One-hundred-million-year-old dinosaur tracks, discovered on the grounds in the early 1990s, are part of the 1.5-acre Hartman Prehistoric Garden, which includes plants from the Cretaceous Period and a 13-foot bronze sculpture of an Ornithomimus dinosaur.

2220 Barton Springs Rd. ℂ **512/477-8672.** www.zilkergarden.org. Free admission. Grounds dawn–dusk. Garden center Mon–Fri 8:30am–4pm; Sat 10am–5pm (Jan–Feb 1–5pm); Sun 1–5pm (sometimes open earlier Sat–Sun for special garden shows; phone ahead). Bus: 30.

Zilker Park ★ ☺ Comprising 347 acres, the first 40 of which were donated to the city by the wealthy German immigrant for whom the park is named, this is Austin's favorite public playground. Its centerpiece is Barton Springs Pool (see "The Top Attractions," earlier in this chapter), but visitors and locals also flock to the Zilker Botanical Garden, the Austin Nature Preserves, and the Umlauf Sculpture Garden & Museum, all described in this chapter. See the "Especially for Kids" and "Staying Active" sections for details about the Austin Nature and Science Center, the Zilker Zephyr Miniature Train, and Lady Bird Lake canoe rentals. In addition to its athletic fields (nine for soccer, one for rugby, and two multiuse), the park hosts a 9-hole disk (Frisbee) golf course and a sand volleyball court.

2201 Barton Springs Rd. ℂ **512/476-9044.** www.ci.austin.tx.us/zilker. Free admission. Daily 5am–10pm. Bus: 30.

ESPECIALLY FOR KIDS

The **Bob Bullock Texas State History Museum** and the **Texas Memorial Museum,** both described in earlier sections, are child-friendly, but outdoor attractions are still Austin's biggest draw for children. There's lots of room for children to splash around at **Barton Springs,** and even youngsters who thought bats were creepy are likely to be converted on further acquaintance with the critters. In addition, the following attractions are especially geared toward children.

Austin Children's Museum ★ This museum will be of interest to children up to 12 years old. It's located in a large space by the trendy 2nd Street shopping district.

Tots enjoy the low-tech but creative playscapes; older kids take on a variety of "creation stations." There's a safe two-story slide and a tinkerer's workshop for those actively inclined, and daily story times at 11am, 1, and 3pm for those who aren't quite so active. Parents will be amused at the replica Austin city landscapes, including the recently introduced Rising Star Ranch, where a Hill Country pond is stocked with wooden musical frogs.

Dell Discovery Center, 201 Colorado St. ✆ **512/472-2499.** www.austinkids.org. General admission $6.50, $4.50 for children 12–23 months, free for children 11 months and under. Tues–Sat 10am–5pm; Sun noon–5pm; donations only Wed 5–8pm, free Sun 4–5pm. Closed Mon and some holidays. Bus: 10, 12, 15, 16, or 64.

Austin Nature and Science Center ★ Bats, bees, and crystal caverns are among the subjects of the Discovery Lab at this museum in the 80-acre Nature Center, which features lots of interactive exhibits. The tortoises, lizards, porcupine, and vultures in the Animal Exhibits—among more than 90 orphaned or injured creatures brought here from the wild—also hold kids' attention. An Eco-Detective trail highlights pond-life awareness. The Dino Pit, with its replicas of Texas fossils and dinosaur tracks, lures budding paleontologists. A variety of specialty camps, focusing on everything from caving to astronomy, are offered from late May through August.

Zilker Park, 301 Nature Center Dr. ✆ **512/327-8181.** www.ci.austin.tx.us/ansc. Donations requested; occasional special exhibits charge separately. Mon–Sat 9am–5pm; Sun noon–5pm. Closed July 4th, Thanksgiving, and Dec 25. Bus: 30.

Austin Zoo This small zoo, some 14 miles southwest of downtown, may not feature the state-of-the-jungle habitats of larger facilities, but it's easy to get up close and personal with the critters here. Most of the animal residents, who range from turkeys and potbellied pigs to marmosets and tigers, were mistreated, abandoned, or illegally imported before they found a home here. It costs $2.50 to board the 1½-mile miniature train for a scenic Hill Country ride, which lets you peer at some of the shyer animals. There are no food concessions here, just plenty of picnic tables.

10807 Rawhide Trail. ✆ **512/288-1490.** www.austinzoo.org. Admission $8 adults, $6 seniors, $5 children ages 2–12, free for children under age 2. Daily 10am–5:30pm. Closed Thanksgiving and Dec 25. Take Hwy. 290 W. to Circle Dr., turn right, go 1½ miles to Rawhide Trail, and turn right.

Splash! Into the Edwards Aquifer The Edwards Aquifer, Austin's main source of water, is fed by a variety of underground creeks filtered through a large layer of limestone. You'll feel as though you're entering one of this vast ecosystem's sinkholes when you walk into the dimly lit enclosure—formerly the bathhouse at Barton Springs pool—where a variety of interactive displays grab kids' attention. Young visitors can make it rain on the city, identify water bugs, or peer through a periscope at swimmers. Although the focus is on the evils of pollution, the agenda is by no means heavy-handed.

Zilker Park, 2201 Barton Springs Rd. ✆ **512/481-1466.** www.ci.austin.tx.us/splash. Free admission. Tues–Sat 10am–5pm; Sun noon–5pm. Bus: 30 (Barton Creek Sq.).

Zilker Zephyr Miniature Train Take a scenic 25-minute ride through Zilker Park on a narrow-gauge, light-rail miniature train, which takes you at a leisurely pace along Barton Creek and Lady Bird Lake. The train departs approximately every hour on the hour during the week and every half-hour on the weekend, weather permitting.

Zilker Park, 2100 Barton Springs Rd. (just across from the Barton Springs Pool). ✆ **512/478-8286.** Admission $3 adults, $2 children 11 and under and seniors, free for infants (under 1) on guardian's lap. Daily 10am–5pm. Bus: 30.

SPECIAL-INTEREST SIGHTSEEING

African-American Heritage

The many contributions of Austin's African-American community are highlighted at **George Washington Carver Museum and Cultural Center,** 1165 Angelina St. (© 512/472-4809; www.ci.austin.tx.us/carver), the first museum in Texas devoted to African-American history. Of interest to many visitors will be its permanent exhibition on the meaning and traditions of "Juneteenth." This is a holiday in Texas, usually celebrated with a parade, picnic, and barbecue, and in some places with a blues concert or hymns. It commemorates June 19, 1865, when Union general Gordon Granger read the Emancipation Proclamation to the public in Galveston, the first time in Texas that the slaves heard of their freedom. Over time, this celebration has become increasingly popular and has spread to other parts of the country, usually through Black Texans who have moved outside the state. Another exhibit, which might still be in place for late 2011 and some of 2012, portrays Austin's African-American community through its neighborhoods, churches, and families.

Less than 2 blocks from the Carver, on the corner of Hackberry and San Bernard streets, stands one of those churches, the **Wesley United Methodist Church.** Established at the end of the Civil War, it was one of the leading black churches in Texas. Diagonally across the street, the **Zeta Phi Beta Sorority,** Austin's first black Greek letter house, occupies the Thompson House, built in 1877, which is also the archival center for the Texas chapter of the sorority. Nearby, at the **State Cemetery** (see "More Attractions," earlier in this chapter), you can visit the gravesite of congresswoman and civil rights leader Barbara Jordan, the first African American to be buried here.

In 1863, during the time of the Civil War, a black freeman, of which there were few in Texas, settled down on the east side of Austin and built a small cabin for himself and his family. He built it near the present-day intersection of I-35 and East 11th Street. His name was Henry Green Madison, and during Reconstruction, he became Austin's first African-American city councilmember. The cabin he built was preserved more by accident than by design and, in 1973, was donated to the city, which moved it to its present site in nearby Rosewood Park at 2300 Rosewood Ave. (© 512/472-6838). There you can see the **Henry G. Madison** cabin and how simple and small it must have been for his family of eight. A contemporary of Madison was Charles Clark, a slave who was emancipated after the Civil War and in 1871 founded a small utopian community of freed blacks just to the west of Austin around what is now West 10th Street. It was called Clarksville and is now a mostly white neighborhood still known by that name.

For a more up-to-date look at the Austin scene, visit **Mitchie's Fine Art & Gift Gallery,** 7801 N. Lamar Blvd. (© 512/323-6901; www.mitchie.com).

STROLLING THE UNIVERSITY OF TEXAS

No ivory tower, the University of Texas is fully integrated into Austin's economic and cultural life. To explore the vast main campus is to glimpse the city's future as well as its past. Here, state-of-the-art structures—including information kiosks that can play the school's team songs—sit next to fine examples of 19th-century architecture. The following tour points out the most interesting spots on campus. You'll probably want to drive or take a bus between some of the first seven sights. (Parking limitations were taken into account in this initial portion of the circuit.) For a walking-only tour, begin at stop 8; also note that stops 2, 6, 12, and 20 are discussed earlier in this chapter, and stop 9 is detailed in the "Organized Tours" section, below.

WALKING TOUR OF THE UNIVERSITY OF TEXAS

START:	**The Arno Nowotny Building.**
FINISH:	**The Harry Ransom Center.**
TIME:	**2 hours, not including food breaks or museum visits.**
BEST TIMES:	**On the weekends, when the campus is less crowded, more parking is available, and the UT Tower is open.**
WORST TIMES:	**Morning and midday during the week when classes are in session and parking is impossible to find. (*Beware:* Those tow-away zone signs mean business.)**

In 1839, the Congress of the Republic of Texas ordered a site set aside for the establishment of a "university of the first class" in Austin. Some 40 years later, when the flagship of the new University of Texas system opened, its first two buildings went up on that original 40-acre plot, dubbed College Hill. Although there were attempts to establish master-design plans for the university from the turn of the 20th century onward, they were only carried out in bits and pieces until 1930, when money from an earlier oil strike on UT land allowed the school to begin building in earnest. Between 1930 and 1945, consulting architect Paul Cret put his mark on 19 university buildings, most showing the influence of his education at Paris's Ecole des Beaux-Arts. If the entire 357-acre campus will never achieve stylistic unity, its earliest section has a grace and cohesion that make it a delight to stroll through.

Though it begins at the oldest building owned by the university, this tour commences far from the original campus. At the frontage road of I-35 and the corner of Martin Luther King, Jr. Boulevard, pull into the parking lot of:

1 The Arno Nowotny Building

In the 1850s, several state-run asylums for the mentally ill and the physically handicapped arose on the outskirts of Austin. One of these was the State Asylum for the Blind, built by Abner Cook around 1856. The Italianate-style structure soon became better known as the headquarters and barracks of General Custer, who had been sent to Austin in 1865 to reestablish order after the Civil War (in shape and size, it actually resembles a barracks). Incorporated into the university and restored for its centennial celebration, the building is now used for administration.

Take Martin Luther King, Jr. Boulevard to Red River, then drive north to the:

2 LBJ Library and Museum

This library and museum (see "The Top Attractions," earlier in this chapter) offers another rare on-campus parking lot. (You'll want to leave your car here

Walking Tour: The University of Texas

Take a Break

1 Arno Nowotny Building
2 LBJ Library and Museum
3 Performing Arts Center
4 Darrell K. Royal/Texas Memorial Stadium
5 Art Building
6 Texas Memorial Museum
7 Santa Rita No. 1
8 Littlefield Memorial Fountain
9 Main Building and Tower
10 Garrison Hall

11 Battle Hall
12 Flawn Academic Center
13 Hogg Auditorium
14 Battle Oaks
15 Littlefield Home
16 Texas Student Union Building
17 The Drag
18 Goldsmith Hall
19 Sutton Hall
20 Harry Ransom Center

while you see sights 3–6.) The first presidential library to be built on a university campus, the huge travertine marble structure oversees a beautifully landscaped 14-acre complex. Among the museum's exhibits is a seven-eighths-scale replica of the Oval Office as it looked when the Johnsons occupied the White House. In the adjoining Sid Richardson Hall are the Lyndon B. Johnson School of Public Affairs and the Barker Texas History Center, housing the world's most extensive collection of Texas memorabilia.

Stroll down the library steps across East Campus Drive to 23rd Street, where, next to the large Burleson bells on your right, you'll see the university's $41-million:

3 Performing Arts Center

This arts center includes the 3,000-seat Bass Concert Hall, the 700-seat Bates Recital Hall, and other College of the Fine Arts auditoriums. The state-of-the-art acoustics at the Bass Concert Hall enhance the sounds of the largest tracker organ in the United States. Linking contemporary computer technology with a design that goes back some 2,000 years, it has 5,315 pipes—some of them 16 feet tall—and weighs 48,000 pounds.

From the same vantage point, to the left looms the huge:

4 Darrell K. Royal/Texas Memorial Stadium

The first of the annual UT–Texas A&M Thanksgiving Day games was played here in 1924. In a drive to finance the original Memorial Stadium, female students sold their hair, male students sold their blood, and UT alum Lutcher Stark matched every $10,000 they raised with $1,000 of his own funds. The upper deck was added in 1972; the end zone was enclosed and the stadium enlarged again in 2008. In the 1990s the name change to honor legendary Longhorns football coach Darrell K. Royal angered some who wanted the stadium to remain a memorial to Texas veterans, and confused others who wondered if Coach Royal was still alive (he is).

Continue west on 23rd; at the corner of San Jacinto, a long staircase marks the entrance to the:

5 Art Building

This used to be the home of the Blanton Museum (see "The Top Attractions," earlier in this chapter); now it is used for classes and to exhibit student art shows.

Walk a short distance north on San Jacinto. A stampeding group of bronze mustangs will herald your arrival at the:

6 Texas Memorial Museum

This monumental art moderne building was designed by Paul Cret, and ground was broken for the institution by Franklin Roosevelt in 1936. Once home to the capitol's original zinc goddess of liberty, which was moved to the Bob Bullock Texas State History Museum along with other historic treasures, this museum now focuses solely on the natural sciences (see "More Attractions," earlier in this chapter).

Exit the building and make your way back to the parking lot of the LBJ Library and your car. Retrace your original route along Red River until you reach Martin Luther

King, Jr. Boulevard. Make a right turn, and at the corner of San Jacinto, on your right you'll see:

7 Santa Rita No. 1

No. 1 is an oil rig transported here from West Texas, where black gold first spewed forth from it on land belonging to the university in 1923. The money was distributed between the University of Texas system, which got the heftier two-thirds, and the Texas A&M system. This windfall has helped make UT the second richest university in the country, after Harvard.

Continue on to University Avenue and turn left. There are public parking spaces around 21st Street and University, where you'll begin your walking tour at the:

8 Littlefield Memorial Fountain

This fountain was built in 1933. Pompeo Coppini, sculptor of the bronze centerpiece, believed that the rallying together of the nation during World War I marked the final healing of the wounds caused by the Civil War. The fountain's style is way over-the-top in a Village People sort of way. The winged goddess Columbia rides on the bow of a battleship sailing across the ocean—represented by three rearing sea horses—to the aid of the Allies. On the deck are two figures representing the Army and the Navy. This fountain is at the beginning of the South Mall. Behind you stands the state capitol.

Directly ahead is the:

9 Main Building and Tower

Walking down the shaded mall, you'll pass several more bronze statues, climb a short flight of stairs, and see before you the university's famous tower. The 307-foot-high structure was created by Paul Cret in 1937. It's a fine example of the Beaux Arts style, particularly stunning when lit to celebrate a Longhorn victory. On the facade, you can read the Inscription: "Ye shall know the Truth . . . and . . . make you free." In the 1970s, the student council proposed that it should be changed to "Money Talks," but the Board of Regents declined. In the top of the tower is a 56-bell carillon, the largest in Texas, which is played on Mondays, Wednesdays, and Fridays for 10 minutes from 12:50 to 1pm. It was from this same tower that Charles Whitman shot and killed 16 people and wounded 31 more on August 1, 1966. The shooting spree ended when he was shot by a policeman. Closed off to the public in 1975 after a series of suicide leaps from its observation deck, the tower reopened for supervised ascensions in 1999 (see "Organized Tours," below). If you climb the staircase on the east (right) side of the tower to the stone balustrade, you can see the dramatic sweep of the entire eastern section of campus, including the LBJ Library.

Sharing the South Plaza with the tower is:

10 Garrison Hall

Garrison Hall is named for one of the earliest members of the UT faculty and is home to the department of history. Important names from Texas's past—Austin, Travis, Houston, and Lamar—are set here in stone. The walls just under the building's eaves are decorated with cattle brands; look for the carved cow skulls and cactuses on the balcony window on the north side.

11 Battle Hall

This building is regarded by many as the campus's most beautiful. Designed in 1911 by Cass Gilbert, architect of the U.S. Supreme Court building, the hall was the first to be done in the Spanish Renaissance style that came to characterize so many of the structures on this section of campus (note the terra-cotta–tiled roof and broadly arched windows). On the second floor, you can see the grand reading room of what is now the Architecture and Planning Library.

From Battle Hall cross the West Mall to:

12 Flawn Academic Center

This building holds the undergraduate technology center, but on the fourth floor is the Leeds Gallery, which often has temporary exhibits. It's also the home to a replica of Erle Stanley Gardner's study. He was a mystery writer and the creator of Perry Mason. In front of the building, Charles Umlauf's *The Torch Bearers* symbolizes the passing of knowledge from one generation to the next.

Behind the Academic Center is:

13 The Hogg Auditorium

This auditorium is another Paul Cret building, designed in the same monumental art moderne mode as his earlier Texas Memorial Museum.

A few steps farther along, you'll come to the trees known as the:

14 Battle Oaks

The three oldest members of this small grove are said to predate the city of Austin itself. They survived the destruction of most of the grove to build a Civil War fortress and a later attempt to displace them with a new Biology Building. It was this last, near-fatal skirmish that earned them their name. Legend has it that Dr. W. J. Battle, a professor of classics and an early university president, holed up in the largest oak with a rifle to protect the three ancient trees.

Cater-cornered from the oak trees is the:

15 Littlefield Home

This mansion was built in high Victorian style in 1894. Major George W. Littlefield, a wealthy developer, cattle rancher, and banker, bequeathed more than $1 million to the university on the condition that its campus not be moved to land that his rival, George W. Brackenridge, had donated. The ostentatious mansion is flanked by a magnificent deodar cedar, which Littlefield had shipped over from its native Himalayas.

Next door to Hogg Auditorium is:

16 Texas Student Union Building

UT's student union building is yet another Paul Cret creation. A staircase leads down to the ground floor, where a long corridor passes by a large food court, eventually ending in the front lobby, where you'll see the information desk and off of which is the **Cactus Cafe,** a popular coffeehouse and music venue (see chapter 15). This bustling student center hosts everything from a bowling alley to a formal ballroom.

17 The Drag

As its name suggests, the Drag is Austin's main off-campus pedestrian strip. Bookstores, fast-food restaurants, and shops line the thoroughfare, which is usually crammed with students trying to grab a bite or a book between classes. On weekends, the pedestrian mall set aside for the 23rd Street Renaissance Market overflows with crafts vendors.

Across the West Mall, opposite the student union stands:

18 Goldsmith Hall

This is one of two adjacent buildings where architecture classes are held. Also designed by Paul Cret, this hall has beautifully worn slate floors and a shaded central courtyard.

Walk through the courtyard and go down a few steps. To your right is:

19 Sutton Hall

This hall was designed by Cass Gilbert in 1918 and is part of the School of Architecture. Like his Battle Hall, it is gracefully Mediterranean, with terracotta moldings, a red-tile roof, and large Palladian windows.

Enter Sutton Hall through double doors at the front and exit straight through the back. You are now facing the:

20 Harry Ransom Center

The Humanities Research Center (HRC) is housed here. The satirical portrait of a rich American literary archive in A. S. Byatt's best-selling novel *Possession* is widely acknowledged to be based on HRC. Walk through the doors to the gallery to view the center's rare Gutenberg Bible, one of just five complete copies in the U.S. You can also see what temporary exhibit is on show.

ORGANIZED TOURS

See chapter 15 for details on touring the *Austin City Limits* studio.

An Amphibious Tour

Austin Duck Adventures   It's a hoot—or should I say a quack? Whether or not you opt to use the duck call whistle included in the tour price to blow at the folks you pass in the street, you'll get a kick out of this combination land-and-sea tour. You'll be transported in a six-wheel-drive amphibious vehicle (originally created for British troops during the Cold War) through Austin's historic downtown and the scenic west side before splashing into Lake Austin. Comedy writers helped devise the script for this 1½-hour tour, so it's funny as well as informative.

Boarding in front of the Austin Convention and Visitors Bureau, 209 E. Sixth St. ✆ **512/4-SPLASH** (477-5274). www.austinducks.com. Tours $26 adults, $24 seniors and students, $16 ages 3–12. Daily tours; times change seasonally; call to check schedule.

Boat Tours

Capital Cruises   From March through October, Capital Cruises plies Lady Bird Lake with electric-powered boats heading out on a number of popular tours. The bat cruises are especially big in summer, when warm nights are perfect for the enjoyable and educational hour-long excursions. The high point is seeing thousands of bats stream out from under their Congress Avenue Bridge roost. Dinner cruises, featuring fajitas from the Hyatt Regency's La Vista restaurant, are also fun on a balmy evening, and the afternoon sightseeing tours are a nice way to while away an hour on the weekend.

Hyatt Regency Lady Bird Lake boat dock. © **512/480-9264.** www.capitalcruises.com. Bat and sightseeing cruises $10 adults, $8 seniors, $5 children 3–12; dinner cruises (including tax and tip) $27–$81, depending on options. Bat cruise daily a half-hour before sunset (call ahead for exact time), weather permitting; sightseeing cruise Sat–Sun at 1pm; dinner cruise Fri–Sun at 6pm. Reservations required for dinner cruises; for bat and sightseeing cruises, show up at the dock a minimum of 30 min. in advance.

Lone Star Riverboat   You'll set out against a backdrop of Austin's skyline and the state capitol on this riverboat cruise and move upstream past Barton Creek and Zilker Park. Along the way, you'll glimpse 100-foot-high cliffs and million-dollar estates. These scenic tours, accompanied by knowledgeable narrators, last 1½ hours. Slightly shorter bat-watching tours leave around half an hour before sunset, so call ahead to check.

South shore of Lady Bird Lake, btw. the Congress Ave. and S. First St. bridges, just next to the Hyatt. © **512/327-1388.** www.lonestarriverboat.com. Scenic and bat tours $10 adults, $8 seniors, $7 children 4–12. Scenic tours Sat–Sun 1pm Mar–Oct only. Bat tours nightly Apr–Oct only; call for exact times.

Segway Tours

Gliding Revolution   These folks offer tours of downtown or East Austin. Tour durations vary between 1 and 3 hours. The company has an office in the Holiday Inn Town Lake on the north shore of Lady Bird Lake by I-35. It also rents kayaks.

20 I-35 N. © **512/699-6051.** www.glidingrevolution.com. Tours $65–$75 adults. Daily tours; call to check schedule.

Segway Nation   This company offers tours of the capitol and downtown areas with various durations and prices, ranging from a 1½-hour tour for $50 to a 2½-hour tour for $65 to $75. Inquire at the Austin Visitor Center for possible discount rates.

1108 Lavaca. © **512/495-9250.** www.segwaynationinc.com. Tours $50–$75 adults. Daily tours; call to check schedule.

Van Tour

Austin Overtures   This 90-minute tour of the city takes you west into the Hill Country and through the heart of central Austin. You can check departure times, make reservations, and buy tickets at the visitor center. Or you can make a reservation on the company's website. This tour is a little lighter on the comedy than the Duck tours; it covers more ground, and it gives more information.

Boarding in front of the Austin Convention and Visitors Bureau, 209 E. Sixth St. © **512/659-9478.** www.austinovertures.com. Tours $25 adults, $21 seniors and military, $17 ages 12 and under. Daily tours; call to check schedule.

Walking Tours

Austin Ghost Tours   If you favor activities that are likely to keep you from sleeping, these tours are for you. Not only are the various outings held in the evening, but they're all concerned with ghouls. The **Ghosts of Austin Downtown Walking Tour** explores the stories of those that even death couldn't separate from downtown, while the tavern-crawl **Haunted Sixth Street Tour** capitalizes on the spirits that liked their spirits (and visitors who like both the spectral and the alcoholic manifestations). Austin Ghost Tours has also teamed up with the Austin Museum of Art for a special 90-minute **Haunted History Walking Tour,** featuring the museum exhibit "The Disembodied Spirit," the Wooten building, the Old Miller Opera House, and the capitol. A variety of other tours are available as well, so be sure to check the website, and then call ahead to make the required reservations.

Tour departure points vary; check ahead. © **512/853-9826.** www.austinghosttours.com. 90-min. Ghosts of Austin and 2-hr. Tours $15–$20. Tour schedules vary; call or check the website.

University of Texas Tower Observation Deck Tour Off-limits to the public for nearly a quarter of a century, the infamous observation deck of the UT Tower (see "Strolling the University of Texas," earlier in this chapter)—where crazed gunman Charles Whitman went on a deadly shooting spree in 1966—was remodeled with a webbed dome and reopened in 1999. Billed as tours, these excursions to the top of the tower are really supervised visits, although a guide gives a short, informative spiel and stays on hand to answer questions. Frankly, it would probably be better if these visits—about 40 minutes long—were half as long and half as expensive (I saw lots of people looking bored after about 10 minutes).

Deck tours are available by reservation only. At present the tower is closed for repairs and isn't expected to open until spring 2011. The tour schedules will probably change. Check the website or phone the numbers listed below.

Note: You are permitted to bring along a camera, binoculars, or a camcorder to take advantage of the observation deck's spectacular, 360-degree view of the city and environs, but you must leave behind everything else, including purses, camera bags, tripods, strollers, and so forth. (Lockers are available at the Texas Union for $1.)

UT Campus, Texas Union Bldg. © **877/475-6633** (outside Austin) or 512/475-6633. www.utexas.edu/tower. Tours $6. Tours are not offered Dec–Feb. Schedules vary according to the academic schedule; late May to late Aug, tours may be offered on Thurs–Fri evenings.

Wild Basin Wilderness Preserve The varied menu of guided and self-guided tours at this preserve on a lovely 227-acre peninsula will keep nature and wildlife lovers happy, night and day. Native plants, birds, arrowheads, and snakes are among the topics covered (though not at the same time) during daylight walks. After dark, there are either moonlight tours (coinciding with the full moon) or stargazing tours 3 or 4 days after the new moon. Call ahead or check the website for exact dates.

805 N. Capital of Texas Hwy. © **512/327-7622.** www.wildbasin.org. Preserve admission $3 adults, $2 seniors and ages 5–12; 2-hour tours $3 adults, $2 ages 5–12, free for children 4 and under. Preserve daily dawn–dusk; office daily 9am–5pm, Sat–Sun 8am–3pm. Hiking tours every weekend, weather permitting; stargazing tours twice monthly, weather permitting, generally 8 or 8:30 to 9:30 or 10pm.

Self-Guided Tours

In addition to the guided walking tours offered by the **Austin Convention and Visitors Bureau** (see below), the ACVB sells MP3 audio tours for $15. These come with a map to guide you and include mellow background music as you navigate from one stop to the next. One tour covers the main attractions of Austin's downtown. The other tour takes you around the most popular live-performance venues in the downtown area.

The visitor center also offers seven self-guided tour booklets, which are free. Five tours (Bremond Block, Hyde Park, Congress Ave. and E. Sixth St., Texas State Cemetery, and Oakwood Cemetery) require foot power alone. The other two (West Austin and O. Henry Trail) combine walking and driving. They make for interesting reading even if you don't have time to follow the routes.

Guided Walks

Enjoyable guided walking **tours** ★★ are offered free of charge by the **Austin Convention and Visitors Bureau (ACVB; ℂ 866/GO-AUSTIN** [462-8784] or 512/478-0098; www.austintexas.org). There are two tours to choose from. Both are downtown; both last approximately 90 minutes; and both depart punctually from the south entrance of the capitol, weather permitting. The tour of the historic Bremond Block takes place on Saturday and Sunday at 11am. The tour of Congress Avenue and East Sixth Street takes place on Thursday, Friday, and Saturday at 9am, and on Sunday at 2pm. Make reservations for the tours at least 24 hours in advance. You can do so by calling the visitor center or by going to the website.

STAYING ACTIVE

BIKING   A city that has a "bicycle coordinator" on its payroll must take biking seriously. Austin publishes a map of city bike routes for the benefit of local bike commuters and those visitors who want to pedal around town. You can download a PDF version of the map or order a hard copy by going to this website: www.ci.austin.tx.us/bicycle/bikemap.htm.

If you want to ride on trails, you have your choice of the mellow hike-and-bike trail around Lady Bird Lake (10 miles), or the more challenging Barton Creek Greenbelt (7.8 miles). Contact **Austin Parks and Recreation,** 200 S. Lamar Blvd. (ℂ **512/974-6700;** www.ci.austin.tx.us/parks), for more information on these and other bike trails. There is also a paved **Veloway,** a 3.1-mile paved loop in Slaughter Creek Metropolitan Park in far South Austin. It is devoted exclusively to bicyclists and in-line skaters.

You can rent bikes and get maps and other information from **University Cyclery,** 2901 N. Lamar Blvd. (ℂ **512/474-6696;** www.universitycyclery.com). A number of downtown hotels rent or provide free bicycles to their guests. For information on weekly road rides, contact the **Austin Cycling Association,** P.O. Box 5993, Austin, TX 78763 (ℂ **512/282-7413;** www.austincycling.org), which also publishes a monthly newsletter, *Southwest Cycling News,* though only local calls or e-mails are returned. For rougher mountain-bike routes, try the **Austin Ridge Riders.** Their website, www.austinridgeriders.com, has the latest contact information.

BIRD-WATCHING   Endangered golden-cheeked warblers and black-capped vireos are among the many species you might spot around Austin. The **Travis Audubon Society** (ℂ **512/926-8751;** www.travisaudubon.org) organizes regular birding trips and even has a rare-bird hot line.

Texas Parks and Wildlife publishes *The Guide to Austin-Area Birding Sites,* which points you to the best urban perches. You should be able to pick up a copy at the Austin Visitor Center or at the offices of any of Austin's parks and preserves (see "More Attractions," earlier in this chapter). Avid birders should also enjoy *Adventures with a Texas Naturalist,* by Roy Bedichek. The author is one of the three friends depicted on the Philosophers' Rock, also listed in the "More Attractions" section, p. 211.

CANOEING   You can rent canoes at **Zilker Park,** 2000 Barton Springs Rd. (ℂ **512/478-3852;** www.fastair.com/zilker), for $10 an hour or $40 all day (daily from Apr–Sept; only weekends, holidays, weather permitting, from Oct–Mar). **Capital Cruises,** Hyatt Regency boat dock (© **512/480-9264;** www.capitalcruises. com), also offers hourly rentals on Lady Bird Lake. If your paddling skills are a bit rusty, check out the instructional courses of UT's **Recreational Sports Outdoor Program** (© 512/471-3116).

FISHING Git Bit (© **512/773-7401;** www.gitbitfishing.com) provides guide service for half- or full-day bass-fishing trips on Lake Travis.

GOLF For information about Austin's five municipal golf courses and to set up tee times, log on to www.ci.austin.tx.us/parks/golf.htm. All but the 9-hole Hancock course offer pro shops and equipment rental, and their greens fees are reasonable. The **Hancock** course was built in 1899 and is the oldest course in Texas. The **Lions** course is where Tom Kite and Ben Crenshaw played college golf for the University of Texas.

HIKING Austin's parks and preserves abound in nature trails; see "Austin Outdoors" in the "More Attractions," section earlier in this chapter for additional information. Contact the **Sierra Club** (© **512/472-1767;** www.texas.sierraclub.org/austin) if you're interested in organized hikes. **Wild Basin Wilderness Preserve** (see "Organized Tours," above) is another source for guided treks, offering periodic "Haunted Trails" tours along with its more typical hikes.

ROCK CLIMBING Those with the urge to hang out on cliffs can call **Mountain Madness** (© **512/329-0309;** www.mtmadness.com), which holds weekend rock-climbing courses at Enchanted Rock, a stunning granite outcropping in the Hill Country. **Austin Rock Gym** (© **512/416-9299;** www.austinrockgym.com) offers two family-friendly indoor climbing facilities, as well as a variety of classes and guided outdoor trips.

SAILING Lake Travis is the perfect place to let the wind drive your sails; among the operators offering sailboat rentals in the Austin area are **Commander's Point Yacht Basin** (© **512/266-2333**) and **Texas Sailing Academy** (© **512/261-6193;** www.texassailing.com). Both offer instruction.

SCUBA DIVING The clarity of the water in Lake Travis varies a good bit. On days when the lake is full and the wind is mild, it's quite good for diving. You can spot boat wrecks and metal sculptures that have been planted on the lake bottom of the private (paying) portion of **Windy Point Park** (© **512/266-3337;** www.windypointpark. com); and Mother Nature has provided the park's advanced divers with an unusual underwater grove of pecan trees. Equipment rentals and lessons are available nearby from **Dive World** (© **512/219-1220;** www.diveworldaustin.com), located at 12129 R.R. 620, #440.

SPELUNKING The limestone country in the Austin area is rife with dark places in which to poke around. In the city, two wild caves you can crawl into with the proper training are **Airman's Cave,** on the Barton Creek Greenbelt, and **Goat Cave Preserve,** in southwest Austin. Check the website of the Texas Speleological Association, www.cavetexas.org, and that of the University Speleological Society, www. utgrotto.org (you don't have to be a student to join), for links to statewide underground attractions. See also chapter 17 for other caves in nearby Hill Country.

SWIMMING The best known of Austin's natural swimming holes is **Barton Springs Pool** (see "The Top Attractions," earlier in this chapter), but it's by no means the only one. Other scenic outdoor spots to take the plunge include **Deep Eddy**

Pool, 401 Deep Eddy Ave., at Lake Austin Boulevard (© **512/472-8546**), and **Hamilton Pool Preserve,** 27 miles west of Austin, off Tex. 71, on FM 3238 (© **512/ 264-2740**).

For lakeshore swimming, consider **Hippie Hollow** (www.co.travis.tx.us/tnr/parks/ hippie_hollow.asp) on Lake Travis, 2½ miles off FM 620, where you can let it all hang out in a series of clothing-optional coves, or **Emma Long Metropolitan Park** on Lake Austin (see "More Attractions," earlier in this chapter).

You can also swim at a number of **free neighborhood pools;** contact the City Aquatics Department (© **512/476-4521**; www.ci.austin.tx.us/parks/aquatics.htm) for more information.

TENNIS   The very reasonably priced **Austin High School Tennis Center,** 2001 W. Cesar Chavez St. (© **512/477-7802**); **Caswell Tennis Center,** 2312 Shoal Creek Blvd. (© **512/478-6268**); and **Pharr Tennis Center,** 4201 Brookview Dr. (© **512/477-7773**), all have enough courts to give you a good shot at getting one to play on. To find out about additional public courts, contact the **Tennis Administration** office (© **512/480-3020**; www.ci.austin.tx.us/parks/tennis.htm).

SPECTATOR SPORTS

College sports are very big, particularly when the **University of Texas (UT) Longhorns** are playing. The most comprehensive source of information on the various teams is www.texassports.com. If you're interested in attending any of these events, go to www.texasboxoffice.com, where you can buy tickets. It's pretty easy. If you would rather do it over the phone, call **UTTM Charge-A-Ticket** (© **512/477-6060**).

BASEBALL   The **University of Texas** baseball team goes to bat February through May at Disch-Falk Field (just east of I-35, at the corner of Martin Luther King, Jr. Blvd. and Comal). Many players from this former NCAA championship squad have gone on to the big time.

Baseball Hall-of-Famer Nolan Ryan's **Round Rock Express,** a Texas Rangers farm club, won the Texas League championship in 1999, their first year in existence (they now compete in the Pacific Coast League). See them play at the Dell Diamond, 3400 E. Palm Valley Rd., in Round Rock (© **512/255-BALL** [2255] or 244-4209; www.roundrockexpress.com), an 8,688-seat stadium where you can choose from box seats or stadium seating; an additional 3,000 fans can sit on a grassy berm in the outfield. Tickets range from about $6 to $12.

BASKETBALL   The **University of Texas** Longhorns and Lady Longhorns basketball teams, both former Southwest Conference champions, play in the Frank C. Erwin, Jr. Special Events Center (just west of I-35 on Red River, btw. Martin Luther King, Jr. Blvd. and 15th St.) November through March. See above for ticket information

FOOTBALL   It's hard to tell which is more central to the success of an Austin Thanksgiving: the turkey or the UT–Texas A&M game. Part of the Big 12 Conference, the **University of Texas** football team often fills the huge Darrell K. Royal/Texas Memorial Stadium (just west of I-35, btw. 23rd and 21st sts., E. Campus Dr., and San Jacinto Blvd.) during home games, played August through November. See above for ticket information.

FORMULA 1 RACING   The Grand Prix circuit might again include the U.S., and if it does, the race will be held in Austin. It's not by any means a done deal, but the process has been moving forward at a brisk clip to get Formula 1 racing here by 2012.

The track would be built south of Bergstrom Airport on a large parcel of undeveloped land. This would be the first track built in the U.S. specifically for Formula 1. Check www.formula1unitedstates.com for current information.

GOLF   The **Triton Financial Classic** (✆ **512/732-2666;** www.tritonclassic. com), previously called the FedEx Kinko's Classic, continues to be played at the Hills Country Club at Lakeway Resort the first week of June. This Austin stop on the PGA's Champions Tour began back in 2003 and has boasted a $1.6-million purse.

HOCKEY   The **Austin Ice Bats** hockey team (✆ **512/927-PUCK** [927-7825]; www.icebats.com) has been getting anything but an icy reception from its Austin fans. This typically rowdy team plays at the Travis County Exposition Center, 7311 Decker Lane (about 15 min. east of UT). Tickets, which run from $10 to $35, are available at any UTTM outlet or from **Star Tickets** (✆ **888/597-STAR** [597-7827] or 512/469-SHOW [469-7469]; www.startickets.com). The team generally plays on weekends, mid-October through late March; a phone call will get you the exact dates and times.

ROLLER DERBY   In 2001, some local women with a taste for mayhem and too much time on their hands formed an amateur women's roller derby league. For those of you who don't remember roller derby (or don't care to), it was a defunct late-night television sport of the '70s, which was celebrated in celluloid by Raquel Welch in that immortal film classic, *Kansas City Bombers.* Two teams in old-style roller skates (not in-line skates) circle a banked track, pushing and elbowing and colliding with each other. Scoring points doesn't really matter all that much. As a sport, it has all the low-brow panache of wrestling, but with less of the good-versus-evil script, and more pure anything-but-wholesome fun.

Attending roller derby bouts quickly became a hip thing to do in Austin, and the league now fields five teams. All the women get in character for their competition and ham it up with as much poor taste as possible. You have the Holy Rollers, the Hell-cats, the Cherry Bombs, and so on. The skyrocketing popularity has led to the formation of leagues in other cities. Whether they are as fun as what goes on in Austin, I can't say. The season lasts from January to October. There are usually two bouts per month, which take place on weekends at the Palmer Event Center. If you want to see some Austin quirkiness and celebrate low-brow culture in a tongue-in-cheek fashion, you will appreciate these events. To see their schedule, check out the **Lonestar Rollergirls** website www.txrd.com. There is now also a flat-track league that is just as fun to watch, called the **Texas Rollergirls** (www.txrollergirls.com). Their season lasts from March through August, with bouts taking place at the Austin Convention Center.

SOCCER   From August through November, you can find the University of Texas women's soccer team competing against the other NCAA teams. In 2008, the team made it into the second round of the NCAA playoffs, losing to Portland 2-0. Home games are played either Friday or Sunday at the Mike A. Myers Stadium and Soccer Field, just northeast of the UT football stadium at Robert Dedman Drive and Mike Myers Drive. See above for ticket information.

SHOPPING IN AUSTIN

V isitors to Austin don't really come for the shopping, but the opportunistic shopper can be rewarded with some wonderful discoveries. Folk art, arts and crafts, music, books—these are the areas where Austin excels. And it's got the rest of the material world pretty well covered, too. As for the shopping experience, I think most will enjoy the helpfulness and lack of artifice shown by salespersons here.

THE SHOPPING SCENE

What follows is a brief description of where the most "Austintatious" shopping can be found. Specialty shops in Austin tend to open around 10am, Monday through Saturday, and close at about 5:30 or 6pm, and many have Sunday hours from noon to 6pm. Malls tend to keep the same Sunday schedule, but Monday through Saturday they don't close their doors until 9pm. Sales tax in Austin is 8.25%.

DOWNTOWN   Most shops are located along several blocks of East Sixth, along Congress Avenue, and along West Second, 1 block off Congress in a shopping district that extends for 3 blocks. If the weather is agreeable, this is an easy area to cover on foot and a good spot for window-shopping. Specialty stores include apparel, interior design, music paraphernalia, hot sauce, and headwear.

SOUTH CONGRESS   Just across the river from downtown begins the SoCo shopping area. Most of the shops are on South Congress, and the majority of these are located up the hill, in a stretch running from the 1200 block to the 2500 block. On the first Thursday of every month, the SoCo merchants sponsor a street festival with music and other entertainment (see "First Thursdays," below). Shops include art galleries, boutiques, bargain antiques stores, and clothing and folk art shops. There are also shops scattered along South Lamar, but they are not concentrated enough to allow for window-shopping, and South Lamar isn't as interesting to navigate as South Congress.

NORTH LAMAR   Just west of downtown (you could almost call it downtown but not quite), in the vicinity of where Fifth and Sixth streets cross Lamar Boulevard, you have a high concentration of one-of-a-kind shops extending for 1 or 2 blocks in any direction. The shops continue, scattered along both sides of Lamar northward up to 12th street. You'll find music, books, clothing, food—all the necessities, plus a lot of extravagance,

Downtown Austin Shopping

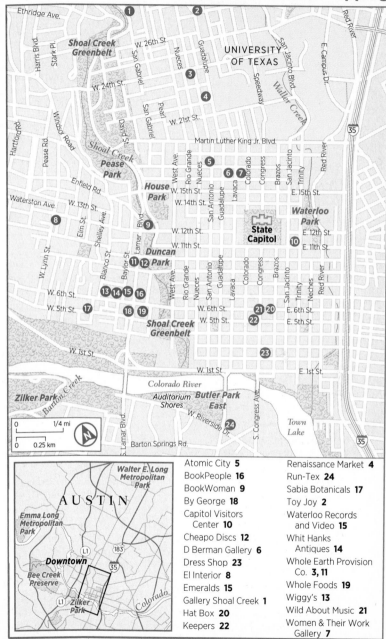

Atomic City **5**
BookPeople **16**
BookWoman **9**
By George **18**
Capitol Visitors
  Center **10**
Cheapo Discs **12**
D Berman Gallery **6**
Dress Shop **23**
El Interior **8**
Emeralds **15**
Gallery Shoal Creek **1**
Hat Box **20**
Keepers **22**

Renaissance Market **4**
Run-Tex **24**
Sabia Botanicals **17**
Toy Joy **2**
Waterloo Records
  and Video **15**
Whit Hanks
  Antiques **14**
Whole Earth Provision
  Co. **3, 11**
Whole Foods **19**
Wiggy's **13**
Wild About Music **21**
Women & Their Work
  Gallery **7**

Greater Austin Shopping

Allen's Boots **25**
Antique Market Place **8**
The Arboretum **2**
Austin Antique Mall **5**
Austin Country Flea Market **7**
Barton Creek Square **18**
Breed & Co. Hardware **16**
Capra & Cavelli **13**
Central Market **15**
Clarksville Pottery & Galleries **15**
Dillard's **9**
The Domain **3**
Eco-Wise **19**
Electric Ladyland **21**
Gateway Shopping Centers **4**
Heritage Boots **20**
Highland Mall **9**
Hill Country Weavers **26**
Lakeline Mall **1**
Neiman Marcus **3**
Neiman Marcus Last Call **28**
Nordstrom **18**
Room Service **12**
Russell Korman **14**
Saks **4**
Sheplers **10**
Spec's Liquor Warehouse **11**
Ten Thousand Villages **24**
Terra Toys **6**
Tesoros Trading Co. **22**
Toy Joy **17**
Whip In Beer and Wine **27**
Yard Dog Folk Art **23**

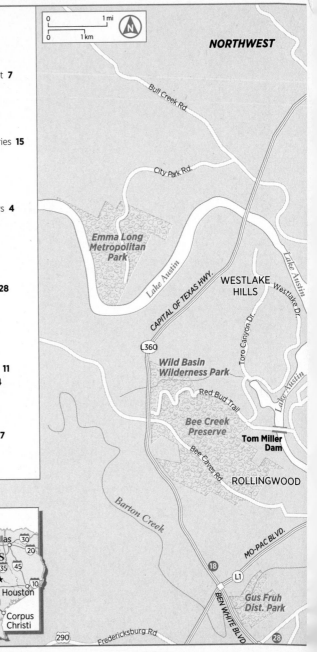

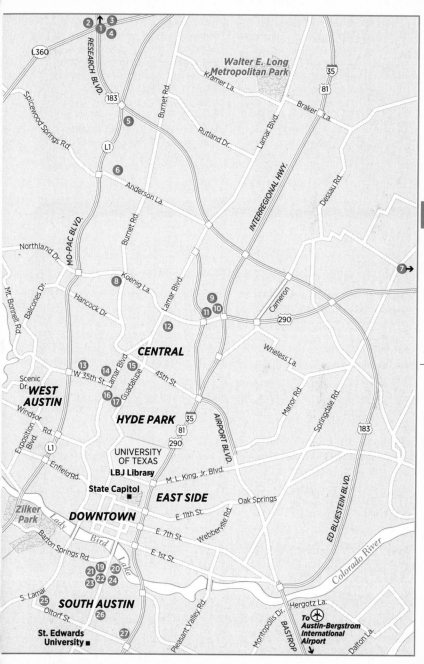

Walter E. Long
Metropolitan Park

WEST
AUSTIN

CENTRAL

HYDE PARK

UNIVERSITY
OF TEXAS
LBJ Library

State Capitol

EAST SIDE

Zilker
Park

DOWNTOWN

SOUTH AUSTIN

St. Edwards
University

To
Austin-Bergstrom
International
Airport

FIRST thursdays

As if there weren't already enough street theater in Austin, the merchants on South Congress Avenue decided a few years back to start hosting a monthly street festival. They began keeping their doors open late and providing food, drinks, and entertainment on the first Thursday of every month. Soon impromptu open-air markets sprang up, and jugglers, drum circles, and of course live bands performed indoors, outdoors, and in between.

First Thursdays have become quite popular for their mix of shopping, entertainment, people-watching, and the surprise factor—you never know what you're going to meet up with. It's also a way for locals to celebrate the approach of the weekend. The street festival occupies about 8 blocks along both sides of South Congress. Traffic along the avenue is not cordoned off, but everyone drives slowly because of the crowds crisscrossing the avenue. It starts around 6pm and runs until 10pm. To find out more, check www.first thursday.info.

too. It's a mixture of chic, quirky, folksy, and artsy. Also located here is Whole Foods' flagship store.

NORTH LAMAR AND 38TH STREET Within a few blocks of this intersection, heading either north on Lamar or west on 38th Street (where it curves south and becomes 35th St.), there is serious shopping. On Lamar, you'll find the shopping center where Central Market's flagship food store is located, surrounded by specialty shops selling cameras, paper goods, cosmetics, jewelry, and pottery. West on 38th are two small shopping centers that host boutiques and specialty stores: 26 Doors and Jefferson Square.

THE DRAG Bordering the university on Guadalupe Street is a stretch of stores selling mostly hip apparel to students: boutiques, beads, books, and an open-air area where hippies sell jewelry, tie-dyed shirts, and such, which for some reason has always had the name Renaissance Market.

NORTHWEST There's no shortage of malls in Austin. In the northwest, three upscale shopping centers, the **Arboretum,** the **Arboretum Market,** and the **Gateway complex** (consisting of the Gateway Courtyard, the Gateway Market, and Gateway Square) have earned the area the nickname "South Dallas." A bit farther north off of Mo-Pac, where it intersects Burnet Road, is the city's newest mall, called the **Domain.**

SOUTH OF AUSTIN Bargain hunters can go farther afield to the huge collection of factory outlet stores just south of San Marcos; see chapter 16 for details.

SHOPPING A TO Z

Antiques

In addition to the one-stop antiques markets listed below, a number of smaller shops line Burnet Road north of 45th Street.

Antique Marketplace For people who like antiques but don't enjoy speaking in hushed tones, the Antique Marketplace offers bargains and treasures in a friendly, relaxed atmosphere. You'll find a little bit of everything: Czech glass, funky collectibles, and expensive furnishings. The store is in a strip mall next to an HEB grocery store at the corner of Burnet and Koenig. 5806 Burnet Rd. © **512/452-1000.**

Austin Antique Mall   You can spend anywhere from five bucks to thousands of dollars in this huge collection of antiques stores. More than 100 dealers occupying a 30,000-square-foot indoor space offer Roseville pottery, Fiesta dishes, Victorian furniture, costume jewelry, and much, much more. 8822 McCann Dr. © **512/459-5900.** www.antiquetexas.com.

Whit Hanks Antiques   More than a dozen independent dealers gather at tony Whit Hanks, just across the street from Treaty Oak. This is Austin's premier outlet for fine antiques. Even if you can't afford to buy anything, it's fun to ogle items from fine crystal and vases to Chinese cabinets and neoclassical columns. 1009 W. Sixth St. © **512/478-2101.** www.whithanksantiques.com.

Art Galleries

D Berman Gallery   This small gallery exhibits local artists working in all kinds of media. Its intimate shows are popular with many in the arts crowd. 1701 Guadalupe St. © **512/477-8877.** www.dbermangallery.com.

Gallery Shoal Creek   Since it opened in 1965, Shoal Creek has moved away from an exclusive emphasis on Western art to encompass work from a wide range of American regions. The focus is on contemporary painting in representational or Impressionist styles—for example, Jerry Ruthven's Southwest landscapes or Nancy McGowan's naturalist watercolors. 2905 San Gabriel St. © **512/454-6671.** www.galleryshoalcreek.com.

Women & Their Work Gallery   Founded in 1978, this nonprofit gallery is devoted to more than visual art—it also promotes and showcases women in dance, music, theater, film, and literature. Regularly changing exhibits have little in common except innovation. This art space often gets the nod for "Best Gallery" from the readers of the *Austin Chronicle*. The gift shop has a great selection of unusual crafts and jewelry created by female artists. 1710 Lavaca St. © **512/477-1064.** www.womenandtheirwork.org.

Bookstores

As might be expected, there are a couple of bookstores in the University of Texas area, on the Drag. The **University Co-Op,** 2244 Guadalupe St. (© **512/476-7211;** www.coop-bookstore.com), opened in 1896, has many volumes of general interest, along with the requisite burnt-orange-and-white Longhorn T-shirts, mugs, and other UT souvenirs.

For a good selection of used and remaindered books, check out **Half-Price Books** at 5555 N. Lamar Blvd. (© **512/451-4463;** www.halfpricebooks.com; four other locations); it also carries CDs, cassettes, DVDs, and videos.

BookPeople   This is one of the largest and best independent bookstores you're likely to find these days. Expanded in the mid-1990s from its New Age roots, but remaining stubbornly quirky and independent, this BookPeople stocks more than 250,000 titles ranging over a wide variety of subjects. It also sells technical videos, books on tape, and gift items (the KEEP AUSTIN WEIRD T-shirt is their bestseller). Lots of intimate sitting areas and an espresso bar prevent this huge store—the largest in Texas—from feeling overwhelming. More than 200 author signings and special events

are held here every year. 603 N. Lamar Blvd. ✆ **800/853-9757** or 512/472-5050. www.book
people.com.

BookWoman   Offering the largest selection of books by and about women in
Texas, this store is also one of the best feminist resource centers, the place to find out
about women's organizations and events statewide. Readings and discussion groups
are regularly held here, too. BookWoman also carries a great selection of T-shirts,
cards, posters, and music. 918 W. 12th St. ✆ **512/472-2785.** www.ebookwoman.com.

Department Stores

Dillard's   This Little Rock–based chain, spread throughout the Southwest, carries
a variety of mid- to high-range merchandise. In Highland Mall, there are two separate
outlets, one focusing on home furnishings and women's clothing, the other devoted
to men's and children's wear. All the stores have western wear shops with good selections of styles. Two other locations are at the Barton Creek Square Mall (✆ **512/327-
6100**) and the Lakeline Mall (✆ **512/257-8740**). Highland Mall. ✆ **512/452-9393.** www.
dillards.com.

Neiman Marcus   Neiman Marcus, a Texas-based chain of department stores long
associated with conspicuous consumption, opened its first full-fledged store in the
Austin area at the Domain shopping center. The store always has items for sale that
are uniquely Texan in a nonstereotypical way. This is high-end retail; if you're seeking
bargains, shop at their Last Call store (see below). The Domain Shopping Center, 3400 Palm
Way, north of Braker Lane, btw. Mo-Pac and Burnet Rd. ✆ **512/719-1200.** www.neimanmarcus.com.

Nordstrom   Now that Nordstrom has come, fashion- and status-conscious Austin
shoppers—the segment of the city not devoted to keeping Austin weird—have much
ground to cover with the 144,000 square feet of floor space that this store fills with
merchandise. It's located in the Barton Creek Square Mall. 2901 S. Capital of Texas Hwy.
✆ **512/691-3500.** www.nordstrom.com.

Saks   Although smaller than many of the other Saks stores, it still offers the high-
tone fashions and accouterments you'd expect, as well as a personal shopper service.
9722 Great Hills Trail. ✆ **512/231-3700.** www.saksfifthavenue.com.

Discount Shopping

Neiman Marcus Last Call ★   Fans of Texas-grown Neiman Marcus will want to
take advantage of Last Call, which consolidates fashions from 27 of the chain's
department stores and sells them here at prices 50% to 75% off retail. New merchandise shipments arrive every week, and not only can you find great bargains, but you
needn't sacrifice the attention for which Neiman Marcus is famous because the staff
here is as helpful as at any other branch, and a personal shopper service is available
as well. Brodie Oaks Shopping Center, 4115 S. Capital of Texas Hwy., at S. Lamar. ✆ **512/447-0701.**
www.neimanmarcus.com.

Ecowares

Eco-wise   It's hard to typecast a shop that sells everything from greeting cards, natural insect repellent, and hand-woven purses to building materials and home decorating
supplies. The common denominator? Everything you'll find here is created with an eye
toward the environment—that is, it's recycled, made from natural fabrics, and/or
chemical free. Staff is knowledgeable and helpful, and customers are passionately

loyal. The store offers baby and wedding-shower registries for earth-friendly brides and grooms or moms and dads. 110 W. Elizabeth St. ✆ **512/326-4474.** www.ecowise.com.

Essential Oils

Sabia Botanicals   All those soothing oils and lotions in their pretty bottles on the shelves seem to whisper, "Buy me, I'll make you feel better." This is aromatherapy central, but along with New Age products, the store also carries old-time herbal lines, such as Kiehl's. 1213 W. Fifth St., Ste. B1. ✆ **512/469-0447.** www.sabia.com.

Fashions

For children's clothing, see **Terra Toys** under "Toys," p. 248.

MEN'S

See also **By George** under "Women's," below.

Capra & Cavelli   Funny radio ads—not to mention hip and classic fashions—draw image-conscious guys (and gals) into this West Austin store. The sales staff knows clothes and is very helpful. There's another store downtown at East Fifth Street and Red River, in the Hilton Hotel. 3500 Jefferson St., Ste. 110. ✆ **512/450-1919.** www.capracavelli. com.

Keepers   This is a fairly conservative men's clothing store. The staff are experts at fitting jackets and suits. The store carries business casual clothing, too, but the emphasis is on expensive, well-cut suits. 515 Congress Ave., Ste. 140. ✆ **512/473-2512.** www. keepersclothing.com.

WOMEN'S

See also **Capra & Cavelli,** under "Men's," above.

By George   These two boutique shops offer an uncommon assortment of designer clothes. The main store, across from Whole Foods, is larger and offers more in the way of cocktail dresses and high heels. It also has a men's department. The South Congress shop (1400 S. Congress; ✆ **512/441-8600**) offers only women's casual wear. 524 N. Lamar Blvd. ✆ **512/472-5951.**

Dress Shop   Boutiques, when they are good, are very personal expressions of the passions and tastes of the owner. The owner of this boutique, Leslie Gandy, likes dresses that make a statement of individuality, whether it be a casual party dress or a formal cocktail dress. 315 Congress Ave. ✆ **512/527-3018.** www.dressshopaustin.com.

Emeralds   It's young, it's hip, it's got Carrie Bradshaw shoes by the dozens, plus racks of outrageous party dresses to wear them with. You can also buy cards, candles, aromatherapy bath salts, and funky jewelry here. 624 N. Lamar Blvd. ✆ **512/476-4496.**

Folk Art & Crafts

El Interior   Nestled in the small cluster of restaurants in the middle of the Clarksville neighborhood is this small, but fun, import shop. The merchandise is collected from the countries of Mexico and Guatemala. Though there are several kinds of crafts for sale, there's an emphasis on textiles and clothing. 1009 W. Lynn St. ✆ **512/474-8680.** www.elinterior.com.

Ten Thousand Villages   This is the local retail outlet for the national nonprofit organization dedicated to fair trade with folk artists, craftsmen, and small farmers from developing nations. This store sells all kinds of merchandise: jewelry, toys, decorative objects, coffee, and chocolate, among many other things. 1317 S. Congress Ave. ℂ **512/440-0440.** www.austin.tenthousandvillages.com.

Tesoros Trading Co.   Now in its new location on trendy South Congress, this folk art store has an incredible variety of objects both large and small from around the world: bronze figurines from Indonesia, *milagro* charms from Mexico, wood cuts from Brazil, talismans from Turkey. You can walk in, intending to spend 15 minutes here, and then get sucked in for a couple of hours. The variety is impressive. The owners operate a wholesale imports business and sell around the country, which allows them to stock their own store with one-of-a-kind pieces they find on their trips. 1500 S. Congress Ave. ℂ **512/447-7500.** www.tesoros.com.

Yard Dog Folk Art   "Outsider" art, created in the deep, rural South, usually by the poor and sometimes by the incarcerated, is not for everyone, but for those interested in contemporary American folk art, this gallery is not to be missed. 1510 S. Congress Ave. ℂ **512/912-1613.** www.yarddog.com.

Food

Austin has become the new frontier of grocery shopping—grocery shopping as aesthetic experience. And the two entities that are busy at work pushing the envelope are **Whole Foods** (headquartered in Austin) and **Central Market.** Both were born in Austin, and both have a vision of ravishing displays of fresh produce, gourmet foods, wines, and delicacies from around the world. I am told by the tourism office that both of these stores are among the most popular tourist attractions in the city.

But for sheer ease of use, and for its being a countercultural artifact, there's Austin's own community grocery store, **Wheatsville Food Co-op,** at 3101 Guadalupe St. (ℂ **512/478-2667**). It's owned and operated by its members, but anyone can shop there. They make the maximum use of their limited floor space, including a good selection of beer and wine and a deli, and have excellent service. Unlike the stores of the future, you're in and out of this one in two shakes of a lamb's tail. The store recently underwent a major expansion and renovation that has it dangerously close to joining the mainstream.

Austin also has an abundance of farmers' markets. Perhaps the most notable of them, **Austin Farmers' Market,** held downtown at Republic Square Park, Fourth Street at Guadalupe, every Saturday from 9am to 1pm March through November (ℂ **512/236-0074**), not only features food products, but also live music, cooking demonstrations, kids' activities, and workshops on everything from organic gardening to aromatherapy.

South Congress Farmers' Market, held Saturday from 8am to 1pm in the parking lot of El Gallo Restaurant, 2910 S. Congress Ave. (ℂ **512/281-4712**), is smaller, but you've got the guarantee that all the goods are locally grown without chemicals.

Central Market ★★   Ah, foodie heaven! Not only can you buy every imaginable edible item at these gourmet megamarkets—fresh or frozen, local or imported—but you also can enjoy quality vittles in the restaurant section, which features cowboy, bistro, Italian, vegetarian—you name it—cuisines. Moreover, prices are surprisingly reasonable. A monthly newsletter announces what's fresh in the produce department, which jazz musicians are entertaining on the weekend, and which gourmet chef is holding forth at the market's cooking school. The newer Westgate Shopping Center branch, 4477 S. Lamar Blvd. (ℂ **512/899-4300**), in South Austin, is as impressive as its history-making sibling north of UT. 4001 N. Lamar Blvd. ☎ **512/206-1000.** www.central market.com.

Whole Foods Market The first link in what is now the world's largest organic and natural foods supermarket chain celebrated its 25th birthday by opening an 80,000-square-foot store near its original downtown location (as well as an adjacent office tower to serve as corporate headquarters). From chemical-free cosmetics to frozen tofu burgers, Whole Foods has long covered the entire spectrum of natural products, and now it's looking to compete with Central Market (see above) in the food-entertainment arena by creating a 600-seat amphitheater, a playscape, gardens, on-site massages, a cooking school, and more. The northwest store in Gateway Market, 9607 Research Blvd. (☎ **512/345-5003**), is a simpler version of the main store. 525 N. Lamar Blvd. ☎ **512/476-1206.** www.wholefoods.com.

Gifts/Souvenirs

See also **Emeralds,** listed under the "Women's" subsection of the "Fashions" section, above.

Capitol Visitors Center The gift shop at the visitor center sells all kinds of Texas memorabilia, including paperweights made from reproductions of the capitol's Texas seal, doorknobs, bookends, and local food products. There are also a variety of educational toys and an excellent selection of historical books. 112 E. 11th St. (southeast corner of capitol grounds). ☎ **512/305-8400.** www.texascapitolvisitorscenter.com.

Wild About Music Austin's obsession with music makes this store possible. All the merchandise is music themed, and much of it is out of the ordinary. Some of it is easy to pack in your suitcase: clothes, accessories, jewelry, books, and musician-designed T-shirts. Other pieces are expensive and bulky, such as posters, musical instruments, and furniture. 115 E Sixth St. ☎ **512/708-1700.** www.wildaboutmusic.com.

Glass & Pottery

Clarksville Pottery & Galleries This emporium, filled with lovely pieces created by local artisans, has long been transplanted from its namesake location in the artsy section of town to a prime spot near Central Market (see "Food," above). You'll find hand-thrown ceramics, blown glass, woodcarvings, and one-of-a-kind gifts, most of which are the work of local artists. Clarksville's contemporary jewelry, especially the engagement and wedding rings, created by local jewelry designers, is very popular. 4001 N. Lamar Blvd., Ste. 200. ☎ **512/454-9079.** www.clarksvillepottery.com.

Hardware & More

Breed & Co. Hardware You don't have to be a power-drill freak to visit Breed & Co. How many hardware stores, after all, have bridal registries where you can sign up for Waterford crystal? This darling of Austin DIY has everything from nails to tropical plants, organic fertilizer, gardening books and cookbooks, pâté molds, and cherry pitters. There's also a branch in the prosperous Westlake Hills area, 3663 Bee Cave Rd. (☎ **512/328-3960**). 718 W. 29th St. ☎ **512/474-6679.** www.breedandco.com.

Jewelry

See also **Tesoros,** under "Folk Art & Crafts," above; and **Clarksville Pottery,** under "Glass & Pottery," above.

Russell Korman   You'd never know it from his current elegant digs, but Russell Korman got his start in Austin's jewelry trade by selling beads on the Drag. Although he's moved on to fine 14-karat gold, platinum, and diamond pieces, along with fine pens and watches—there's an experienced watchmaker on the premises—his store still has a considerable collection of more casual sterling silver from Mexico. Prices are competitive, even for the most formal baubles. 3806 N. Lamar Blvd. © **512/451-9292.** www.russellkormanjewelry.com.

Malls/Shopping Centers

The Arboretum   The retail anchor of the far northwest part of town is a shopping center so chic that it calls itself a market, not a mall. This two-level collection of outdoor boutiques doesn't include any department stores, but it does have a Barnes & Noble Superstore and a huge Pottery Barn. You'll find your basic selection of yuppie shops—everything from upscale clothing stores to a cigar humidor. The second floor features art galleries, a custom jeweler, and crafts shops. Dining options, including a Cheesecake Factory, Thundercloud Subs (a local chain of sandwich shops), and an outlet for Amy's—Austin's local favorite ice cream—tend to be on the casual side. 10000 Research Blvd. (Hwy. 183 and Loop 360). © **512/338-4437.** www.shopsimon.com.

Barton Creek Square   Set on a bluff with a view of downtown, Barton Creek tends to be frequented by upscale Westsiders; the wide-ranging collection of more than 180 shops is anchored by Nordstrom, Dillard's, Foley's, Sears, and JCPenney. One of the newest malls in Austin, it's refined and low-key, but the presence of Frederick's of Hollywood and Victoria's Secret lingerie boutiques makes one wonder if the daytime soaps might not be onto something about the bored rich. At least they've got a sense of humor: There's also a jewelry store called Filthy Rich of Austin. 2901 S. Capital of Texas Hwy. © **512/327-7040.** www.bartoncreeksquare.com.

The Domain   The newest shopping center in town, this one didn't open for business without stirring up a hornet's nest of controversy from some rather generous tax rebates that the city council unwisely bestowed on the developers. This mall brings a lot of upmarket stores to town, including Tiffany, Burberry, Louis Vuitton, and Calypso. The mall is anchored by Macy's and Neiman Marcus. It's located in north Austin, off Mo-Pac, between Braker Lane and Burnet Road. 11410 Century Oaks Terrace. © **512/795-4320.** www.simon.com.

Gateway Shopping Centers   Comprising three not-so-distinct shopping areas, the Gateway Courtyard, the Gateway Market, and Gateway Square, this large, open complex includes mainly national chains such as Crate & Barrel, REI, Old Navy, and CompUSA. There are also branches of Austin-based stores, including Run-Tex and Whole Foods Market, discussed individually in this chapter. 9607 Research Blvd. at Hwy. 183 and Capital of Texas Hwy. © **512/338-4755.** www.simon.com.

Highland Mall   Austin's first mall, built in the 1970s, has fallen on hard times. A couple of the anchor stores are gone, and the occupancy level of the small retailers has declined—all of this despite the fact that this mall remains the most centrally located mall in Austin. This might be changing, though. The owners have reached an agreement with Austin Community College to lease space for classrooms. This in turn could bring more foot traffic and life to the mall and allow Highland to reverse its fortunes. 6001 Airport Blvd. © **512/454-9656.** www.highlandmall.com.

Lakeline Mall   This mall serves a suburban public in a far northwest location. It's notable for an attention-grabbing design, featuring lots of colorful murals and detailed reliefs of the city. The shops, including Foley's, Dillard's, Mervyn's, Sears, JCPenney, Brookstone, the Bombay Company, and Best Buy, are not nearly so unusual, but there are some interesting smaller shops, from Dollar Tree, where everything costs a buck, to the Stockpot, with state-of-the art cookware. 11200 Lakeline Mall Dr., Cedar Park. ✆ **512/257-SHOP** (7467). www.lakelinemall.com.

Markets

Austin Country Flea Market Every Saturday and Sunday year-round, more than 550 covered spaces are filled with merchants selling all the usual flea market goods and then some—new and used clothing, fresh herbs and produce, electronics, antiques. This is the largest flea market in central Texas, covering more than 130 paved acres. There's live music every weekend—generally a spirited Latino band—to step up the shopping pace. 9500 Hwy. 290 E. (4 miles east of I-35). ✆ **512/928-2795** or 928-4711; www.austincountry.citymax.com.

Renaissance Market Flash back or be introduced to tie-dye days at this hippie crafts market, where vendors are licensed by the City of Austin (read: no commercial schlock). Billed as the only continuously operated, open-air crafts market in the United States, it's theoretically open daily 8am to 10pm, but most of the merchants turn up only on the weekends. You'll find everything from silver jewelry and hand-carved flutes to batik T-shirts. Many of the artisans come in from small towns in the nearby Hill Country. W. 23rd St. and Guadalupe St. (the Drag). ✆ **512/397-1456.**

Music

Cheapo Discs In spite of being an import, Cheapo has carved out a niche in the hearts of Austin music lovers. It's *the* place to buy, sell, and trade new and used CDs, and thanks to the knowledgeable (if often surly) staff, there are always treasures to be found in its half-acre of bins. 914 N. Lamar Blvd. ✆ **512/477-4499.** www.cheapotexas.com.

Waterloo Records and Video Carrying a huge selection of sounds, Waterloo is always the first in town to get the new releases. If they don't have something on hand, they'll order it for you promptly. They love looking for arcane stuff. The store has a popular preview listening section, offers compilation tapes of Austin groups, and sells tickets to all major-label shows around town. It also hosts frequent in-store CD-release performances by local bands. The staff is knowledgeable and helpful. There's a video annex just west of the record store (✆ **512/474-2525**) and, for purists, a vinyl section. 600A N. Lamar Blvd. ✆ **512/474-2500.** www.waterloorecords.com.

Outdoor Gear

Run-Tex Owned by the footwear editor for *Runner's World* magazine—and serving as the official wear test center for that publication—this store not only has a huge inventory of shoes and other running gear, but also does everything it can to promote healthful jogging practices, even offering free running classes and a free injury-evaluation clinic. The staff will make sure any footwear you buy is a perfect fit for your feet and running style. There's a larger Run-Tex in Gateway Market, 9901 Capital of Texas Hwy. (✆ **512/343-1164**); a location at 2201 Lake Austin Blvd. (✆ **512/477-9464**); and a related WalkTex at 4001 N. Lamar Blvd. (✆ **512/454-WALK** [454-9255]). But this downtown store is best: It's near that runner's mecca, Town Lake. 422 W. Riverside Dr. ✆ **512/472-3254.** www.runtex.com.

The Whole Earth Provision Co.   Austin's large population of outdoor enthusiasts flocks to this store to be outfitted in the latest gear and earth-friendly fashions. If you wouldn't think of hiking without a two-way radio or a Magellan positioning navigator, you can find them here. The Austin-based chain also carries gifts, housewares, educational toys, and travel books. There are additional locations at 1014 N. Lamar Blvd. (📞 **512/476-1414**) and Westgate Shopping Center, 4477 S. Lamar Blvd. (📞 **512/899-0992**). 2410 San Antonio St. 📞 **512/478-1577.** www.wholeearthprovision.com.

Textile Arts

Hill Country Weavers   This store has the largest selection of yarns in Texas. Also basket supplies, dyes, spinning wheels, and felting supplies, but it's really the selection and variety of yarns, many made by independent artisans, that cause lots of visitors to Austin to seek out this store. The de facto center of the local weaving and knitting community, this store is often the scene of some kind of social gathering. 1701 S. Congress Ave. 📞 **512/707-7396.** www.hillcountryweavers.com.

Toys

Atomic City   Playthings—including a sizable collection of vintage metal wind-up toys—are just one component of the merchandise at this funky, eclectic store in a deceptively prim-looking house near the University of Texas. You'll also find a sizable collection of cult classic film and TV memorabilia and, in the back, hundreds of styles of shoes and boots for the ultrahip rockabilly crowd. It's all a bit surreal—but in a good way. 1700 San Antonio St. 📞 **512/477-0293.**

Terra Toys   This toy store is a rare find. Its owner knows exactly what makes a toy a classic. She has assembled an excellent inventory of beautiful and imaginative toys from around the world. The store is large and was expanded in 2010. It carries a large selection of children's books, classics and the newest bestsellers, as well. If you are looking for something particular in a toy, I recommend you visit Terra Toys. It's located in north-central Austin, off Lamar Boulevard, in the West Anderson Plaza shopping center. The store also carries a variety of miniatures, train sets, games, and kites. And it has a separate department for children's clothing. 2438 W. Anderson Lane. 📞 **800/247-TOYS** (247-8697) or 512/445-4489. www.terratoys.com.

Toy Joy   This store, close by campus, sees more college students than children, so its selection of games and toys is slanted toward bigger kids. But it carries a lot of items that will be popular with both kinds of customers, including a good number of small items that would make excellent gifts. 📞 **512/320-0090.** www.toyjoy.myshopify.com.

Vintage

Electric Ladyland/Lucy in Disguise   Feather boas, tutus, flapper dresses, angel wings, and the occasional gorilla suit overflow the narrow aisles of Austin's best-known costume and vintage clothing outlet. The owner, who really *does* dress like that all the time, is a walking advertisement for her fascinating store. You'll find floral-print dresses and bold-striped shirts, lots of costume jewelry, outrageous Western belt buckles, and the most bodacious selection of sunglasses you've ever seen. 1506 S. Congress Ave. 📞 **512/444-2002.**

Room Service   This is one of those fun stores where you're never quite sure what you'll find. The owner stocks clothing and home furnishings from the 1950s and '60s, funky jewelry, and assorted other artifacts. It's always worth a few chuckles, and if you tire of the merchandise here, there are a couple of neighboring stores in this old strip of shops that have similar wares. 107 E. North Loop Blvd. ✆ **512/451-1057.**

Western Wear

Allen's Boots   Name notwithstanding, Allen's sells a lot more than just footwear. Come here too for hats, belts, jewelry, and other boot-scootin' accouterments, and bring the young 'uns, too. This store, in now trendy SoCo—which explains the appearance of tie-dyed KEEP AUSTIN WEIRD T-shirts with the Allen's logo—has been around since 1970. 1522 S. Congress St. ✆ **512/447-1413.** www.allensboots.com.

Hat Box   Though this place sells hats of various styles, from pork pie to bowlers, its specialty is cowboy hats—custom shaped, painted, and even "dirt" hats. These last are the stiff canvas light-weight hats that are a common sight, but these have been darkened with dirt and charcoal and then sealed. Walking around Austin, you'll see quite a few of them, especially among the night prowlers. 115 E. Sixth St. ✆ **512/476-1203.** www.hatbox.com

Heritage Boots   The thing about cowboy boots is that it's a lot easier to find the perfect fit when they are handmade than when they are mass production. Fit, of course, is everything, and you can get lucky with a commercial brand, but more often than not, you don't, and the boots never quite shapes to the foot. Eventually they get relegated to the back corner of your closet. Not the case with boots sold here. These are all made by hand using the best materials by the shop's own boot makers. The boots start around $350 and vary in price depending on the amount of decorative stitching on the uppers. Jerry, the owner, sells only the boots that his craftsmen make. He knows his boots to the last detail, and he spends time with his customers to make sure that they walk away with exactly the right boot for them. 1200 S. Congress St. ✆ **512/326-8577.** www.heritageboot.com.

Sheplers   Adjacent to Highland Mall, the huge Austin branch of this chain of Western-wear department stores has everything the well-dressed urban cowboy or cowgirl might require. If you're already back home and you get a sudden urge for a concho belt or bolo tie, the mail-order and online business can see you through any cowpoke-fashion crisis. 6001 Middle Fiskville Rd. ✆ **512/454-3000** or 800/835-4004 (mail order). www.sheplers.com.

Wine & Beer

See also **Central Market** and **Whole Foods Market** in "Food," p. 244.

Spec's Liquor Warehouse   A recent arrival to Austin, this store is a member of a Houston chain of liquor stores, noted for discounted prices. The selection of wines and beers is large. Cigars are available, too, at low prices. There's also a selection of gourmet and deli foods from around the world, but these aren't quite so economical. One satellite location is in southwest Austin, in the Sunset Valley area, at 4960 Hwy. 290 W. (✆ **512/366-8260**). Another is in northwest Austin, near the Arboretum mall, at 10515 N. Mo-Pac Expwy. (✆ **512/342-6893**). The central location is near the Highland Mall shopping center. 5775 Airport Blvd., # 100. ✆ **512/366-8300.** www.specs online.com.

Whip In Beer and Wine 🏷️   Beginning life as a convenience store just off the freeway, this place doesn't have much in the way of atmosphere. What it does have is an amazing selection of beer: At a conservative estimate, Whip In has almost 400

different types of brews at any given time, and even more come Oktoberfest or other special beer-producing seasons. In 2003, one of the members of the family that owns Whip In opened **Travis Heights Beverage World,** which features a terrific selection of wines and spirits of all varieties, and weekly wine and spirit tastings. It's right next door to the Whip In at 1948 I-35 S.(© **512/440-7778;** www.travisheightsbev-world.com). 1950 I-35 S., Woodland Ave. exit on southbound service road. © **512/442-5337.** www.whipin.com.

Wiggy's If liquor and tobacco are among your vices, Wiggy's can help you indulge in high style. In addition to its extensive selection of wines (more than 1,500 in stock) and single-malt scotches, this friendly West End store also carries a huge array of imported smokes, including humidified cigars. Prices are reasonable, and the staff is very knowledgeable. The newer location at 1104 N. Lamar Blvd. (© **512/479-0045**) is smaller and doesn't have the same selection as the main store. 1130 W. Sixth St. © **512/474-WINE** (9463).

AUSTIN AFTER DARK

Entertainment in Austin starts with live music. In fact, you might get your first taste of it before you even pick up your bags at the airport, where the city offers 11 concerts per week to serenade travelers. Live music is what this city is known for. Austin's music scene is fluid; there's a lot of mixing of styles and genres, some well known, such as country and rock hybrids, others more incongruous, such as punk and bluegrass. The level of virtuosity is impressive. Many famous musicians, such as the Dixie Chicks and Shawn Colvin, call Austin home and frequently perform here. But there are also many lesser-known but great performers, who are content to stay in Austin and enjoy a comfortable and modest level of success.

Another aspect of the live music scene here is that it's inexpensive. Some really good bands play for tips on weekdays and for starving-artist pay at other times. This has been true for years, and it makes you feel that the city is getting a lot more from this arrangement than it's giving. Not that Austin doesn't try to support its local musicians. Social groups organize benefit concerts, and the city and some companies offer lots of free concerts to promote the local talent.

Keep an eye out for performances by checking out the ***Austin Chronicle*** and **XLent,** the entertainment supplement of the *Austin American-Statesman*. Both are available in hundreds of outlets every Thursday.

For information about what's happening in the other performing arts, you should check out the website www.nowplayingaustin.com. This site is a joint project of the Austin Creative Alliance and the city. It has a comprehensive, well organized calendar of events for all the performing arts, and includes museum shows as well. At this site you can get info and buy tickets through its "Austix" link. If you would rather use the phone, call the **Austix Box Office** (✆ **512/474-8497**). Whether you buy online or by phone, the tickets can be picked up at the event, or at the Austix office, in the city's Visitor Center at 209 E. Sixth Street. Sometimes Austix offers discount tickets and sometimes half-price, last-minute tickets. There is a small fee for using the service, which goes to support the performing arts.

Austin's principal venue for the performing arts is the **Long Center,** which hosts symphony concerts, operas, and the ballet performances (see below). The University of Texas has several performance venues as well, including the large Bass Concert Hall. Other venues are spread out across the city, including many local theaters, some quite small.

AUSTIN city limits

PBS's longest-running television program (it first aired in 1975), **Austin City Limits** has showcased such major talent as Lyle Lovett, Willie Nelson, Garth Brooks, the Dixie Chicks, and Phish. Originally pure country, it has evolved to embrace blues, zydeco, Cajun, Tejano—you name it. The show is taped live, from August through December, sometimes through February. For 2011, the program will begin taping shows at the new Moody Theater downtown, part of the W Hotel and Residences development, at West Second Street and Lavaca. Getting free tickets for the tapings will still be the same hit-or-miss method that it's always been. Despite the fact that the new theater is much larger, the producers of the show are going to keep the audiences small to retain the intimate feel that they had at the old studio, which accommodated only 320 people. Log on to **www.austin citylimits.org** for details of how to get tickets, or phone the show's hot line at ☎ **512/475-9077.**

The new theater's full name is **Austin City Limits Live at the Moody Theater** (☎ **877/435-9849;** www.acl-live.com). When it's fully occupied, the theater will hold 2,700 people. It plans to stage 100 to 160 events a year, apart from the Austin City Limits tapings. To see the calendar of events and get tickets, go to the website.

The other branded endeavor is the **Austin City Limits Music Festival,** a 3-day outdoor event with multiple stages and many, many performers representing a mix of established artists and up-and-coming talent. The concert festival debuted in September 2002 and has been extremely popular since its inception. Each year it becomes more of a happening, with acts arriving early to make surprise appearances in clubs around town. In 2010, the festival sold out quickly at $155 per ticket. There were more than 100 bands playing on eight stages. Check the website for the bands who have played the festival in the past, and what bands are booked for the next festival. In the last couple of years, the dates of the festival have shifted around between September and October. The 2011 festival dates will be September 16 to September 18. It's usually still warm, though not hot, at that time of year. Festival organizers and the city have worked together to make sure that the Zilker park land, site of the festival, is well sodded. Still, you might want to dress in cool clothes and take a hat. This event is beginning to resemble South by Southwest (S×SW; see the "Label It Successful: Austin's S×SW" box, below), but without the stuffy conference part. For information on past and future festivals, log on to **www.aclfestival.com.**

THE PERFORMING ARTS

With completion of the **Long Center for the Performing Arts** (☎ **512/457-5500;** www.thelongcenter.org), Austin now has a respectable venue for its symphony orchestra, opera, and ballet performances, and for visiting performances as well. The new hall, set on the south shore of Lady Bird Lake, was designed to take advantage of its location. A raised terrace framed by a circular colonnade looks out over the lake, to the downtown skyline. The grand concert hall, named after Michael and Susan Dell, seats 2,400 people and is grand indeed. It is a modern version of the classic concert hall, using vertical space to accommodate seating. Seats are positioned

Austin After Dark

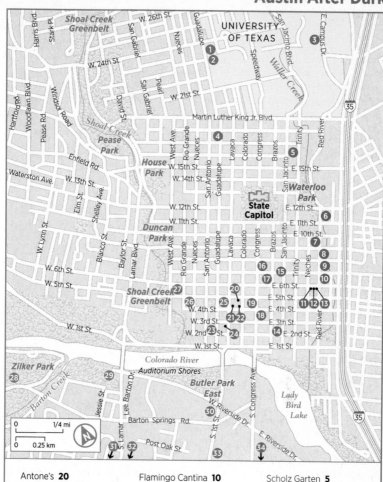

Antone's **20**
Broken Spoke **32**
Cactus Cafe **1**
Cedar Door **14**
Club de Ville **7**
Continental Club **34**
Dog & Duck Pub **4**
The Driskill **17**
Elephant Room **18**
Emo's **10**
Esther's Follies **12**
Fado **21**

Flamingo Cantina **10**
Ginger Man **24**
Jovita's **33**
La Zona Rosa **26**
Long Center **30**
Málaga **23**
Mother Egan's **27**
Paramount Theater **16**
The Parish **15**
Rainbow Cattle Co. **25**
The Red Eyed Fly **9**
Saxon Pub **31**

Scholz Garten **5**
Speakeasy **19**
Stubb's Bar-B-Q **8**
Symphony Square **6**
Texas Performing Arts
  Center and Bass
  Concert Hall **3**
Texas Union Film Series **2**
Velveeta Room **13**
Zach Theater **29**
Zilker Hillside Theater **28**

relatively close to the stage, and multitiered balconies wrap around the walls. A studio theater hosts smaller performances and seats around 200 people. Free tours of the Long Center are held every Wednesday at noon. You can buy tickets for performances directly through the Long Center website or through www.nowplayingaustin.com.

The University of Texas has six theaters, which are managed by its own organization: **Texas Performing Arts** (📞 **512/471-2787;** www.texasperformingarts.org). It attracts major roadshows, including Broadway musicals, pop singers, and classical music ensembles. Of the six theaters, the largest is Bass Hall, which accommodates 2,900 people. You can buy tickets directly through the website or through www.now playingaustin.com.

Opera & Classical Music

Austin Chamber Music Center   The Austin Chamber Music Center is a local organization, which includes members of the symphony orchestra and the university music school, that performs a wide range of compositions in small ensembles, usually quartets. Concerts usually take place in churches or at private residences to small audiences. Performances may include works by anyone from a classical composer such as Mozart to a modern composer such as Glen Gould to a tango composer such as Astor Piazzolla. The best way to find the concerts is to check the center's website (www.austinchambermusic.org) or www.nowplayingaustin.com. 3814 Medical Pkwy. 📞 **512/454-7562** or 454-0026.

Austin Lyric Opera   This small, professional opera company, founded in 1985, presents three productions a year. These performances are held at the Long Performing Arts Center. For the 2010–11 season, the company will perform Verdi's *La Traviata,* Rossini's *The Italian Girl in Algiers,* and a contemporary work called *Flight* by Jonathan Dove. 901 Barton Springs Rd. 📞 **512/472-5992.** www.austinlyricopera.org.

Austin Symphony   The symphony orchestra performs a range of classic and modern works. The season runs from September to May. It also has a Pops series in the fall and winter, which features the most accessible works of classic music, as well as old show tunes from Broadway and music from light opera. Most of these performances are held at the Long Center; a few are held at another auditorium called the **Riverbend Centre** (📞 **512/327-9416;** www.riverbendcentre.com). It's located in Westlake Hills at 4214 N. Capital of Texas Hwy. In June and July, every Wednesday from 9:30 to about 11:30am, kids can try out various orchestral instruments in the symphony's version of a petting zoo. This is held at Symphony Square, a grouping of historic buildings at the intersection of Red River and 11th Street. These are situated around an outdoor amphitheater built of limestone. The buildings date from 1871 to 1877. Waller Creek runs between the seats and the stage of the amphitheater. 1101 Red River St. 📞 **888/4-MAESTRO** (623-7876) or 512/476-6064. www.austinsymphony.org. Tickets $19–$48.

Theater

Founded in 1932, **Zach Theatre** (📞 **512/476-0541** [box office] or 476-0594; www.zachtheatre.org) is one of the oldest arts organizations in Austin. It produces plays for its two theaters in South Austin; just off of Lamar Boulevard is the John E. Whisenhunt Arena at 1510 Toomey Rd., and directly behind it is the theater-in-the-round Kleburg at 1421 W. Riverside Dr.

Other theaters in town tend toward the smaller and, in some cases, more offbeat. These include the intimate **Hyde Park Theatre,** 511 W. 43rd St. (📞 **512/479-PLAY** [479-7529; box office] or 479-7530; www.hydeparktheatre.org), focused on

Austin writers, actors, and designers. It's the venue for the Short Fringe performances at the annual 5-week-long FronteraFest, the largest fringe theater/performance art festival in the Southwest. At the thriving theater department at St. Edward's University, the **Mary Moody Northern Theatre,** 3001 S. Congress Ave. (© **512/448-8484** [box office] or 448-8483; www.stedwards.edu/hum/thtr/mmnt.html), gets support for its performances from a variety of professional directors and guest actors.

East Austin is the home of many experimental performance and film venues. The most established is the **Vortex,** 2307 Manor Rd. (© **512/478-LAVA** [5282]; www. vortexrep.org), home to the Vortex Repertory Company. You can tell by the titles alone—*The Dark Poet's Binge,* say, or *St. Enid and the Black Hand*—that you're well into the fringe. Another, venue in East Austin is **Salvage Vanguard Theater** (© **512/474-7886;** www.salvagevanguard.org), at 2803 Manor Rd. It, too, has its own company, which performs mostly contemporary works. Others to look out for are the **Off Center,** 2211 Hidalgo St. (© **512/567-7833;** www.rudemechs.com), and the **Blue Theater,** 916 Springdale Rd. (© **512/927-1118;** www.bluetheater.org). The latter hosts such annual events as the full-length FronteraFest performances and Flicker Fest film screenings.

Dance

The two dozen professional dancers of **Ballet Austin** (© **512/476-2163** [box office] or 476-9051; www.balletaustin.org) perform such classics as *The Nutcracker* and *Swan Lake,* as well as more avant-garde pieces of the trendsetting *Director's Choice* series, which pairs the work of various contemporary choreographers with the music of popular local Latin musicians and singer-songwriters. When in town, the troupe performs at the Long Center.

Free Entertainment

The amount of free live music offered here is almost absurd. There are several free concert series. One is **Live from the Plaza,** which is sponsored by the city to showcase local musicians. Performances are most Fridays at noon, in front of City Hall, at 301 W. Second St. Other concert series include the **Ensemble Concerts,** which are held every Sunday from June through August at 7:30pm on the grounds of the Long Center. The ensembles are formed of members of the symphony orchestra and play classical and jazz pieces. In May and June, there are free **Wednesday night concerts** at Waterloo Park, at 15th and Trinity streets. These begin at 7:30pm. Bands range from rock and reggae to Latin and country-and-western. Every other Wednesday night from June through August, **Blues on the Green** is held at Zilker Park Rock Island, 2100 Barton Springs Rd., sponsored by radio station **KGSR** (www.kgsr.com). This series can attract some major bands. Check the website or the local paper for who's playing. Shady Grove, one of the restaurants on Barton Springs Road (see chapter 12), offers a series of free outdoor concerts called **Shady Grove Unplugged.** They take place in the restaurant's large shaded patio every Thursday in the spring and summer at 7pm. Acts include popular local and touring bands, such as James McMurtry, the Derailers, Jimmy LaFave, the South Austin Jug Band, Ruthie Foster, and Ray Wilie Hubbard. Check the restaurant's website: www.theshadygrove.com.

Other places to hear free music include **Central Market** (www.centralmarket.com/Stores/Austin-Central.aspx), which has live music three times a week at both its central and south locations. **Whole Foods Market** (www.wholefoodsmarket.com), at Fifth Street and Lamar, has the **Music at the Market** series taking place on Thursdays from 6 to 7:30pm. Also, bands are always playing at First Thursdays on South Congress (see "First Thursdays" in chapter 14).

From mid-July through late August, the **Beverly F. Sheffield Zilker Hillside Theater,** across from Barton Springs Pool, hosts a summer musical (Zilker Theater Productions; ☎ 512/479-9491; www.zilker.org). Started in the late 1950s, this is the longest-running series of its type in the United States. The summer **Austin Shakespeare Festival** is often held at the theater, too; for up-to-date information, call ☎ 512/454-BARD (454-2273) or log on to www.austinshakespeare.org. More than 5,000 people can perch on the theater's grassy knoll to watch performances. If you can, take something to sit on, such as a blanket or a lawn chair.

THE CLUB & MUSIC SCENE

Music was always important to life in Austin, but it became a big deal in the early '70s with the advent of "progressive country" (aka redneck rock). Local boy Willie Nelson became its principal proponent, along with several other Austin musicians. And the Armadillo World Headquarters, a music hall known for hosting all the '60s rock bands, became the center of events and symbolized the marriage of country with counterculture. The city has since become an incubator for a wonderfully vital, cross-bred alternative sound that mixes rock, country, folk, blues, punk, and Tejano. Although the Armadillo is now gone, live music in Austin continues to thrive in bars all across central Austin.

While **Sixth Street** is well known to many outsiders and is home to some good bars, just as popular but less famous is the **Warehouse District,** which has more glitz than grunge. And for those wanting exposure to more of the local sound, there are cheap dives just off Sixth, on **Red River Street** (see "Navigating Austin's Downtown Bar Scene" for a short guide for downtown barhopping). And then there are the many venues that don't fall inside these districts, like the Continental Club and the Saxon Pub. All in all, there's a lot to explore. Have fun and poke around. You might come across the next Janis Joplin, Stevie Ray Vaughan, or Jimmie Dale Gilmore, to name just a few who were playing local gigs here before they hit the big time. When big events occur, such as S×SW (see "Label it Successful—Austin's S×SW" below), the Republic of Texas Biker Rally (June), or the Custom Car and Hot Rod Show (Jan), things get a little crazy and barhopping becomes impossible, but walking Sixth Street is still highly entertaining.

NAVIGATING AUSTIN'S downtown bar scene

Austin's downtown bars are concentrated in three areas called Sixth Street, the Warehouse District, and Red River. When people talk of **Sixth Street,** they are referring to a 5-block portion of East Sixth, from Congress Avenue to Red River. This strip has all kinds of bars, from noisy saloons that cater to college students and offer $1 beer nights, such as the **Aquarium** and the **Library,** to a piano bar **(Pete's Dueling Pianos),** where the crowd is older and the volume of the music much lower. The best thing you can do is just walk the street and see what you like. You're apt to hear cover bands, Irish folk music, hip-hop, and Latin, to name just a few of the sounds.

Red River Street, between Sixth and 10th streets, is for those seeking out the local, underground music scene. You'll pass by a collection of bars that are less commercial and, frankly, don't look like much, but are where Austinites and music aficionados, mostly in their 20s and 30s, go to hear local bands of various stripes. Bars such as the **Red Eyed Fly** (see listing below) will mix blues, country, and metal bands; **Beerland** will usually have something "indie-garagey-punky"; **Room 710** something hard,

metal, or punk. Farther down the street are **Club de Ville** and **Mohawk,** which might have just about anything, including low cover charges in the range of $3 to $10, depending on the night. The one exception is **Stubb's** (see listing below), which is a large venue that signs name touring acts as well as some of the most popular local bands, and their cover charges are correspondingly higher.

The **Warehouse District** is west of Congress Avenue and extends from Second to Fifth streets, and from Congress Avenue to Guadalupe, encompassing 9 square blocks. It's more of a social scene with less emphasis on live music. It will work for those who want to have a drink and perhaps some food in attractive surroundings. Again, the best thing to do would be to stroll around until you see something that fits your mood. For the beer drinker, there are bars, such as the **Ginger Man** (at 301 Lavaca), a bar with an astonishing array of beers from around the world. On the tony side would be a cocktail bar called **Qua** (213 W. Fourth St.). **Málaga,** a tapas bar listed below, would be in the same category.

Note: Categories of clubs in a city known for crossover are often very rough approximations, so those that completely defy typecasting are dubbed "eclectic." Cover charges range from $5 to $15 for well liked local bands. Note, too, that in addition to the clubs detailed below, several of the restaurants discussed in chapter 12, including **Threadgill's** (p. 197) and **Artz Rib House** (p. 191), offer live music regularly.

Folk & Country

Broken Spoke ★★   This is one of the great country music dance halls. It dates back to 1964, when people would come out here to two-step across the large wood-plank floor. It hasn't changed much, except for the occasional busload of tourists that stops by. It's a lot of fun and well worth the effort of dragging your potential dance partner out of the cozy hotel room. This is Austin, so you don't have to be all duded up for dancing here. Granted, boot scootin' is nice to do with real boots, but lots of people show up in sneakers and Hawaiian shirts. Photos of Hank Williams, Tex

Ritter, and other country greats line the walls of the club's "museum." You can eat in a large, open room out front (the chicken-fried steak can't be beat), or bring your long necks back to a table overlooking the dance floor. 3201 S. Lamar Blvd. © **512/442-6189.** www.brokenspokeaustintx.com. Cover $5–$15.

Jovita's Jovita's is part Mexican restaurant, part nightclub, part Mexican-American cultural center. The food is okay, not great, but it's quite the place to sip a margarita while watching some of the best acts in town—mostly country but also some Latin groups. 1619 S. First St. © **512/447-7825.** www.jovitas.com. Cover $5–$10.

Jazz & Blues

Antone's ★ Although Willie Nelson and crossover country-and-western bands such as the Austin Lounge Lizards have been known to turn up at Clifford Antone's place, the club owner's name has always been synonymous with the blues. Stevie Ray Vaughan used to be a regular, and when such major blues artists as Buddy Guy, Etta James, or Edgar Winter venture down this way, you can be sure they'll either be playing Antone's or stopping by for a surprise set. Clifford Antone died recently, and the response by the blues community was a large outpouring of performances to honor the man. Look for the club to continue the same trajectory set out by its former owner. 213 W. Fifth St. © **512/320-8424.** www.antones.net. Cover $8–$35 (depending on performer).

Elephant Room This downtown bar is a great setting for listening to jazz—a cozy, softly lit chamber in the basement of one of Congress Avenue's old buildings. You have to be purposeful to get here because the Elephant Room entrance is a small door with a tiny sign, and the club isn't on Sixth or in the Warehouse District. The club lines up first-class acts, mostly contemporary jazz. The best night to go is on a weeknight when the bar is less crowded. 315 Congress Ave. © **512/473-2279.** www.elephantroom.com. Cover $5–$15.

Latin & Reggae

Flamingo Cantina The Flamingo attracts local and touring acts in all subgenres of reggae—dance hall, ska, rocksteady, and dub—as well as a range of local Latin bands and DJs. Lounge around one of several bars and open-air decks when you're not sitting on the comfy carpeted bleachers listening to the performers. 515 E. Sixth St. © **512/494-9336.** www.flamingocantina.com. Cover $5–$20.

Rock

Emo's This is one of Austin's best known clubs with a reputation for signing up bands that are on their way up, which makes many groups covet a gig here. The music tends to be alternative forms of rock, pop, hip-hop, and anything that seems to be different and original. It's all about the music here, not the decor. There's an urban-jungle feel to the place, much of which is outdoors, and the public seems to like it that way. There are two stages, each with its own entrance (one on Sixth, the other on Red River). Both areas connect to a biergarten of sorts in the middle of the block. Emo's attracts a mostly young crowd and many off-duty musicians. 603 Red River St. © **512/477-EMOS** (512/477-3667). www.emosaustin.com. Cover $5–$12.

The Red Eyed Fly A good representative of the clubs along Red River, the Fly signs up about 90% local bands of all kinds. There's nothing fancy about the club. The first part is a lounge with a pool table, a bar, a jukebox, and some furniture in varying degrees of decay; the back is where the bands perform and where you pay a cover charge to see them. It's an outdoor stage bordering Waller Creek. The crowd is mostly young and stands around with beers in hand or dances to the music in a way that's hard to describe—other than to say that it's very Austin. 715 Red River St. ℂ **512/474-1084.** www.redeyedfly.com. Cover $5–$10.

Singer-Songwriter

Cactus Cafe ★   A small, dark cavern with great acoustics and a fully stocked bar, UT's Cactus Cafe is home-away-from-home for a lot of singer-songwriters. There's a crowd of regulars who come here to see the likes of solo artists such as Alison Krauss and Suzanne Vega, along with well-known acoustic combos. The adjacent **Texas Union Ballroom** (ℂ **512/475-6645**) draws larger crowds with such big names as the Dixie Chicks. Texas Union, University of Texas campus (24th and Guadalupe sts.). ℂ **512/475-6515.** www.utexas.edu/student/txunion/ae/cactus. Cover $10–$35.

Eclectic

Carousel Lounge   In spite of (or maybe because of) its out-of-the-way location and bizarre circus theme—complete with elephant and lion-tamer murals and an actual carousel behind the bar—the Carousel Lounge is a highly popular local watering hole. You never know what will turn up onstage—this place has hosted everything from smaller musical acts to belly dancers. 1110 E. 52nd St. ℂ **512/452-6790.** Cover up to $5.

Continental Club ★   This Austin institution showcases rock, rockabilly, country, Latino, and new wave sounds. So many local acts have played here on their way to fame, and so many already famous acts will occasionally return, that it's worth your while to check out this small, dark club on South Congress. With high stools and a pool table in the back room, it feels much more like a neighborhood bar than a major venue, which is the lure of the place. It's got the best happy hour music in town. The club also operates a gallery club in the upstairs of the building next door. It features smaller acts and often has no cover. 1315 S. Congress Ave. ℂ **512/441-2444.** www.continentalclub.com. Cover $5–$20.

La Zona Rosa ★★   Another Austin classic, LZR has departed from its funky roots to go a bit upmarket, featuring bigger names and bigger covers than in the past. But the venue has remained the same—a renovated garage brightly painted with monsters and filled with kitschy memorabilia—and this is still a fun place to listen to good bands, from the Gourds to Mose Allison to Greg Allman and Friends. 612 W. Fourth St. ℂ **512/263-4146,** 888/597-STAR (597-7827), or 512/469-SHOW (469-7469) for tickets. www.lazonarosa.com. Tickets $8–$12 local acts, $20–$50 national acts.

The Parish   Formerly called "The Mercury," this upstairs club on Sixth Street is known locally as a great place to hear live music in a range of genres—hip-hop, rock,

Started in 1987 as a way to showcase unsigned Texas bands, **South by Southwest (S×SW)** soon became *the* place for fledgling musicians from around the world to come and perform their music in front of music-industry bigwigs. In the mid-1990s, S×SW started a film and interactive (digital and Internet) media festival, which begins a few days before the music festival. It, too, has grown considerably over the years.

S×SW's music festival is held during UT's spring break, usually the third week of March. Programs might include as many as 60 panels and workshops and 900 musical appearances at more than 40 venues around town. Check the website at **www.sxsw.com** or call © **512/467-7979.** Wristbands for the 4-day event, which allow access to all the venues, usually run from $150 to $810 for the walk-up Platinum rate, which affords access to all of the conference and better access to bars. Even with a wristband, it can be difficult or impossible to see some bands. Every year a few bands will get some buzz before the festival and attract too big a crowd for the venue. Still, with 40 bands playing at any given time, chances are you'll find something you like.

funk, reggae, Latin, and electronic. 214 E. Sixth St. © **512/478-6372.** www.theparishroom.com. Tickets $5–$12 local acts, $13–$20 national acts.

Saxon Pub   Look for the oversize knight in suit of armor on South Lamar Boulevard to find this iconic club that gets country, rock, and blues performers, big and small. The crowd is older and more laid-back, and the volume is lower than at most of the Sixth Street bars. Check the calendar on the club's website, and you'll find performers who rarely play in such a small venue. This is a very comfortable place to catch great bands performing. 1320 S. Lamar Blvd. © **512/448-2552.** www.thesaxonpub.com. Cover $5–$15.

Speakeasy   The walk down a dark alley in the Warehouse District to reach this multilevel club is all part of the 1920s Prohibition theme, which, mercifully, is not taken to an obnoxious extreme. Lots of dark wood and red velvet drapes help create a swanky atmosphere. Walk up two flights of narrow stairs to enjoy a drink or dance on the romantic Evergreen terrace. Lately the club has been signing some good Latin bands, mellow rock bands, and the occasional funk band. 412 Congress Ave. © **512/476-8086.** www.speakeasyaustin.com. Cover $5–$15.

Stubb's Bar-B-Q   Within the rough limestone walls of a renovated historic building, you'll find great barbecue and country Texas fare and three friendly bars—plus terrific music, ranging from singer-songwriter solos to hip-hop open mics to all-out country jams. Out back, the Waller Amphitheater hosts some of the bigger acts that come to Austin. See chapter 12 also for Stubb's Sunday gospel brunches. 801 Red River St. © **512/480-8341.** www.stubbsaustin.com. Cover $6–$25.

Comedy Clubs

Cap City Comedy   Top-ranked on the stand-up circuit, Cap City books nationally recognized comedians such as Dave Chappelle, Carlos Mencia, and Bobcat Goldthwait. The cream of the crop turn up on Friday and Saturday, of course, but you'll find plenty to laugh at (including lower cover charges) the rest of the week. Performances

If it's 3am and you have a hankering for a huge stack of pancakes to soak up the excess alcohol you shouldn't have downed, Austin has you covered. Austin's all-night cafes offer funky atmosphere and large quantities of hippie food. In addition to the usual cafe offerings, you can get local favorites, including Tex-Mex items such as *migas,* breakfast tacos, vegetarian versions of traditional Texas fare, and large creative salads.

One of the earliest on the scene and still hugely popular is **Kerbey Lane,** 3704 Kerbey Lane (✆ **512/451-1436;** www.kerbeylanecafe.com). Sunday mornings, locals spill out on the porch of the comfortable old house, waiting for a table so they can order the signature "pancakes as big as your head." Musicians finishing up late-night gigs at the Continental Club usually head over to the **Magnolia Cafe South,** 1920 S. Congress Ave. (✆ **512/445-0000;** www.cafemagnolia.com). On nice nights, enjoy the Love Veggies sautéed in garlic butter or the Deep Eddy burrito on an outdoor deck. Both cafes are open 24 hours daily. Kerbey Lane has three other locations, and Magnolia Cafe has one clone; but the originals are far more interesting.

are nightly at 8pm with additional performances Friday and Saturday at 10:30pm. You can find who's performing by checking the website www.nowplayingaustin.com. 8120 Research Blvd., Ste. 100. ✆ **512/467-2333.** www.capcitycomedy.com. Tickets $4.50–$25.

Esther's Follies   You might miss a couple of the punch lines if you're not in on the latest twists and turns of local politics, but the no-holds-barred Esther's Follies doesn't spare Washington, either. It's satirical, irreverent, and very Austin. Performances are Thursday, at 8pm; Friday through Saturday, 8 and 10pm. 525 E. Sixth St. ✆ **512/320-0553.** www.esthersfollies.com. Tickets $18–$23; $2 off for students and seniors.

Velveeta Room   For one-stop comedy consumption, go straight from Esther's to the Velveeta Room next door, a deliberately cheesy club serving more generic stand-up, local and national, as well as an open mic. Open-mic night is Thursday at 10pm; performances Friday and Saturday are 9:30 and 11pm. 521 E. Sixth St. ✆ **512/469-9116.** www.thevelveetaroom.com. Tickets $5–$10.

THE BAR SCENE
British & Irish Pubs

Dog & Duck Pub   This drinking spot captures the comfy, worn-in feel of pubs in the U.K. A lot of regulars and a lot of happy faces can be seen here, drinking pints of their favorite brews, several of which are imported from the mother country. Sit outside at the outdoor picnic tables or roam indoors past the dartboards and the bar area, to find some of the cozier nooks and crannies. Though the Dog & Duck goes out of its way to evoke the feel of a British public house, it can't escape its Austin roots; something can be said for the authentic taste of the bangers and mash, but that's not necessarily a good thing. 406 W. 17th St. ✆ **512/479-0598.** www.doganddduckpub.com.99.

Fado   This Irish pub in the Warehouse District looks surprisingly like the genuine article. The regulars can even be seen following soccer matches from the old country on large television screens. On weekend nights, local bands play on the small outdoor

15

AUSTIN AFTER DARK

The Bar Scene

stage. The food, however, is a New World departure from Irish pub grub—it's international, with burgers, quesadillas, and the like. 214 W. Fourth St. © **512/457-0172.** www.fadoirishpub.com.

Mother Egan's   The weekday happy hour is animated by lively, friendly banter and a general atmosphere of bonhomie, while on the weekends, the bar welcomes patrons from the open-air artists' market next door. There's no shortage of classic pub entertainment, either, with a mix of TV football, live music in the singer-songwriter vein, and tournaments for trivia. The Irish classics (corned beef and cabbage, shepherd's pie, and so on) and American pub grub are crowd pleasers, too. 715 W. Sixth St. © **512/478-7747.** www.motheregansirishpub.com.

Gay Bars

Oilcan Harry's   Its name notwithstanding—it's known locally as the Can—this slick Warehouse District bar attracts a clean-cut, upscale, mostly male crowd. Consistently voted Austin's Best Gay Club by readers of the *Austin Chronicle,* this is the place to go if you're looking for a buttoned-down, Brooks Brothers kind of guy. There's dancing, but not with the same frenzy as at many of the other clubs. 211 W. Fourth St. © **512/320-8823.** www.oilcanharrys.com.

Rainbow Cattle Co.   This is Austin's prime gay country-western dance hall. It's about 75% male, but also attracts a fair share of lesbian two-steppers, especially on Thursday, which is Ladies Night. 305 W. Fifth St. © **512/472-5288.** www.rainbowcattleco.com.

A Historic Bar

Scholz Garten ★   Since 1866, when councilman August Scholz first opened his tavern near the state capitol, every Texas governor has visited it at least once (and many quite a few more times). In recent years, Texas's oldest operating bar was sold to the owners of the popular Green Mesquite BBQ, giving it new life. The extensive menu now combines barbecue with German favorites, such as bratwurst and sauerkraut, and jagerschnitzel. This place is packed during Longhorn football games or when some other special university event is happening; otherwise it's generally a quiet spot to drink a beer out in the biergarten. On Thursdays in the spring and fall, when the weather holds, a group of talented amateurs get together to play old-style brass band songs for the crowd—a Scholz's tradition. All in all, a great place to drink in some Austin history. 1607 San Jacinto Blvd. © **512/474-1958.** www.scholzgarten.net.

A Local Favorite

Cedar Door   Think "Cheers" with a redwood deck in downtown Austin. In spite of the fact that it keeps changing location—it's moved four times in its 26-year history—the Cedar Door remains Austin's favorite dumpy bar, drawing a group of regulars ranging from hippies to journalists and politicos. The beer's cold and the drinks are strong. The signature cocktail is the Mexican martini. If you're smart, you'll limit yourself to one. 201 Brazos St. © **512/473-3712.** www.cedardooraustin.com.

> **Impressions**
>
> *There is a very remarkable number of drinking and gambling shops [in Austin], but not one bookstore.*
> —Frederick Law Olmsted, *A Journey Through Texas,* 1853

A Piano Bar

The Driskill   Sink into one of the plush chairs arrayed around a grand piano and enjoy everything from blues to show tunes in the upper-lobby bar of this newly opulent historic hotel. A pianist accompanies the happy hour hors d'oeuvres (nightly 5–7pm), but the ivory thumping gets going around 8pm Tuesday through Saturday. 604 Brazos St. ✆ **512/391-7162.** www.driskillgrill.com/bar.html.

A Wine & Tapas Bar

Málaga   Come to this sleek spot to sip fine wines at good prices—50 selections by the glass—and nibble Spanish appetizers (the swordfish bites are especially tasty). 440 W. Second St. ✆ **512/236-8020.** www.malagatapasbar.com.

FILMS

Not surprisingly, you can see more foreign films in Austin than anywhere else in the state. In the university area, the largest concentration of art films can be found at the **Texas Union Film Series,** UT campus, Texas Union Building and Hogg Auditorium (✆ **512/475-6656**). **Alamo Drafthouse,** 1120 S. Lamar Blvd. (✆ **512/707-8262;** www.originalalamo.com), is an Austin original that combines "dinner and a movie"

---

celluloid AUSTIN

Austin has long had an undercover Hollywood presence. During the past 3 decades, more than 90 films were shot in the city and its vicinity. But you'd be hard-pressed to identify Texas's capital in any of them. Because it has such a wide range of landscapes, Austin has filled in for locations as far-flung as Canada and Vietnam.

The city has less of an identity crisis behind the camera. It first earned its credentials as an indie director–friendly place in 1982, when the Coen brothers shot *Blood Simple* here. And when University of Texas graduate Richard Linklater captured some of the loopier members of Austin's denizens in *Slackers*—adding a word to the national vocabulary in the process—Austin arrived on the *cinéaste* scene. Linklater is often spotted around town with Robert Rodriguez, who shot all or part of several of his films (*Alienated, The Faculty,* and the *Spy Kids* series) in Austin,

and with Quentin Tarantino, who owns property in town. Mike Judge, of *Beavis and Butthead* and *King of the Hill* fame, lives in Austin, too.

Of the many cinematic events held in town, October's **Austin Film Festival** is among the more interesting. Held in tandem with the Heart of Films Screenwriters Conference, it focuses on movies with great scripts. For current information, contact the Austin Film Festival, 1604 Nueces, Austin, TX 78701 (✆ **800/310-FEST** [310-3378] or 512/478-4795; fax 512/478-6205; www.austinfilmfestival.com). And the comelately film component of S×SW (see "Label It Successful—Austin's S×SW" earlier in this chapter) gets larger every year. Panelists have included Linklater and John Sayles, whose film *Lone Star* had its world première here.

See also chapter 18 for information on the Austin Gay and Lesbian International Film Festival.

into a one-stop affair. The owners have taken over old movie theaters and refitted the seating in order to add counter space for patrons. They provide a menu of basic food and drinks, including beer and wine, ordered and delivered straight to your seat. The staff make custom film shorts before the feature presentation. Other locations include Alamo Village, 2700 W. Anderson Lane (north central), and Alamo Lake Creek, 13729 Research Blvd. (far north). There is a downtown location, in the old Ritz Theater at 320 E. Sixth St.

SIDE TRIPS FROM AUSTIN

I f you're looking for a quick day trip out of town, or if you're arriving to Austin by car from Dallas, Houston, or San Antonio, this chapter is for you. With just a short drive or detour, or perhaps no detour at all, you can, for instance, find one-of-a-kind world-famous barbecue, see a bit of small-town Texas that's not the least bit touristy, canoe on a clear river under tall cypress trees, hike in a pine forest, or shop in a Texas-size outlet mall.

SMALL TOWNS & TEXAS BARBECUE

More so than chili con carne or chicken-fried steak, barbecue can justly claim to be the quintessential Texas food. Not only is it highly prized in all corners of the state, but barbecue is also the recipient of contributions from just about every major culture and ethnic group that came to Texas. Everyone lent a hand in its creation—cowboys and Indians, Mexicans and Germans, Anglos and African Americans. And it took every one of those contributions to perfect the technique of combining meat, fire, and smoke into a rare sensory delight. It also created a rich lore surrounding barbecue, lots of traditions, and, of course, endless debate over such important matters as wet or dry, direct or indirect heat, and sauce or no sauce.

City vs. Country

Before I tackle such complex and weighty issues, it's important to note that Austin is at the center of a constellation of small towns famous for their barbecue. Here you'll find the real deal. Franklin's BBQ, off I-35, has the most traditional, uncompromising style. But if you can leave the city, you will find small-town barbecue, where the slower rhythms of life and the importance of tradition apply to the cooking of barbecue.

Another advantage small towns have is the lack of clean-air ordinances, because to create old-time barbecue you need lots of smoke. City barbecue is leaning more and more on the use of commercial cookers, which have improved over the years, but they still can't match the character of barbecue cooked using wood. Wood is the fuel of choice, not charcoal, because charcoal burns too cleanly. The moisture and sap in the wood create the smoke that gives the meat its flavor and creates the pink line running just below the surface of the meat. This line is produced when nitrogen dioxide in the smoke reacts with the myoglobin in the meat. If

EXPERIENCING CENTRAL TEXAS barbecue

In Texas, barbecue varies from region to region. In central Texas, the traditional "dry" method is most often used. (A dry rub is applied to the meat, which isn't marinated or basted. Then the meat is cooked for many hours using indirect heat.) This method produces a delicious crust on the meat, which is different from Kansas City or Carolina barbecue. As to which style is best, you be the judge.

Barbecue joints in central Texas will cook a variety of meats, but there are three constants: brisket, spareribs (pork), and sausage. All other meats, such as beef ribs, pork chops, turkey, and chicken might be offered, but are not considered essential. When ordering brisket, you'll often be asked if you want it lean or fatty. Try the fatty. Another hallmark of Texas barbecue is the sauce—a sweet and spicy tomato-based concoction. There is a debate in Texas as to whether good barbecue needs sauce or not, to which there is no definitive answer as it is entirely a matter of personal taste. Almost all barbecue joints will offer sauce, and the customers are free to use it or not.

In Texas, barbecue is always served with plain white bread (anything else would be too highfalutin'), onions, and pickles. Popular side dishes include chili beans, potato salad, and cole slaw. Often the barbecue is served on butcher paper (as plates would also be too highfalutin'). Most small towns sell barbecue by weight—prices run about $7 to $10 per pound for the mainstays: ribs, sausage, and brisket.

It's important to note that barbecue is traditionally eaten early, to allow ample time for digestion. Many small town barbecue joints close by 6pm, and many run out of meat long before then. And one more thing to remember when heading to these small towns for barbecue: Bring cash. Credit cards are often not accepted.

the brisket has been cooked with a wood fire in a proper pit, the line will be redder and deeper than on brisket cooked in a commercial smoker.

Lockhart

This little town 30 miles south of Austin is the most famous town in Texas for barbecue. If you have but one shot to try real barbecue, this is the place you should go. From Austin, take Hwy. 183 south. Try to leave before 4pm to avoid traffic. If you're headed to Austin from San Antonio, you can make a little detour at San Marcos. Follow Hwy. 80 E. to Martindale, then Hwy. 142 to Lockhart.

Lockhart has three important barbecue joints. Perhaps the most famous (and a personal favorite) is **Kreuz Market.** It's located north of downtown at 619 N. Colorado St. (© **512/398-2361**). Hours are Monday to Saturday 10:30am to 8pm. As you enter Lockhart (coming from Austin) on Hwy. 183, you'll come to a flyover. Take the last right before the flyover, and you'll practically be in the parking lot.

Once you walk through the doors, head to the pit room in back. A sign on the wall reads like an edict: NO SALAD. NO SAUCE. NO CREDIT CARDS. This is one of the few places that refuses to provide sauce. A lot of barbecuers agree with this position in theory but aren't about to chase off those customers who like sauce. The guys here just don't care. Once you buy your barbecue, head to the large dining room where you can buy drinks and what few side dishes are available. The sides are few and not very

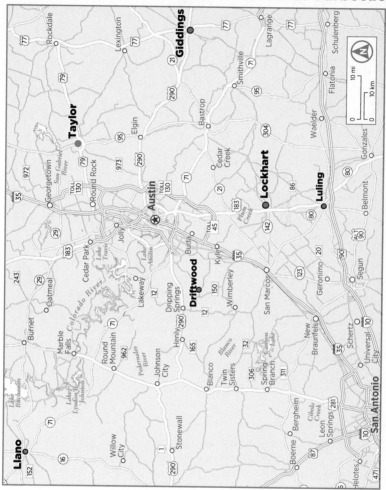

good, but the meat is amazing. With one bite of the brisket or the ribs, you'll understand what Central Texas barbecue is all about. The sausage is spicy and coarsely ground. For some it's too fatty, but I love it.

If you want sauce with your barbecue, head to **Black's Barbecue** (© **512/398-2712**), at 215 N. Main St. It's located 3 blocks north of the town square. You'll see signs pointing the way as you enter Lockhart. In addition to excellent barbecue and a tangy sauce, Black's also offers well-prepared side dishes. Food is served daily from 10am to 8pm.

Your third option is **Smitty's Market** (© **512/398-9344**), at 208 S. Commerce, a half-block south of the town square. It's open Monday to Saturday from 7am to 6pm. Even if you eat elsewhere, make a point of strolling into Smitty's just to see the smoke-caked pit room. This is the original location of Kreuz Market. The family parted ways 15 years ago—one side kept the original location while the other side kept the name. The recipes are about the same in both places, but I think the quality of the meat is a little better at the new place. While you're walking off your meal, take a spin around the town square and county courthouse, which was renovated in 2000. It's a distinctive building with mansard roofs on the corners and strangely shaped decorative towers in the center and on the north and south sides. Small, struggling businesses and empty storefronts make up the main square, which is indicative of the state of the local economy. Barbecue may be the town's economic engine.

Luling

This town is 16 miles south of Lockhart. It's actually a bit closer to San Antonio than Austin. And, if you're traveling between Houston and San Antonio, it's but a short detour off I-10. The place to go is **Luling City Market** (© 830/875-9019), at 633 E. Davis, where Hwy. 183 crosses the railroad tracks. As with other barbecue joints, first you buy your barbecue in the pit room, before getting your sauce, drinks, and side dishes in the dining room. Only beans and potato salad are available. In my opinion, the ribs and the brisket are the best of the offerings. The dry rub on the ribs gives them a slightly crispy texture, and the brisket melts in your mouth. Luling City Market is open Monday to Saturday 7am to 6pm. You can walk off your meal by strolling down Davis Street to the Oil Museum. Both the museum and the town are described in greater detail in chapter 9.

Driftwood

Seventeen miles southwest of Austin is the tiny town of Driftwood and its famous barbecue joint, the **Salt Lick** (© 512/858-4959). Take Hwy. 290 west. As you pass through Oak Hill, keep to your left when the highway forks. After you pass the fork, make a left on to FM 1826 at the third traffic light. Drive 13 miles to the Salt Lick. It will be on your right, and Camp Ben McCulloch will be on your left. The address is 18001 FM 1826, but that's not going to help you much, and it's not important, because you can't miss the place. If you're in the vicinity of San Marcos, continue north on I-35 and exit Kyle, taking Hwy. 150 W. Stay on 150 until you get to FM 1826, then turn right.

The Salt Lick is open daily 11am to 10pm. It can get crowded on weekends when Austinites come down with their ice chests full of beer, which they drink while waiting for a table. (Beer can't be sold because this part of Hays County is dry.) The Salt Lick cooks its barbecue differently from standard local practice. It uses an open stone pit, direct heat, and basting. In Texas, this is often called "cowboy style." If you prefer Kansas City–style barbecue, you'll like this place. The meat gets a good smoky flavor, but leans more heavily on the sauce—it's rich and tangy and a favorite with the locals. The setting is charming and rustic, in a long rambling building filled with picnic tables. There's a screened porch area, which is pleasant when the weather is mild. Food is served in individual portions or all-you-can-eat family style. The cole slaw, potato salad, and beans are good, as are the desserts.

Llano

Llano is 75 miles northwest of Austin, which is too far to go just to get some barbecue, when there are great places closer by. But if you're already up in the Highland Lakes area, in the vicinity of Lake Buchanan, you can take advantage of your proximity and enjoy some barbecue at **Cooper's** (✆ 325/247-5713). It's located at 604 W. Young (Hwy. 29). Like the Salt Lick, Cooper's uses the direct-heat method, and the same comments apply. The brisket is the star of the show. Cooper's is open daily from 10:30am to 8pm.

Taylor

Northeast of Austin is the town of Taylor. It's about a 35-mile trip. Take I-35 north to Round Rock, then Hwy. 79 E. This is the home of a famous barbecue joint called **Louie Mueller's** (✆ 512/352-6206), at 206 W. Second St., open Monday through Saturday from 10am to 6pm. If you're on your way to Austin from Dallas, it's only a 16-mile detour. Barbecue is cooked with the indirect heat method in an impressive pit. The rub uses a lot of black pepper, and combined with the smoke, makes a wonderful black crust on the brisket. The restaurant is large and old-fashioned and smells of smoke that's been wafting through here for 50 years.

Giddings

If you're coming from Houston on Hwy. 290, you won't have to make any detour whatsoever to have some excellent barbecue at **City Meat Market** (✆ 979/542-2740). It's located in downtown Giddings at the intersection with Hwy. 77 (aka Austin St.), in an old-fashioned brick storefront. You can't miss it. This place is also a market that sells fresh meat, despite the fact that it's also been selling barbecue for about 50 years. It's open Monday to Friday from 7:30am to 5:30pm and Saturdays from 7:30am to 4pm, but most of the barbecue is gone by 1 or 2pm. The owner tells me that people can call ahead to reserve meat. This place cooks a delicious pork shoulder, which I recommend. Giddings is 55 miles east of Austin. While digesting your meal, you can walk down Austin Street for a block in order to view the Lee County courthouse, built in the 1890s. It was designed by J. Riely Gordon, the same architect who built the courthouses in San Antonio, New Braunfels, and Gonzales. He loved to use Romanesque elements, which emphasize solidity and gravity—virtues one would like to associate with the administration of justice.

Lexington

Also in Lee County is the town of Lexington, home of **Snow's Barbecue** (✆ 979/542-8189), at 516 Main. From Hwy. 290, take Hwy. 77 north for 20 miles (from Austin, take Hwy. 290 to FM 696; you see a sign pointing the way to Lexington). Snow's is open only on Saturday, from 8am until noon. This inconvenience is made worse by the fact that it often sells out of meat before 10am. It became a destination bbq joint after *Texas Monthly* food editors dubbed it the best in Texas, and so it draws the serious aficionados from across the state. In truth, the cooking is excellent, especially the brisket, and would be well worth the effort and timing needed to get there were it not in the heart of barbecue country, which offers so many excellent options.

So what is the best bbq in central Texas? That depends on the day in question and perhaps the alignment of the stars, and of course, on your own taste. I prefer the traditional dry method, with its smoky, peppery crust. On some days, I show up at a bbq joint at the exact moment when the meat is just perfect, and the smoky taste is at its height but before the meat has had a chance to dry out. On other days, I'm not so lucky. But, of the places mentioned above, I think those in Lockhart, Luling, and Lexington are the ones where that magical moment is most likely to occur.

In the 1980s, the stretch of Interstate 35 between Austin and San Antonio was dubbed "The Golden Corridor." Since then, the area has lived up to its name—with commerce exploding along the way, linking more closely each year such booming little towns as Buda (pronounced "Byoo-dah") and Kyle, with its charming downtown. San Marcos is known as a fun college town and shopping mecca, and New Braunfels is an old German settlement turned busy modern town.

SAN MARCOS

The interstate highway connecting Austin and San Antonio roughly traces a boundary between the Hill Country to the west and the coastal prairie to the east. This relatively narrow strip of land extending from north of Austin to south of San Antonio is dotted with natural springs, which were formed when the uplifting that produced the Edwards Plateau and the Hill Country opened fissures in the limestone substrate along the Balcones fault line. Rainwater on the plateau seeps into these cracks and flows underground for many miles before bubbling back up to the surface at the lower elevation of this boundary zone.

Some of the largest of these springs are found in San Marcos, 26 miles south of Austin. These springs and the wildlife they attracted were probably what brought the first human inhabitants to the region, some 12,000 years ago. Archaeological evidence points to continuous settlement along these springs in one form or another, prompting local scholars to boast that San Marcos is the oldest continuously inhabited site in the Western Hemisphere. Temporary home to two Spanish missions in the late 1700s, as well as to the Comanche and Apaches, this area was eventually inhabited by Anglo settlers in the middle of the 19th century. Now host to Texas State University–San Marcos (formerly Southwest Texas State), the alma mater of LBJ, San Marcos has the laid-back feel of a college town. It's also fast becoming a bedroom community of Austin, only half an hour away.

Just 15 miles farther south, toward San Antonio, is the town of New Braunfels, which has several attractions for visitors, including caverns, a large waterpark, tubing on a river, and a classic country dance hall (in Gruene). New Braunfels is described in chapter 9.

What to See & Do

Before arriving in San Marcos, you pass through two small towns, Buda, a corruption of the Spanish word for widow, *viuda*) and Kyle. These are old towns that now are almost entirely bedroom communities for Austin and have lost any distinctive character that they may have had.

But in Buda, you'll find one of those destination stores for outdoor gear called **Cabela's** (© 512/295-1100; www.cabelas.com). You'll see signs marking the exit (220), and can see the store from the highway. It's a cavernous structure with an indoor waterfall, a large aquarium area, and a diorama of the African savanna. It sells a lot of gear to hunters, fishermen, campers, and kayakers, as wells as clothing and footwear.

To get to San Marcos, take exit 206 and turn right on to Aquarena Springs Drive. This will lead you directly to Spring Lake, which is filled entirely by natural springs.

The waters are astonishingly clear and maintain a constant temperature of 72°F (22°C). On the lake's shore sits the **Aquarena Center ★★**, 921 Aquarena Springs Dr. (© **512/245-7570;** www.aquarena.txstate.edu). An exemplar of tourist trends, it was a somewhat cheesy theme park, once home to Ralph the Swimming Pig, until it was purchased in the mid-1990s by Texas State University, which spent $16 million to convert it into an environmental research center (no swimming permitted in the lake). Glass-bottom boat tours, which allow you to view the lake's rare flora and fauna, cost $9 for adults, $7.50 for seniors 55 and older, and $6 for children ages 4 to 15. These enjoyable tours run on a regular schedule, depending on the season. In addition, there are environmental tours (2 weeks' advance arrangement required), an endangered species exhibit, a natural aquarium, hikes, and a boardwalk over the wetlands, where more than 100 species of birds have been spotted. You can also visit the log home of Gen. Edward Burleson, who built the dam that created Spring Lake to power his gristmill.

Spring Lake is the headwaters of the **San Marcos River,** which from here crosses under I-35 and begins its winding course down to the Gulf of Mexico. If you want to get wet, the river is your best option; it's probably the cleanest river in Texas. Common activities include tubing, kayaking, and canoeing. Log on to www.sanmarcos-river.org to find out about conservation measures taken by the San Marcos River Foundation. Tubing is possible from May through mid-September: The local **Lions Club** (© **512/396-LION** [396-5466]; www.tubesanmarcos.com) rents inner tubes and operates a river shuttle at City Park. Check the website for a schedule and rates.

Tip: You can also tube the Guadalupe River in nearby New Braunfels. See chapter 9 for a full discussion of where to tube in central Texas.

For canoeing or kayaking, a great outfitter is **TG Canoes & Kayaks** (© **512/353-3946;** www.tgcanoe.com) at 402 Pecan Park Dr. They provide watercraft, gear, and transportation. Most of the popular trips are downstream from San Marcos, closer to Luling. The best time for kayaking is in September and October, after the summer vacation season, when the crowds are gone. If you would like to take a class in kayaking, contact **Olympic Outdoor Center** (© **512/203-0093**) before your trip. The center teaches a white-water course. The class takes place at Rio Vista Park, a section of the river where the city has created some small rapids for the benefit of kayakers. This newly refurbished park is also an attractive place to go swimming in the calm pool of water above the rapids. Rio Vista is on the west side of I-35, not far from the San Marcos Visitor's Center, mentioned below.

If you would like to see some of the town, take a stroll around **Courthouse Square.** San Marcos, like Kyle and Buda, has seen rapid growth in the last 30 years, which has produced little of interest for visitors. Downtown and the university hold most the attractions.

San Marcos is the seat of Hays County, named after John Coffee Hays, whose bronze statue stands by the courthouse. Hays led a wild life as a Texas Ranger, explorer, surveyor, and lawman. He was one of the earliest members of the Texas Rangers and fought many skirmishes with Mexicans, Apaches, and Comanche in the Hill Country and South Texas. During the Mexican War (1846–48), he and his comrades gained national fame for their exploits in several battles, including the siege of Monterrey. The newspaper accounts of these battles were what really began the myth and lore of the Texas Rangers. When peacetime returned, Hays explored several routes between Austin and El Paso, and later traveled to California during the Gold Rush and was hired as sheriff of San Francisco to bring law and order to that unruly boomtown. In the statue, Hays is shown on horseback gripping a Colt revolver. Hays and another Texas Ranger, Samuel Walker, were instrumental in the development of the Colt revolver, working closely with Samuel Colt, testing some of his early models, and giving valuable input on how they could be improved.

Around the square are several old storefronts in various stages of restoration. One building facing the square is the **State Bank and Trust Building,** dating back to the late 1800s. It was robbed by the Newton Gang in 1924 and (most likely) by Machine Gun Kelly in 1933. San Marcos's entire downtown area is listed in the National Register of Historic Places. Also facing the square from across Guadalupe Street is a small museum documenting LBJ's early years. It concentrates on his childhood and has old newspapers and photos of San Marcos and the region. Admission to the **LBJ Museum of San Marcos** (© 512/353-3300; www.lbjmuseum.com) is free. For more information on what to see in San Marcos, go to the **Visitor's Center** at 617 I-35, on the west side of the highway (© 512/393-5930). Hours are Monday to Saturday from 9am to 5pm and Sunday from 10am to 4pm.

Texas State University's Albert B. Alkek Library is home to some of the state's most important literary artifacts, as well as to a good gallery specializing in photographs. The **Wittliff Collections,** on the seventh floor of the library, at 601 University Dr. (© 512/245-2313; www.thewittliffcollections.txstate.edu), showcases materials donated by the region's leading filmmakers, musicians, and wordsmiths. You might see anything from a 1555 printing of the journey of Spanish adventurer Cabeza de Vaca to a songbook created by an 11-year-old Willie Nelson to the costumes worn by Tommy Lee Jones and Robert Duvall in *Lonesome Dove.* (The collection was founded by screenwriter Bill Wittliff, who wrote the script for that TV miniseries as well as for *Legends of the Fall* and *A Perfect Storm.*) The collection is generally open to the public Monday, Tuesday, and Friday 8am to 5pm, Wednesday and Thursday 8am to 7pm, Saturday 10am to 5pm, and Sunday 1 to 6pm, but hours change with university holidays and breaks. It's a good idea to call ahead to confirm. Another part of the collections, the **Southwestern & Mexican Photography Collection,** focuses on the photographic works of this region from the 19th century to the present. Its holdings include the works of many famous photographers, including Ansel Adams, Edward Curtis, Alvarez Bravo, and Annie Leibovitz.

When the Balcones Fault was active some 30 million years ago, an earthquake created the cave at the center of **Wonder World,** 1000 Prospect St., off Bishop (© 877/492-4657 or 512/392-3760; www.wonderworldpark.com). You might not want to visit this much-hyped attraction. The petting farm, for example, is essentially a tram ride through an enclosure of depressed-looking deer. A tour of the cave eventually takes you to the so-called Anti-Gravity House, where you can see water flowing upward. The cave is okay, but there are better ones, such as Natural Bridge Caverns (discussed in chapter 9). And the Anti-Gravity House is just tacky. This attraction is open daily from June through August from 8am to 8pm; Monday through Friday from 9am to 5pm, Saturday and Sunday from 9am to 6pm the rest of the year; it is closed Christmas Eve and Christmas. Tickets for the entire park cost $20 for adults, $15 for kids 6 to 12, and $7.50 for children 3 to 5.

OUTLET SHOPPING

The other attraction that brings people to San Marcos is the outlet shopping mall. There are actually two of them, but they're right next to each other a couple of miles south of downtown San Marcos, on the east side of the highway (exit 200): **Tanger**

Factory Outlet Center (© 800/408-8424 or 512/396-7446; www.tangeroutlet. com) and the larger and tonier **Prime Outlets** (© 800/628-9465 or 512/396-2200; www.primeoutlets.com). Among the almost 150 stores, you'll find everything from Dana Buchman, Anne Klein, and Brooks Brothers to Coach, Samsonite, and Waterford/Wedgwood. There's also a Saks Fifth Avenue outlet.

Where to Stay & Dine

The **Crystal River Inn,** 326 W. Hopkins, San Marcos, TX 78666 (© 888/396-3739 or 512/396-3739; www.crystalriverinn.com), offers something for everyone. It's located a few blocks from the courthouse. Nine rooms and three suites, beautifully decorated with antiques, occupy a large 1883 Victorian main house and two smaller houses behind it. All three houses have character. The four guest rooms in the main house are decorated more traditionally, while the four in the Thomas house are more contemporary and eclectic. Those in the Rock house fall somewhere in between. Rates, which range from a low of $105 for a room during the week to a high of $175 for a two-bedroom suite on the weekend, include a full breakfast. The innkeepers have been running this B&B for years and are quite good at it. They even host murder-mystery weekends, which are elaborately scripted and enthusiastically acted. Other than this place, most of the lodging is along the highway, where there are more than a dozen hotel/motels.

If while you're walking around the courthouse you get a bit hungry, try the **Café on the Square** (© 512/396-9999) at 126 N. LBJ. It's not fine dining, but it's reliable, has good service, is open for breakfast, lunch, and dinner, and has bargain prices. It offers burgers, sandwiches, Tex-Mex, and a few local standards, such as fried catfish.

If you're looking for something more upscale, go to **Palmer's,** 216 W. Moore (© 512/353-3500; www.palmerstexas.com), just off Hopkins Street. Here you can eat outside in an attractive courtyard or inside in one of the wood-paneled dining rooms. This is a comfortable restaurant with good seating, and it doesn't get very noisy. The cooking is contemporary American, which the owners call Hill Country cuisine. To be sure, they use local providers whenever possible, and add a Texas twist to some of their standards. Main courses include grilled chops soaked in brine and topped with a habañero-honey sauce. There's also a good tortilla soup, which is vegetarian. Palmer's is known for its desserts, including Key lime and chocolate satin pies, and especially its margaritas. The restaurant is open for lunch and dinner daily, and meals are moderate to expensive.

A Literary Aside

Pulitzer Prize–winning author Katherine Anne Porter, best known for her novel *Ship of Fools,* spent most of her childhood just a few miles south of Buda, in the town of Kyle. In 2001, the **1880 Katherine Anne Porter House,** 508 W. Center St. (© 512/268-6637; www.english.txstate.edu/kap), was dedicated and opened to the public, as well as to a visiting writer chosen by the Texas State University–San Marcos. The house, which was restored and furnished with period antiques, hosts Porter's works and a collection of her photographs. There's no admission charge, but you need to call ahead for an appointment.

LOST pines

Thirty miles southeast of Austin lies an ecological anomaly—a pine forest surrounded on all sides by prairie. It is the last remnant of an extensive pine forest that once extended all the way from Piney Woods of East Texas. This one patch of forest has survived because the soils in this one area are rich in iron, which favors the growth of pine trees over the grasses of the surrounding prairie. It is very hilly, which also marks a difference with the surrounding land. Located within the forest is **Bastrop State Park** (© **512/321-2101;** www.tpwd.state.tx.us/spdest/findadest/parks/bastrop), which offers plenty of hiking trails, a golf course, a swimming pool, campsites, and cabins (which must be reserved by phone well in advance: © **512/389-8900**). Mountain biking is not permitted, but

the park road, which extends to a nearby park, is one of the most popular bike rides in Texas. This park is situated just off Hwy. 71, which is one of the main roads between Austin and Houston. Also located in this pine forest is **Hyatt Regency Lost Pines Resort and Spa** (© **512/308-1234;** www.lostpines.hyatt.com), which is a family-oriented resort in the same style as the Hyatt Regency Hill Country Resort on the outskirts of San Antonio (see chapter 4). It's located on the banks of the Colorado River and offers such activities as kayaking and canoeing, as well as horseback riding. Rates for a standard room run from $250 to $325, depending on the day of week and time of year. Promotional rates and packages are often available.

If what you're looking for is beauty, I think the prettiest place to eat in San Marcos is on the outdoor deck of the **Saltgrass Steakhouse** (© **512/396-5255**) at 211 Sessoms Dr., just off Aquarena Drive. It's a one-of-a-kind setting, perched out over Spring Lake right where it feeds into the river. This is a chain restaurant, and the food isn't of the highest quality, but if you stick to the steaks or chops, you'll be fine. If you're on Aquarena Springs, drive past the Aquarena Center and make a right turn just after it crosses the river. The restaurant will be immediately on your right.

Nearby Wimberley

From San Marcos, you can take a quick trip into the Hill Country by driving to the town of Wimberley. From central San Marcos, you can leave town via Moore Street. Wimberley is a scattered community, with a dense little commercial center. The center of town is located on the banks of the Blanco River, some 15 miles northwest of San Marcos. Texans from different parts of the state treat it as a weekend getaway and patronize a varied collection of bed-and-breakfasts—it's a favorite setting for family reunions. In addition to the countryside, shopping for antiques and art objects is one of the main attractions here. From April through December, the first Saturday of each month is **Market Day,** a large crafts gathering on Lion's Field; check www.visitwimberly.com/marketdays for additional information.

If you like artsy-craftsy (and, especially, country cutesy) stuff, you could spend all day browsing the shops and boutiques on and near the town square. But one of the most interesting places to visit, **Wimberley Glass Works,** is on the highway halfway between San Marcos and Wimberley (R.R. 12 at Hugo Rd.). The showroom is full of beautiful, vibrantly colored works of art. And many of the creations are made for sconce and pendant lighting and show off their colors all the more when lit from within. Behind the showroom is the studio where during regular business hours from Tuesday to Saturday you can see demonstrations and watch glass blowers at work. Of the places to stay in Wimberley, nicest is the **Blair House Inn,** 100 Spoke Hill Rd., Wimberley, TX 78676 (© **877/549-5450** or 512/847-1111; www.blairhouseinn. com). It's a luxury property on 85 Hill Country acres, offering eight spacious rooms and three separate cottages in a Texas limestone ranch complex. With a cooking school on the premises, you know the breakfasts—and dinners, offered to outsiders as well as guests every Saturday night—are going to be good. Rates run $150 to $209 for double rooms, $244 to $289 for the cottages. The cooking classes and dinners are popular with Austinites (and others), so book in advance if you want to attend.

For information about other places to stay, eat, or shop in Wimberley, contact the **Chamber of Commerce,** 14100 R.R. 12, just north of the town square (© **512/ 847-2201;** www.wimberley.org).

TOURING THE TEXAS HILL COUNTRY

A rising and falling land of rivers, lakes, springs, and caverns, the Hill Country is one of Texas's prettiest regions—especially in early spring, when wildflowers daub it with every pigment in nature's palette. Dotted with old dance halls, country stores, quaint Teutonic towns—more than 30,000 Germans emigrated to Texas during the great land-grant years of the Republic—and birthplace to one of the U.S.'s most colorful presidents, the region also lays out an appealing mosaic of the state's history.

San Antonio lies at the southern edge of the Hill Country; Austin at its eastern edge. The Interstate highway I-35, which connects the two cities, parallels a line of steep hills known as the Balcones Escarpment. These hills divide the coastal prairie from the Edwards Plateau, which extends for hundreds of miles north and west of San Antonio and Austin; the part closest to these cities is called the Hill Country. The extra 1,200 feet of elevation makes the climate a little drier and milder in summer than San Antonio or Austin.

In the 19th century, many German and Czech settlers arrived in the area fleeing the social upheavals in Europe. They established small towns that now dot the land and add a little contrast to the prevailing cowboy culture. The mild climate, rolling hills, and abundant springs attract visitors to this part of the state, with summer camps, guest ranches, and resorts serving a public that comes here to enjoy the outdoors.

The state government sells maps of different regions of the state for wildlife enthusiasts. The two that cover the Hill Country are called **Heart of Texas–Wildlife Trails.** There's an east and a west region. You can download sections of the maps at www.tpwd.state.tx.us/wildlifetrails. They offer loop routes covering a variety of the region's natural attractions and are available at several local visitor centers. You can also order the maps online for $2 each by going to www.tcebookstore.org or calling 𝄐 888/900-2577.

BOERNE

From San Antonio, the quickest route to the Hill Country is I-10 northwest to Boerne (rhymes with "journey"). Boerne is only 30 miles away, but before you get there, you'll pass another attraction—Cascade Caverns. It makes for an interesting visit, but if you would rather hold off for a bit, you can see a better one, **Cave Without a Name,** which lies north of Boerne (see below).

Boerne is the seat of Kendall County and has more than 6,000 residents. It was founded in 1849 by German settlers who had come to Texas to form a utopian community in an area northwest of Austin. That community disintegrated, partly owing to poor location. This wasn't a problem for Boerne, located on the banks of Cibolo Creek. In fact, it actually got a reputation for having a healthful environment and by the 1880s became a popular health resort. Boerne was named for German political writer, Ludwig Börne (1786–1837), whose ideas resonated with many Germans in the turbulent 1840s, including those who settled here.

Despite being so close to San Antonio, Boerne has retained its small-town atmosphere. One of the things it's known for is the **Boerne Village Band,** an old-time brass band that occasionally holds concerts in the gazebo on the main plaza and bills itself as the oldest continuously operating German band in the world outside Germany (it first tuned up in 1860). Boerne is also known for its collection of 19th-century limestone buildings in the old downtown area. These buildings include a small historical museum, boutiques, and restaurants. Most are along the *Hauptstrasse,* or main street, which is also decorated with old-fashioned lampposts and German street signs. Here, you'll find lots of crafts and antiques shops.

From I-10, you will enter town on South Main Street. It then becomes the *Hauptstrasse* farther along. But before that, you will pass the **Boerne Visitors Center,** 1407 S. Main (turn right into the Wal-Mart parking lot and look for a building on your right), Boerne, TX 78006 (© **888/842-8080** or 830/249-7277; www.visitboerne.org).

What to See & Do

In Boerne the main event is shopping in the stores along the *Hauptstrasse.* But there's quite a bit to do outside of town. On the southeast edge of Boerne is the **Cibolo Nature Center,** City Park Road, off Hwy. 46 E. next to the Kendall County Fairgrounds (© **830/249-4616;** www.cibolo.org). It's parkland with good hiking trails, which take you to four distinct ecosystems (grassland, marshland, woodland, and river bottom), where you can enjoy viewing some very pretty countryside. If you prefer golf, at the other end of town is **Tapatio Springs Golf Course,** Johns Road exit off I-10 W. (© **800/999-3299** or 830/537-4611; www.tapatio.com).

Farther afield, you can visit **Cascade Caverns** (© **830/755-8080;** www.cascadecaverns.com); 3 miles south of Boerne on I-10, take exit 543, and drive a little over 2 miles east. This active cave boasts huge chambers, a 100-foot underground waterfall, and comfortable walking trails; guides provide 45-minute to 1-hour interpretive tours every 30 minutes. It's open Memorial Day through mid-August daily 9am to 5pm; the end of August through the end of May Monday through Friday 10am to 4pm, Saturday and Sunday 9am to 4pm (during off season, call ahead for tour times). Admission is $16 adults, $8 children ages 4 to 11.

Another, more impressive cavern because of its variety of features, greater amount of living rock, and the number of chambers is the **Cave Without a Name,** 325 Kreutzberg Rd., 12 miles northeast of Boerne (© **830/537-4212;** www.cavewithoutaname.com). Hour-long tours of six large chambers are offered throughout the day. The chambers are well lit and display plenty of features and living rock. Open Memorial Day through Labor Day daily 9am to 6pm; off season daily 10am to 5pm. Admission $16 adults, $8 children ages 6 to 12.

The Texas Hill Country

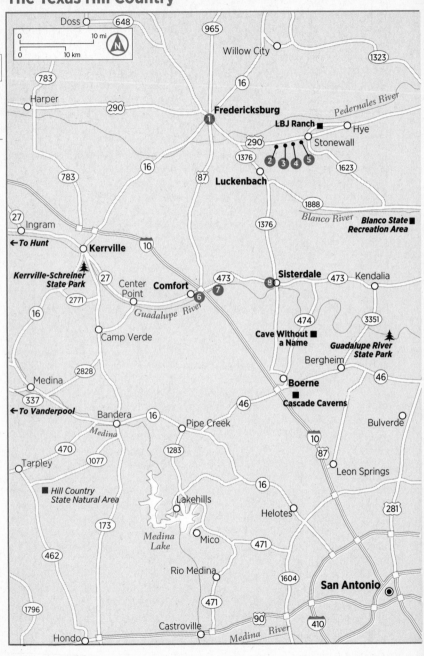

Doss 648

965

0 — 10 mi
0 — 10 km
N

783

Willow City

1323

16

Harper

290

Fredericksburg **1**

Pedernales River

LBJ Ranch ■ Hye

16

290

Stonewall

1376

2 **3** **4** **5**

1623

87

Luckenbach

1888

Blanco River

Blanco State ■
Recreation Area

1376

27 Ingram

←To Hunt

Kerrville

10

Kerrville-Schreiner
State Park

473

Sisterdale 473 Kendalia

9

27 Center
Point

Comfort

6 **7**

2771

Guadalupe River

474

Cave Without ■
a Name

3351

Guadalupe River
State Park

16

Camp Verde

Bergheim

46

2828

Medina

337

←To Vanderpool

Bandera

16

Pipe Creek

Boerne ■
■ Cascade Caverns

46

Bulverde

10

87

470

Medina

1283

1077

Tarpley

173

Hill Country
State Natural Area ■

Lakehills

Leon Springs

16

281

Helotes

462

Medina
Lake

Mico

471

Rio Medina

1604

San Antonio ◉

1796

Castroville

471

90

410

Hondo

Medina River

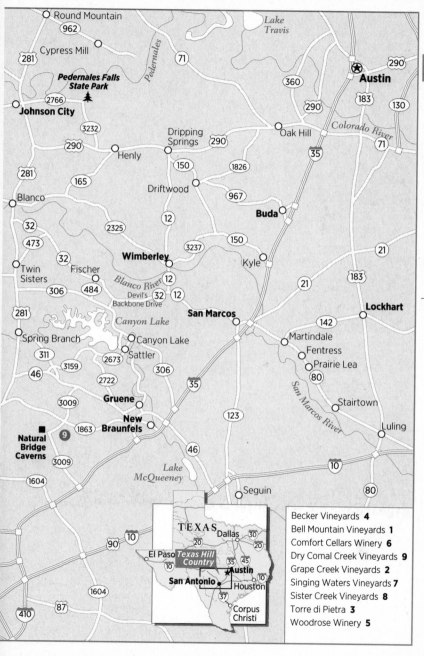

Round Mountain
962
Cypress Mill
281
*Pedernales Falls
State Park*
Pedernales
2766
Johnson City
3232
Dripping
Springs
290
290
Henly
150
281
165
1826
Blanco
Driftwood
967
32
473
2325
12
Buda
32
Wimberley
3237
150
306
484
12
Kyle
Twin
Sisters
Fischer
Blanco River
Devil's
Backbone Drive
32
12
21
183
281
Canyon Lake
San Marcos
Lockhart
Spring Branch
311
Canyon Lake
142
Martindale
Fentress
3159
2673
Sattler
306
Prairie Lea
80
46
2722
35
San Marcos River
Stairtown
3009
Gruene
123
Luling
1863
**New
Braunfels**
46
10
**Natural
Bridge
Caverns**
9
3009
80
1604
*Lake
McQueeney*
Seguin

*Lake
Travis*

290
Austin
183
290
130
Colorado River
360
290
71
35
71

90
10
TEXAS
Dallas
30
20
20
El Paso
*Texas Hill
Country*
35
45
10
★ **Austin**
San Antonio ●
10
Houston
1604
37
87
Corpus
Christi
410

Becker Vineyards **4**
Bell Mountain Vineyards **1**
Comfort Cellars Winery **6**
Dry Comal Creek Vineyards **9**
Grape Creek Vineyards **2**
Singing Waters Vineyards **7**
Sister Creek Vineyards **8**
Torre di Pietra **3**
Woodrose Winery **5**

THE HILL COUNTRY wine trail

Wine-tasting jaunts through the Hill Country are becoming more and more popular. Though most people don't know it, Texas has an old connection to wine-making and viticulture. Domesticated grapes first came to Texas in the late 16th century when Franciscan friars brought them from Mexico for cultivation at the Spanish missions. From the missions, the cultivation of grapes spread to the general populace and continued be practiced long after Texas separated itself from Mexico. In fact, during the 1870s a Texan grape grower, Thomas Munson, saved the French winemaking industry by shipping to France a number of root stocks that were resistant to the disease phylloxera, which had ravaged the vineyards of France and central Europe. The French were able to graft their own varietals to these root stocks and save their vineyards from ruin.

Viticulture in Texas would surely have kept developing had it not been for Prohibition, which was more disastrous than any plague. Not until the 1970s was grape growing able to reestablish itself. At first it grew in fits and starts, but then took off in the 1990s. In the Hill Country, small wineries now number more than 30. They can be visited at any time of year, but spring and fall are perhaps best. There are several wineries in and around Fredericksburg that are open to the public throughout the week, but the rest open their tasting rooms only on weekends. For more information about Hill Country Wineries, see www.texaswine trail.com.

Between New Braunfels and Boerne, you will find:

- **Dry Comal Creek Vineyards** (*©* 830/855-4076; www.dry comalcreek.com), at 1471 Herbelin Rd., is just off Hwy. 46 between New Braunfels and Bulverde. It's known for being one of the first wineries to highlight a local varietal called Black Spanish, a descendant of the cuttings brought from Mexico long ago by Franciscan friars. Available are red and white wines made with this grape and a wonderful port. Also of note is the bone-dry French Colombard.

Between Boerne and Fredericksburg:

- **Sister Creek Vineyards** (*©* 830/324-6704; www.sistercreekvine yards.com), in Sisterdale, close to the intersection of R.R. 473 and FM 1376, is in a gloriously rough-hewn old cotton gin that dates from 1885. You can stroll through some of the fermentation rooms and see the large vats and oak barrels used in the production of the wine. The winery employs traditional French techniques but is as down-home as the building it occupies.

- **Comfort Cellars Winery** (*©* 830/995-3274; www.comfortcellars.com), at 723 Front St., in the town of Comfort, has a full range of wines from dry to sweet, but the latter are what sells the most, including an intriguing orange chardonnay and what the owner calls sweet rojo (red).

- **Singing Water Vineyards** (*©* 830/995-2246; www.singingwater vineyards.com) is located 2 miles east of Comfort at 316 Mill Dam Rd. The winery is best known for its sauvignon blanc and a merlot/cabernet blend.

In the Fredericksburg area:

- **Fredericksburg Winery** (*©* 830/990-8747; www.fbgwinery.com) is on Fredericksburg's Main Street. It's run by three brothers who are rebels in the wine-making business. Visitors will always find something out of the ordinary, and the wines available for tasting are always changing.

- **Bell Mountain Vineyards** (© 830/685-3297; www.bellmountainwine.com) is located 14 miles north of Fredericksburg off Hwy. 16. The tasting room at the vineyard is open only on Saturday. A trip there can be combined with an outing to Enchanted Rock. But the vineyard has opened a tasting room on Fredericksburg's Main Street, above the Rathskeller Restaurant.

- **Grape Creek Vineyard** (© 820/644-2710; www.grapecreek.com). Ten miles east of town on Hwy. 290, in the direction of Stonewall, are four beautiful vineyards loosely bunched together. Grape Creek is one of them—situated on a hilltop with a panoramic vista that you can enjoy from beneath a copse of old oak trees. Try the cabs and the Fumé blanc.

- **Torre di Pietra** (© 830/744-2829; www.texashillcountrywine.com) is another impressive winery with an inviting terrace. The cab/syrah/Sangiovese blends are what most people go for.

- **Becker Vineyards** (© 830/644-2681; www.beckervineyards.com) is probably the Hill Country's most famous vineyard. The tasting room is within an old-style stone barn, and the old bar was taken from a saloon in San Antonio. It grows classic French varietals with which it makes some skillfully produced cabernet and Viognier, among many others.

- **Woodrose Winery** (© 830/644-2539; www.woodrosewinery.com) has another beautiful outdoor setting for sampling the wines. The cabernet sauvignon is popular.

In the Northern Hill Country and Lakes:

- **Flat Creek Vineyards** (© 512/267-6310; www.flatcreekestate.com) is on the north side of upper Lake Travis. From Austin take Hwy. 183 (avoid getting on the toll road) to Cedar Park and go west on RM 1431 for 14 miles, then left on Singleton Bend Road (there's a sign). This is one of the grandest of Hill Country vineyards, with a large tasting room offering wide vistas of rolling terrain. The winery produces a lot of wine using grapes from outside the state. Only a few of the wines here use locally grown grapes.

- **Pillar Bluff Vineyards** (© 512/556-4078; www.pillarbluff.com) is the treasure for those who stay on Hwy. 183 all the way to Lampasas (66 miles from Austin), and then take FM 1478 west, to these two small wineries owned by twin brothers Gill and Bill Bledsoe. Gill Bledsoe produces an interesting white merlot, a full-flavored cabernet, and a medium dry port, among other wines.

- **Texas Legato** (© 512/556-9600; www.texaslegato.com) is within sight of Pillar Bluff; this winery, owned by Bill Bledsoe, produces merlot and Malbec wines.

- **Alamosa Wine Cellars** (© 325/628-3313; www.alamosawinecellars.com) is 25 miles west of Lampasas, near the tiny town of Bend. The owners have been careful to select varietals that they believe have the best chance of producing outstanding wines when grown in Texas. Try the Tempranillo, which is bottled under the label "El Guapo," the Viognier, and a fruity Grenache.

A TASTE OF alsace IN TEXAS

Just 20 miles west of San Antonio (via U.S. 90 W.), Castroville has become something of a bedroom community for San Antonio, but the center of town retains its heritage as an old Alsatian community. Henri Castro, a Portuguese-born Jewish Frenchman, received a 1.25-million-acre land grant from the Republic of Texas in exchange for his commitment to colonize the land. He founded it on a scenic bend of the Medina River in 1842. Second only to Stephen F. Austin in the number of settlers he brought over, Castro recruited most of his 2,134 immigrants from the Rhine Valley, especially from the French province of Alsace. A few of the oldest citizens still can speak Alsatian, a dialect of German, though the language is likely to die out in the area when they do.

Get some insight into the town's history at the **Landmark Inn State Historic Site,** 402 E. Florence St., Castroville, TX 78009 (℗ 830/931-2133; www.tpwd. state.tx.us/park/landmark), which also counts a nature trail, an old gristmill, and a stone dam among its attractions. The park's centerpiece, the **Landmark**

Inn, offers eight simple rooms decorated with early Texas pieces dating up until the 1940s.

For a delicious taste of the past, visit **Haby's Alsatian Bakery,** 207 U.S. 90 E. (℗ 830/931-2118), owned by the Tschirhart family since 1974 and featuring apple fritters, strudels, stollens, breads, and coffeecakes. Open Monday to Saturday 5am to 7pm.

For additional information, contact the **Castroville Chamber of Commerce,** 802 London St., P.O. Box 572, Castroville, TX 78009 (℗ **800/778-6775** or 830/538-3142; www.castroville.com), where you can pick up a walking-tour booklet of the town's historic buildings, as well as a map that details the local boutiques and antiques shops (they're not concentrated in a single area). It's open 9am to noon and 1 to 3pm Monday through Friday.

Note: Downtown Castroville tends to close down on Monday and Tuesday, and some places are shuttered on Wednesday and Sunday as well. If you want to find everything open, come on Thursday, Friday, or Saturday.

For hiking or swimming, you can visit **Guadalupe River State Park** (℗ 830/438-2656; www.tpwd.state.tx.us/park/guadalup). It's 13 miles east of Boerne in the direction of New Braunfels. Take Hwy. 46 to P.R. 31; the turnoff is clearly marked. The park includes 4 miles of river frontage at a particularly attractive section of the river above Canyon Lake. There are a number of great swimming spots and some hiking trails that lead through some beautiful and rugged hill country. Keep an eye out and you might spot white-tailed deer, coyotes, armadillos, or even a rare golden-cheeked warbler. Camping is available (make reservations using the website). Often the park rangers offer a 2-hour interpretive tour of a nearby natural area (inquire ahead of time). The park is open daily from 8am to 10pm, and the entrance fee is $7, free for kids age 12 and under.

Where to Stay

A small, picturesque hotel fronting the main plaza is **Ye Kendall Inn,** 128 W. Blanco, Boerne, TX 78006 (℗ **800/364-2138** or 830/249-2138; www.yekendallinn.com), which opened as a stagecoach lodge in 1859. The rooms ($110–$130) and suites ($140–$200) are decorated in various styles. Historic cabins ($160–$180) transported to the grounds are available, too. For more economical lodging, try a room at the **Bourne Vistro Country Inn** (✆ 830/249-9563; www.boernevistro.com). It has small rooms ($69–$79) arranged like an old-fashioned motor court.

Where to Dine

The **Limestone Grille**, in **Ye Kendall Inn** (see above), 128 W. Blanco (✆ 830/249-9954), offers an atmospheric dining room and New American cuisine. It's open for lunch Monday through Saturday, dinner Tuesday to Saturday, brunch only Sunday; entrees are moderate to expensive. The more casual **Bear Moon Bakery,** 401 S. Main St. (✆ 830/816-BEAR [816-2327]), is ideal for a hearty breakfast or light lunch. Organic ingredients and locally grown produce enhance the flavor of the inventive soups, salads, sandwiches, and wonderful desserts. It's open Tuesday to Saturday 6am to 5pm, Sunday 8am to 4pm, and is inexpensive. A fun place for lunch or dinner is the **Dodging Duck Brewhaus** (✆ 830/248-DUCK [248-3825]), at 402 River Rd. It's on Cibolo Creek and has a welcoming outdoor dining area in front. The food is mainly sandwiches, soups, steaks, and a bit of seafood. There are normally four different local brews to choose from, or you can order a sampler. Prices are moderate.

BANDERA

Bandera is a small town of 1,000 inhabitants 30 miles west of Boerne. Take Hwy. 46 west to Hwy. 16 and turn right. Bandera began as a lumber camp in 1853, harvesting cypress trees along the Medina River for making shingles. It's now a popular getaway for city folk to come and enjoy rodeos and other cowboy activities. It's the seat of Bandera County, and a commercial center for all the surrounding guest ranches and working ranches. Bandera isn't a pretty town, like Fredericksburg, but its unassuming, genuine feel grows on you. A lot of the buildings are rustic affairs that would never meet the building standards of big cities. The interiors have a certain rough-cut, unpolished look to them. In this, they are a reflection of the general attitude of the natives, who are open and friendly and have that unhurried pace which denotes a life unfettered by schedulers and smartphones.

What to See & Do

Interested in delving into the town's roots? Pick up a self-guided tour brochure of historic sites—including **St. Stanislaus** (1855), the country's second-oldest Polish

---

Fantastic Foliage

Locals make annual pilgrimages to **Lost Maples State Natural Area** (✆ 830/966-3413 [info] or 512/389-8900 [reservations]; www.tpwd.state.tx.us) to see the best display of colorful fall foliage to be found in the Lone Star State. Covering 2,174 scenic acres north of Vanderpool on the Sabinal River, the area attracts more than 200,000 visitors each year and is a popular place for Sunday drives, hiking, biking, and camping under magnificent big-tooth maple trees. The stunning area can be jampacked and traffic-filled in the fall (go on weekdays if you can), but nobody seems to mind—the colors are worth it to see autumn in its full glory. Fall colors usually peak in early November, and reservations are necessary that time of year for overnight stays.

parish—at the **Bandera County Convention and Visitors Bureau,** 1206 Hackberry St., Bandera, TX 78003 (© **800/364-3833** or 830/796-3045; www.bandera cowboycapital.com), open weekdays 9am to 5pm, Saturday 9am to 2pm. Or explore the town's living traditions by strolling along Main Street, where a variety of crafters work in the careful, deliberate style of yesteryear. Shops include **Kline Saddlery** (© **830/522-0335;** www.klinesaddlery.com), featuring belts, purses, briefcases, and flask covers as well as horse wear; the **Stampede** (© **830/796-7650**), a good spot for Western collectibles; and **Love's Antique Mall** (© **830/796-3838**), a one-stop shopping center for current local crafts as well as things retro. Off the main drag, buy beautiful customized belt buckles, spurs, and jewelry at **Hy O Silver,** 1107 12th St. (© **830/796-7961;** www.hyosilver.com). Naturally, plenty of places in town, such as the **Cowboy Store,** 302 Main St. (© **830/796-8176**), can outfit you in Western duds.

Bandera holds its major rodeos on Memorial Day weekend and on Labor Day weekend, but you can find a smaller rodeo just about any week in between. Ask around when you get there, or try the visitor center.

THE GREAT OUTDOORS

Most people come to Bandera to do some horseback riding. This is easy to arrange. Many guest ranches offer horseback rides for day-trippers, and the going rate is about $35 to $40 an hour. But it's even easier and more cost effective if you elect to stay at a guest ranch (see below). This is one of the best ways to experience some of the beautiful country out there.

One place that offers ample room for horseback riding is the **Hill Country State Natural Area** (© 830/796-4413; www.tpwd.state.tx.us/park/hillcoun). It's 10 miles southwest of Bandera and is the largest state park in Texas. It has about 40 miles of trails for the use of riders, hikers, and mountain bikers. A few adjacent ranches can provide mounts. You can locate one through the Bandera Visitors Bureau. Be sure to take water along because none is available at the park.

A visit to the nonprofit **Brighter Days Horse Refuge,** 682 Krause Rd., Pipe Creek, about 9 miles east of Bandera (© 830/510-6607; www.brighterdayshorse refuge.org), will warm any animal lover's heart. The price of admission to this rehabilitation center for abandoned and neglected horses is a bag of carrots or apples; donations are also very welcome.

Another set of activities involves the pretty little Medina River, which runs right by the town. There are a couple of outfitters who rent tubes and kayaks. One is the **Bandera Beach Club Kayak & Tube Rental,** 1106 Cherry St. (© **830/796-7555**). Another is the **Medina River Company** (no phone), at 1307 N. Main St., next to the Longhorn Saloon at the north end of town. You'll see a big sign. Swimming is another option; there are a couple of good swimming spots just upstream from the town. In that part of the river, the current is usually slow, but check it before you decide to go swimming.

Going fishing is possible, but not quite so easy to do. First, you need to obtain a fishing license. A single-day license for a nonresident is $16. Visitors can buy one at Boyle's Market (© 830/796-3861) at 1002 Main St. **Bandera County Park at Medina Lake** (© 800/364-3833; www.wildtexas.com/parks/medinalk.php; take Hwy. 16 to R.R. 1283) allows fishing, but you have to have your own gear because there's no regular outfitter in town. But if you do, you can hook crappie, white or black bass, and especially huge yellow catfish; the public boat ramp is on the north side of the lake, at the end of P.R. 37.

If you feel like taking a hike, you also have several options. The closest is **Bandera Park** (© 830/796-3765). It's a 77-acre green space within the city limits where you can stroll along the River Bend Native Plant Trail or picnic by the Medina River. Slightly farther away is the Hill Country State Natural Area, mentioned above. But to hike through some particularly beautiful country, especially during autumn, head west about 40 miles to **Lost Maples State Natural Area** (© 830/966-3413; www.tpwd.state.tx.us/park/lostmap). Take Hwy. 16 to Medina, then R.R. 337 to Vanderpool, then R.R. 187 to the park.

Staying at a Guest Ranch

Accommodations in this area range from rustic cabins to upscale B&Bs, but if you're looking for lots of activities to do, stay at one of Bandera's many guest ranches (you'll find a full listing of them, as well as of other lodgings, on the Bandera website). Most of these places are big enough that you can get away from everybody and enjoy the countryside. It's much easier to do this at a guest ranch than at a state park, because the state parks are crowded, and, for the most part, are relatively small compared to the size of the state. Note that most of them have a 2-night (or more) minimum stay. You wouldn't want to spend less time at a dude ranch, anyway. Expect to encounter lots of European visitors, who flock to these places.

Rates at each of the following are based on double occupancy and include three meals, two trail rides, and most other activities.

At the **Dixie Dude Ranch,** P.O. Box 548, Bandera, TX 78003 (© 800/375-YALL [375-9255] or 830/796-7771; www.dixieduderanch.com), a longtime favorite retreat, you're likely to see white-tailed deer or wild turkeys as you trot on horseback through a 725-acre spread. The down-home, friendly atmosphere keeps folks coming back year after year. Rates are $135 per adult per night.

Tubing on the Medina River and soaking in a hot tub are among the many activities at the **Mayan Ranch,** P.O. Box 577, Bandera, TX 78003 (© 830/796-3312 or 460-3036; www.mayanranch.com), another well-established family-run operation ($150 per adult). The ranch provides plenty of additional Western fun for its guests during high season—things like two-step lessons, cookouts, hayrides, singing cowboys, or trick-roping exhibitions.

The owner of **Silver Spur Guest Ranch,** 9266 Bandera Creek Rd., Bandera, TX 78003 (© 830/796-3037 or 460-3639; www.ssranch.com), used to be a bull rider, so the equestrian expertise of the staff is especially high ($135 per adult). So is the comfort level. The rooms in the main ranch house and the separate cabins are individually decorated, with styles ranging from Victorian pretty to country rustic. The ranch, which abuts the Hill Country State Natural Area, also boasts the region's largest swimming pool, some roaming buffalo, and a great kids' play area.

Twin Elm Guest Ranch, 810 FM 470, Bandera, TX 78003 (© 830/796-3628; www.twinelmranch.net) features a variety of horseback rides through different terrain and plenty of fun on the river, too ($145 per adult, assuming double occupancy).

Where to Stay & Dine

If you opt not to stay at a guest ranch, there's an inexpensive motel in Bandera, the **River Oak Inn,** 1203 Main St. (© 830/796-7751). It's a motel with simple rooms, some of which are decorated with large murals. For most of the year, rates are between $60 and $70.

Dining in Bandera is downright cheap. You should stick to country cooking and Tex-Mex. **O.S.T.** (© **830/796-3836**), named for the Old Spanish Trail that used to run through Bandera, has been open since 1921. It retains the feel of an old place with wooden paneling, framing, and furniture. Along one side of the main dining room is a bar with saddles for bar stools. It opens at 6am every day for breakfast and closes around 9pm. It serves burgers and Tex-Mex, and is known the chicken-fried steak platter. Check out the John Wayne room, which is covered in photos and old movie posters of "the Duke."

Brick's River Cafe, 1105 Main St. (© **830/460-3200**), is behind the River Oak Inn at the north end of town. It serves up down-home country standards such as chicken-fried steak, fried catfish, and liver and onions. The menu includes green salads, too, and plenty of vegetable side dishes. There's a deck perched in back (half enclosed, half open-air) from which you can look out over the Medina River. It's open daily for lunch and dinner.

Mi Pueblo, 706 Main St. (© **830/796-8040**), offers a large variety of Tex-Mex cooking, including fajitas and some good green enchiladas. It's open for all three meals.

Some Local Honky-Tonks

If you spend the night in town, you can go honky-tonkin' pretty easily. Bandera seems to have a high bar-per-capita ratio. And after a night of doing this, you'll have a pretty good idea of what locals consider the proper ambience for having a drink. First, it must be a study in rusticity—nothing should be shiny or polished. Second, there must be a lot of rough-cut wood, a solid-looking wooden bar, old beer signs, and a mounted head or two. And, third, it has to be semi-exposed to the elements, preferably with a patio area attached. If you're in town on an off night, all the better. You can chew the fat in peace with some of the other patrons. On weekends, there's usually live music, so come prepared to dance.

One popular joint is **Arkey Blue's Silver Dollar Bar,** 308 Main St. (© **830/796-8826**). Arkey is a well-known figure in Texas country music and has written many songs for and played with some of the biggest names in the state, including Willie Nelson. It's a downstairs bar, below the Bandera General Store. Sawdust is strewn on the floor to provide a better surface for boot scootin'. On a table in one of the corners, you can see where Hank Williams, Sr., carved his name.

Just down the street is the **Bandera Saloon,** 401 Main St. (© **830/796-3699**), aka the Chicken Coop, because it used to have chicken wire in place of windows. It has live music on Wednesdays, Fridays, and Saturdays, anything from rockabilly to Western swing.

Another favorite drinking hole is the **Longhorn Saloon,** 1307 Main St. (© **830/796-3600**). It's another ramshackle affair with exposed, rough-cut wood framing and siding. On weekends, there's live music, always country. One of the owners is Clint Black's brother, and sometimes he and his brothers minus Clint will play some tunes for the audience. It can draw a lively crowd.

En Route to Kerrville

There are two ways to get from Bandera to Kerrville. If you like to drive and aren't in a hurry, take the longer route (37 miles), Hwy. 16 through Medina. It's a nice curvy road through some beautiful country—new-growth forest, river-bottom lands, and rolling ranch land. But if it has been raining, avoid this route because it has too many

Lavender Fields Forever

You may equate Texas with cattle trails, but in the Hill Country, folks like to gush about the lovely lavender trail that cuts a pretty path through these hills. Not so long ago, local winemakers and farmers realized the Texas soil is much like that of the French countryside in Provence and that lavender, like grapes, grows well in the Hill Country. Today, lavender fields at farms and low-water crossings. These flood easily, and flash floods are a serious matter in the Hill Country. In Medina, you can make a stop at **Love Creek Orchards Cider Mill and Country Store** (© **800/449-0882** or 830/589-2588; www.lovecreekorchards. com) on the main street. You can buy apple pies, apple cider, apple syrup, apple butter, apple jam, and apple ice cream—you can even have an apple sapling shipped back home. If you're in the mood for more substantial food, there's a restaurant out back that serves burgers.

Texas wineries are so popular that visitors come to see and smell the pretty plants, buy fragrant soaps and other lavender products, and enjoy lavender-inspired dinners and parties. Each spring, local growers host a Lavender Trail festival, with special weekend events, activities, and lavender farm-to-table dinners. Texas trails never smelled so sweet!

The main highway to Kerrville is Hwy. 173, which passes through **Camp Verde,** the former headquarters (1856–69) of the short-lived U.S. Army camel cavalry. There's little left of the camp, but you can tour the **1877 General Store and Post Office** (© **830/634-7722**), purveying camel memorabilia and artifacts. This route is only 26 miles.

KERRVILLE

With a population of close to 25,000, Kerrville is the largest town in the Hill Country. It's a popular retirement and tourist area without either the cowboy aura of Bandera or the quaintness of Fredericksburg, but it's on the way to many places in the Hill Country, including Fredericksburg and the upper Guadalupe River. Most of the available activities center on the river, parts of which are very scenic and lined with large cypress trees. The town was founded in the 1840s by Joshua Brown, from Gonzales, Texas, who was attracted to the region by these cypress trees, which he hoped to mill into roof shingles. (Before the arrival of industry, all Central Texas rivers were lined by cypress trees. The wood was in high demand because it resists rot.) Brown was a friend of Maj. James Kerr, who first established Gonzales, and was one of the founding fathers of Texas independence. (Kerr died in 1850 and never actually saw the town and county named after him.)

Beginning as a rough-and-tumble camp, Kerrville soon became a ranching center for longhorn cattle and, more unusually, for Angora goats, eventually turning out the most mohair in the United States. In the later part of the 19th century, one man, Capt. Charles A. Shreiner (1838–1927), built an empire based on commerce, ranching, and banking. His family is prominent and still active in the city's affairs, and you'll see the family name all around town. In the 1920s, Kerrville became noted for its healthful climate and began to draw youth camps, sanitariums, and retirees. The area surrounding the town has, in the last 20 years, seen a construction boom of weekend

old england FINDS THE OLD WEST

Several attractions, some endearingly offbeat, plus beautiful vistas along the Guadalupe River, warrant a detour west of Kerrville. Drive 5 miles from the center of town on Hwy. 27 W. to reach tiny **Ingram.** Take Hwy. 39 W. to the second traffic light downtown. After about a quarter-mile, you'll see a sign for the Historic Old Ingram Loop, once a cowboy cattle driving route and now home to rows of **antiques shops, crafts boutiques,** and **art galleries** and **studios.**

Back on Hwy. 39, continue another few blocks to the **Hill Country Arts Foundation** (© **800/459-4223** or 830/367-5121; www.hcaf.com), a complex comprising two theaters, an art gallery, and studios where arts-and-crafts classes are held. Every summer since 1948, a series of musicals has been offered on the outdoor stage.

Continue 7 miles west on Hwy. 39 to the junction of FM 1340, where you'll find **Hunt,** which pretty much consists of a combination general store, bar, and restaurant that would look right at home in any Western. *Surprise:* There's a replica of **Stonehenge** sitting out in the middle of a field. It's not as large as the original, but this being Texas, it's not exactly diminutive, either. A couple of reproduction Easter Island heads fill out the ancient mystery sculpture group commissioned by Al Shepherd, a wealthy eccentric who died in the mid-1990s. The same road continues on, following the course of the upper Guadalupe and is one of the most pleasant drives in the state.

houses for people living as far away as Houston or Dallas. Kerrville has not been able to keep up with the increase in traffic created by these visitors, so traffic jams sometimes occur. Try to plan your trip such that you arrive in Kerrville during the week.

What to See & Do

You can stop at the **Kerrville Visitors Center,** 2108 Sidney Baker, Kerrville, TX 78028 (© **800/221-7958** or 830/792-3535; www.kerrvilletexascvb.com), for brochures and to get answers. It's open weekdays 8:30am to 5pm, Saturday 9am to 3pm, Sunday 10am to 3pm.

Tip: If you're planning to come to Kerrville around Memorial Day weekend, when the huge, 18-day **Kerrville Folk Festival** kicks off and the **Official Texas State Arts and Crafts Fair** is held, book far in advance. If you're not planning to attend, and you're in the Hill Country during these dates, give a wide berth to Kerrville or you'll get caught in the traffic.

The pleasantest part of the downtown area is that part around Earl Garrett and Water streets, where you'll find a variety of restaurants and shops, many selling antiques and/or country-cutesy knickknacks. You'll also find Capt. Charles Schreiner's impressive mansion, built of native stone by Alfred Giles. It's now home to the **Hill Country Museum,** 226 Earl Garrett St. (© **830/896-8633**). At present the museum is closed for remodeling, but that's not much of a loss—the collection of artifacts that it held, a collection of 19th-century furniture and clothing, was difficult to tie to early life in the Hill Country. On one side of the mansion is the original location of the Schreiner Mercantile Company, where Capt. Schreiner began making his fortune. On the opposite side of the mansion is the 1935 post office, now the **Kerr**

Arts & Cultural Center, 228 Earl Garrett St. (© **830/895-2911;** www.kacc kerrville.com), which holds several galleries.

At the south end of town is the **Museum of Western Art** (formerly the Cowboy Artists of America Museum), 1550 Bandera Hwy. (© **830/896-2553;** www.museum ofwesternart.org). If you like modern Western art, from the mid–20th century to the present, then you'll like this museum. Open Tuesday to Saturday 10am to 4pm. Admission is $7 adults, $6 seniors, $5 children ages 9 to 17, free for 8 and under. Just outside of town is the **Kerrville-Schreiner Park,** 2385 Bandera Hwy. (© **830/257-5392;** www.kerrville.org/index.asp?NID=318), a 500-acre green space with 7 miles of hiking trails, as well as swimming and boating on the Guadalupe River. Campsites and small cabins are available for guests. Call the number for more information or to make reservations.

A Nearby Ranch

You'll need a reservation to visit the **Y.O. Ranch,** 32 miles from Kerrville, off Hwy. 41, Mt. Home, TX 78058 (© **800/YO-RANCH** [967-2624] or 830/640-3222; www. yoranch.com). Originally comprising 550,000 acres purchased by Charles Schreiner in 1880, the Y.O. Ranch is now a 40,000-acre working ranch known for its exotic wildlife (1½- to 2-hr. tours cost $35 per person) and Texas longhorn cattle. A variety of overnight accommodations are available, too, but you should know that this ranch isn't the same as a guest ranch. Many of the activities here revolve around hunting, and there are fewer of the elements normally associated with guest ranches.

Where to Stay

The **Y.O. Ranch Resort Hotel and Conference Center,** 2033 Sidney Baker, Kerrville, TX 78028 (© **877/YO-RESORT** [967-3767] or 830/257-4440; www.yoresort. com)—not near the Y.O. Ranch (see above), but in Kerrville itself—offers large and attractive Western-style quarters. Its Branding Iron dining room features big steaks as well as Continental fare, and the gift shop has a terrific selection of creative Western-theme goods. Double rooms range from $79 to $129, depending on the season.

Inn of the Hills Resort, 1001 Junction Hwy., Kerrville, TX 78028 (© **800/292-5690** or 830/895-5000; www.innofthehills.com), looks like a motel from the outside, but it has the best facilities in town, including tennis courts, three swimming pools, a putting green, two restaurants, a popular pub, and free access to the excellent health club next door. Rates for double rooms range seasonally from $100 to $135.

The **Sunset Inn and Studio,** 124 Oehler Road St. (off FM 479), Mountain Home, TX 78058 (© **877/739-1214** or 830/866-3336; www.sunsetinn-studio. com), offers two rooms for guests with full breakfasts. The inn and artist studio are a mile off I-10, 3 miles east of "downtown" Mountain Home and 14 miles from Kerrville. This is a great place to relax. The property has longhorn cattle and miniature donkeys that the guests can feed and pet. At dusk, the owners offer a retreat time to sit out and enjoy the evening with some refreshments. Dinner can be had if you reserve ahead of time. Room rates are $130.

Where to Dine

Set in a restored 1915 depot with a lovely patio out back, **Rails,** 615 Schreiner (© **830/257-3877**), is an attractive spot for lunch or dinner. The menu features fresh salads, Italian panini sandwiches, and a small selection of hearty entrees.

bats ALONG A BACK ROAD TO FREDERICKSBURG

If you missed the bats in Austin, you've got a second chance to see some in an abandoned railroad tunnel supervised by the Texas Parks and Wildlife Department. From Comfort, take Hwy. 473 N. for 5 miles. When the road winds to the right toward Sisterdale, keep going straight on Old Hwy. 9. After another 8 or 9 miles, you'll spot a parking lot and a mound of large rocks on top of a hill. During the season (May–Oct), you can watch as many as three million Mexican free-tailed bats set off on a food foray around dusk. There's no charge to witness the phenomenon from the Upper Viewing Area, near the parking lot; it's open daily. If you want a closer view and an educational presentation lasting

about 30 minutes to an hour, come to the Lower Viewing Area, open from Thursday through Sunday ($5 adults, $3 seniors, $2 children 6–16). There are 60 seats, filled on a first-come, first-served basis. Contact the **Old Tunnel Wildlife Management Area** (© 830/990-2659; www.tpwd.state.tx.us/wma) to find out when its occupants are likely to flee the bat cave, as well as other information.

Even if you don't stop for the bats, this is a wonderfully scenic route to Fredericksburg. You won't see any road signs, but have faith—this really will take you to town, eventually. You're likely to spot grazing goats and cows and even some strutting ostriches.

Francisco's, 201 Earl Garrett St. (© **830/257-2995**), in the old Weston building at the corner of Earl Garret and Water streets, offers New American cooking with Mexican accents. It has attractive indoor and outdoor dining.

Taking Time Out for Comfort

The direct route from Kerrville to Fredericksburg (25 miles) is Hwy. 16 N., but by taking Hwy. 27 east you can pass through Comfort, a small German town. It has been said that the freethinking German immigrants who founded the town in 1852 were originally going to call it Gemütlichkeit—a more difficult-to-pronounce native version of its current name—when they arrived at this welcoming spot after an arduous journey from New Braunfels. The story is apocryphal, but it's an appealing explanation of the name, especially as no one is quite sure what the truth is.

The rough-hewn limestone buildings in the center of Comfort may contain the most complete 19th-century business district in Texas. Noted San Antonio architect Alfred Giles designed some of the offices. These days, most of these structures, and especially those on High Street, host high-quality (and high-priced) antiques shops. More than 30 dealers gather at the **Comfort Antique Mall,** 734 High St. (© **830/995-4678**). The nearby complex of antiques shops known as **Comfort Common,** 717 High St. (© **830/995-3030;** www.thecomfortcommon.com), also doubles as a bed-and-breakfast. If you're in town Thursday to Sunday from 11am to 3:30pm, combine shopping and noshing at **Arlene's Café and Gift Shop,** 426 Seventh St., just off High Street (© **830/995-3330**). The tasty soups, sandwiches, and desserts are freshly made on the premises.

The **Comfort Chamber of Commerce,** on Seventh and High streets (© **830/995-3131**), has very limited hours, but who knows—you might be lucky enough to

arrive when it's open. Alternatively, try the **Ingenhuett Store,** 830–834 High St.
(© **830/995-2149**), owned and operated by the same German-American family
since 1867. Along with groceries, outdoor gear, and sundries, the store carries maps
and other sources of tourist information.

FREDERICKSBURG

Fredericksburg is a town of 10,000 inhabitants located just about 75 miles from
either San Antonio or Austin. It's noted for a picturesque main street, with old-time
storefronts and sidewalk canopies, in the tradition of small-town Texas. It's also
known for its German heritage, serving as the center of a large German farming community. These days, the farmers are known for the peaches they grow (available at
orchards and roadside stands May–July), and more recently, their vineyards. Fredericksburg is the hub of the Hill Country wineries. See the "Hill Country Wine Trail"
box (p. 280).

The town serves as a weekend escape for city dwellers. It has lots of bed-and-
breakfasts and guesthouses, as well as hotels and motels. Many visitors come for the
shopping and to relax, and perhaps taste some wine. Others come to explore the surrounding countryside, including nearby Enchanted Rock, the Hill Country's most
famous geological feature.

Fredericksburg was founded in 1846, when Baron Ottfried Hans von Meusebach
took 120 settlers in ox-drawn carts from the relative safety of New Braunfels to this
site in the wild lands of the frontier. He named the settlement for Prince Frederick
of Prussia. Meusebach negotiated a peace treaty with the Comanche in 1847, claim-
ing to be the only one in the United States that was honored. The settlement prospered during the California Gold Rush, as it was the last place travelers could get
supplies on the southern route, until the town of Santa Fe, New Mexico. Fredericksburg is the seat of Gillespie County.

What to See & Do
IN TOWN

For a virtual preview, go to **www.fredericksburg-texas.com**. Once you're in town,
the **Visitor Information Center,** 302 E. Austin St., Fredericksburg, TX 78624
(© **888/997-3600** or 830/997-6523), can direct you to the many points of interest
in the town's historic district. It's open weekdays 8:30am to 5pm, Saturday 9am to
noon and 1 to 5pm, Sunday noon to 4pm.

While walking around town, you're likely to see some very small frame houses
(usually having only two rooms). Called **Sunday Houses,** they were built by German
farmers in the 19th century, whose fields were too far from Fredericksburg to allow
them to live in town. These simple dwellings were meant to be a humble *pied-à-terre*
for use on market days, Sundays, and holidays. You'll also notice many homes built in
the Hill Country version of the German *fachwerk* design, made out of limestone with
diagonal wood supports.

On the town's main square, called Market Square, is an unusual octagonal **Vereins Kirche (Society Church).** It's actually a replica (built in 1935) of the original
1847 building. The original was the first public building in Fredericksburg. It was
built to be a church where both Lutheran and Catholic Germans could hold services,
and as such, was a symbol of unity for the early pioneers. It originally stood on Main
Street until the 1890s, when it had decayed to the point where it had to be torn down.

The replica shows how primitive the original construction had been. Inside is a historical exhibit of the town, which can be viewed in a half-hour. It's open 10am to 4pm Monday to Saturday, 1 to 4pm Sunday. The Vereins Kirche is operated by the Historical Society, which also maintains the **Pioneer Museum Complex,** 309 W. Main St. Admission to either museum is valid for the other. The cost is $5 for adults, $3 for students 6 to 17 years old, and free for children 5 and under. The Pioneer Museum consists of the 1849 Kammlah House (which was a family residence and general store until the 1920s), as well as the barn and the smokehouse. Later, other historical structures were moved onto the site. These include a one-room schoolhouse and a blacksmith's forge. The complex is open Monday to Saturday 10am to 5pm, Sunday 1 to 5pm. For information on both places and on the other historical structures in town, phone 𝓒 **830/997-2835** or log on to www.pioneermuseum.com.

The 1852 Steamboat Hotel, originally owned by the grandfather of World War II naval hero Chester A. Nimitz, is now part of the **National Museum of the Pacific War ★★,** 311 E. Austin St. (𝓒 **830/997-4379;** www.nimitz-museum.org), a 9-acre Texas State Historical Park and the world's only museum focusing solely on the Pacific theater. It just keeps expanding and getting better. In addition to the exhibits in the steamboat-shaped hotel devoted to Nimitz and his comrades, there are also the Japanese Garden of Peace, a gift from the people of Japan; the Memorial Wall, the equivalent of the Vietnam wall for Pacific War veterans; the life-size Pacific Combat Zone (2½ blocks east of the museum), which replicates a World War II battle scene; and the George Bush Gallery, where you can see a captured Japanese midget submarine and a multimedia simulation of a bombing raid on Guadalcanal. Indoor exhibits are open daily from 9am to 5pm but are closed Thanksgiving and Christmas. Adult admission is $12; seniors, military, and veterans $10; students pay $6; and children 5 and under enter free.

If you're interested in saddles, chaps, spurs, sheriffs' badges, and other cowboy-bilia, visit **Gish's Old West Museum,** 502 N. Milam St. (𝓒 **830/997-2794**). A successful illustrator for Sears & Roebuck, Joe Gish started buying Western props to help him with his art. After more than 40 years of trading and buying with the best, he has gathered a very impressive collection. Joe opens the museum when he's around (he generally is), but if you don't want to take a chance, phone ahead to make an appointment.

NEARBY

A visit to the **Wildseed Farms ★,** 7 miles east on Hwy. 290 (𝓒 **830/990-1393;** www.wildseedfarms.com), will disabuse you of any naive notions you may have had that wildflowers grew wild. At this working wildflower farm, from April through July, beautiful fields of blossoms are harvested for seeds that are sold throughout the world. During the growing season, for $5 you can grab a bucket and pick bluebonnets, poppies, or whatever's blooming when you visit. There are a gift shop and the Brew-Bonnet beer garden, which sells light snacks. Entry to the grounds, open 9:30am to 6pm daily, is free, but you'll have to pay ($4 adults, $3.50 seniors and kids ages 4–12) to visit the latest addition, the Butterfly Haus, featuring pretty flitters native to Texas.

North of town is **Enchanted Rock State Natural Area ★★** (𝓒 **325/247-3903;** www.tpwd.state.tx.us/park/enchantd), a 640-acre site with a dome of solid pink granite that was pushed up to the surface by volcanic uplifting. Take FM 965 north for 18 miles. You'll know when you get there. It's a stark sight that shares nothing

ATTRACTIONS ●
Enchanted Rock State Natural Area **13**
Gish's Old West Museum **2**
Lady Bird Johnson Municipal Park **16**
Market Square **5**
National Museum of the Pacific War **10**
Pioneer Museum Complex **3**
Vereins Kirche **5**
Wildseed Farms **15**

DINING ◆
Altdorf Biergarten **4**
Cabernet Grill **6**
Fredericksburg Brewing Co. **8**
Friedhelm's Bavarian Inn **1**
Hilda's Tortilla Factory **7**
Hill Top Cafe **14**
Navajo Grill **11**
The Nest **12**
Rather Sweet Bakery & Cafe **11**

THE HISTORIC DISTRICT

in common with the surrounding hills. The dome (known geologically as a batholith) is almost 600 feet high. To hike up and down on the trail takes about an hour. The creaking noises that emanate from it at night—likely caused by the cooling of the rock's outer surface—led the area's Native American tribes to believe that evil spirits inhabited the rock. The park is open daily 8am to 10pm; day-use entrance fees are $7 adults and free for children 12 and under. Tent sites in the vicinity of the parking lot cost $15 to $17. There are primitive backpack sites 1 to 3 miles away, which cost $10 to $12. Each site can accommodate up to four people. All campers will need to pay the day-use entrance fee, too. *Tip:* Though the park is fairly large, the parking lot is not, and as soon as it fills, no more visitors are admitted. On weekends, if you get there by 10am, you shouldn't have a problem. When going to Enchanted Rock, I suggest you get an early start, and before you leave town, stop by **Hilda's Tortilla Factory** (see "Where to Dine," below) to load up on breakfast tacos that you can eat either on the way there or in the parking lot once you've entered the park. Don't worry if you see a line of customers extending out Hilda's door. It moves quickly.

SHOPPING

In town, there are more than 100 specialty shops, many of them in mid-19th-century houses, which feature work by Hill Country artisans. You'll find candles, lace coverlets, cuckoo clocks, hand-woven rugs, even dulcimers. At **Homestead,** 230 E. Main St. (© **830/997-5551;** www.homesteadstores.com), a fashionable, three-story home furnishings emporium, European rural retro (chain-distressed wrought-iron beds from France, for example) meets contemporary natural fabrics. Dog owners can pamper their pets at **Dogologie,** 148-B W. Main St. (© **830/997-5855;** www.dogologie. com), carrying everything the fashionable canine might need. For something less effete, check out **Texas Jack's,** 117 N. Adams St. (© **830/997-3213;** www.texas jacks.com), which has outfitted actors for Western films and TV shows, including *Lonesome Dove, Tombstone,* and *Gunsmoke.* This is the place to stock up on red long johns. **Chocolat,** 251 W. Main St. (© **800/842-3382** or 830/990-9382; www.liquid chocolates.com), is like no other chocolate shop you've visited. The owner, Lecia Duke, is an architect by training but later found out that she got more satisfaction working with chocolate. She has mastered an old-world technique for encasing any alcohol in chocolate by manipulating the sugar in the liquor to form a thin cocoon around the liquid. This method is practiced nowhere else in the U.S. and by only a handful of small chocolate makers in Europe. In her store, you'll find a wide variety of chocolates, with and without spirits.

Becoming increasingly well-known via its mail-order business is the **Fredericks-burg Herb Farm,** 405 Whitney St. (© **800/259-HERB** [259-4372] or 830/997-8615; www.fredericksburgherbfarm.com), just a bit south of town. You can visit the flower beds that produce salad dressings, teas, fragrances, and air fresheners (including lavender, one of the area's major crops these days), and then sample some of them in the on-site restaurant (lunch only; moderate), B&B, and day spa. The herb farm is building 14 guest cottages modeled on the traditional Fredericksburg Sunday houses. At press time, 6 of the 14 cottages were open, the remainder expected to open by midsummer 2011. The newly opened state-of-the-art spa, with eight treatment rooms, makes use of the lotions and gels made on the farm.

Where to Stay

Fredericksburg is well known for having more than 300 bed-and-breakfasts and *gas-tehauses* (guest cottages). If you choose one of the latter, you can spend the night in anything from an 1865 homestead with its own wishing well to a bedroom above an old bakery or a limestone Sunday House. Most *gastehauses* are romantic havens complete with robes, fireplaces, and even spas. And, unlike the typical B&B, these places ensure privacy because either breakfast is provided the night before—the perishables are left in a refrigerator—or guests are given coupons to enjoy breakfast at a local restaurant. *Gastehauses* run anywhere from $120 to $200. Most visitors reserve lodgings through one of the main booking services: **First Class Bed & Breakfast Reservation Service,** 909 E. Main (✆ **888/991-6749** or 830/997-0443; www.fredericksburg-lodging.com); **Gästehaus Schmidt,** 231 W. Main St. (✆ **866/427-8374** or 830/997-5612; www.fbglodging.com); **Absolute Charm,** 709 W. Main St. (✆ **866/244-7897** or 830/997-2749; www.absolutecharm.com); and **Main Street B&B Reservation Service,** 337 E. Main (✆ **888/559-8555** or 830/997-0153; www.travelmainstreet.com). Specializing in the more familiar type of B&B is **Fredericksburg Traditional Bed & Breakfast Inns** (✆ **800/494-4678;** www.fredericksburgtrad.com).

For something less traditional, consider the **Roadrunner Inn** (✆ **830/997-1844;** www.theroadrunnerinn.com), a modern B&B at 306 E. Main St., above a boutique. It has very large, uncluttered rooms furnished with a mix of mod and industrial. Rates start at $130.

If you would rather stay in a hotel, the **Hangar Hotel,** 155 Airport Rd., Fredericksburg, TX 78624 (✆ **830/997-9990;** www.hangarhotel.com), has large, comfortable rooms. It banks on nostalgia for the World War II flyboy era. Located at the town's tiny private airport, as its name suggests, this hotel hearkens back to the 1940s with its clean-lined art moderne–style rooms, as well as an officer's club (democratically open to all) and retro diner. The re-creation isn't taken too far: Rooms have all the mod-cons. Rates—which include one $5 "food ration," good at the diner, per night—run from $120 on weekdays to $170 on weekends. For bargain rates, the old **Frederick Motel** (✆ **800/996-6050;** www.frederick-motel.com), at 1308 E. Main St., offers rates from $40 to $100 and, on weekends, includes full breakfast.

See also Rose Hill Manor, in the nearby town of Stonewall, reviewed in the "Lyndon B. Johnson Country" section, below.

Where to Dine

Fredericksburg's dining scene is diverse, catering to the traditional and the trendy alike. For breakfast or lunch, a jewel of a place is **Rather Sweet Bakery & Cafe,** 249 E. Main St. (✆ **830/990-0498**). Rebecca Rather, the owner, is a noted cookbook author, who makes everything from scratch using the freshest ingredients, including homegrown herbs and vegetables. The bakery is open Monday through Saturday until 5pm, but the cafe stops serving lunch at 2pm. For breakfast takeout, you should try **Hilda's Tortilla Factory** (✆ **830/997-6105**) at 149 Tivydale Rd. (at S. Adams St.). This place serves good tacos on fresh-made flour tortillas. "El Especial" has poblano, eggs, beans, bacon, and tomatoes. Be sure to ask for a couple of packs of green sauce.

If you don't mind driving 10 miles, a great place to go for dinner (or for lunch on the weekend) is the **Hill Top Café** (✆ **830/997-8922;** www.hilltopcafe.com), right on Hwy. 87 to Mason. This was an old country gas station that was converted into a restaurant by John and Brenda Nichols. John used to be a member of a legendary Austin band, Asleep at the Wheel. He usually plays music on Friday and Saturday evenings. Brenda runs the kitchen, and the food is well-prepared—American with a smattering of Greek and Cajun dishes. Reservations are highly recommended.

GOING BACK (IN TIME) TO luckenbach

About 11 miles southeast of Fredericksburg on R.R. 1376, but light-years away in spirit, the town of **Luckenbach** (pop. 25) was immortalized in song by Waylon Jennings and Willie Nelson. The town pretty much consists of a dance hall and a post office/general store/bar. But it's a very mellow place to hang out. Someone's almost always strumming a guitar, and on weekend afternoons and evenings, Jerry Jeff Walker or Robert Earl Keen might be among the names who turn up at the dance hall. Tying the knot? You can rent the dance hall—or even the entire town. Call (© **830/997-3224** for details. And to get a feel for the town, log on to www.luckenbachtexas.com.

Whenever you visit, lots of beer is likely to be involved, so consider staying at the **Full Moon Inn,** 3234 Luckenbach Rd., Fredericksburg, TX 78624 ((© **800/997-1124** or 830/997-2205; www.luckenbachtx.com), just half a mile from the action on a rise overlooking the countryside. The best of the accommodations, which range in price from $125 to $200, is the 1800s log cabin, large enough to sleep four.

If you've come to Fredericksburg for German food, you can try **Altdorf Biergarten,** 301 W. Main St. ((© 830/997-7865), open Wednesday to Monday for lunch and dinner, Sunday for brunch; and **Friedhelm's Bavarian Inn,** 905 W. Main St. ((© 830/997-6300), open Tuesday to Sunday for lunch and dinner, both featuring moderately priced, hearty schnitzels, dumplings, and sauerbraten, and large selections of German beer.

Also on Main, the **Fredericksburg Brewing Co.,** 245 E. Main St. ((© 830/997-1646), offers typical pub food with a few lighter selections. The beer is quite good. Try the Pioneer Porter or the Peace Pipe Pale Ale, both of which have won awards. It's open daily for lunch and dinner; prices are moderate.

Local foodies like to roost in the **Nest,** 607 S. Washington St. ((© 830/990-8383; www.thenestrestaurant.com), which features New American cuisine in a lovely old house Thursday through Monday evenings; meals are expensive. Equally popular and a bit more cutting edge, the contemporary-chic **Navajo Grill,** 803 E. Main St. ((© 830/990-8289; www.navajogrill.com), offers food inspired by New Orleans, the Southwest, and occasionally the Caribbean. It's open nightly for dinner and on Sunday for brunch, and meals are expensive.

Another popular dinner spot is the **Cabernet Grill,** 2805 Hwy. 16 S. ((© 830/990-5734), which focuses on Texas wines and local produce from area ranches and farms, such as quail and striped bass. Dinner is served Monday through Saturday. Entrees range from moderate to expensive. During the week, it offers a lunch buffet that runs $10. Attached to the restaurant is **Cotton Gin Village** ((© 830/990-5734; www.cottenginvillage.com), a collection of rustic cabins with eight large and comfortable rooms that have all the modern conveniences. These generally run between $150 and $200 a night.

Nightlife

Yes, Fredericksburg's got nightlife, or at least what passes for it in the Hill Country. Some of the live music action takes place a bit outside of the center of town. On Fridays and Saturdays at the Hill Top Café, John Nichols jams with friends starting at about 7pm. Luckenbach (see above) also hosts lots of good bands.

And lately, Fredericksburg's main (and side) streets have also come alive with the sound of music—everything from rockabilly and jazz to oompah—especially from Thursday through Saturday nights. An offshoot of the Luckenbach Dancehall, **Hondo's on Main,** 312 W. Main St. (© **830/997-1633**), also tends to feature Texas roots bands. Check with the Visitor Information Center for a complete weekly listing.

LYNDON B. JOHNSON COUNTRY

Fifty miles west of Austin is Johnson City, where the forebears of the 36th president settled almost 150 years ago. LBJ grew up here, and you can visit his boyhood home. After he became president, he did much of his work from his ranch in this area, which you can also visit. The two sites are 13 miles apart. Both are worth viewing, and if you have the flexibility, I recommend that you see the boyhood home first. This will provide context that will make the visit to the "Texas White House" all the more interesting. With travel time and meals, viewing both sites will take most of a day. Even if you're not usually drawn to the past, you're likely to be intrigued by the picture of LBJ that emerges, and how his life was both a reflection of his times and the seed of change.

LBJ National Historical Park

Johnson City is a small farming town named for James Polk Johnson, LBJ's first cousin once removed. From Austin, take U.S. 290 west. From San Antonio, take Hwy. 281 north. These two roads will join about 4 miles south of Johnson City. Continue on Hwy. 281 until you get to the town, and U.S. 290 splits off to the left and becomes the town's main street. After a few blocks, turn left onto G Street, and straight ahead you'll see the visitor center for the **Lyndon B. Johnson National Historical Park** (© **830/868-7128**). Ask to be in the next tour of the **Boyhood Home ★**, and while you're waiting, take a look at the exhibits: a timeline of LBJ's life and an explanation of the Great Society legislation. Since the tours are frequent, you probably won't have time to see either of the movies shown in the auditoriums, but you can do so after your tour.

The small white clapboard structure where the family lived from 1913 is an eye-opener. Though LBJ's family was not well to do, they were by no means poor by local standards, yet it's striking to see how they lived. LBJ's father, Sam Ealy Johnson, Jr., experienced some hard times but was a community leader and for a while a state legislator. His wife, Rebekah, was a rarity for the Hill Country, a college-educated woman (she was much more educated than her husband). Seeing the house and learning about LBJ's early life, you can start connecting all the dots that led the future politician to push for rural electrification and eventually the transformative project called the Great Society.

After the tour, you can walk over to the **Johnson Settlement,** where LBJ's grandfather, Sam Ealy Johnson, Sr., and his great-uncle, Jessie, engaged in successful cattle speculation in the 1860s. The rustic dogtrot cabin out of which they ran their business is still intact.

The Boyhood Home, visitor center, and Johnson Settlement are all open 8:45am to 5pm daily except Christmas, Thanksgiving, and New Year's Day. Admission is free.

The Boyhood Home can be visited only by tours, offered every half-hour, from 9 to 11:30am and 1 to 4:30pm.

State Park & LBJ Ranch

Continue west on Hwy. 290 for 13 miles, and just before the town of Stonewall you'll see signs for **Lyndon B. Johnson State Park** and the **LBJ Ranch ★**. The first is operated by the Texas Parks and Wildlife Department (© **830/644-2252;** www.tpwd.state.tx.us/park/lbj), and the ranch by the National Park Service (© **830/868-7128;** www.nps.gov/lyjo). You need to go to the state park visitor center first, so that you can get a free visitor's permit to visit the LBJ Ranch and a CD for the self-guided driving tour (having a CD player in your car makes the trip a bit more fun) of the 600 acres of ranch that are part of the land donated to the national park. It remains a working ranch, as you will see in the tour. Crossing over the Pedernales River and through fields of phlox, Indian paintbrush, and other wildflowers, you can see why Johnson used the ranch as a second White House, and why, discouraged from running for a second presidential term, he came back here to find solace and, eventually, to die. A reconstruction of the former president's modest birthplace lies close to his (also modest) final resting place, shared with five generations of Johnsons.

Lady Bird Johnson spent about a third of her time at the Ranch before her death in 2008. After her death, the park service began giving tours of the 7,500-square-foot ranch house. The tour of the house is the only thing that costs money ($2). So far, five rooms can be viewed, but there are plans to include more rooms once they are ready (which means refurnishing them to look as they did ca. 1965). Once more of the house is opened up for the tour, the price will probably rise, too. The tour really brings home what a colorful character LBJ was and how different the 1960s were.

Not far from the state park visitor center is the **Sauer-Beckmann Living History Farm,** where you'll find period-costumed "occupants" giving visitors a look at typical Texas-German farm life at the turn of the 20th century. Chickens, pigs, turkeys, and other farm animals roam freely or in large pens, while the farmers go about their chores, which might include churning butter, baking, or feeding the animals. The midwife who attended LBJ's birth grew up here. Interesting in the same way as Colonial Williamsburg, but much less known (and thus not as well funded), this is a terrific place to come with kids. Nearby are nature trails, a swimming pool (open only in summer), and lots of covered picnic spots. The park also keeps a small number of bison for visitors to view. *Tip:* It's best to visit the Sauer-Beckmann farm after you've seen the LBJ ranch, especially if it's late in the day. You don't want to run the risk of being bumped from the last tour of the house for the day.

All state park buildings, including the visitor center, are open daily 8am to 5pm; the Sauer-Beckmann Living History Farm is open daily 8am to 4:30pm. The Nature Trail, grounds, and picnic areas are open until dark every day. All facilities in both sections of the park are closed Thanksgiving, Christmas, and New Year's Day.

Where to Dine

The surest bet is **Ronnie's Ice House Barbecue,** 211 Hwy. 281, just south of 290 (© **830/868-7553**). But he usually runs out of meat by 1pm. Your next best bet is the **Silver K Café**, at the corner of Main and F Street (© **830/868-2911**). For lunch, they have soups, salads, and sandwiches. For dinner, they have a full menu. Prices range from moderate to expensive. If you prefer something on the go, visit **Whittington's,** 602 Hwy. 281 S. (© **877/868-5501**), known for its beef and turkey jerky.

Outside of Johnson City, the place to dine—and to bed down—is close by the LBJ Ranch, in Stonewall. **Rose Hill Manor,** 2614 Upper Albert Rd., Stonewall, TX 78671 (℃ **877/ROSEHIL** [767-3445] or 830/644-2247; www.rose-hill.com), is a reconstructed Southern manse. Light and airy accommodations—four in the main house, and six in separate cottages—are beautifully but comfortably furnished with antiques. All offer porches or patios and Hill Country views. Rates run from $155 to $179 on weekdays, and $199 to $249 on weekends. The inn's New American cuisine, served Wednesday through Sunday evenings in an ultraromantic dining room, is outstanding. Reservations are essential; prices are expensive.

If you're heading on to Austin, take a short detour from U.S. 290 to **Pedernales Falls State Park,** 8 miles east of Johnson City on F.R. 2766 (℃ **830/868-7304;** www.tpwd.state.tx.us/park/pedernal). When the flow of the Pedernales River is high, the stepped waterfalls that give the 4,860-acre park its name are impressive.

THE NORTHERN LAKES

One of the nice things about touring these lakes is that you have to take it slow: The roads that wind around them force you to meander rather than beeline it to your destination. And, of course, engaging with that water—whether submerging in it or just gazing at it—is the reason most people come here. For additional information about where to kayak, sail, swim, or fish, check with the chambers of commerce and visitor centers listed in this section.

From Austin, it's 48 miles northwest on Hwy. 71 to the town of **Marble Falls,** known for two natural features, only one of which still exists. The cascades for which the town was named once descended some 20 feet along a series of marble ledges, but they were submerged when the Max Starcke Dam, which created Lake Marble Falls, was completed in 1951. (You can occasionally get a peek at the falls when the Lower Colorado River Authority lowers the water level to repair the dam.) The town's other natural claim to fame is the still very visible Granite Mountain, from which the pink granite used to create the state capitol in Austin was quarried.

VIEWING bluebonnets & OTHER WILDFLOWERS

Of its many names—*lupinus subcarnosus, lupinus texensis,* buffalo clover, wolf flower, even *el conejo*—bluebonnet is the most descriptive. And when the official state flower of Texas puts in an appearance, starting in March and peaking in April, hordes of people descend on the Hill Country to ogle and photograph the fields of flowers.

To enjoy the bluebonnets and other wildflowers, you must be flexible. When the conditions are perfect, they can be blooming everywhere, but sometimes the rains don't fall where they should. In 2010, the northern Hill Country had few wildflowers for lack of rain. Greater numbers were seen in the southern parts, and even more were blooming in the coastal prairies south and east of Austin and San Antonio.

For up-to-date info on where to find the best views of wildflowers in central Texas, contact the **Wildflower Hotline** (aka the National Wildflower Research Center in Austin) at ℃ **512/929-3600.**

The main reason most people come to Marble Falls these days is its three parks and two lakes (Lake LBJ lies a little upstream), but it's also pleasant to wander around the center of town, where there are a number of historic homes, antiques shops, and the Old Oak shopping complex.

One of the town's other attractions is also the place to get details on what to see and do in the area: The **Marble Falls/Lake LBJ Visitor Center,** 801 Hwy. 281 (✆ **800/759-8178** or 830/693-4449; www.marblefalls.org), is located in the Historic Depot Building, built to serve the railroad spur used to transport granite to Austin. The visitor center is open Monday to Friday from 8am to 5pm.

Trains no longer make it to Marble Falls, but they do go to **Burnet,** some 14 miles to the north. The Austin Steam Train Association restored the five rail coaches and the 1916 locomotive that you can board for the **Hill Country Flyer Steam Train Excursion** (✆ **512/477-8468;** www.austinsteamtrain.org), a leisurely 33-mile ride from Cedar Park, a northwest suburb of Austin. The train runs Saturday and Sunday March through May, Saturday only June to November, and selected December evenings. Fares are $28 adults, $25 seniors, and $18 for children 13 and under in coach with no heat or A/C; or $33, $30, and $23, respectively, with heat or A/C; and $43, $39, and $27, respectively, for a lounge car ticket. (On some days, the train only goes half the distance and is called the Bertram Flyer, and the tickets are correspondingly cheaper.) The train makes one trip per day—departure times vary, so call or check the website.

The train makes a 3-hour layover on Burnet's historic town square, which, with its impressive courthouse—not to mention its collectibles shops and cafes—is also a good spot for visitors who drive into town to explore. (***Beware:*** A gunfight is staged at 2:30pm on most Saturdays when the train comes in.) Burnet grew up around a U.S. Army post established in 1849, and you can still visit the **Fort Croghan Grounds and Museum,** 703 Buchanan Dr. (Hwy. 29 W.; ✆ **512/756-8281;** www. fortcroghan.org), home to several historic outbuildings and more than 1,200 historic artifacts from around the county. Admission is free; the museum is open April through August, Thursday through Saturday, from 10am to 5pm. In the same complex is the **Burnet Chamber of Commerce** (✆ **512/756-4297;** www.burnetchamber. org). Here, among other things, you can find out why Burnet calls itself the Bluebonnet Capital of Texas. The chamber is open 8:30am to 5:30pm Monday through Friday.

Some 11 miles southwest of Burnet, **Longhorn Cavern State Park,** Park Road 4, 6 miles off U.S. 281 (✆ **877/441-CAVE** [441-2283] or 830/598-CAVE [598-2283]; www.longhorncaverns.com), has as its centerpiece one of the few river-formed caverns in Texas. Its past visitors include Ice Age animals, Comanche Indians, Confederate soldiers, and members of the Civilian Conservation Corps, who, in the 1930s, built the stairs that descend into the main room. The cave's natural and human history is detailed on narrated tours—the only way you can visit—that last about an hour and a half; they're offered from Labor Day to Memorial Day Monday to Thursday at 11am, 1, and 3pm, Friday to Sunday from 10am to 4pm every hour on the hour. In summer, tours run every day on the hour from 10am to 4pm. Admission is $13 adults, $12 for seniors and teens, and $8 ages 2 to 12.

Continue north on Park Road 4, beyond where it intersects with R.R. 2342, and you'll reach **Inks Lake State Park,** 3630 Park Rd. 4 W. (✆ **512/793-2223;** www. tpwd.state.tx.us/park/inks), offering some 1,200 acres of recreational facilities on and adjacent to the lake for which it's named: hiking trails, canoe and paddle-boat rentals, swimming, fishing—even golf on an 18-hole course. Don't miss Devil's Waterhole,

The Northern Lakes

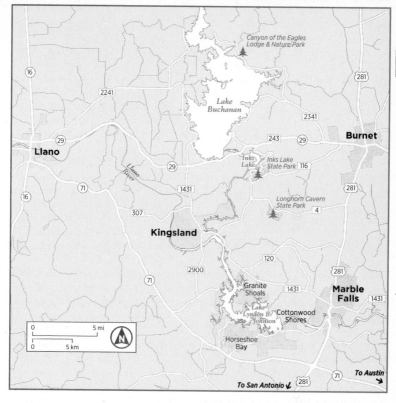

flanked by pink granite boulders and a waterfall. You can canoe through it, hike to it, or just view it from a scenic overlook on Park Road 4.

   Those with limited time might want to skip Inks Lake in favor of the oldest, most remote, and largest of the Highland Lakes, the 32-mile-long **Lake Buchanan**. The best way to see it—and the highlight of any trip to this area—is the **Vanishing Texas River Cruise ★★** (© **800/4-RIVER-4** [474-8374] or 512/756-6986; www.vtrc. com), which departs from the Canyon of the Eagles Lodge & Nature Park (see "Where to Stay & Dine," below), at the end of R.R. 2341 on the lake's north shore (call for directions, or check the website). The lake's banks are still startlingly pristine (though private development may soon make the "vanishing" part of the cruise's name too true), and no matter what time of year you come, you're bound to see some wildlife. From November through March, bald eagles troll the skies, while the rest of the year wild turkeys and deer abound. These expertly narrated tours, which offer a lot of historical as well as natural information, vary season by season; prices range from about $20 for adults for the basic 2½-hour naturalist tours to $33 for sunset dinner cruises ($30 for children ages 2–12). Reservations are recommended.

Where to Stay & Dine

Rustic lakeside cabins and small motels dot this entire area, but two lodgings stand out. If you head 15 miles east of Marble Falls on FM 1431, you'll reach the town (such as it is) of Kingsland and the **Antlers,** 1001 King St., Kingsland, TX 78639 (✆ **800/383-0007** or 916/388-4411; www.theantlers.com), a restored turn-of-the-20th-century resort occupying 15 acres on Lake LBJ. You've got a choice of bedding down in one of six antiques-filled suites in the 1901 railroad hotel, as President William McKinley did ($140–$160); in one of three colorful converted train cabooses ($120) or a converted railroad coach ($150–$160), parked on a piece of original track; or in one of seven appealing cabins scattered around the grounds ($140–$250). Some of the accommodations sleep four or six people comfortably, and one of the lodges accommodates up to eight. Activities include strolling several nature trails, boating or fishing on the lake, or browsing the antiques shop in the main hotel building. For fortification, cross the road to the **Kingsland Old Town Grill,** a good place for steak, regular or chicken-fried. Look eerily familiar? This 1890s Victorian house served as the film set for the original *Texas Chainsaw Massacre.*

Opened in 1999 on 940 acres owned by the Lower Colorado River Authority—most of it still wilderness preserve—the **Canyon of the Eagles Lodge & Nature Park,** 16942 R.R. 2341, Burnet, TX 78611 (✆ **800/977-0081** or 512/756-8787; www.canyonoftheeagles.com), is ideal for those seeking serious escape. You can indulge in the Lake Buchanan excursions or adventures described in the previous section, hike the property's trails, stargaze at the lodge's observatory, or just kick back on your porch and watch birds flitting by. The **Canyon Room** restaurant offers everything from Fredericksburg bratwurst to pecan-crusted trout. Rates for the rooms, which are country-style rustic but feature such conveniences as phones (in case your escape is not *that* serious) and, in the Cottage Rooms, minifridges and microwaves, range from $130 to $170. A minimum of 2 nights is required for popular weekends, but you wouldn't want to stay less time than that anyway.

In addition to the Kingsland Old Town Grill and the Canyon Room—the latter has the advantage of being BYOB and the disadvantage of being far from most everywhere if you're not staying at the lodge—I'd recommend another place in Marble Falls, for a change of pace. **Blue Bonnet Cafe,** 211 Hwy. 281 (✆ **830/693-2344;** www.bluebonnetcafe.net), first opened its doors in 1929 and has received accolades for its down-home country food—chicken-fried steak, pot roast, fried okra. It's open every day for breakfast and lunch, and serves dinner every day except Sunday. Prices are inexpensive to moderate.

If you're in the mood for barbecue and you're in the vicinity of Llano, you can stop by a well-known joint called **Cooper's,** where the Wootan family has been smoking big meat in a big pit forever, at 505 W. Dallas St. (© **325/247-5713;** www.coopers bbq.com). For more information on Texas barbecue and Cooper's, see "Small Towns & Texas Barbecue" in chapter 16. Cooper's is open daily 10:30am to 7pm. Prices are moderate.

PLANNING YOUR TRIP TO SAN ANTONIO & AUSTIN

18

Because San Antonio and Austin offer so many options, it can be daunting to begin planning your trip. Whether touring the Alamo is your priority or you're determined to sample barbecue in every small town on the outskirts of Austin, this chapter will provide you with the tools you'll need to make the most of your time in Central Texas. See below for information on getting around both cities, as well as quick, on-the-ground resources.

GETTING THERE: SAN ANTONIO

By Plane

The **San Antonio International Airport** (airport code SAT; 📞 **210/ 207-3411;** www.ci.sat.tx.us/aviation) is 7 miles north of downtown. It is compact, well marked, and has two terminals. Among its various amenities are a postal center, ATM, foreign-currency exchange, game room, and well-stocked gift shops. Advantage, Alamo, Avis, Budget, Dollar, Enterprise, Hertz, National, and Thrifty all have rental-car desks at both of the airport terminals.

Attention visitors to the U.S. from abroad: Some major airlines offer transatlantic or transpacific passengers special discount tickets under the name **Visit USA,** which allows mostly one-way travel from one U.S. destination to another at very low prices. Unavailable in the U.S., these discount tickets must be purchased abroad in conjunction with your international fare. This system is the easiest, fastest, cheapest way to see the country. Inquire with your air carrier.

GETTING INTO TOWN FROM THE AIRPORT

Loop 410 and U.S. 281 S. intersect just outside the airport. If you're renting a car here (see "By Car," in "Getting Around: San Antonio," below), it should take about 15 to 20 minutes to drive downtown via U.S. 281 S.

Most of the hotels within a radius of a mile or two offer **free shuttle service** to and from the airport (be sure to check when you make your reservation). If you're staying downtown, you'll most likely have to pay your own way.

VIA Metropolitan Transit's bus no. 5 is the cheapest ($1.10) way to get downtown. The trip should take from 40 to 50 minutes. You need exact change.

SATRANS (✆ **800/868-7707** or 210/281-9900; www.saairportshuttle.com), with a booth outside each of the terminals, offers shared van service from the airport to the downtown hotels for $18 per person one-way, $32 round-trip. Prices to other destinations vary; call or check the website for specifics. Vans run from about 7am until 1am; phone 24 hours in advance for van pickup from your hotel.

There's a **taxi** queue in front of each terminal. Airport taxis will cost about $25 for downtown destinations.

By Bus

The Greyhound bus line (✆ **800/231-2222** or 210/270-5824; www.greyhound.com) and its affiliates handle all the bus travel between cities in Texas. The Greyhound station in San Antonio is downtown at 500 N. St. Mary's St.

By Car

For listings of the major car-rental agencies in San Antonio, please see "Renting," below. If you're visiting from abroad and plan to rent a car in the United States, keep in mind that foreign driver's licenses are usually recognized in the U.S., but you should get an international one if your home license is not in English.

If you plan to rent a car in the United States, you probably won't need the services of an additional automobile organization. If you're planning to buy or borrow a car, automobile-association membership is recommended. **AAA** (American Automobile Association; ✆ **800/222-4357;** www.aaa.com) is the country's largest auto club and supplies its members with maps, insurance, and, most important, emergency road service. The cost of joining runs from $71 to $124 for singles and from $97 to $178 for two members, but if you're a member of a foreign auto club with reciprocal arrangements, you can enjoy free AAA service in America.

San Antonio is fed by four interstates (I-35, I-10, I-37, and I-410), three U.S. highways (U.S. 281, U.S. 90, and U.S. 87), four state highways (Tex. 16, Tex. 211, Tex. 151, and Tex. 1604), and several Farm-to-Market (FM) roads. In San Antonio, I-410 and Hwy. 1604, which circle the city, are referred to as Loop 410 and Loop 1604. All freeways lead into the central business district; U.S. 281 and Loop 410 are closest to the airport.

San Antonio is 975 miles from Atlanta; 1,979 miles from Boston; 1,187 miles from Chicago; 1,342 miles from Los Angeles; 1,360 miles from Miami; 527 miles from New Orleans; 1,781 miles from New York; 1,724 miles from San Francisco; and 2,149 miles from Seattle. The distance to Dallas is 282 miles, to Houston 199 miles, and to Austin 80 miles.

The most cost-effective, convenient, and comfortable way to travel around the United States is by car. The interstate highway system connects cities and towns all over the country; in addition to these high-speed, limited-access roadways, there's an extensive network of federal, state, and local highways and roads. The Texas state highway system is one of the best in the U.S., as it is funded with oil revenues.

For information on car rentals and gasoline (petrol) in San Antonio, see "Fast Facts: San Antonio" later in this chapter.

By Train

Trains leave from the depot at 350 Hoefden St. (✆ **210/223-3226**) in downtown San Antonio. Call ✆ **800/USA-RAIL** (872-7245), or log on to www.amtrak.com for current fares, schedules, and reservations. The Sunset Limited leaves for Orlando via Houston and New Orleans three times a week at 11:55pm. It departs for Los Angeles at 7am three times a week. The Texas Eagle departs for Chicago via Austin and Dallas daily at 7am.

GETTING THERE: AUSTIN

By Plane

Austin-Bergstrom International Airport (✆ **512/530-ABIA** [2242]; airport code **AUS**) opened in 1999 on the site of the former Bergstrom Air Force Base, just off Hwy. 71 (Ben White Blvd.) and only 8 miles southwest of the capitol. For more information about the airport, go to www.ci.austin.tx.us/austinairport.

GETTING INTO TOWN FROM THE AIRPORT

Taxis from the major companies in town usually form a line outside the terminal, though occasionally you won't find any waiting. To ensure off-hour pickup in advance, phone **American Yellow Checker Cab** (✆ **512/452-9999**) before you leave home. The ride between the airport and downtown costs around $25.

If you're not in a huge rush to get to your hotel, **SuperShuttle** (✆ **800/BLUE-VAN** [258-3826] or 512/258-3826; www.supershuttle.com) offers minivan service to hotels and residences. Prices range from $14 one-way ($24 round-trip) for trips to a downtown hotel, to $14 ($24 round-trip) for trips to a central hotel, to $18 ($26 round-trip) for trips to a hotel in the northwestern part of town. The drawback is that you often must share your ride with several others, who may be dropped off first. You don't have to book in advance for pickups at the airport, but you do need to phone 24 hours ahead of time to arrange for a pickup when you're leaving town.

For $1, you can go from the airport to downtown or the university area on a city bus called the **Airport Flyer** (no. 100). It runs until about midnight. The passenger pickup is outside the arrival gates, close to the end of the concourse. Buses depart about every 40 minutes. You can grab a route schedule from the city's visitor information office, by the baggage carousels. Or you can download it from the website **Capital Metro Transit** (✆ **512/474-1200** or TTY 385-5872; www.capmetro.org). It's also available at ABIA's website (www.ci.austin.tx.us/austinairport); just click on "Ground Transportation." See also the "By Bus" section, below, and "By Bus" in "Getting Around: Austin," later in this chapter, for additional information.

Most of the major car-rental companies—Advantage, Alamo, Avis, Budget, Dollar, Hertz, National, and Thrifty—have outlets at the airport; see "Car Rentals" in the "Getting Around: Austin" section, later in this chapter, for details. The trip from the airport to downtown by car or taxi takes about 20 minutes, much more if you're headed to north Austin. During rush hour, there are often backups all along Hwy. 71. Be sure to allow extra time when you need to catch a flight.

By Bus

You'll also be going through San Antonio if you're traveling east or west to Austin via **Greyhound,** 916 E. Koenig Lane (© **800/231-2222** or 512/458-4463; www. greyhound.com). There are approximately nine buses between the two cities each day, with one-way fares running around $19.

By Car

Austin is 941 miles from Atlanta; 1,899 miles from Boston; 1,107 miles from Chicago; 1,377 miles from Los Angeles; 1,326 miles from Miami; 494 miles from New Orleans; 1,701 miles from New York; 1,741 miles from San Francisco; and 2,188 miles from Seattle. The distance to Dallas is 202 miles, to Houston 165 miles, and to San Antonio 80 miles. **I-35** is the north-south approach to Austin; it intersects with **Hwy. 290,** a major east-west thoroughfare, and **Hwy. 183,** which also runs roughly north-south through town. For those staying on the west side of Austin, **Loop 1** is helpful. Locally it's known as Mo-Pac.

To get to Austin from Dallas/Fort Worth, take I-35 south. The trip will take 3 to 4 hours. From Houston you have a choice, and both take about the same time (3 hr.): Take Hwy. 290 west or take I-10 west toward San Antonio, and then north on Hwy. 71, just after you pass the town of Columbus.

For information on car rentals and gasoline (petrol) in Austin, see "Fast Facts: Austin" later in this chapter.

By Train

Amtrak provides service west to Los Angeles (via San Antonio, El Paso, and Tucson) on the Texas Eagle, which departs at 6:30pm. **Amtrak,** 250 N. Lamar Blvd. (© **800/872-7245** or 512/476-5684; www.amtrak.com) is downtown. In the opposite direction, the Texas Eagle provides daily service to Chicago via Dallas, Forth Worth, Little Rock, and St. Louis. Departures are at 9:30am.

GETTING AROUND: SAN ANTONIO

Like other Sunbelt cities, San Antonio has a relatively compact downtown nucleus, encircled by old neighborhoods and commercial areas, which then give way to wide stretches of suburbia. Most visitors will have an easy time finding their way around the downtown area. For the rest of the city, they need only a general understanding of the freeway system and the locations of the major attractions that lie outside the center of town. The rest can be gleaned upon arrival. North of downtown, and not very far away, are the airport, several museums, and many of the best dining spots. To the southeast are the old Spanish missions. SeaWorld is on the far west side, and Six Flags Fiesta Texas theme park is in the far northwest.

I find that the freeways are laid out in a fairly reasonable pattern, and they're easy to use so long as you have a map. But you can avoid the freeways by using the main avenues and streets that crisscross the area. A map would be absolutely essential for this, and you should be aware that there are a few large, enclosed areas of town occupied by military installations, which you have to drive around. San Antonio and the military have a long relationship. Among members of the Army and Air Force, San Antonio is often referred to as Military City, and it is a favorite location for retired military personnel.

By Car

If you're staying in central San Antonio you can get by without a car if you're confining your activity to the amusements of the central city. You can take a bus or a taxi to the museums in north-central San Antonio. A car saves time and taxi fares when you want to stay or travel farther afield to such attractions as the theme parks and shopping districts in the suburbs. In downtown San Antonio, the pattern of one-way streets is a bit confusing and slow going. It's more enjoyable to park your car and walk or take the bus, which is easy to use in the downtown area.

As for highway driving, pay attention. Because of the many convergences of major freeways in the area—described in the "Main Arteries & Streets" section, below—you can find yourself in an express lane headed somewhere you really don't want to go. Don't let your mind wander; watch signs carefully, and be prepared to make quick lane changes.

Rush hour lasts from about 7:30 to 9am and 4:30 to 6pm Monday through Friday. The crush may not be bad compared with that of Houston or Dallas, but it's getting worse all the time. Because of San Antonio's rapid growth, you can also expect to find major highway construction or repairs going on somewhere in the city at any given time. For more info, log on to the Texas Department of Transportation's website at **www.dot.state.tx.us**.

RENTING San Antonio is a convention town. You need to reserve a rental car ahead of your visit. Nothing really above the usual requirements is necessary. When choosing a rental that fits your budget, don't forget to take taxes into account. In San Antonio, the tax for rentals at the airport is 16%, elsewhere in town 11%.

Here's a quick list of the rental agencies in San Antonio: **Advantage** (© 800/777-5500; www.advantagerentacar.com), **Alamo** (© 800/327-9633; www.alamo.com), **Avis** (© 800/331-1212; www.avis.com), **Budget** (© 800/527-0700; www.budget.com), **Dollar** (© 800/800-4000; www.dollarcar.com), **Enterprise** (© 800/325-8007; www.enterprise.com), **Hertz** (© 800/654-3131; www.hertz.com), **National** (© 800/CAR-RENT [227-7368]; www.nationalcar.com), and **Thrifty** (© 800/367-2277; www.thrifty.com) all have desks at both of the airport terminals. **Hertz** is also represented downtown at the Marriott Rivercenter at Bowie and Commerce (© 210/225-3676).

Almost all the major car-rental companies have their own discount programs. Your rate will often depend on the organizations to which you belong, the dates of travel, and the length of your stay. Some companies give discounts to AAA members, for example, and some have special deals in conjunction with various airlines or telephone companies. Prices are sometimes reduced on weekends (or midweek). Call as far in advance as possible to book a car, and always ask about specials.

The basic insurance coverage offered by most car-rental companies, known as the **Loss/Damage Waiver (LDW)** or **Collision Damage Waiver (CDW),** can cost as much as $20 per day. It usually covers the full value of the vehicle with no deductible if an outside party causes an accident or other damage to the rental car. You will probably be covered in case of theft as well. If you are at fault in an accident, however, you will be covered for the full replacement value of the car but not for liability. Most rental companies will require a police report in order to process any claims you file, but your private insurer will not be notified of the accident.

The car-rental companies also offer additional liability insurance (if you harm others in an accident), personal accident insurance (if you harm yourself or your passengers), and personal effects insurance (if your luggage is stolen from your car). If you have insurance on your car at home, you are probably covered for most of these "unlikelihoods." If your own insurance doesn't cover rentals, or if you don't have auto insurance, you should consider the additional coverage (keeping in mind that the car-rental companies are liable for certain base amounts).

Check out **Breezenet.com,** which offers domestic car-rental discounts with some of the most competitive rates around. Also worth visiting are **Orbitz, Hotwire.com, Travelocity,** and **Priceline,** all of which offer competitive online car-rental rates.

International visitors should note that insurance and taxes are almost never included in quoted rental car rates in the U.S. Be sure to ask your rental agency about additional fees for these. They can add a significant cost to your car rental.

If you're visiting from abroad and plan to rent a car in the United States, keep in mind that foreign driver's licenses are usually recognized in the U.S., but you may want to consider obtaining an international driver's license.

Most rental agencies will give you a small map of San Antonio that's good only for general orientation. For anything more than that, you'll need to get a city map. Both **Rand McNally** and **Gousha**'s maps of San Antonio are reliable; you'll find one or the other at most gas stations, convenience stores, drugstores, bookstores, and newsstands.

San Antonio lies at the southern edge of the Texas Hill Country and is mostly flat. Streets, especially those in the old parts of town, are jumbled, while a number of the thoroughfares leading in and out of town follow old Spanish trails or 19th-century wagon trails.

MAIN ARTERIES & STREETS Most of the major roads in Texas meet in San Antonio, where they form a rough wheel-and-spoke pattern. There are two loops: I-410 circles around the city, coming to within 6 to 7 miles of downtown in the north and east, and as far out as 10 miles in the west and south; and Hwy. 1604 forms an even larger circle with a 13-mile radius. The spokes of the wheel are formed by highways I-35, I-10, I-37, U.S. 281, U.S. 90, and U.S. 87. Occasionally two or three highways will merge onto the same freeway, which will then carry the various designations. For example, U.S. 90, U.S. 87, and I-10 converge for a while in an east-west direction just south of downtown, while U.S. 281, I-35, and I-37 run together on a north-south route to the east; I-10, I-35, and U.S. 87 bond for a bit going north-south to the west of downtown.

Among the most major of the minor spokes are Broadway, McCullough, San Pedro, and Blanco, all of which lead north from the city center into the most popular shopping and restaurant areas of town. Fredericksburg goes out to the Medical Center from just northwest of downtown. You may hear locals referring to something as being "in the Loop." That doesn't mean it's privy to insider information, but rather, that it lies within the circumference of I-410. True, this covers a pretty large area, but with the spreading of the city north and west, it's come to mean central.

Downtown is bounded by I-37 to the east, I-35 to the north and west, and U.S. 90 (which merges with I-10) to the south. Within this area, Durango, Commerce, Market, and Houston are the important east-west streets. Alamo on the east side and Santa Rosa (which turns into S. Laredo) on the west side are the major north-south streets. **Note:** A lot of the north-south streets change names midstream (or, I should say, mid-macadam). That's another reason, besides the confusing one-way streets, to consult a map carefully before attempting to steer your way around downtown.

LOCATING AN ADDRESS   Few locals are aware that there's any method to the madness of finding downtown addresses, but in fact, directions are based on the layout of the first Spanish settlements—back when the San Fernando cathedral was at the center of town. Market Street is the north-south divider, and Flores separates east from west. Thus, South St. Mary's becomes North St. Mary's when it crosses Market, with addresses starting from zero at Market going in both directions. North of downtown, San Pedro is the east-west dividing line, although not every street sign reflects this fact.

There are few clear-cut rules like this in Loop land, but on its northernmost stretch, Loop 410 divides into east and west at Broadway, and at Bandera Road, it splits into Loop 410 north and south. Keep going far enough south, and I-35 marks yet another boundary between east and west. Knowing this will help you a little in locating an address, and explains why, when you go in a circle around town, you'll notice that the directions marked on overhead signs have suddenly completely shifted.

PARKING   San Antonio is one of those rare cities that has plenty of parking, even downtown. Within a few blocks of all sites of interest, you'll find open-air parking lots. Most of these work by the hour and the day. There's usually no attendant. You pay at a kiosk (keep on hand plenty of bills of lower denominations and make sure you put your money into the slot that corresponds to your parking space). Rates run from $5 to $10 per day, though the closer you get to the Alamo and the River Walk, the more expensive they become. Prices tend to go up during special events and summer weekends, so a parking lot that ordinarily charges $6 a day is likely to charge $9 or more. Out in suburbia, all parking is free and usually plentiful.

By Bus

San Antonio's public transportation system is visitor-friendly and fares are inexpensive. **VIA Metropolitan Transit Service** offers regular bus service for $1.10, with an additional 15¢ charge for transfers. You'll need exact change. Call ℭ **210/362-2020** for transit information, check the website at **www.viainfo.net**, or stop in one of VIA's many service centers, which you can find by checking the website. The most convenient for visitors is the downtown center, 260 E. Houston St. (ℭ **210/475-9008**), open Monday to Friday 7am to 6pm, Saturday 9am to 2pm. A helpful bus route is the no. 7, which travels from downtown to the San Antonio Museum of Art, Japanese Tea Garden, San Antonio Zoo, Witte Museum, Brackenridge Park, and the Botanical Garden. It is particularly geared toward tourists. *Tip:* During large festivals, such as Fiesta and the Texas Folklife Festival, VIA offers many Park & Ride lots that allow you to leave your car and bus it downtown.

In addition to its bus lines, VIA offers four convenient downtown streetcar routes that cover all the most popular tourist stops and run with great frequency. Designed to look like the turn-of-the-20th-century trolleys used in San Antonio until 1933, the streetcars cost the same as buses (exact change required; drivers carry none). The trolleys, which have signs color-coded by route, display their destinations.

If you're planning to spend most of the day exploring downtown and other parts of the city, your best option is to buy a day pass for $4. You can by them at the service centers, such as the one mentioned above.

BY TAXI

Cabs are available outside the airport, near the Greyhound and Amtrak terminals (only when a train is due, however), and at most major downtown hotels, but they're next to impossible to hail on the street; most of the time, you'll need to phone for one in advance. The best of the taxi companies in town (and also the largest, as it represents the consolidation of two of the majors) is **Yellow-Checker Cab** (✆ **210/222-2222**), which has an excellent record of turning up when promised. The base charge on a taxi is $2; add $2.15 for each mile (plus a fuel charge if gasoline is over $3 per gallon).

ON FOOT

Downtown San Antonio is a treat for walkers, who can walk from one tourist attraction to another or stroll along a beautifully landscaped river. Traffic lights have buttons to push to make sure the lights stay green long enough for pedestrians to cross without putting their lives in peril. Jaywalking is a ticketable offense but is rarely enforced.

GETTING AROUND: AUSTIN

In 1839, Austin was laid out in a grid on the northern shore of the Colorado River, bounded by Shoal Creek to the west and Waller Creek to the east. The section of the river abutting the original settlement is now known as Town Lake, and the city has spread far beyond its original borders in all directions. The land to the east is flat Texas prairie; the rolling Hill Country begins on the west side of town.

By Car

Driving in Austin is a bit of a challenge for visitors. Highways are rife with signs that suddenly insist LEFT LANE MUST TURN LEFT or RIGHT LANE MUST TURN RIGHT—generally positioned so they're noticeable only when it's too late to switch. I-35—nicknamed "the NAFTA highway" because of the big rigs speeding up from Mexico—is mined with tricky on-and-off ramps and, around downtown, a confusing complex of upper and lower levels; it's easy to miss your exit or find yourself exiting when you don't want to. The rapidly developing area to the northwest, where Hwy. 183 connects I-35 with Mo-Pac and the Capital of Texas Highway, requires particular vigilance, as the connections occur very rapidly. There are regular lane mergers and sudden, precipitous turnoffs.

A number of major downtown streets are one-way; many don't have street signs or have signs so covered with foliage they're impossible to read. Driving is particularly confusing in the university area, where streets like "32½" suddenly turn up. Multiply the difficulties at night, when you need super vision to read the ill-lit street indicators.

Nervous? Good. Bett'er you're a bit edgy than lost or injured. Consult maps in advance and, when driving around the university or downtown, try to gauge the number of blocks before turns so you won't have to be completely dependent on street signs. You can also check the Texas Department of Transportation's (TxDOT) website, www.dot.state.tx.us, for the latest information on road conditions, including highway diversions, construction, and closures.

CAR RENTALS   If you're planning to travel at a popular time, it's a good idea to book as far in advance as you can, both to secure the quoted rates and to ensure that you get a car.

Advantage (© 800/777-5500; www.arac.com), **Alamo** (© 800/327-9633; www. alamo.com), **Avis** (© 800/831-2847; www.avis.com), **Budget** (© 800/527-0700; www. budget.com), **Dollar** (© 800/800-4000; www.dollarcar.com), **Hertz** (© 800/654-3131; www.hertz.com), **National** (© 800/227-7368; www.nationalcar.com), and **Thrifty** (© 800/367-2277; www.thrifty.com) all have representatives at the Austin airport.

Lower prices are usually available for those who are flexible about dates of travel or who are members of frequent-flyer or frequent-hotel-stay programs or of organizations such as AAA or AARP. Car-rental companies are eager to get your business, so they're as likely as not to ask whether you belong to any group that will snag you a discount, but if the clerk doesn't inquire, it can't hurt to mention every travel-related program you're a member of—you'd be surprised at the bargains you might turn up.

Try checking out **Breezenet.com,** which offers domestic car-rental discounts with some of the most competitive rates around. Also worth visiting are **Orbitz, Hotwire.com, Travelocity,** and **Priceline,** all of which offer competitive online car-rental rates.

MAIN ARTERIES & STREETS I-35, forming the border between central and East Austin (and straddling the Balcones Fault Line), is the main north-south thoroughfare; Loop 1, usually called Mo-Pac (it follows the course of the Missouri–Pacific railroad, although some people like to say it got its name because it's "mo' packed"), is the westside equivalent. Hwy. 290, running east-west, merges with I-35 where it comes in on the north side of town, briefly reestablishing its separate identity on the south side of town before merging with Hwy. 71 (which is called Ben White Blvd. btw. 183 and Lamar Blvd.). Hwy. 290 and Hwy. 71 split up again in Oak Hill, on the west side of town. Not confused enough yet? Hwy. 2222 changes its name from Koenig to Northland and, west of Loop 360, to Bullcreek, while, in the north, Hwy. 183 is called Research Boulevard. (Looking at a map should make all this clear as mud.) Important north-south city streets include Lamar, Guadalupe, and Burnet. If you want to get across town north of the river, use Cesar Chavez (once known as First St.), 15th Street (which turns into Enfield west of Lamar), Martin Luther King, Jr. Boulevard (the equivalent of 19th St., and often just called MLK), 38th Street, or 45th Street.

FINDING AN ADDRESS Congress Avenue was the earliest dividing line between east and west, while the Colorado River marked the north and south border of the city. Addresses were designed to move in increments of 100 per block, so that 1500 N. Guadalupe, say, would be 15 blocks north of the river. This system still works reasonably well in the older sections of town, but breaks down where the neat street grid does (look at a street map to see where the right angles end). All the east-west streets were originally named after trees native to the city (for example, Sixth St. was once Pecan St.); most that run north and south, such as San Jacinto, Lavaca, and Guadalupe, retain their original Texas river monikers.

STREET MAPS The maps available for no cost at the Austin Convention and Visitors Bureau, as well as at many car-rental companies at the airport, should help you locate major landmarks. For more detail, you can buy street maps at convenience stores, pharmacies, and bookstores.

DRIVING RULES Unless indicated, right turns are permitted on red after coming to a full stop. Seat belts and child-restraint seats are mandatory in Texas (www.txdps. state.tx.us/director_staff/public_information/carseat.htm).

PARKING   Unless you have legislative plates, you're likely to find the selection of parking spots downtown extremely limited during the week (construction isn't making the situation any better); as a result, lots of downtown restaurants offer valet parking (with hourly rates ranging $4–$6). There are a number of lots around the area, costing anywhere from $5 to $7 per hour, but the most convenient ones tend to fill up quickly. If you're lucky enough to find a metered spot, it'll run you 75¢ per hour, with a 2-hour limit, so bring change. Although there's virtually no street parking available near the capitol before 5pm during the week, there is a free visitor garage on 15th and San Jacinto (2-hr. time limit).

   In the university area, trying to find a spot near the shopping strip known as "the Drag" can be just that. However, cruise the side streets and you're eventually bound to find a pay lot that's not filled. The two most convenient on-campus parking garages are located near San Jacinto and East 26th streets and off 25th Street between San Antonio and Nueces. There's also a (free!) parking lot near the LBJ Library, but it's far from the central campus. Log on to **www.utexas.edu/parking** for additional places to drop off your car.

By Train

In spring of 2010, Cap Metro began light rail service between downtown and the bedroom communities in the north. This was a relatively inexpensive way to introduce light rail to the city by using existing train track. The downside is that the train doesn't follow the preferred routes. Worse, the train only runs during commuting times, making it an impractical choice for visitors.

By Bus

Austin's public transportation system, **Capital Metropolitan Transportation Authority** (www.capmetro.org), operates more than 50 bus lines and features low fares. New fares were established in 2010. A single fare on a Cap Metro bus is $1. A day pass costs $2; an express day pass to/from various Park & Ride lots costs $4. You'll need exact change or fare tickets to board the bus. Day passes are a good option because they're more flexible. It costs the same as a round-trip and allows you to ride as many buses as you want for that day. Tell the bus driver you're buying a day pass before you insert your money in the machine.

   Call ✆ **800/474-1201** or 512/474-1200 from local phones for point-to-point routing information. You can also pick up a schedule booklet at any H-E-B or Fiesta grocery store; at stores and hotels throughout the downtown area; or at the Cap Metro Transit Store, 323 Congress Ave., first floor.

   There used to be a free shuttle bus circulating through downtown known as a "'Dillo," but, alas, no more.

FAST FACTS: SAN ANTONIO

Area Code   The telephone area code in San Antonio is **210.**

Automobile Organizations   Auto clubs will supply maps, suggested routes, guidebooks, accident and bail-bond insurance, and emergency road service. The **American Automobile Association (AAA)** is the major auto club in the United States. If you belong to an auto club in your home country, inquire about AAA reciprocity before you leave. You may be able to join AAA even if you're not a member of a reciprocal club; to inquire, call AAA (✆ **800/222-4357**). AAA is actually an organization of regional auto clubs, so look under "AAA Automobile Club" in the White Pages of the telephone directory. AAA has a nationwide emergency road service telephone number (© **800/AAA-HELP** [222-4357]).

Business Hours   Banks are usually open Monday to Friday 9am to 5pm, Saturday 9am to 1pm. Drive-up windows are open 7am to 6pm Monday to Friday, and 9am to noon on Saturday. Office hours are generally weekdays from 9am to 5pm. Shops tend to be open from 9 or 10am until 5:30 or 6pm Monday to Saturday, with shorter hours on Sunday. Most malls are open Monday to Saturday from 10am to 9pm, Sunday from noon to 6pm.

Car Rentals   See "By Car," under the earlier "Getting Around: San Antonio" section.

Climate   See "When to Go," in chapter 2.

Crime   San Antonio is a safe city. Violent crime occurs less frequently than in the average American city. In fact, of the 32 largest cities in the U.S., San Antonio ranked the eighth safest according to a firm that sorts through crime data for the United States. Still, you will want to avoid tempting fate by keeping off the low-traffic areas of the River Walk at night, and staying close to groups of other people. You also need to protect yourself from the opportunistic thief, especially purse-snatchers in the downtown area. Take care not to leave your possessions unattended on a chair at a restaurant or bar, and when walking around the downtown area at night, keep them tucked under your arm.

The other most common areas for visitors, the Monte Vista and King William neighborhoods, are usually safe to stroll around in late at night, but the same cannot be said for the area south of King William, which closes down early and doesn't have many pedestrians at night.

Customs   San Antonio has an international airport with Customs inspectors, but most visitors will have already passed through Customs at another port of entry. The only regularly scheduled international flights into San Antonio originate in Mexico and a couple of Central American countries.

Dentist   To find a dentist near you in town, contact the San Antonio District Dental Society, 3355 Cherry Ridge, Ste. 214 (© **210/732-1264**).

Disabled Travelers   Disabled travelers will find the same facilities that are present in other major American cities thanks to the federal laws governing accessibility, specifically the Americans with Disabilities Act, which continues to be revised with new standards for design added in 2010, and the Air Carrier Access Act. Local cab companies and mass transit agencies offer service to travelers with disabilities.

Almost all public establishments (including hotels, restaurants, museums, and so on, but not including certain National Historic Landmarks), and at least some modes of public transportation provide accessible entrances and other facilities for those with disabilities.

San Antonio has worked hard to make itself friendlier to wheelchair users. The River Walk Trolley Station, for example, was built with a large elevator to transport people down to the water. Contact the **San Antonio Department of Public Works** (© **210/207-7245,** voice and TTY) for additional information, or log on to the website of San Antonio's Disability Access Office (www.sanantonio.gov/ada). At this website you can get maps that show River Walk access points and downtown parking places.

If you're not bringing your own car, several taxis have been equipped with lifts and ramps; **Yellow Cab** (© **210/222-2222**) has the most. For more information about their accessible taxis go its website, www.yellowcabsa.com, and click on the wheelchair accessible icon. The downtown trolleys and 100% of the public buses are now accessible. For **VIA Trans Disabled Accessibility Information,** phone © **210/362-2240,** or click on the "Accessible Service" section of **www.viainfo.net.**

If you have any doubt about the accessibility of certain destinations, check out the Weekender section of the *San Antonio Express-News,* which includes accessibility symbols for restaurants, theaters, galleries, and other venues.

Doctors   For a referral, contact the Bexar County Medical Society at 6243 I-10 W., Ste. 600 (📞 **210/301-4391;** www.bcms.org), Monday through Friday from 8am to 5pm.

Driving Rules   See "Getting Around: San Antonio," earlier in this chapter.

Drugstores   Most branches of CVS (formerly Eckerd) and Walgreens, the major chain pharmacies in San Antonio, are open late Monday through Saturday. There's a CVS downtown at 211 Losoya/River Walk (📞 **210/224-9293**). Call 📞 **800/925-4733** to find the Walgreens nearest you; punch in the area code and the first three digits of the number you're phoning from and you'll be directed to the closest branch.

Electricity   Like Canada, the United States uses 110–120 volts AC (60 cycles), compared to 220–240 volts AC (50 cycles) in most of Europe, Australia, and New Zealand. If your small appliances use 220–240 volts, you'll need a 110-volt transformer and a plug adapter with two flat parallel pins to operate them here. Downward converters that change 220–240 volts to 110–120 volts are difficult to find in the United States, so bring one with you.

Embassies & Consulates   All embassies are located in the nation's capital, Washington, D.C. Some consulates are located in major U.S. cities, and most nations have a mission to the United Nations in New York City. If your country isn't listed below, call for directory information in Washington, D.C. (📞 **202/555-1212**), or log on to **www.embassy.org/embassies**.

The embassy of **Australia** is at 1601 Massachusetts Ave. NW, Washington, DC 20036 (📞 **202/797-3000;** www.austemb.org). There are consulates in New York, Honolulu, Houston, Los Angeles, and San Francisco.

The embassy of **Canada** is at 501 Pennsylvania Ave. NW, Washington, DC 20001 (📞 **202/682-1740;** www.canadianembassy.org). Other Canadian consulates are in Buffalo (New York), Detroit, Los Angeles, New York, and Seattle.

The embassy of **Ireland** is at 2234 Massachusetts Ave. NW, Washington, DC 20008 (📞 **202/462-3939;** www.irelandemb.org). Irish consulates are in Boston, Chicago, New York, San Francisco, and other cities. See their website for a complete listing.

The embassy of **New Zealand** is at 37 Observatory Circle NW, Washington, DC 20008 (📞 **202/328-4800;** www.nzemb.org). New Zealand consulates are in Los Angeles, Salt Lake City, San Francisco, and Seattle.

The embassy of the **United Kingdom** is at 3100 Massachusetts Ave. NW, Washington, DC 20008 (📞 **202/588-7800;** www.britainusa.com). Other British consulates are in Atlanta, Boston, Chicago, Cleveland, Houston, Los Angeles, New York, San Francisco, and Seattle.

Emergencies   For police, fire, or medical emergencies, dial 📞 **911.**

Family Travel   The San Antonio edition of the free monthly *Our Kids* magazine includes a calendar that lists daily local activities oriented toward children. You can read it online at **http://sanantonio.parenthood.com**; order it in advance from 8400 Blanco, Ste. 201, San Antonio, TX 78216 (📞 **210/349-6667**); or find it in San Antonio at H-E-B supermarkets, Wal-Mart stores, Hollywood Video, and most major bookstores.

To locate accommodations, restaurants, and attractions that are particularly kid-friendly, refer to the "Kids" icon throughout this guide.

Gasoline (Petrol)   Petrol is known as gasoline (or simply "gas") in the United States, and petrol stations are known as both gas stations and service stations. Gasoline costs almost half as much here as it does in Europe (about $2.80 per gallon at press time), and taxes are already included in the printed price. One U.S. gallon equals 3.8 liters or .85 imperial gallons.

Holidays Banks, government offices, post offices, and many stores, restaurants, and museums are closed on the following legal national holidays: January 1 (New Year's Day), the third Monday in January (Martin Luther King, Jr., Day), the third Monday in February (Presidents' Day), the last Monday in May (Memorial Day), July 4th (Independence Day), the first Monday in September (Labor Day), the second Monday in October (Columbus Day), November 11 (Veterans Day/Armistice Day), the fourth Thursday in November (Thanksgiving Day), and December 25 (Christmas). Also, the Tuesday following the first Monday in November is Election Day and is a federal government holiday in presidential-election years (held every 4 years, and next in 2012).

Hospitals The main downtown hospital is **Baptist Medical Center,** 111 Dallas St. (© **210/297-7000**). **Christus Santa Rosa Health Care Corp.,** 519 W. Houston St. (© **210/704-2067**), is also downtown. Contact the **San Antonio Medical Foundation** (© **210/614-3724**) for information about other medical facilities in the city.

Hot Lines Contact the National Youth Crisis Hot Line at © **800/448-4663;** Rape Crisis Hot Line at © **210/349-7273;** Child Abuse Hot Line at © **800/252-5400;** Mental Illness Crisis Hot Line at © **210/227-4357;** Bexar County Adult Abuse Hot Line at © **800/252-5400;** and Poison Control Center at © **800/764-7661.**

Information See "Visitor Information," below.

Internet & Wi-Fi If you have your own computer, access points for the Internet abound in San Antonio. Most likely you'll be able to use the hotel or bed-and-breakfast where you'll be staying. If you are seeking to avoid a charge for the service, you can go to a **public library.** The downtown branch (© **210/207-2500**) is at 600 Soledad St., at the corner of Navarro, in the northern section of downtown. It offers laptops for use in the library, which make use of the free Wi-Fi. Most coffee shops in downtown San Antonio offer free Internet access.

Legal Aid If you are "pulled over" for a minor infraction (such as speeding), never attempt to pay the fine directly to a police officer; this could be construed as attempted bribery, a much more serious crime. Pay fines by mail, or directly into the hands of the clerk of the court. If accused of a more serious offense, say and do nothing before consulting a lawyer. Here the burden is on the state to prove a person's guilt beyond a reasonable doubt, and everyone has the right to remain silent, whether he or she is suspected of a crime or actually arrested. Once arrested, a person can make one telephone call to a party of his or her choice. Call your embassy or consulate.

LGBT Travelers San Antonio has a large, but not exceedingly visible, gay and lesbian population. To get info about activities, check out the website www.outinsanantonio.com. It has columns, blogs, and a calendar of events, all of which give one a pretty good idea of what the local gay community is involved in and how to connect with it. Another source of information is **QSanAntonio** (www.qsanantonio.com). It's mainly a news site with a large business listings section. If you stay at the **Painted Lady Inn,** a lesbian-owned bed-and-breakfast at 620 Broadway (© **210/220-1092**), you can also find out all you want to know about the local scene. In addition, the **Esperanza Peace & Justice Center,** 922 San Pedro (© **210/228-0201;** www.esperanza center.org), often screens films or has lectures on topics of interest to gay, lesbian, and transgender travelers.

Libraries San Antonio's main library is located downtown at 600 Soledad Plaza (© **210/207-2500**). See "More Attractions," in chapter 6 for details.

Liquor Laws The legal drinking age in Texas is 21. Under-age drinkers can legally imbibe as long as they stay within sight of their legal-age parents or spouses, but they need to be prepared to show proof of the relationship. Open containers are prohibited in public and in vehicles. Liquor laws are strictly enforced; if you're concerned, check www.tabc.state.tx.us for the entire Texas alcoholic beverage code. Bars close at 2am.

Lost Property Be sure to tell all of your credit card companies the minute you discover your wallet has been lost or stolen and file a report at the nearest police precinct. Your credit card company or insurer may require a police report number or record of the loss. Most credit card companies have an emergency toll-free number to call if your card is lost or stolen; they may be able to wire you a cash advance immediately or deliver an emergency credit card in a day or two. Visa's U.S. emergency number is ✆ **800/847-2911** or 410/581-9994. American Express cardholders and traveler's check holders should call ✆ **800/221-7282.** MasterCard holders should call ✆ **800/307-7309** or 636/722-7111. For other credit cards, call the toll-free number directory at ✆ **800/555-1212.**

If you need emergency cash over the weekend when all banks and American Express offices are closed, you can have money wired to you via **Western Union** (✆ **800/325-6000;** www.westernunion.com).

Mail At press time, domestic postage rates were 29¢ for a postcard and 44¢ for a letter. For international mail, a first-class letter of up to 1 ounce costs 98¢ (75¢ to Canada and 79¢ Mexico); a first-class postcard costs the same. For more information, go to **www.usps.com** and click on "Calculate Postage."

If you aren't sure what your address will be in the United States, mail can be sent to you in your name, c/o General Delivery, at the main post office of the city or region where you expect to be. (Call ✆ **800/275-8777** for information on the nearest post office.) The addressee must pick up mail in person and must produce proof of identity (driver's license, passport, and so on). Most post offices will hold your mail for up to 1 month, and are open Monday to Friday from 8am to 6pm, and Saturday from 9am to 3pm.

Generally found at intersections, mailboxes are blue with a red-and-white stripe and carry the inscription U.S. MAIL. If your mail is addressed to a U.S. destination, don't forget to add the five-digit postal code (or zip code), after the two-letter abbreviation of the state to which the mail is addressed. This is essential for prompt delivery.

Mobile Phones To have the use of a cellphone while visiting San Antonio, the easiest thing to do is buy a cheap prepaid cellphone. These are for sale in various outlets, but the cheapest and easiest way to get a phone is probably through the local H-E-B grocery stores. This chain has entered into business with a local company called **Pocket Wireless** (www.pocket.com), which has other independent outlets. Go to the website for locations, or go to www.heb.com to use a store locator.

Money & Costs The most common bills are the $1 (a "buck"), $5, $10, and $20 denominations. There are also $2 bills (seldom encountered), $50 bills, and $100 bills (the last two are usually not welcome as payment for small purchases).

Coins come in seven denominations: 1¢ (1 cent, or a penny); 5¢ (5 cents, or a nickel); 10¢ (10 cents, or a dime); 25¢ (25 cents, or a quarter); 50¢ (50 cents, or a half-dollar); the gold-colored Sacagawea coin, worth $1; and the rare silver dollar.

Newspapers & Magazines The *San Antonio Express-News* is the only mainstream source of news in town.

Passports **For Residents of Australia:** You can pick up an application from your local post office or any branch of Passports Australia, but you must schedule an interview at the passport office to present your application materials. Call the **Australian Passport Information Service** at ✆ **131-232,** or visit the government website at www.passports.gov.au.

For Residents of Canada: Passport applications are available at travel agencies throughout Canada or from the central **Passport Office,** Department of Foreign Affairs and International Trade, Ottawa, ON K1A 0G3 (✆ **800/567-6868;** www.ppt.gc.ca).

WHAT THINGS COST IN SAN ANTONIO	US$
Taxi from the airport to the city center	30.00
Streetcar ride between any two downtown points	1.10
Local telephone call	0.50
Long-neck beer	4.00
Double at Westin Riverwalk Inn (very expensive)	360.00
Double at Drury Inn & Suites Riverwalk (moderate)	150.00
Double at Best Western Sunset Suites (inexpensive)	135.00
Lunch for one at Rosario's (moderate)	12.00
Lunch for one at Twin Sisters (inexpensive)	7.00
Dinner for one, without wine, at Las Canarias (very expensive)	60.00
Dinner for one, without beer, at La Fonda on Main (moderate)	16.00
Dinner for one, without beer, at Schilo's (inexpensive)	10.00
Adult admission to the Witte Museum	7.00
Ticket to the San Antonio Symphony	20.00–80.00
Ticket to a Spurs game	50.00–100.00

Note: Canadian children who travel must have their own passport. However, if you hold a valid Canadian passport issued before December 11, 2001, that bears the name of your child, the passport remains valid for you and your child until it expires.

For Residents of Ireland: You can apply for a 10-year passport at the **Passport Office,** Setanta Centre, Molesworth Street, Dublin 2 (ⓒ **01/671-1633;** www.irlgov.ie/iveagh). Those under age 18 and over age 65 must apply for a 3-year passport. You can also apply at 1A South Mall, Cork (ⓒ **021/272-525**) or at most main post offices.

For Residents of New Zealand: You can pick up a passport application at any New Zealand Passports Office or download it from their website. Contact the **Passports Office** at ⓒ **0800/225-050** in New Zealand or 04/474-8100, or log on to www.passports.govt.nz.

For Residents of the United Kingdom: To pick up an application for a standard 10-year passport (5-year passport for children under age 16), visit your nearest passport office, major post office, or travel agency, or contact the **United Kingdom Passport Service** at ⓒ **0870/521-0410** or search its website at www.ukpa.gov.uk.

Police Call ⓒ **911** in an emergency. For non-emergency calls, dial ⓒ **311.**

Post Office The city's most convenient post office for visitors is at 615 Houston St., at North Alamo Street, in the San Antonio Federal Building.

Safety The crime rate in San Antonio has gone down in recent years, and there's a strong police presence downtown (in fact, both the transit authority and the police department have bicycle patrols); as a result, muggings, pickpocketings, and purse-snatchings in the area are rare. Still, use common sense as you would anywhere else: Walk only in well-lit, well-populated streets. Also, it's generally not a good idea to stroll south of Durango Avenue after dark.

Senior Travel For museums and attractions, you can expect most senior discounts to run between 5% and 15%.

Smoking Smoking is prohibited in all public buildings and common public areas (that includes hotel lobbies, museums, enclosed malls, and so on). A new ordinance, to become effective in August 2011, will limit smoking indoors and in public spaces, allowing it only in some bars, on designated restaurant patios, and on the River Walk and Alamo Plaza.

Taxes The sales tax here is 8.25%, and the city surcharge on hotel rooms increases to a whopping 16.75%.

Taxis Call **Yellow-Checker Cab** (© **210/222-2222**).

Time Zone San Antonio and Austin (and all of the rest of Texas except for the El Paso area) are in the Central Time zone. The continental United States is divided into **four time zones:** Eastern Standard Time (EST), Central Standard Time (CST), Mountain Standard Time (MST), and Pacific Standard Time (PST). Alaska and Hawaii have their own zones. For example, noon in New York City (EST) is 11am in Chicago (CST), 10am in Denver (MST), 9am in Los Angeles (PST), 8am in Anchorage (AST), and 7am in Honolulu (HST).

Daylight saving time is in effect from 2am on the second Sunday in March through 2am on the first Sunday in November, except in Arizona, Hawaii, the U.S. Virgin Islands, and Puerto Rico. Daylight saving time moves the clock 1 hour ahead of standard time.

Tipping Tips are a very important part of certain workers' income, and gratuities are the standard way of showing appreciation for services provided. (Tipping is certainly not compulsory if the service is poor!) In hotels, tip **bellhops** at least $1 per bag ($2–$3 per bag if you have a lot of luggage) and tip the **chamber staff** $1 to $2 per day (more if you've left a disaster area for him or her to clean up). Tip the **doorman** or **concierge** only if he or she has provided you with some specific service (for example, calling a cab for you or obtaining difficult-to-get theater tickets). Tip the **valet-parking attendant** $1 every time you get your car.

In restaurants, bars, and nightclubs, tip **service staff** 15% to 20% of the check, tip **bartenders** 10% to 15%, tip **checkroom attendants** $1 per garment, and tip **valet-parking attendants** $1 per vehicle.

As for other service personnel, tip **cabdrivers** 15% of the fare; tip **skycaps** at airports at least $1 per bag ($2–$3 per bag if you have a lot of luggage); and tip **hairstylists** and **barbers** 15% to 20%.

Toilets You won't find public toilets or "restrooms" on the streets in most U.S. cities, but they can be found in hotel lobbies, bars, restaurants, museums, department stores, railway and bus stations, and service stations. Large hotels and fast-food restaurants are probably the best bet for good, clean facilities. If possible, avoid the toilets at parks and beaches, which tend to be dirty; some may be unsafe. Restaurants and bars in resorts or heavily visited areas may reserve their restrooms for patrons. Some establishments display a notice indicating this. You can ignore this sign or, better yet, avoid arguments by paying for a cup of coffee or a soft drink, which will qualify you as a patron.

Visas For information about U.S. visas, go to **http://travel.state.gov** and click on "Visas." Or go to one of the following websites:

Australian citizens can obtain up-to-date visa information from the **U.S. Embassy Canberra,** Moonah Place, Yarralumla, ACT 2600 (© **02/6214-5600**) or by checking the U.S. Diplomatic Mission's website at **http://usembassy-australia.state.gov/consular**.

British subjects can obtain up-to-date visa information by calling the **U.S. Embassy Visa Information Line** (© **0891/200-290**) or by visiting the "Visas to the U.S." section of the American Embassy London's website at **www.usembassy.org.uk**.

Irish citizens can obtain up-to-date visa information through the **Embassy of the USA Dublin,** 42 Elgin Rd., Dublin 4, Ireland (© **353/1-668-8777**), or by checking the "Consular Services" section of the website at **http://dublin.usembassy.gov**.

Citizens of **New Zealand** can obtain up-to-date visa information by contacting the **U.S. Embassy New Zealand,** 29 Fitzherbert Terrace, Thorndon, Wellington (© **644/472-2068**), or get the information directly from the "For New Zealanders" section of the website at **http://wellington.usembassy.gov**.

Visitor Information San Antonio Visitor Information Center (© 210/207-6748) is at 317 Alamo Plaza, across from the Alamo. For transit information, call © **210/362-2020;** call © **210/226-3232** for time and temperature.

FAST FACTS: AUSTIN

Area Code The telephone area code in Austin is **512.**

Business Hours Banks are usually open Monday to Friday 9am to 5pm, Saturday 9am to 1pm. Drive-up windows are open 7am to 6pm Monday to Friday, and 9am to noon on Saturday. Office hours are generally weekdays from 9am to 5pm. Shops tend to be open from 9 or 10am until 5:30 or 6pm Monday to Saturday, with shorter hours on Sunday. Most malls are open Monday to Saturday from 10am to 9pm, Sunday from noon to 6pm.

Car Rentals See "By Car," under the earlier "Getting Around: Austin" section.

Climate See "When to Go," in chapter 2.

Crime Morgan Quitno, a firm that sifts through national crime data, ranks Austin as the fourth safest of America's 32 largest cities, and for the visitor, it's probably even safer. There have been few reports of violence directed toward tourists in Austin in the last 5 years. Still, you need to exercise caution. In the most popular parts of downtown, the number of people on the streets and the prominent police presence keep it very safe. Most assaults have occurred on the fringes of these areas when people were walking back to their cars. This is usually not a problem for visitors who are staying in the downtown hotels.

Areas outside of downtown are largely safe, except perhaps for East Austin, where it's not a good idea to walk around alone at night. The area around the University of Texas campus does attract a criminal element, but it focuses mostly on theft and burglary of vehicles.

Customs Austin has an international airport, but the presence of Customs agents there is solely for charter and private flights. There are no regularly scheduled international flights, so almost all international visitors will have entered the United States through some other point of entry.

Disabled Travelers There's an active **Americans with Disabilities Act (ADA)** office in Austin. Its website, www.ci.austin.tx.us/ada, has lots of useful links. You can also call © **512/974-3256** or 974-1897 if you have questions about whether any of the hotels or other facilities you're curious about are in compliance with the Act. All the large downtown hotels maintain accessible rooms and parking, and most of the large hotels in the outlying areas do as well.

All of Austin's public buses are equipped with lifts to make them accessible. Also, as mandated by ADA, it maintains paratransit service. To contact CapMetro about accessible services, call $\mathbb{C}$ **512/478-9647** or go to the website: www.capmetro.org/riding/accessibleservices.asp. For taxi service for wheelchair users, call Yellow Cab's service line ($\mathbb{C}$ **512/452-9999**), and make it clear that you need a wheelchair-accessible cab, or order a cab through the Web page: www.yellowcabaustin.xohost.com, and click on wheelchair access.

Doctors The Medical Exchange ($\mathbb{C}$ **512/458-1121**) and **Seton Hospital** ($\mathbb{C}$ **512/324-4450**) both have physician referral services.

Driving Rules See "Getting Around: Austin," earlier in this chapter.

Drugstores You'll find many Walgreens, CVS, and Randalls drugstores around the city; most H-E-B grocery stores also have pharmacies. Several Walgreens are open 24 hours. Have your zip code ready and call $\mathbb{C}$ **800/925-4733** to find the Walgreens branch nearest you.

Embassies & Consulates All embassies are located in the nation's capital, Washington, D.C. Some consulates are located in major U.S. cities, and most nations have a mission to the United Nations in New York City. If your country isn't listed below, call for directory information in Washington, D.C. ($\mathbb{C}$ **202/555-1212**), or log on to **www.embassy.org/embassies**.

The embassy of **Australia** is at 1601 Massachusetts Ave. NW, Washington, DC 20036 ($\mathbb{C}$ **202/797-3000;** www.austemb.org). There are consulates in New York, Honolulu, Houston, Los Angeles, and San Francisco.

The embassy of **Canada** is at 501 Pennsylvania Ave. NW, Washington, DC 20001 ($\mathbb{C}$ **202/682-1740;** www.canadianembassy.org). Other Canadian consulates are in Buffalo (New York), Detroit, Los Angeles, New York, and Seattle.

The embassy of **Ireland** is at 2234 Massachusetts Ave. NW, Washington, DC 20008 ($\mathbb{C}$ **202/462-3939;** www.irelandemb.org). Irish consulates are in Boston, Chicago, New York, San Francisco, and other cities. See their website for a complete listing.

The embassy of **New Zealand** is at 37 Observatory Circle NW, Washington, DC 20008 ($\mathbb{C}$ **202/328-4800;** www.nzemb.org). New Zealand consulates are in Los Angeles, Salt Lake City, San Francisco, and Seattle.

The embassy of the **United Kingdom** is at 3100 Massachusetts Ave. NW, Washington, DC 20008 ($\mathbb{C}$ **202/588-7800;** www.britainusa.com). Other British consulates are in Atlanta, Boston, Chicago, Cleveland, Houston, Los Angeles, New York, San Francisco, and Seattle.

Emergencies Call $\mathbb{C}$ **911** if you need the police, the fire department, or an ambulance.

Family Travel For families visiting Austin, one of the best resources is a free publication called Austin Family. You can find it at local restaurants and grocery stores. It comes out once a month, and though much of it is not directed at visitors, there is a good monthly calendar of events. You can also see the online version at www.austinfamily.com.

Gasoline Petrol is known as gasoline (or simply "gas") in the United States, and petrol stations are known as both gas stations and service stations. Gasoline costs almost half as much here as it does in Europe (about $2.80 per gallon at press time), and taxes are already included in the printed price. One U.S. gallon equals 3.8 liters or .85 imperial gallons.

Hospitals **Brackenridge,** 601 E. 15th St. ($\mathbb{C}$ **512/324-7000**); St. David's, 919 E. 32nd St., at I-35 ($\mathbb{C}$ **512/397-4240**); and **Seton Medical Center,** 1201 W. 38th St. ($\mathbb{C}$ **512/324-1000**), have good and convenient emergency-care facilities.

Hot Lines Crisis Hot Line (☎ **512/472-4357**); Poison Center (☎ **800/764-7661**); Domestic Violence Crisis Hot Line (☎ **512/928-9070**); Sexual Assault Crisis Hot Line (☎ **512/440-7273**).

Internet & Wi-Fi If you have your own computer, many access points for the Internet exist in Austin. Most likely you'll be able to use the hotel or bed-and-breakfast where you'll be staying. If you are seeking to avoid a charge for the service, you can go to a public library. Almost every coffee shop in Austin offers free Internet access. See chapter 12 for several locations. If you're not carrying a computer, your best option is the public library.

Legal Aid If you are "pulled over" for a minor infraction (such as speeding), never attempt to pay the fine directly to a police officer; this could be construed as attempted bribery, a much more serious crime. Pay fines by mail, or directly into the hands of the clerk of the court. If accused of a more serious offense, say and do nothing before consulting a lawyer. Here the burden is on the state to prove a person's guilt beyond a reasonable doubt, and everyone has the right to remain silent, whether he or she is suspected of a crime or actually arrested. Once arrested, a person can make one telephone call to a party of his or her choice. Call your embassy or consulate.

LGTB Travelers A university town and the most left-leaning enclave in Texas, Austin is generally gay-, lesbian-, bisexual-, and transgender-friendly. To find out about clubs in addition to those listed in chapter 15 (Oilcan Harry's and Rainbow Cattle Co.), log on to www.austin.gaycities.com. **Book Woman,** 5501 North Lamar #A-105 (☎ **512/472-2785;** www.ebookwoman.com) is the best place to find gay and lesbian books and magazines, as well as the Austin Gay and Lesbian Yellow Pages. A good online resource for gay travelers is www.outinaustin.com. It includes feature stories about local events and has a lot of business listings.

Established in 1987, the annual **Austin Gay and Lesbian International Film Festival,** held in September, debuts works by gay, lesbian, bisexual, and transgender filmmakers from throughout the world. Log on to www.agliff.org for additional information, or call ☎ **512/302-9889.**

Libraries Downtown's Faulk Central Library, 800 Guadalupe St. (☎ **512/974-7400**), and adjoining Austin History Center, 810 Guadalupe St. (☎ **512/974-7480**), are excellent information resources. To find the closest local branch, log on to **www.ci.austin. tx.us/library**.

Liquor Laws The legal drinking age in Texas is 21. Under-age drinkers can legally imbibe as long as they stay within sight of their legal-age parents or spouses, but they need to be prepared to show proof of the relationship. Open containers are prohibited in public and in vehicles. Liquor laws are strictly enforced; if you're concerned, check www.tabc.state.tx.us for the entire Texas alcoholic beverage code. Bars close at 2am.

Lost Property Be sure to tell all of your credit card companies the minute you discover your wallet has been lost or stolen and file a report at the nearest police precinct. Your credit card company or insurer may require a police report number or record of the loss. Most credit card companies have an emergency toll-free number to call if your card is lost or stolen; they may be able to wire you a cash advance immediately or deliver an emergency credit card in a day or two. Visa's U.S. emergency number is ☎ **800/847-2911** or 410/581-9994. American Express cardholders and traveler's check holders should call ☎ **800/221-7282.** MasterCard holders should call ☎ **800/307-7309** or 636/722-7111. For other credit cards, call the toll-free number directory at ☎ **800/555-1212.**

WHAT THINGS COST IN AUSTIN

	US$
Taxi from the airport to downtown	20.00
Double at the Four Seasons (very expensive)	380.00
Double at the Holiday Inn Austin Town Lake (moderate)	159.00
Double at the Austin Motel (inexpensive)	90.00
Lunch for one at the Roaring Fork (expensive)	17.00
Lunch for one at Shady Grove (inexpensive)	8.00
Dinner for one, without drinks, at Jeffrey's (very expensive)	72.00
Dinner for one, without drinks, at Vivo (moderate)	18.00
Dinner for one, without drinks, at the Iron Works (inexpensive)	9.00
Soft drink at restaurant	1.50
Cup of espresso	3.50
Admission to Texas State History Museum	5.00
Roll of ASA 100 Kodacolor film, 36 exposures	7.50
Movie ticket	9.00
Austin Symphony ticket	30.00

If you need emergency cash over the weekend when all banks and American Express offices are closed, you can have money wired to you via **Western Union** (© **800/325-6000;** www.westernunion.com).

Mail   At press time, domestic postage rates were 29¢ for a postcard and 44¢ for a letter. For international mail, a first-class letter of up to 1 ounce costs 98¢ (75¢ to Canada and 79¢ Mexico); a first-class postcard costs the same. For more information, go to **www.usps.com** and click on "Calculate Postage."

If you aren't sure what your address will be in the United States, mail can be sent to you in your name, c/o General Delivery, at the main post office of the city or region where you expect to be. (Call © **800/275-8777** for information on the nearest post office.) The addressee must pick up mail in person and must produce proof of identity (driver's license, passport, and so on). Most post offices will hold your mail for up to 1 month, and are open Monday to Friday from 8am to 6pm, and Saturday from 9am to 3pm.

Generally found at intersections, mailboxes are blue with a red-and-white stripe and carry the inscription u.s. mail. If your mail is addressed to a U.S. destination, don't forget to add the five-digit postal code (or zip code), after the two-letter abbreviation of the state to which the mail is addressed. This is essential for prompt delivery.

Money & Costs   The most common bills are the $1 (a "buck"), $5, $10, and $20 denominations. There are also $2 bills (seldom encountered), $50 bills, and $100 bills (the last two are usually not welcome as payment for small purchases).

Coins come in seven denominations: 1¢ (1 cent, or a penny); 5¢ (5 cents, or a nickel); 10¢ (10 cents, or a dime); 25¢ (25 cents, or a quarter); 50¢ (50 cents, or a half-dollar); the gold-colored Sacagawea coin, worth $1; and the rare silver dollar.

Newspapers & Magazines   The daily *Austin American-Statesman* (www.austin360.com) is the only large-circulation, mainstream newspaper in town. The *Austin Chronicle* (www.auschron.com), a free alternative weekly, focuses on the arts, entertainment, and politics. Monday through Friday, the University of Texas publishes the surprisingly sophisticated *Daily Texan* (www.dailytexanonline.com) newspaper, covering everything from on-campus news to international events.

Passports **For Residents of Australia:** You can pick up an application from your local post office or any branch of Passports Australia, but you must schedule an interview at the passport office to present your application materials. Call the **Australian Passport Information Service** at 📞 **131-232,** or visit the government website at www.passports.gov.au.

For Residents of Canada: Passport applications are available at travel agencies throughout Canada or from the central **Passport Office,** Department of Foreign Affairs and International Trade, Ottawa, ON K1A 0G3 (📞 **800/567-6868;** www.ppt.gc.ca). ***Note:*** Canadian children who travel must have their own passport. However, if you hold a valid Canadian passport issued before December 11, 2001, that bears the name of your child, the passport remains valid for you and your child until it expires.

For Residents of Ireland: You can apply for a 10-year passport at the **Passport Office,** Setanta Centre, Molesworth Street, Dublin 2 (📞 **01/671-1633;** www.irlgov.ie/iveagh). Those under age 18 and over age 65 must apply for a 3-year passport. You can also apply at 1A South Mall, Cork (📞 **021/272-525**) or at most main post offices.

For Residents of New Zealand: You can pick up a passport application at any New Zealand Passports Office or download it from their website. Contact the **Passports Office** at 📞 **0800/225-050** in New Zealand or 04/474-8100, or log on to www.passports.govt.nz.

For Residents of the United Kingdom: To pick up an application for a standard 10-year passport (5-year passport for children under age 16), visit your nearest passport office, major post office, or travel agency, or contact the **United Kingdom Passport Service** at 📞 **0870/521-0410** or search its website at www.ukpa.gov.uk.

Police Call 📞 911 in an emergency. The non-emergency number for the Austin Police Department is 📞 311.

Post Office The city's main post office is located at 8225 Cross Park Dr. (📞 **512/342-1252**); more convenient for visitors are the Capitol Station, 111 E. 17th St., in the LBJ Building; and the Downtown Station, 510 Guadalupe St. For information on other locations, phone 📞 **800/275-8777.**

Safety Austin has been ranked one of the five safest cities in the United States, but that doesn't mean you can throw common sense to the wind. It's never a good idea to walk down dark streets alone at night, and major tourist areas always attract pickpockets, so keep your purse or wallet in a safe place. Although Sixth Street itself tends to be busy, use caution on the side streets in the area.

Senior Travel Senior travel isn't has highly promoted in Austin as it is in many other destinations. Austin doesn't receive many "winter Texans," who come down from the northern U.S. fleeing the cold. Still, you'll find standard senior discounts at most attractions, such as the museums and recreational facilities, but most often, it amounts to only $1 or $2 discount.

Austin's Old Bakery and Emporium, 1006 Congress Ave. (📞 **512/477-5961;** www.ci.austin.tx.us/parks/bakery1.htm), not only sells crafts and baked goods made by seniors, but also serves as a volunteer center for people over 50. It's a good place to find out about any senior activities in town.

Smoking Smoking is prohibited in all public buildings and common public areas (that includes hotel lobbies, museums, enclosed malls, and so on). It's also prohibited in enclosed bars or enclosed bar areas of restaurants. But it is permitted in open-air bar areas.

Taxes The tax on hotel rooms is 15%. Sales tax, added to restaurant bills as well as to other purchases, is 8.25%.

Taxis Call **American Yellow Checker Cab** (© 512/452-9999).

Time San Antonio and Austin (and all of the rest of Texas except for the El Paso area) are in the Central Time zone. The continental United States is divided into **four time zones:** Eastern Standard Time (EST), Central Standard Time (CST), Mountain Standard Time (MST), and Pacific Standard Time (PST). Alaska and Hawaii have their own zones. For example, noon in New York City (EST) is 11am in Chicago (CST), 10am in Denver (MST), 9am in Los Angeles (PST), 8am in Anchorage (AST), and 7am in Honolulu (HST).

Daylight saving time is in effect from 2am on the second Sunday in March through 2am on the first Sunday in November, except in Arizona, Hawaii, the U.S. Virgin Islands, and Puerto Rico. Daylight saving time moves the clock 1 hour ahead of standard time.

Tipping Tips are a very important part of certain workers' income, and gratuities are the standard way of showing appreciation for services provided. (Tipping is certainly not compulsory if the service is poor!) In hotels, tip **bellhops** at least $1 per bag ($2–$3 per bag if you have a lot of luggage) and tip the **chamber staff** $1 to $2 per day (more if you've left a disaster area for him or her to clean up). Tip the **doorman** or **concierge** only if he or she has provided you with some specific service (for example, calling a cab for you or obtaining difficult-to-get theater tickets). Tip the **valet-parking attendant** $1 every time you get your car.

In restaurants, bars, and nightclubs, tip **service staff** 15% to 20% of the check, tip **bartenders** 10% to 15%, tip **checkroom attendants** $1 per garment, and tip **valet-parking attendants** $1 per vehicle.

As for other service personnel, tip **cabdrivers** 15% of the fare; tip **skycaps** at airports at least $1 per bag ($2–$3 per bag if you have a lot of luggage); and tip **hairstylists** and **barbers** 15% to 20%.

Transit Information Call Capital Metro Transit (© 800/474-1201, or 512/474-1200 from local pay phones; TTY 385-5872).

Useful Telephone Numbers Get the time and temperature by dialing © 512/476-7744.

Visitor Information The Austin Visitor Center (© 866/GO-AUSTIN [462-8784]) is at 209 E. Sixth St.

AIRLINE WEBSITES

Major U.S. Airlines

(*flies internationally as well)

AirTran Airways
www.airtran.com

American Airlines*
www.aa.com

Continental Airlines*
www.continental.com

Delta Air Lines*
www.delta.com

JetBlue Airways
www.jetblue.com

Midwest Airlines
www.midwestairlines.com

Northwest Airlines
www.nwa.com

United Airlines*
www.united.com

US Airways*
www.usairways.com

Major International Airlines

Aeroméxico
www.aeromexico.com

Air Canada
www.aircanada.com

Air India
www.airindia.com

Air New Zealand
www.airnewzealand.com

British Airways
www.british-airways.com

Emirates Airlines
www.emirates.com

Qantas Airways
www.qantas.com

South African Airways
www.flysaa.com

Virgin Atlantic Airways
www.virgin-atlantic.com

WestJet
www.westjet.com

Index

See also Accommodations and Restaurant indexes, below.

General Index

A

AAA (American Automobile Association), 305
  San Antonio, 313–314
Accommodations. *See also* Accommodations Index
  Austin and environs, 164–180
    best, 3–4, 165–166
    budget choices, 165
    Central Austin, 173–175
    for extended stays, 173
    Northwest, 175–178
    San Marcos, 273
    South Austin, 171–173
    Westlake/Lake Travis, 178–180
    Wimberley, 275
  the Hill Country
    Bandera, 285–286
    Boerne area, 282–283
    Fredericksburg, 294–295
    guest ranches, 285, 289
    Kerrville, 289
    Luckenbach, 296
    northern lakes, 302
  San Antonio and environs, 46–65
    best, 3–4, 48–49
    Corpus Christi, 152–153
    downtown, 46–56
    family-friendly, 58
    Fort Sam Houston area, 60
    King William Historic District, 47, 56–59
    Monte Vista Historic District, 59–60
    New Braunfels and Gruene, 143–144
    North Central (near the airport), 64–65
    Port Aransas, 152–153
    West/Northwest, 61
Actors Theater of San Antonio, 129
Addresses, finding
  Austin, 312
  San Antonio, 310
Adelante Boutique (San Antonio), 123
Advantage car rentals
  Austin, 312
  San Antonio, 308
Adventures with a Texas Naturalist (Bedichek), 232

African Americans
  Austin sights and attractions, 223
  Juneteenth
    Austin, 31
    San Antonio, 29
Airman's Cave (Austin), 233
Airport Flyer (Austin), 306
Airports
  Austin, 306
    accommodations, 180
  San Antonio, 304
    accommodations near, 64–65
Air travel, San Antonio, 304–305
A Journey Through Texas (Olmsted), 18, 23
Alameda Theater (San Antonio), 106, 107
Alamo Antique Mall (San Antonio), 118
Alamo car rentals
  Austin, 312
  San Antonio, 308
Alamodome (San Antonio), 131
Alamo Drafthouse (Austin), 263
Alamo Drafthouse Westlakes (San Antonio), 136
Alamo Fiesta (San Antonio), 123
Alamo Heights area (San Antonio), 38, 102
  restaurants, 82–84
  sightseeing, 94–95, 102
The Alamo (movie, 1959), 92
The Alamo (movie, 2004), 92
The Alamo (San Antonio), 15–17, 42–43
  movies about, 92
  sightseeing, 87–88, 108
Alamosa Wine Cellars (near Lampasas), 281
Alamo Movies (Thompson), 92
Alamo Quarry Market (San Antonio), 124
Alamo Sightseeing Tours (San Antonio), 113
Alamo-The Price of Freedom (movie), 92
Allen's Boots (Austin), 249
All Hat & No Cattle (Dingus), 23
American Automobile Association (AAA), San Antonio, 313–314
American Indians, 14, 20
Americans with Disabilities Act (ADA), 320
American Yellow Checker Cab (Austin), 306, 325
Amphibious tour, Austin, 229
Amtrak, 307
Amy's ice cream (Austin), 190
Annexation of Texas, 21
Antique Marketplace (Austin), 240–241
Antiques
  Austin, 240–241
  Comfort, 290
  San Antonio and environs, 118
  Gonzales, 145

Antone's (Austin), 258
Aquarena Center (San Marcos), 271
Aquarium, San Antonio
  Zoological Gardens and, 102
The Arboretum (Austin), 246
Area code
  Austin, 320
  San Antonio, 313
Arkey Blue's Silver Dollar Bar (Bandera), 286
Armadillo Christmas Bazaar (Austin), 32
Arneson River Theatre (San Antonio), 129
The Arno Nowotny Building (Austin), 224
Art and artists
  Austin Fine Arts Festival, 31
  San Antonio, 28, 29
  First Fridays, 98
Art Building (University of Texas at Austin), 226
Art galleries and museums, Austin and environs
  commercial galleries, 241
  San Marcos, 272
Arthouse at Jones Center (Austin), 211
Art Museum of South Texas (Corpus Christi), 151
Art museums and galleries
  Austin and environs
    Arthouse at Jones Center, 211
    Austin Museum of Art-Downtown, 211–212
    Austin Museum of Art-Laguna Gloria, 215
    Blanton Museum of Art, 210
    Elisabet Ney Museum, 216
    MEXIC-ARTE Museum, 213
    Moore/Andersson Compound, 216
    outdoor art, 220
    Umlauf Sculpture Garden & Museum, 215
  Kerrville, 289
  San Antonio and environs, 97
    Art Museum of South Texas (Corpus Christi), 151
    ArtPace, 97
    Blue Star Contemporary Art Center, 101
    commercial Galleries, 118
    Marion Koogler McNay Art Museum, 43, 94–95
    New Braunfels Museum of Art & Music, 142
    San Antonio Museum of Art, 43–44, 94
ArtPace (San Antonio), 97, 118
Arturo's Sports Bar & Grill (San Antonio), 134

Asian Cultures Museum (Corpus Christi), 151
AT&T Center (San Antonio), 131
AT&T Championship (San Antonio), 116
Atomic City (Austin), 248
Attractions and sightseeing
　Austin and environs, 204–232
　　Central Austin, 210, 216–218
　　downtown, 204–208, 211–215
　　East Side, 218–219
　　for kids, 221–222
　　organized tours, 229–232
　　outdoors, 219–221
　　parks and gardens, 220–221
　　South Austin, 209, 215
　　top attractions, 204–211
　　West Austin, 215–216
　Kerrville and environs, 291–292, 294
　San Antonio and environs, 87–113
　　Alamo Heights area, 94
　　Corpus Christi, 147–148
　　downtown, 87–94, 97–101
　　Hispanic heritage, 106–108
　　for kids, 104
　　King William Historic District, 88, 92–94
　　for military history buffs, 106
　　New Braunfels, 140–141
　　organized tours, 112–113
　　parks and gardens, 103–104
　　South Side, 95–96
　　strolling downtown, 108–113
　　top attractions, 87–97
Austin, Lake, 219
Austin, Stephen F., 19
Austin American-Statesman, 251, 323
Austin American-Statesman Bat Hotline, 208
Austin Antique Mall, 241
Austin-Bergstrom International Airport, 306
Austin Chamber Music Center, 254
Austin Children's Museum, 221–222
Austin Chronicle, 251, 323
Austin Chronicle Hot Sauce Festival, 31
Austin City Limits, 252
Austin City Limits Live at the Moody Theater, 252
Austin City Limits Music Festival, 32, 252
Austin Convention and Visitors Bureau (ACVB)
　guided walking tours, 232
　self-guided tours, 231–232
Austin Country Flea Market, 247
Austin Cycling Association, 232

Austin Dam, 22
Austin Duck Adventures, 229
Austin Farmers' Market, 244
Austin Film Festival, 32, 263
Austin Fine Arts Festival, 31
Austin Gay and Lesbian International Film Festival, 322
Austin Ghost Tours, 230–231
Austin High School Tennis Center, 234
Austin History Center, 322
Austin History Center/Austin Public Library, 211
Austin Ice Bats, 235
Austin Lyric Opera, 254
Austin Museum of Art-Downtown, 211–212
Austin Museum of Art-Laguna Gloria, 215
Austin Nature and Science Center, 222
Austin Nature Center, 220
Austin Overtures, 230
Austin Ridge Riders, 232
Austin Rock Gym, 233
Austin Shakespeare Festival, 256
Austin Symphony Orchestra (Austin), 31, 254
Austin 360 (website), 8–9
Austin Zoo, 222
Austix Box Office, 251
Australia
　embassy and consulates, 315
　passports, 317
　visas, 319
Avis car rentals
　Austin, 312
　San Antonio, 308
A Wall of History (San Antonio), 88
Aztec Theater (San Antonio), 107, 130

B
Bajo sextos, 134
Ballet Austin, 255
Bambinos Boutique (San Antonio), 122
Bandera, 45, 283–287
　rodeos, 116
Bandera Beach Club Kayak & Tube Rental, 284
Bandera County Convention and Visitors Bureau, 284
Bandera County Park at Medina Lake, 284
Bandera Park, 285
Bandera Saloon, 286
Baptist Medical Center (San Antonio), 316
Barbecue (BBQ)
　Austin and environs, 26, 265
　　Austin restaurants, 182, 188, 191, 199, 201, 202
　　small-town restaurants, 265–269
　San Antonio restaurant, 73

Barbed wire, 12
Bars
　Austin, 257, 261–263
　San Antonio, 135–136
Barton Creek Square (Austin), 246
Barton Springs Pool (Austin), 12, 159, 209, 221, 233
Baseball
　Austin, 234
　Corpus Christi, 148, 152
　San Antonio, 115
Basketball
　Austin, 234
　San Antonio, 115–116
Bass Concert Hall (Austin), 226
Bastrop State Park, 274
Bat Conservation International (Austin), 208
Bates Recital Hall (Austin), 226
Bats
　Austin, 159, 208
　near Fredericksburg, 290
Battle Hall (University of Texas at Austin), 228
Battle Oaks (University of Texas at Austin), 228
Beaches
　Matagorda Bay, 150
　Mustang Island State Park, 152
Becker Vineyards, 281
Bed-and-breakfasts (B&Bs), San Antonio, 49
Bedichek, Roy, 232
Beethoven Halle and Garten (San Antonio), 130
Bell Mountain Vineyards (near Fredericksburg), 281
Bergheim Campground, 115
Bermuda Triangle (San Antonio), 133
Beverly F. Sheffield Zilker Hillside Theater (Austin), 256
Biking
　Austin, 232
　Bastrop State Park, 274
　San Antonio, 113–114
Bird, Sarah, 24, 25
Bird-watching
　Austin, 232
　coastal plains, 148, 151
Blanton Museum of Art (Austin), 158, 210
Bluebonnets, 299
Blues on the Green (Austin), 256
Blue Star Bike Shop (San Antonio), 114
Blue Star Brewing Company Restaurant & Bar (San Antonio), 135
Blue Star Contemporary Arts Center (San Antonio), 101, 118
Blue Theater (Austin), 255
Blunn Creek (Austin), 220

Boating. *See* Canoeing;
  Kayaking; Rafting; Sailing
Boat tours and cruises
  Austin, 229–230
  San Antonio, 113
    Vanishing Texas River Cruise
      (Lake Buchanan), 301
Bob Bullock Texas State History
  Museum (Austin), 158
The Bob Bullock Texas State
  History Museum (Austin), 210
Boerne, 44, 276–283
Boerne Village Band, 277
Bonham Exchange (San
  Antonio), 133–135
BookPeople (Austin), 241–242
Books, recommended
  Austin, 24–25
  San Antonio, 23–24
Bookstores, Austin, 241–242
BookWoman (Austin), 242, 322
Boot Hill (San Antonio), 126
Boots, Austin, 249
Botanical gardens
  San Antonio, 103–104
  Zilker Botanical Garden
    (Austin), 221
Botanicas, San Antonio, 124
Boyhood Home of Lyndon B.
  Johnson (Johnson City), 297
Brackenride (San Antonio), 114
Brackenridge (Austin), 321
Brackenridge Eagle (San
  Antonio), 103
Brackenridge Park (San
  Antonio), 103, 114
Brammer, Billy Lee, 25
Brandon, Jay, 24
Braunig Lake (San Antonio), 114
Brauntex Performing Arts
  Theatre (New Braunfels), 144
Breed & Co. Hardware (Austin),
  245
Breezenet.com, 309
Bremond Block (Austin), 212
Brighter Days Horse Refuge
  (near Bandera), 284
Brindles Awesome Ice Cream
  (San Antonio), 85
Broken Spoke (Austin), 257–258
Buchanan, Lake, 301
Buckhorn Saloon & Museum (San
  Antonio), 98
Buda, 270
Budget car rentals
  Austin, 312
  San Antonio, 308
Burnet, 300
Burnet Chamber of Commerce,
  300
Business hours
  Austin, 320
  San Antonio, 314
Bussey's Flea Market (San
  Antonio), 126
Bus tours, San Antonio, 113

Bus travel
  Austin, 307, 313
  San Antonio, 305, 310
By George (Austin), 243

C
Cabela's (Buda), 270
Cabs
  Austin, 325
  San Antonio, 305, 311, 319
Cactus Cafe (Austin), 259
Cadillac Bar & Restaurant (San
  Antonio), 135
Caffé Medici (Austin), 203
Calaveras Lake (near San
  Antonio), 114
Calendar of events
  Austin, 30–32
  San Antonio, 28–30
Camp Verde, 287
Canada
  embassy and consulates, 315
  passports, 317–318
Canoeing
  Austin, 232–233
  Inks Lake State Park, 300–301
  San Antonio, 115
  San Marcos, 271
Canyon Lake (near San Antonio),
  114
Canyon of the Eagles Lodge &
  Nature Park (Burnet), 302
Canyon Springs (San Antonio), 114
Cap City Comedy (Austin), 260
Capital Cruises (Austin),
  229–230
  canoe rentals, 233
Capital Metropolitan
  Transportation Authority
  (Austin), 306, 313
Capitol Visitors Center (Austin),
  212, 245
Capra & Cavelli (Austin), 243
Carnival Brasileiro (Austin), 30
Carousel Lounge (Austin), 259
Car rentals
  Austin, 306, 311–312
  San Antonio, 308
Car travel
  Austin, 307, 311
  Corpus Christi, 147
  San Antonio, 305–306, 308
Carver Community Cultural
  Center (San Antonio), 130
Casa Navarro State Historic Site
  (San Antonio), 98, 112
Casa Salazar (San Antonio), 118
Casbeers at the Church (San
  Antonio), 132
Cascade Caverns (near Boerne),
  277
Castroville, 45, 282
Castroville Chamber of
  Commerce, 282
Caswell Tennis Center (Austin),
  234
Cave Without a Name (Boerne),
  277

Cedar Creek (San Antonio), 114
Cedar Door (Austin), 262
Cellphones, 317
Central Austin, 155
  accommodations, 173–175
  coffeehouses, 203
  restaurants, 195–198
  sights and attractions,
    210–211, 216–218
Central Market
  Austin, 244–245
  San Antonio, 123
Central Texas Oil Patch Museum
  (Luling), 147
Centro Alameda cultural zone
  (San Antonio), 106
Charles Anthony Jewelers (San
  Antonio), 123
Cheapo Discs (Austin), 247
Chicken-fried steak, 26–27
Children, families with
  Austin, 321
    hotels, 179
    restaurants, 197
    sights and attractions,
      221–222
  San Antonio, 315
    accommodations, 48, 58
    entertainment, 129
    restaurants, 81
    shopping, 122, 126
    sights and attractions,
      96–97, 103, 104
Children's Museum, San Antonio,
  105
Chili con carne, 26
  San Antonio, 75
Chocolat (Fredericksburg), 294
Christus Santa Rosa Health Care
  Corp. (San Antonio), 316
Chuy's Christmas Parade
  (Austin), 32
Cibolo Nature Center (Boerne),
  277
Cinco de Mayo Music Festival
  (Austin), 31
Cinemas
  Austin
    Austin Film Festival, 32
    cinemas, 263–264
  San Antonio
    movies about the Alamo,
      92
    cinemas, 107, 136
    San Antonio CineFestival,
      28
    Wings, 104
Cisneros, Sandra, 24
City of Austin Nature Preserves,
  220
Civil War, 16–17, 21
Clarksville (Austin), 155
Clarksville Pottery & Galleries
  (Austin), 245
Classical music
  Austin, 254
  San Antonio, 128–129

Clothing (fashions)
Austin, 243
vintage, 248–249
San Antonio, 122–123
Western wear, 126
Club and music scene
Austin, 256–261
San Antonio, 131
Coffeehouses, Austin, 203
Collision Damage Waiver (CDW), 308
Comal County Courthouse (New Braunfels), 140
Comedy
Austin, 260–261
San Antonio, 133
Comfort Antique Mall, 290
Comfort Cellars Winery, 280
Comfort Chamber of Commerce, 290–291
Comfort Common, 290
Commander's Point Yacht Basin (Austin), 233
Concepción (San Antonio), 95
Congress Avenue (Austin), 154–155
Conjunto, San Antonio, 134
Tejano Conjunto Festival, 28–29
Conservation Plaza (New Braunfels), 141
Contemporary Art Month (San Antonio), 29
Continental Club (Austin), 162, 259
Convention and Visitors Bureau (San Antonio), 28
Cool Arrows (San Antonio), 134
Copano Bays, 147
Corpus Christi, 147–153
Corpus Christi Hooks, 148, 152
Country music
Austin, 257–258
San Antonio, 131–132
Courthouse (Gonzales), 145
Courthouse Square (San Marcos), 271
Covert Park at Mount Bonnell, 219
Cowboy Store (Bandera), 284
Crafts/folk art
Austin, 243–244
San Antonio, 118
Crime
Austin, 320
San Antonio, 314
Crossroads of San Antonio Mall, 124
Cuisine and food, 26–27
Austin
restaurants by cuisine, 182–183
Saveur Texas Hill Country Wine and Food Festival, 31
San Antonio, 29
restaurants by cuisine, 68–69
tours, 34

Currency and currency exchange, 317
Current, 128
Customs regulations
Austin, 320
San Antonio, 314

D

Daily Texan, 324
Dance performances, Austin, 255
Darrell K. Royal/Texas Memorial Stadium (Austin), 226
Daylight saving time, 319, 325
Dazed and Confused (film), 214
D Berman Gallery (Austin), 241
Deep Eddy Pool (Austin), 233
Dell Computer Corporation, 23
Dentists, San Antonio, 314
Department stores
Austin, 242
San Antonio, 122
Devil's Waterhole, 300–301
Diez y Seis
Austin, 31
San Antonio, 29
Dillard's (Austin), 242
Dingus, Anne, 23
Dining. *See also* **Restaurant Index**
Austin and environs, 181
barbecue. *See* Barbecue (BBQ)
best, 4–5, 182
Central Austin, 195–198
coffeehouses, 203
by cuisine, 182–183
downtown, 184–188
East Side, 198–199
late-night, 261
musical brunches, 202
Northwest, 200–201
San Marcos, 273
South Austin, 188–193
West Austin, 193–194
Westlake/Lake Travis, 201–202
the Hill Country, 295–296
Bandera, 286
Boerne area, 283
Kerrville, 289–290
Lyndon B. Johnson Country, 298
northern lakes, 302–303
San Antonio and environs, 66–86
Alamo Heights area, 82–84
best, 4–5, 67–68
categories of restaurants, 67
Corpus Christi, 153
by cuisine, 68–69
King William and Southtown, 76–78
New Braunfels and Gruene, 144

Disabled travelers
Austin, 320–321
San Antonio, 314–315
Discount shopping, Austin, 242
Discovery Architectural Antiques (Gonzales), 145
Dive World (Austin), 233
Doctors
Austin, 321
San Antonio, 315
Dog & Duck Pub (Austin), 261
Dogologie (Fredericksburg), 294
Dollar car rentals
Austin, 312
San Antonio, 308
Dolphin cruises, Corpus Christi, 150
The Domain (Austin), 246
Doolin, Elmer, 104
Downtown
Austin, 154
accommodations, 166–171
restaurants, 184–188
shopping, 236
sights and attractions, 204–208, 211–215
San Antonio, 35
accommodations, 46–56
restaurants, 69–75
shopping, 117
sights and attractions, 87–94, 97–101
strolling, 108–113
walking, 311
The Drag (Austin), shopping, 240
The Drag (University of Texas at Austin), 229
Dress Shop (Austin), 243
Driftwood, 268
The Driskill (Austin), 212, 263
Driving rules, 312
Drugstores
Austin, 321
San Antonio, 315
Dry Comal Creek Vineyards (between New Braunfels and Bulverde), 280
Dyeing O' the River Green Parade (San Antonio), 28

E

East Side (Austin), 155
restaurants, 198–199
sights and attractions, 218–219
Eating and drinking, 26–27. *See also* **Restaurant Index**
Austin
restaurants by cuisine, 182–183
Saveur Texas Hill Country Wine and Food Festival, 31
San Antonio, 29
restaurants by cuisine, 68–69
tours, 34
Eco-wise (Austin), 242–243

1877 General Store and Post Office (Camp Verde), 287
Eisenhauer Road Flea Market (San Antonio), 126
Electricity, 315
Electric Ladyland/Lucy in Disguise (Austin), 248
Elephant Room (Austin), 258
Elisabet Ney Museum (Austin), 216
Embassies and consulates, 315
Emeralds (Austin), 243
Emergencies
  Austin, 321
  San Antonio, 315
Emma Long Metropolitan Park (Austin), 220–221, 234
Emo's (Austin), 258
Empire Theater (San Antonio), 107, 130
Enchanted Rock State Natural Area (near Fredericksburg), 115, 292, 294
Ensemble Concerts (Austin), 255
Enterprise car rentals, San Antonio, 308
Entertainment and nightlife
  Austin, 251–264
    bars, 257, 261–263
    club and music scene, 256–261
    comedy, 260–261
    free entertainment, 255–256
    performing arts, 252–256
    theater, 254–255
  the Hill Country, 296
    Bandera, 286
    Boerne, 277
  San Antonio and environs, 128–136
    bars, 135–136
    classical music, 128–129
    club and music scene, 131–135
    major arts venues, 129–131
    movies. See Movies
    New Braunfels and Gruene, 144–145
    theater, 129
Esperanza Center (San Antonio), 136
Essential oils, Austin, 243
Esther's Follies (Austin), 261

F

Fado (Austin), 261–262
Fairview Park (Austin), 155
Fall Jazz Festival (Austin), 31
Families with children
  Austin, 321
    hotels, 179
    restaurants, 197
    sights and attractions, 221–222

San Antonio, 315
  accommodations, 48, 58
  entertainment, 129
  restaurants, 81
  shopping, 122, 126
  sights and attractions, 96–97, 103, 104
Farmer's markets, Austin, 244
Fashion (clothing)
  Austin, 243
    vintage, 248–249
  San Antonio, 122–123
    Western wear, 126
Faulk Central Library (Austin), 322
Faust Hotel (New Braunfels), 140
Festivals and special events
  Austin, 30–32
  San Antonio, 28–30
Fiesta San Antonio, 28
Fiestas Navideñas (San Antonio), 29
Films
  Austin
    Austin Film Festival, 32
    cinemas, 263–264
  San Antonio
    about the Alamo, 92
    cinemas, 107, 136
    San Antonio Cine-Festival, 28
    Wings, 104
Finesilver Gallery (San Antonio), 118
First Class Bed & Breakfast Reservation Service (Fredericksburg), 295
First Fridays (San Antonio), 98
First Thursdays (Austin), 240
Fishing
  Austin, 233
  Bandera, 284
  San Antonio and environs, 114
  Port Aransas, 150
Flamingo Cantina (Austin), 258
Flat Creek Vineyards (Lake Travis), 281
Flatonia, 146
Flawn Academic Center (University of Texas at Austin), 228
Flea markets, San Antonio, 126
Flea Mart (San Antonio), 126
Flightpath (Austin), 203
Flipnotics (Austin), 203
Floores Country Store (San Antonio), 131–132
Folk art and crafts
  Austin, 243
  San Antonio, 118
Folk music, Austin, 257–258
Food and cuisine, 26–27
  Austin
    restaurants by cuisine, 182–183
    Saveur Texas Hill Country Wine and Food Festival, 31

San Antonio, 29
  restaurants by cuisine, 68–69
  tours, 34
Food carts and trucks, Austin, 181, 195
Food stores and markets
  Austin, 244
  San Antonio, 123
Football, Austin, 234
Ford Holiday River Parade and Lighting Ceremony (San Antonio), 29
Formula 1 racing, Austin, 234–235
Fort Croghan Grounds and Museum (Burnet), 300
Fort Sam Houston area (San Antonio)
  accommodations, 60
  sightseeing, 102
Fort Sam Houston Museum (San Antonio), 102
Fort Sam Houston (San Antonio), 17, 38, 102
Fredericksburg, 290, 291–297
Fredericksburg Herb Farm, 294
Fredericksburg Traditional Bed & Breakfast Inns, 295
Fredericksburg Winery, 280–281
Free or almost free activities
  Austin, 5–6
  San Antonio, 5
French Legation Museum (Austin), 218
Friedrich Wilderness Park (Milsa), 115

G

Gabriel's (San Antonio), 127
Galería Ortiz Contemporary (San Antonio), 118
Galleries and art museums
  Austin and environs
    Arthouse at Jones Center, 211
    Austin Museum of Art-Downtown, 211–212
    Austin Museum of Art-Laguna Gloria, 215
    Blanton Museum of Art, 210
    Elisabet Ney Museum, 216
    MEXIC-ARTE Museum, 213
    Moore/Andersson Compound, 216
    outdoor art, 220
    Umlauf Sculpture Garden & Museum, 215
  Kerrville, 289
  San Antonio and environs, 97
    Art Museum of South Texas (Corpus Christi), 151
    ArtPace, 97

Galleries and art museums (cont.)
Blue Star Contemporary Art Center, 101
commercial Galleries, 118
Marion Koogler McNay Art Museum, 43, 94–95
New Braunfels Museum of Art & Music, 142
San Antonio Museum of Art, 43–44, 94
Gallery Shoal Creek (Austin), 241
Garcia Art Glass, Inc. (San Antonio), 118
Gardens and parks
Austin, 220–221
San Antonio, 103–104
Garrison Hall (Austin), 227
Gasoline, 315–316
Austin, 321
Gateway Shopping Centers (Austin), 246
Gavin Metalsmith (San Antonio), 123
Gay and lesbian travelers
Austin, 322
bars, 262
San Antonio, 133, 316
Gebhardt, William, 26, 75
General Store and Post Office (Camp Verde), 287
George Washington Carver Museum and Cultural Center (Austin), 223
Ghost Tours, Austin, 230–231
Giddings, 269
Gifts and souvenirs
Austin, 245
San Antonio, 123
Ginger Man (Austin), 257
Gish's Old West Museum (Fredericksburg), 292
Git Bit (Austin), 233
Gliding Revolution (Austin), 230
Goat Cave (Austin), 220
Goat Cave Preserve (Austin), 233
Goldsmith Hall (University of Texas at Austin), 229
Golf
Austin, 233, 235
Boerne, 277
San Antonio, 114, 116
Gonzales, 145–146
Governor's Mansion (Austin), 212–213
Grape Creek Vineyard (near Fredericksburg), 281
Gray Line Tours, 34
The Great Texas Coastal Birding Trail, 148
Greyhound
Austin, 307
San Antonio, 305
Grocery stores, Austin, 187
Gruene, 141–143, 163
Gruene Hall, 144

Gruene River Company, 142
Guadalupe Cultural Arts Center (San Antonio), 107, 130
Guadalupe River, 115, 143, 288
tubing, 142
Guadalupe River State Park (near Boerne), 115, 282
Guenther House (San Antonio), 92
Guest ranches, Bandera, 285
The Guide to Austin-Area Birding Sites, 232
Guide to Puro San Antonio, 108
Guinness World Records Museum (San Antonio), 105

H

Haby's Alsatian Bakery (Castroville), 282
Half-Price Books (Austin), 241
Halloween (Austin), 32
Hamilton Pool Preserve (near Austin), 234
The Handbook of Texas Online (website), 8
Harrell, Jacob, 19
Harrigan, Stephen, 24
Harry Ransom Humanities Research Center (Austin), 216, 229
Hat Box (Austin), 249
Haunted History Walking Tour (Austin), 231
Heart of Texas-Wildlife Trails, 276
HemisFair Park (San Antonio), 103, 110
Henne Hardware (New Braunfels), 140
Henry, O., 23–25
O. Henry Museum (Austin), 213–214
Henry G. Madison cabin (Austin), 223
Heritage Boots (Austin), 249
Heritage Village (New Braunfels), 141
Hertz car rentals
Austin, 312
San Antonio, 308
Hey Cupcake! (Austin), 190, 195
Highland Lakes (near Austin), 219
Highland Mall (Austin), 246
High-tech companies, 22–23
Hike-and-Bike Trail (Austin), 159
Hiking
Austin, 233
Bandera, 285
Guadalupe River State Park (near Boerne), 282
San Antonio, 115
The Hill Country, 276–303
Bandera, 283–287
Boerne, 276–283
Fredericksburg, 291–297
Kerrville, 287–291

Lyndon B. Johnson Country, 297–299
the northern lakes, 299–303
wineries, 280–281
Hill Country Arts Foundation (Ingram), 288
Hill Country Flyer Steam Train Excursion (Burnet), 300
Hill Country Museum (Kerrville), 288
Hill Country State Natural Area, 284
Hill Country Weavers (Austin), 248
Hippie Hollow (Austin), 234
Hispanic people and heritage
Austin, 213
San Antonio
history, 14–15
music, 28–29, 31, 134
shopping, 118, 122, 124
sights and attractions, 106
Spanish Governor's Palace, 100
special events and festivals, 28, 29
Historic Texas Tours (near San Antonio), 34
History
Austin, 19–22
today, 12–14
San Antonio, 10–19
today, 11–12
Hockey, Austin, 235
The Hogg Auditorium (University of Texas at Austin), 228
Holidays, 28, 316
The Holy Cacao (Austin), 195
Homestead (Fredericksburg), 294
Hondo's on Main (Fredericksburg), 297
Horseback riding, Bandera, 284
Horse racing, San Antonio, 116
Hospitals
Austin, 321
San Antonio, 316
Hotels. See also Accommodations Index
Austin and environs, 164–180
best, 3–4, 165–166
budget choices, 165
Central Austin, 173–175
for extended stays, 173
Northwest, 175–178
San Marcos, 273
South Austin, 171–173
Westlake/Lake Travis, 178–180
Wimberley, 275
the Hill Country
Bandera, 285–286
Boerne area, 282–283
Fredericksburg, 294–295
guest ranches, 285, 289
Kerrville, 289
Luckenbach, 296
northern lakes, 302

San Antonio and environs, 46–65
    best, 3–4, 48–49
    Corpus Christi, 152–153
    downtown, 46–56
    family-friendly, 58
    Fort Sam Houston area, 60
    King William Historic District, 47, 56–59
    Monte Vista Historic District, 59–60
    New Braunfels and Gruene, 143–144
    North Central (near the airport), 64–65
    Port Aransas, 152–153
    West/Northwest, 61
Hot lines
    Austin, 322
    San Antonio, 316
Houston, Sam, 15–16, 19, 20
Howl at the Moon Saloon (San Antonio), 135
Huebner Oaks Shopping Center (San Antonio), 125
Hugman, Robert H. H., 18–19
Hunt, 288
Hyde Park (Austin), 155, 216–217
Hyde Park Theatre (Austin), 254–255
Hy O Silver (Bandera), 284

I

Ice cream
    Austin, 190
    San Antonio, 85
Ice hockey, San Antonio, 116
IMAX Theater Rivercenter (San Antonio), 42, 105
Ingenhuett Store (Comfort), 291
Ingram, 288
Inks Lake State Park, 300–301
Institute of Texan Cultures (San Antonio), 99
Instituto Cultural Mexicano/Casa Mexicana (San Antonio), 107
Insurance, car-rental, 308–309
Interior (Austin), 243
International Accordion Festival (San Antonio), 29
International visitors, car-rental insurance, 309
Internet access
    Austin, 322
    San Antonio, 316
Ireland
    embassy and consulates, 315
    passports, 318
    visas, 320
Itineraries, suggested
    Austin, 158–163
    San Antonio, 39–45
        the best in 1 day, 39–43
        the best in 3 days, 44–45
Ivins, Molly, 24

J

Jacob Schmidt Building (New Braunfels), 140
Jailhouse (Gonzales), 145
Japanese Tea Garden (San Antonio), 103
Jazz and blues
    Austin, 31, 258
    San Antonio, 29, 133
Jazz'SAlive (San Antonio), 29
Jerry Jeff Walker's Birthday Weekend (Austin), 30
Jewelry
    Austin, 245–246
    San Antonio, 123
Jiménez, Flaco, 134
Johnson, Lady Bird, 298
Johnson City, 297
Johnson Settlement (Johnson City), 297
Jones, Anson, 20–21
Joplin, Janis, 26
Josephine Theatre (San Antonio), 129
Joske's (San Antonio), 110
Jovita's (Austin), 258
Jump-Start Performance Company (San Antonio), 129
Juneteenth
    Austin, 31
    San Antonio, 29

K

Katherine Anne Porter House (Kyle), 273
Kathleen Sommers (San Antonio), 123
Kayaking
    Bandera, 284
    Corpus Christi, 150
    San Marcos, 271
Keepers (Austin), 243
Kerr Arts & Cultural Center (Kerrville), 289
Kerrville, 286–291
Kerrville Folk Festival, 288
Kerrville-Schreiner Park, 289
Kerrville Visitors Center, 288
KGSR (Austin), 256
Kids
    Austin, 321
        hotels, 179
        restaurants, 197
        sights and attractions, 221–222
    San Antonio, 315
        accommodations, 48, 58
        entertainment, 129
        restaurants, 81
        shopping, 122, 126
        sights and attractions, 96–97, 103, 104
Kids Junction Resale Shop (San Antonio), 126

King William Historic District (San Antonio), 35, 38, 44
    accommodations, 47, 56–59
    restaurants, 76–78
    sightseeing, 88, 92–94
Kitchenware, San Antonio, 124
Kite Festival (Austin), 30
Kline Saddlery (Bandera), 284
Kristkrindle Markt (San Antonio), 130

L

Lady Bird Johnson Wildflower Center (Austin), 158, 209
Lady Bird Lake, 219
    cruises, 229–230
La Gran Posada (San Antonio), 29
Laguna Madre (North Padre Island), 150–151
Lake Austin, 219
Lake Buchanan, 301
Lakeline Mall (Austin), 246–247
Lake Travis (Austin)
    accommodations, 178–180
    restaurants, 201–202
    sailing, 233
Lakeway (Austin), 155
Lamar, Mirabeau Buonaparte, 19, 20
The Landing (San Antonio), 133
Landmark Inn State Historic Site (Castroville), 282
The Land of Was (San Antonio), 118
Laurie Auditorium (San Antonio), 130
Lavender farms, 287
La Villita National Historic District (San Antonio), 43, 92–93, 110
La Villita (San Antonio), 118
Lay of the land, 32–33
La Zona Rosa (Austin), 259
LBJ Library and Museum (Austin), 158, 210–211, 224, 226
LBJ Museum of San Marcos, 272
LBJ National Historical Park (Johnson City), 297–298
Legal aid, 316
    Austin, 322
Le Midi Bar (San Antonio), 135
Leon Springs Dancehall (San Antonio), 132
Lexington, 269
Lexington, USS (Corpus Christi), 147, 148
LGBT travelers
    Austin, 322
        bars, 262
    San Antonio, 133, 316
Libraries
    Austin, 322
    San Antonio, 316
Lincoln Heights (San Antonio), 38

GENERAL INDEX

Lindheimer Home (New Braunfels), 141
Liquor laws, 316–317, 322
Little City (Austin), 203
Littlefield Home (University of Texas at Austin), 228
Littlefield Memorial Fountain (Austin), 227
Little's Boots (San Antonio), 126
Live from the Plaza (Austin), 255
Llano, 268–269
Lockhart, 266–268
Lodging. See also Accommodations Index
  Austin and environs, 164–180
    best, 3–4, 165–166
    budget choices, 165
    Central Austin, 173–175
    for extended stays, 173
    Northwest, 175–178
    San Marcos, 273
    South Austin, 171–173
    Westlake/Lake Travis, 178–180
    Wimberley, 275
  the Hill Country
    Bandera, 285–286
    Boerne area, 282–283
    Fredericksburg, 294–295
    guest ranches, 285, 289
    Kerrville, 289
    Luckenbach, 296
    northern lakes, 302
  San Antonio and environs, 46–65
    best, 3–4, 48–49
    Corpus Christi, 152–153
    downtown, 46–56
    family-friendly, 58
    Fort Sam Houston area, 60
    King William Historic District, 47, 56–59
    Monte Vista Historic District, 59–60
    New Braunfels and Gruene, 143–144
    North Central (near the airport), 64–65
    Port Aransas, 152–153
    West/Northwest, 61
Lone Star Riverboat (Austin), 230
Lonestar Rollergirls (Austin), 235
Long Barrack (San Antonio), 88
Long Center for the Performing Arts (Austin), 251, 252, 254
Longhorn Cavern State Park (near Burnet), 300
Longhorn Saloon (Bandera), 286
Los Patios (San Antonio), 125
Loss/Damage Waiver (LDW), 308
Lost Maples State Natural Area, 283, 285
Lost property
  Austin, 322–323
  San Antonio, 317

Louis Tussaud's Waxworks & Ripley's Believe It or Not (San Antonio), 104
Love Creek Orchards Cider Mill and Country Store (Medina), 287
Love Puppies Brownies (Austin), 195
Love's Antique Mall (Bandera), 284
Lucchese Gallery (San Antonio), 126–127
Luckenbach, 296
Luling, 146–147, 268
Lyndon B. Johnson Country, 297–299
Lyndon B. Johnson National Historical Park (Johnson City), 297
Lyndon B. Johnson State Park (near Stonewall), 298

M

McAllister Park (San Antonio), 114
McFarlin Tennis Center (San Antonio), 115
Madison, Henry G., cabin (Austin), 223
Magik Theatre (San Antonio), 129
Mail
  Austin, 323
  San Antonio, 317
Main arteries and streets
  Berlin, 312
  San Antonio, 309
Main Building and Tower (University of Texas at Austin), 227
Main Plaza (Plaza de Las Islas; San Antonio), 111
Main Street B&B Reservation Service (Fredericksburg), 295
Majestic Theatre (San Antonio), 107, 130, 131
Málaga (Austin), 257, 263
Malls and shopping centers
  Austin, 246–247
  San Antonio, 124–125
Maps
  Austin, 312
  San Antonio, 309
Marble Falls, 299–300, 302
Marble Falls/Lake LBJ Visitor Center, 300
Marion Koogler McNay Art Museum (San Antonio), 43, 94–95
Market Day (Wimberley), 274
Markets
  Austin, 247
  San Antonio, 125
Market Square (San Antonio), 39, 93, 112
  indoor markets, 125

Mary Moody Northern Theatre (Austin), 255
Matagorda Bay, 150
Matagorda Island, 150
Mayfield Park (Austin), 220
Medina, 287
Medina Lake (near Bandera), 114
Medina River, 284
Medina River Company (Bandera), 284
Melissa Guerra (San Antonio), 79, 124
Menger Bar (San Antonio), 135
The Menger Hotel (San Antonio), 110
Mexican Americans
  Austin, 213
  San Antonio
    history, 14–15
    music, 28–29, 31, 134
    shopping, 118, 122, 124
    sights and attractions, 106
    Spanish Governor's Palace, 100
    special events and festivals, 28, 29
MEXIC-ARTE Museum (Austin), 213
Michelob ULTRA Riverwalk Mud Festival (San Antonio), 28
Michener, James, 25
Military Plaza (Plaza de Armas; San Antonio), 111
Miss Congeniality (movie), 92
Mission Drive-In (San Antonio), 136
Missions, San Antonio, 95–96
Mission San Antonio, 14–15. See also The Alamo (San Antonio)
Mission Trails (San Antonio), 113
Mobile phones, 317
Monarch Collectibles (San Antonio), 126
Money and costs, 317, 323
Monte Vista Historic District (San Antonio), 38
  accommodations, 47–48, 59–60
  restaurants, 78–82
Moonlight Prowl Tours (Austin), 218
Moonlight Towers (Austin), 214
Moore/Andersson Compound (Austin), 216
Mother Egan's (Austin), 262
Mountain Madness (Austin), 233
Movies
  Austin
    Austin Film Festival, 32
    cinemas, 263–264
  San Antonio
    about the Alamo, 92
    cinemas, 107, 136
    San Antonio CineFestival, 28
    Wings, 104
Mozart's (Austin), 203

Museo Alameda (San Antonio), 99

Museum of Science and History (Corpus Christi), 151

Museum of Texas Handmade Furniture (New Braunfels), 141

Museum of Western Art (Kerrville), 289

Music
classical
Austin, 254
San Antonio, 128–129
country
Austin, 257–258
San Antonio, 131–132
eclectic
Austin, 259–260
San Antonio, 132–133
jazz and blues
Austin, 31, 258
San Antonio, 29, 133
rock
Austin, 258–259
San Antonio, 132
Tejano (San Antonio), 134

Musical brunches, Austin, 202

Music stores, Austin, 247

Mustang Island State Park, 152

MySanAntonio.com, 8

N

Naeglin's Bakery (New Braunfels), 140

NAFTA (North American Free Trade Agreement), 11–12

Nanette Richardson Fine Art (San Antonio), 118

National car rentals
Austin, 312
San Antonio, 308

National Museum of the Pacific War (Fredericksburg), 292

Native Americans, 14, 20

Natural Bridge Caverns (near New Braunfels), 138

Natural Bridge Wildlife Ranch (near New Braunfels), 138

Nature preserves, Austin and environs, 219–220

Neighborhoods
Austin, 154–155
San Antonio, 35, 38–39

Neill-Cochran Museum House (Austin), 217

Neiman Marcus (Austin), 242

Neiman Marcus Last Call (Austin), 242

Nelson, Willie, 23

New Braunfels, 137–144, 163
nearby caverns, 138
sights and attractions, 140–141

New Braunfels Chamber of Commerce, 140

New Braunfels Live (radio show), 142

New Braunfels Museum of Art & Music, 142

New Braunfels Railroad Museum, 140

New Braunfels's Landa Park, 143

Newspapers and magazines
Austin, 323
San Antonio, 317

New World Wine and Food Festival (San Antonio), 29

New Zealand
embassy and consulates, 315
passports, 318
visas, 320

Nightlife and entertainment
Austin, 251–264
bars, 257, 261–263
club and music scene, 256–261
comedy, 260–261
free entertainment, 255–256
performing arts, 252–256
theater, 254–255
the Hill Country, 296
Bandera, 286
Boerne, 277
San Antonio and environs, 128–136
bars, 135–136
classical music, 128–129
club and music scene, 131–135
major arts venues, 129–131
movies. See Movies
New Braunfels and Gruene, 144–145
theater, 129

Nordstrom (Austin), 242

North Central (San Antonio), 38–39
accommodations, 64–65

North Lamar (Austin), shopping, 236, 240

North Star Mall (San Antonio), 125

Northwest
Austin, 155
accommodations, 175–178
restaurants, 200–201
shopping, 240
San Antonio, 38
accommodations, 61–64
restaurants, 84–86

O

Off Center (Austin), 255

Official Texas State Arts and Crafts Fair (Kerrville), 288

O'Gorman, Juan, 103

O. Henry Museum (Austin), 213–214

O. Henry Museum Pun-Off (Austin), 31

Oilcan Harry's (Austin), 262

Oktoberfest (San Antonio), 29

Old Bakery and Emporium (Austin), 214

Old Pecan Street Spring Arts and Crafts Festival (Austin), 31

Old Settlers Music Festival (Austin), 31

Old Tunnel Wildlife Management Area (near Fredericksburg), 290

Olmos Park (San Antonio), 38

Olmsted, Frederick Law, 18, 23

Olympic Outdoor Center (San Marcos), 271

Opera, Austin, 254

Organized tours, San Antonio, 112–113

Our Kids magazine (San Antonio), 315

Outdoor activities
Austin, 232–234
best, 7
Bandera, 284–285
San Antonio and environs, 113–115
Corpus Christi, 150–151

Outdoor gear, Austin, 247–248

P

Pace Picante Sauce, 12

Padre Island National Seashore, 150–151

Papa Jim's (San Antonio), 124

Paramount Theatre (Austin), 255

Paris Hatters (San Antonio), 127

The Parish (Austin), 259–260

Parking
Austin, 313
San Antonio, 310

Parks and gardens
Austin, 220–221
San Antonio, 103–104

Paseo del Río (River Walk, San Antonio), 19, 42, 111
sightseeing, 93–94

Passports, 317–318, 324

Pearl Brewery (San Antonio), 79

Pecan Valley (San Antonio), 114

Pedernales Falls State Park (near Johnson City), 299

Pegasus (San Antonio), 133

Performing Arts Center (University of Texas at Austin), 226

Petrol, 315–316
Austin, 321

Petticoat Junction (San Antonio), 133

Pharr Tennis Center (Austin), 234

Philosophers' Rock (Austin), 220

Phoenix Saloon (Gruene), 144

Phoenix Saloon (New Braunfels), 140

Pillar Bluff Vineyards (Lampasas), 281

Pioneer Museum Complex (Fredericksburg), 292

Pioneer Village (Gonzales), 146

Planning your trip
Austin
getting around, 311–313
getting there, 306–307
holidays, 28
San Antonio, 304
getting around, 307–311
getting there, 304–306
seasons and weather, 27
Plaza de Armas (Military Plaza; San Antonio), 111
Plaza de Las Islas (Main Plaza; San Antonio), 111
Police
Austin, 324
San Antonio, 318
Port Aransas
accommodations, 152–153
fishing, 150
Porter, Katherine Anne, 273
Post offices
Austin, 324
San Antonio, 318
Prime Outlets (San Marcos), 162, 273
Pumpjack Tour (Luling), 147

Q

Qua (Austin), 257
Quadrangle (San Antonio), 102
Quarry (San Antonio), 114

R

Rafting, San Antonio, 115
Rainbow Cattle Co. (Austin), 262
Real estate bubble, Austin, 13
The Red Eyed Fly (Austin), 258–259
Red Eye Regatta (Austin), 30
Red River District (Austin), 155
Red River Street (Austin), 257
Regal Fiesta Stadium 16 (San Antonio), 136
Reid, Jan, 24
Renaissance Market (Austin), 247
Republic of Texas, 15, 16, 19, 21
Republic of Texas Biker Rally (Austin), 31
Responsible travel, 33
Restaurants. *See also* **Restaurant Index**
Austin and environs, 181
barbecue. *See* Barbecue (BBQ)
best, 4–5, 182
Central Austin, 195–198
coffeehouses, 203
by cuisine, 182–183
downtown, 184–188
East Side, 198–199
late-night, 261
musical brunches, 202
Northwest, 200–201
San Marcos, 273
South Austin, 188–193

West Austin, 193–194
Westlake/Lake Travis, 201–202
the Hill Country, 295–296
Bandera, 286
Boerne area, 283
Kerrville, 289–290
Lyndon B. Johnson Country, 298
northern lakes, 302–303
San Antonio and environs, 66–86
Alamo Heights area, 82–84
best, 4–5, 67–68
categories of restaurants, 67
Corpus Christi, 153
by cuisine, 68–69
King William and Southtown, 76–78
New Braunfels and Gruene, 144
Retama Park (San Antonio), 116
Return of the Chili Queens (San Antonio), 29
Richards, Ann, 16
Riordan, Rick, 24
Rio San Antonio Cruises, 113
Ripley's Haunted Adventure (San Antonio), 105
Riverbend Centre (Austin), 254
Rivercenter Comedy Club (San Antonio), 133
Rivercenter Mall (San Antonio), 125
River cruises. *See* Boat tours and cruises
River sports, San Antonio, 115
Riverwalk, Live from the Landing **(San Antonio),** 133
River Walk (Paseo del Río; San Antonio), 19, 42, 111
sightseeing, 93–94
Rock climbing, Austin, 233
Rockin' R River Rides (Gruene), 142
Rock music
Austin, 258–259
San Antonio, 132
Rockport Adventures, 150
Rodeos
Austin, 30
San Antonio, 28, 116
Roller derby, Austin, 235
Rollingwood (Austin), 155
Room Service (Austin), 248–249
Round Rock Express (Austin), 234
Run-Tex (Austin), 247
Russell Korman (Austin), 246

S

Sabia Botanicals (Austin), 243
Safety
Austin, 324
San Antonio, 318

Sailing, Austin, 233
Saint (San Antonio), 133
St. Joseph's Catholic Church (San Antonio), 110
St. Stanislaus (Bandera), 283–284
Saks Fifth Avenue
Austin, 242
San Antonio, 122
Salute! (San Antonio), 133
Salvage Vanguard Theater (Austin), 255
San Angel Folk Art (San Antonio), 122
San Antonio Arts & Cultural Affairs, 128
San Antonio Bed & Breakfast Association, 47
San Antonio Botanical Garden, 43, 103–104
San Antonio Central Library, 99
San Antonio Children's Museum, 105
San Antonio CineFestival, 28
Sanantonio.citysearch.com, 9
San Antonio Conservation Society, 88
San Antonio Convention and Visitors Bureau, accommodations, 48
San Antonio Department of Public Works, 314
San Antonio Express-News, 128
San Antonio Golfing Guide, 114
Sanantonio.gov, 9
San Antonio Hispanic Chamber of Commerce, 107–108
San Antonio IMAX Theater Rivercenter, 105
San Antonio International Airport, 304
San Antonio Medical Foundation, 316
San Antonio Missions, 115
San Antonio Missions National Historical Park, 44, 95–96
San Antonio Museum of Art, 43–44
San Antonio Rampage, 116
San Antonio River, 18–19
San Antonio Spurs, 115–116
San Antonio Stock Show and Rodeo, 116
San Antonio Symphony, 128–129
San Antonio Theater Coalition, 129
San Antonio Visitor Information Center, 87
San Antonio Zoological Gardens and Aquarium, 102
San Fernando Cathedral (San Antonio), 39, 42, 100, 111
San Francisco de la Espada (San Antonio), 96
San José (San Antonio), 96
San Juan Capistrano (San Antonio), 96
San Marcos, 162, 270–275

San Marcos River, 271
  tubing, 142
San Pedro Creek (San Antonio), 112
San Pedro Playhouse (San Antonio), 129
Santa Anna, Antonio López de, 15
Santa Rita No. 1 (Austin), 227
SAS Shoemakers (San Antonio), 122
Satel's (San Antonio), 122
SATRANS (San Antonio), 305
Sauer-Beckmann Living History Farm (near Stonewall), 298
SAVE (San Antonio Vacation Experience), 47
SAVE San Antonio discount book, 87
Saveur Texas Hill Country Wine and Food Festival (Austin), 31
Saxon Pub (Austin), 260
Schlitterbahn (Gruene), 142–143
Scholz Garten (Austin), 262
Schultze House Cottage Garden (San Antonio), 103
Scuba diving, Lake Travis, 233
Sea kayaking. See Kayaking
Seasons, 27
SeaWorld San Antonio, 97
SeaZar's Fine Wine & Spirits, 127
Segway Nation (Austin), 230
Segway tours
  Austin, 230
  San Antonio, 113
Selena, 134
Senior travel
  Austin, 324
  San Antonio, 319
Seton Medical Center (Austin), 321
Shady Grove Unplugged (Austin), 256
Shakespeare Festival, Austin, 256
Sheplers (Austin), 249
Sheplers Western Wear (San Antonio), 127
Shiner, 146
Shiner beer, 146
Shoes, San Antonio, 122
Shopping
  Austin and environs, 236–250
    First Thursdays, 240
    neighborhoods, 236, 240
  San Marcos, 272–273
  the Hill Country
    Bandera, 284
    Fredericksburg, 294
    Medina, 287
  San Antonio, 117–127
    best, 6
    neighborhoods, 117
Shopping centers and malls
  Austin, 246–247
  San Antonio, 124
The Shops at La Cantera (San Antonio), 125

Side trips
  from Austin, 265–275
    Lockhart, 266–268
  from San Antonio, 137–153
    Corpus Christi and environs, 147–153
    Flatonia, 146
    Gonzales, 145–146
    Luling, 146–147
    nearby caverns, 138
    New Braunfels and Gruene, 137–144
    Shiner, 146
Sierra Club, 233
Sights and attractions
  Austin and environs, 204–232
    Central Austin, 210, 216–218
    downtown, 204–208, 211–215
    East Side, 218–219
    for kids, 221–222
    organized tours, 229–232
    outdoors, 219–221
    parks and gardens, 220–221
    South Austin, 209, 215
    top attractions, 204–211
    West Austin, 215–216
  Kerrville and environs, 291–292, 294
  San Antonio and environs, 87–113
    Alamo Heights area, 94
    Corpus Christi, 147–148
    downtown, 87–94, 97–101
    Hispanic heritage, 106–108
    for kids, 104
    King William Historic District, 88, 92–94
    for military history buffs, 106
    New Braunfels, 140–141
    organized tours, 112–113
    parks and gardens, 103–104
    South Side, 95–96
    strolling downtown, 108–113
    top attractions, 87–97
Silver Dollar (San Antonio), 133
Singing Water Vineyards (near Comfort), 280
Sister Creek Vineyards (Sisterdale), 280
Si Texas Tours (Bandera), 34
Six Flags Fiesta Texas (San Antonio), 96–97
Sixth Street (Austin), 214–215
Sloan/Hall (San Antonio), 123
Smoking, 133, 319, 324
Soccer, Austin, 235
Sophienburg Museum (New Braunfels), 141
South Austin, 155
  accommodations, 171–173
  coffeehouses, 203

restaurants, 188–193
  sights and attractions, 209, 215
South by Southwest (SxSW) Music and Media Conference & Festival (Austin), 30, 260
South Congress Farmers' Market, 244
South Congress Street (SoCo; Austin), 13, 155
  shopping, 236
South Side (San Antonio), 38
  sightseeing, 95–96
Southtown Arts and Entertainment District (San Antonio), 132
Southtown (San Antonio), 38
  restaurants, 76–78
Southwestern & Mexican Photography Collection (San Marcos), 272
Southwest School of Art and Craft (San Antonio), 100
Spanish Governor's Palace (San Antonio), 39, 100, 112
Speakeasy (Austin), 260
Special events and festivals
  Austin, 30–32
  San Antonio, 28–30
Spec's Liquor Warehouse (Austin), 249
Spectator sports
  Austin, 234–235
  San Antonio, 115–116
Spelunking, Austin area, 233
Spider House (Austin), 203
Splash! Into the Edwards Aquifer (Austin), 222
Splashtown (San Antonio), 105
Spoetzl brewery (Shiner), 146
Sports and outdoor activities
  Austin, 232–234
  Bandera, 284–285
  San Antonio, 113–115
Stampede (Bandera), 284
Starkey Properties (Port Aransas), 152
Star of Texas Fair and Rodeo (Austin), 30
Star Tickets (Austin), 235
Starving Artist Show (San Antonio), 28
State Bank and Trust Building (San Marcos), 272
State Capitol (Austin), 158, 204, 208
Statesman Capitol 10,000 (Austin), 30
Steves Homestead Museum (San Antonio), 88, 92, 101
Stevie Ray Vaughan Statue (Austin), 220
Stock Show and Rodeo (San Antonio), 28
Stonehenge, replica of (Hunt), 288

GENERAL INDEX

Stone Oak Park (San Antonio), 103
Stonewall, 298, 299
Stone Werks Cafe and Bar (San Antonio), 135
Street maps, Austin, 312
Stubb's Bar-B-Q (Austin), 260
Sunday Houses (Kerrville), 291
Sunken Garden Theater (San Antonio), 131
Sunset Station (San Antonio), 131
SuperShuttle (Austin), 306
Sutton Hall (University of Texas at Austin), 229
Swig Martini Bar (San Antonio), 136
Swimming, Guadalupe River State Park (near Boerne), 282
Swimming holes and pools
    Austin, 233–234
    San Antonio, 115

T

Tackle Box Outfitters (New Braunfels), 114
Tanger Factory Outlet Center (San Marcos), 162, 272
Tapatio Springs Golf Course (Boerne), 277
Tarrytown (Austin), 155
Taxes
    Austin, 325
    San Antonio, 319
Taxis
    Austin, 325
    San Antonio, 305, 311, 319
Taylor, 269
Tejano Conjunto Festival (San Antonio), 28–29
Tejano music, 134
Tennis
    Austin, 234
    San Antonio, 115
Ten Thousand Villages (Austin), 243–244
Terra Toys (Austin), 248
Terrell Hills (San Antonio), 38
Tesoros Trading Co. (Austin), 159, 244
Texan vocabulary and phrases, 16–17, 302
Texas Book Festival (Austin), 32
Texas Department of Transportation, website, 8
Texas Folklife Festival (San Antonio), 29
Texas Jack's (Fredericksburg), 294
Texas Legato (near Lampasas), 281
Texas Memorial Museum (Austin), 217, 226
Texas Memorial Stadium (Austin), 226
Texasmonthly.com, 9
Texas Outside (website), 8
Texas Performing Arts (Austin), 254

Texas Rollergirls (Austin), 235
Texas Sailing Academy (Austin), 233
Texas Ski Ranch (near New Braunfels), 143
Texas State Aquarium (Corpus Christi), 147–148
Texas State Cemetery (Austin), 218–219
Texas Stories (Henry), 23
Texas Student Union Building (University of Texas at Austin), 228
Texas Toast Culinary Tours, 34
Texas Union Ballroom (Austin), 259
Texas Union Film Series (Austin), 263
Texas Union Information Center (Austin), 218
Tex-Mex food, 26
Tex-Mex restaurants
    Austin and environs, 191, 192, 194, 198, 199, 202
    San Antonio and environs, 74, 76, 78, 80, 81
    Corpus Christi, 153
Tex's Grill (San Antonio), 136
TG Canoes & Kayaks (San Marcos), 271
Theater
    Austin, 254–255
    San Antonio, 129
Thompson, Frank, 92
Thrifty car rentals
    Austin, 312
    San Antonio, 308
Ticketmaster, San Antonio, 128
Time to Write (Henry), 23
Time zones, 319, 325
Tiny Texas Houses (Luling), 146
Tipping, 319, 325
Toilets, San Antonio, 319
Tomb Rider 3D (San Antonio), 105
Too Good to Be Threw (San Antonio), 126
Torre di Pietra, 281
Tours, 34
Tower of the Americas (San Antonio), 43, 101
Toy Joy (Austin), 248
Toys, Austin, 248
Traffic, Austin, 13
Train travel
    Austin, 307, 313
    San Antonio, 306
Transit information, Austin, 325
Travis, Lake (Austin),
    accommodations, 178–180
    restaurants, 201–202
    sailing, 233
Travis Audubon Society (Austin), 232
Travis Heights (Austin), 155
Travis Heights Beverage World (Austin), 250

Treaty Oak (Austin), 215
Tres Rebecas (San Antonio), 122
Triton Financial Classic (Austin), 235
Trolley tours, San Antonio, 113
Tubing, 142
    Bandera, 284
    San Antonio and environs, 115, 143
Tycoon Flats (San Antonio), 133

U

Umlauf Sculpture Garden & Museum (Austin), 215
United Kingdom
    embassy and consulates, 315
    passports, 318
    visas, 320
University Co-Op (Austin), 241
University Cyclery (Austin), 232
University of Texas at Austin, 13, 21, 22, 217–218
    spectator sports, 234, 235
    theaters, 254
    Tower Observation Deck Tour, 231
    walking tour, 223–229
U.S. Army Medical Department Museum (San Antonio), 102
USS *Lexington* (Corpus Christi), 147, 148
UTTM Charge-A-Ticket, 234

V

Valero Texas Open (San Antonio), 116
Vanishing Texas River Cruise (Lake Buchanan), 301
Van tours (Austin), 230
Vaughan, Stevie Ray, 26
    Statue (Austin), 220
Veloway (Austin), 232
Velveeta Room (Austin), 261
Vereins Kirche (Fredericksburg), 291–292
Verizon Wireless Amphitheater (San Antonio), 131
VIA Metropolitan Transit (San Antonio), 305, 310
VIA Trans Disabled Accessibility Information (San Antonio), 314–315
Villa Finale (San Antonio), 88, 101–102
Visas, 319–320
Visitor information
    Austin, 325
    San Antonio, 320
Visitsanantonio.com, 9
Visit USA, 304
Vocabulary and phrases, Texan, 16–17, 302
Vortex (Austin), 255

W

Walking tours
  Austin, 230–232
  University of Texas at
    Austin, 223–229
  downtown San Antonio,
    108–113
Waller, Edwin, 20
Warehouse District (Austin), 155,
  257
Waterloo Records and Video
  (Austin), 162, 247
Watermelon Thump (Luling), 147
Waterparks, San Antonio, 115
Watersports, Gruene, 142–143
Waxy O'Connors Irish Pub (San
  Antonio), 136
Weather, 27
Websites, best, 8–9
Wednesday night concerts
  (Austin), 255–256
Wesley United Methodist Church
  (Austin), 223
The West (San Antonio), 39
West Austin, 155
  restaurants, 193–194
  sights and attractions,
    215–216
Westcave Preserve (Dripping
  Springs), 220
Western Union, 317, 323
Western wear
  Austin, 249
  San Antonio, 126–127
Westin La Cantera (San
  Antonio), 114
West Lake (Austin), 155
Westlake (Austin), restaurants,
  201–202
Westlake Hills (Austin), 155
  accommodations, 178–180
West Side (San Antonio), 97
  accommodations, 61–64
Whataburger Field (Corpus
  Christi), 148
Wheatsville Food Co-op
  (Austin), 244
Wheelchair accessibility
  Austin, 320
  San Antonio, 314–315
Whip In Beer and Wine (Austin),
  249–250
White Rabbit (San Antonio), 132
Whit Hanks Antiques (Austin),
  241
The Whole Earth Provision Co.
  (Austin), 248
Whole Foods Market (Austin),
  162, 244, 245
Whooping crane cruises (Corpus
  Christi), 150
Whooping cranes, 151
Wi-Fi access
  Austin, 322
  San Antonio, 316

Wiggy's (Austin), 250
Wild About Music (Austin), 245
Wild Basin Wilderness Preserve,
  231, 233
Wildflower Hotline, 299
Wildflowers, 299
  Lady Bird Johnson
    Wildflower Center (Austin),
    158, 209
Wildseed Farms (near
  Fredericksburg), 292
Wimberley, 274–275
Wimberley Glass Works,
  274–275
Windsurfing, Laguna Madre
  (North Padre Island), 150–151
Windy Point Park (Austin), 233
Wines and wineries
  Austin, 249
  the Hill Country, 280–281
  San Antonio, 127
Wine Tours of Texas (Austin), 34
Witte Museum (San Antonio), 95
Wittliff Collections (San Marcos),
  272
Women & Their Work Gallery
  (Austin), 241
Wonder World (San Marcos), 272
Woodrose Winery, 281
Woody's Sports Center (Port
  Aransas), 150
Worldwinds Windsurfing (Padre
  Island National Seashore), 151

X

XLent, 251

Y

Yard Dog Folk Art (Austin), 244
Yellow-Checker Cab (San
  Antonio), 311, 314
Y.O. Ranch (Mt. Home), 289

Z

Zach Theatre (Austin), 254
Zeta Phi Beta Sorority (Austin),
  223
Zilker Botanical Garden (Austin),
  221
Zilker Park (Austin), 221
  canoeing, 232–233
Zilker Park Tree Lighting
  (Austin), 32
Zilker Preserve (Austin), 220
Zilker Zephyr Miniature Train
  (Austin), 222
Zinc (San Antonio), 136
Zoos
  Austin, 222
  San Antonio Zoological
    Gardens and Aquarium, 102

Accommodations— San Antonio and environs

Balinese Flats (Port Aransas),
  153
Beckmann Inn and Carriage
  House, 57
Best Western Sunset Suites-
  Riverwalk, 54
Bonner Garden, 59
Brackenridge House, 57–58
Bullis House Inn, 60
Crockett Hotel, 54
Doubletree Hotel San Antonio
  Airport, 64–65
Drury Inn & Suites San Antonio
  Riverwalk/Drury Plaza
  Riverwalk, 54–55
Emily Morgan, 52–53
The Fairmount, 53
Faust Hotel (New Braunfels), 143
George Blucher House (Corpus
  Christi), 152
Gruene Apple Bed and
  Breakfast, 144
Gruene Mansion Inn, 143–144
Hilton San Antonio Hill Country
  Hotel and Spa, 58, 64
Holiday Inn Express-Riverwalk
  area, 55
Homewood Suites by Hilton,
  55, 58
Hoope's House (Rockport), 152
Hotel Contessa, 49
Hotel Havana, 55
Hotel Valencia Riverwalk, 49–50
Hyatt Regency Hill Country
  Resort and Spa, 58, 61
Hyatt Regency San Antonio on
  the River Walk, 50
The Inn at Craig Place, 59
Jackson House, 56–57
King William Manor, 58–59
La Quinta Inn & Suites San
  Antonio Airport, 65
Lighthouse Inn (Rockport), 152
Marriott Plaza San Antonio, 53
Marriott Rivercenter, 50
Menger Hotel, 53–54
Mokara Hotel & Spa, 52
O'Brien Hotel, 56
O'Casey's Bed & Breakfast, 58,
  59–60
Ogé House and Pancoast
  Carriage House, 57
Omni Corpus Christi Hotel, 152
Omni La Mansión del Río, 50, 52
Omni San Antonio, 58, 64
Prince Solms Inn (New
  Braunfels), 143
Riverwalk Vista, 56
Ruckman Haus, 60

San Antonio Airport Hilton, 65
Sea Shell Inn (Corpus Christi), 152
St. Anthony Hotel, 56
Tarpon Inn (Port Aransas), 152
Westin La Cantera, 58, 61, 64
Westin Riverwalk Inn, 52, 58

Accommodations— Austin

The Adams House, 175
Austin Folk House, 173–174
Austin Motel, 172
Barton Creek Resort, 178, 179
Blair House Inn (Wimberley), 275
Crystal River Inn (San Marcos), 273
Doubletree Guest Suites Austin, 169, 179
Doubletree Hotel Austin, 174
The Driskill, 166
Extended Stay America Downtown, 173
Four Seasons Austin, 166, 168, 179
Habitat Suites, 174
Hampton Inn & Suites Austin-Downtown, 170
Hawthorn Suites, 165
Hilton Austin, 169
Hilton Austin Airport, 180
Holiday Inn Austin, 179
Holiday Inn Austin Town Lake, 170–171
Homestead Studio Suites Austin-Downtown, 173
Hostelling International-Austin, 172–173
Hotel Saint Cecilia, 171
Hotel San José, 172
Hyatt Regency Austin, 168
Hyatt Regency Lost Pines Resort and Spa, 274
InterContinental Stephen F. Austin, 169–170
Kimber Modern Boutique Hotel, 171–172
Lake Austin Spa Resort, 178–179
Lakeway Inn, 179–180
La Quinta Inn-Capitol, 171
Mansion at Judges Hill, 173
Omni Austin, 168–169
Renaissance Austin Hotel, 175
Sheraton Austin, 170
Star of Texas Inn, 175
Staybridge Suites, 178
Studio 6, 165
W Austin, 169

Accommodations— the Hill Country

Absolute Charm (Fredericksburg), 295
The Antlers (Kingsland), 302

Bourne Vistro Country Inn (Boerne), 283
Cotton Gin Village (Fredericksburg), 296
Dixie Dude Ranch (Bandera), 285
Frederick Motel (Fredericksburg), 295
Full Moon Inn (Luckenbach), 296
Gästehaus Schmidt (Fredericksburg), 295
Hangar Hotel (Fredericksburg), 295
Inn of the Hills Resort (Kerrville), 289
Landmark Inn (Castroville), 282
Mayan Ranch (Bandera), 285
River Oak Inn (Bandera), 285
Roadrunner Inn (Fredericksburg), 295
Rose Hill Manor (Stonewall), 299
Silver Spur Guest Ranch (Bandera), 285
Sunset Inn and Studio (Kerrville), 289
Twin Elm Guest Ranch (Bandera), 285
Ye Kendall Inn (Boerne), 282
Y.O. Ranch Resort Hotel and Conference Center (Kerrville), 289

Restaurants—San Antonio and environs

Acenar, 73
Aldo's (San Antonio), 84–85
Azuca, 76
Biga on the Banks, 69
Bistro Vatel, 82
Bohanan's, 69–70
Boudro's, 72
Casa Rio, 74
Cascabel, 77
Chris Madrids, 81
Ciao Lavanderia, 83
County Line, 73
Demo's, 80
The Filling Station, 77
Frederick's, 82
Gristmill River Restaurant & Bar (Gruene), 144
Guenther House, 77–78
Huisache Grill (San Antonio), 144
Il Sogno, 78–79
La Gloria, 80
La Playa (Corpus Christi), 153
La Playa Mexican Grille (Corpus Christi), 153
Las Canarias, 70
Latitude 28°02' (Rockport), 153
Le Midi, 72
Liberty Bar, 76
Little Rhein Steak House, 70
Los Barrios, 80–81
Los Comales (Rockport), 153
Luling City Market, 146, 268

Madhatters, 78, 81
Mi Tierra, 74, 93
Myron's (New Braunfels), 144
New Braunfels Smokehouse, 144
Olmos Pharmacy, 81, 84
Ostra, 70, 72
Paesano's Riverwalk, 72–73
Paloma Blanca, 83
Rolando's Super Tacos, 81–82
Rosario's, 76–77
Sandbar, 79
Schilo's, 74–75, 81
Silo, 83
Sushi Zushi, 73
Thai Restaurant, 85
Tip Top Cafe, 85–86
Tito's, 78
Tre Trattoria, 84
Twin Sisters, 75
Van's, 84
Venetian Hot Plate (Corpus Christi), 153
Water Street Seafood Company (Corpus Christi), 153
Zinc, 73–74

Restaurants— Austin

Artz Rib House, 191
Asti, 195
Black's Barbecue (Lockhart), 267
Café on the Square (San Marcos), 273
Casa de Luz, 191
Chez Nous, 184
Chez Zee, 200
Chuy's, 191
Cipollina, 194
City Meat Market (Giddings), 269
Clay Pit, 186
Cooper's (Llano), 269
County Line on the Hill, 201–202
Curra's Grill, 191–192
Eastside Cafe, 198
East Side King, 199
Eddie V's Edgewater Grille, 200
El Naranjo, 187–188
El Sol y La Luna, 188
Flip Happy Crepes, 195
Fonda San Miguel, 196
Franklin Barbecue, 199
Gristmill River Restaurant & Bar, 163
Güero's, 192
Gumbo's, 184
Hoover's, 198
House Pizzeria, 196
Hudson's on the Bend, 201
Hula Hut, 194
Hut's Hamburgers, 188
Hyde Park Bar & Grill, 196
The Iron Works, 188
Jeffrey's, 193
Jo's, 203
Kerbey Lane, 261
Kreuz Market (Lockhart), 266–267

La Traviata, 184
Louie Mueller's (Taylor), 269
Luling City Market, 268
Magnolia Cafe South, 261
Manuel's, 186–187
Matt's El Rancho, 192
The Mighty Cone, 195
Mother's Café & Garden, 197–198
Musashino, 200
The Oasis, 202
Olivia, 188–189
Palmer's (San Marcos), 273
Ranch 616, 187
Roaring Fork, 158, 184, 186
Saltgrass Steakhouse (San Marcos), 274
Salt Lick (Driftwood), 268
Shady Grove, 159, 193
Smitty's Market (Lockhart), 267–268
Snow's Barbecue (Lexington), 269
South Congress Cafe, 159, 192–193
Stubb's Bar-B-Q, 202
Tacos, 195
Threadgill's, 197

Threadgill's World Headquarters, 202
Titaya's, 197
Uchi, 189–190
Vaquero Cocina, 195
Vespaio & Enoteca Vespaio, 190
Vivo, 198–199
Zocalo, 194
Z'Tejas Southwestern Grill, 201

Restaurants—the Hill Country

Altdorf Biergarten (Fredericksburg), 296
Arlene's Café and Gift Shop (Comfort), 290
Bandera Mi Pueblo, 286
Bear Moon Bakery (Boerne), 283
Blue Bonnet Cafe (Marble Falls), 302
Brick's River Cafe (Bandera), 286
Cabernet Grill (Fredericksburg), 296
Canyon Room, 302
Cooper's (Llano), 303
Dodging Duck Brewhaus, 283
Francisco's (Kerrville), 290
Fredericksburg Brewing Co. (Fredericksburg), 296
Friedhelm's Bavarian Inn (Fredericksburg), 296
Hilda's Tortilla Factory (Fredericksburg), 294, 295
Hill Top Café (Fredericksburg), 295
Kingsland Old Town Grill, 302
Limestone Grille (Boerne), 283
Navajo Grill (Fredericksburg), 296
Nest (Fredericksburg), 296
O.S.T. (Bandera), 286
Rails (Kerrville), 289
Rather Sweet Bakery & Cafe (Fredericksburg), 295
Ronnie's Ice House (Johnson City), 298
Silver K Café (Johnson City), 298
Whittington's (Johnson City), taxi, 298